Neo-Confucian Studies
SPONSORED BY THE REGIONAL SEMINAR IN NEO-CONFUCIAN STUDIES
COLUMBIA UNIVERSITY

Principle and Practicality

Essays in Neo-Confucianism
and Practical Learning

Wm. Theodore de Bary and Irene Bloom, Editors

New York   Columbia University Press   1979

Library of Congress Cataloging in Publication Data
Main entry under title:
Principle and practicality.
  (Neo-Confucian Studies)
  Includes bibliographical references and index.
  1. Neo-Confucianism—Addresses, essays, lectures.
2. Practice (Philosophy)—Addresses, essays, lectures.
3. China—History—Ming dynasty, 1368–1644—Addresses,
essays, lectures. 4. Japan—History—Tokugawa period,
1600–1868—Addresses, essays, lectures. I. De Bary
William Theodore, 1919–   II. Bloom, Irene.
III. Series.
B127.N4P74   181'.09'512   78-11530
ISBN 0-231-04612-X
ISBN 0-231-04613-8 pbk.

Columbia University Press
New York   Guildford, Surrey

*This book is dedicated by his fellow conferees
to the senior member of the conference*
OKADA TAKEHIKO
*in tribute to his great contribution to the study
of Neo-Confucianism and to his important role in
a continuing tradition of Confucian cultivation
and scholarship*

Neo-Confucian Studies

Preface

This volume continues the work of earlier conferences devoted to a reassessment of Chinese thought in the premodern period. It is a sequel to *Self and Society in Ming Thought* (1970) and *The Unfolding of Neo-Confucianism* (1975), which focused on the late Ming-early Ch'ing years as a new phase in the maturation of Chinese thought and culture. In the mid-seventeenth century, with the conquest of the native Ming dynasty by the invading Manchus, we have a major turning point by which to measure change and continuity in the handing on of Confucian tradition.

Earlier in the same century, however, another foreign people had appropriated this revitalized tradition by less violent means, with the importation to Japan and sponsorship by the Tokugawa regime of Neo-Confucian philosophy. This made the Japanese heirs, and indeed co-executors along with the Chinese and Koreans, of the full legacy of Sung-Ming thought.

On Japanese soil, as on Korean, old continuities were resumed and familiar ideas took root, but new growth too sprang from the transplanted tree as it spread out beyond accustomed limits. Thus it is only in the context of East Asian history as a whole that the full reach of Neo-Confucianism and the larger implications of its teachings can be grasped.

Owing to the modern maledictions pronounced upon this tradition, much of the good it had done was interred with its bones and is waiting to be rediscovered. For those who seek anew to explore the entire range of its mature development and to gauge the true limits of Neo-Confucian thought, what the Japanese were able to make of it in the Tokugawa period has great value for comparative study.

The papers presented here treat one important theme in Neo-Confucian thought—its claim to be "real" or "practical," or to have a sure hold on reality by virtue of its demonstrable application to basic human needs. As those needs changed, so did the responses of Neo-Confucian thinkers, whether as advisers to the ruling class, as influential teachers of the educated elite, or as independent speculative philosophers. In these responses we find material for the comparative study of a living tradition acting out its values in different historical and cultural settings. Each of the studies presented here contributes to our understanding of this comparative development, though neither singly nor together can they claim to establish new guidelines for comparative study. At best, they only complicate the problem in ways that are necessary if we are to progress beyond the simplistic notions about Neo-Confucianism and modernization that have prevailed in the past.

Comparative study is always an approximation, but it is nonetheless indispensable. At this point what we can hope to achieve, building on the studies of China in the preceding volumes, is to extend the investigation to Japan and establish the larger record, by opening up possibilities previously discounted and identifying relationships so far ignored. To do more than this we shall need further study of eighteenth- and nineteenth-century thought in China and Japan and of the whole Korean development of Neo-Confucianism and "practical learning" (*sirhak*).

The participants in this project wish to acknowledge the assistance of the following in arranging the conference and publishing the results: the Subcommittee on Chinese Thought and Religion of the American Council of Learned Societies, for its support of conference expenses from funds of the Ford Foundation; Professor Chung-ying Cheng and the University of Hawaii, for their hospitality in June 1974; to Professors Abe Yoshio, Wing-tsit Chan, and Wei-ming Tu, for their valuable contributions to the conference discussions; Professors Robert Wargo, Valdo Viglielmo, Carol Gluck, and Samuel Yamashita, for virtuoso performances as simultaneous interpreters; Professors Hiroshi Miyaji, Robert Wargo, David Dilworth, and Samuel Yamashita, for major assistance in the translation of papers; Professor Yoshito Hakeda, for advice in the reading of Japanese texts; Ms. Jeanette Hsü, for her contribution of manuscript calligraphy; Ms. M. Theresa Kelleher, for expert and painstaking help in the preparation of the manuscript. The editors also wish to express their gratitude to Professor Philip B. Yampolsky, Director of the East Asian Library, Columbia University, for generously sharing his extraordinary bibliographic knowledge and patiently helping to resolve innumerable questions of fact, translation, and style.

Explanatory Note
and Abbreviations Used

Chinese philosophical terms often elude precise translation into English. The problem, apart from obvious differences of linguistic structure and conceptual category, has to do with a conservatism that attends the use of philosophical vocabulary. The extent to which meanings and intentions change is sometimes obscured by the relative constancy of the terminology employed to clothe them. A given term or phrase may be retained over the course of centuries and used in a variety of contexts; its nuance or even its basic connotation may change considerably over time or gain new accretions of meaning as successive generations of thinkers allude, directly or tacitly, to earlier uses of the term. Thinkers who are contemporary with one another frequently differ in their understanding of a given term, sometimes openly disagreeing about how it is to be interpreted and sometimes passing over a significant difference in silence. This would appear to be part of the reason that Chinese, and especially Neo-Confucian, philosophical terms typically convey a richness, and, in some cases, an ambiguity of meaning and association which no single English term can accurately convey.

In this volume the Chinese term *shih* (Japanese, *jitsu*) conveys just such a variety of senses. Often it carries the connotation of "practicality," but there are also contexts in which the emphasis is rather on solidity, substantiality, or reality, and, in these cases, alternate renderings are offered, with the Chinese or Japanese term indicated in romanized form. Similarly, with the important term *ching* (*kei*), meaning reverence and/or seriousness, the romanized form is given in parentheses to call attention to the original term with all its fullness of meaning.

The phrase *ch'iung-li* (*kyūri*), meaning the fathoming or plumbing of principle, is particularly difficult to render in translation because of the wide range of meanings which attach to it in various contexts. Where the use of the term suggests emphasis on the interior pursuit of principle within the individual mind or consciousness, the translation "plumbing principle" has been favored here; where the context suggests emphasis on the empirical investigation of principles in the exter-

ix

nal world, the same term has been translated as "exhaustive exploration of principle." Needless to say, this solution represents a compromise and entails the unfortunate risk of obscuring in translation an ambiguity which might more appropriately be preserved if a consistent and yet faithful rendering could be found.

The term *t'i-jen* (*tainin*) and the term *tzu-te* (*jitoku*) also pose problems in translation. They occur both separately and in combination, the former generally conveying the sense of incorporating a given truth, perception, or reality into oneself through personal experience, the latter, the sense of discovering moral principles or the Way within one's own person. For *t'i-jen*, the translation "personal experience" has frequently been employed, while *tzu-te* has in most cases been rendered "self-realization." Again, the romanized forms of the terms have been provided for the sake of clarity.

Unless the context dictates a change in the convention, the romanized Chinese form of a term is given first in each case, followed by the Japanese form.

Abbreviations of Chinese and Japanese titles are identified at the first appearance, except in the case of the following standard works or editions:

MJHA	*Ming-ju hsüeh-an*
NKBT	*Nihon koten bungaku taikei*
NRI	*Nihon rinri ihen*
NST	*Nihon shisō taikei*
SPPY	Ssu-pu pei-yao
SPTK	Ssu-pu ts'ung-k'an
ST	*Shushigaku taikei*
TSCC	Ts'ung-shu chi-ch'eng

Contributors

IRENE BLOOM is a Lecturer in East Asian Languages and Cultures at Columbia University, where she has also been a Fellow in the Society of Fellows in the Humanities. Her particular interests are in classical Confucianism and in Sung and Ming Neo-Confucianism and she is currently working on a Confucian reader.

CHUNG-YING CHENG is Professor of Philosophy at the University of Hawaii and works in the fields of Chinese philosophy, comparative philosophy, and American logical philosophy. He has published studies in classical Chinese logic, Confucianism, and Neo-Confucianism, including a book, *Tai Chen's Inquiry into Goodness* (1969). He is the founder and editor of the *Journal of Chinese Philosophy* and founder and president of the International Society for Chinese Philosophy. He is currently working on studies of the *Book of Changes* and of Chu Hsi.

JULIA CHING is Associate Professor of Philosophy and East Asian Studies at Yale University and has also taught at Australian National University and Columbia University. She is the author of several books, including *To Acquire Wisdom: The Way of Wang Yang-ming* (1976) and *Confucianism and Christianity* (1977).

WM. THEODORE DE BARY is John Mitchell Mason Professor of the University at Columbia University, where he has also served as Vice President and Provost. A former President of the Association for Asian Studies, he is the editor and co-author of *Sources of Chinese Tradition, Sources of Japanese Tradition, Sources of Indian Tradition, The Buddhist Tradition, Self and Society in Ming Thought* and, most recently, of *The Unfolding of Neo-Confucianism*.

DAVID A. DILWORTH is Professor of Philosophy at the State University of New York at Stony Brook. He has worked in the fields of modern Japanese philosophy and comparative philosophy and has published translations of *An Encouragement of Learning* by Fukuzawa Yukichi (1969) and *Fundamental Problems of Philosophy: The World of Action and the Dialectical World* by Nishida Kitarō (1970). With J. Thomas Rimer, he has recently published an edition of *The Historical Literature of Mori Ōgai* (2 vols., 1977).

IAN JAMES MC MULLEN is University Lecturer in Japanese at Oxford University. He was educated at Cambridge University where he obtained his doctorate for a thesis entitled, "Kumazawa Banzan: The Life and Thought of a Seventeenth-century Japanese Confucian." He has written several articles on Japanese Confucianism of the Tokugawa Period and is at present preparing a monograph on Kumazawa Banzan's commentary on the *Tale of Genji*.

MINAMOTO RYŌEN is Professor at the Research Institute for Japanese Culture at Tohoku University in Sendai, Japan. He is the author of *Tokugawa gōri shisō no keifu* (The Genealogy of Rationalistic Thought in the Edo Period, 1972), *Tokugawa shisō shōshi* (A Short History of Ideas in the Tokugawa Period, 1973), and *Giri to Ninjō* (1974). He is currently writing a book on *jitsugaku* thought.

OKADA TAKEHIKO is Emeritus Professor of Chinese at Kyūshū University in Fukuoka, Japan. A Doctor of Literature from the same university, he is the author of numerous books and articles in Japanese on Neo-Confucian thought in China and Japan, including *Zazen to seiza* (Zen Meditation and Quiet Sitting, 1965) and *Ō Yōmei to Minmatsu no jugaku* (Wang Yang-ming and Late Ming Confucianism, 1970), and *Sō Min tetsugaku josetsu* (Introduction to Sung-Ming Philosophy, 1977). He edited the 1970 reprint of the 1473 edition of the *Chu Tzu yü-lei* (Recorded Conversations of Chu Hsi) and has been a major contributor to the *Yōmeigaku taikei* (Compendium of Wang Yang-ming Studies) and *Shushigaku taikei* (Compendium of Chu Hsi studies) series.

YAMASHITA RYŪJI is a graduate of Tokyo University and is now Professor of Chinese Philosophy in the Faculty of Letters of Nagoya University, specializing in Sung and Ming thought and in Japanese thought of the Tokugawa period. His principal works include *Yōmeigaku no kenkyū* (Studies of the Wang Yang-Ming School in China and Japan, 1971, 2 vols.) and *Daigaku-Chūyō* (The Great Learning and the Mean) in *Zenshaku kanbun taikei* (Compendium of Chinese Classics Translated into Japanese, vol. 3, 1974).

Contents

Principle and Practicality
Essays in Neo-Confucianism and Practical Learning

In all the world there are no concrete forms without their ordering principles and no principles without concrete forms. If there is a concrete form to be investigated, there will be its principle inherent in it. Thus with Heaven-and-earth there are their regulating principles, and with bodily forms there are the principles of their natures and feelings. . . . If one leaves out concrete forms in the search for principles, one inescapably falls into vain and empty theories. This is not the real, practical learning of our Confucian school. The reason why the Great Learning taught men to investigate things and extend knowledge is that principles are found in things. Thus scholars should have the solid ground of reality on which to exert their efforts and not chase off into the realms of empty nothingness.

> Chen Te-hsiu (1178–1235)
> leading exponent of Neo-Confucian
> philosophy after Chu Hsi

Wm. Theodore de Bary

Introduction

When Fukuzawa Yukichi, a pioneer of Westernization in nineteenth-century Japan, wished to convert his Confucian-educated countrymen to the superiority of the new scientific learning from the West, he argued the case for it in terms of its greater usefulness and practicality. The old learning, he said, consisted merely of "knowing difficult characters, reading difficult old books, and composing poetry." Pleasant though these diversions might be, they were useless in everyday life. "Thus the kind of learning we should work at now is *jitsugaku*[a]—practical learning which is close to men's everyday lives. The other unpractical kind of learning we can ignore for the time being."[1]

The distinction made here between practical and unpractical learning was one long used by the Confucians themselves, and its rhetorical effect for Fukuzawa depended upon that fact. As Carmen Blacker has said,

Jitsugaku was the useful, solid, practical knowledge conducive to what they [the Confucians] conceived to be the proper end and object of learning. *Kyogaku*[b] was the empty, useless learning which diverted men from that end. . . . It was in their conception of what precisely was useful knowledge that they differed. To the Confucianists knowledge was "useful" if it helped man to follow his moral Way. To the *keimō*[c] men [advocates of Western-style Enlightenment] it was useful if it increased his knowledge of the external world and thereby helped to raise him to a higher rung on the ladder of progress.[2]

1

Another Meiji period spokesman for Western-style enlightenment, Tsuda Mamichi,[d] contrasted the new *jitsugaku* to the "empty learning" of both Confucianism and Buddhism. According to Tsuda, *jitsugaku* "advocates principles of reality which are verified by real forms and judged by actual things."[3]

These statements, expressive of the nineteenth-century Japanese progressives' state of mind and the need they felt to break sharply with the old learning, speak for their own time and its dilemmas, not for a past from which they have already been considerably distanced. Their view of the old learning is foreshortened, and when Tsuda refers to Confucianism and Buddhism together as "empty learning," he ignores the distinction once clearly drawn by Neo-Confucians between their "practical learning" and the "empty learning" of Buddhism and Taoism. Nor could he have recalled that earlier Neo-Confucians, thinking of their own practical learning being opposed to the Buddhist view of the external world as illusory, had advocated in terms similar to his "principles of reality which are verified by real forms and judged by actual things."

The great Neo-Confucian Chu Hsi had indeed pursued learning which "helped man to follow his moral Way" but he had also affirmed the reality of the external world as a manifestation and confirmation of that Way. This is not to say, of course, that Chu's world or his principles coincided with Tsuda's, but only that there had been a more positivistic and practical side to Chu's philosophy to which Tsuda remained, unknowingly, the heir. Moreover, as will be shown in the pages which follow, faithful followers of Chu Hsi in Ming China and Tokugawa Japan had already traversed more than half the distance to the point where Fukuzawa and Tsuda took up their westward journey. From these Neo-Confucians, in fact, their Meiji successors received the intellectual formation and orientation to the world which helped set them on their course.

The aim of this book is not to retrace the long trail up from Chu Hsi in twelfth-century China to Fukuzawa Yukichi in nineteenth-century Japan, but to establish some landmarks in earlier Neo-Confucian thought from which to survey and measure the progress of this practical learning as it moved to play a role in Japan's modernization. Like Fukuzawa and Tsuda, most historians have treated *jitsugaku*, with its rationalistic and empirical tendencies and its growing interest in science, technology, and social reform, as a movement which arose in opposition to Neo-Confucianism, and broke away from it, helping to free the Japanese mind from a medieval, metaphysical outlook and reorient it toward a modern, "humanistic" and secular outlook. Some indeed have taken the appearance in Japan of this new learning, and its absence in China, as a sign of the latter's persistent inability to emancipate itself from the dead hand of Neo-Confucianism.

In questioning this view, and attempting to show that many of the roots of practical learning are to be found in Neo-Confucianism itself, we are not simply stating a truism—that no historical movement is wholly new or unindebted to its past. Rather, we are suggesting that these two movements are inseparable phases in a larger historical process in premodern Chinese and Japanese thought—a process of continuing, irrepressible growth rather than a period of prolonged, festering stagnation.

Though the present study is limited to certain key figures and concepts in Ming China and early Tokugawa Japan, and does not attempt to follow the matter down into the nineteenth century, it can serve as a means of exploring on a comparative basis some of the issues which have arisen in interpreting later developments. In this light, Japanese *jitsugaku* emerges as only one aspect of a wider practical learning engendered by Neo-Confucianism wherever it spread, including Korea with its *sirhak* counterpart to *jitsugaku*.

To take this broader appoach we must first disabuse ourselves of any lingering notion that Neo-Confucianism played only the reactionary role of a rigid, constraining dogma, standing in the way of progress. Often in studies of modernization an over-simplified version of Neo-Confucian "orthodoxy" has been set up as the foil for modern David's scientific triumph over a stolid medieval Goliath. Thus one of the tasks confronting this series of conferences has been to understand better the actual complexities of that orthodoxy and on this basis to reconsider the nature of practical learning's alleged incompatibility with it. To do this properly requires us to place both of these phenomena—orthodoxy and practical learning—in the larger context of Neo-Confucian thought as a whole.

At earlier conferences in the Chinese thought series I have tried to identify the reformist tendencies underlying Neo-Confucianism and also to characterize some of the attitudes and ideas which enabled it to spread and develop in premodern China, Japan, and Korea. More recently, the conference on Ming thought has brought to light the lively and variegated growth of Neo-Confucian thought from the fifteenth to seventeenth centuries, well after the initial articulation of the so-called

"Ch'eng-Chu" orthodoxy in the twelfth and thirteenth centuries. In this process Ch'eng-Chu "orthodoxy" itself underwent change, and at the subsequent conference on seventeeth-century Chinese thought these internal transmutations proved to be increasingly significant for the new thought and scholarship appearing in early Ch'ing China and Tokugawa Japan.

Pursuing the same line of inquiry we shall seek here a better understanding of how both Neo-Confucianism and practical learning may be interpreted in such broad historical and comparative terms as "humanism" and "secularism," and in the development from "medieval" to "modern" thought. These characterizations in turn relate to patterns of continuity and discontinuity, and of orthodoxy and heterodoxy, which may be traced through the evolving use of central concepts like principle (*li; ri*) and ether (*ch'i; ki*);[e] "real" or "practical" (*shih; jitsu*) and "empty" or "unreal" (*hsü; kyo*).[f] In this tracing we are led to discover, I believe, not only a more complex interweaving of thought trends in Neo-Confucianism than has usually been recognized, but also a greater degree of continuity in growth from old to new, and between the Chinese and Japanese varieties.

HUMANISM AND SECULARISM IN THE CONFUCIAN REVIVAL

Let us begin with "humanism" and "secularism," which are often considered to be essential characteristics of "modern" thought, and therefore key criteria for the passage from medieval thought to modern. What significance have these terms for Neo-Confucianism, in a tradition already identified as humanistic and secular from its inception? In what sense could Neo-Confucianism become still more humanistic than earlier Confucianism, or "modern" thought in China and Japan be still more humanistic than Neo-Confucianism? That there was no simple progression or unilinear path followed by Neo-Confucianism is the conclusion to which these studies seem to lead. On the contrary, they suggest that secularization was accompanied by the rise of new religious attitudes, and that from the confluence of earlier humanisms emerged new spiritualities. With Neo-Confucianism the most perceptible shift toward a new secularism probably occurred well before the modern era, in the eleventh century. The subsequent development of new and deeper forms of humanism came about not only through the opening up of new dimensions of social experience in an ever more complex society and culture, but also through the regeneration of traditional ideals and the reconsecration of secular activities.

Thus, the religious element in Confucianism, while subject to significant change in its "classical," "medieval," and "premodern" phases, instead of suffering gradual attenuation or displacement, came to be, like Chinese agriculture or Japanese art, more and more intensively cultivated, more refined, and more richly hybridized. Where the spiritual is seen as the most distinctively "human" aspect of man, and the secular is viewed as sacred, there can be a deepening and broadening of spirituality in the midst of secular change. In such a context, the movement from "medieval" to "modern" cannot be taken simply as one from the sacred to the secular or from the metaphysical to the material, but rather must be seen as a complex ramification and interaction of individual and social needs; moral, intellectual, and religious concerns; rational and intuitive methods.

In this respect there are significant comparisons to be made with the humanism of the Renaissance in Europe, and I have found it useful to consider basic Neo-Confucian concepts in relation to the "Renaissance Concepts of Man" which Paul Kristeller has identified in his Wimmer and Arensberg lectures, referred to below.

What we call Neo-Confucianism emerged from a revival of Confucian learning in the eleventh century A.D. after almost a millennium of Buddhist dominance. Against the background of a religion viewed by its critics as transcendental, life-denying, and asocial, the new movement sought to reassert indigenous Chinese social and cultural values as expressed in the Confucian classics. In this sense we may speak of Neo-Confucianism as a movement, similar to the Renaissance in Europe, which brought a notable revival of classical learning. While there are important differences between classical Greek and Confucian humanism, especially in regard to their relative potential for scientific learning of a theoretical sort, what is common to both the Neo-Confucian revival and the Renaissance is the rediscovery of the learning of antiquity as embodying perennial human values or models which can serve as an inspiration and guide for the present.

There are three ways in which this rediscovery of classical learning and the Confucian Way may be considered humanistic. One is Neo-Confucianism's reassertion of basic ethical values defined in terms of personal relationships within the family and community, having individual, social, and cosmic dimensions. Here the Confucians sought to reconcile the egalitarian claims of a common humanity with the need for a hierarchy of values, which they saw as a natural and essential outgrowth of man's civilizing activity and also as indispensable to the maintenance of any social order.

A second humanistic and secular aim of the Confucian revival was the "restoration" (fu-ku)[g] of the ancient political and social order as described, and somewhat idealized, in the classics. This was embodied in a program for the reconstruction of all governmental, economic and educational institutions. Major efforts at political reform took place in the eleventh century under the slogan of a "restoration of the ancient order." These efforts culminated in the famous New Laws of Wang An-shih, prime minister from 1069–76, but subsided thereafter.

Thirdly, the restoration movement was accompanied by an effort at literary reform to revive the so-called "ancient literature" or "classical style" (ku-wen),[h] which stressed a return to the simplicity, directness, and vigor of classical prose as contrasted to the elegant and highly refined parallel-prose style of the T'ang Dynasty (seventh to tenth centuries). Underlying this movement was a belief that the reform of ethics and social institutions depended upon the effective communication of values through a more genuine and expressive prose style. In contrast to Buddhism's skepticism in regard to language as expressive of truth, the Neo-Confucian movement was humanistic in its reaffirmation of the value of literature as an essential human activity.

The flowering of literature in manifold form during and after the Sung dynasty is evidence enough of the cultural vitality of this movement. More than this, however, the literary renaissance itself gave early impetus to the Confucian revival in the late T'ang and early Sung periods, rather than being merely an outgrowth, or by-product, of philosophical and religious change. Indeed, what Professor Kristeller has said about the Western Renaissance in this regard is equally true of the Confucian revival:

Leaving aside a number of important specific ideas which are the property of individual humanists rather than of the entire movement, the main contribution of Renaissance humanism seems to lie in the tremendous expansion of secular culture and learning which it brought about in the areas of literature, historiography, and moral thought.[4]

Professor Kristeller's underscoring of the relationship of the "humanities" to the Renaissance could also be taken as descriptive of its Chinese counterpart:

Later in the fourteenth century and during the fifteenth century, Renaissance scholars began to use the term "humanities" (*studia humanitatis*) for the disciplines they studied, taught, and liked. The term, borrowed from Cicero and other ancient writers . . . came to signify . . . grammar, rhetoric, poetry, history, and moral philosophy. The fact that the term "humanities" was applied to these subjects . . . expresses the claim that these studies are especially suitable for the education of a decent human being and, hence, are, or should be, of vital concern for man as such.[5]

The most influential of the Neo-Confucian philosophers and scholars, Chu Hsi, used the term *tao wen hsüeh*[1] (from the classic of the *Mean*) to express the same idea as was conveyed by "*studia humanitatis*" in the Western Renaissance. By *tao wen hsüeh* Chu described that aspect of the "Study of the Way" which was particularly concerned with scholarly and literary pursuits, in contrast to moral cultivation and social action. It was learning relevant to the humane concerns of the Confucian Way, and took many of the same forms as the *studia humanitatis*.

Thus in the eleventh-century Confucian concept of revival or restoration—a return to the ancient way—there is a fundamental likeness to the Renaissance return to a classical heritage which was also considered to embody humanistic values and studies. What remains to be clarified in the Chinese case is its specifically Buddhist background. On the one hand, this reaffirmation of humane values took on a special quality as a reaction against Buddhism; on the other, certain characteristic features of Neo-Confucianism showed the influence of Buddhism. The net result, then, was a humanistic revival which did not so much result in a decline of spirituality as in a transformation of it.

Dealing first with the reaction *against* Buddhism, I also touch on a significant difference between the Chinese revival and the European Renaissance. The latter, according to Professor Kristeller, emerges out of medieval Christianity and does not openly disavow it, whereas Neo-Confucianism starts with an explicit repudiation of Buddhism, and its debts to the latter remain largely unacknowledged.

Where Neo-Confucianism reasserted basic ethical values, Buddhism was seen as inimical to such values and even a threat to civilized life. From one point of view, Buddhism itself may be thought of as "humanistic" insofar as it seeks to deal with the fundamental human condition of suffering, impermanence, egoism, and illusion. From the Neo-Confucian standpoint, however, Buddhism undermined human values by stressing their relativity, transitoriness, and insubstantiality. Again, where Buddhism sought to deliver man from attachment to the ephemeral and illusory, to transcend change and the painful contingencies of the moral sphere, Neo-Confucianism saw change, not as threatening destruction, loss, and disillusionment, but as containing the potentiality for meaningful life, growth, and maturation. The latter values in turn were affirmed and sustained by the Neo-Confucians on the basis of defined codes of conduct, bodies of learning, and social institutions conducive to human life. Buddhism, if it did not finally deny these values and institutions, at least negated them in the process of passing beyond the karmic sphere of intellectual and moral involvement. Its essential indifference to human relations and social ethics did not preclude tolerance of given value systems, or even qualified acceptance of them, but it did effectively cut the metaphysical ground out from under any positive and final assertion of rational, moral or social imperatives. This Buddhist skepticism the Confucians could not but reject and resist as antithetical to a "humane" human order.

The Neo-Confucian rejection of Buddhism on social grounds is implicit in the first objection. There could be no "restoration" of the ideal social order if there were no basis for it in the moral sphere, and no social morality could be positively affirmed on the shaky ground of Buddhism's essential indeterminism. Similarly, Buddhism's radical critique of culture and its distrust of the intellect led to a process of social and cultural deconditioning which Buddhism insisted upon as a prerequisite to self-discovery and the realization of Buddhahood. To the Neo-Confucians no serious, humane literature could be produced or sustained in the face of such withering skepticism or such indifference to cultural values.

There is finally another affinity to the Western Renaissance implied in the Confucian affirmation of human life and growth just alluded to. From its inception, Neo-Confucianism saw the Way as a dynamic life-force. Sung thinkers quoted the *Book of Changes* to the effect that the essence of the Tao was creativity—its life-producing, life-renewing (*sheng-sheng*)[j] power. "Renaissance" as "rebirth" comes close to the meaning of *sheng-sheng* as life-giving and life-renewing. Though syntactically the Chinese term could not be applied to a particular historical movement like the Sung revival to designate it as a "Renaissance," the centrality of this conception is confirmed by the recurrent theme of renewal in Neo-Confucian social and cultural reform, which suggests that its essential spirit was not too different from that of the Renaissance in Europe.[6]

In the Chinese case, however, the persistent growth and pervasiveness of state power loomed larger on the intellectual scene, and in keeping with Confucian priorities political and social reform commanded greater immediate attention. Not that this was totally lacking in Renaissance Europe—in the vision of a new Rome, in the political humanism and civic patriotism of fourteenth-century Florence, in More's *Utopia* and in sixteenth-century French humanism, there is an approximation of the Chinese ambition to restore the classical age of the Three Dynasties and achieve the Great Society—but there is nothing to match the broad scale of the actual reform movement or the strenuous attempt to remold the Sung dynastic state and redirect it toward humanitarian goals.[7]

It is commonly believed that the historical movement from the medieval to the modern age in Europe brought a shift in thinking away from the supra-mundane, and that the Renaissance issued in a growing process of secularization. Professor Kristeller, however, cautions against too simplistic an interpretation of that process, when he says that ". . . Renaissance thought was more 'human' and more secular, although not necessarily less religious, than medieval thought."[8]

In the case of China we observe at the outset of the Confucian revival a powerful secularizing trend. Indeed its initial effort to mobilize human thought and energies for a radical restructuring of society made the secular state a central focus of Neo-Confucian thought. There was also at this time a reintensification of the trend toward an ever more centralized civil bureaucratic regime, which by the eleventh century brought China politically to the threshold of the "early modern" period, as some historians have designated it.

Parallel to this development, however, we find new spiritualities and new mysticisms replacing the old, and new forms of humanism developing their own religious manifestations. Thus we discover in China a counterpart to what Professor Kristeller describes as the "strongly religious and theological context" of humanism in the Italian Renaissance, as well as striking similarities to the humanists Ficino and Pico who "share with their humanist predecessors . . . a profound concern with man and his dignity; but . . . develop this notion within a framework that was completely absent in the earlier humanists, that is, they assign to man a distinctive position within a well-developed metaphysical system of the universe, and they define and justify man's dignity in terms of his metaphysical position."[9]

In China, such metaphysical speculation developed as one aspect of the Confucian revival in the eleventh century, but was at first overshadowed in importance by the heroic effort to remake society. The model of human cultivation which had exemplified man's active social conscience in this early phase of the restoration is memorably expressed in the statesman Fan Chung-yen's definition of the Confucian noble man (chün-tzu)[k] as one who was "first in worrying about the world's troubles and last in enjoying its pleasures." Here the significant contrast was to the Buddhist goal of nirvana as a spiritual state characterized by peace of mind and freedom from anxiety, or the ideal of the bodhisattva who helped others achieve that state. Fan's noble man, instead of renouncing the world, surrendered his own peace of mind and accepted the demands of a troubled human conscience actively responding to the needs of man.

This heroic ideal—plausible perhaps in the daylight dreams of a new golden age—lost some of its heady quality as political reform foundered on the shoals of bureaucratic factionalism, fiscal difficulties, and military crises. Despite their access to power and the benevolent patronage of Sung rulers, the Sung Confucians had encountered human limitations in the executing of their grand designs. Lest disillusionment end in indifference, apathy or despair, Chu Hsi, in the twelfth century, readjusted and reordered his human priorities. The consequence was his intensification of the effort to articulate a Neo-Confucian metaphysics and to develop a practical system of spiritual and intellectual cultivation, centering on the ideal of the sage, such as I have described in the Unfolding of Neo-Confucianism.

In this process, Neo-Confucianism developed features with a strong resemblance to those Professor Kristeller describes as central themes of Renaissance thought: the dignity of man, the immortality of the soul, the unity of truth. Each of these has a close counterpart in the central doctrines of Neo-Confucianism. Though the second theme is expressed in terms quite foreign to Confucianism, e.g., immortality of the soul, the Neo-Confucians had a religious or mystical view of the self as united with all creation in such a way as to transcend its finite limitations. This is found most characteristically in Neo-Confucian accounts of the attainment of sagehood as an experience of the realization of the true self, based on the doctrine that "humaneness unites man with Heaven-and-Earth and all things."

Although a key feature of Neo-Confucian thought, highlighted in our recent studies of Ming and later seventeenth-century Chinese thought, the nature and importance of this conception of the self, and its relevance to the questions before us are still not generally appreciated. Developing out of the earlier Confucian idea of the unity of Heaven and Man, this view was perhaps most eloquently and memorably expressed in the famed "Western Inscription" of Chang Tsai:[1]

Heaven is my father and Earth my mother. Even such a small creature as I finds an intimate place in their midst. Therefore that which fills the universe I regard as my body and that which guides the universe I regard as my nature. All people are my brothers and sisters, and all things are my companions. . . .

One who knows the principles of transformation will skillfully carry forward the undertakings of Heaven-and-Earth, and one who penetrates spirit to the highest degree will skillfully carry out their will. . . .

Wealth, honor, blessings and benefits are meant for the enrichment of my life. Poverty, humble station and sorrow are meant to help me to fulfillment.

In life I follow and serve Heaven-and-Earth. In death I will be at peace.[10]

According to this Neo-Confucian view, man in his essential nature is identical with all nature (Heaven-and-Earth) and of the same substance as all things. Theoretically, this identity is based on the equating of man's nature or "humaneness" with the life force itself. As we have seen, the fundamental characteristic of the Way is its creativity or productivity, and man too is seen as creative in his very essence.

On this basis one can understand the Neo-Confucian view of the unity of truth as the unity of the principles of all things converging in the Supreme Ultimate. Such a unity was thought to be realizable in the mind-and-heart (hsin)[m] of man through the conjoining of an ideal moral nature with a dynamic physical nature. In developing their metaphysics, the Neo-Confucians, while combating what they believed to be serious errors in Buddhism and Taoism, were prepared to assimilate those of their concepts and practices which they considered reconcilable with

their own conception of man, including contemplative practices as well
as spiritual ideals.

THE NEO-CONFUCIAN SYNTHESIS OF SCHOLARSHIP AND SPIRITUALITY

In the school of Chu Hsi the balance between intellectual and
moral/spiritual cultivation is stated in terms of the "investigation of things
and the plumbing of principle" (ko-wu ch'iung-li),[n] and "abiding in reverence" (chü-ching).[o] For generations of scholars in China and Japan these
were mottoes which summed up the twin aims of the Ch'eng-Chu
school. Chu Hsi also spoke of devoting "half the day to book-learning
(tu-shu)[p] and half to quiet-sitting (ching-tso)."[q] Though his commitment
to the latter was qualified by admonitions against any form of quietism
—Chu recommended a wide range of intellectual, moral, and religious
disciplines to his followers—these two together, book-learning and quiet-
sitting, became accepted in the minds of many Neo-Confucian schoolmen as giving a working definition to the search for principle and the
practice of reverence.

Nowhere is the pervasive influence of Buddhism and Taoism on Chinese spirituality so apparent as in the adoption of quiet-sitting by the
Neo-Confucians, who stood in such strong opposition to them philosophically. It is unlikely that Chu Hsi himself spent half his time in
quiet-sitting, but for him to speak of half the day being spent in contemplative activity gave it a compelling endorsement and wide acceptability. In consequence, Neo-Confucian cultivation became, as I have
explained elsewhere,[11] to a remarkable and unprecedented degree, self-
centered, that is, focused on the individual and carried on in relative
isolation. As a further consequence, this meditative practice led to a deep
interiorization of Confucian cultivation and created an expectation that
some culminating inner experience of self-realization might be achieved
by it.

Despite the philosophical differences among later Neo-Confucians,
especially as regards the dualism of principle and ether or material force,
quiet-sitting was widely engaged in by those schooled in the idea that the
search for principle, even among external things, eventually aimed at the
convergence of objective learning and subjective experience in the con-

templative mind. It became the principal meditative practice through which moral "effort" (kung-fu)[r] was applied to the issuance of conscious thought and will from the subconscious or quiescent ("unexpressed" wei-fa)[s] state of mind, and the practitioner sought to overcome the division of self and non-self, subject and object, or internal and external, through an experience of the unity of principle. This culminating experience of the Supreme Ultimate as both microcosm and macrocosm reconciled the two irreducible aspects of the Way reflected in human nature: its rational, normative, and static aspects with its non-rational, indeterminate, and dynamic aspects.

What emerges from the Sung development then is a wide range of ideas and disciplines, answering to both secular and spiritual needs, upon which the Chinese, and later the Japanese, might draw as these became relevant to their own concerns.

It is significant, however, that Chu Hsi's philosophy, while broadly comprehensive in its synthesis of human experience on several levels, was relatively non-political. It recognized the obligation to serve in government, but dealt with this mainly in terms of the personal ethics of such service (the personal responsibility of the ruler, the personal relationship of minister to ruler, etc.) and had almost nothing to say in its basic primers about political systems, institutions or methods as such.

This reflects neither a lack of interest in politics on Chu Hsi's part nor a lack of awareness of the actual complexities of the problems of government, but rather a deep pessimism with regard to the possibilities for systematic reform. The Northern Sung reformers had failed to restore the "feudal" institutions of the sage-kings, based on personal and familial relationships, or to modify substantially the centralized, bureaucratic structures and impersonal processes of the dynastic system. Chu himself could neither approve the existing order, nor could he on the other hand hope for restoration of the ancient order. He prepared to live with an inescapable situation and rise above it.

Thus, reluctant acceptance of the existing order, rather than commitment to, or consecration of it characterized Chu Hsi's view of the dynastic system. And to this austere philosophy his later adherents generally subscribed. Whether they were involved politically or uninvolved, their goal was to achieve purity of moral character and lofty transcendence of spirit; they did not put their hopes in social programs or political success. Hence, to the extent that scholarship and spirituality, book-learning and quiet-sitting, characterized the orthodox Chu Hsi school, they implied a critical attitude, intellectually and morally, and a detached one spiritually, toward the established bureaucratic order. For this they were criticized by others, and indeed ridiculed, for their pedantry and preciosity.

In Japan, Neo-Confucianism met a different historical destiny, but suffered in the end a similar fate. Though Sung culture and philosophy were already quite accessible to the Japanese by the fourteenth century, Neo-Confucianism did not soon come into its own. There was curiosity about Sung texts and the new metaphysics, but in the great age of Buddhist faith and spirituality spanning the Kamakura and Ashikaga periods, the Buddhist clergy dominated the cultural scene; the Zen monks who served as the purveyors of Chinese learning were careful to present Sung philosophy as an essentially secular teaching, assigned a limited and subordinate role. Only in the sixteenth century did political and social changes create a new, more receptive climate for it, first as the possible answer to the chaos of the Warring States period, and second, after the rise to dominance of the Tokugawa, as an answer to the need for a unified ideology and ethos which would transcend regional and religious differences.

It is not our task here to discuss the historical changes which then occurred in Japan, but we cannot fail to note two significant points. One is the shift in concern which can fairly be described as a movement from a "medieval" spirituality to a premodern secularism, insofar as Buddhism yielded its position of intellectual dominance to Neo-Confucianism.[12] This shift roughly corresponds to the earlier Confucian revival in eleventh-century China. There is a further similarity to the Chinese case in that social and political change brought a new emphasis on civil, and increasingly bureaucratic, rule as opposed to the previous dominance of the military. Nevertheless, the problems of the new Tokugawa polity were sufficiently different—and indeed quite substantially so—from those of Sung China that the specific content of Sung social and political reforms had little relevance for the Japanese. Hence, although we can speak of a new secular outlook generating a powerful interest in Neo-Confucianism, and of a strong intellectual reaction against Buddhism, as occurred earlier in the Sung, the new Tokugawa regime, which proceeded to consolidate its own feudal power in its own way, found an ideological use for Ch'eng-Chu Neo-Confucianism which it could not serve in China. Its ethic based on personal relations found a certain plausibility as a rationale for the Tokugawa regime's feudal pattern of personal and familial relations that it had not had for the bureaucratic regime in China.

MAIN TYPES OF NEO-CONFUCIAN ORTHODOXY

In Professor Masao Maruyama's *Studies in the Intellectual History of Tokugawa Japan*, Neo-Confucianism is presented as a closed and unvarying system of thought which had served as the orthodoxy of an unchanging dynastic state in China. Influenced by an Hegelian (and what subsequently became a Marxian) view of Chinese history and the state as stagnant and unchanging, Professor Maruyama abstracts from Chu Hsi's philosophy and presents a highly structured model of Neo-Confucian orthodoxy which corresponds closely to the pattern of an authoritarian state and social order.

It is a view lent some credence both by the long association of Confucianism with the Chinese state, and that state's efforts to define Confucian orthodoxy for its own purposes. This is especially true of Neo-Confucianism, a mature and highly developed form of the teaching, which grew up alongside of, and indeed in the shadow of, a similarly mature and highly developed system of state power. By extension from this relative stability of dynastic institutions a similar fixity of Neo-Confucian doctrine was often assumed.

In Maruyama's view, however, such a monolithic system was ill-adapted to the different historical situation of Japan. Dynamic and undergoing constant change, Japanese society would never conform for long to such a rigid pattern. The outcome of any attempt to impose such an orthodoxy on Japan was predictable: Neo-Confucianism could only break up and disintegrate. Its rigidity could not withstand the shocks of Japan's tectonic instability, and the restless Japanese would not hold still for such a static world view.

Even in the Chinese case, however, the comparative stability of dynastic institutions was insufficient to guarantee the integrity or fixity of state orthodoxy. It is true that for over half a millennium, from the Ming to the Manchus, the civil service examinations were perpetuated with remarkably little change, with Chu Hsi nominally installed as the authoritative interpreter of the classics. Despite this, however, the leading seventeenth-century scholar Ku Yen-wu fulminated at length over the

infiltration and subversion of the examinations by the heterodox teachings of Wang Yang-ming and his school. At this point one may discern
the helplessness of any formal system, however firmly entrenched, to
resist by simple inertia the spread of vital thought processes set in motion,
not so much by heterodox thinkers, as by "orthodox" philosophers themselves. Wang Yang-ming, after all, was both a traditionalist and a reformer, struggling with the problems left him by Chu Hsi. Even Chu
Hsi's philosophy, non-conformist in respect to the official view of his
time, won acceptance as orthodox in spite of the establishment.

In the Japanese case, moreover, the specific forms of Neo-Confucianism which became influential in the seventeenth century did not
themselves represent a direct inheritance from the Sung. The Chu Hsi
School, despite its later reputation for rigidity, had grown and in some
ways changed. It may have "sat still" but did not stand still. More than
just a dogma serving the purposes of the state, or a hierarchical system
upholding the status quo, it was a system of ideas inspiring further
thought, reflection and reinterpretation. The Japanese exposure to it in
the sixteenth and seventeenth centuries was strongly affected by the more
developed forms in which Neo-Confucian teachings reached them from
Ming China and Korea.

A main purpose of our conference has been to focus attention on these
later formulations, and the papers in this volume deal with major specific
examples. Here I wish to underscore certain general features of the
changes which had taken place, inasmuch as seventeenth-century Neo-
Confucianism in Japan tends to recapitulate Ming thought—learning and
"catching-up" with the latest developments from abroad as the Japanese
have so often done throughout their history.

In Ming China, Neo-Confucian orthodoxy appeared in not just one
but three distinguishable types. First, there was the official state orthodoxy or ideology, which adopted Ch'eng-Chu doctrine chiefly in the
form of commentaries on the classics as a standard for civil service examinations, and promulgated selected Sung texts as authoritative doctrine
while ignoring much else in Chu Hsi's teaching.

Second, there was the philosophical orthodoxy upheld by non-official
schools which identified themselves with Ch'eng-Chu teaching and practice, engaging most notably in the combination of scholarly study and
mind-cultivation (especially quiet-sitting) referred to above. Often the exponents of this second type of philosophical orthodoxy were critical of

prevailing attitudes or at odds with the state authority, as Chu Hsi himself had often been. Thus we find non-conformity to the official system or to current convention as a not infrequent feature of this kind of orthodoxy; Wu Yü-pi[t] in the early Ming and the neo-orthodoxy of the Tung-lin school in the late Ming are examples of this.[13]

Third, there was the sense of orthodoxy upheld by many later Confucians who did not identify the authentic tradition with either the state system or the Ch'eng-Chu school as a sectarian doctrine, and yet, as spokesmen for what they considered to be the mainstream of Neo-Confucian thought, argued for a broader and more liberal view of orthodoxy. This group included many who criticized the Ch'eng-Chu school for its want of political activism and commitment. Admittedly, this third view was less fixed and doctrinaire, but it remains an identifiable alternative tradition *within* the Neo-Confucian movement. Liu Tsung-chou[u] and Huang Tsung-hsi[v] exemplify this in the seventeenth century, and it would be granting too much to his critics not to allow some such claim to Wang Yang-ming, who sought to fulfill the aims of the Sung school and believed himself to be faithful to the import of Chu Hsi's mature thought. We may also include Lin Chao-en[w] (1517–1598) in this classification; while an avowed syncretist, he based himself on the Neo-Confucian mental discipline (*hsin-fa*)[x] and ethical system, and conceded nothing on the score of orthodoxy.[14] Lin's continuing influence in Japan constitutes a link between the various forms of more and less orthodox *shingaku*[y] from Fujiwara Seika[z] to Nakae Tōju[aa] and Ishida Baigan.[ab].

Within both the second and third types we find individual thinkers whose doctrinal emphases or interpretations give a different tone or direction to these philosophical orthodoxies as they pass from one generation to another. And the same is true of their passage to Japan, where all three of the above types of orthodoxy reappear. First, there is the Chu Hsi orthodoxy which became established doctrine through its sponsorship by the Tokugawa shogunate or Bakufu. The same texts are given authoritative status as in the Ming: the Ch'eng-Chu commentaries on the Four Books and Five Classics; to a somewhat lesser degree, the *Great Compendium on Human Nature and Principle* (*Hsing-li ta-ch'üan*)[ac] containing selected texts of the Sung masters on metaphysics, ethical and spiritual cultivation, and ritual matters; *Reflections on Things at Hand* (*Chin-ssu lu*);[ad] the *Elementary Learning* (*Hsiao-hsüeh*);[ae] and the *Outline and Digest of the General Mirror* (*T'ung-chien kang-mu*),[af] Chu Hsi's edited and condensed version of the general history of China by Ssu-ma Kuang.[ag]

As the term "*Bakufu*"[ah] indicates, however, the Tokugawa maintained an essentially hereditary military government, and this difference from the civil bureaucratic system of Ming and Ch'ing China suggests a need for distinguishing between these two types of official Neo-Confucian orthodoxy. For this purpose, the Chinese type might be termed "Mandarin orthodoxy," inasmuch as it represented the ideology and ethos of the bureaucratic Mandarin class and its formal mastery for purposes of the civil service examinations constituted an important qualification for entrance into the ranks of officialdom. In Japan, this examination system did not exist except barely in name, and the largely hereditary officers of the military government or feudal aristocracy did not actually depend on such mastery for their status or success. Neo-Confucian texts served rather as the basis of the curriculum in the official schools at Edo and in the various domains, and for the training of the Confucian advisers and teachers employed by feudal rulers. To identify this type of official teaching we might use the term "Bakufu orthodoxy," distinguishing the military and feudal character of its political setting from the more bureaucratic and meritocratic Mandarin orthodoxy of China. Illustrative of the Japanese case is the hereditary nature of the Hayashi family's position as the official teachers of the Bakufu—something unthinkable in China.

There is much irony in both situations, of course, as regimes so diverse adopted the Ch'eng-Chu texts for educational purposes while largely ignoring the political views of the Ch'eng brothers and Chu Hsi. In China, as a consequence, the texts became enshrined in a bureaucratic examination and recruitment system, of which most Neo-Confucians did not theoretically approve, and in Japan the teaching was entrusted to professional Confucians who had a very limited political role, and were precluded, by the very feudal system they upheld as the ideal, from any kind of political activism.

Both Mandarin and Bakufu orthodoxies held in common, not only basic Neo-Confucian texts but also traditional forms of canonization and ritual observance associated with Confucian temples in both countries. The enshrinement of Confucian sages and worthies was another mode of upholding values for general emulation, and thus, of propagating official doctrine. In Japan, where the incentives of an official reward system channeling education along orthodox lines and attracting ambitions into well-defined roles were lacking, the ceremonial aspects had relatively greater importance as educational instruments.

Even so, Bakufu orthodoxy, as compared to Mandarin, was probably less pervasive in influence, less routine in its workings, and less uniform in its effects. It operated more through personal relationships, at first quite informal, rather than through institutional arrangements. Hence, even among official orthodoxies sharing certain traditional ritual observances and a common scriptural basis, there are significant differences in their institutional setting and style.

As a reflection of these institutional differences, there is also in Japan a somewhat different relationship between the official orthodoxy and the philosophical orthodoxy. The Japanese setting gave more scope to the individual teacher or school as educators and less to routine preparation for examinations as a system. In this circumstance, accidents of personal history and preference came more into play. Sometimes indeed they had a decisive influence on what was taught, what was thought, and what was pursued in the way of scholarly studies. The two leading figures in the original Tokugawa establishment of Neo-Confucianism, Fujiwara Seika and Hayashi Razan,[ai] despite their own teacher-disciple relationship, contrasted markedly in personality and outlook. They also responded quite differently to ideas reaching Japan from Korea at the turn of the sixteenth and seventeenth centuries, as the researches of Professor Abe Yoshio[aj] and others have indicated.

Professor Abe identifies these two types as parallel transmissions of Neo-Confucianism down through the Tokugawa period, the one stressing principle (ri) and the other ether (ki). In the former case, however, principle is not to be understood as static, abstract or rational principle, but as the unitary principle or the dynamic integration of the conscious mind. As such it comes to function as a powerful religious or mystical element, generating a moral and spiritual energy which flows down through this line of transmission into the late Tokugawa period. By contrast, the rationalistic tendency sometimes identified with principle (ri) is actually to be found more often associated with the empirical study of principles in their concrete physical manifestation and, here too, in a dynamic, developmental state.

In terms of the twin Neo-Confucian aims of "exploring or plumbing principle" and "abiding in reverence," we can see how these two strains of Tokugawa thought might evolve, not so much from separate lines of pedagogical transmission, as from the further exploration and adaptation of polar values in the Ch'eng-Chu teaching itself. Principle, having both its objective and subjective aspects, might be studied or pursued in relation to the differentiated worlds either of physical nature or of human affairs, in which case *ch'iung-li/kyūri* could well mean "exploring principle," with the emphasis on extensive investigation, wide experience or broad learning; or it might be pursued in depth, subjectively or experientially, in which case it could be understood as "plumbing principle," stressing the attainment of truth through a more profound interiority or reflective contemplation, whether active or passive. By the same token, "abiding in reverence" could represent an intense concentration, dwelling on the unity of principle, in which case it might become a powerful force activating the individual psyche; or it could express the sense of communion with cosmic forces and the human community as manifestations of the Way, with somewhat less stress on the individual's self-mastery. If, however, Tokugawa thinkers exhibit these differing tendencies in varying degrees, it is usually in some combination which still reflects these basic polarities.

Finally, we note that these alternative interpretations of Ch'eng-Chu teaching have an equal claim to "orthodoxy," as represented by its founding fathers in Japan, Seika and Razan. Each fulfills in different ways the possibilities inherent in the Ch'eng-Chu synthesis. In consequence of this fruitful duality Neo-Confucian orthodoxy in the Tokugawa Bakufu could serve to engender a wide range of Confucian activities in the seventeenth and eighteenth centuries, much as Mt. Hiei with its Tendai synthesis of Buddhist philosophy and religious practice had served earlier as the fountainhead of the new movements which dominated the medieval period.

Most previous characterizations of the so-called "Chu Hsi orthodoxy" in Japan, like Maruyama's, have assumed that it was "pure" at the start of the Tokugawa period—with connotations of dogmatic "purity" and a "medieval" conformity to one fixed authority—and that it subsequently became modified or undermined by modernizing tendencies.[15] In fact, Chu Hsi orthodoxy was pure mainly in the sense of being faithful to the ambiguities of the Neo-Confucian tradition and carrying forward the development of the two main lines of thought which had already appeared in Ming China.[16] It was already furnished with many of the elements of criticism and reevaluation which have been misconceived heretofore as being antithetical to Neo-Confucianism rather than as being in a state of dynamic tension within it.

Though both had Tokugawa sanction, the two main lines of transmission of Ch'eng-Chu philosophy were not confined within the official Hayashi school. Yamazaki Ansai's[ak] school carried on the orthodox "school of the mind" under the patronage of a branch of the Tokugawa family in the Aizu domain, and Ishida Baigan propagated a popular form of this shingaku among the townspeople. Both in its "samurai" and its "commoner" forms this teaching exhibited the strain of rigorism which had become a mark of Ch'eng-Chu orthodoxy in its spiritualistic and moralistic discipline, formally practiced in both the Ansai (Kimon)[al] and Baigan (Sekimon)[am] schools through quiet-sitting.

The continuing importance of this moralistic and spiritualistic type of Neo-Confucian orthodoxy is shown in its sharp interaction with the alternative transmission of a more intellectualized Neo-Confucianism and empirical scholarship, and also in its activist ideology at the end of the Edo period. In fact, both the moralistic and the intellectual tendencies have an element of "practicality"—the one experiential and the other empirical—and neither can be lost sight of in any discussion of Neo-Confucianism and practical learning.

Alongside these trends—"orthodox" in the first and second senses cited above—grew up the brand of shingaku which considered itself, and not the Chu Hsi school, the authentic orthodoxy according to the broader canons of the third type. This movement became identified with the Neo-Confucianism of Wang Yang-ming, but as represented by Nakae Tōju it emerged directly out of and in reaction to the Chu Hsi teaching. Tōju, in effect, rediscovered Wang Yang-ming only after making his own exodus from the formalistic disciplines of the mind along the same spiritual path Wang had travelled in the Ming. While this school was true to much the same sense of "practical learning" as Ch'eng-Chu shingaku, it was less sympathetic to the Ch'eng-Chu ideals of broad learning and empirical investigation on the one hand, and to the practice of reverence through quiet-sitting on the other. Perhaps nowhere else do we find the complementary relation (as contrasted with the antithetical relation) of the "real" (shih; jitsu) and the "empty" (hsü; kyo) so well illustrated as in Professor Yamashita's paper on the practical learning of Nakae Tōju, nor so clear an example of the parallel working out in China and Japan of one type of inner logic in the Ch'eng-Chu synthesis.

Included in these transmissions of Neo-Confucian thought to and within Japan are three active ingredients: one is the original complex of Ch'eng-Chu teaching; another is the extension, clarification, and refor-

Wm. Theodore de Bary

mulation of this teaching in the hands of Ming Chinese and Yi dynasty Korean thinkers; and the third is their continuing development in Japanese hands. We must bear in mind, however, that none of these elements existed in unmixed form, and there was no direct or pure transmission of Chu Hsi philosophy at the beginning of the process. One cannot say that "to present the views of the Tokugawa Chu Hsi scholars would merely be to repeat the statements of the Chinese Chu Hsi philosophers."[17] Before proceeding further, therefore, we do well to review the later trends in Ming thought upon which this hybrid Neo-Confucianism drew.[18]

THE LIVING LEGACY OF MING THOUGHT

I cite for this purpose the following broad trends in the Ming which are essential background elements in the Tokugawa and sometimes intrude directly upon the scene through specific books and thinkers which made a particular impression on the Japanese. These trends include:

1. A decline in rationalistic metaphysics in favor of personal experience of the truth in practice (t'i-jen),[an] including various formal practices, e.g., "quiet-sitting," which fostered a sense of interiority, self-consciousness, and individualism.
2. Emphasis on actual experience (shih-chien)[ao] which involved testing truths in daily life and responding to the needs of one's own time and place by drawing upon traditional values as relevant to the present. Hence:
3. Awareness of the needs of the present and immediate utility (jih-yung).[ap]
4. Awareness of the contemporary situation as irreversibly different from the past, thus heightening the sense of history (especially the distinctive features of recent history) as contrasted to idealization of the past.
5. Vitalism and a sense of the unfailing creativity (sheng-sheng) of Heaven-and-earth.
6. Increasing emphasis on the reality of the physical world (ch'i) and physical self (ch'i-chih),[aq] expressed philosophically in a monism of ch'i and intellectually in the study of principles inhering in concrete forms (e.g., the kind of naturalism and

empiricism seen in Lo Ch'in-shun[ar] (1465–1547) as just one example out of many).

7. A critical rationalism which reflects the influence of both Buddhist skepticism and Neo-Confucian detachment on scholarly inquiry and empirical studies, and also the kind of Weberian "rationality" implicit in Wang Yang-ming's view of knowledge as a process of continuing experience and reevaluation.

8. A deeper humanism, with the above-mentioned critical rationalism helping to overcome some of the more ethnocentric, rigoristic tendencies in early Neo-Confucianism, and encouraging an openness to new experience and a search for the common spiritual and moral ground among religions.

9. A syncretic trend which, in asserting the complementarity and respective contributions of the Three Teachings, helped also to redefine what was most essential in Confucianism.

10. As part of the processes of redefinition implied in 2, 4, and 9, a return to the original essence of Confucianism, away from Sung metaphysics and back to the personal example and teaching of Confucius.

11. A tendency for the original theistic element in the classical Confucian concept of Heaven to reassert itself as against the pantheistic metaphysics of Chu Hsi. (This tendency in late Ming thought proved to have special significance not only for Christianity but for early Tokugawa Confucianism.)

12. A continuing, more intensive study of the classics, both as models (literary and social) and as sources of authority appealed to in philosophical disputes, with a consequent refinement of text criticism reflecting the new awareness of historical, linguistic, and philosophical change.

These attitudes are more fully dealt with in *Self and Society in Ming Thought* and *The Unfolding of Neo-Confucianism*. The list above is meant only to identify specific ways in which Neo-Confucianism grew and changed as it lived out its own values. The combined and cumulative effect of these trends was to fulfill the original impulses of the movement, but carrying certain of these tendencies to their logical conclusions sometimes disturbed the balance of Chu Hsi's synthesis and created great tensions within it.

Against this background we can appreciate how the Neo-Confucian sense of the real and the practical (shih), and of practical experience (shih-chien) might undergo change and development over the centuries. For the Neo-Confucian, the "real" or "practical" was understood, or given a working definition, in relation to other values in the system. One of these, as we have seen, was literary or scholarly study, a value for the Confucian but not an end in itself; carried to an extreme of stylistic refinement or bookish learning, it became divorced from central human concerns and removed from reality. Thus real or practical learning could be juxtaposed to a major component of the cultural tradition as a countervailing effort to redeem it from elegant irrelevancy or vapid pedantry.

In *The Unfolding of Neo-Confucianism*, I have attempted to explain the relationships of both complementarity and opposition between *shih* (real, substantial) and *hsü* (empty). [19] *Hsü*, "emptiness" had for the early Neo-Confucian a useful ambivalence and was not simply a pejorative term. On the positive side it was associated with the prime virtue of reverence (*ching*)[as], in one sense signifying an undifferentiated awe or respect for Heaven and its benign, creative power. Corresponding to this sense of *ching* as reverence was the "empty" reflective state of mind characterized by selfless detachment, openness, and receptivity, and a supra-moral, mirror-like objectivity, which reflected the unconditioned, open-ended aspect of the Supreme Ultimate as infinite (*wu-chi*).[at] The practice of quiet-sitting aimed at achieving such mirror-like receptivity and objectivity, without any preconceptions or distortions. Thus the emptiness of contemplative detachment associated with *ching* could be seen as a precondition for either intellectual objectivity or selfless action. [20] In another sense, however, *ching* connoted intellectual and moral seriousness, attentiveness, or concentration. Corresponding to this was the state of mind characterized as *shih*—"solid," "substantial" or "full" of principles. This latter stood in opposition to Taoist vacuity (*hsü*) and Buddhist emptiness (*k'ung*),[au] both of which were seen as amoral and asocial, that is, as a spurious emptiness flawed by the ulterior motive of self-deliverance from the sufferings of the human world.

Shih, meaning substantial or solid, at first stressed the moral solidity of principles as the prime reality and also the practicality of moral values based on human relations. Later, under the influence of the trends listed above, it came increasingly to emphasize both the experiential and empirical aspects of principles as seen in things and affairs. The receptivity or objectivity which had from the beginning represented a not insignificant value of Neo-Confucianism could then have a different value depending upon the context. And the context differed in the two main lines of Neo-Confucian thought, as well as among different thinkers, depending upon the aspect or the order of principles they were dealing with—ranging from the moral to the supra-moral, and from the practical and empirical to the theoretical or speculative.

In general, however, we may say that the real or solid learning (*shih-hsüeh; jitsugaku*) nurtured by Neo-Confucianism represented a broad spectrum of possibilities, each of which tended to become differentiated from the others as it was explored further. Chu Hsi's own studies were most comprehensive, and could be considered exemplary of real or substantial learning in the several senses of moral solidity, rational coherence, practical effectiveness, and experiential or empirical verification. But as later scholars and thinkers pursued these aims in different historical and cultural situations, it became increasingly difficult to maintain the balance between these different elements of practical learning, and almost impossible to sustain the cultural burden of the past while keeping pace with the demands of historical change, dimly perceived as these often were.

One can detect a shift in the center of gravity from an early emphasis on moral substantiality and metaphysical truth to the pursuit of objective, empirical investigation serving utilitarian ends. Indeed, our translation of *shih-hsüeh/jitsugaku* as practical learning tends to resolve the ambiguity between moral substantiality and functional practicality in favor of the latter, reflecting a broad, long-term trend which perhaps valued tangible benefits more than philosophical fruits. But for the exploratory purposes of our conference it has been more appropriate to preserve, and indeed cultivate, the ambiguity.

The complexities and subtleties of the problem, both as regards Neo-Confucianism and practical learning, are typified by Fujiwara Seika, who, at the outset of the Neo-Confucian movement in Japan, recapitulated in his own life and personal synthesis the successive developments in Sung and Ming Neo-Confucianism: 1) as a former Zen monk, he represents the abandonment of a medieval religiosity for a new spirituality with a strong ethical emphasis; 2) as a sufferer from the violent final paroxysm of the Warring States period, he feels a compelling need for a philosophy and way of life on which to establish peace and construct a new polity; 3) as a consequence both of his personal situation and his exposure to the works of Ming thinkers, he stresses practical utility in everyday life and the subjection of all learning to the test of personal experience; 4) as both ex-Zen monk and Confucian convert, he expresses the need for a synthesis of religious and moral disciplines which would reconcile the claims of moral duty and spiritual freedom (*ching/kei* as both seriousness or concentration on the one hand, and undifferentiated reverence on the other); and 5) as one involved in the international relations of his day (with China, Korea, Annam, and the West), he manifests the universalistic drive to find the common human ground in all teachings and thus to arrive at a deeper humanism.

Seika's synthesis is all the more remarkable in one who stands at the inception of the movement in Japan rather than at its climax or culmination. As a personal achievement his synthesis is indeed impressive. Yet it falls short of attaining a full catholicity or perfect balance among the elements in Chu Hsi's synthesis, and it was left to his follower Hayashi Razan to develop the broad range of scholarly activities, empirical studies, and official duties which had equally been concerns of Chu Hsi.

Seika's conversion to Neo-Confucianism arose from his increasing conviction that it represented "real" or "practical" learning, in contrast to the "emptiness" and insubstantiality of Zen. "The Buddhists take the nature to be empty. . . . We Confucians take it to be real, to be principle, as in the saying [of the *Mean*]: 'what Heaven decrees is called nature,' which is the unmanifest state."[21] The basis for this view lay in Neo-Confucianism's moral concept of man's nature, its applicability to human relations, and its daily utility. But Seika was also aware that the subjective intentions of the individual had a determining effect on what would prove to be "real":

Even the study of "empty words," if pursued with a view to self-discipline and the governance of men so that its effects extend to concrete things and affairs, may represent real action and not mere empty talk. Conversely even the study of "real action" (*jikkō no gaku*)[av], if it is merely given lip-service and superficial thought and is not subjected to the test of practical experience of one's own, becomes empty words and not real action.[22]

In this passage one may see the criterion for practical learning being set by Seika, as it was by other Neo-Confucians of his persuasion, in terms of personal motivation and effective action rather than bookish learning or scholarly investigation. On the basis of this criterion we can understand how even the contemplative practice of quiet-sitting might have been viewed as a valid exercise, preparatory to effective action and more "practical" than any amount of book-learning. Actually, however, Seika's real or practical learning has little to show for itself in terms of either empirical studies or direct political action, and one might even argue that quiet-sitting was not, after all, very far removed from *zazen*[aw] as a practical method. Nevertheless, in the total context of Neo-Confucian humanism and the broad spectrum of values it sought to reconcile, we can still appreciate the historical contribution made by Seika in adapting the latest developments in Ming thought to the many Japanese uses of *jitsugaku* in the seventeenth century.

The studies gathered here present examples of Neo-Confucian thought in China upon which the Japanese drew for their practical learning, and also emerging trends among the thinkers (and schools) of early Tokugawa Neo-Confucianism who sought to articulate what for them was most real, most substantial, and most practical in the teaching. In this process the Japanese demonstrated how readily they could take advantage of their access to Chinese writings of the Ming period and to developments in Korea. As so often in the past, they proved themselves avid learners, entering wholeheartedly into the experience of others and going on to appropriate and adapt it to their own needs.

Previously, the complexity of this process has been underestimated, and misleading conclusions have been drawn from an over-simplified version of early Japanese Neo-Confucianism. Hence, one might well be wary of any generalizations on the subject. As guidelines for further inquiry, however, one may consider the following conclusions drawn from studies reported on here:

First, when the Japanese turned their main attention to Neo-Confucianism, they assimilated quickly not only the original Ch'eng-Chu teaching, but also much that had subsequently emerged in the later conflicted development of Neo-Confucian thought. Their value commitments were made with some awareness of the ambiguities attached and the issues in dispute.

Second, as a reflection of this receptivity and catholicity, Japanese Neo-Confucianism came to exhibit many of the same trends and characteristics pointed to above in the thought and scholarship of the Ming period. Beyond testifying to the remarkable replicative powers of the Japanese, these shared characteristics are suggestive of underlying continuities and a pattern of growth within the Neo-Confucian system which asserted themselves even in the very different historical circumstances of To-kugawa Japan. One can point to distinctive Japanese aspects in any such development, but their singularity can be seen and appreciated only against the background of the comparable Chinese experience.

Third, because Neo-Confucianism was less authoritarian and doctri-naire than has been commonly supposed, far more self-critical, and more productive of dynamic reactivity within the system, one must be con-scious of the give-and-take and of the contending values that compete for attention within the system. Conflict and controversy cannot in them-selves be taken as signs of disaffection or deviation from Neo-Con-fucianism as a whole.

Fourth, once we recognize the existence of alternatives within the tradition, as well as different phases in the development of its central val-ues, we can appreciate how the spread of Neo-Confucianism to Japan presented opportunities for fuller growth in certain areas of thought and scholarship, which the Japanese took to more eagerly than the Chinese.

The case studies which follow are illustrative of these points. Lo Ch'in-shun, the subject of Irene Bloom's paper, is an example of a major Ch'eng-Chu thinker and a principal alternative to Wang Yang-ming in his time, whose influence blossomed out in Japan after he had been largely lost sight of in seventeenth-century China. Lo's brand of ortho-doxy—a revisionist view sympathetic toward Chu Hsi, but constructively critical of him—contributed to the growth in Japan of a practical learning with strong empirical and naturalistic tendencies.

If Lo Ch'in-shun represents a type of orthodox learning in China with an emphasis on objective or empirical rationality, the "Sung" school of the early Ch'ing, which found Lo's critical rationalism uncomfortable, developed along lines more characteristic of the alternative orthodoxy represented in the early Ming by Hu Chü-jen[ax] (1434–1484). The Sung school in late seventeenth-century China has been characterized in one earlier study as marked by an extreme subjective idealism and psycholo-gical interiorization, and in another study by its "pragmatic" and "prac-tical" quality.[23] At variance though these two interpretations might ap-pear to be, they are probably not mutually exclusive; as noted in Seika's case, the psychological discipline (hsin-fa) of the Ch'eng-Chu school had been conceived as both a prelude to moral action and as a retrospection upon it. But the suggestion that this system in China is worlds apart from Tokugawa Confucianism, and that its peculiarly inverted or involuted quality is to be explained by the repressive character of Ch'ing absolutism in a highly centralized autocracy,[24] seems gratuitous when one recognizes the existence in Japan of a close parallel to this moral discipline and spiritual training in Seika himself, as well as in Yamazaki Ansai and Ishida Baigan. These schools exhibited both the introverted and extroverted forms of Ch'eng-Chu teaching. To this extent, they shared a common legacy with Chinese Neo-Confucians but in circumstances so different systemically from the Chinese case as to render the social and political setting of either country a negligible factor in accounting for the common methods of thought and self-cultivation.

Another significant parallel is to be found in the case of Yen Yüan[ay] (1635–1704), long known for his outright rejection of the Ch'eng-Chu system and his advocacy of a practical learning that stressed "pragmatic" action. Chung-ying Cheng attempts herein to show the affinities that exist between both Chu Hsi and Wang Yang-ming and the type of practical learning which ostensibly broke away from them. Professor Cheng's line of argument, stressing the continuities amid the discontinuities of Neo-Confucian thought, is not without relevance to a parallel Japanese development in the so-called school of Ancient Learning (Kogaku)[az]. In the latter case there is a comparable break with the Ch'eng-Chu system of self-cultivation but the Ancient Learning carries forward, as Yen Yüan does not, the "broad-learning," empirical study, and critical rationality engendered by Neo-Confucianism as one aspect of its practical learning.

In both cases, Yen Yüan and the Kogaku, we observe a fundamentalist reaction to Neo-Confucianism in the urge to return to the classical sources of Confucianism as found in both the original texts and the irreducible ethical teachings of the school. Chu Shun-shui, the Chinese expatriate and Ming loyalist who is usually considered the Neo-Confucian godfather of the Mito school in Japan, appears in Julia Ching's study as combining these seemingly opposed attitudes; he was both a follower of the orthodox Ch'eng-Chu school and a fundamentalist whose Neo-Confucian sense of "reverence" or "seriousness" (ching) eschewed the metaphysical speculation of the Sung and devoted itself to the more practical forms of education. In thus pursuing only the practical side of Chu Hsi's teaching, Shun-shui was a typical product of the late Ming (as indeed was Yen Yüan himself) with its preference for concrete action over metaphysical speculation.

Interpretations of Japanese Confucianism have sometimes seen it as expressing a similar preference—spoken of as a "typical" Japanese penchant for action over abstraction and for the concrete over the universal. The case of Chu Shun-shui, however, warns us away from any such facile differentiations between Chinese and Japanese attitudes. There was nothing un-Chinese about Chu or the late Ming style of anti-metaphysical thought which he brought to Japan. If it proved congenial to the Japanese, this in itself evidences a convergence of needs and interests, not a basic divergence in outlook.

The same Confucian virtues, it is true, may have become invested with different values according to the varying social and political circumstances of China and Japan. The loyalism, for example, which Chu, as a symbol of Ming resistance to the Manchus, imparted to the Japanese, no doubt developed differently in the hands of the Mito school than it could in any Ch'ing school under a foreign dynasty or in any society and culture which lacked the vital traditions of clan loyalty still prevailing in Tokugawa Japan. If, however, we are tempted to view this as evidence that the Japanese stressed loyalty to the ruler over filial piety, or that the Chinese, conversely, placed filial piety ahead of political loyalties, such simple contrasts are belied by the cases treated here. Chu Shun-shui, as a Ming loyalist, is not untypical of the Chinese scholars of his time. On the other hand, the Japanese Nakae Tōju, though perhaps not so exclusively motivated by filial devotion to his mother as pious legend would have it, did find in filial piety the primary basis for Confucian reverence, and in turn established the latter as the ground of moral action.

As Professor Yamashita traces the development of Tōju's thought, it becomes apparent that Tōju, instead of simply reflecting the teaching of Wang Yang-ming with which he is usually identified, actually followed his own course of evolution out of the Ch'eng-Chu system, working up to Wang in his excursus from Chu Hsi at the same time that he worked back to Wang through study of his late Ming followers. From either direction, Tōju sought a way out of the more rationalistic and rigid demands of the formalized Ch'eng-Chu system to the underlying sources of Neo-Confucian religiosity as a wellspring of moral action.

A circumstance in Japan which lent itself to this religious development was the lively presence of Shinto tradition. Tōju's own involvement with religion, however, arose from more than simply local circumstance or native tradition. In the Wang Yang-ming school there had continued to be a close relation between religious transcendence and ethical action, that is between "emptiness" (*hsü*) as a creative detachment or vital spirituality on the one hand, and realism or practicality (*shih*) as a commitment to positive action on the other. In this respect the theistic influences and moral activism which Tōju received from the late Ming were quite compatible with Shinto worship, and the two tended to be mutually reinforcing.

In his preface to *Studies in the Intellectual History of Tokugawa Japan*, Professor Masao Maruyama expressed doubts about his own earlier assumption that early Tokugawa Confucianism was as unadulterated as if it had just arrived from China, thus overlooking its genuinely Japanese characteristics:

It is, of course, true that Yamazaki Ansai and his school *claimed* a fierce orthodoxy in their exposition of Chu Hsi's doctrines. . . . But whether or not their own outlook, or their choice of texts or of emphasis, coincided *objectively* with those of Chu Hsi is an entirely different matter. For all their subjective intentions one might, ironically, see the Ansai school precisely as a characteristic illustration of the distance between Japanese Neo-Confucianism and that of China. . . . However, if one starts by bringing out much more clearly how much not only Ansai's Confucianism, but also that of Hayashi Razan who stands right at the very point of departure of Tokugawa Confucianism, rested on essentially revisionist interpretations, one would arrive at a version of Tokugawa intellectual history rather considerably different from the perspective of this book. [25]

Some of the studies presented here do offer such "revisionist interpretations" and new perspectives on Tokugawa intellectual history, but it would be unfortunate if they left one with only a choice of radically opposed Chinese and Japanese alternatives. Both Razan and Ansai represent plausible interpretations of Chu Hsi's philosophy and at the same time variant adaptations of it to the Japanese scene. Ansai's "fierce orthodoxy" has its counterpart in other Ch'eng-Chu schoolmen of China and Korea, and draws upon an authentic strain of idealistic, moralistic rationalism in Chu Hsi's teaching. At the same time, Ansai pays due tribute, as Professor Okada's paper shows, to the need for textual evidence and a close familiarity with the relevant sources, which Chu Hsi too would have insisted upon. None of this, however, prevented the Ansai school from developing its own brand of Japanese nationalism or from selectively emphasizing such doctrines of self-sacrificing loyalty as "the highest duty is to fulfill one's allotted function (*taigi meibun*)[ba]"—a doctrine which does not figure prominently, if at all, in the Neo-Confucian orthodoxies of China. One could argue from this that the *taigi meibun* theory is peculiarly Japanese. More reasonably, however, one could take it as a distinctive Japanese formulation of a religious/moral attitude which finds diverse expression both within and among the cultural traditions sharing the Neo-Confucian legacy.

Later this same religious and moral dynamism was to be a significant force in the thinking of the activists at the end of the Tokugawa period who are referred to in Professor Dilworth's paper. Though it has not been within the scope of the present work to pursue this later development, the renewed vitality and influence of both the Chu Hsi (*Shushi*) and Wang Yang-ming (*Ōyōmei*) schools in nineteenth-century Japan suggest that the practical learning of Neo-Confucianism survived not only in the form of a protoscientific empirical rationalism but also as a radical moral activism which was no less significant a factor in Japan's modernization.

Against this background it is clear that the relation between a changing Neo-Confucianism and an evolving practical learning is not a simple one, but rather a matter of growing complexity over time. Initially almost a synonym for Neo-Confucianism, practical learning became increasingly identified with one or another of its component values or activities as each claimed a higher priority on men's attentions or a greater relevance to the needs of the age. One such prime value in practical learning was moral solidity and practicality. Another was social applicability. Still another was intellectual substantiality, as rational speculation was subject to confirmation by extensive inquiry, broad learning, and concrete evidence.

Both separately and together these tendencies underwent development in the hands of successive thinkers and schools. Each new growth exhibits continuities with, as well as discontinuities from, the past, and since there is no fixed reference point or finished form which can serve as the basis for comparison, it becomes problematical indeed as to what remains "Neo-Confucian" in the successive stages or products of this process.

If there is any criterion which may be usefully applied to such judgments, however, it must be the test of balance, integration, and wholeness. Reality for the Neo-Confucian was to be attained through an integrative process of self-realization based on a synthesis of humanistic (especially philosophical) studies, social action, and personal praxis. To find the unifying thread, the balancing mean, the underlying value or the all-embracing conception remained the fundamental aim of Neo-Confucian teaching. Here the prime symbols are the Sage, as microcosm, model of human integrity, and exemplar of self-fulfillment in action; and the Way, as macrocosm, overarching unity, and ultimate process. As the separate values in the Neo-Confucian synthesis underwent their own development in constantly changing and ever more complex historical and cultural circumstances, their meaning and validity were also tested in relation to such unifying conceptions, which were themselves subject to reformulation in the light of new experiences and modes of perception.

In these studies we have only made a beginning at uncovering and understanding that process. To comprehend further how it relates to the profound challenges of contact with the West and the shocks experienced by modern China and Japan, is a challenge which demands fuller study. Here at least one may find a broader perspective, as well as new inner dimensions, in which to examine it.

34   Wm. Theodore de Bary

NOTES

1. Carmen Blacker, *The Japanese Enlightenment* (Cambridge: Cambridge University Press, 1964), p. 51.
2. *Ibid.*
3. Thomas R. H. Havens, *Nishi Amane and Modern Japanese Thought* (Princeton: Princeton University Press, 1970), p. 167.
4. Paul Oskar Kristeller, *Renaissance Concepts of Man and Other Essays* (New York: Harper Torchbooks, 1972), p. 127.
5. *Ibid.*, p. 7.
6. See Etienne Balazs, *Political Theory and Administrative Reality in Traditional China* (London: School of Oriental and African Studies, University of London, 1965), p. 14; also William S. Atwell, "From Education to Politics: The Fu She," in Wm. Theodore de Bary et al., *The Unfolding of Neo-Confucianism* (New York: Columbia University Press, 1975).
7. Cf. Hans Baron, "Secularization of Wisdom and Political Humanism in the Renaissance," *Journal of the History of Ideas* (1960), 21:144–48.
8. Kristeller, *Renaissance Concepts*, p. 2.
9. *Ibid.*, p. 9. There are, of course, also differences among these conceptions in other respects, as is brought out by Frederic Wakeman, Jr. in his *History and Will* (Berkeley: University of California Press, 1973), pp. 80–81.
10. Adapted from Wing-tsit Chan, *A Source Book in Chinese Philosophy* (Princeton: Princeton University Press, 1963), pp. 497–98.
11. Cf. de Bary, *Unfolding*, pp. 14, 162–72.
12. Cf. Ishida Ichirō, *Fujiwara Seika, Hayashi Razan, Nihon shisō taikei*[bb] (NST), 28:471.
13. See my introduction to *Unfolding*, pp. 19–23, 28.
14. See Judith Berling, *The Uniting of the Ways: The Syncretic Thought of Lin Chao-en*, Columbia University Ph.D. dissertation (Ann Arbor: University Microfilms, 1976), pp. 92–94, 286–87.
15. Cf. Albert Craig's reformulation of the Maruyama thesis in "Science and Confucianism in Tokugawa Japan," in Marius B. Jansen, *Changing Japanese Attitudes Toward Modernization* (Princeton: Princeton University Press, 1965), pp. 155–56.
16. Masao Maruyama, *Studies in the Intellectual History of Tokugawa Japan* (Princeton: Princeton University Press, 1975), p. 33. By failing to take into account the intervening formulations of Lo Ch'in-shun, Yi T'oegye, Lin Chao-en and others who influenced Seika and Razan, Maruyama interprets as pure Chu Hsi thought what has actually undergone considerable development in other hands, and the real issues at stake are sometimes missed. Maruyama concludes that "Razan did no more than present simple explanations of Chu Hsi philosophy" (p. 35), but some of the passages he cites from Seika and Razan as reflecting "the distinctive features of the Chu Hsi school" are virtual quotations from Lin Chao-en of the late Ming. When Ishida cites

the same passages as evidence of the influence on Seika of the Wang Yang-ming school, the confusion is apparent. Actually Lin's *hsin-fa* represents the kind of *hsin-hsüeh* which he synthesized as the common ground between Chu and Wang, so that both Maruyama and Ishida can be both right and wrong! Cf. Ishida Ichirō, *Fujiwara Seika, Hayashi Razan* (NST ed.), 28:420, 440–41.

17. Cf. Maruyama, *Intellectual History*, p. 33.
18. The points which follow are based on my discussion in *Unfolding*, esp. pp. 196–204.
19. Cf. de Bary, *Unfolding*, pp. 184–87.
20. Tomoeda Ryūtarō, *Shushi no shisō keisei*,[bc] (Tokyo: Shunjū-sha, 1969), pp. 58–59.
21. Wajima Yoshio, *Nihon Sōgakushi no kenkyū*[bd] (Tokyo: Yoshikawa kōbun-kan, 1962), p. 296.
22. Fujiwara Seika, "Kokon i-anjo," *Seika sensei bunshū*[be] (NST ed.), 28:82.
23. Jansen, *Changing Japanese Attitudes*, pp. 278–79; Wing-tsit Chan, "The Hsing-li ching-i and the Ch'eng-Chu School of the Seventeenth Century," in de Bary, *Unfolding*, pp. 543–72.
24. Cf. Jansen, *Changing Japanese Attitudes*, pp. 278–79.
25. Maruyama, *Intellectual History*, pp. xxxv-xxxvi.

GLOSSARY

a	実学	am	石門
b	虚学	an	體認
c	啓蒙	ao	実踐
d	津田眞道	ap	日用
e	理氣	aq	氣質
f	実虚	ar	羅欽順
g	復古	as	敬
h	古文	at	無極
i	道文学	au	空
j	生生	av	実行の学
k	君子	aw	坐禪
l	張載	ax	胡居仁
m	心	ay	顔元
n	格物窮理	az	古学
o	居敬	ba	大義明分
p	讀書	bb	石田一郎，藤原惺窩，林羅山，日本思想大系
q	靜坐	bc	友枝龍太郎，朱子の思想形成
r	工夫	bd	和島芳男，日本宋学史の研究
s	未發	be	藤原惺窩，古今医案序，惺窩先生文集
t	吳與弼		
u	劉宗周		
v	黃宗羲		
w	林兆恩		
x	心法		
y	心学		
z	藤原惺窩		
aa	中江藤樹		
ab	石田梅岩		
ac	性理大全		
ad	近思錄		
ae	小学		
af	通鑑綱目		
ag	司馬光		
ah	幕府		
ai	林羅山		
aj	阿部吉雄		
ak	山崎闇斎		
al	崎門		

Chung-ying Cheng

Practical Learning in Yen Yüan, Chu Hsi and Wang Yang-ming

AMBIVALENCE OF PRACTICALITY IN CONFUCIANISM

Confucianism as a philosophy is practically motivated. It is *intended* to apply to practical life and to achieve the moral transformation of man and society. It is therefore practical versus theoretical, where the latter term implies concern merely with theory and speculation. But if one asks whether traditional Confucianism was utilitarian or practical in the sense of leading to the pursuit of modern science or technology, or contributing to social progress and economic advancement, the answer would seem to be negative. Despite the doctrine of the investigation of things (*ko-wu*)[a] and the extension of knowledge (*chih-chih*)[b] in the *Great Learning (Ta-hsüeh)*[c], neither classical Confucianism nor the Neo-Confucianism of the Sung and Ming periods led to the development—whether practical or theoretical—of modern science. The Japanese Sinologist Hattori Uno-kichi flatly stated that Confucianism is neither utilitarian nor positivistic.[1] He maintained that classical Confucianism and Neo-Confucianism in general justify righteous action in terms of virtuous motivation rather than in terms of utility. These remarks point to an apparent ambivalence concerning "practicality" in Confucian philosophy; Confucian philosophy is practical in the sense of being concerned with morality, social interaction, and political activity, but it is not practical in the sense

37

of being concerned with economy and technology. If we may call practicality in the former sense moral practicality and practicality in the latter sense utilitarian practicality, we may say that Confucian philosophy in general is a philosophy of moral practicality but not of utilitarian practicality.

In light of this proposed distinction between two types of practicality in Confucian philosophy, we may first explain "practical learning" (shih-hsüeh)[d] as a phase of Confucian development and then investigate the extent to which it endorses utilitarian practicality and criticizes moral practicality and how it relates or reconciles both. In this article I wish to consider these problems in light of the writings and systems of Chu Hsi[e] (1130–1200) and Wang Yang-ming[f] (1472–1529), who are, as a matter of historical irony, both the source of shih-hsüeh and the target of attack by shih-hsüeh. It is also noteworthy that in the course of Confucianism's development there were some Confucians who conscientiously sought to promote utilitarian practicality at the expense of moral practicality. Hence we have an ambivalence concerning practicality in Confucian thought.

WHAT IS SHIH-HSÜEH?

"Practical learning" (shih-hsüeh) developed in the seventeenth century from a genuine critique of the main currents of Sung and Ming Neo-Confucianism. Even though Chu Hsi and Wang Yang-ming belonged to different schools of thought, they were grouped together as one antipode of practical learning. To understand what practical learning is, and how it developed, it would be best to concentrate on its exposition in the doctrines of Yen Yüan[g] (1635–1704) and Kung Tzu-chen[h] (1792–1841), for Yen Yüan is well-known as a strong critic of Sung and Ming Neo-Confucianism and Kung Tzu-chen as an advocate of enlightened economic philosophy in late Ch'ing Confucianism.

Throughout Yen Yüan's philosophical writings the idea of shih[i] is central and predominant. Shih is not only a matter of moral *practice* or the accomplishment of *actual* deeds, but also a very fundamental principle of the universe—a principle of reality to be witnessed in the activities of all things. He traced this philosophy of shih to pre-Confucian sage-rulers and related what they said and did to their contributions of shih in the universe as well as in society. He said:

Before Confucius and Mencius all those to whom Heaven and Earth gave birth in order to direct the course of events were engaged in practical thinking (language) and practical action (*shih-wen shih-hsing*)[j] and were devoted to developing things of substance and real use (*shih-t'i shih-yung*)[k]. They were thus able to create actual deeds (*shih-chi*)[l] for Heaven and Earth so that people were peacefully settled and production abounded.[2]

This reference to *shih* in thinking (language), action, substance, and use gives a very rich meaning to the term. *Shih* is to be exhibited in all spheres of life; *shih* leads to visible benefits in society; and finally, *shih* is derived from Heaven-and-Earth and is intended to be the path of truth and righteousness. It is in these contexts of *shih* that we can define *shih-hsüeh*. *Shih-hsüeh*, or practical learning, is the learning of thinking (speaking) and doing, both internally with regard to the principle (substance) and externally with regard to the application (use) of principle to produce results beneficial to society at large. Though Yen Yüan himself nowhere suggested this explanation of *shih-hsüeh* as such, there is no doubt that this represents his essential view.

In most cases Yen refers to *shih-hsüeh* as a *verb* phrase rather than as a *noun* phrase. *Shih-hsüeh* is not *practical* learning but learning vigorously through *practice* and for the purpose of practice. In this sense of *shih*, Yen Yüan also speaks of *shih-chiao*[m] or teaching vigorously through actual deeds for the purpose of practice.[3] What one learns or what one teaches is something which satisfies the *needs* of people and society as explained above. In fact, Yen Yüan specified concretely what he considered to be the content of *shih-hsüeh* (as a verb phrase) in his frequent references to the three matters (*san-shih*)[n] and six functions (*liu-fu*)[o] of Yao[p] and Shun,[q] and the six virtues (*liu-te*),[r] six practices (*liu-hsing*),[s] and six arts (*liu-i*)[t] of the Duke of Chou[u] and Confucius. The three matters refer to the rectification of virtue (*cheng-te*),[v] the strong protection of life (*hou-sheng*),[w] and the development of ability (*li-yung*)[x] mentioned in the *Book of Documents* (*Shang-shu*).[y] The six functions (of government) are functions pertaining to the offices of warfare, agriculture, economy, storage, fire and water control, as well as general works mentioned in the *Rites of Chou* (*Chou-li*).[z] The six virtues apparently refer to humaneness (*jen*),[aa] righteousness (*i*),[ab] wisdom (*chih*),[ac] decorum (*li*),[ad] loyalty (*chung*),[ae] and integrity (*hsin*).[af] The six practices appear to refer to language (*wen*),[ag] action (*hsing*),[ah] loyalty (*chung*),[ai] integrity (*hsin*),[aj] filial piety (*hsiao*),[ak] and respect toward elder brothers (*ti*).[al] Finally, the six arts refer to the learning of rites (li),[am] the learning of music (yüeh), [an] the learning of archery (hsieh),[ao] the learning of charioteering (yü),[ap] the learning of history (shu),[aq] and the learning of numbers (shu).[ar]

Though all these subjects had their historically-defined content, when Yen Yüan mentioned them he clearly had logically distinct disciplines in mind. The three matters of the Book of Documents are the guiding principles for his shih-hsüeh. The six arts are applications of these principles in the education of a person. Performance of the six functions is, of course, to be expected from a government and its functionaries.[4] But these delineate areas in which the Confucian scholar should place himself. The six virtues and the six practices are matters of moral practicality which are as important as the utilitarian practicality of the six arts and the six functions. They are all important in the actual ordering of Heaven-and-Earth (shih wei t'ien-ti)[as] and nourishing of the ten thousand things (shih yu wan-wu).[at][5] Borrowing the categories of "inner" and "outer" frequently used in Confucian philosophy, we may describe the six arts and six functions as pertaining to the outer activities of a person and the six virtues and six practices as pertaining to the inner cultivation of a person. We may further suggest that what we call utilitarian practicality pertains to the outer requirements of learning while what we call moral practicality pertains to the inner requirements of learning. Understood in these terms, we can see that Yen Yüan set forth a clearly adumbrated program of shih-hsüeh, in which learning (hsüeh) was pursued both for the purpose of shih[au] and toward the goal of shih. This is the thesis of his essay (Ts'un-hsüeh pien)[av] (On Preserving Learning):

[I] authored the essay "On Preserving Learning" to illuminate the way of the three matters, six functions, six virtues, six practices and six arts of Yao and Shun, the Duke of Chou and Confucius. My main purpose was to point out that the Way (truth) does not lie in the text of the Shih [ching] and the Shang [shu] and that learning does not lie merely in understanding and awakening through reading but that one should follow the Confucian school in acquiring wide knowledge and in restraining oneself through ritual so that one can substantially study (shih-hsüeh) and actually practice what one learns, without idleness throughout one's life.[6]

From this solid ground of shih-hsüeh thus defined and described, Yen Yüan launched his criticism of Buddhism, Taoism, and the Neo-Confucianism of Chu Hsi, Wang Yang-ming, and their followers. He attacked them for their doctrine of emptiness (k'ung)[aw] and their attempt to "cut off all practical learning" (tuan-chin shih-hsüeh).[ax]

Yen Yüan contrasted *shih-hsüeh* with the "learning of letters" (*wen*)[ay] on the one hand and with the "absence of learning" (*yeh*)[az] on the other. The learning of letters is the study of conventional, empty, and soulless texts and dogmas, of meditation manuals, or of commentaries and compositions to meet the requirements of the civil service examinations. The content of such learning was considered by Yen Yüan to be dominated by the canonized teachings of Sung and Ming Neo-Confucianism and to contain Ch'anist ideas associated with Wang Yang-ming and the Taoists as well as the Buddhists. These teachings were branded as contrary to *shih* because, in Yen's eyes, they were different from what was practiced by the sage-kings, Confucius, and Mencius, and irrelevant to the needs of life and society. On the other hand, the absence of learning is a state in which learning and civilization are abused and abandoned. In this light, practical learning stands out as a logically necessary and substantially sound form of inquiry and investigation. It is not confined to the superficial recitation of dogmas for the purpose of pleasing authority or seeking appointment in the government. It is not useless, body-weakening and mind-emaciating word-exercises. And it is not empty metaphysical talk of quiet-sitting which does not contribute to reforming the affairs of state and society. Rather it is the search for knowledge of things which one can apply in actual life for the advancement of the social good or at least for the strengthening of one's own spirit and body. It involves study of the fundamental principles of history and the cosmos in the original Confucian texts as well as in the original spirit of the sage-kings and Confucius.[7]

Yen Yüan established an historical perspective on the need for practical learning. He thought that if there were too much learning of letters in a society, the people of that society might rebel against it and overreact by way of violence and suppression of the thought, education, and culture which are associated with letters (*wen*). *Shih-hsüeh*, therefore, is required in order to prevent the irrational overthrow of culture due to an excessive concern with letters; its development is intended to forestall such an historical crisis. From this perspective practical learning represents a genuine mean between too much learning of letters and the complete abandonment of civilization. If promoted in a timely manner, it will meet the needs of society and history.[8] This seems to suggest a characterization of two domains of *shih-hsüeh*. For one thing, *shih-hsüeh* is the learning of *shih*[i] as contrasted to *hsü*[ba] (empty), implying the mere study of words and meditation on texts. For another, *shih-hsüeh* concerns things (*wu*)^{bb} and affairs (*shih*)^{bc} and therefore knowledge and technology (*i*)^{bd} bearing on things. It is also learning for the purpose of practice and working for the good of society.

Yen Yüan, as he himself testified, worked on the doctrines of the Ch'eng brothers and Chu Hsi when he was thirty. But three years later, after his grandmother passed away, he was awakened to the truth of Mencius' doctrine of the goodness of human nature, and he decided that the teachings of Chu Hsi and the Ch'eng brothers were not genuinely Confucian. It was then that he started to formulate his doctrine of *shih-hsüeh*. Though he frequently referred to the Neo-Confucian dialogues of Ch'eng-Chu and Lu-Wang, he chose to criticize and comment explicitly on the views of the Ch'engs and Chu Hsi in his *Ts'un-hsüeh pien* and his *Ts'un-hsing pien*^{be} (On Preserving the Nature). Generally Yen approved of Chu Hsi's criticisms of the Buddhists, the Taoists, and the school of Lu Hsiang-shan (and thus, by implication of the school of Wang Yang-ming). But he insisted that the Ch'eng brothers and Chu Hsi themselves were not exempt from the charges of emptiness, triviality, speculativeness, arrogance, and non-practicality which they levelled at the Lu school.[9] The following quotation gives a sample of such criticism of Chu Hsi:

If we compare the theory and practice of Chu Hsi with those of the classical Confucians, we see that they are radically different. It may appear that Chu Hsi is too strong on *chih*^{bf} (knowledge of theory) and too weak on practice. But in point of fact, [Chu Hsi] is weak not only on practice (*shih-hsing*),^{bg} but also on theory . . . We must deplore (his doctrine of) quiet-sitting (*ching-tso*)^{bh} and mental concentration (*chu-ching*)^{bi} as it leads to quietude and uselessness (*chi-shou wu-yung*)^{bj}.[10]

In order to accentuate his teaching of *shih-hsüeh*, Yen transformed the well-known motto of the Han Confucian, Tung Chung-shu,^{bk} "Follow righteousness without pursuing utility; illumine the Way without calculating the success" into "Follow righteousness in order to pursue the utility; illumine the Way in order to calculate the success."[11] Evidently, what Yen refers to as utility (*li*)^{bl} and actual results (*kung*)^{bm} are things that bear on the actual improvement and advancement of social welfare in terms of the functioning of government and the contribution of individuals. They form the subject matter of Yen Yüan's utilitarian practicality of *shih-hsüeh*.

In order to give a more contemporary meaning to what Yen Yüan called *shih-hsüeh*, one may look at his list of important subjects of study in the curriculum of an educational academy.[12] There are four categories of subjects 1) the humanities: writing, music (arts), history, arithmetic, astronomy, geography, etc.; 2) the martial arts: strategies of the Yellow Emperor, Chiang T'ai-kung,[bn] and Sun Wu,[bo] defense and attack tactics, warfare on water and land, archery and charioteering, shooting and boxing, etc.; 3) the classics and history: the thirteen classics, dynastic histories, edicts, memorials, poetry, and (Confucian) prose, etc.; and 4) technology and science: study of water, study of fire, engineering, geometry, etc. Hou Wai-lu[bp] suggests that the first category corresponds to pure science; the second, to military science; the third, to social science; and the last, to technical science.[13] That these categories exclude metaphysical subjects such as the study of *li*[bq] (principle) is also striking. Lest we be misled by a description of practical learning which excludes metaphysical studies, we may recall that, in practice, Yen Yüan did not ignore philosophical or metaphysical thinking. He developed a metaphysics[14] of practical learning in order to encourage as well as to justify the concern with and promotion of practical learning.

About one hundred and fifty years later Kung Tzu-chen succeeded Yen Yüan in promoting the development of practical learning as a cure for the social and political evils of his time. Kung was more violent and direct in attacking the politics and society of his time because his time had seen more troubles arising from administrative callousness and social stagnation. Though he did not single out the Neo-Confucianism of the Sung period as a target of attack, he strongly criticized the examination system (*k'o-chü*),[br] which was largely based on the Sung learning, at least in part on the ground that it stifled talent and led to nothing but plagiarism and empty talk.[15] Kung did not openly acknowledge any indebtedness to either the Chu Hsi or Che-tung schools. His writings are characterized by constant references to classical sources and a relative lack of interest in Sung scholarship, a fact which may reflect the influence of the Ch'ing textual style (*hsün-ku hsüeh*)[bs] practiced by his maternal grandfather Tuan Yü-tsai.[bt] More than Yen Yüan, Kung focused his attention on matters of economic and social reform for the well-being of the people and thus advanced a strong utilitarian philosophy to meet the challenge of his time, a philosophy which anticipated the doctrine of enriching the nation and strengthening the army (*fu-kuo ch'iang-ping*)[bu] advocated by Yen Fu[bv] (1853–1921) at the end of the nineteenth century. With the object of enriching the people, he promoted the redistribution of land, the breaking of commercial monopolies, and the lowering of taxation.[16] With the object of strengthening the army, he suggested the establishment of provincial administration for the Western Regions of China and promoted migration from inland areas to the Western Regions.[17]

Though the term "practical learning" was not much used, in Kung we see two important features of practical learning in the nineteenth century. First, with the waning of the thought of the Chu Hsi school, practical learning came to be tied up with the development of the Kung-yang learning (*Kung-yang hsüeh*)[bw] in the New Text school (*chin-wen hsüeh-p'ai*).[bx] Though we cannot elaborate here on the history of the struggle between the New Text school and the Old Text school (*ku-wen hsüeh-p'ai*),[by] it is apparent that from the end of the seventeenth century until the end of the eighteenth century the search for universal and deep meaning in the Confucian classics lent itself to the search for applications of the classics to the political and economic problems of the time, and thus to the rejection of the historical and textual philological research endorsed by the Old Text school. Kung Tzu-chen distinguished three stages in the history of Confucian learning. The first stage he called the stage of order; the second, the stage of disorder; and the third, the stage of disintegration. With regard to the stage of order, he said:

This way of harmony and happiness between the ruler and his ministers and the people, this study of the sage-kings and Confucian writings in order to bring out truth, and this actual establishment of social and political order are indeed one.[18]

His distinction of these stages of Confucian learning led to K'ang Yu-wei's[bz] (1858–1927) theory of "three periods," again based on the Kung-yang learning. This means that practical learning was still embedded in and justified on the ground of classical Confucian writings. Second, a study of Kung's time and of subsequent Chinese history shows that economic, social, and political conditions in China and aggressive pressures exerted on China by the Western powers combined to create a crisis which led to the ever-growing criticism and abandonment of Sung and Ming Neo-Confucianism on the one hand, and to the ever-increasing need for practical learning as a means of national and cultural survival on the other.

To summarize briefly, practical learning in the seventeenth and eighteenth centuries was not a simple phenomenon but had its own development and combined many factors. It ran counter to earlier Neo-Confucian philosophy and yet was related to it in complex ways. It was also a product of the crisis of eighteenth-century China. It therefore has both a theoretical and an historical significance. Accordingly, any study of practical learning must specify in which respect it is to be understood.

CAN ONE DEDUCE SHIH-HSÜEH FROM LI-HSÜEH?[ca]

Even though Yen Yüan's shih-hsüeh resulted from a strong reaction against Sung and Ming Neo-Confucian philosophy, it is nevertheless not clear in what fundamental way his shih-hsüeh is incompatible with Neo-Confucian philosophy. I wish to show that in the case of Chu Hsi and Wang Yang-ming shih-hsüeh is not theoretically incompatible with their philosophies, and that, given appropriate conditions, shih-hsüeh might, in fact, have been generated from their philosophies. But this is not to say that the Chu school or the Wang school saw the possibility of this generation, or that it could have taken place in the absence of external stimuli, or without the criticism of certain tendencies in the doctrines of Chu and Wang which inhibited the development of shih-hsüeh. Thus we can understand shih-hsüeh as having originated in Neo-Confucianism, but having produced no radical change of a theoretical nature in its metaphysics or ethics.

In the case of Chu Hsi, it can be shown that, in spite of his metaphysical speculation concerning li (principle) and ch'i[cb] (material force or vital nature), his philosophizing about how to investigate things in terms of knowing li, and his predilection for bookish knowldege without sufficient stress on practical application in life and society, the essentials of practical learning are present in his views and in this sense generable from his philosophy. Thus it can be shown that the attack on Chu Hsi's Neo-Confucian philosophy (Chu-hsüeh) by the later practical learning school cannot be philosophically valid if, by Chu-hsüeh, Chu Hsi's own philosophy is intended. It will also be clear that it does require a special cognitive focusing to derive shih-hsüeh from Chu-hsüeh and that, historically, in the absence of such special cognitive focusing on the part of Sung and Ming Neo-Confucians, shih-hsüeh failed to develop from Chu-hsüeh. As explained above, shih-hsüeh presupposes an understanding of shih, a concern with the problem of shih, and a responsiveness to the social needs of the time. It was only the social and political changes in the eighteenth century that made possible the special focusing required for developing *shih-hsüeh* from *Chu-hsüeh.*

To appreciate how *shih-hsüeh* is potentially present in Chu Hsi, we shall first of all focus on the similarity between *shih-hsüeh* and *Chu-hsüeh* in their common criticisms of impractical, irrelevant, and empty subjects of learning and study. As we have seen, advocates of practical learning regarded textual criticism and the study of letters and prose for the purpose of the civil service examinations not only as a waste of time, but as a pursuit which resulted in weakening the will of the mind. Similarly, Chu Hsi endorsed the view that the study of prose and textual criticism for the purpose of the civil examinations was of no value for attaining the truth. Thus he said:

What is called learning starts with being an intellectual (*shih*) and continues in learning to become a sage. I-ch'uan[cc] (Ch'eng I) says one can learn three ways: learn prose, learn textual criticism, and learn the doctrine of Confucius. If one wishes to understand truth (*tao*),[ed] there is no other way but learning the doctrine of Confucius.[19]

Chu Hsi deplored the degrading effects of learning for the sake of passing the civil examinations, which deprived men of a higher purpose in life and precluded the concentration of mind on the search for principle and righteousness. Chu Hsi keenly observed that the study of prose writing for civil examinations was demoralizing. The innate sense of righteousness in a man disintegrated, and selfishness and personal gain became the goal of life. He said:

Thus in regard to learning ancient and present things, and in regard to matters of right and profit, one will fail to make a distinction and will fail to see what is proper and what should be done. Thus even though a person may be well-read and expert in literary composition, this will merely serve to harm his mind. One must reverse this. Then one can talk about the right method of learning.[20]

Chu was similarly opposed to empty talk and empty thinking which did not focus on actual and useful matters of life. By this he meant far-flown thinking which is not applied to life and practice or is inapplicable to society. It was on this ground and on the ground of their failure to give up their attachment to self-interest that Chu Hsi opposed Buddhism and Taoism and strongly defended Confucianism as the most just and balanced doctrine for man. He said:

In learning one should not become far-flown and high-sounding. One need only pay attention to one's words and conduct (practice) so that one will be substantial. Nowadays when scholars talk of truth (tao), they only talk of principle (li), but do not talk of things (shih); they only talk of mind, but do not talk of body. The talk is profound, but there is no evidence for its truth. It lapses into emptiness and heterodoxy.[21]

In saying this, Chu Hsi of course did not mean to reject inquiry into li as a proper subject of study. Rather, he was suggesting that when one studies li one should study it in connection with concrete affairs and things. This was what he called shih. "Profound" thinking divorced from concrete affairs and things and separated from practice was, according to Chu, nothing but "high illusion" (kao-huan).[ce22] It is evident that practical learning is directly opposed to high illusion.

A positive account of Chu Hsi's theory of learning and knowing will bring out even more clearly the affinity between Chu's teaching and practical learning. A first principle of Chu Hsi's theory of learning is that learning must embody reference to actual reality and must incorporate and command practice. In other words, learning is not something to be separated from the intimate concerns of one's nature, nor from things that one may use in developing one's nature or in realizing the principles of things. Chu Hsi was opposed to mere practice without the learning of principle just as he was opposed to mere learning of principle without practice. Thus he said:

If one has understanding but does not practice what one understands, then one's understanding has no use. It is empty understanding only. If one merely does things without understanding, then doing things will have no goal, it is blind activity only.[23]
Knowing and practice are mutually dependent, as eyes without feet cannot walk, feet without eyes cannot see. In terms of priority, knowing should be first. In terms of importance, practice should be more important.[24]

Thus learning is clearly conceived by Chu to have the objective of applying to life and concrete reality and yielding results useful to society or to one's self-realization. In this perspective, learning for Chu should be practical and concrete (shih), just as it should be for Yen Yüan. Specifically, Chu Hsi defined learning as "[That process] in which one seeks knowledge and know-how where one does not know or where one lacks know-how."[25] If one has known something or learned a certain ability to do something, one can put one's knowledge and one's ability into practice. This was what Chu called "review of one's learning (hsi)".[cf26] Both learning and the "review of learning" are comprehensive and unlimited in scope and thus do not exclude anything which the practical learning *admits* or promotes. Thus Chu Hsi said:

In learning it is vitally important frequently to review what one learns. It should always be uppermost in one's mind and thinking. There is nothing that one should not learn, no time at which one should not learn, nowhere that one should not learn.[27]

Perhaps one difficulty with this approach to learning is that it is too broad and diffuse, lacking a point of focus and thus a sense of urgency. The issue therefore is not that it does not include the subjects of practical learning but rather that it does not single out the subjects of practical learning for special attention.

Another difficulty of this approach to learning is in connection with Chu Hsi's constant reference to the study of the ideas and writings of ancient sages. In this sense learning is more retrospective than prospective. It is in practice, though not in principle, very much confined to Confucian subjects of learning, such as how to develop one's nature and how to pacify the world and serve the ruler in a correct and upright way. If that is the practical usefulness intended by Chu Hsi, then there is indeed a contrast between the goals and methods of Chu Hsi's learning and those of practical learning as represented by Yen Yüan and Kung Tzu-chen. Whereas Chu Hsi wished to see learning aim at self-cultivation and the making of a sage, the paramount end of practical learning as a whole was the strengthening of the state. It was therefore a delimitation of the Confucian theory of learning through self-cultivation as promoted in Chu Hsi's philosophy. Chu Hsi characterized his theory of learning in the framework of the *Great Learning*:

If one reads, exhaustively explores principles, and broadly studies the prescribed teachings of sages and worthies in the past and the present, the learning will be practically useful.[28]

Learning is not identical with reading. But without reading one could not know the way of learning. The sages only teach man to make sincere his intentions, rectify his mind, cultivate his person, regulate his family, govern well the state, and pacify the world. What is called learning is to learn this. Without reading, one does not know how to cultivate his person, or how to regulate his family or govern the state.[29]

Since learning is conceived to be guided by the principles of the *Great Learning*, it is apparent that learning cannot be as freely extended as was originally intended by Chu Hsi. When taken together, Chu Hsi's theory of *li* and his integrated theory of *ko-wu* (investigation of things) and *chih-chih* (extension of knowledge) yielded a conception of learning such that ultimately learning becomes a matter of seeking understanding of *li*, not a practice of life to promote useful results, as Chu Hsi appears to claim. Chu Hsi's stress on learning to understand *li* cannot be underestimated. This stress, I believe, constituted an obstacle for the school of practical learning which they criticized severely and ultimately rejected. Consider the following statements of Chu Hsi:

It is through learning that one encounters *li* in one's life. Without learning one will not be able to see *li* in its perfection, in its large scope, and in its accurate detail.[30]

If one's mind becomes familiar with learning, then one naturally will see wherein *li* lies. If one's mind becomes familiar with learning, then one's mind will be subtle and perceptive. If one's mind does not see *li*, it is because one's mind is still crude.[31]

Once Chu Hsi introduces this theory of *li*, his general doctrine of learning becomes removed from his original idea of practical applicability to life and society. This is so because *li* is considered to be basically inherent in one's mind. *Li* is the nature which a person's mind becomes aware of in the process of his learning. Learning therefore ultimately serves the purpose of achieving self-awakening in a person. Self-awakening, while an important aspect of sagehood, is nevertheless subject to Buddhistic interpretations.

Learning does not grow outside but is originally innate in oneself. Yao and Shun derived it from their nature, and *li* was not lost. T'ang and Wu returned to it, losing it somewhat but succeeding in restoring it to one's good nature. Learning is only restoring *li* to one's old nature (*fu ch'i chiu-hsing*).[cg][32]

If learning is only "restoring *li* to one's old nature," then learning cannot really be directed toward the outside, and thus remains metaphysical as well as moralistic. Thus learning has its main effect in transforming one's temperament (*ch'i-chih*)[ch] so that one can enter the truth (*tao*). Chu Hsi advised:

In the beginning of one's learning with great effort, one should inquire and think and practice, then one can transform one's temperament and enter the *tao*.[33]

Learning then becomes inward and a matter of cultivating one's character, not outward and a matter of transforming the society into an eco-
nomically better one.

"Practice" (*hsing*), in Chu Hsi's usage, is a matter of close observation
of *li* in life, not a devotion to seeking solutions for the social problems of
the time. It is therefore neither genuinely "practical" (*shih*) practice nor
practice of *shih* in its social and economic sense. Certain difficulties may
have prevented Chu Hsi's doctrine of learning from actually developing
into practical learning, and may, in fact, have created serious misunder-
standings and caused Chu Hsi's followers or commentators to espouse a
doctrine or adopt a practice which the advocates of the later practical
learning criticized. We must, nevertheless, do justice to Chu Hsi's theory
of learning by recognizing its original intent and its flexible scope, which
are highly compatible with the theory and practice of practical learning.
We must reiterate that, given suitable social stimulation, it is conceivable
that Chu Hsi's theory of learning would have been conducive to the development of practical learning. As evidence for this assertion we may
again quote Chu Hsi to indicate his understanding that learning includes
practical and useful studies and incorporates precisely the subjects which
practical learning earnestly sought to promote.

In talking about learning and studying for governing oneself and others, there are
many things to learn. As to astronomy, geography, the principles of rites and
music, military science, and penal codes, all are subjects of study characterized
by practical usefulness. The study of them is not outside what one should do. In
ancient times men were taught the six arts (*liu-i*) in order to develop their minds.
They were taught just for this purpose. When compared with empty word-play
and document-compiling, the great merit of the former and the great demerit of
the latter cannot be measured.[34]

Of particular interest in this passage is Chu Hsi's mention of the six
arts as subjects of teaching and learning. No one will doubt that these
words could have been written by a staunch advocate of practical learning
such as Yen Yüan or Kung Tzu-chen.

Though Chu Hsi used the word *shih* on many occasions and in many
contexts, such as, "Sincerity is *shih*" (*ch'eng shih shih*),[ci] and "Sincerity is
the principle of actuality" (*ch'eng shih li yeh*),[cj][35] he generally meant by
shih the truthful principle or the real principle of things. *Shih* in this
sense is clearly tied up with his doctrine of *li*. But to my knowledge there
are at least two occasions when Chu Hsi used the term *shih-hsüeh* not in

connection with the study of *li*, but in a context which suggests that *shih-hsüeh* connotes social and political application. In a memorial to the throne written, when he was sixty-seven years old, in connection with his proposal to compile and edit the ancient documents on rites (*li*), the *I-li*, [ck] he said: "By compiling and editing these, we may expect to preserve what is deserved so that it may last forever, and so that students of the future may know *shih-hsüeh*. Sometime it may serve as an aid to the establishment of institutions for the society and state." [36] And on another occasion Chu Hsi remarked:

If one takes passing the civil service examination as a means for supporting one's parents and undertakes no learning for one's cultivation, it shows that one lacks a good ideal. If one considers passing the examination as hindering *shih-hsüeh*, would he also consider it as hindering eating and drinking? This merely shows one's lack of an ideal. [37]

Thus, *shih-hsüeh* is clearly intended to bear on the ordering of society and the governing of the state, and therefore acquires a sense which is not remote from *shih-hsüeh* in Yen Yüan's philosophy. In this connection it is interesting to note that Chu Hsi is the first major Neo-Confucian to apply the significant and suggestive term *shih-hsüeh*. [38]

HOW PRACTICAL-MINDED WAS CHU HSI IN HIS POLITICAL LIFE?

Chu Hsi had a long and eventful political career of forty-seven years, but it appears that he did not wield any significant power or influence in national affairs. On the contrary, he frequently became a target of abuse and persecution for those who opposed his teachings or his orthodox Confucian approach, characterized by a sense of righteousness, candor, and public-mindedness. [39] There are two important facts in Chu Hsi's political career which are worthy of special mention and explanation. First, Chu was in a general way very much concerned with establishing schools for higher learning. During his administration of Nan-k'ang[cl] between 1179 and 1180, Chu undertook to restore the White Deer Grotto Academy and caused it to flourish. He was also known for his relief work, including the establishment of a communal loan granary as a measure for relieving famine. This shows that Chu Hsi was an able and competent administrator who always had the economic and moral welfare of the people in mind. Second, Chu was not slow to petition the throne for political reform on matters which he regarded to be of national importance. In his memorials he was very candid and voiced his views on many affairs in the interests of the government and people. His attempt in his *Wu-shen feng-shih*cm Petition of 1187 to rectify weaknesses of the Emperor is well-known. He acted as a teacher and guide to the throne but chose to retire when his advice remained unheeded.

It is clear that Chu Hsi generally put into practice what he believed in good faith and that he truly acted as a conscientious Confucian statesman both in relation to his ruler and to the people under his care. To say this is to say that he was practical-minded and not merely a speculative philosopher. One may also conclude that his learning and philosophy of *li* did not prevent him from taking a practical attitude toward the concrete affairs of society which was consonant with the utilitarian practicality of *shih-hsüeh*.

In order to determine whether Chu Hsi's philosophy actually contains the utilitarian practicality of *shih-hsüeh*, one should inquire into what Chu Hsi thought about methods of government and what ideas he had regarding the managing of government. If by the utilitarian practicality of *shih-hsüeh* we ultimately mean ordering the state, stabilizing the society, and benefiting the people through economic welfare and educational guidance, then our assessment of Chu Hsi's political thought should to a large extent determine our assessment of whether his learning and philosophy possessed this practicality or not.

It is true that Chu Hsi's attitude toward practice is not a utilitarian one. He subscribed to Tung Chung-shu's maxim, "Follow righteousness without pursuing the utility; illumine the Way without calculating the success." In this view, to follow (do) righteousness is part of knowing righteousness which does not require procuring actual benefit; and to illumine the Way is part of understanding the Way which does not require demonstration in social, political, or economic success. Chu cautioned that:

One should carry out one's plans in a fair and upright way; whether they succeed or not is decided by Heaven. Some men in the past succeeded not because they had intelligence, but because of coincidence. All unnecessary devices, efforts, and intricate calculations are of no help, and are all in vain.[40]

This attitude toward action of course does not mean that Chu Hsi was completely indifferent to consequences. But it does mean that he thought one should do his best and not let the possibility of failure deter him from doing so. It also implies that one should employ righteous methods for arriving at a righteous goal. Yet these two principles should not be construed as implying that once motivation and actual practice are rectified practical consequences are not relevant in judging the value of a teaching or a doctrine.

Chu Hsi took governing a state as a serious matter. He seems to have been suggesting three basic measures for achieving good government. First, he urged that ministers should "invite the able and sagely, reject the vicious and crooked, and open their minds to all men under Heaven in order to secure order under Heaven."[41] Second, he urged that the ruler should be unselfish and public-minded and rectify his mind so that he could listen and get close to the righteous and separate himself from the small man. And finally he believed that, "Learning and clarifying the true meanings and principles of things will enlighten the minds of the people and enable more people to know principles, and thus one need not worry about failure in government."[42]

Chu Hsi truly followed Confucius when he asserted that, in order to govern well, one has to start with rectifying one's mind and making sincere one's intentions.[43] But when he held that one should investigate things and extend knowledge by clarifying principles, he not only advanced the thesis of the *Great Learning* but promoted his own thesis of learning *li*. Chu Hsi concluded that government depends on the existence of good persons and that a good system is not sufficient.[44] In this regard he was not conservative and did not accede to the ancients on the question of what is good, but defended what is good on its own merits. Thus, when questioned about it, he did not defend the well-field system (*ching-t'ien chih*)[cn] or the system of feudal establishment (*feng-chien*).[co]

In his own philosophical remarks, Chu Hsi showed great concern with concrete matters of administration. Here I will merely give a few illustrations from his sayings. In regard to the role of magistrate, he said:

If one takes the job of a county magistrate, it is proper for one to administer legal justice, eliminate robbery and theft, encourage farming, and suppress indecent activities.[45]

Chu Hsi similarly showed great sensitivity to what was needed in terms of public measures for the benefit of the state and the society. In regard to the economic burden of the people in his time, he said:

Today people are poor because the subsistence of the army is a financial burden
[for people]. [The government should] adopt the policy of settling soldiers to cultivate land in order to lighten the burden of the people.[46]

He also recommended adoption of other measures for improving the
economy:

Today [the people are] poor. [In order to mend the situation,] the government
should correctly check the land ownership so that taxes are correctly levied.
[When the government] knows the correct income from taxes, it can plan its
budget on the basis of the revenue and eliminate waste as well as wipe out taxes of
incorrect title. This will save the people from poverty. If the government does not
recognize that the people belong to the government as they would to one's own
self, this is lack of kindness [toward the people].[47]

In regard to famine due to drought, he said:

To set up relief is no panacea; one needs to plan irrigation. [Without irrigation,]
relief is not a solution.[48]

In regard to the contemporary military situation, Chu Hsi exhorted the
ruler to rectify himself and make an effort to lead the soldiers in strengthening military power against the foreign invaders.[49] Finally, as we have
noted, Chu laid great stress on educational matters and urged the establishment of schools to achieve the transformation of social mores and
thereby the basis for good government.

A special note must be added concerning the relation between *Chu-
hsüeh* and the Che-tung[cp] (the Yung-k'ang[cq] and the Yung-chia[cr]) schools
in order to clarify the meaning of *shih-hsüeh* in Chu's usage. Ch'en
Liang[cs] (1143–1194), of the Yung-k'ang school, urged the adoption of
political and economic measures for strengthening the state and procuring power in the spirit of the Han and T'ang. This was clearly a utilitarian doctrine which Chu Hsi criticized for its lack of stress on righteous
motivation or on sagely cultivation of oneself. Yeh Shih[ct] (1150–1223) of
the Yung-chia school was more moderate in his advocacy of utility, as he
based this advocacy on the ground of social institutions conforming to
Neo-Confucian doctrines. But he still regarded Chu Hsi's principle,
"Follow righteousness without pursuing utility; illumine the Way without
calculating success" (in the words of Tung Chung-shu) as too impractical
and unrealistic.[50] The contrast between Chu Hsi's idea of *shih-hsüeh* and
that of the Che-tung schools brings out the non-utilitarian, if not anti-
utilitarian, character of Chu's concern with practical affairs in his learning and philosophy.

IS WANG YANG-MING'S *HSIN-HSÜEH*^{cu} INCOMPATIBLE
WITH *SHIH-HSÜEH?*

Even though advocates of practical learning in the seventeenth and
eighteenth centuries criticized the Wang Yang-ming school as empty and
Ch'an-dominated, there is scarcely any explanation given as to how
Wang Yang-ming and his learning should be evaluated from the point of
view of *shih-hsüeh*. Again, the problem of understanding what constitutes
practicality (*shih*) may have more than one answer. Apparently, for Wang
Yang-ming, *shih* does not mean utility and profit; in fact, Wang rejected
practicality in this sense. Neither does *shih* mean the application of principles to things, for Wang recognized no separate existence of principles
apart from the concrete uses of them. Nor does *shih* mean simply a concern with the affairs of society and state as it did for Chu Hsi; Wang
Yang-ming aimed at something more fundamental than such a simple
concern with the affairs of society and state. In what follows, I shall
explain what Wang explicitly rejected as not practical (*shih*) and what he
accepted as practical. I shall suggest that his philosophy of the unity of
knowledge and action and the fulfillment of the innate knowledge of
goodness forms an essential dimension of practicality. I shall also indicate
that the practical learning of the seventeenth century should be considered a spiritual heir of Wang's practicality, despite the fact that no acknowledgment was ever made to Wang by the *shih-hsüeh* advocates.

First of all, Wang contrasted *shih* with *ming*^{cv} (name) and thus pin-
pointed the dominant meaning of *shih* as actual or real and as what has
actually been done. He said:

In learning, the great weakness is love of name . . . Name contrasts with actuality (*shih*). The more one is concerned with actuality, the less one is concerned
with name.[51]

The concept of *shih* is related to the concept of revealing or realizing innate knowledge of goodness in one's life. It is something inside oneself
and yet universal among men. It does not entail success in one's political
career or in one's intellectual enterprise, but it leads one to be a sagely
man, a man who truly realizes his nature and the nature of others. Conversely, the "name" signifies something on the surface and has no root in
one's true self. It is thus limited to "external" success or achievement that
is of no use to one's self-cultivation. Clearly, Wang Yang-ming rejected
"name" not only in the sense of renown, but also in the sense of knowl-

edge, education, literary ability or scholarship. For all of these may serve the purpose of seeking utility and self-interest and may therefore become obstacles to the attainment of goodness. He said:

The wide scope of one's erudition will only make one proud, the great amount of one's knowledge will merely cause one to practice evil, the large expanse of one's understanding will only cause one to be disputatious, the richness of one's prose will merely help one to disguise one's deception.[52]

Specifically, Wang rejected the study of textual criticism and flowery prose, and in this respect he was in substantial agreement with the advocates of *shih-hsüeh*. But it is noteworthy that Wang went one step further than the school of practical learning in that, while it attached great importance to knowledge of things, Wang doubted that seeking knowledge of things and learning principles would ever preserve one's true insight into the goodness of one's nature. For this reason Wang rejected Chu Hsi's doctrine of seeking principles. Wang called his own learning the "learning of sagehood" (*sheng-hsüeh*)[cw] and sometimes even spoke of *hsin-hsüeh* (the learning of mind). The question now is how this learning of sagehood or *hsin-hsüeh* can be regarded as containing or presenting a dimension of practicality.

The essence of Wang's philosophy is that one should endeavor to become a sage, a man who regards Heaven-and-Earth and all men and things as a unity of close relationship, and thus as deserving of his care and love. In more specific terms, the goal of a man's education is to attain harmony and achieve the well-being of all people so that the goodness of the universe will be realized in them through him. This requires a person to be thoroughly unselfish and thoroughly enlightened as to his true nature, the nature of others, and the world. He must restore and retain a mind of universal sympathy toward other people, and he must act in accordance with equity and fairness. In other words, he must also be thoroughly enlightened so that he is able to arrive at right perceptions and judgments about what can and should be done.

According to Wang, the beginning point of being unselfish is also the beginning point of being enlightened, and thus, being unselfish and being enlightened are mutually interdependent and are simultaneously derived from the same root nature and capacity of man. This capacity he referred to, following Mencius, as *liang-chih*[cx] (the innate knowledge of goodness). *Liang-chih* is innate in every man and is therefore both universal among men and particular and proper to each individual man. It is also the ultimate quality of man issuing from Heaven-and-Earth and can be aptly identified with the illumined virtue (ming-te)[cy] in the Great Learning and sincerity (ch'eng)[cz] in the Mean. Though liang-chih is universal among men and is proper to a particular man, great effort and attention are needed to preserve the activity and awareness of liang-chih in a person, and even greater effort and attention are required to bring liang-chih to bear in every affair of life. However, with constant and continuous cultivation of liang-chih, one will be able to achieve a mentality of unselfishness and an enlightened vision in one's judgments and actions. It is in this sense that a person can be said to be learning to be a sage or applying his mind correctly. This is what Wang calls fulfilling liang-chih (chih liang-chih).[da] It is a doctrine of learning to maintain one's uprightness and clarity and one's rationality and goodness even under the most adverse conditions.

Wang Yang-ming clearly saw the learning of sagehood in the above sense as a most practical undertaking, and it is undeniable that this learning, given its philosophical presuppositions, is indeed practical in the sense of involving the consideration of achieving goodness for the person and the society.[53] But the learning of sagehood—through retaining and developing liang-chih—is not only practical in the sense of realizing goodness in oneself and society; it is also practical in another sense as defined by Wang's doctrine of the unity of knowledge and action (chih hsing ho-i).[db] Wang held that knowledge and action must not be regarded as two separate things, but should instead be conceived as ultimately unified in their generation and completion. This is a great insight into the nature of knowledge and the nature of practice. As Wang pointed out, "Knowledge is the plan (chu-i)[dc] of action, action is the effort (kung-fu)[dd] of knowledge; knowledge is the beginning of action and action is the completion of knowledge."[54] This view underscores the intentionality of knowing (chih) and practicing (hsing) as well as their dynamic and dialectical relationship to one another, which is most obvious in political, social, and moral activities. With his assertion of the unity of knowledge and action, he brought to light a fundamental dimension of mind, namely, the practicality (in the sense of act or action) of mind. According to Wang,

Whenever one genuinely knows, there is action; whenever one acts perceptively, there is knowledge. The task of knowledge and action cannot really be separated.

It is only because in later days scholars give separate attention to them and thus lose sight of the original substance of knowledge and action that I advocate their unity and simultaneous advance. True knowledge is for the sake of action and, without action, knowledge cannot be called knowledge. [55]

The important point about Wang's thesis on the unity of *chih* and *hsing* is that *chih* and *hsing* are originally one and are never intended to be separated. If one looks into the metaphysical ground of this original unity of knowledge and action, one can clearly see that this ground is found in the existence of *liang-chih*, which every man inherits from Heaven. *Liang-chih* is not only the defining quality of the morally good mind and nature, but also the source of practicality in perceptive and cognitive activities. This is to say that mind premises every perceptive and cognitive act on an act of volition and desire, so that knowledge inevitably points to action which is, in turn, the satisfaction or completion of the whole act of mind. That mind is such as described is an essential part of Wang's doctrine of mind and *liang-chih*. In conjunction with Wang's theory of *chih liang-chih*, this doctrine also underscores Wang's idea of learning as learning to become a sage who will fulfill or bring about goodness in man and society. [56]

In the above, we have analyzed the notion of practicality in Wang's philosophy and theory. We can see that this morally and metaphysically significant notion of practicality is not the same practicality which the later philosophers of *shih-hsüeh* advocated, for in their view, the doctrines of mind and *chih liang-chih* lead only to empty talk and idle thinking and therefore controvert the practicality of *shih-hsüeh*. They justified their valuation by pointing to the Ch'anist followers of the Wang school. For Wang Yang-ming, however, there is a sense of practicality articulated in his doctrines of mind and *chih liang-chih*, which is more fundamental than the practicality of *shih-hsüeh*, yet not incompatible with it. Practicality (act or action of mind) in this sense is the source of all practicalities and unifies as well as evaluates all other practicalities. Thus, on the basis of this fundamental practicality of mind, Wang objected to the tendency to ignore moral practicality in advancing utilitarian practicality and the failure to develop an attitude of moral practicality before developing one of utilitarian practicality. Once moral practicality was developed, Wang was, apparently, ready to accept utilitarian practicality as a means for promoting an orderly and materially prosperous society. For example, he said in relation to the function of the school in antiquity:

The sole objective of the school was to perfect virtue. But people differed in their capacities, some excelling in rites and music, some in government and education, others in public works and agriculture. On the basis of their perfected virtue, they were sent to school, further to refine their abilities.[57]

One might therefore conclude that, when we take the essentials of Wang's philosophy into consideration, *shih-hsüeh* could have a proper place in his philosophy and that, even though the later *shih-hsüeh* is not directly derivable from Wang's philosophy, it is highly relevant for understanding his philosophy.

PRACTICALITY IN THE POLITICAL CAREER OF WANG YANG-MING

In personality and in practice Wang Yang-ming was a motivated and active person. Even though he was versatile in his abilities and had pursued many subjects of study, he sought study and learning as a way of fulfilling his deep aspiration to reach for truth and existential-intellectual satisfaction. In fact, a close examination of his biography shows that the knowledge and learning he acquired were direct results of his efforts to fulfill this aim. His philosophy of mind and *chih liang-chih* is therefore a crystallization of intellectual inquiry as well as a reflection on wisdom born of his life experience in adversity and hardship.

Though in his early career he studied many "impractical" subjects such as Taoism and Buddhism, which may in some way have continued to influence his Confucian thinking in the later period of his life, for twenty-nine years Wang concentrated primarily on practical affairs and the practical learning of his time. Among the practical affairs which commanded his attention, none is more noteworthy than his preoccupation with military studies. At the age of twenty-six, he became alarmed about border conflicts and started to study closely the classics of the military arts. His interest in participating in contemporary politics for the purpose of improving government and strengthening the state also became dominant in this period. After obtaining the *chin-shih*[de] degree in 1500, at the age of twenty-eight, Wang, for the next twenty-nine years until his death proved to be extremely tough-minded in politics. He also achieved much military success for the government. For himself, he succeeded in advancing his doctrine and thinking in a most energetic manner and taught many disciples in the school of thought that he established.

Here I am unable to give an account of Wang's political career sufficiently detailed to testify adequately to the rich and not uncharacteristic practicality of his career. My purpose in mentioning his career is merely to point out that Wang's teaching of practicality was borne out by his practice of what he taught and was, in fact, to a large measure inspired by his experiences in political life. In his practice, Wang was not only not opposed to the spirit of practical learning which developed after his own time but, rather, he indirectly contributed to the need that was later felt for *shih-hsüeh*. But, for all his utilitarian practicality in his military and political activities, Wang never gave up moral practicality as the basis and guiding principle of his career and activities. This should explain why his political and military practice often led to personal disasters in spite of his achievements.

There are three things to be said about Wang's political career which reflect Wang's moral practicality and the relevance of his analysis of practical affairs in his time. In the first place, he wrote a memorial on border affairs (*Pien-wu shu*)[df] at the age of twenty-eight. This memorial shows his active concern with national security and his sincere hope to increase the efficacy of the military. His proposal for seeking talent, organizing the army, extending the cultivation of land, and adopting a code of discipline, etc., entails sound measures and reveals a practical but correct mind at work.

Secondly, Wang was good at the administration of local government. In his term as magistrate of Lu-ling[dg] county, at the age of thirty-nine, he brought real peace and order to the locality and won fame for being a capable administrator. His organizational and governmental ability was also demonstrated in his military pacification of southern Kiangsi[dh] and Ssu-t'ien in Kwangsi.[di] His relief and reform policies for local government introduced a solid foundation into those troubled areas. This was reflected in his drafting of the "Covenant for Governing the South Kiangsi Area" (*Nan-Kan hsiang-yüeh*)[dj] and the "Memorial on Pacifying the Localities in Order to Secure Lasting Peace" (*Ch'u-chih p'ing-fu ti-fang i t'u chiu-an shu*)[dk] [58]

Finally, Wang Yang-ming showed great dexterity and tactical acumen in leading military campaigns and expeditions. He was assigned to three different military operations against rebels and bandits, and in short periods successfully and effectively accomplished his assignments. In 1517–18 he quelled unrest in the southern Kiangsi area. In 1520 he put down the Shen Hou[dl] rebellion. In 1528, one year before his death, he pacified the turbulent Kwangsi border regions.

These three things in Wang's political career suffice to show that Wang, as a Neo-Confucian, did not hesitate to deal with practical affairs in a practical way as guided by his practical philosophy of moral cultivation. In this regard Wang is comparable to Chu Hsi, although he engaged himself in many more practical activities than Chu Hsi did.

CONCLUDING REMARKS

We have shown in our examination and analysis of practicality in the philosophy of Yen Yüan that practicality can have many meanings. In its most relevant sense, as a movement in seventeenth- and eighteenth-century China, *shih-hsüeh* is the learning of things in response to the social needs of the time. We have also shown that practical learning (*shih-hsüeh*) can be theoretically traced to the theory and practice of Chu Hsi and Wang Yang-ming. Even though *shih-hsüeh* was ostensibly promoted and developed at the expense of *Chu-hsüeh* (the school of Chu Hsi) and *Wang-hsüeh* (the school of Wang Yang-ming), in reality, the doctrines and careers of both Chu Hsi and Wang Yang-ming incorporated a deep concern for meeting social problems and contained elements congenial to the teachings of *shih-hsüeh*. A strong case can, in fact, be made for the view that it was because of the acceptance of moral practicality in the doctrines of Chu and Wang that the utilitarian practicality of *shih-hsüeh* received its philosophical and moral justification and sanction. This is amply borne out by the fact that most of the advocates of *shih-hsüeh* unambiguously subscribed to the fundamental Confucian tenet that good government must concentrate on bringing well-being to the people. Yen Yüan is clearly a paradigm of this Confucian commitment, and Kung Tzu-chen with his advocacy of Kung-yang learning, is no less an exemplar of this Confucian political belief. We have also shown that Chu Hsi's philosophy can be conceived as having provided a basis for *shih-hsüeh*, and that Wang Yang-ming's theory of the unity of knowledge and action constituted an important basis for incorporating *shih-hsüeh* into government and society. The political careers of Chu and Wang further testify to the vigor and ability of Confucians in applying their doctrines to actual human needs, qualities which inspired many practitioners of *shih-hsüeh* in the China of the eighteenth and nineteenth centuries. While observing that Chu Hsi and Wang Yang-ming can be thought of as having given rise to *shih-hsüeh* both in theory and practice, we must at the same time recognize that when new circumstances gave rise to new social needs their ideas had reached their limits. An awareness of the limited scope of their ideas relative to the new circumstances led to the vigorous development of *shih-hsüeh* to replace them.

NOTES

1. Hattori Unokichi, *Ju-chia yü tang-tai ssu-hsiang*[dm] (Confucianism and Contemporary Thought) (Taipei, 1964), pp. 19–55.
2. Yen Yüan, *Ts'un-hsüeh pien* (On Preserving Learning) (Shanghai: Commercial Press, 1937 reprint) *chüan 1, Shang T'ai-ts'ang Lu Fu-t'ing hsien-sheng shu.*[dn]
3. *Ibid., chüan* 1; "Ming-ch'in."[do]
4. See Li Kung's *Ch'ou wang pien,*[dp] as mentioned in Hou Wai-lu's *Chung-kuo tsao-ch'i ch'i-meng ssu-hsiang shih*[dq] (History of the Early Enlightenment Thought of China) (Peking: People's Publishing Co., 1956), p. 381. It is clear that Li, as Yen's disciple, has given a more explicit account of Yen's views.
5. Yen Yüan, *Ts'un-hsüeh pien, Shang T'ai-ts'ang Lu Fu-t'ing hsien-sheng shu,* 1:9 (consec. pagin.).
6. *Ibid.*
7. *Ibid., Ts'un-hsüeh pien,* 1:12.
8. Yen Yüan once spoke of *shih-hsüeh* in the following terms: "If Heaven does not abandon me, I will enrich the earth with seven words: reclaim land, equalize land ownership, [and] conduct water irrigation. I will strengthen the world with six words: make people soldiers, make officials generals. I will pacify the world with nine words: select talent [for] government, rectify laws [and] norms, promote rites [and] music." See *Yen Hsi-chai hsien-sheng nien-p'u*[dr] (Chronological Biography of Master Yen Hsi-chai [Yen Yüan]).
9. Yen Yüan, *Ts'un-hsüeh pien,* 3:37.
10. *Ibid.,* p. 49.
11. See Yen Yüan's *Ssu-shu cheng-wu*[ds] (Corrections of Interpretations of the Four Books), part 1.
12. See *Hsi-chai chi-yü*[dt] (Record of Peripheral Writings of Hsi-chai), *chüan* 2, in *Chang-nan shu-yüan chi*[du] (Taipei: Yi-wen Book Co., 1955), vol. 22.
13. See Hou Wai-lu, *Chung-kuo tsao-ch'i ch'i-meng ssu-hsiang shih,* pp. 331 ff.
14. See my article, "Reason, Substance, and Human Desires in Seventeenth-Century Neo-Confucianism," in Wm. Theodore de Bary, ed., *The Unfolding of Neo-Confucianism* (New York: Columbia University Press, 1975), pp. 469–509.
15. See *Ting-an wen-chi*[dv] (Collected Essays of [Kung] Ting-an), *chüan* 2.
16. *Ibid., chüan* 2 and part 1.
17. *Ibid.,* part 2.
18. Kung Tzu-chen, "I-ping chih chi chu-i,"[dw] 6 (Essays in the Year of I-Ping, 6) in *Ting-an wen-chi, chüan* 1.
19. Quoted from Chang Po-hsing,[dx] *Hsü Chin-ssu lu*[dy] (Sequel to *Reflections on Things at Hand*) (Taipei: Shih-chieh shu-chü) 2:36 (consec. pagin.).
20. *Ibid.,* 2:56–57.
21. *Ibid.,* p. 35.

22. *Ibid.*, p. 41.
23. *Ibid.*, p. 37.
24. *Ibid.*, p. 38.
25. *Ibid.*, p. 37.
26. *Ibid.*
27. *Ibid.*, p. 36.
28. *Ibid.*, p. 37.
29. *Ibid.*, p. 39.
30. *Ibid.*, p. 45.
31. *Ibid.*, p. 44.
32. *Ibid.*, p. 45.
33. *Ibid.*, p. 43.
34. *Ibid.*, p. 47.
35. See *Chu Tzu yü-lei* (Recorded Conversations of Chu Hsi) 6:3b and 16:9b.
36. See Wang Mou-hung,^{dz} *Chu Tzu nien-p'u*^{ea} (Chronological Biography of Chu Hsi) (Taipei: Commercial Press, 1971), p. 221.
37. Quoted in *Hsü Chin-ssu lu*, p. 133.
38. In a personal communication Wing-tsit Chan pointed out that Lu Hsiang-shan, a contemporary of Chu Hsi, also used the term *shih-hsüeh* in a sentence which suggests *shih-hsüeh* as a verb phrase. "[One should] single-mindedly concentrate on genuine learning and [should] not spend time in empty talk (*i-i shih-hsüeh pu-shih k'ung-yen*)^{eb}." *Hsiang-shan ch'üan-chi* (SPPY ed.), 12:4a. Professor Chan also pointed out that this usage of *shih-hsüeh* is of a later date than Chu Hsi's usage.
39. See the informative article by Conrad M. Schirokauer, "Chu Hsi's Political Career: A Study in Ambivalence," in Arthur F. Wright and Denis Twitchett, eds., *Confucian Personalities* (Stanford: Stanford University Press, 1962), pp. 162–88. See also Wang Mou-hung, *Chu Tzu nien-p'u.*
40. Quoted in *Hsü Chin-ssu lu*, p. 175.
41. *Ibid.*, p. 177.
42. *Ibid.*, p. 181.
43. *Ibid.*, p. 154.
44. *Ibid.*, p. 162. Chu Hsi says, "Institutions are easy to talk about, but all depends on whether there are good people to carry out good institutions."
45. Quoted in *Hsü Chin-ssu lu*, p. 151.
46. *Ibid.*, p. 164.
47. *Ibid.*, p. 193.
48. *Ibid.*, p. 189.
49. See the text of the *Wu-shen feng-shih* Petition in Fan Shou-k'ang,^{ec} *Chu Tzu chi ch'i che-hsüeh*^{ed} (Chu Hsi and His Philosophy) (Taipei: K'ai-ming shu-tien, 1964), pp. 282–91.
50. Cf. Chu Hsi's saying in *Hsü Chin-ssu lu*, p. 175.
51. Quoted from *Ch'uan-hsi lu*^{ee} (Instructions for Practical Living), part I, section 105. See also Wing-tsit Chan, trans., *Instructions for Practical Living*

and *Other Neo-Confucian Writings* by *Wang Yang-Ming* (New York: Columbia University Press, 1963), p. 67.

52. Quoted from his essay *Pa-pen sai-yüan lun*[ef] (Pulling Up the Root and Stopping Up the Source) in *Ch'uan-hsi lu*, part 2. See also Chang Hsi-chih[eg], *Yang-ming hsüeh-chuan*[eh] (Record of Learning of [Wang] Yang-ming), (Taipei: Chung-hua shu-chü, 1961), pp. 173 ff., and Chan, *Instructions*, pp. 117–24.

53. See his essay *Ta-hsüeh wen*[ei] (Inquiry on the *Great Learning*), in *Wang Wen-ch'eng kung ch'üan-shu*[ej] (Complete Works of Wang Yang-ming), Kuo-hsüeh chi-pen ts'ung-shu ed., Book 10, ch. 26, which discusses realization of one's virtue by loving and getting close to people.

54. *Ch'uan-hsi lu*, part 1, section 5. See also Chan, *Instructions*, p. 11.

55. *Ibid.*, part 2, section 133. See also Chan, *Instructions*, p. 93.

56. See Wang's essay *Ta-hsüeh wen*.

57. Quoted from Wang's essay, *Pa-pen sai-yüan lun* in *Ch'uan-hsi lu*, part 2. See also Chan, *Instructions*, pp. 119–20.

58. *Wang Wen-ch'eng kung ch'üan-shu*, Book 6, ch. 14, pp. 77 ff., and Book 7, ch. 17, pp. 93 ff.

GLOSSARY

a	格物	am	禮	by	古文學派
b	致知	an	樂	bz	康有爲
c	大學	ao	射	ca	理學
d	實學	ap	御	cb	氣
e	朱熹	aq	書	cc	伊川（程頤）
f	王陽明	ar	數	cd	道
g	顏元	as	實位天地	ce	高幻
h	龔自珍	at	實育萬物	cf	習
i	實	au	實	cg	復其舊性
j	實文實行	av	存學編	ch	氣質
k	實体實用	aw	空	ci	誠是實
l	實績	ax	斷盡實學	cj	誠實理也
m	實敎	ay	文	ck	儀禮
n	三事	az	野	cl	南康
o	六府	ba	虛	cm	戊申封事
p	堯	bb	物	cn	井田制
q	舜	bc	事	co	封建
r	六德	bd	藝	cp	浙東
s	六行	be	存性編	cq	永康
t	六藝	bf	知	cr	永嘉
u	周公	bg	實行	cs	陳亮
v	正德	bh	靜坐	ct	葉適
w	厚生	bi	主敬	cu	心學
x	利用	bj	寂守無用	cv	名
y	尚書	bk	董仲舒	cw	聖學
z	周禮	bl	利	cx	良知
aa	仁	bm	功	cy	明德
ab	義	bn	姜太公	cz	誠
ac	智	bo	孫武	da	致良知
ad	禮	bp	候外廬	db	知行合一
ae	忠	bq	理	dc	主意
af	信	br	科學	dd	功夫
ag	文行	bs	訓詁學	de	進士
ah	忠信	bt	段玉裁	df	邊務疏
ai	孝悌	bu	富國強兵	dg	廬陵
aj		bv	嚴復	dh	江西
ak		bw	公羊學	di	廣西思田
al		bx	今文學派	dj	南贛鄉約

dk 處置平復地方以圖久安疏
dl 宸濠
dm 服部宇之吉，儒家與當代思想
dn 上太倉陸桴亭先生書
do 明親
dp 瘳忘編
dq 中國早期啟蒙思想史
dr 顏習齋先生年譜
ds 四書正誤
dt 習齋記餘
du 漳南書院記
dv 定盦文集
dw 乙丙之際箸議
dx 張伯行
dy 續近思錄
dz 王懋竑
ea 朱子年譜
eb 一意實學不事空言
ec 范壽康
ed 朱子及其哲學
ee 傳習錄
ef 拔本塞源論
eg 張希之
eh 陽明學傳
ei 大學問
ej 王文成公全書

Irene Bloom

On the 'Abstraction' of Ming Thought: Some Concrete Evidence from the Philosophy of Lo Ch'in-shun[a]

> "It is possible that upon catching the fish, one forgets
> the fish trap, and that upon catching the rabbit, one
> forgets the snare. But is it reasonable to boast about
> catching the fish and the rabbit and then turn around
> and find fault with the trap and the snare for having
> gotten in the way?"
>
> -Lo Ch'in-shun

A standard criticism of Ming thought, repeated over and over again by Ch'ing scholars and modern historians, is that it was "abstract." Liang Ch'i-ch'ao's[b] summary of the intellectual milieu of the early Ch'ing began, "Having inherited the very abstract Ming thought (ch'eng Ming-hsüeh chi k'ung shu),[c] men [of the Ch'ing period] grew tired of it and one after another turned to something profoundly concrete (fan yü shen shih)[d]."[1] The notion of the "abstraction" of Ming thought has become a theme almost without variations and, as so often happens, the very repetition of the idea has lent a certain cumulative weight to the indictment.

Rarely, however, has a detailed explanation been offered for the meaning of the word "abstract" in this context. While the use of the term k'ung[e] in its Buddhist connotation refers to emptiness and vacuity as an ultimate ontological reality, its use by later critics of Neo-Confucianism appears usually to be non-philosophical, and in some cases even anti-philosophical, in nature. The criticism of Ming thought by Ch'ing thinkers and their successors as "empty" or "abstract" generally directs attention to what has been commonly understood as an excessive concern with ontological issues and a concomitant detachment from urgent social

69

and economic problems—in other words, from the "practical" realities of human life. Interestingly, the critics have not been noticeably inclined to specific or substantive analysis of the deficiencies (or excesses) of the Ming thinkers in this regard, nor have many been at pains to describe in detail the theories that are under attack. Apparently the vulnerability of Ming thinkers to the charge of "abstraction" has been sufficiently obvious that closer scrutiny of the problem as evidenced in particular schools and currents of thought has been considered unnecessary. But, as any charge often made and seldom questioned eventually invites reconsideration, and as the recurrence of the term "abstract" poses some interesting philosophical problems, there would seem to be warrant for further examination of the issue of "abstract" versus "concrete" learning in terms of specific cases in Ming intellectual history. In what follows some aspects of the philosophy of Lo Ch'in-shun are considered in this light.

The primary purpose here will be expository rather than critical. However, the attempt to assess the charge of "abstraction" as it might apply to one exemplar of Ming orthodoxy impels us to confront several critical questions, notably: 1) the degree of continuity or discontinuity between Sung and Ming and between Ming and Ch'ing styles of learning; 2) the problem of "creativity" in the Ming; 3) the significance of a new emphasis in sixteenth-century thought on ch'i, or material force; 4) the implications of the new philosophical interests of the mid- and late Ming for subsequent developments in the thought of Ch'ing China and Tokugawa Japan; and 5) the relation between the "abstract" philosophy associated with Neo-Confucian metaphysical inquiries and the emergence of new modes of thought which came to be associated with "practical learning" in both China and Japan. Whether or not genuine progress can be made here toward providing answers to such questions, the hope is that at least their general relevance may be underscored. The philosophical achievements of Lo Ch'in-shun were considerable, and even one such example may serve to illustrate the fact that the conventional labels that have attached to Ming thought may be misleading and, particularly, that casual judgments about its allegedly abstract character are in many respects problematic.

LO CH'IN-SHUN AND THE *K'UN-CHIH CHI*[f]

A native of T'ai-ho *hsien* in Kiangsi, Lo Ch'in-shun was born on December 25, 1465.[2] Having placed third in the metropolitan examinations of 1493, he was accorded the rank of Hanlin compiler. By 1502, he had been promoted to be Director of Studies at the State University in Nanking, where he served together with Chang Mou[g] (1436–1521) until 1504. Late in 1504 Lo requested an extended leave in order to care for his father, and, although the request was officially denied, he determined to remain at home regardless. Apparently angered by this assertion of independence, the notorious eunuch Liu Chin[h] (d. 1510) saw to it that Lo was deprived of both rank and office in 1508. Lo's self-imposed withdrawal from official life at this time spared him some of the bitterness experienced by his great contemporaries, Wang Yang-ming[i] (1472–1529), exiled by the same Liu Chin to Kuei-chou, and Wang T'ing-hsiang[j] (1474–1544), who also suffered exile at Liu's instigation. After remaining in retirement for two years, Lo was restored to his previous post in 1510, following the execution of Liu Chin in that year.

From this point on he received numerous promotions in rapid succession, being appointed Vice Minister of the Court of Imperial Sacrifices in 1511, Junior Vice Minister of Personnel in Nanking in 1515, and Senior Vice Minister in 1519. In 1521 he was appointed Senior Vice Minister of Personnel in Peking, and in 1522 he was elevated to the position of Minister of Personnel in Nanking. Upon the death of his father in 1523, he began the observance of mourning. When at the end of the mourning period he was recalled to office, first as Minister of Rites and subsequently as Minister of Personnel, he twice declined, a decision which Lo's biography in the *Ming-shih*[k] attributes to an unwillingness to be associated with Chang Ts'ung[l] (1475–1539) and Kuei O[m] (d. 1531), whose influence in the government dated from this time.[3]

After his request for retirement was finally granted in 1527, Lo spent the remaining twenty years of his life at home in quiet study and reflection. During this time he engaged in detailed study not only of the classical canon, the works of the Sung Neo-Confucians, and the writings of earlier Ming writers such as Wu Yü-pi[n] (1392–1469), Hu Chü-jen[o] (1434–1484), and Ch'en Hsien-chang[p] (1428–1500), but later of Buddhist texts as well. The results of his studies were recorded in the *K'un-*

chih chi (Notes on Knowledge Painfully Acquired), which first appeared in an edition of two *chüan* in 1528, when Lo was sixty-three. Additional *chüan* were completed in 1531, 1533, and 1538, and still another was added in 1546, the year before his death. His death came on May 13, 1547 at the age of eighty-two. Lo was given the title of Grand Guardian of the Heir Apparent and the posthumous name of Wen-chuang,[q] and in 1724 his tablet was placed in the Confucian temple.

All accounts of Lo Ch'in-shun's life testify to his intense seriousness and scrupulous sense of personal integrity, qualities which seem to have guided his intellectual life as well as his official career. Huang Tsung-hsi's[r] (1610–1695) biographical account in the *Ming-ju hsüeh-an*[s] (Philosophical Records of Ming Confucians) conveys a sense of his austere dedication to scholarly pursuits.

When he dwelled at home he arose at dawn every day, dressed himself correctly, and went up to the Hall for the Study of Antiquity (*Hsüeh-ku lou*),[t] followed by his disciples. After receiving their greetings and obeisances, he sat in a dignified posture and engaged in study. Even when he dwelled alone, he was not careless in his demeanor. He was frugal in his diet, had no pavilions or garden houses, and employed no music when he entertained.[4]

Frequently cited by biographers, including Kao P'an-lung[u] (1562–1626) of the Tung-lin[v] school of the late Ming,[5] is a tribute paid by Lin Hsi-yüan[w] (*chin-shih*, 1517) who wrote, "From his initial service in the Han-lin, to his service as a minister, his conduct both in and out of office was like pure gold and precious jade. One could find no flaws."[6]

Lo's own descriptions of his life and work are characterized by candor and humility. The fact that the *K'un-chih chi* was first published when he was in his sixties and that he subsequently undertook to rework and refine the views elaborated in the first two *chüan* attests both to a sense of personal reserve and to a conviction that intellectual and spiritual growth are achieved at the cost of diligence and painstaking effort. The title of the work is itself suggestive: it recalls the passage in the *Mean* (XX: 9) which counsels, "Some are born with knowledge (*huo sheng erh chih chih*);[x] some attain it through study (*huo hsüeh erh chih chih*);[y] and some acquire it only after painstaking effort (*huo k'un erh chih chih*)."[z] Evidently this experience of *k'un*,[aa] or painstaking effort, conditioned all of Lo's inquiries. As Wang Yang-ming's philosophical endeavors came to maturity through the "hundred deaths and thousand sufferings"[7] of his active personal life, so it would seem that Lo's efforts were rewarded only after long years of uncertainty and self-doubt.

Before turning to the philosophical views elaborated in the *K'un-chih chi*, it may be useful to comment briefly on the nature of the text and what we may expect to learn from it. Not surprisingly, the work does not offer a systematic or sustained discussion of particular problems and themes; rather it is a loosely organized collection of notes and reflections recorded over the course of twenty years or more. Much of it is composed of reading notes in which Lo sets forth his critical reactions to books he has read. The tone throughout is lively and argumentative, and yet there is also a mellowness, an autumnal quality to the work. Lo is revealed as a scholar of remarkable erudition, given to meticulous accuracy in his textual research[8] and highly consistent development of his philosophical positions.

These positions would seem to have been carefully thought out by 1528, when the first two *chüan* of the *K'un-chih chi* were completed. He reworked them in later years but did not make substantive changes, nor can his relative emphases be said to have shifted discernibly. Careful reading of the *Ch'uan-hsi lu*[ab] (Instructions for Practical Living) indicates clearly that it can provide evidence of Wang Yang-ming's philosophical development and of the fact that Wang's perspective did change considerably in his later years.[9] But the *K'un-chih chi* is not a comparable document. Inasmuch as it contains only Lo's mature thought, we cannot approach it with the expectation of finding similar evidence of intellectual development in progress. Professor Yamashita Ryūji[ac] has observed, after the most detailed and perceptive scrutiny of both the *Ch'uan-hsi lu* and the *K'un-chih chi*, that there is reason to believe that Lo, when commenting on the writings of his contemporaries, put down his thoughts on a given work soon after he encountered it.[10] In this sense, the *K'un-chih chi* represents Lo's direct responses to current issues and doctrines, and it is possible to get some clues about the evolution of Wang Yang-ming's thought by taking note of where in the *K'un-chih chi* a particular idea or formulation of Wang's was criticized or commented on by Lo. But since, as Professor Yamashita demonstrates, there is no evidence that Lo was directly influenced by Wang in his own doctrinal formulations,[11] knowledge of this fact helps us more in interpreting the *Ch'uan-hsi lu* than in adding to our understanding of the *K'un-chih chi* itself. Lo's temperament was no doubt more reserved, his habit of mind more deliberate, and his students and potential recorders fewer, so that we are left in the end with only what in Neo-Confucian terms might be described as his "settled views" or final conclusions.

Virtually all that is known about the background of the *K'un-chih chi* and the intellectual preparation of its author derives from a brief autobiographical reflection, included almost as an aside in a passage given over mainly to a critique of Lu Hsiang-shan[ad] (1139–1193). Lo explains that he had in his earlier years been drawn to Ch'an[ae] Buddhism. He describes a meditative experience which at the time he had taken for enlightenment, but which he later recognized more accurately as "a vision" (*kuang-ching*),[af] elusive and unreliable. Then some time after the experience of the "vision," while he was employed at the State University in Nanking, he began a program of extensive reading in classical texts, in the course of which he gradually came to very different conclusions about the nature of reality and of knowledge. As he put it, "I spent several decades engaged in the most earnest effort. Only when I approached the age of sixty did I finally attain insight into the reality of the mind and the nature and truly acquire the grounds for self-confidence."[12] Lo's exposure to and interest in Ch'an are hardly unusual for a Neo-Confucian thinker, for a great many, including Chu Hsi[ag] himself, had experiences that were in some ways similar. More remarkable are the clarity with which he later delivered his judgment about the ultimate limitations of meditative discipline and the intense devotion with which he committed himself to intellectual cultivation. Chu Hsi had favored a form of cultivation in which appropriate attention was given to both quiet-sitting (*ching-tso*)[ah] and textual study (*tu-shu*).[ai] Lo, who was concerned about a disparity between a "vision" of the oneness of all being and the objective reality of oneness in nature itself, put virtually all his emphasis on intellectual cultivation. He too appears to have practiced quiet-sitting on occasion as a means of personal cultivation,[13] and, like so many Neo-Confucians, remained convinced that intellectual cultivation culminates and is perfected in a profound spiritual awareness. But, for him, intellectual achievement was the basis for a necessary objectivity that allowed one to attain an accurate perspective on the self and the natural world as a whole.

Lo's own intellectual achievement came to fulfillment out of the long, silent years of study and effort, and yet, as evidence concerning the particular course that he followed during these decades is lacking, there is no way in which his progress can be traced, no way that we can watch him at work. What can be inferred on the basis of the available textual evidence is that after his own experience with Ch'an, Lo went back to the Ch'eng-Chu tradition and developed his philosophy on the basis of an intellectual perspective that had earlier been fostered by Chu Hsi (1130–1200). It is an interesting reflection on Ming "orthodoxy" and indeed on the whole complex phenomenon of orthodoxy in the Neo-Confucian tradition that, though he was impelled, after some twenty years of study, to revise substantially a number of the primary metaphysical formulations of Ch'eng I[aj] (1033–1107) and Chu Hsi, as well as their views on human nature and the goals of cultivation, he could without any sense of ambivalence or contradiction consider himself to have remained faithful to the tradition in terms of its underlying intellectual and spiritual orientation. Seeing the tradition from within, Lo apparently did not find in philosophical orthodoxy the kind of doctrinal rigidity often ascribed to it by critics who approach it from without. What he did find in the Ch'eng-Chu tradition was a particular kind of scholarly rigor and a conviction about the indiscerptible relation between intellectual and spiritual concerns, and to this rigor and this relation he remained deeply committed.

It may be noted that, while Chu Hsi had done more than any other thinker to promote the kind of scholarly rigor which was important to Lo, when it came to several important doctrinal formulations, Lo's unqualified approval was reserved for Ch'eng Hao[ak] (1032–1085). This was apparently because of the monistic tendency in Ch'eng Hao's thought and because of a complex view of human nature which, in Lo's judgment, avoided some of the problems that attached to the views of Ch'eng I and Chu Hsi. Ch'eng I and Chu Hsi came in for respectful criticism for their philosophical dualism, while the early Ming thinkers whose work he studied, notably Hsüeh Hsüan[al] (1389–1464) and Hu Chü-jen, were taken to task on this score with equal incisiveness and less reserve. The fact that this kind of nonconformity in respect to significant issues and interpretations is found within the Ch'eng-Chu school itself is evidence of the vitality and flexibility of the tradition and suggests that it is unhistorical to discuss "the Neo-Confucian concept of principle" or "the Neo-Confucian view of human nature" as if these were static and unchanging philosophical constants. Liang Ch'i-ch'ao and other writers of his period at times refer to "Sung-Ming *li-hsüeh*"[am][14] as if a system of Sung thought had been inherited intact by the Ming thinkers, and yet the evidence is very much to the contrary. Lo, for example, retained certain intellectual and spiritual values which had their origin in the Sung period, while in other respects his views were closer to those of classical Confucianism. At the same time, elements were introduced which had little apparent precedent in the earlier tradition. In particular, certain of the ideas about knowledge adumbrated in the *K'un-chih chi* were new and indicative of the changing values and concerns of the mid-Ming period—a time when the questions that were being asked about the criteria for knowledge and the determination of its proper objects were more searching than in any previous period in Chinese thought.

LO CH'IN-SHUN AND THE PHILOSOPHY OF *CH'I*

One term of tremendous importance in the history of Chinese philosophy in general and Ch'ing philosophy in particular goes almost without mention in Liang Ch'i-ch'ao's *Intellectual Trends in the Ch'ing Period (Ch'ing-tai hsüeh-shu kai-lun)*[an]. This is the term *ch'i*,[ao] or, as it is most often translated, material force. It is interesting that Liang never discussed the implications of a philosophy of *ch'i*, not even in connection with his account of Wang Fu-chih[ap] (1619–1692) or Tai Chen[aq] (1724–1777), both of whom are known for their emphasis on *ch'i*. The omission is the more curious when one considers that it was primarily by virtue of an emphasis on *ch'i* that an otherwise disparate group of Ch'ing thinkers was united; Huang Tsung-hsi, Ku Yen-wu[ar] (1613–1682), Wang Fu-chih, Yen Yüan[as] (1635–1704), Li Kung[at] (1659–1733) and Tai Chen, for example, whatever philosophical differences they had among themselves, were at one in denying the reality of *li*,[au] or principle, as independent of *ch'i*. Not only does the philosophy of *ch'i* represent an intellectual trend of the Ch'ing period, it represents one of the dominant trends and one without which Ch'ing empiricism might conceivably not have developed at all. For empiricism has no proper object until full and independent reality is accorded to concrete things, and its method is inevitably thwarted until the problem of causality is approached as distinct from the concerns of ethics.

The philosophy of *ch'i*, which involved just such a change in metaphysical and epistemological perspective, had its origin in the Ming period, and the first of the Ming thinkers to develop it consciously and deliberately was Lo Ch'in-shun.[15] Whether one opts with Professor Abe Yoshio[av] to call Lo's philosophy revolutionary[16] or, alternatively, prefers to interpret it as reformist, depends upon whether one chooses to concentrate on the relation between Chu Hsi's view and Lo Ch'in-shun's or on a more purely philosophical criterion.[17] In either case the fact remains that, although committed to the general intellectual and spiritual orientation of the Ch'eng-Chu school, Lo separated himself from Ch'eng I and Chu Hsi by rejecting their theory of *li* and *ch'i* and virtually all of its implications and shifting the primary focus of his philosophical interest from *li* to *ch'i*.[18] It could hardly have been coincidental that he was also prompted to consider some basic questions about the nature of knowledge and to make at least preliminary steps toward developing a critical epistemology.

Chu Hsi's theory of *li* and *ch'i* has been discussed elsewhere with much more thoroughness and expertise than is possible here.[19] What bears stating, however, is that, while Chu Hsi might not have allowed that his theory amounted to a dualism, it could hardly qualify as monism in any but the most elaborately qualified and even anomalous definition of that term. Chu had repeatedly clarified his view that *li* and *ch'i* could not exist in isolation (*li wei ch'ang li yü ch'i*)[aw].[20] However, he also believed that it followed from the premise that *li* is above form (*hsing erh shang*)[ax] and *ch'i* is within form (*hsing erh hsia*)[ay] that *li* could be considered prior (*hsien*)[az] and *ch'i* posterior (*hou*)[ba].[21] As against the formlessness (*wu hsing*)[bb] of principle, which was seen as perfect, he found material force to be coarse (*ts'u*)[bc] and marked by impurities (*yu cha tzu*)[bd].[22] Because *li* was understood as prior and perfect, it could be abstracted from *ch'i*, and for this reason Chu could speak of the relation of *li* and *ch'i* from several perspectives and, on occasion, represent *li* as the origin or source (*pen*)[be] of living things.[23]

The priority of principle was asserted in such statements as, "Fundamentally, principle and material force cannot be spoken of as prior or posterior. But if we must trace their origin, we are obliged to say that principle is prior."[24] And, "There is principle before there is material force. But it is only when there is material force that principle finds a place to settle."[25] Its superiority was stressed in numerous statements in which principle was identified with the Way and the nature, which are permanent and enduring, while material force was associated with finite physical beings, which are subject to integration and disintegration. For example, "The nature of man and things is nothing but principle and cannot be spoken of in terms of integration and disintegration. That which integrates to produce life and disintegrates to produce death is material force."[26] Principle and material force were at times represented as "two things" (erh wu)[bf],[27] the former being conceived as the moving force or controlling power that determined the specific character of the latter, as the ontological visitor that regulated its life.

This dualistic view of li and ch'i was also among the determinants of Chu Hsi's theory of human nature, for the excellence of the original nature, which was identified with principle, was thought to be compromised in varying degrees by its association with physical substance, understood as the individual allotment of material force. Just as li could be considered prior to ch'i in the sense that it was "above form," so the nature was accorded priority, as, for example, when Chu Hsi stated that, "Before material force exists, there is already the nature. There is a time when material force does not exist, but the nature is eternal."[28] One of the central problems in Sung thought was to find a way to deal conceptually with the matter of evil, or of moral obliquity, and it was of the utmost consequence that Chang Tsai[bg] (1020–1077), Ch'eng I, and Chu Hsi all found the explanation for the existence of evil in terms of this compromise between ideal principle and real physical substance, i.e., between the original nature which is pure and perfectly good and the physical nature which harbors the "selfish human desires."

Differences among individuals were, in Chu Hsi's view, ascribed to an inequality in the material force with which they were endowed at birth, so that the ideal nature was conditioned by the physical portion with which it happened to be associated:

The nature of all men is good, and yet there are those who are good from their birth and those who are evil from their birth. This is because of the difference in material force with which they are endowed. The revolutions of the universe consist of countless variety and are endless. But these may be seen: If the sun and moon are clear and bright, and the climate temperate and reasonable, the man born at such a time and endowed with such material force, which is clear, bright, well-blended, and strong, should be a good man. But if the sun and moon are darkened and gloomy, and the temperature abnormal, all this is evidence of violent material force. There is no doubt that if a man is endowed with such material force, he will be a bad man. The objective of learning is to transform this material endowment.[29]

The problem of ethical cultivation, for Chu Hsi, was thus to transform a given material endowment so that the purity of principle would no longer be obstructed.

One other implication of Chu Hsi's theory of *li* and *ch'i* is in the area of his theory of knowledge. This is a subject of considerable complexity and importance which can be treated here in only the most preliminary and suggestive fashion. Even so, it should emerge quite clearly when the Sung view as represented by Chu Hsi is juxtaposed against the Ming view represented by Lo Ch'in-shun that a gradual change was underway within the "orthodox" school. For Chu Hsi, principle, the primary object of knowledge, had both ontological and ethical reality. That is, a statement about principle had equal reference to truth and goodness, though more often than not, it seems, the emphasis was on the latter. There can be little doubt, for example, that when Chu Hsi observed that, "What is right is the Principle of Nature, and what is wrong is in violation of the Principle of Nature,"[30] he was suggesting that the overriding reason to seek knowledge of the Principle of Nature was that such knowledge provided the key to moral judgments and action. Ch'eng I had retained the confidence that, "Things and the self are governed by the same principle. If you understand one, you understand the other, for the truth within and the truth without are identical."[31] There is every reason to believe that Chu Hsi accepted this view and that, if anything, his concept of mind was such as to favor an even more reliable introspection. As he said, "The mind embraces all principles and all principles are complete in this single entity, the mind."[32] "The Way exists everywhere, but how are we to find it? Simply by returning to the self and discovering it within one's own nature and function."[33] Again and again the inner life is stressed as the appropriate point of reference for both virtue and knowledge.

In their reaction against Buddhist quietism, the Sung masters were deeply concerned with reaffirming an effective moral relation between the inner self and the outer world, and a balance between internal and external cultivation was often urged. Yet there are often signs of a wariness on the part of Chu Hsi, as well as other Sung thinkers, toward the outer, physical world. Once when discussing learning, Chu Hsi expressed regret over his "past defect of emphasizing fragmentary and isolated details" and "the faults of forgetting the self, chasing after material things, leaving the internal empty, and greedily desiring the external."[34] He followed by alluding to Ch'eng I's statement that, "One must not allow the myriad things in the world to disturb him. When the self is established, one will naturally understand the myriad things in the world."[35] The moral law is most vividly present in and accessible to the mind, and the goal of establishing the self requires first that the mind be rendered perfectly pure, calm and collected. While a potentially "disturbing" diversity is displayed in the external or superficial aspects of things, it is possible through an effort of the mind to work through the transitory and ephemeral to achieve integration. When Ch'eng I spoke of "understanding" or "apprehending" (te)[bh] the myriad things of the world, what he seems to have had in mind was one's moral disposition toward things, or one's capacity to achieve integration. As this kind of integrative knowledge was profoundly moral, the need to make a clear distinction between ethical and epistemological questions did not really arise.

The corollary of this profound concern with the moral disposition was that sensory perception tended to be deprecated to a certain degree, as when Chu Hsi invoked Chang Tsai's injunctions against relying too much on sense knowledge as a means of understanding "things in the world":

The mind is not like a side door which can be enlarged by force. We must eliminate the obstructions of selfish desires, and then it will be pure and clear and able to know all. When the principles of things and events are exhaustively explored, penetration will come as a sudden release. Heng-ch'ü[bi] [Chang Tsai] said, "Do not allow what is seen or heard to fetter the mind." "By enlarging one's mind one can enter into all things in the world." This means that if penetration is achieved through moral principles, there will be penetration like a sudden release. If we confine [the mind] to what is heard and seen, naturally our understanding will be narrow.[36]

Here it is not the validity or reliability of sense perception that is questioned, but its ultimate significance. Whereas Western philosophers were frequently concerned with problems stemming from the contradictory nature of sense impressions,[37] Sung thinkers were more likely to ask what to them were more basic questions about whether knowledge accumulated by the senses was the sort that really mattered or whether, on the contrary, it might under some circumstances count as a distraction. Their most urgent concerns, again, tended to be moral rather than epistemological.

It is characteristic of the particular kind of dualism to which Ch'eng I and Chu Hsi subscribed that they conceived of the most significant operation of the mind as a kind of uniting of subject and object, a penetration by the mind to the essence (or principle) of a thing, as distinct from mere acquaintance with its superficial or ephemeral aspect.[38] This kind of penetration is achieved, as Chu Hsi put it in the passage quoted above, "through moral principles" and is comparable to "a sudden release." The chief criterion for this kind of mental operation is that selfish desires be eliminated and the mind be made pure. Evidently, what Chu Hsi was discussing was the mind in its conative rather than its cognitive function. "To know all" in a cognitive sense is clearly beyond the realm of human possibility, but it is also beyond the realm of moral necessity. Chu Hsi was primarily concerned with a perceived relation between subject and object. What mattered was the realization that when the mind is pure and clear it is capable of sympathetic identification with all things and, through this, the requirements of ethical universalism are served.

It has been observed of St. Augustine's theory of knowledge that,

The chief defect which compels the mind to press on from . . . the knowledge of physical objects to the contemplation of the Ideas is the presence of impermanence. The intellect perceives above the flux of visible things and above human minds a system of unchangeable truths. And the *res intelligibles* which are open to the grasp of intellectual insight are not merely formal propositions, they are the constitutive principles of things. Endowed with the power of "illumination" the mind may descry beyond space and time the source of Ideas.[39]

Leaving aside the much debated question of whether in metaphysical terms there is an appropriate comparison to be made between Platonic Ideas, medieval universals, and the Chinese concept of principle,[40] and confining ourselves for the moment to the matter of epistemology, we may note that impermanence was regarded as a kind of "defect" by the Sung Neo-Confucians as well. And their profound concern to get beyond the accidental and particular to the necessary and universal had a decisive influence on their theory of knowledge. In the Chinese case, this deep awareness of impermanence may, ironically, have been the most enduring element in their experience of Buddhism, prompting Sung Neo-Confucians to look beyond "the flux of visible things" to the permanence and perfection of principle.[41]

The view that principle was prior and material force posterior seems to have reflected an uneasiness about change and process and the finitude of individual beings which was not really characteristic of classical Confucianism.[42] The epistemological consequences of this were considerable. So long as principle and material force were understood as separate entities, the one absolute and the other conditional in its reality, a high valuation would in all likelihood not be placed on detailed scrutiny of facts or on empirical confirmation. The compulsion was always to penetrate to a higher truth which would integrate or unite all phenomenal reality. For all the importance attached by Sung thinkers, especially Chu Hsi, to the discipline of "the investigation of things" (ko-wu)[bj] much of its significance lay in the fact that investigation could amplify and deepen knowledge of the higher truth of principle, though this principle might also be known more immediately and directly as an internal reality.[43]

It was suggested at the outset that the change that began in the mid-Ming period had to do with a heightened interest in the complexity of concrete facts. Whether this interest should properly be seen as a cause or an effect of the philosophical developments which will be described here remains open to question. What can be said with reasonable certainty, however, is that virtually all of the elements of Chu Hsi's thought on *li* and *ch'i* as it has just been summarized, except for the acceptance of the terms *li* and *ch'i* as valid philosophical concepts, were discarded by Lo Ch'in-shun. Before exploring the issues as Lo framed them and the actual language he used, a few general comments about the attendant philosophical change may be in order.

Already in mid-Ming times, Chu Hsi's *li-hsüeh* was being modified in various ways by thinkers who concentrated their attention on *ch'i* rather than on *li*. This fact has considerable significance for the characterization of Ming thought, the phenomenon of Ming "orthodoxy," and the overall continuities and discontinuities in the Chinese intellectual tradition. It should become apparent, for example, that Joseph Levenson was not on firm ground in arguing in his now famous essay on "The Abortiveness of Empiricism in Early Ch'ing Thought" that Sung and Ming criticisms of Chu Hsi's *li-hsüeh* "came from the far side of idealism, from the subjective-idealist *hsin-hsüeh*[bk] of Lu Hsiang-shan and Wang Yang-ming,"[44] and that a philosophy of *ch'i* came to the fore only with the change in philosophical tide which occurred in early Ch'ing times. The argument as advanced by Professor Levenson was that there were two great critical movements against Chu Hsi's *li-hsüeh*, an idealistic Sung-Ming trend which emphasized mind as against principle, and a naturalistic Ch'ing trend which concentrated on material force in contrast to principle. However, Lu Hsiang-shan is fairly styled an idealist only if that term is accorded a specifically Chinese definition, and, as several scholars have shown, the controversy between Chu and Lu is not very accurately represented as one of *li-hsüeh* as against *hsin-hsüeh*.[45] It is questionable, therefore, that Lu was offering a fundamental criticism of Chu's concept of *li*. Such a criticism did arise, however, during the Ming period, and it came first from within the Ch'eng-Chu school itself, from one of Chu's own followers. It is significant that, in fact, the philosophy of *ch'i* originated in the early sixteenth century and not, as Professor Levenson suggested, in the mid-seventeenth century, and that it came first from the heart of "orthodoxy," for, as Levenson would have been the first to agree, questions concerning chronology and the provenance of ideas are far from inconsequential to a fair assessment of intellectual continuities and discontinuities.

Lo Ch'in-shun dismissed the view that principle is in any sense prior to material force. He also rejected the view that it is superior to material force or that it is appropriate to distinguish principle and material force on the basis that only the latter is subject to integration and disintegration. He argued that principle was not to be understood as a "regulating power" (*chu-tsai*)[bl] within material force. Principle was not a "thing" (*wu*)[bm] but, more accurately, a "term" or "designation" (*ming*)[bn] for the way things are in actual fact, for the working of nature. Talking about "principle" is a way of talking about actual, perceptible reality. Lo answered a critical Neo-Confucian question, "what is principle?" in the following way:

That which penetrates Heaven and earth, enduring from past to present, is nothing other than material force, which is unitary. Material force is originally one but follows an endless cycle of movement and tranquillity, going and coming, opening and closing, rising and falling. Having become increasingly obscure, it then becomes manifest; through being manifest, it reverts to obscurity. It is the warmth and coolness and the cold and heat of the four seasons, and the birth, growth, gathering in and preservation of all living things. It is the people's daily life and social relations and the success and failure, gain and loss in human affairs. That which for all the multitudinousness and complexity cannot be disturbed, and which is so even without our knowing why it is so, is called principle. From the beginning principle is not a separate entity which depends on material force for its existence, nor is it something which "attaches to material force and thus operates."[46]

When he asserted that principle is "not a separate entity which 'attaches to material force and thus operates,' " Lo was alluding to and explicitly contradicting Chu Hsi, who had effectively summarized a particular view of causality in the statement, "Principle attaches to material force and thus operates."[47] Lo's statement was in effect a denial that there was any causal or determinative power associated with principle. Principle was the pattern itself, the actual reality, rather than the origin or cause of what is true of the natural process. He went on to elaborate what he believed to be a view of principle and the Supreme Ultimate more in conformity with classical conceptions than that of Chu Hsi:

There are some who because of the phrase, "There is in the changes the Supreme Ultimate,"[48] suspect that the transformations of yin and yang have a single entity that acts as a regulating power among them. This is not the case. "Change" is a collective name for the two primary forces, the four secondary forms, and the eight trigrams. The Supreme Ultimate is a collective name for all principles taken together. When [Confucius] said, "There is in the changes the Supreme Ultimate," he meant that manifold diversity takes its origin from a single source. This was then extended to the process of "production and reproduction"[49] to clarify that the dispersal of the single source produces manifold diversity. This is certainly the working of nature, its unregulated regularity, and not something that can be sought in the tangible realm.[50]

Following this discussion Lo went on to contrast the view of principle and material force held by Ch'eng Hao with the views of Ch'eng I and Chu Hsi. His conclusion was that only Ch'eng Hao had dealt with the problem "in truly subtle fashion."[51] He found distinct problems or inconsistencies inherent in the views of both Ch'eng I and Chu Hsi. Lo particularly faulted Chu Hsi's statements that, "Principle and material force are definitely two things,"[52] that, "Principle is strong and material force is weak,"[53] and that, "It is only when there is material force that principle finds a place to settle."[54] All of these statements suggested a dualism of li and ch'i, and, for this dualism, which Lo believed was without classical precedent, he was intent on substituting the monistic view that material force is the fundamental reality of the universe, while principle is the designation for its "unregulated regularity" or spontaneous order.

Principle is no more nor less than the pattern, or to use Joseph Needham's term, the "organization"[55] which may be observed in the operations of material force, though as Lo is careful to point out, its reality is not a function of our perception of it. As there is no such thing in Lo's view as a universal in the sense of a distinct entity present within each of the myriad individual things, there is also no absolute in the sense of a regulating power that defines and governs their operations and interactions. The Supreme Ultimate becomes a "term" or "collective name" for all principles taken together. When Lo refers to the Supreme Ultimate he has in mind a designation for the sum total of what is invariably true of the natural process. It is something to be observed and verified; it cannot be known a priori or from limited experience, however profound.

While Lo objected to Chu Hsi's philosophy of principle, he was even more pointedly critical of the early Ming Confucian, Hu Chü-jen, in whose philosophy principle, understood as a metaphysical absolute and supreme ethical norm, was stressed even more strongly than it had been in the philosophy of Chu Hsi.[56] Hu himself had been among the most prominent adherents of the Ch'eng-Chu school in the fifteenth century and was known as a man of the most austere dedication to Confucian ethical standards. However, while admiring Hu's personal integrity and moral fiber, Lo found himself deeply at odds with him intellectually and observed:

The discussion of reverence in the *Chü-yeh lu*[bo] (Record of Occupying One's Sphere of Activity) is very thorough, and it was because [Hu Chü-jen] embodied it in himself that his discussion of it was very personal and affecting. He also devoted his attention to "the exhaustive exploration of principle *(ch'iung-li)*,[bp] but in this case he seems to have been lacking in thoroughness. For example, he said, "*Ch'i* is what is produced by *li*," and, again, "The Way of man is produced by harmony and righteousness." Again, "That which brings about the Supreme Harmony is the Way." "First there is *li* and then there is *ch'i*." But anyone who reads the "Great Appendix" [to the *Book of Changes*] will see for himself whether [Hu's] theories agree with it or not.[57]

Lo went on to lament a loss of balance in the Ch'eng-Chu school of the early Ming, concluding that,

Although Chu Hsi regarded *li* and *ch'i* as two things, his statements were characterized by the utmost breadth and balance. None of his successors reached the same standard in their speculations, and so these qualities have been lost. For example, the *Hsing-shu*[bq] (Book on the Nature) by Yü Tzu-chi[br58] is an extreme case. He says, "*Ch'i* can lend beauty to *li*. Will not *li* save *ch'i* from decline?" On one occasion I happened to remark that I had not realized *li* and *ch'i* offered each other so much charitable assistance.[59]

Two standards are applied in Lo's critique of Hu Chü-jen and Yü Yu. The first is the standard of consistency with the classical conception of principle as found in the *Book of Changes*. The second is the standard of internal balance and cogency. The concept of "universal principle" (*t'ien-hsia chih li*)[bs] in the "Great Appendix" to the *Book of Changes* is not elaborately developed in that work,[60] and it is not suggested that Lo was either consciously or effectively repudiating the philosophical developments of the Sung period and reverting to a purely classical conception. Rather, what is suggested is that Lo's understanding of principle was essentially naturalistic and that his discussions of *li* and *ch'i* in the *K'un-chih chi* reflect an impulse to reduce, simplify, and clarify the notion of principle so that it would be more in keeping with his own understanding of a more naturalistic concept of principle found in the *Book of Changes*. The problem of internal consistency and cogency was also of great concern to him, possibly because his own habit of mind was rigorous, and he could see in a thinker like Yü Yu a tendency to become lost in jejune philosophical exercises.

A somewhat different view of the relation between principle and material force had been advanced by Hsüeh Hsüan. As has been noted above, Chu Hsi had said that the fact that principle was originally unimplicated in physical form indicated that it was prior to material force, which existed within physical form. As he put it, "When spoken of as being before or after physical form, is there not the difference of priority or posteriority?"[61] Hsüeh Hsüan differed with Chu Hsi to the extent that he repeatedly denied that principle could be considered prior to material force. For example, he said, "Principle only exists within material force (*li chih tsai ch'i shang*)[bt] and there can be no distinction of prior or posterior."[62] Again,

Someone said, "Before Heaven and earth existed there was this principle. There was this principle and then there was this material force."

I would say that principle and material force cannot be distinguished as prior or posterior. Before Heaven and earth existed, when the forms of Heaven and earth had not yet been completed, the material force that was to become Heaven and earth existed as an undifferentiated mass, and, there being neither pause nor interruption, principle was contained within material force.[63]

Here Hsüeh Hsüan was directly, if discreetly, disavowing Chu Hsi's view, since the statement he had chosen to contradict, the source of which went unidentified by Hsüeh, is among the opening lines of the first *chüan* of the *Chu Tzu yü-lei*.[bu][64] Hsüeh also stated, "Material force is limitless (*wu-ch'iung*)[bv]; principle is also limitless."[65]

To Lo's mind, however, this view was still flawed by a dualistic tendency, so while he unreservedly praised Hsüeh's personal integrity and a conception of scholarship that he found particularly illuminating, he remained honestly skeptical about what he felt to be certain lapses on the subject of *li* and *ch'i*:

It says in the [*Tu-shu*] *lu*[bw] (Record of My Reading), "Principle and material force are inseparable, and therefore it is said, 'Concrete things are the Way, and the Way is also concrete things.' "[66] This statement is correct. But I can only be skeptical in respect to [Hsüeh Hsüan's] repeated attempts to prove the theory that material force is characterized by integration and disintegration but that principle is not characterized by integration and disintegration. For if one were so characterized and the other were not, the separation between them would be considerable. How could one then say that, "Concrete things are the way and the way is also concrete things"? Wen-ch'ing[bx] [Hsüeh Hsüan] always regarded principle and material force as two things, and therefore the occasional contradiction inevitably showed up in his words.

Principle, being subtle, profound, and mysterious, is very difficult to discuss, and if one misses the truth by the slightest bit, there will be no way to avoid contradictions . . . It is my view that the integration of material force is itself the principle of integration and that the disintegration of material force is itself the principle of disintegration. Inferentially, [one may know that] it is the same in the growth and decline of all creation and in the beginning and end of all affairs and things. If it is discussed in these terms, [the nature of principle] will be naturally clear, and there will be no contradiction.[67]

Hsüeh Hsüan had evidently been holding fast to one aspect of Chu Hsi's theory of *li* and *ch'i*, the idea of principle as a timeless reality, immune to change. He parted from Chu Hsi by affirming that principle and material force are one rather than two and denying that principle is prior or superior to material force. Yet the fact that he did not entirely abandon the Sung view in all its aspects is illustrated by his statement that, "Material force is constantly changing and varied; principle is forever fixed and immutable."[68] It may be significant that, after the idea of the priority and superiority of principle had lapsed, the last vestiges of dualism in the thought of this early Ming adherent of the Ch'eng-Chu school survived in his defense of the immutability of principle. It is as if the tenure of Buddhist assumptions could not quite be revoked, and the "defect" of impermanence remained for a time a continuing cause for Neo-Confucian concern.

Other explanations for the Sung dichotomy of *li* and *ch'i* have been advanced, and on distinguished authority,[69] but the explanation that seems most cogent in philosophical terms is that the dualism was formulated as part of the Neo-Confucian response to and reaction against Buddhism. It is instructive that for nearly five centuries the Neo-Confucian reaction against Buddhism had been characterized by implicit acceptance of its warnings about change and impermanence, and a corresponding Neo-Confucian conviction that the metaphysical and moral bases of order and stability required constant attention. As late as the first half of the fifteenth century, Hu Chü-jen, an implacable foe of Buddhism, had maintained a view of principle and material force that was more explicitly dualistic than Chu Hsi's had been, while Hsüeh Hsüan, having modified Chu's view in several important respects, still clung to the perception of principle as a constant, beyond time and change. Less than a century later, Lo Ch'in-shun, possibly reacting against the thought of Hu Chü-jen,[70] denied that the refuge of an immutable principle apart from the flux of concrete things was defensible.

The common tendency in the thought of Chu Hsi, Hsüeh Hsüan, and Hu Chü-jen was a view of principle as the perfect and perduring element that exists unaltered by the integration and disintegration of material force. Principle, for them, was essentially timeless and permanent. For Lo, principle had neither priority nor permanence. It was itself the immutably mutable, the phenomenon of regularity within process, the inevitability and reliability of change as it affects and conditions concrete things. However, whereas in Buddhist terms, the recognition of change and impermanence implied the negative consequence that there could be no enduring self and its corollary that universality is discovered in the condition of suffering, in Lo's terms, change implied dynamism, vitality, and the constant process of renewal in the natural order. In his view,

Principle is only the principle of material force. It must be observed in the phenomenon of revolving and turning of material force. The successive process of going and coming is the phenomenon of revolving and turning. The fact that coming inevitably follows going, and going follows coming, is so even without our knowing why it is so, offering the semblance of a single entity acting as a regulating power within things and causing them to be as they are. This is what we designate as principle. [The statement in the "Great Appendix" to the Book of Changes,] "There is in the changes the Supreme Ultimate," refers to this. If one gains a clear understanding of this phenomenon of revolving and turning, one will find that everything conforms to it.[71]

Here are the elements of a consistent monism of ch'i in which principle is regarded as the pattern of change and development characteristic of the operations of material force.

It is particularly in respect to his emphasis on the concrete things of the phenomenal world and his active interest in the processes of change in nature that Lo's philosophy of *ch'i* contrasts so strikingly with that of Chang Tsai. The nature of Chang Tsai's philosophy of *ch'i* and the philosophical influences that it reflects constitute an important subject in the intellectual history of the Sung period and cannot be explored in detail here.[72] However, it is essential both to an understanding of the thought of Lo Ch'in-shun and an appreciation of the complex intellectual currents that were playing out in the Ming period to recognize that, unlike his contemporary Wang T'ing-hsiang, Lo in no sense considered himself a follower of Chang Tsai. Wang T'ing-hsiang, like the early Ch'ing thinker, Wang Fu-chih, had criticized Chu Hsi's theory of *li* and *ch'i* and defended Chang Tsai's view as a powerful and convincing alternative.[73] But Lo Ch'in-shun's disagreement with Chang was, if anything, more pronounced than his disagreement with Chu.

Briefly, it may be observed that Chang Tsai conceived of the Supreme Vacuity (*t'ai-hsü*)[by] as "the original substance of *ch'i* in its formless state" (*wu-hsing ch'i chih pen-t'i*).[bz][74] In one sense he regarded the Supreme Vacuity, *ch'i*, and the individual things of the phenomenal world as the same actuality in different states. In another sense he was inclined to distinguish the primal source or undifferentiated *ch'i* from the living beings and things of the actual world and to see the latter as representing a kind of falling away from a more fully integrated or unified and hence more perfect state of existence. This tendency to distinguish finite, differentiated reality from the formless infinitude of the Supreme Vacuity explains in part Chang Tsai's distinction between the nature of Heaven and earth (*t'ien-ti chih hsing*),[ca] which was understood to be pure and perfect, and the physical nature (*ch'i-chih chih hsing*),[cb] which was seen as flawed.[75] Lo's rejection of a distinction between the nature of Heaven and earth and the physical nature will be discussed more fully below. Here it must be observed that underlying his rejection of this distinction was his refusal to accept the notion that there was any such transcendent reality as the Supreme Vacuity, out of which finite reality emerged and into which it would ultimately be subsumed.

From Lo's standpoint Chang's thought too harbored a dualistic tendency:

In the passage from Master Chang's *Cheng-meng*[cc] (Correcting Youthful Ignorance), "From the Supreme Vacuity, there is Heaven . . ."[76] *li* and *ch'i* are regarded as two things. I do not doubt the depth 'of his inquiry, but his language is arbitrary and forced and fails to convey the natural principle of the nature and destiny.[77]

Chang had gone on in this passage of the *Cheng-meng* to say that:

From the transformation of material force, there is the Way. In the integration (*ho*)[cd] of the Supreme Vacuity and material force, there is the nature. And in the integration of the nature and consciousness, there is the mind.[78]

For Lo, the very notion of integration suggested a dualism, since only things that were originally distinct or separate could be spoken of as "integrating" or "combining." The implication of Lo's remark was that Chang Tsai's concept of the Supreme Vacuity, while explicitly identified by Chang with *ch'i*, was in some respects closer to Chu Hsi's concept of *li* than it was to Lo's own concept of *ch'i*. As the original, underlying reality of existence, it was perfect, enduring, infinite, and, in an ultimate sense, beyond change.

Another criticism Lo made of Chang Tsai was directed at his concept of the "transformation of *ch'i*," which Lo felt revealed unmistakable evidence of Buddhist influence:

In the *Cheng-meng* it says: "Whether integrated or disintegrated, it is my body just the same. One is qualified to discuss the nature of man when he realizes that 'death is not annihilation.' "[79] It also says, "In its disintegrated state, *ch'i* is scattered and diffuse. Through integration, it forms matter, thereby giving rise to the manifold diversity of men and things. Yin and yang follow one another in endless succession, thereby establishing the great norms of Heaven and earth."[80]

Now human beings and things experience life and death, but from the point of view of the universe, ten thousand aeons remain the same. When material force becomes integrated, a thing comes to life. Assuming physical form, the thing exists. When there is this thing, there is this principle. Upon the dispersal of its material force, the thing dies and finally reverts to nothingness. When there is no longer this thing, there is no longer this principle. How could there be this socalled "death without annihilation"? If in the natural course of the universe, the ten thousand aeons remain the same, what death and life, existence and annihilation could there be?

If one adopts the analogy of a tree, human beings and things are the flowers and leaves, while Heaven and earth are the trunk and roots. When the flowers fade and the leaves wither, they are blown away and scattered. The spirit of life of the trunk and roots is as before, but how can what is blown away and scattered have any further connection with the trunk and roots? Can one say that they are not annihilated? In referring to this statement of Chang Tsai's, Master Chu said that, "This leads to [viewing reality] as a great process of transmigration."[81] But Chang Tsai held to this view with great tenacity and did not realize his mistake was of this kind.[82]

Lo took the position that an individual life was finite and that annihilation was final. Chang Tsai would no doubt have found a disturbing starkness in the analogy of the tree, with its trunk and roots enduring, while its leaves and flowers are blown away and forever scattered. Were modern interpretive categories to be interjected, the crucial contrast between them might be discovered in Chang's idealistic belief in a "unity of substances" as against Lo's essentially naturalistic interest in a "continuity of natural processes."[83] With Lo, the focus had shifted from what is timeless and beyond change to the process of change itself.

This shift, so clearly indicated in Lo's critique of Chang, is of great importance in the context of the Neo-Confucian encounter with Buddhism, above all for the evidence it affords of a change in the way the issues were framed. Lo, as he developed his philosophy of ch'i, was no longer laboring to find Neo-Confucian answers to Buddhist philosophical problems— e.g., the absorbing problem of eternalism versus nihilism—but instead was primarily engaged in rethinking the problems themselves, drawing on earlier Neo-Confucian speculative efforts but also consciously tapping traditional Confucian sources. Certainly by mid-Ming times attitudes toward Buddhism had changed, as indicated both by the nature of the critiques that were being written in some quarters and the way in which Buddhist concepts were being assimilated and applied in others.[84] Different as they were as personalities and as thinkers, Lo Ch'in-shun and Wang Yang-ming, for example, both show signs of having come more fully to terms with Buddhism at a philosophical level than their predecessors in the Sung, Yüan, and early Ming ever had. It could hardly have been coincidental that both also came to adopt a philosophy of ch'i. One explanation for the change of direction in the mid-Ming period might well be that, having come to terms with Buddhism philosophically, Lo and Wang and their successors could then go on to redirect their attention to other concerns and to concrete things.

NATURE AND HUMAN NATURE

The concern for concrete things had many ramifications. Among the intellectual consequences of Lo Ch'in-shun's philosophy of ch'i was an understanding of human nature which differed markedly from Chu Hsi's. Having rejected the notion that principle and material force were distinguishable as "two things," Lo followed by refusing to allow a distinction between an original nature (*pen-jan chih hsing*),[ce] associated with principle, and a physical nature (*ch'i-chih chih hsing*), bound up with material force. The nature is one. Lo was persuaded that by discussing "the nature conferred by Heaven" (*t'ien-ming chih hsing*)[cf] as if it were opposed to "the physical substance" (*ch'i-chih*),[cg] Chang Tsai and Ch'eng I had proffered "two names for one thing," which in his view amounted to obscuration.[85]

He also criticized Chu Hsi's statement that, "The physical nature is the entirety of the Supreme Ultimate descended into the physical substance."[86] In a sense, this objection is reminiscent of one characteristically raised by the nominalists of medieval Europe against the idea of the entirety of a hypothetical universal being present in any given particular. But Lo's objection was not a strictly logical one such as had been raised by Peter Abelard against the doctrine of extreme realism or by William of Ockham against the subtle modification of that doctrine by Duns Scotus. Nor was he especially concerned with the status of universals as a logical problem. Rather, he was set on establishing one crucial point of ontology—namely, that there could be no universals apart from particulars, no *li* prior or superior to *ch'i*. And he was too careful an observer of the nuances of language to have overlooked the fact that Chu Hsi's choice of the word "descended" (*to*)[ch] in this context expressed, however inadvertently, a dualistic assumption.

Lo refused to admit such a dualism. Presumably alluding to a famous statement concerning the nature attributed to Ch'eng Hao,[87] he wrote:

Material force and the nature are one thing; there is only the difference that one is above form and the other is within form. Nourishing the nature is nourishing material force, and nourishing material force is nourishing the nature.[88]

Material force is the concrete and the nature the concretizing aspect of a single, integral reality. And because he understood reality as fundamentally undivided, it was no contradiction for him to maintain that "material force and the nature are one," and at the same time to endorse Ch'eng I's identification of the nature with principle. However, it had taken him some time and rethinking of terms to reach this conclusion. As he described it,

Chu Hsi once said that Ch'eng I's statement, "The nature is the same as principle," would be "the basis for pronouncements on the nature for countless future generations."[89] When I began my efforts I often endeavored to achieve personal experience of this statement, but for all my striving to achieve personal experience, there were aspects I could penetrate and others I could not. It went on that way for a number of years, and in the end I was unable to achieve a consistent solution. I suspected that this statement of Ch'eng I's was somehow incomplete and feared that Chu Hsi's statement too had been exaggerated so that it was difficult to believe without hesitation.

Then I put the matter aside for a time and took up the words principle and material force, examining one against the other and attempting to achieve personal experience. But for all my striving to achieve personal experience, there were again aspects I could penetrate and others I could not. Again this continued for several years, and, as before, I could not achieve a consistent solution.

I became extremely disheartened. I felt that my intelligence was limited, and I began to fear that in the end I would never succeed in my efforts. I was inclined to give up until suddenly I remembered the words, "Although one is dull, he will [through unremitting effort] surely become intelligent."[90] I could no longer give up but went back and applied myself to Ch'eng I's words, going over them again and again without putting them aside.

One day I experienced an enlightenment in respect to the words, "Principle is one; its particularizations are diverse (li-i fen-shu)."[ci 91] I turned to myself and verified this in regard to my own body and mind and then, by extension, in regard to other people. I verified it in connection with yin and yang and the five agents and, again, I verified it in connection with birds and beasts and with plants and trees. I found that everything conformed to it, and thus I began to feel overwhelming self-confidence and to realize that the words of these two gentlemen [Ch'eng I and Chu Hsi] would not lead me astray.

That I should go so far as to say this is not a matter of personal conceit. For I have often noticed that when in the writings of our [Confucian] school, the idea that "the nature is principle" is considered to be incorrect, it is simply because the word "principle" is difficult to understand, and it is often regarded as something that is obstructed by material force. As soon as [the critics] notice the lack of conformity, they assume that the statements of our Confucian predecessors are unworthy of credence . . .[92]

Just when he is reconfirming his confidence in Ch'eng I and Chu Hsi and defending them against the criticisms of detractors (presumably of the Wang Yang-ming school), Lo's own differences with Ch'eng and Chu become the more apparent. There can be no doubt that when he wrote,

"the word 'principle' is difficult to understand," he was tactfully expressing his disagreement with Chu Hsi, as Chu had been a proponent of the
theory that principle is obstructed by impure material force.[93] Unlike
Ch'eng I and Chu Hsi, Lo used the term "principle" to refer exclusively
to the recurrent aspect in the transformations of material force—the "organization" or regularity which may be discerned in the natural process.
Once principle had been so defined, and, essentially, taken out of the
moral sphere, Lo's use of the formula *hsing chi li*[cj] ("the nature is principle") represented a different order of philosophical statement.

While Lo did not get involved in the logical problems that so absorbed
the nominalists of medieval Europe, he expressed concern that the Sung
scholars' account of the phenomenon of individuation placed a great deal
of weight on accidental differences in *ch'i* without their having shown
commensurate interest in *ch'i* in and of itself. In their terms it was *li* that
was essential and invariant, while the *li* of human nature or of animal
nature was individuated through the external, adventitious forms associated with *ch'i*. In Lo Ch'in-shun's view, as in Peter Abelard's, the
qualities that serve to define a thing must be intrinsic to its nature, not
external to it. Lo came to this view not through an effort in logic, however, but through a process of simplification which seems to have taken
him back toward a more naturalistic concept of principle such as had
been current in Chinese thought prior to its transformation under the influence of Buddhism. In the course of his reflections on human nature
he found that the dichotomy of an essential *li* and an accidental *ch'i* was
unconvincing in that it was unnatural. He dismissed it in favor of a view
that was at once monistic and naturalistic and, concomitantly, discarded
the distinction between an ideal and a physical nature:

. . . In the Sung there emerged Ch'eng I, Chang Tsai, and Chu Hsi, who used
different terms to explain the question of what was the nature endowed by
Heaven and what was the physical nature. They formulated their theories with
reference to Confucius and Mencius and verified them in terms of the human
emotions, so that they were in this respect complete. But to a single nature they
applied two names. Although [Ch'eng I] said, "it is wrong to regard [the nature
and material force] as two,"[94] he was not yet able to see them as one. In the end
the doubts of scholars were not resolved, so that right down to the present their
endless debates are carried on in the world. And can one blame them?

I had pursued the problem day and night in an attempt to achieve personal experience. I had devoted years to it when suddenly one day it seemed to me that I

had understood it in its entirety. I submit that the wondrous truth of the nature and endowment is summarized in the expression, "Principle is one; its particularizations are diverse (*li-i fen-shu*)." [95] This is simple and yet complete, concise and yet utterly penetrating. [The operation of principle] owes nothing to artificial constraint or compulsion, and by its nature it surely cannot be changed.

Upon coming into existence and being endowed with material force, human beings and things are one in principle. After having attained physical form, they are diverse in their particularizations. That their particularizations are diverse is entirely in accordance with natural principle, for principle, which is unitary, always exists in diverse particularizations. This is the explanation for the wondrous truth of the nature and endowment . . .[96]

Just as the phrase *hsing chi li* had one meaning for Ch'eng I and another for Lo, so the phrase *li-i fen-shu* was interpreted differently in accordance with Lo's own concept of *li*. The aphorism is one that has found a place in the writing of almost every adherent of the Ch'eng-Chu tradition down to and including Tseng Kuo-fan,[ck97] though with varying significance in different contexts. While he applied the phrase in different ways, Ch'eng I had first enunciated it in an ethical context in the course of distinguishing Confucian ethics, in which universal and particular claims were balanced, from Mohist ethics, which enjoined universal love on utilitarian grounds as a most practical form of sublimation.[98] Lo's use of the phrase was primarily ontological.[99] As the quotations offered above indicate, he attached a great deal of importance to it because, as he interpreted it, it enabled him to resolve the Sung dualism of *li* and *ch'i* without, in consequence, having to resign from the Ch'eng-Chu school. Its peculiar usefulness was that it allowed him, mutatis mutandis, to account for the fact of individuation and the whole spectrum of phenomenal diversity naturalistically, without recourse to anterior judgments about the ethical quality of *ch'i*. His criticism of Ch'eng I and Chu Hsi was that their distinction between "the nature endowed by Heaven" and "the physical nature" was arbitrary and in a sense unnatural; it reflected just such a tendency to account for ethical potential (or its frustration) in terms of the varying quality of *ch'i*.

As Lo interpreted the phrase *li-i fen-shu*, the distinction between an ideal nature and a physical nature was unnecessary. Principle is originally one, and in this sense it is universal. In the simplest terms, it is the propensity of all living things to conform to an orderly process of change and development. Once having attained physical form and become discrete individuals, things differ both in form and in principle, and the nature or principle of a discrete individual impels it to complete its own life cycle or destiny. This is equally true of man and of other living things. It is an interesting consequence of the revised attitude toward *ch'i* that the distinction between human nature and the nature of other living beings tended to be perceived in terms of formal and species differences rather than in terms of the ethical quality (or relative purity) of *ch'i*. Among the more important consequences of the revised understanding of principle was the recognition that human nature had ontological reality, while ethical value inhered not in the nature itself but in knowledge of the nature. For Lo, the nature was less a substance, as A. C. Graham indicates it had been for Ch'eng I, and, to a more limited extent, for Chu Hsi as well,[100] and more a veridical object.

In identifying the nature with principle Ch'eng I had been asserting, in effect, that the goodness of the nature exists as an ideal essence within individuals. The statement, as made by him, was strongly ethical in its implications, for he was sanctioning a particular kind of ethical striving by confirming that the human endowment included this pure component and that, despite the impediments of material force, the purity might be recovered. In his identification of the nature with principle Lo Ch'in-shun had in mind not an essential goodness or purity but the spontaneous tendency of all beings to follow the internal dictates of their own natures. Since principle was, for him, the dynamic aspect of material force, the fact of recurrence in its transformations, his concept of the nature was also of a dynamic pattern characteristic of individual beings rather than of an ideal essence within them. This was why, in contrast to Ch'eng I and Chu Hsi, who were always conscious of a tension between the nature and the human feelings and desires, Lo regarded the feelings and desires as qualities of the nature, as visible signs of an invisible reality. As he said,

The fact that man has desires definitely derives from Heaven (or Nature). Some are necessary and cannot be repressed, and some are appropriate and cannot be changed. If those that are irrepressible all conform to the principle of what is appropriate, how can they be bad? It is only heedlessly giving way to the passions, indulging the desires, and not knowing how to turn back [to the proper course] that is evil. Confucians of the past often spoke about eliminating or checking human desires, and the means by which they would prevent unrestraint had to be severe. But their language seems overly emphatic. The desires, together with pleasure, anger, sorrow, and joy, are qualities of the nature. Can pleasure, anger, sorrow and joy also be eliminated?[101]

When Lo argued that the desires, together with pleasure, anger, sorrow and joy, are qualities of the nature, he claimed to be arguing on classical authority. [102] But this was not a pro forma argument only, and there was more involved than a dispassionate defense of passion. When he concluded by asking rhetorically whether pleasure, anger, sorrow and joy could be eliminated, he was suggesting that one must begin by observing what is "natural" in actual human behavior rather than by seeking an ideal model of the selfless man.

This reaction against the more rigorous demands of the Sung scholars for effacing the desires may be understood as another sign that Lo had reckoned more fully with Buddhism than had his predecessors, who had been more subject to the influence of Buddhist psychology and perhaps more quietistically inclined. One might offer the same general interpretation for the new attitude toward the feelings and desires that was emerging at about the same time in the Wang Yang-ming school. But as important as the reaction itself, is the question of what prompted it and what the new attitude implied in each case. Wang Yang-ming took a more affirmative view of the human emotions than had Lu Hsiang-shan, as is evidenced in statements such as, "When the seven feelings follow their natural courses of operation, they are all functions of innate knowledge and cannot be distinguished as good or evil . . . When there is an attachment to the seven feelings we call them selfish desires, and they become obscurations to innate knowledge." [103] As Professor Yamashita Ryūji has observed, "Yang-ming's approval of the feelings and desires had to do with their issuing from the natural mind of human beings and not with his view of *li* and *ch'i* as an integral unity." [104] It would appear that, as Professor Yamashita has suggested, Lo's affirmation of the human desires was directly related to his view of *li* and *ch'i* and to his determination to concentrate on actual individuals and things in the real and immediate world of human experience.

The distinction, though subtle, is valid. Wang's more affirmative view of the human feelings was expressed in terms of an interest in innate knowledge, the source of moral potential which was recognized to exist in every human being. Lo's revised attitude toward the desires derived at least in part from his particular interest in *ch'i* and his belief that ethical judgments apply to thought or conduct, but not to material force itself. In his view, anything that is natural or that derives from Nature has its own validity; the human feelings and desires, being natural, cannot be extinguished or eliminated, but only regulated and channelled. The defense of the human desires is one example of a tendency to start with what is observably true of actual, existing things and to proceed from there.

By way of putting Lo Ch'in-shun's view of human nature into perspective as an expression of the evolution of Neo-Confucian thought in the mid-Ming period, the following interpretation may be offered. Lo was suggesting, in effect, that the theoretical systems elaborated by "Confucians of the past" were too rigid, too abstract, as it were, and did not take concrete human realities adequately into account. His argument, reduced to its simplest form, was that the Sung concept of principle had been an abstraction which had come to seem unnatural. The distinction between an ideal nature, associated with *li*, and a physical nature, associated with *ch'i*, was the basic abstraction, and the denial of human feelings and desires on the ground that they were contrary to principle was its corollary. For Wang Yang-ming, the abstraction was manifested in the Sung concept of sagehood, and his modification of it was expressed in the assertion that, "In innate knowledge and innate ability, men and women of simple intelligence and the sage are equal."[105] Though the philosophical implications were different, it might be argued that for both Lo and Wang the tension between an ideal world and the real world of ordinary experience was eased.

Though both Wang and Lo may be said to have reacted against the abstract character of Sung thought where "abstract" is understood to imply some degree of detachment from the observable realities of ordinary human experience, neither went so far as to reject abstract thought where "abstract" is understood to mean a speculative concern with metaphysical issues. In registering their differences with Ch'eng I and Chu Hsi, both confirmed that, philosophically speaking, the Sung thinkers had left unfinished business. It was not that the enterprise of Sung philosophy was invalid but that certain of the assumptions of the Sung thinkers about nature and human nature were in need of revision. A similar impulse to revise and modify applied in the area of epistemology.

THE NATURE OF KNOWLEDGE AND THE KNOWLEDGE OF NATURE

Ch'eng I's affirmation that, "When the self is established, one will naturally understand the myriad things in the world,"[106] reflected a remark-

able assurance about the accessibility of knowledge; from the ethical condition of the self being established, he proceeded to the intellectual
consequence of the myriad things being understood. Ch'eng I had not
been inclined to make a clear distinction between ethical and epistemological concerns, and the kind of understanding he had in mind apparently involved not so much cognitive knowledge as a sympathetic
identification on the part of the morally disciplined individual with the
whole of nature through an extension of ethical consciousness. Nor did
the "investigation of things" as understood by Ch'eng I and Chu Hsi necessarily involve an empirical approach to reality or even a genuine interest in nature per se. One might say that they looked to nature with an eye
to sagehood, since the investigation of external reality was to serve above
all to provide corroboration of the internal reality of principle. This was
why it was possible for Ch'eng I to hold that essentially the same result
could be attained either through internal or external cultivation and, so
long as there was no loss of mental poise, through a broad or a concentrated program of study.

Oriented as they were toward the goal of principle as an integrative reality, the primary criterion of knowledge for Ch'eng I and Chu Hsi was
whether it was profound or superficial, morally edifying or stultifying.
Though all Neo-Confucians might agree on this as an ultimate standard,
other criteria began to be introduced by Ming thinkers, apparently in
conjunction with the philosophy of ch'i. In line with his revised concept
of principle, Lo Ch'in-shun began to move toward other criteria for
knowledge, chief among them being generality, consistency, and verifi-
ability—standards more appropriate to the observation of dynamic developmental tendencies within and among things than to a search for their
ultimate ontological reality. The transition was only beginning in the
Ming period, and Lo's formulation of the criteria for knowledge must be
considered rudimentary. However, as standards were elaborated and refined by Ch'ing thinkers of the seventeenth and eighteenth centuries and
by Tokugawa thinkers of the same period, a critical spirit came to the
fore. In marking the emergence of that spirit in one of its earlier manifestations, it becomes possible to gain some insight into continuities within
the Neo-Confucian tradition which might otherwise go unnoticed.

One of the ways in which the new spirit manifested itself in the early
sixteenth century was in a revised attitude toward sense perception.
Ch'eng I and Chu Hsi, who had been given to making ethical judgments

about the relative quality of the original endowment of *ch'i*, were naturally inclined to entertain certain reservations about the physical body
and the sense organs associated with it. But when *ch'i* was accepted as
morally neutral (i.e., as formally "diverse" rather than qualitatively
"pure" or "impure") such reservations lost much of their hold. Having
resolved the Sung dualism of *li* and *ch'i* and concluded that *ch'i* did not
represent an obstruction to *li*, Lo discarded the belief that, "the knowledge obtained through hearing and seeing is not the knowledge obtained
through the moral nature."[107] This latter view was one of the epistemological consequences of the dualistic thinking of the Sung and gradually began to drop out of currency as Buddhism came under philosophical attack and monistic theories gained acceptance in the Ming.

At no point in the *K'un-chih chi* is sense perception deprecated relative
to moral knowledge or contrasted with knowledge of higher truth. In fact,
Lo was at some pains to try to refute the Buddhist idea that knowledge of
absolute reality was distinct from and, in fact, opposed to sense perception, the former unitary and integrative and the latter fragmentary and
delusive. His argument was directed at the Buddhists when he wrote,
"There are those who say that the truth (*dharma*, *fa*)[cl] is separate from
seeing, hearing, knowing and understanding. How can they be conscious
of something apart from seeing, hearing, knowing and understanding?"[108] The notion that the mind had a potential for knowledge
independent of the senses was from his point of view altogether
untenable:

[The Buddhists] consider the knowledge of the mind (*hsin-shih*)[cm] as fundamental
and the knowledge associated with the six senses (*liu-shih*)[cn] as secondary. Their
terminology is not at fault, but inquiry into the realities indicates that there is no
such thing as sense knowledge apart from the knowledge of the mind. Nor is it a
matter of the unity of the mind being divided in the six senses. When one sees
something, the entirety [of the mind] is involved in the eye. When one hears
something, the entirety [of the mind] is involved in the ear. When one speaks,
the entirety [of the mind] is involved in the mouth, and when one moves, the
entirety [of the mind] is involved in the body. (I have selected just these four
examples in the interests of simplicity and comprehensibility.)[109] This is precisely
the principle which is referred to [in the "Great Appendix to the *Book of Changes*]
where it speaks of [the mind's] "being stimulated and then penetrating."[110]
Viewed in this way, the mind and the senses are obviously one. How can one
divide them into two and associate one part with truth and the other with
delusion?[111]

Similarly, he argued with Ou-yang Te^{co} (1496–1554), a leading disciple of Wang Yang-ming, over his suggestion that innate knowledge (*liang-chih*)^{cp} might be considered distinct from sense perception:

There cannot be two kinds of human knowledge. Mencius' original idea was that that which people know without having to reflect is called innate (*liang*).^{cq112} It was not that he spoke of another kind of knowledge apart from this.

Now if one takes knowing commiseration, knowing shame and dislike, knowing deference, and knowing right and wrong to be "innate knowledge" (*liang-chih*) and the knowledge involved in seeing, hearing, speaking and acting to be "consciousness" (*chih-chüeh*)^{cr}, are these really two kinds of knowledge? When people see, hear, speak and act, they usually do so without reflection. As a drum sounds on being struck, so we respond immediately to stimuli. What is different in the case of the arising of commiseration, shame and dislike, deference, and the sense of right and wrong? The arising of the "four beginnings" [of virtue] is always related to seeing, hearing, speaking, and acting. The sense of right and wrong is expressed through one's mouth, reverence is expressed through one's demeanor, dislike for an offensive odor is expressed through covering the nose. When one sees a child about to fall into a well, one immediately rushes headlong to save it. What is the difference between the perception and the response? Knowledge is unitary, and nowhere in the writings of our sages and worthies are arbitrary distinctions made.^{113}

Lo insisted that it was through Buddhist influence that a distinction between sense perception and knowledge of the absolute had gained currency but that the distinction was both unwarranted and untraditional. He implied that Neo-Confucians who made a similar distinction between moral knowledge and sense perception revealed their own susceptibility to Buddhist influence. It would be highly misleading were one to argue that, in removing the stigma that had attached to sense perception, Lo had adopted a thoroughgoing empiricism. But at least one of the negative conditions for an empiricism was met when reservations about the value or significance of sense experience were effectively dispelled.

Another element in Sung theories of knowledge that apparently derived from the dualism of *li* and *ch'i* was the tacit assumption that the highest knowledge, being knowledge of principle, was also knowledge of the unperceived. Chang Tsai, for example, understood the most excellent operation of the mind to involve a process of enlargement to enable it to "embody" all things in the universe (*t'i t'ien-hsia chih wu*).^{cs114} Chu Hsi, in commenting on Chang's idea, observed that, "Although we have not attained to that standard [i.e., of enlarging the mind to the utmost], we must still learn to say that beyond the senses there is a realm of principle which cannot be seen or heard. If we have not learned so much, how can the mind be extended?"[115] There are other statements in Chu Hsi's writings and conversations which imply that principle may be at least indirectly perceived, but in general when a particular kind of mental process is prescribed as appropriate to arriving at the realm of principle, verbs of perception are not preferred. The general attitude of the Sung thinkers toward sense experience has been adumbrated above; here another reason for their reluctance to rely on sense data for obtaining the highest truth is suggested—namely, the status of principle as unperceived truth.

In this respect too attitudes began to change during the Ming, and Lo Ch'in-shun's view is again illustrative. He specified that principle must be perceived as an aspect of material force.

> Principle must be identified in the context of material force (*li hsü chiu ch'i shang jen ch'ü*)[ct], and yet to identify material force with principle (*jen ch'i wei li*)[cu] would be incorrect. The distinction between the two is very slight, and hence it is difficult to explain. Rather we must perceive it within ourselves and understand it in silence. To speak of "identifying principle in the context of material force" or of "identifying principle with material force" amounts to two different statements, and there is a clear distinction between them. If this is not apparent, there is no point in explaining further.[116]

The observation that "principle must be identified in the context of material force" was at variance with Chu Hsi's view that, "beyond the senses there is a realm of principle which cannot be seen or heard." Lo had argued at the outset that, "principle is only the principle of material force," and the conclusion he drew in epistemological terms was that principle could not be abstracted as a separate realm but had always to be identified in the context of concrete things in the sensible world. Since the distinction between a thing and its nature or way of being was in his terms "very slight" (unlike the separation between opposing physical and spiritual realms), direct observation of actual things was the appropriate mode of discovery of principle. Lo did not reject spiritual consciousness, but neither did he see sense experience and spiritual consciousness as mutually exclusive or conflicting modes. For him, employing the senses to know the concrete things of the world was a legitimate pursuit in itself and an essential prerequisite to higher forms of integration.

A third respect in which Lo's epistemological perspective differed from that of several of his predecessors in the Sung was in the far greater emphasis that he placed on intellectual cultivation. In his article "Epistemological Methods in Chinese Philosophy," E. R. Hughes described the epistemology of the Ch'eng-Chu school as "personal illumination following a long period of arduous study plus commensurate ethical practice plus concentrated meditation."[117] There may be grounds for questioning whether such a methodology is quite as "clear" and "cogent" as Professor Hughes suggested,[118] or even whether it should strictly be called a distinct epistemology. But as a general description of the Sung approach to knowledge it seems faultless. It aptly expresses how deeply interfused intellectual and ethical concerns were in the minds of many Sung scholars and suggests how disinclined they were to specify what the relation might be between the two. Given the Sung context, there was no particular need for them to do so, since their primary concern was to combat Buddhist skepticism with a reassertion of the practicality of moral knowledge and a reaffirmation of Confucian confidence in the efficacy of individual moral action in all spheres of active life.

In the Ming period, particularly from the sixteenth century onward, the challenge of Buddhism tended to be perceived in different terms;[119] in this context Lo and others, including his contemporary Wang T'ing-hsiang, began to reemphasize a skeptical spirit. Several also sought to define more clearly the relation between intellectual and moral cultivation and to establish a reliable order of approach. This insistence on a reliable order of approach became the central problem of Lo's thought and one that he worked out in considerable detail in the process of developing his critique of Buddhism. Through years of study he had come to the view that the problem with Buddhist enlightenment was that it was possibly real but necessarily unreliable. He did not doubt that there were those who actually experienced enlightenment, nor was he insensitive to its cognitive implications, but as a Confucian, he worried that the experience as he had known it was elusive and ultimately unproductive, that the perception of non-duality could not of itself be sustained so as to be rendered serviceable. He argued, in effect, that it is one thing to see the world and everything in it as one in a momentary flash of inspiration. This was certainly within the capacity of "the mind's spiritual intelligence" (jen-hsin chih shen-ming).[cv] It was another thing to know the world in a veridical sense on the basis of a study of its principles of change and development. The former can be understood as a kind of mental clarity or illumination which may be attained through meditative discipline. The latter is knowledge of the nature of things, achieved only through an intellectual process of study and observation.

Lo repeatedly returned in the *K'un-chih chi* to the necessary distinction between the mind as an active subject and the nature as its veridical object. When he wrote that, "Buddhist learning is on the whole involved with perceiving the mind rather than with perceiving the nature,"[120] he was indicting the Buddhists for excessive concern with the mind's subjective function and neglect of the world's objective reality. He noted that the denial of the self could paradoxically generate an antithetical preoccupation with the very subjective consciousness that was being called into question, an observation which then seems to have become the point of departure for his own theory of knowledge.

Lo attributed to the Ch'eng brothers the revival of the doctrine of the "investigation of things" from the *Great Learning* as a corrective for the Buddhist tendency to excessive emphasis on interiority. His analysis of what was happening in intellectual life in the eleventh century was that:

At that time Ch'an was flourishing, and students were often deeply immersed in theories of "clarifying the mind and perceiving the nature." They no longer applied their minds to the principles of Heaven and earth and the myriad things, and so they constantly fell into partiality and were deluded about the self . . . The Ch'eng brothers were deeply distressed about this, and so they expounded the text of the *Great Learning* and explained the idea of the investigation of things. Their idea was to enable students to give equal attention to external things and the self, harmonize inner and outer, and correlate subject and object. This was the profound way in which they saved people from error and brought them into the great Mean . . .[121]

The object of Chang Tsai's ethical cultivation had been to "enlarge" the mind so that it could "embody" or sympathetically unite with all things in the universe, the necessary condition being the end of egotism. Though similarly motivated, Ch'eng I had made more of a place for intellectuality in the process of cultivation by his attention to the "investigation of things." Chu Hsi further extended the claims of intellectuality, and, as Professor Wing-tsit Chan has observed, Chu's "completion of Neo-Confucianism" must be understood in terms of his selection of "investigating the principles of things" as the "first and foremost" task of cultivation.[122] As a follower of Chu Hsi in the Ming, Lo Ch'in-shun resolutely defended intellectuality, abandoning the meditative practices of the Sung thinkers and emphasizing the investigation of things almost exclusively. His interpretation of "investigation" also involved a more decisive commitment to the observation of the external world. In a continuation of the passage quoted immediately above he wrote:

This principle as it exists in the world proceeds from unity to the myriad things without any artificial compulsion, and when the many reconverge into the one, it allows for no selfish constraint. Thus in "seeking in oneself" there is nothing better than to begin with one's own nature and feelings.[123] If one has perceived something there but finds that it is not applicable when extended to external things, it is not ultimate principle. Seeking it in external things, there is no difference in respect to birds and beasts or plants and trees. If one has perceived something there but refers back to one's own mind and finds any incongruity, it is not ultimate principle. Only when one has clear insight into the wondrous consistency which is such that there is absolutely no difference between subject and object, and that, despite the immense variety of particular forms, there is no possibility of confusion, can the task of the investigation of things and the extension of knowledge be considered complete. But this can only be accomplished through genuine and unremitting effort over a long period of time.[124]

In contrast to empirical observations, which ordinarily require confirmation, moral intuitions may be complete and contained, and if the goal of cultivation is, as Chang Tsai understood it, to attain unity with the mind of Heaven or to achieve the perfection of ethical consciousness, there is nothing to be tried or tested. The standard may be purely internal. But Ch'eng I and Chu Hsi had already turned their attention outward, seeking to find a more objective basis for the relation of inner and outer reality, and Lo was still more explicit in looking for the truth of oneness as a factual reality characteristic of nature itself and not of consciousness only. His idea of confirming the principle discerned in one's own nature and feelings through the observation of external reality and, conversely, of confirming the realities of nature through one's personal experience, suggests both an intellectual assurance in confronting the phenomenal diversity of nature and a more critical attitude toward the process of understanding principle than had been current in Sung times. In his terms "ultimate principle" (chih-li)^{cw} represented a level of generality in which individual differences would be subsumed. It would be discovered through comparative observation and critical scrutiny, or, to use his preferred definition of the ko in ko-wu, by "penetrating everywhere with no omissions."[125]

The insistence that an "ultimate principle" must be tested and that a generality will be invalidated as an "ultimate principle" if it is disconfirmed through conflicting evidence may be seen to reflect the emergence of a critical spirit *prior* to the development of a critical method. However, the emergence of this spirit in the Ming is itself interesting because it indicates the important implications of the revised attitude toward principle as the pattern of organization in material force. As Professor Minamoto[cx] observes in his article appearing in this volume, this revision was possibly the most crucial shift in emphasis to occur within the Chu Hsi school during the Ming and early Tokugawa periods.[126] Lo's skepticism had a precedent in Chu Hsi's own attitude toward the classics and textual study,[127] but here the range of critical scrutiny was extended to other areas of inquiry as well, including issues of law, taxation, and landholding, which had a direct bearing on public policy. The transition from Lo's insistence on the need to confirm the reality of an "ultimate principle" to Kaibara Ekken's[cy] (1630–1714) concern with a critical method, as described by Professors Okada[cz] and Minamoto, was no doubt an important step, as was the extension of active interest to the world of nature per se, but it may also be seen as a natural and even a logical one.

CONTINUITIES AND DISCONTINUITIES

At this point it is appropriate to pick up a loose thread in the argument: the consideration of chronology and the provenance of ideas. Here it may be observed that Joseph Needham seems to slight the scope and significance of the philosophy of *ch'i*, particularly in the matter of epistemology, when he describes it as "a great reverse movement" against the supposedly "idealist" doctrine of Wang Yang-ming and his followers, "which, though accepting the philosophy of Chu Hsi as the highest orthodoxy, tended to criticise him for not being materialistic enough."[128] It has already been pointed out in reference to Joseph Levenson's analysis of Ch'ing empiricism that the origins of this "empiricism" were actually considerably earlier. In directing his attention primarily to the Ch'ing thinkers, beginning with Wang Fu-chih, Professor Needham, like Professor Levenson, seems to neglect the fact that the philosophy of *ch'i* was in the fullest sense a Ming product.[129] It should also be observed that Lo Ch'in-shun was an older contemporary of Wang Yang-ming, and while the exact nature of the mutual influence between the two remains unclear, there is ample textual evidence to show that Lo's formulation of the philosophy of *ch'i* represented *not* a reaction against Wang but an attempt to resolve the problems he felt had been left unresolved by his own forbears in the Ch'eng-Chu school. It may also be somewhat misleading to suggest that the "naturalist" thinkers of the Ch'ing accepted the philosophy of Chu Hsi as "the highest orthodoxy" because such a statement tends to underestimate the degree of flexibility and change within the tradition. The Ch'ing thinkers whom Professor Needham describes as "naturalists" differed from Chu Hsi in many respects and said so openly and unequivocally. Finally, it is highly debatable whether the philosophy of *ch'i* is aptly described as "materialism."

This, in fact, may be the nub of the problem. It seems likely that because the philosophy of *ch'i* has been styled "materialism," it has been assumed (the dialectical mode being as attractive as it is) that it must have come into being as a reaction against a philosophical "idealism." Since the latter term could plausibly, if inaccurately, be applied to the Wang Yang-ming school, a neat conceptual schema seemed to be available for the interpretation of changing intellectual styles. But the realities would appear to have been more complex. Even if the term "materialism" were carefully qualified and provisionally allowed as a description for the philosophy of *ch'i*, there would remain the problem of explaining the wide currency of the philosophy of *ch'i*, particularly in the latter part of the sixteenth century, in terms of the idealist/materialist dichotomy.

Lo Ch'in-shun and Wang T'ing-hsiang, who, as we have seen, were among the earliest proponents of a philosophy of *ch'i*, were followed by a number of other Ming scholars who also showed signs of rejecting a philosophy that accorded priority to *li* and concentrating instead on *ch'i* as the fundamental reality of the universe. The trend of thought represented by these scholars was, to my knowledge, first recognized by Yamanoi Yū[da][130] and subsequently studied in detail by Yamashita Ryūji.[131] The Ming thinkers cited by Professor Yamanoi include Wang Tao[db] (1476–1523), Chiang Hsin[dc] (1483–1559), Wei Chiao[dd] (1483–1543), Liu Pang-ts'ai[de] (a disciple of Wang Yang-ming, dates unknown), Wang Chi[df] (1498–1583), Lü K'un[dg] (1536–1618), T'ang Hou-cheng[dh] (1538–1619), Yang Tung-ming[di] (1548–1624), Sun Shen-hsing[dj] (1565–1636), and Liu Tsung-chou[dk] (1578–1645). Yamanoi also identified among the Ch'ing proponents of the philosophy of *ch'i*, Ch'en Ch'ueh[dl] (1604–77), Huang Tsung-hsi, Wang Fu-chih, Yen Yüan, Li Kung, and Ch'eng T'ing-tsu[dm] (1691–1767). He saw the culmination of this trend of thought in the philosophy of Tai Chen.

It will be noted that, besides Lo, an adherent of the Ch'eng-Chu tradition, and Wang T'ing-hsiang, an admirer of Chang Tsai, the list of Ming thinkers includes followers of Wang Yang-ming. Recent studies by Yamashita Ryūji and others suggest that there is also reason to include Wang himself, since, in the later development of his thought, *li* and *ch'i* are affirmed as one in line with an understanding of *liang-chih* as an integral whole.[132] The implications of the focus on the immediate and concrete by members of the Wang Yang-ming school are explored in other articles in this volume; here this development is mentioned only in order to establish that the philosophy of *ch'i* represented a broadly based movement in the sixteenth century and that Lo Ch'in-shun's espousal of it did not represent an isolated case. Secondly, it should be apparent from the inclusion of followers of Wang Yang-ming among those tending toward a philosophy of *ch'i* that what was involved in the shift from a philosophy of *li* to a philosophy of *ch'i* could not have been simply a "materialist" reaction against an "idealist" philosophy of mind, since to impute to "idealist" thinkers the adoption of a "materialist" premise would entail obvious semantic difficulties.

Finally, it may be observed that the philosophy of *ch'i* involved not one strand of thought but several and that it originally arose not as a reaction against one of the major Neo-Confucian schools but as a development within both of them. Lo Ch'in-shun regarded himself as no less Confucian and no less an adherent of the Ch'eng-Chu tradition because he disagreed with Chu Hsi over *li* and *ch'i*, and this fact suggests that, for him, and doubtless for other Ming Neo-Confucians as well, the commitment to a specific metaphysical doctrine was far less crucial to the continuity of the Neo-Confucian tradition than the perspective on man and society which was at its heart.

ALTERNATIVE VIEWS OF ORTHODOXY

From the foregoing it should be apparent that Lo Ch'in-shun's own conception of orthodoxy did not involve strict or literal adherence to the doctrinal formulations of his Sung predecessors. For Lo, "orthodoxy" did not require the acceptance of specific doctrines of Chu Hsi's about *li* and *ch'i*, the Supreme Ultimate, or human nature, any more than "orthodoxy" for the late Ming painter and critic Tung Ch'i-ch'ang[dn] (1555–1636) meant routinely repainting the masterpieces of Tung

Yüan.[do] Rather, orthodoxy involved a particular sense of discipline and of tradition—a characteristically intellectual perspective, a conscious focusing on intellectual continuities, and a developed appreciation for the relevance of the cumulative experience of the past for the efforts and concerns of the present. A commitment to orthodoxy implied, for Lo, rigor but not rigidity, and his conclusion about his own relation to the Sung thinkers was at one point expressed this way:

Although the learning of the Ch'eng brothers and Chu Hsi might be called complete (chih),[dp] in their own minds, they certainly never considered it complete. How do I know this? When Ch'eng I's Commentary on the Book of Changes[dq] was finished, he would show it to no one. When someone asked him about it, he said, "In my own opinion my vital powers have not yet declined, and I still hope to see some slight improvement."[133] When Master Chu was nearing the age of seventy he lamented that he was "still not able to see everything clearly."[134] They truly had insight into the inexhaustibility of moral principles, and in their minds they could not be contented. Nor were they simply being modest in what they said.

I have taken up all of the writings of Ch'eng I and Chu Hsi and sought their finest essence, reading them over and over again without stop. It is only in the case of the words of Ch'eng Hao that I feel not the slightest doubt. The writings and conversations of Ch'eng I and Chu Hsi are numerous, and they often probe the furthest depths and attain the utmost subtlety. Both sides of an argument are explored to the fullest. The reason that I have doubts is that I have yet to see that they achieve a final integration. Can this be called "still not seeing everything clearly"? To search their statements for what is not yet integrated can only be done by one who genuinely honors and trusts them. This is why I devote all my mind to this and dare not be neglectful.[135]

There is no reason to believe that Lo's devotion was prompted by either superficial tact or political expedience. Many passages in the K'un-chih chi indicate that he did have the most genuine respect for Chu Hsi's intellectual integrity and his commitment to sustained and careful inquiry. This was why in his letter of 1520 to Wang Yang-ming Lo defended Chu both for his textual study and scholarly perspective and criticized Wu Ch'eng (1249–1333) for contraposing textual study (which implied acknowledgment of indebtedness to the collective wisdom of the past) and personal enlightenment (which supposed reliance on individual apprehension of truth). Wu Ch'eng had claimed that he experienced enlightenment only *after* he had given up the kind of textual study advocated by Chu Hsi, and Wang Yang-ming had applauded Wu's recognition that truth was to be discovered as an interior reality. Lo questioned not the claim to enlightenment or the high value assigned to the individual mind but rather the suggestion that the study had been without its ultimate rewards. He maintained that the past, personal or historical, could not be denied but that it was available to the present in the measure that it could be consciously absorbed and utilized for present purposes. This was the context of his observation that, "It is possible that upon catching the fish one forgets the fishtrap and that upon catching the rabbit one forgets the snare. But is it reasonable to boast about catching the fish and the rabbit and then turn around and find fault with the trap and the snare for having gotten in the way?"[136] The allusion to Chuang Tzu was, if ironic, nonetheless genial. This was hardly a narrow or defensive attitude toward orthodoxy.

By contrast, a considerably more introverted or defensive attitude toward orthodoxy became prevalent during the Ch'ing period, and the fate of the K'un-chih chi in the early eighteenth century serves as an example of this defensiveness. When Chang Po-hsing[dr] (1652–1725), one of the leaders of the "Sung school" in the early eighteenth century, edited the K'un-chih chi for inclusion in the Cheng-i-t'ang ch'üan-shu[ds] (Complete Library of the Hall of Rectifying the Way), the compendium of "orthodox" writings representing the period from the Sung to Chang's own time, he expunged virtually all of the passages in which Lo had elaborated his philosophy of ch'i and all of those in which he had directly criticized Chu Hsi. Chang's editorial disposition, which obviously guided his approach to the writings of other orthodox writers of the Ming as well,[137] was perhaps anticipated by the attitude of another Ch'ing adherent of the Sung school, Lu Lung-ch'i[dt] (1630–1693), who had written, "Master Chu was the one who continued Confucius and clarified the Six Classics. That which is not the Way of Confucius should be destroyed. Therefore that which is not the Way of Master Chu should be destroyed."[138] Whatever the reasons for such an attitude toward the role of Chu Hsi and for the tendency to define orthodoxy in narrower terms, it is clear that the balance of appreciation and skepticism exemplified by several Ming adherents of the orthodox tradition no longer prevailed among Ch'ing writers, for whom "orthodoxy" came to refer to fidelity to certain doctrinal requirements rather than to a sense of an evolving tradition. Professor Ying-shih Yü[du] has suggested that the great eighteenth-century thinker Tai Chen may have been influenced by Lo Ch'in-shun in his attitudes toward *li* and *ch'i*, human nature, and the human desires.[139] Yet, significantly, whereas Lo saw himself within the orthodox fold, Tai finally felt compelled to reject the Ch'eng-Chu tradition and to present his own views not as a revision or an extension of orthodoxy, but as a repudiation of it.

The work of Professor Abe Yoshio serves to show very clearly that the later career of orthodoxy in Japan was quite different. This was at least partly because the tradition, which was reintroduced into Japan in the late sixteenth century by way of Korea—through Korean editions of Chinese works and the mediation of several prominent Korean Neo-Confucians—divided almost from the beginning into two distinct schools or trends of thought.[140] The first, identified with the philosophy of *ch'i*, came to be associated with such thinkers as Hayashi Razan[dv] (1583–1657), Kaibara Ekken, and Kinoshita Jun'an[dw] (1621–1699). The second, identified with the philosophy of *li*, which had been developed in Korea in the school of Yi T'oegye[dx] (1501–1570), came to be associated in Japan with Yamazaki Ansai[dy] (1618–1682) and his followers in the Kimon[dz] school, and Ōtsuka Taiya[ea] (1677–1750) and his followers in the Kumamoto[eb] school. According to Professor Abe, the understanding of what principle was and what relation it had to material force represented the essential difference between these two tendencies or schools of thought in the early Tokugawa period. He suggests that the strongly intellectual and empirical orientation of the thinkers who adopted a philosophy of *ch'i* was a direct consequence of their perception of *ch'i* as the underlying reality of the universe, whereas the ethical and religious orientation of those who espoused a philosophy of *li* was a consequence of their conviction that behind the individual concrete things of the world lay the more fundamental and enduring reality of principle.

On the basis of his study of the intellectual developments of the early Tokugawa period, Professor Abe has shown that the Neo-Confucian philosophical works which were most influential in Japan in the mid-seventeenth century were Yi T'oegye's *Ch'eon myeong toseol*[ec] (Explanation of the Diagram of the Mandate of Heaven) and his autobiographical *Chasŏngnok*[ed] (Record of Self-Examination), works which deeply inspired Yamazaki Ansai and several of his followers, including Satō Naokata[ee] (1650–1719) and Asami Keisai[ef] (1652–1711), and Lo Ch'in-shun's *K'un-chih chi*, which helped to recast the philosophical perspective of Hayashi Razan and several of his intellectual descendants. The *K'un-chih chi* was hand-copied by Razan, apparently from a Korean edition, [141] and later printed in Japanese woodblock editions of 1658, 1661, and 1704. While the assessment of patterns of intellectual influence is inevitably difficult, it is clear from the evidence assembled by Professor Abe that the *K'un-chih chi* was read soon after its first printing in Japan by a number of prominent scholars, including Kaibara Ekken, who commented appreciatively on the work in his own *Taigiroku*[eg] (Grave Doubts), Andō Seian[eh] (1622–1701) and the influential leader of the Ancient Learning (*Kogaku*)[ei] school, Itō Jinsai[ej] (1627–1705), who also came to adopt a philosophy of *ch'i*. Since the text was so important to Hayashi Razan, it may also have been read by other disciples, including, for example, Yamaga Sokō[ek] (1622–1685). Professor Abe has observed that the implications of Lo's monism of *ch'i* and his concern for objective investigation were particularly great for a scholar like Ekken who went on to extend the scope of "investigation" to the world of nature as well as military science, law and philology. [142]

Abe's conclusions concerning the significance of Lo Ch'in-shun's thought in Japan are as follows:

Lo Ch'in-shun pointedly criticized and broadly modified Chu Hsi's philosophy of *li* and *ch'i* and the mind and the nature, established a philosophy which can aptly be described as a monism of *ch'i*, and restyled the Sung philosophy which negated the desires into one which affirmed the desires. He sharply attacked the idealism of both the Lu-Wang school and Ch'an Buddhism and further developed the rationalist and objectivist aspect of the Chu Hsi school, through which he opened the road which led to the rationalist thought of the modern world. [143]

Interestingly, such a conclusion could not have been drawn on the basis of an assessment of Lo's influence in China alone, where the later career of philosophical orthodoxy was less expansive. That it could be aptly drawn on the basis of an assessment of his influence in Japan points up the deeper problem of why the philosophical potential of the Chu Hsi school was in certain important respects more fully realized in Japan than in China itself, and suggests any number of questions about the potential of ideas as against their actualization in a given historical context.

Professor Abe himself has examined the general question of why Confucian studies were so active in the Tokugawa period in terms of the social structure and political environment of seventeenth- and eighteenth-century Japan, which set it apart from both Ch'ing China and Yi Korea. He observes, for example, that the fact that the social status of

Tokugawa Confucians was generally lower than that of their Chinese and Korean counterparts seems to account for their greater interest in and influence among the lower orders of society, that the political alternatives associated with the dual authority of the Bakufu and the imperial court allowed for greater dynamism in political thought, and that the autonomy of the Japanese *han* encouraged the employment of Confucian thinkers, particularly those skilled in practical learning. [144] These elements, he suggests, contributed to the rather flexible attitudes of Japanese Confucians toward traditional values, the variety in their views of value, and the overall vitality of Confucian thought, which enabled it to serve, both ideologically and practically, as the basis of modernization in Japan. [145]

Returning to the particular problem of differing developments within Neo-Confucian orthodoxy, another potentially significant difference may lie in the relatively greater openness of Japanese thinkers of the seventeenth and eighteenth centuries to the enterprise of philosophy. As has been observed above, Lo Ch'in-shun's thought, though informed by an interest in the concrete, nonetheless retained a place for the abstract, where "abstract" is understood to mean essentially speculative. This interest in speculative thought and openness to questions about the world, nature, and human nature were part of the earlier Ch'eng-Chu tradition in which Confucian thought had been brought into creative tension with Buddhism. In thinkers like Kaibara Ekken, that tradition was continued and developed with no sign of the intellectual introversion that marked Ch'eng-Chu thought in the late seventeenth and early eighteenth centuries in China. This striking difference suggests that another important line of future research lies in more detailed inquiry into the relation between the Ch'eng-Chu school and the school of evidential research in eighteenth-century China, and between the wing of the Japanese Chu Hsi school which was oriented toward empirical investigation and the emergent school of Ancient Learning, itself apparently less resolutely disposed against abstract or speculative philosophy than its Chinese counterpart, the school of Han Learning.

NOTES

1. Liang Ch'i-ch'ao, *Ch'ing-tai hsüeh-shu kai-lun* (Hong Kong: Chung-hua shu-chü, 1963), p. 20. Translation adapted from Immanuel C. Y. Hsü, trans., *Intellectual Trends in the Ch'ing Period* (Cambridge: Harvard University Press, 1959), p. 45.

2. Except as otherwise indicated, all biographical information is drawn from Lo's chronological autobiography, *Cheng-an lü-li chi*[el] in *K'un-chih chi hsü-pu*[em] (1622 ed.), 7:11b–28b.

3. *Ming-shih* (Kuo-fang yen-chiu yüan ed.) (Taipei: 1962), 282:3169.

4. Huang Tsung-hsi, *Ming-ju hsüeh-an* (SPPY ed.), 47:1a.

5. According to Heinrich Busch, Kao P'an-lung apparently felt some affinity for Lo, and, like Lo, adopted a monistic philosophy in which *li* and *ch'i* were regarded as aspects of one reality. See *The Tung-lin Academy and its Political and Philosophical Significance* (Ann Arbor: University Microfilms, 1954), pp. 189–92.

6. Quoted in "Lo Wen-chuang kung chuan,"[en] in *Kao Tzu i-shu*[eo] (1764 ed.; Princeton University Library), 10A:6b.

7. *Wang Wen-ch'eng kung ch'üan-shu*[ep] (SPTK ed.), preface, p. 15a. Cited in Wing-tsit Chan, trans., *Instructions for Practical Living and Other Neo-Confucian Writings by Wang Yang-ming* (New York: Columbia University Press, 1963), Introduction, p. xxxvi.

8. Lo's critique of Wang Yang-ming's scholarship in the latter's essay, "Chu Tzu wan-nien ting-lun" and its preface is an example. The critique is found in his letter of 1520 to Wang, in *K'un-chih chi fu-lu*,[eq] 5:1a–7a.

9. In *Yōmeigaku no kenkyū*[er] (Studies on the Wang Yang-ming school), vol. 2 (Tokyo: Gendai jōhōsha, 1971), Yamashita Ryūji discusses the significance of the change between the earlier and later periods in Wang Yang-ming's thought, the latter having been characterized by the development of the doctrine of the extension of innate knowledge (*chih liang-chih*[es].) See especially pp. 108–15.

10. *Ibid.*, p. 111.

11. *Ibid.*, especially pp. 108–12. Professor Yamashita's argument is tightly reasoned and based both on his own careful study of the texts of the *Ch'uan-hsi lu* and the *K'un-chih chi* and on the work of Imai Usaburō[et] in "Zensho-bon Denshūroku kō"[eu] (A Study of the Complete Text Edition of the *Instructions for Practical Living*), in *Shibun*[ev] (1945), vol. 27, nos. 7–9. The subject is too complex to allow for brief summation, but part of the argument is as follows: "In the first two *chüan* of the *K'un-chih chi* he [Lo Ch'in-shun] reacts to the early period of Yang-ming's thought in the *Ch'uan-hsi lu*, Part I, and the words 'innate knowledge' (*liang-chih*) are not mentioned even once. Consequently we can see that at the time of the writing of the first two *chüan* of the *K'un-chih chi*, Lo Ch'in-shun did not know of the later thought of Wang Yang-ming, i.e., he did not know of the absolutism of innate

knowledge and the distinctive thought that made principle and material force two aspects of innate knowledge. . . . However one reconstructs it, his reading of the Letter in Reply to Lu Yüan-ching [which contains Wang's famous statement that, 'principle is the order according to which material force operates; material force is the functioning of principle'] seems to have been after 1526. The fact that in his second letter to Wang Yang-ming [written in 1528] he finally brought up his doubts concerning the theory of innate knowledge enables us to conclude that his reading of the original text of the *Ch'uan-hsi lu*, Part II must have been around 1528. For this reason I believe that we see no influence at all in the first two *chüan* of the *K'un-chih chi* [completed in 1528 on the basis of work begun around 1505]" (p. 112).

12. *K'un-chih chi*, 2:41. This and subsequent citations refer to the *chüan* and to the sections in which the *chüan* were divided by Lo Ch'in-shun.

13. There is one reference which would suggest this in a poem on his study entitled, "Hsüeh-ku lou ko"[ew] (Song on the Hall for the Study of Antiquity) in *Lien-Lo feng-ya*[ex] (Poems from the Schools of Lien-hsi and Lo-yang) (*Cheng-i-t'ang ch'üan-shu* ed.), 9:4a–b. The line reads, "Now and then I practice quiet-sitting to preserve my mind and nourish my nature."

14. At some points Liang distinguishes Sung and Ming thought (generally in the course of attributing to Ming thinkers excessive abstractness or insufficient attention to textual study) and at others he tends to equate them, as in speaking of "Sung-Ming *li-hsüeh*." See, for example, *Ch'ing-tai hsüeh-shu kai-lun*, pp. 3, 6.

15. This is the judgment of Yamanoi Yū in his study, "Min Shin jidai ni okeru 'ki' no tetsugaku"[ey] (The Philosophy of "Ch'i" in the Ming and Ch'ing Periods), in *Tetsugaku zasshi*[ez] (1951), 66(711):94.

16. Abe Yoshio, "Nissen Min ni okeru shuriha shukiha no keifu to sono toku-shitsu"[fa] (The Genealogy and Special Characteristics of the School of *Li* and the School of *Ch'i* in Japan, Korea, and Ming [China]) in *Chōsen Gakuhō*[fb] (1959), 14:427.

17. In *The Unity of Philosophical Experience* (New York: Scribner's, 1937), Etienne Gilson draws a distinction between "pure ideas" which tend to give rise to philosophical revolutions and "concepts" which are "born reformers that never lose touch with reality" (p. 68). Were a criterion like Gilson's adopted, there would be few revolutionaries in the history of Chinese thought, and Lo Ch'in-shun would hardly be counted among them.

18. Lo's philosophy is referred to throughout as a "philosophy of *ch'i*" or a "monism of *ch'i*," though there is some disagreement among scholars as to the appropriateness of either designation. Alfred Forke in *Geschichte der neuren chinesischen Philosophie* (Hamburg: De Gruyter, 1938) considered Lo Ch'in-shun, Yang Tung-ming, Yeh Tzu-ch'i[fc], Wu Ju-hsü,[fd] and Wang Wen-lu[fe] as "realistic monists" (pp. 332–47). Yamanoi Yū (" 'Ki' no tet-sugaku," p. 99) disagrees about the applicability of the term "monist" in the case of Lo and Yang, but he does not specify his reasons for doing so. Yamashita Ryūji's view is that, "To call Lo Ch'in-shun's thought a 'philoso-

phy of *ch'i* in the sense that it criticizes Chu Hsi's 'philosophy of *li*' is not necessarily wrong, but we must note that his viewpoint differs both from Chang Tsai's 'philosophy of *ch'i*' and from Wang T'ing-hsiang's 'philosophy of *ch'i.*' I think that in order to draw attention to the fact that Lo Ch'in-shun's thought is not a 'philosophy of *ch'i*' in the sense of making *ch'i* prior and *li* posterior, it might be more appropriate to call it a 'philosophy of *li* and *ch'i* as integrated.' Its special characteristic is that it concentrates solely on the world and the things in it and has nothing whatever to do with a world prior to or transcending this one." *Yōmeigaku no kenkyū,* 2:78. Professor Yamashita's distinction between Chang Tsai's "philosophy of *ch'i*" and Lo's is an important one. My own reservations about describing Lo's philosophy as one in which *li* and *ch'i* are "integrated" is that this may still imply an original separation between the two. Like Professor Yamashita (*Yōmeigaku no kenkyū,* 2:124), I see Lo's philosophy as essentially nominalist in its implications and conclude that it is important that any designation applied to his philosophy should make it clear that *li* and *ch'i* are in his view never separate in any sense. Since *li* is seen as the pattern in the operations of *ch'i,* the designation "philosophy of *ch'i*" or "monism of *ch'i*" seems appropriate.

19. See especially Wing-tsit Chan, "The Evolution of the Neo-Confucian Concept of *Li* as Principle," in *Tsing-hua Journal of Chinese Studies* (February 1964), n.s. 4(2):123–48. Reprinted in *Neo-Confucianism, Etc.: Essays by Wing-tsit Chan* (Hanover, N.H.: Oriental Society, 1969), pp. 45–87. Ch'ien Mu[ff] includes an extended section on Chu Hsi's view of *li* and *ch'i* in his *Chu Tzu hsin hsüeh-an*[fg] (A New Scholarly Record of Chu Hsi) (Taipei: San-min shu-chü, 1971), 1:238–62. This section concludes with some quotations from Lo Ch'in-shun's critique of Chu Hsi's theory and remarks by Ch'ien Mu concerning Lo's understanding of Chu. Professor Ch'ien (pp. 260–62) criticizes Lo for having dealt with only "one side" of Chu's theory, the dualistic side.

20. E.g., *Chu Tzu yü-lei* (Classified Conversations of Master Chu) (Taipei: Cheng-chung shu-chü, 1970 reprint of the 1473 ed.), 1:2a.

21. *Ibid.,* 1:2a–b.

22. *Ibid.,* 1:2b.

23. *Ibid.,* 1:1b.

24. *Ibid.,* 1:2b. Translation by Wing-tsit Chan in A *Source Book in Chinese Philosophy* (Princeton: Princeton University Press, 1963), p. 634.

25. *Chu Tzu yü-lei,* 4:8a. Translation adapted from Chan, *Source Book,* p. 637.

26. Letter in Reply to Liao Tzu-hui[fh] in *Chu Tzu wen-chi*[fi] (Collection of Literary Works by Master Chu Hsi) (SPPY ed.), published under the title *Chu Tzu ta-ch'üan*[fj] (Complete Literary Works of Master Chu Hsi), 45:19b. Chan, *Source Book,* p. 637.

27. Letter to Liu Shu-wen[fk] in *Chu Tzu wen-chi,* 46:24a.

28. *Chu Tzu ch'üan-shu*[fl] (Complete Literary Works of Master Chu Hsi) (1714 ed.), 42:18b. Translation adapted from Chan, *Source Book,* p. 618.

29. *Chu Tzu ch'üan-shu,* 43:4b. Translation adapted from Chan, *Source Book,* pp. 624–25.

30. *Chu Tzu ch'üan-shu*, 2:2a. Chan, *Source Book*, p. 606.
31. *I-shu*[fm] (Written Legacy), 18:8b in *Erh Ch'eng ch'üan-shu*[fn] (Complete Works of the Two Ch'engs) (SPPY ed.). Chan, *Source Book*, p. 563. Ch'eng I uses two verbs here, both translated by Professor Chan as "understand." In neither case does he use the word *chih*[fo] but in the first instance *ming*[fp] and in the second, *hsiao*.[fq]
32. *Chu Tzu ch'üan-shu*, 2:4b. Chan, *Source Book*, p. 606.
33. *Ibid.*, 42:13a. Chan, *Source Book*, p. 617.
34. *Ibid.*, 1:30a. Chan, *Source Book*, p. 605.
35. *Ibid.* The original statement appears in *I-shu*, 6:2a. The verb here translated as "understand" is *te*.[fr]
36. *Chu Tzu ch'üan shu*, 44:13a–b. Chan, *Source Book*, p. 630.
37. It is certainly possible to find examples of concern with perceptual problems on the part of Chinese thinkers as well; however, this is an area which was of greater interest to Taoists than to Confucians. Even so, the interest of Taoists in problems of perception seems in general to have been of a different sort. One may be permitted a certain skepticism about Joseph Needham's suggestion that the interest of the tenth-century Taoist T'an Chiao[fs] in the substantive factors determining sense experience may be seen as "an anticipation of Locke's distinction between primary and secondary qualities some eight centuries before him." *Science and Civilisation in China*, (Cambridge: Cambridge University Press, 1956), 2:451. When T'an Chiao compared an owl which sees well at night with a hen which sees well in daylight, one may assume that the problem of perception did not occupy him in the same way that it would a Western empiricist. He was presumably not searching for the conditions under which truth can be indubitably known but rather pointing up in good Taoist fashion the relativity of truth. According to D. W. Hamlyn, Western empiricism beginning with Locke is founded on the confidence that "perception is at some point or other indubitable." Hamlyn, *The Theory of Knowledge* (Garden City: Doubleday Anchor Books, 1970), p. 35. This view would probably be uncongenial to most Taoists, and the whole area of inquiry would in all likelihood have been found unrewarding by most Sung Neo-Confucians.
38. See, for example, Ch'eng I's statement in *I-shu*, 25:2a, that, "The knowledge that comes through hearing and seeing is not the knowledge associated with the moral nature. When one thing comes into contact with another, the knowledge derived is not from within. This is what is meant by extensive learning and much ability today. The knowledge obtained from the moral nature does not depend on seeing and hearing." Translation adapted from Chan, *Source Book*, p. 570.
39. Meyrick H. Carré, *Realists and Nominalists* (Oxford: Oxford University Press, 1967), p. 7.
40. This question is discussed by Fung Yu-lan, *A History of Chinese Philosophy*, Derk Bodde, trans. (Princeton: Princeton University Press, 1953), 2:482, 507, 542; O. Graf, *Djin-si lu* (Tokyo: Sophia University Press, 1953), 1:66, 77, 255; Carsun Chang, *The Development of Neo-Confucian Thought* (New

York: Bookman Associates, 1957), 1:260–64; Joseph Needham, *Science and Civilisation*, 2:475.

41. Many writers have made reference to the influence of Buddhism on Chinese epistemology. Needham's comment (*Science and Civilisation*, 2:423) is that, "Behind all these points of tentative contact between Buddhist ideas and the developing interest in the sciences of Nature there lay the fact that Buddhism had introduced to China a wealth of highly sophisticated discussions concerning logic and epistemology." However, this observation is made in passing, and, to my knowledge, the full implications of this important and many-faceted topic have yet to be explored in detail.

42. In a classic article, "La Pénétration du Bouddhisme dans La Tradition Philosophique Chinoise," in *Cahiers d'Histoire Mondiale*, vol. 3 (1956) Paul Demiéville has considered the evolution of the concept of *li* (principle) from its original sense in early Chinese thought through the end of the Han as a principle of order or distribution, to the Sung Neo-Confucian understanding of *li* as a metaphysical absolute. The evolution of the concept is seen as a Neo-Confucian response to a highly elaborated Buddhist metaphysics. It might also be viewed more particularly as a complex reaction to the Buddhist idea of impermanence, an attempt to discover an ethical and ontological constant that would be beyond "integration and disintegration." Apart from an analysis of the concepts of *li* and *ch'i* in Sung thought, the question of the attitude of the Sung thinkers toward impermanence might also be approached through an exploration of their views on reincarnation. This is a subject touched on, though briefly, by A. C. Graham in *Two Chinese Philosophers: Ch'eng Ming-tao and Ch'eng Yi-ch'uan* (London: Lund Humphries, 1958), pp. 90–91.

43. Ch'eng I's statements on this subject vary somewhat, but the following dialogue in *I-shu*, 19:1a (Chan, *Source Book*, p. 568) is not atypical: "Question: 'In the investigation of things, should these be external things or things within our nature and function?' Answer: 'It does not matter. All that is before our eyes is nothing but things, and all things have principle. For example, from that by which fire is hot or water is cold to the relations between ruler and minister, and father and son, are all principle."

44. Joseph R. Levenson, "The Abortiveness of Empiricism in Early Ch'ing Thought," in *Confucian China and Its Modern Fate* (Berkeley: University of California Press, 1965), 1:3–4.

45. This point was persuasively made by Wei-ming Tu in "Some Reflections on Chu Hsi's Intellectual Debate," paper presented at the University Seminar on Oriental Thought and Religion, Columbia University, March 1, 1974.

46. *K'un-chih chi*, 1:11.

47. *Chu Tzu ch'üan-shu*, 49:4b.

48. "Great Appendix" to the *Book of Changes*. In *Chou I cheng-i*[fn] (SPPY ed.), 7:17a.

49. *Ibid.*, 7:8a.

50. *K'un-chih chi*, 1:11.

51. *Ibid.*
52. See above, note 27.
53. *Chu Tzu yü-lei*, 4:13b.
54. *Chu Tzu yü-lei*, 4:8a.
55. Needham, *Science and Civilisation*, 2:472 ff.
56. This is the opinion of Yamashita Ryūji in *Yōmeigaku no kenkyū*, 2:64–65. Ch'ien Mu concludes his extended section on Chu Hsi's theory of *li* and *ch'i* in his *Chu Tzu hsin hsüeh-an*, 1:238–62, with quotations from Lo's critique of Hu Chü-jen and Hsüeh Hsüan, suggesting (p. 260) that it was really to their theories that Lo was reacting rather than to those of Chu Hsi himself. It may be noted, however, that the views of Hu and Hsüeh were recognized by Lo to be different from those of Chu. In *K'un-chih chi*, 2:51, he also distinguished between Chu Hsi's views and those of his successors, observing, "Although Master Chu regarded *li* and *ch'i* as two things, his statements were characterized by the utmost breadth and balance. None of his successors reached the same standard in their speculations, and so these qualities have been lost."
57. *K'un-chih chi*, 2:51.
58. Yü Yu^fu (1465–1528). He was Hu Chü-jen's son-in-law. For an account of him see *Ming-ju hsüeh-an*, ch. 3.
59. *K'un-chih chi*, 2:51.
60. "Great Appendix" to the *Book of Changes*. In *Chou I cheng-i*, 7:3a.
61. *Chu Tzu yü-lei*, 1:2b. Chan, *Source Book*, p. 634.
62. Hsüeh Hsüan, *Tu-shu lu* (1826 ed. in 11 ch.), 4:15b.
63. *Tu-shu lu*, 3:2a.
64. *Chu Tzu yü-lei*, 1:1a.
65. *Tu-shu lu*, 3:13a, 6:3a.
66. *Tu-shu lu*, 6:5b. The statement that, "Concrete things are the Way, and the Way is also concrete things," is usually attributed to Ch'eng Hao. See *I-shu*, 1:3b.
67. *K'un-chih chi*, 2:46.
68. *Tu-shu lu*, 4:25b.
69. Joseph Needham's conclusion on this subject in *Science and Civilisation*, 2:482, is as follows; "At bottom Chu Hsi remained a dualist, in the sense that matter-energy [*ch'i*] and organisation [*li*] were coeval and of equal importance in the universe, 'neither afore nor after other,' though the residue of belief in some slight 'superiority' on the part of the latter was extremely difficult to discard. I take it that the reason for this was unconsciously social; since in all forms of society of which the Neo-Confucians could conceive, the planning, organising, adjusting administrator, was socially superior to the farmer and artisan occupied with and hence the representatives of, Chhi. If Chu Hsi could have liberated himself fully from this prejudice he would have anticipated by eight hundred years the standpoint of organic materialism with its dialectic and integrative levels." Professor Needham's association of *li* with administrators and *ch'i* with farmers and artisans is open to some question,

particularly in light of Chu Hsi's repeated assertion that principle is equally endowed in all human beings. It may also be observed that the "superiority" of *li* was only one aspect of Chu Hsi's theory; he also ascribed to it logical priority and immutability. To account for all of these elements in the concept of *li* on the basis of a socio-economic analysis would be difficult, and to account for the many changes in the concept during the Ming period and the variety of views held by different Ming thinkers solely or even primarily in terms of the increasingly fluid status system of the Ming would be even more problematical.

70. See above, note 56.
71. *K'un-chih chi*, 3:40.
72. Yamashita Ryūji has provided a thoughtful analysis of the reasons for Lo's disagreement with Chang Tsai and the relation of Chang's thought to that of Chou Tun-i in *Yōmeigaku no kenkyū*, 2:68–73.
73. See especially Wang T'ing-hsiang's essay, "Heng-ch'ü li-ch'i pien"[fv] (Chang Tsai's Explanation of *Li* and *Ch'i*) in Hou Wai-lu[fw], *Wang T'ing-hsiang che-hsüeh hsüan-chi*[fx] (Selections from the Philosophy of Wang T'ing-hsiang) Taipei: Ho-Lo t'u-shu ch'u-p'an she, 1973 reprint), pp. 176–77. Whether, despite his approbative attitude, Wang's own philosophy of *ch'i* was actually fundamentally similar to that of Chang Tsai is another considerably more complex issue which must be reserved for separate consideration.
74. *Cheng-meng*, "T'ai-ho"[fy] chapter, section 2, in *Chang Tzu ch'üan-shu*[fz] (Complete Writings of Chang Tsai) (SPPY ed.), 2:2a.
75. *Cheng-meng*, "Ch'eng-ming"[ga] chapter, section 21, in *Chang Tzu ch'üan-shu*, 2:18b–19a.
76. *Cheng-meng*, "T'ai-ho" chapter, section 9, in *Chang Tzu ch'üan-shu*, 2:3b.
77. *K'un-chih chi*, 2:22.
78. *Cheng-meng*, "T'ai-ho" chapter, section 9, in *Chang Tzu ch'üan-shu*, 2:3b. Translation adapted from Chan, *Source Book*, p. 504.
79. *Cheng-meng*, "T'ai-ho" chapter, section 4, quoting *Tao-te ching*[gb], section 33, in *Chang Tzu ch'üan-shu*, 2:2a. Chan, *Source Book*, p. 501.
80. *Ibid.*, section 15 in *Chang Tzu ch'üan-shu*, 2:4b. Cf. translation by Chan in *Source Book*, p. 505.
81. Chu Hsi's commentary in *Chang Tzu ch'üan-shu*, 2:1b.
82. *K'un-chih chi*, 2:33.
83. Following the distinction proposed by John Herman Randall, Jr. in *Nature and Historical Experience: Essays in Naturalism and the Theory of History* (New York: Columbia University Press, 1958), p. 205.
84. Lo Ch'in-shun's own critique of Buddhism forms a major part of the *K'un-chih chi*, and the greater part of the third *chüan* of the work is given over to it. Unlike many of the Sung Neo-Confucians, who were inclined to attack Buddhism primarily from an ethical standpoint, Lo criticized Buddhism on more broadly philosophical grounds and on the basis of a thorough acquaintance with Buddhist texts and commentaries. For aspects of the assimilation of Buddhism by Confucian thinkers, see Araki Kengo[gc], "Confucianism and

Buddhism in the Late Ming," in Wm. Theodore de Bary, ed., *The Unfolding of Neo-Confucianism* (New York: Columbia University Press, 1975), pp. 39–66.

85. *K'un-chih chi*, 1:14.
86. *K'un-chih chi*, 1:15. Chu Hsi's statement appears in *Chu Tzu wen-chi*, 61:24a in a letter in response to Yen Shih-heng.[gd] See the discussion of this passage in Ch'ien Mu, *Chu Tzu hsin hsüeh-an*, 1:450–51.
87. In *I-shu*, 1:7b. Ch'eng Hao had said, " 'What is inborn is called the nature.' Nature is the same as material force and material force is the same as nature. They are both inborn." See Chan, *Source Book*, pp. 527–28.
88. *K'un-chih chi*, 1:23. Wang T'ing-hsiang also approved of this statement of Ch'eng Hao's. See the first part of his *Ya-shu*[ge] (Pure Words) in Hou Wai-lu, *Wang T'ing-hsiang che-hsüeh hsüan-chi*, p. 87. Wang Yang-ming also alluded to it in part 3 of the *Ch'uan-hsi lu*. See Chan, *Instructions*, pp. 208–9.
89. *Chu Tzu yü-lei*, 93–8b, quoting Ch'eng I in *I-shu*, 22A:11a.
90. *Mean*, XX: 21.
91. *I-ch'uan wen-chi*, 5:12b.
92. *K'un-chih chi*, 3:37.
93. See, for example, *Chu Tzu ch'üan-shu*, 43:2b. "Nature is principle only. However, without the material force and concrete stuff of the universe, principle would have nothing in which to inhere. When material force is received in its state of clearness, there will be no obscurity or obstruction and principle will express itself freely. If there is obscurity or obstruction, then in its operation of principle, the Principle of Heaven will dominate if the obstruction is small and human selfish desire will dominate if the obstruction is great. From this we know that original nature is perfectly good." Translation by Chan in *Source Book*, pp. 623–24.
94. *I-shu*, 6:2a.
95. See above, note 91.
96. *K'un-chih chi*, 1:14.
97. See Carsun Chang, *The Development of Neo-Confucian Thought*, 2:396.
98. *I-ch'uan wen-chi*,[gf] 5:12b. See also Chu Hsi's reflections on the ethical implications of the phrase *li-i fen-shu* in his commentary on Chang Tsai's "Western Inscription" in *Chang Tzu ch'üan-shu*, 1:7a.
99. However, Lo also used the phrase in an ethical sense in at least one context. *K'un-chih chi*, 1:74.
100. A. C. Graham, *Two Chinese Philosophers*, p. 48.
101. *K'un-chih chi*, 2:14.
102. Chiefly, the "Record of Music" in the *Book of Rites*. See James Legge, trans., *Li Chi: Book of Rites* (New Hyde Park: University Books, 1967), 2:96.
103. Chan, *Instructions*, p. 229.
104. Yamashita Ryūji, *Yōmeigaku no kenkyū*, 2:96.
105. Chan, *Instructions*, p. 108.
106. *I-shu*, 6:2a. See above, note 35.

107. A statement of Ch'eng I in *I-shu*, 25:2a.

108. *K'un-chih chi*, 3:3.

109. This is Lo Ch'in-shun's original note.

110. "Great Appendix" to the *Book of Changes*. In *Chou I cheng-i*, 7:14b.

111. *K'un-chih chi*, 3:8.

112. Alludes to *Mencius*, VIIA, 15:i.

113. Letter [of 1534] to Ou-yang Te, in *K'un-chih chi fu-lu*, 5:16a–22a.

114. *Chang Tzu ch'üan-shu*, 2:21a.

115. J. Percy Bruce, trans., *Chu Hsi's Philosophy of Human Nature* (London: Probsthain, 1922), p. 179.

116. *K'un-chih chi*, 2:35.

117. E. R. Hughes, "Epistemological Methods in Chinese Philosophy," in Charles A. Moore, ed., *Essays in East-West Philosophy* (Honolulu: University of Hawaii Press, 1951), p. 72, note 16. The article is reprinted in Charles A. Moore, ed., *The Chinese Mind* (Honolulu: University of Hawaii Press, 1967).

118. *Ibid.*, p. 63. Professor Hughes's statement was that, "the Sung era produced among its various methodologies one clear and, along its own line, cogent methodology, namely that of the Ch'eng-Chu school."

119. See Araki Kengo, "Confucianism and Buddhism in the Late Ming," especially pp. 45–50.

120. *K'un-chih chi*, 1:5.

121. *K'un-chih chi*, 1:7.

122. Wing-tsit Chan, "Chu Hsi's Completion of Neo-Confucianism," in *Études Song* (1973), ser. 2, no. 1, p. 87.

123. Alluding to Ch'eng I's statement in *I-shu*, 17:1b.

124. *K'un-chih chi*, 1:7.

125. *K'un-chih chi*, 1:10. Lo derived his definition from Lü Tsu-ch'ien[gg] (1137–1181), who spoke of "penetrating the 'three primal powers' with no omissions" (*t'ung san-chi erh wu-chien*).[gh] See *Tseng-hsiu Tung-lai Shu-shuo*[gi] (Lü Tsu-ch'ien's Revised and Expanded Explanations of the *Book of History*) (in *Chin-hua ts'ung-shu*[gj]), 26:8b.

126. This volume, pp. 377–78 and 416–18.

127. See Wing-tsit Chan, "Chu Hsi's Completion of Neo-Confucianism," especially pp. 83–85.

128. Needham, *Science and Civilisation*, 2:510.

129. In a section subtitled, "The Search for a Monistic Philosophy," Professor Needham mentions several Ming thinkers, including Lo Ch'in-shun, Yang Tung-ming, and Kao P'an-lung, but suggests that "These men were all consciously in opposition to the tradition of metaphysical idealism which had come to a climax with Wang Yang-ming about +1500." *Science and Civilisation*, 2:506.

130. Yamanoi Yū, " 'Ki' no Tetsugaku," pp. 94–99.

131. Yamashita Ryūji, *Yōmeigaku no kenkyū*, 2:115–22.

132. *Ibid.*, p. 95.

133. *I-ch'uan hsien-sheng nien-p'u*[gk] (Chronological Biography of Master Ch'eng I), in *I-shu*, Appendix,[gl] p. 12a. In *Ts'ui-yen*[gm] (Pure Words) 1:26a it is indicated that Ch'eng I was over seventy when he made this statement.

134. *Chu Tzu yü-lei*, 104:10b.

135. *K'un-chih chi*, 1:13.

136. For example, Hsüeh Hsüan's *Tu-shu lu* suffered a similar fate at Chang's hands; however, in Hsüeh's case the distortion was less because his own differences with Chu Hsi on this point were less profound.

137. *San-yü-t'ang wen-chi*[gn] (Collection of Literary Works of the Hall Dedicated to the Three Fish) (1701 ed.), 9:11a-b. Cited in Wing-tsit Chan, "The *Hsing-li ching-i* and the Ch'eng-Chu School," in de Bary, *Unfolding*, p. 554.

138. Personal communication.

139. See Professor Abe's seminal study, *Nihon Shushigaku to Chōsen*[go] (The Chu Hsi School in Japan and [its relation to] Korea) (Tokyo: Tokyo daigaku shuppankai, 1965), especially pp. 491–534.

140. *Ibid.*, pp. 514–20.

141. *Ibid.*, pp. 523–24.

142. *Ibid.*, p. 503.

143. Abe Yoshio, "Development of Neo-Confucianism in Japan, Korea and China: A Comparative Study," in *Acta Asiatica* (1970), 19:16–39, especially pp. 31–39.

144. *Ibid.*, p. 39.

GLOSSARY

a	羅欽順	am	宋明理學	by	太虛
b	梁啟超	an	清代學術概論	bz	無形氣之本體
c	承明學極空疏	ao	氣	ca	天地之性
d	返於沈實	ap	王夫之	cb	氣質之性
e	空	aq	戴震	cc	正蒙
f	困知記	ar	顧炎武	cd	合
g	章懋	as	顏元	ce	本然之性
h	劉瑾	at	李塨	cf	天命之性
i	王陽明	au	理	cg	氣質
j	王廷相	av	阿部吉雄	ch	墮
k	明史	aw	理未嘗離乎氣	ci	理一分殊
l	張璁	ax	形而上	cj	性即理
m	桂萼	ay	形而下	ck	曾國藩
n	吳與弼	az	先	cl	法
o	胡居仁	ba	後	cm	心識
p	陳獻章	bb	無形	cn	六識
q	文莊	bc	粗	co	歐陽德
r	黃宗羲	bd	有渣滓	cp	艮知
s	明儒學案	be	本	cq	艮
t	學古樓	bf	二物	cr	知覺
u	高攀龍	bg	張載	cs	體天下之物
v	東林	bh	得	ct	理須就氣上認取
w	林希元	bi	橫渠	cu	認氣為理
x	或生而知之	bj	格物	cv	人心之神明
y	或學而知之	bk	心學	cw	至理
z	或困而知之	bl	主宰	cx	源了圓
aa	困	bm	物	cy	貝原益軒
ab	傳習錄	bn	名	cz	岡田武彥
ac	山下龍二	bo	居業錄	da	山井湧
ad	陸象山	bp	窮理	db	王道
ae	禪	bq	性書	dc	蔣信
af	光景	br	余子積	dd	魏校
ag	朱熹	bs	天下之理	de	劉邦采
ah	靜坐	bt	理只在氣上	df	王畿
ai	讀書	bu	朱子語類	dg	呂坤
aj	程頤	bv	無窮	dh	唐鶴徵
ak	程顥	bw	讀書錄	di	楊東明
al	薛瑄	bx	文清	dj	孤愼行

dk 劉宗周
dl 陳確
dm 程廷祚
dn 董其昌
do 董源
dp 至
dq 伊川易傳
dr 張伯行
ds 正誼堂全書
dt 陸隴其
du 英時余
dv 林羅山
dw 木下順庵
dx 李退溪
dy 山崎闇齋
dz 崎門
ea 大塚退野
eb 熊本
ec 天命圖說
ed 自省錄
ee 佐藤直方
ef 淺見絅齋
eg 太疑錄
eh 安東省庵
ei 古學
ej 伊藤仁齋
ek 山鹿素行
el 整菴履歴記
em 困知記續補
en 羅文莊公傳
eo 高子遺書
ep 王文成公全書
eq 困知記附錄
er 陽明學の研究
es 致良知
et 今井宇三郎
eu 全書本伝習錄考
ev 斯文
ew 學古樓歌
ex 濂洛風雅
ey 明清時代におけ

ez 哲学雑誌
fa 日鮮明における
主理派主氣派の
系譜とその特質
fb 朝鮮學報
fc 葉子奇
fd 吳儒須
fe 王文祿
ff 錢穆
fg 朱子新學案
fh 廖子晦
fi 朱子文集
fj 朱子大全
fk 劉叔文
fl 朱子全書
fm 遺書
fn 二程全書
fo 知
fp 明
fq 曉
fr 得
fs 譚峭
ft 周易正義
fu 余祐
fv 横渠理氣辯
fw 侯外廬
fx 王廷相哲學選集
fy 太和
fz 張子全書
ga 誠明
gb 道德經
gc 荒木見悟
gd 嚴時亨
ge 雅述
gf 伊川文集
gg 呂祖謙
gh 通三極而無間
gi 增修東萊書說
gj 金華叢書
gk 伊川先生年譜

る「氣」の哲学
gl 遺書附錄
gm 粹言
gn 三魚堂文集
go 日本朱子學と朝鮮

Wm. Theodore de Bary

Sagehood as a Secular and Spiritual Ideal in Tokugawa Neo-Confucianism

As a long-standing ideal of human fulfillment in the Chinese tradition, sagehood had taken on new life in Sung Neo-Confucianism and was to do so again when Sung and Ming teachings reached Tokugawa Japan. For the early Neo-Confucians "The Way of the Sages" had represented the sage as the ideal ruler and teacher of antiquity, whose humane government stood in contrast to the flawed reality of the later dynastic system. Another function of the sage in this teaching had been as the primal source of authority, the fountainhead of the True Way and the progenitor of the orthodox succession. In the Ch'eng-Chu school, however, the most signal role of the sage was as the model for the self-cultivation of the individual. In this he was no lofty and remote figure in the past, no hazy abstraction, but an attainable goal in a post-Buddhist age that required a secular model for immediate emulation, a Vimalakirti with a social conscience and political vocation. It was particularly under this latter aspect that sagehood could become a plausible ideal for the scholars and samurai of seventeenth-century Japan.

Students of the Sung school in later times and in different circumstances could still be deeply impressed by the ideals and personal qualities of the Sung masters as Chu Hsi described them in his *Reflections on Things at Hand,* notably combining an active involvement in human affairs with a serenity of spirit born of disciplined and tested commitment to the Way. Along with Chu's *Reflections,* inspiration came from Chou

127

Tun-i's lofty idealizations of the sage in his speculations on the *Changes*, Chang Tsai's mysticism of the human order in the *Western Inscription*, Chu's own account of his spiritual growth through his dialogues with Li T'ung, and above all his assurance that sustained study and practice could culminate in a profound experience of the meaning of life and a personal communion with Heaven and earth and all things. All of these became powerful inducements for later generations to take up the Confucian way of life.

Models such as the Sung masters and a systematic method for emulating them were what attracted converts to Neo-Confucianism more than metaphysical theories. The doctrines indeed had life and significance only as a philosophy of human nature which could lead to the attainment of sagehood. For example, Wu Yü-pi,[a] a leader of the Ch'eng-Chu school in the early Ming, notes how deeply impressed he was by the ability of Li T'ung,[b] Chu Hsi's teacher, to master his own unruly impulses and passionate nature, and how important this realization was in persuading Wu of the practicability of Li's method for achieving sagehood. Similarly, late Ming followers of this method were attracted by the power of Wu's own example, in the absence of any singular philosophical contribution on his part.

But experience in practice also meant working to achieve sagehood in new conditions from age to age, and seeing it with different eyes. As something to be realized for oneself, sagehood was less of a defined concept than an experience subject to varying interpretations. Upheld as a model for general emulation, it could lead to frustration or disappointment as well as to heroic achievement. The life stories of Ming and Ch'ing scholars are replete with such experiences.

In its Sung formulation, the conception of sagehood combined human activities as comprehensive and diverse as the manifold interests of Sung thinkers, but most notably broad learning, scholarly mastery of the classics and literature, a humane concern for one's fellowman, and dedication to public service. These activities were carried on in a spirit of reverence for all life, a grave and respectful manner that was to be balanced by a natural and spontaneous enjoyment of life, and an elevation of mind which transcended the petty problems of the world while yet dealing effectively with them. An open and magnanimous spirit and a graciousness of style were particularly admired and cultivated.

In the climate of those times, however, there was an expectation that the state of sagehood could be, as we have seen, personally realized and experienced. No doubt in part as a reflection of residual Buddhist and Taoist influence, this was often expressed in terms of achieving a kind of illumination or enlightenment in which one attained personal identification with the ultimate reality as both Supreme Norm (*t'ai-chi*),[c] and Infinite (*wu-chi*),[d] or in which one experienced the unity of one's humaneness (*jen*)[e] with Heaven and Earth and all things. Li T'ung interpreted this experience of the "unity of principle and the diversity of its particularizations" as a liberating self-discovery which produced a sense of spiritual freedom and spontaneity. In the Ming many orthodox Ch'eng-Chu schoolmen adopted Chu Hsi's suggestion that half the day be spent in studying books and half in quiet-sitting, while others challenged its practicability.[1] Ch'en Ti[f] (1541–1617), a pioneer in classical phonology but also a rare example of a Confucian military man, wondered how Chu Hsi could have achieved such feats of scholarship if he had really spent half his time in quiet-sitting.[2]

From this one could well speculate as to the changed conditions of life in Ming China which rendered less plausible the specific Sung model of sagehood and less practicable perhaps its method of achievement. This is indeed a question worthy of study by historians of thought, but one should be aware that Chu Hsi himself had raised similar questions regarding Li T'ung's investment of time in quiet-sitting. He supposed that such a contemplative life was possible only for someone like Li who avoided taking office and was not preoccupied with the administration of affairs.[3] Thus Chu recognized that individual circumstances might well condition the practice of any such method, and yet this did not preclude for him acceptance of the sagely ideal.

Similar questions must be faced in dealing with the development of Japanese Neo-Confucianism. Among the wide range of relevant cases, I shall confine myself here to the founders of that movement, and to the School of Ancient Learning (*Kogaku*),[g] which has been seen as the turning point in regard to the indigenization or rejection of Neo-Confucianism, its involvement in processes of modernization and its relationship to "practical learning." Further, I shall attempt to bring into focus both the elements of continuing adaptation within Neo-Confucianism and the central conception of the sage which, as its integrating ideal, must be seen as the crucial testing ground for allowable variation or incompatible change in the system.

THE NEO-CONFUCIAN SYNTHESIS OF FUJIWARA SEIKA

Fujiwara Seika[h] (1561–1619), besides exhibiting a remarkable philosophical breadth and depth, was extraordinary in his capacity to synthesize the diverse strains of Neo-Confucian thought coming to Japan at this time. In general, one may characterize his teaching as centered on a tradition of mind cultivation and spiritual discipline which underlay both the Ch'eng-Chu school and the so-called Lu-Wang school of the mind. Both of these were indeed "schools of the mind," as Seika well recognized, but this fact has since become obscured by the attention given to rationalist tendencies in the Ch'eng-Chu school of principle (li-hsüeh)[i] and its seeming antithesis in Lu-Wang "intuitionism," rather than being viewed as a matter of differing emphasis between two schools which shared the rational and intuitive approaches in different ways.

As we have seen, there is an intended ambivalence in Neo-Confucian teaching between reason and intuition, objective and subjective learning, observation or contemplation of the world and active involvement in it. A balance was sought among the intellectual, moral and spiritual claims on one's self-cultivation. Values and facts, the principles of things conceived in both normative and descriptive terms, were seen as complementary or converging aspects of truth. Yet for all this, the tensions among them were very real, whether in self-cultivation, philosophical speculation or scholarship. Seika's effort to achieve a personal synthesis of these elements was not uninfluenced by centuries of debate in China and Korea over such issues in Ch'eng-Chu doctrine. New access to the work of Yi T'oegye,[j] the commanding figure in Chu Hsi orthodoxy in Korea, and also to that of the Ch'eng-Chu school philosopher Lo Ch'in-shun[k] and the syncretist Lin Chao-en[l] in Ming China, was an historical development of crucial significance for both Seika and Razan, and for many other Neo-Confucians in Japan, as Professor Abe and others have shown.[4]

T'oegye's synthesis of Ch'eng-Chu teachings stressed the moral and spiritual aspects of principle as subjectively realized in the mind. Seika was strongly drawn to this view, though for him, as for most Neo-Confucians, it was not an issue of mutually exclusive principles, since he affirmed the need to apprehend principle in both the mind and things.[5] To Seika indeed an essential mark of Confucian orthodoxy was its hold on the proper balance between the unity and diversity of principle, or in other words, between unitary principle in the mind and the manifold principles found in affairs and things as the differentiated world of facts and events came into being through the individuating and actualizing agency of ether or material force (ch'i; ki).[m]

As Seika said to Hori Kyōan:[n]

The True Way of learning in making ethical distinctions, takes "the unity of principle and the diversity of its particularizations" (li-i fen-shu)[o] as its basis. There is a unity of principle pervading the multiplicity of things and facts. Between self and things there should be no separation. To insist only on the unity of principle is to follow in the way of Buddha with his leveling of things and his purely expediential view of them, or in the way of Mo Tzu with his undifferentiated universal love. [On the other hand] to dwell exclusively on the particularity of things inevitably leads to the egoism of Yang Chu. Unable directly to benefit from the personal instruction of the sages, we turn to their books and enter into their minds so that we may be converted to the truth of "the unity of principle and the diversity of its particularizations" and free ourselves from all error and defect.[6]

Seika believed in the possibility of latter-day saints and sages, and the sages he has in mind here are the Sung masters. When he speaks of "the unity of principle and the diversity of its particularizations," he invokes a doctrine which came to him from Chang Tsai and Ch'eng I through Chu Hsi's teacher, Li T'ung.[7] In Chu Hsi's Dialogues with Yen-p'ing (Yen-p'ing ta-wen),[p] a text republished in Korea with commentary by T'oegye and a work particularly significant for Seika, this expression appears to represent the quintessence of the Confucian experience of truth as expounded by Li T'ung and as exemplified by Li's lofty and pure character.[8] The personal realization (t'i-jen)[q] of this truth was described by Li T'ung as "a total realization of oneness" (hun-jan i-t'i),[r] and by Chu Hsi as a "sudden and total penetration of the pervading unity" (huo-jan kuan-t'ung),[s] a holism overcoming the dichotomies of internal and external, subject and object, one and many, latent and manifest nature.[9]

As a method or exercise (kung-fu; kufū)[t] most conducive to the attainment of this illumination, Li T'ung favored quiet-sitting, and Seika, adopting this practice, saw it as the prime means for the personal realization of truth in an experience of enlightenment which Li T'ung had described as "untrammeled spontaneity" (sa-lo; sharaku)[u] and which he (like Li T'ung) sharply distinguished from the amorality of Zen.[10] In such an experience Seika found a basis for reconciling the divergent philosophies of Chu Hsi and Wang Yang-ming. Though this can be characterized as an eclectic view, Seika's profound personal synthesis of these teachings, manifested in his notable independence of mind and strength of character, belies any suspicion of a facile or soft-minded eclecticism on his part, and stands instead as an impressive example of the integrative power of Neo-Confucian cultivation.[11]

In this way Seika became identified with one basic strain of Ch'eng-Chu orthodoxy as transmitted through Yi T'oegye. It reflected the specific character of a Korean orthodoxy markedly religious in tone. Its aims are summed up in the expression "abiding in reverence and plumbing principle" (*chü-ching ch'iung li; kyokei kyūri*).[v] "Abiding in reverence" is a term we have seen deriving from Ch'eng I and Chu Hsi, whose combination of moralistic and rationalistic tendencies justifies using for *ching* ("reverence"), the alternative translations of "seriousness," "concentration" or "devotion." In practice, for T'oegye and Seika, the method of "abiding in reverence" was chiefly the quiet-sitting so strongly recommended by Li T'ung. Along with it came, from T'oegye to Seika, a philosophical formulation meant to clarify the metaphysical basis of self-cultivation. This formulation dealt with the accepted Neo-Confucian equation of human nature and principle. On the one hand, it identified the "four seeds or sprouts" of virtue (spoken of by Mencius as the basis of the goodness of human nature) with principle, and on the other, it explicitly identified the "seven emotions" (*ch'i-ch'ing*)[w] with the physical nature of man (*ch'i-chih*).[x][12] Since these emotions were seen as the source of selfish desires and a potentiality for evil, a practical implication of the doctrine for those engaged in quiet-sitting was to employ it as a kind of self-watchfulness over evil thoughts and impulses associated with the physical, sensual nature. In the stilled mind man's original nature or principle, unobstructed by disturbing psycho-physical activity, emerged clearly as the effortless controller of the mind-and-heart—principle in this state being conceived as naturally dominant over ether.

According to the recent studies of Professor Kanaya Osamu,[y] Seika's rigorism was reinforced by the specific influence of the Ming syncretist Lin Chao-en (1517–1598), whose system of mind-culture became for Seika a discipline to purge the mind of the "stain of worldly desires." "*Butsu* or worldliness is dust [on the mirror of the mind]. As the mirror becomes clear and bright when no speck of dust dirties it, so lucid wisdom will come to us if we renounce the worldliness of our mind."[13] Professor Kanaya stresses that for Seika, as for Lin Chao-en, this mental discipline was strongly oriented toward moral activism and away from quietistic contemplation, and the same is true of the influence of Lin on other thinkers like Nakae Tōju[z] and Kumazawa Banzan.[aa]

From this one can see how attitudes associated very early with the practice of quiet-sitting might engender a strong tendency toward puritanism. Though not a necessary deduction from Chu Hsi's philosophical position, neither was it without some basis in Chu's doctrine concerning the physical nature. T'oegye's theory of the "four sprouts of virtue and the seven emotions"[ab] served simply to formulate in more explicit terms a puritanical view which in China very early became associated with Ch'eng-Chu orthodoxy and was already present or latent in Li T'ung's teaching.[14] T'oegye's formulation heightened this tendency, and communicated to certain Japanese "orthodox" Neo-Confucians a "reverence" with a moralistic and puritanical "seriousness" about it. Indeed, recent studies of specific late Ming influences on early Tokugawa thought and ideology,[15] including those of Lin Chao-en and the *Ming-hsin pao-chien*,[ac] have reinforced the view that Japanese Neo-Confucianism exhibited an intense theistic and moralistic quality which is not wholly identifiable with Chu Hsi's philosophy, but only expresses certain tendencies or options available within it.

RATIONALISM AND EMPIRICISM IN THE ORTHODOXY OF HAYASHI RAZAN

Hayashi Razan (1583–1657), on the other hand, rejected T'oegye's view, adopting an alternative one of Ming provenance, likewise with a history of philosophical and polemical dispute attaching to it. The debate in Korea had given prominence to the views of the Ming thinker Lo Ch'in-shun and his work, the *K'un-chih chi*,[ad] freely translatable as "Knowing Pains" but more literally "Record of Knowledge Attained through Painful Effort." Lo's view of the physical nature is discussed in this volume by Irene Bloom, and his influence in Japan has been described by Professor Abe.

Lo represented a strong counter-trend in the Ming and within the Ch'eng-Chu school itself, resisting the idea that the physical nature was evil and asserting that principle, including human nature, could not exist apart from its actual embodiment or manifestation in ether (physical or psychical *ch'i*). Wang Yang-ming had said something similar when he spoke of principles not existing apart from the mind, but Lo questioned the subjectivity of Wang's view and stressed instead the objective "investigation of principle in things and affairs." By emphasizing the reality of ether and the physical nature, Lo countered the tendency to think of the desires as anything but natural. Hence, his view may be termed "naturalistic" insofar as he affirmed the reality of man's actual nature and the necessity of accepting it as sharing in the goodness of the moral nature. At the same time, since ether was the individuating and concretizing agent in the actual world, Lo's philosophy directed attention to the principles in things as concrete facts to be observed. In this sense his view may be said to have a strong empirical bent, establishing the need for evidential inquiry.[16]

Though this naturalism and empiricism were increasingly in evidence as a general trend of late Ming thought, its emergence within the Ch'eng-Chu school is significant. Lo believed that he was only amending and not revoking the essential Ch'eng-Chu tradition, which he sought to defend against an excess of moralistic idealism. A major point in the Neo-Confucian case against Buddhism had been its reaffirmation of the physical world. In accepting Lo's view, Razan had no reason to believe that Lo was anything but faithful to the original Neo-Confucian intention, or that his contribution was other than a needed clarification of what Chu Hsi had meant. At the same time we recognize it as a clarification which led in one possible direction out of several. Indeed, Lo's empirical approach was a possibility which Wang Yang-ming himself had recognized in Chu Hsi and consciously reacted against, i.e., the possibility of a value-free objectivity in regard to external matters, or "the investigation of things good and evil purely as external objects."[17] In resisting this tendency, Wang claimed that he was actually following Chu Hsi's own thought to the revised conclusions Chu Hsi ultimately arrived at.

Razan's identification with Lo Ch'in-shun arose from two objective needs in his own situation. One was the need for a strong stand against Buddhism, which had dominated shogunal courts for centuries and was virtually an established religion. To serve as an adviser to the Shogun Razan had to submit to the tonsure and serve as if he were a monk. This indignity for a Confucian made Razan all the more appreciative of Lo Ch'in-shun's keen critique of Buddhism, which exhibited both a sophistication and an articulateness Razan must have envied.

Secondly, Razan's strongest qualification was his encyclopedic learning. It was his stock of knowledge that Ieyasu found so impressive and so useful to the Tokugawa administration.[18] Lo's philosophy likewise underscored the value of a knowledge of facts as well as texts, and in this it fulfilled the aim of Chu Hsi to achieve "broad learning" (*po-hsüeh*).[ae] Razan's own activities as a cultural and diplomatic adviser to the shogunate extended to a wide variety of fields, and his published works reflected his interest in law, diplomacy, military affairs, medicine, pharmacopoeia and herbology, religion, philosophy and institutional and cultural history. Professor Abe's studies bring out the impetus Razan gave to his disciples' wide range of scholarly activities and research, including empirical studies in the natural sciences.[19]

Moreover, Razan had a strongly rationalistic and skeptical cast of mind and reserved judgment on many questions pending further evidence. Far from being a credulous fanatic in the service of a blind orthodoxy, he demonstrated a questioning attitude and insatiable curiosity in regard to many points which others took on faith or accepted authority. Thus Lo's philosophy, which set a high value on objective learning and evidential research, was well suited to the presentation of Chu Hsi's teaching under two of its aspects most likely to meet the needs of both Razan's temperament and situation.

Behind these differences in received transmissions, there were differences in the personal backgrounds and temperaments of Seika and Razan which affected their respective philosophical approaches. Seika was retiring and introverted. After spending almost a lifetime in the practice of Zen, even after his conversion to Neo-Confucianism he was drawn to the mental and spiritual disciplines which constituted the *shingaku*[af] of the Chu Hsi school, especially in the form of quiet-sitting and in Lin Chao-en's Taoistic method of practicing the *I-ching's* "stilling in the back" (*ken pei*).[ag] Razan's more extroverted personality, which had never been subdued by the practice of *zazen*, did not take to quiet-sitting, was diffident about the non-rational elements in the Chu Hsi school, and felt more at home in studies of a rationalistic and empirical sort.[20]

In an essay on "Tokugawa Feudal Society and Neo-Confucian Thought," Professor Ishida Ichirō[ah] has sought to correct two misconceptions among modern scholars: first, that Neo-Confucianism was merely an ethical system with a strong secular orientation; and second, that its moralistic tendency inhibited the development of an interest in natural science and empirical research.[21] Ishida points to the pervasive religious element in Neo-Confucianism, centering on the concept of Heaven, and he simultaneously affirms the Tokugawa Confucianists' philosophical disposition toward a naturalistic empiricism and "love of scientific learning."[22] He offers a detailed account of Confucian religiosity toward Heaven, which was combined with a scholarly interest in secular problems and scientific study. These he encompasses in a characterization of "Chu Hsi-Confucianism" as a secularized medieval religion.[23]

According to Ishida, there was a close correspondence between this religion, the basic principle of which was the sovereignty of Heaven governing all things through natural law, and the fundamental reality of Tokugawa feudal society.

Japanese Chu Hsi-Confucianism emphasized the power of Heaven not only because this idea was germane to Chu Hsi-Confucianism as it was originally formulated, but also because it was inherently demanded by the ideals and reality of Tokugawa society. The life experience of the people who lived under the absolute autocracy of the feudal system was such as to enable them to respond sympathetically to the doctrines of Chu Hsi-Confucianism even though these were of foreign origin. . . . [It] met a need of the times by giving formal expression to the life experience of feudal society.[24]

Professor Ishida's explanation of the ideological uses of Neo-Confucianism in Tokugawa Japan gives a good account of those aspects of the teaching which offered a rationale for the exercise of feudal power. However, his attempt to link Neo-Confucian "secular religion" to the "consciousness of feudal life (particularly in the castle towns)," and to see it as giving "formal expression to the life experience of feudal society" and becoming the "supporting 'theology' of the Tokugawa system,"[25] is subject to some qualification. Neo-Confucianism served much the same functions in the very different political and social circumstances of China and Korea. The Japanese castle town and its highly structured hereditary feudal relationships were worlds apart from the egalitarian peasant mentality of China's Chu Yüan-chang[ai] and the meritocratic, bureaucratic system he set up as founding father of the Ming dynasty and as sponsor of the official Neo-Confucian orthodoxy. Nevertheless, Neo-Confucian ethical constants could provide a plausible rationale for order and authority in both cases. To the extent that they affirmed the universality and immutability of values attaching to human relationships and saw all life as governed by a rational structure of static, unchanging norms, Neo-Confucianism upheld a view which could be invoked in behalf of elements in almost any authority system—and equally, we might add, in behalf of challenges to the status quo for failing to meet these norms.

Hayashi Razan, however, as the intellectual leader and founder of the Bakufu orthodoxy, was a Neo-Confucian who largely followed Lo Ch'in-shun's Ming reformulation of Ch'eng-Chu philosophy, which paid primary allegiance not to static norms and principles but to the dynamic, psycho-physical element of *ch'i* (*ki*) and to objective principles as found in a world of change and growth. At times he questioned the existence of a metaphysical "Supreme Norm" (*t'ai chi; taikyoku*),[c] was puzzled over the prominent place given to it and to the dubious concept of an unconditioned ultimate reality (*wu-chi*)[d] in Chu Hsi's *Reflections on Things at Hand* (*Chin-ssu lu*),[aj] and showed a persistent skepticism in regard to the supposedly authoritative example of the ancient sages in China and the accounts of the Divine Emperors in Japan.[26]

The same factors must be borne in mind when one generalizes about the absoluteness of the moral and political imperatives of Chu Hsi orthodoxy in the early Tokugawa period. What gave Bakufu orthodoxy its absolute quality was, in fact, the unquestioned success, power and authority of the regime in its early years. The official ideology received a sanction from this irresistible force which could not have been derived from the inherent fitness of Chu Hsi's philosophy to the historical situation. Nor was it likely to remain unquestioned if the critical inquiry and scholarly study represented by Razan were allowed any scope.

Two Strains of Neo-Confucian Thought

Indeed Razan was no anomaly in this respect. The attitude of skeptical questioning and critical inquiry which came down to him from Chu Hsi and Lo Ch'in-shun (among others) was carried on by several of Razan's disciples, including Kaibara Ekken[ak] and Yamaga Sokō.[al] Similarly, with Razan's emphasis on the dynamic ether (*ki*) and on principle (*ri*) as an objective rather than a subjective reality—this attitude too became a vital current in Japanese Neo-Confucianism, and watered the seeds of independent thought in the next generation.[27] The view of some writers that Bakufu orthodoxy was exclusively concerned with upholding normative principles (*li*) does not take into account the ambiguities of the situation, as reflected, for example, in the matter-of-fact, but unexpected, observation of Professor Abe concerning Yamaga Sokō, that "since he was a disciple of Hayashi Razan, it is quite understandable that he denied Chu Hsi's *li* philosophy."[28] How, we ask, could Razan be spoken of as rejecting Chu Hsi's *li* philosophy? To answer this one must go beyond the usual view of Razan as simply an adherent of Chu Hsi or an upholder of principle, and recognize that what Abe actually refers to is the view of *li* as transcendent principle immanent in the mind, whereas Razan, by contrast, stressed the objective study of principles in things.

The point of these observations is not to deny that Neo-Confucian orthodoxy or Ch'eng-Chu philosophy could provide the Bakufu with normative concepts and hierarchical structures which might serve as a rationale for its own rule and give meaning to the life-experience of Japanese in a feudal social structure. It is rather to highlight the indubitable and indeed seminal role of attitudes of mind no less central than these to Neo-Confucian thought: the inclination to raise questions and attempt answers on an evidential basis, and the ability to challenge as well as to accept established authority, both intellectual and political. In this, Neo-Confucianism had a capacity for self-criticism which also gave it the power of continued growth.

Whatever one's view of the uses of ideology and the abuses of Confucian philosophy, Seika and Razan indubitably functioned in two familiar Neo-Confucian roles: as critics of Buddhism, and as proponents of secular society and culture. It was an accident of history that Chu Yüan-chang, the founder of Ming orthodoxy, and these two Japanese leaders of the Neo-Confucian movement were alike in being ex-monks and tending to be anti-clerical. But it was not accidental that the Tokugawa, seeking to build a new and more unified secular order, turned to a humanism which offered a positive attitude toward human society, an ethical system on which stable social relations could be built, and a body of learning which could help civilize the feudal, military class. Thus Ishida is certainly correct in considering the Bakufu's choice of Neo-Confucianism to be no accident of history.[29] This is shown by the parallel between early Sung China and early Tokugawa Japan. In both periods, as we have observed, there was a new emphasis on civil, as opposed to military, rule, and on a secular order as contrasted to the clerical dominance of Buddhism. And in both periods Neo-Confucianism responded to the trend.

Nevertheless, as Ishida says, the new humanism was not without an important religious or spiritual dimension. Instead, however, of being

identified simply with reverence for external authority, it is most genuinely expressed in the type of spirituality found in the Neo-Confucian
school(s) of the mind, represented initially by Seika. What we have then
are parallel strains of Neo-Confucian thought: one, emerging from
Seika's spiritual cultivation, was centered on the experience of the unity
of principle in active contemplation (or contemplative action), and the
other, stemming from Razan, was more rational, scholarly, and intellectual and more given to the study of both human society and natural
science.

Given these divergent strains of Neo-Confucian "orthodoxy," reflecting
the range of human activity and experience comprehended in Chu Hsi's
system, it became all the more important that its power of synthesis could
be concretely exemplified in the unifying conception of the sage. Thus
what happens to the conception of sagehood under the influence of these
historical developments is a crucial indicator of Neo-Confucianism's ability to contribute to or adapt to change.

YAMAGA SOKŌ AND THE "DEAD-WOOD" OF THE SUNG SAGE

Yamaga Sokō (1622–1685), best known for his contributions to the art
of war and the ethics of the warrior class, was also a Confucian scholar
with broad intellectual interests, reflecting the Chu Hsi tradition of
"broad learning" which his teacher, Hayashi Razan, carried on. Respon-
sive to many of the needs of his own time, Sokō nevertheless thought in a
Neo-Confucian context and his writings show a continuing preoccupation with the central problems of that teaching, expecially the meaning
and significance of the sage.

Sokō's autobiography (*Haisho zanpitsu*)[am] describes his spiritual odys-
sey and the doubts he experienced, like many Neo-Confucians before
him, until he found the teaching which could become for him a way of
life. His early education was in the Ch'eng-Chu school and, as he came
to realize later, very "Chinese." It was also a very "catholic" training,
including both orthodox book-learning and religious discipline. The latter he identified as the practice of "sustained reverence" (*jikei; ch'ih-
ching*)[an] manifested mainly in the form of quiet-sitting. Apparently, he
found the latter too constraining, and wondered whether it was not mak-

ing him too grave, over-serious, and withdrawn. Turning to Taoism and Buddhism, especially as synthesized in Zen, he found that their mystical insights provided greater access to spiritual freedom and spontaneity.[30] These were values the Neo-Confucians themselves had recognized, and at this stage of his development Sokō found them immensely liberating.

In pursuing an "inexpressible state of selfless purity and mystical freedom," however, Sokō became aware that it took him away from society, not into it. His continued search for a practicable, livable "way" for the Japanese of his time, led him back to both the original teachings of the Confucian classics and the original Japanese way of life in Shinto, from which he derived a simplified system of basic ethics that would serve as a kind of least-common-denominator adaptable to any social station or situation in life, whether that of the samurai, townsman or peasant. He succinctly stated his conclusions in a little primer, *The Essence of the Sage's Teaching (Seikyō yōroku)*[ao] (1666), the contents and organization of which follow Neo-Confucian lines,[31] as if it were a highly abbreviated and revised version of Chu Hsi's *Chin-ssu lu* or the *Hsing-li ta-ch'üan*[ap] of the Ming, but with each topic discussed in the simplest fashion.

In the opening passage, Sokō goes straight to the central issue, the model of the sage, which he redefines in everyday terms. There is no set form, way, style or practice of sagehood; the sage's true teaching consists in the ordinary practice of virtue in human relations, the regular pursuit of learning as it pertains to everyday needs and functions. It involves attainment of the Mean in daily life, not the cultivation of special states of mind or the discussion of philosophical subtleties.[32]

Chu Hsi had revamped the conception of sagehood by humanizing and secularizing it in contemporary Sung terms. Sokō now deflates this re-mythologized ideal for not offering a workable model for his own times. He goes on in this brief work, and in his other recorded utterances, to affirm the importance of the sages' example while inveighing against precisely those two pursuits which we recognize as most characteristic of the Sung school—the scholarly study of texts or book-learning, and the practice of quiet-sitting. Both of these Sokō sees as removing the practitioner from real life and drawing him away from his social responsibilities.[33]

Nothing, of course, could have been further from the minds of the Sung masters themselves, who, given their social and cultural situation and the spiritual climate of their times, thought of both scholarly study and contemplative practice as the ideal preparation for dealing with human affairs. Moreover, the methods Chu Hsi prescribed were believed practicable for even "a young lad in an isolated village," if only he aspired to sagehood.[34]

Yet what the Sung masters conceived as a universally valid model—and it did indeed exert a remarkably wide appeal—took for granted much that was the natural property of only the Sung scholar-official class. As members of the leisured gentry, many of them had the time and means to engage in scholarly study and quiet-sitting as ordinary men did not, even though the ordinary man might aspire to them. Sokō, on the other hand, a samurai with a strong sense of duty and a calling to a much more active life, identifies these pursuits with the kind of cultural refinement or polite learning which Confucius had said one might engage in if he had the "energy left over for it,"[35] after he had met his primary obligation to society. Without differentiating the historical situations, his and the Sung masters', Sokō prescribes in equally universal terms, moralistically condemning these Sung preoccupations as irresponsible and effete, an insidious intrusion of Buddho-Taoist quietism and escapism.

The tone and language of Sokō's critique, and indeed his basic standpoint, we recognize as Neo-Confucian. He applies to the Sung masters their own criteria for what was "real" or "practical" learning. And if he does this from an altered historical perspective, this was no more than Ming Neo-Confucians had done with the Sung conception of sagehood as they adapted it to their own social and cultural requirements, still affirming the goal but recasting the model to render it plausible and achievable for every man. Indeed, Sokō's critique of the sitting sage of the Sung is quite reminiscent of the Ming Confucian Ch'en Ti, whose experience of military life and involvement in specialized scholarly research rendered the Sung conception less practicable as a model of self-cultivation.

A main target of Sokō's attack was the notion that one might, through quiet-sitting, contemplate one's nature in its quiescent state. This he likened to the "direct apprehension of one's own nature" in Zen.[36] For Sokō, man's moral nature, as Mencius had defined it, consisted in the innate seeds or sprouts of goodness which, if cultivated and acted upon, would become perfected in true humanity. Sokō's was a dynamic conception of the nature and principle, which could only be fulfilled or realized in action.[37] There being no such thing as a static principle or quiescent nature, whatever principle one attained to in quiet-sitting was to him (using Chu Hsi's own language) like the "principle of dead and withered wood."[38]

Here again Sokō's critique is a familiar one, strongly resembling earlier Ming objections to the Sung view from the standpoint of the vitalistic trend mentioned above. At the same time, Sokō points to some differences between Chu Hsi and several of his predecessors in this regard. Chou Tun-i, with his teaching of quiescence and his Unconditioned Supreme Reality (wu-chi erh t'ai-chi)[aq]; Chang Tsai with his Supreme Vacuity (t'ai-hsü)[ar]; and the Ch'eng brothers with their attempt to experience the nature in its unmanifest state (wei-fa chih chung)[as] through quiet-sitting—these and others in the Sung school had engendered a pervasive quietism which Chu Hsi at first had resisted, according to Sokō, but to which he eventually succumbed when he resorted to the distinction between man's Heavenly moral (static) nature and his physical (active) nature.[39]

For Sokō, as for Lo Ch'in-shun and others in the Ming, there could be no moral nature of man apart from the physical nature, just as there could be no principle apart from things and affairs. On this account too Sokō decried the Sung tendency to curb or suppress human desires, seeing the latter as powerful creative forces which it was the sage's duty to nurture and satisfy. To what extent Sokō was familiar with, or influenced by, seventeenth-century Chinese thinkers who held the same view is difficult to judge. Given his own antecedents in Razan and Lo, and the live issue which was already emerging in contemporary Japanese literature over the conflict between human feelings (ninjō)[at] and Confucian ethical principles or duties (giri),[au] one need not presuppose external influences in order to account for Sokō's attitude. Rather, it appears as a natural conjunction of Japanese sensibilities with the internal evolution of Neo-Confucian thought in both China and Japan.

Sokō's affirmation of physical desires and his denunciation of the "Sung" school for suppressing them, have been cited by some writers as a "modern," "humanistic" element in his thought. Professor Ishida, however, sees this interpretation as based on a misconception. He says:

In Chu Hsi-Confucianism seeking after the satisfaction of one's desires is good or bad depending upon whether or not it is permitted by the social (Heaven's) order. A distinction is made between desire which is permitted by Heaven (public desire) and desire which is merely personal (private desire). Some students of Tokugawa intellectual history have claimed that the school of Neo-classical Confucianism (*Kogaku*)[g] arose in opposition to Chu-Hsi-Confucianism, because the latter denied the fulfillment of human desires. This is incorrect. . . .

Hayashi Razan explained that man is not human without sexual desire and appetite for food. . . . Every man, even the sage, is subject to the seven passions of joy, anger, sorrow, fear, love, hate and desire. . . . To deny sexuality is to deny Heaven's creative will, and prevents man's fulfilling his obligation to reproduce. Sexual activity within the limits imposed by the social order assists Heaven's creative work and is permitted by Heaven.[40]

Here Ishida clearly has Razan on his side, and yet this does not suffice to settle the matter. For Razan (and Kaibara Ekken, whom Ishida also cites in this connection)[41] bespeaks only one orthodox view of the matter, and one which Sokō himself reflects, as a fundamental Neo-Confucian assertion of the goodness of man's physical nature as well as of his moral nature. A differing view—and the real target for Sokō—can be found in the alternative transmission of Neo-Confucian orthodoxy which came through T'oegye and Seika. Though it did not explicitly assert that man's physical nature or desires were evil, its curbing of the desires through the practice of quiescence had the effect, as we have already seen, of engendering a strict and puritanical view among many orthodox Neo-Confucians and especially Yamazaki Ansai,[av] the bête noire of Kogaku scholars. Sokō we know had personally engaged in this discipline and later reacted strongly against it. He speaks from experience and not from conjecture or misconception. And we know too that Razan, in the passage quoted by Ishida, alludes specifically (though without attribution) to T'oegye's formulation concerning the "seven passions" as identified with the physical nature in opposition to the moral nature, and then rebuts it from the same standpoint as Lo Ch'in-shun.[42] Sokō then is not overturning Neo-Confucianism but upholding one side of that tradition against another.

Here is a clear-cut case in which the discussion of Neo-Confucian orthodoxy must take into account the alternatives which existed, and the continuing dialogue and controversy which were carried on *within* this complex, evolving tradition. As it happens, too, it is a case in which foreign influences can be seen quite definitely at work, and the precise identification of them is essential to a clarification of the issues.

While recognizing the specific influences on Neo-Confucianism which render Sokō's criticism plausible, we may also note how the original Neo-Confucian affirmation of man's physical nature, which Professor

Ishida correctly assesses, had taken such an ironic turn. Far from viewing human nature as evil, the Neo-Confucians had thought to assert its goodness; indeed, in their zeal to refute the Buddhist view of man's original nature as beyond good and evil, the Ch'eng-Chu school had even committed themselves to an unprecedented degree to Mencius' position concerning its goodness—a doctrine repeatedly invoked against any surreptitious Buddhist influence. How then did the Sung school end up being attacked by Sokō for its "Buddhistic" view of man's nature and human desires?

The explanation seems to lie in a curious distortion of the two basic Neo-Confucian positions: one affirming the reality of moral values in the sense of their enduring truth and immutability (as against the Buddhist view of universal impermanence), and the other affirming the reality of the physical world and man's physical nature (as against the Buddhist view of them as a source of delusion). The sphere of pure and unchanging moral values was metaphysical, i.e., transcending the karmic sphere and not subject to essential loss or destruction in time. Constant human values were seen as reembodied and actualized in different times and places down through the ages. The Ch'eng-Chu school affirmed both of these aspects of man's nature, the moral and the physical, the ideal and the actual, and, as Professor Ishida asserts, Hayashi Razan too reaffirmed them.

In Chu Hsi's system of mind-cultivation, however, a distinction was made between the mind's pure and objective reflection of immutable moral principles when there was no ego-involvement in its perception (i.e., when the mind-and-heart was still and unmoved by the will) and its active realization of these principles in practice. Chu's method sought on the one hand to compose the mind to achieve a mirror-like receptivity, in which moral values were objectively reflected, and on the other hand, to follow through with an effort of the will in practical activity which was free of ulterior selfish motives. There would then be no discrepancy between the ideal and the actual.[43]

For Sokō, and other Neo-Confucian critics of the Sung school in Ming and Ch'ing China, the implication of this method that selfish motives were bad was unacceptable. It seemed to imply that the actual self was evil. Hence, they repudiated Chu Hsi's distinction between the metaphysical and physical natures, as also between metaphysical principles and actual values, and in the process they also abandoned the Ch'eng-

Chu conception of the sage as the perfect embodiment of the active integration of metaphysical principles in human activity. For Sokō, principles existed only in their differentiated state, and instead of it being possible to unite all principles in one discrete experience of sagehood, the fulfillment of man's humanity could only take place through a gradual process of integration, matching or adjusting the individual's aspirations and desires with the objective requirements of his own situation in life, as based on experience or empirical study.

To some recent writers, this stress on a person's actual nature and individuality, as contrasted to his conformity with a universal and transcendent ideal, is one of the marks of Sokō's modernity. Before accepting this conclusion, however, we would do well to note that Sokō defined this individuality largely in terms of one's station, function or physical condition in life; that is, in relation to the external world and especially society.

It is a crucial point, for while Sokō emphasized the functional definition of the individual in terms of his social relations and responsibilities ("All things have their own uses and each use has its principle; hence its use is its principle."), there is much evidence in Sokō's writing that his repeated attacks on Sung subjectivism were directed against the individual subjectivity which, from another point of view, could be seen as a potential source of modern individualism. Thus, for instance, Sokō expressed his dissatisfaction with the Neo-Confucian concept of individual fulfillment or self-realization as expressed in Mencius' "finding the way in oneself" (tzu-te).[aw][44] This had been, from Li T'ung through the Ming thinkers, Ch'en Hsien-chang,[ax] Wang Ken, and on to Li Chih in the sixteenth century, a developing theme of an individualistic and liberal (if not indeed libertarian) strain in Ming Neo-Confucian thought.[45] The experience of self-transcendence, of rising above the limitations of past experience and present circumstances, was understood as a miraculously creative and unpredictable process. But Sokō, if his autobiography is any indication, had already grown distrustful of such "liberating" experiences and no doubt also of the individualism which in the Ming sprang from this intense subjectivity. It may then be that there is something more "alive" here in the "dead-wood" of the Sung sage than Sokō would have wished.

Sokō does not, however, wholly remove the sage from the scene as an archetype of self-cultivation. Sagehood remains a possibility to be achieved by the individual, with his undeniable physical needs and irre-

pressible desires, through the process of extending his knowledge of objective principles and facts and interacting with the totality of the dynamic forces defining his individual existence. This is not a possibility
which derives from his being endowed potentially with the principles of
all things, nor is there any unitary principle by which, through a combination of "broad learning" (i.e. book-learning) and interior contemplation, he could comprehend all principles and achieve unity with all
things in an experience of sudden illumination.[46] But if this latter is impossible for Sokō, and if for everyone to achieve the fullness of sagehood
is quite improbable, nonetheless, by following the objective example of
the sages and their teachings every man can achieve self-realization
(makoto)[ay] as a participant in the total moral economy of Heaven-and-
earth.[47]

It would be equally erroneous, however, to conclude from Sokō's functional or utilitarian view of the individual that his is a purely secular
man, without a religious dimension. Neo-Confucian "reverence" remains for Sokō an essential value but it is directed outward in the form of
respect for Heaven-and-earth and the objective standards exemplified in
the ritual system of the sages. Moreover the rituals, for Sokō, also extend
to the Shinto traditions of Japan. In this respect his religiosity has a theistic quality that contrasts with the undifferentiated, rationalized "reverence" of the Ch'eng-Chu school which recognized no external object of
devotion but was largely internalized.[48]

Allowing for these differences in emphasis and thrust, Sokō's own synthesis remains essentially an internal realignment of Neo-Confucian values, with an admixture of those elements increasingly evident in later
Neo-Confucian thought: empirical study, practical activity, everyday utility, and a syncretic humanism. Much as he challenged the Sung model
of the sage, he did not fail to recognize the multi-dimensional character
of human experience which it was meant to embody. Accordingly, "real"
or "practical" learning was for him many-sided, extending to military
science, Western learning and Shinto, along with a "neo-classical" reformulation of the central conception of the sages' teaching. But it was now
grounded in the actual social process to a degree not achieved by his
Neo-Confucian predecessors in seventeenth-century Japan.

ITŌ JINSAI: FROM DEAD SERIOUSNESS TO
LIFE-AFFIRMING LOVE

Though a commoner, and quite different from Sokō in terms of social background, Itō Jinsai[az] (1627–1705), a slightly younger contemporary of his, shared with Sokō a common inheritance as a second-generation Neo-Confucian, and he also experienced a remarkably similar spiritual and intellectual development. Whatever the social disadvantages which attached to his being a townsman of Kyoto, the cultural advantages of the capital afford him easy access to the new teaching, and though largely self-taught, he immersed himself quickly in its depths and complexities. There he encountered much the same difficulties and trials which had tested others before him.

One did not need to be enrolled in an official school or to aspire to be of some service as a samurai in order to feel the powerful attractions of Sung philosophy. Jinsai found himself drawn to the same texts which by then had become standard works of Neo-Confucian teaching, books which had impressed generations of scholars in different places, times and social situations: Chu Hsi's lucid commentaries on the Confucian classics, his *Reflections on Things at Hand* (*Chin-ssu lu*), a systematic guide to the achievement of sagehood; and the *Great Compendium of Human Nature and Principle* (*Hsing-li ta-ch'üan*), with its wide-ranging speculations on the universe and human life.[49] But of special significance to us is the fascination for him of Chu Hsi's *Dialogues with Yen-p'ing*, which we recognize as having had a similar appeal for Fujiwara Seika and no doubt for the same reason: it offered a method of self-cultivation which seemed both concrete and comprehensive and held out the prospect of lofty spiritual achievement like that which Chu Hsi described so admiringly in Li T'ung.

This strong religious attraction in Neo-Confucianism is indicated by Itō's taking the pen-name at this time of Keisai, which conveyed a sense of dedication to a life of reverence or seriousness (*kei*).[ba][50] (It had been the pen-name before of Hu Chü-jen[bb] (1434–1484), who was probably the most religiously orthodox of Ming Ch'eng-Chu schoolmen.) By the age of twenty-nine or thirty, however, Itō had changed the name to Jinsai, indicating a new commitment to humaneness or love (*jin*) as his highest ideal. From this process we learn something of the intensity with which Jinsai had devoted himself to his study of Chu Hsi (reminiscent of Wu Yü-pi, Ch'en Hsien-chang, Hu Chü-jen and others in the Ming). We learn too of how disenchanted he had eventually become with his former ideal. As in the case of Sokō, what had first recommended itself as a demanding discipline and austere dedication to lofty goals eventually generated a reaction against its very puritanism and rigidity. And from this experience of disillusionment with the Sung model, style, and practice of sagehood a familiar pattern emerged. Thus as Jinsai sought to articulate the intellectual and philosophical consequences of his new stance he could draw upon the earlier work of a Ming Neo-Confucian, Wu T'ing-han,[bc] who like Lo Ch'in-shun, represented a brand of Neo-Confucian teaching which stressed ether as the prime reality.[51]

From this new vantage point, Jinsai saw the "reverence" or "seriousness" of the Sung school as a deadening, life-denying attitude in much the same way as Sokō had spoken of the Sung masters as searching out the "principle of dead and withered wood."

Learning should seek to discover living principles; it should not be concerned with the preservation of dead principles. Withered grass, dried roots, metal and stone, pottery and tile—these are dead objects. Their being is fixed; nothing can be added or subtracted. But for man it is otherwise. If he does not advance, he must surely withdraw; if he does not withdraw, he must surely advance. For him there is not a moment of fixity [but only ceaseless movement]. It cannot be for him as it is for dead things.

Therefore what the noble man esteems is not so much being without fault as being able to reform oneself. The old men of the Sung school, however, take a cautious and calculating, inch-by-inch, pinch-penny attitude toward things. They are restrained and reserved, lest they give anyone the chance to find so much as a miniscule fault in their behavior. Therefore they are severely handicapped in their own power to do good, and they cannot appreciate magnanimity in others or a warm open-heartedness. This is what I call recognizing dead principles, but not recognizing live principles.[52]

Chu Hsi, according to Jinsai, had stressed reverence or seriousness as the root and basis of all things, as the beginning and end of the sages' teaching, and as the guide or ruler of the mind.[53] He thus made of it the supreme virtue. Seeing every act of man as having value implications and consequences, the Ch'eng-Chu school had indeed enjoined upon man a strict conscientiousness both in every single action and in the total ordering of one's life and conduct. This was the aspect of Neo-Confucian reverence which called for a life-and-death seriousness and a grave attention to each matter at hand, as contrasted to the spiritual openness and receptivity which was meant to serve as the necessary complement to moral seriousness. In the experience of Jinsai, apparently, this prime Neo-Confucian value had become distorted and developed into a deadly seriousness, fretful prudery, and a totally introverted cast of mind, recalling Sokō's description of it in the *Haisho zanpitsu* as making him also too grave, over-serious and withdrawn.[54]

Nor was this purely a matter of Jinsai's or Sokō's personal experience, but a recognized pattern of behavior in the Chu Hsi school. Professor Yamashita cites the following anecdote concerning Nakae Tōju in his *Life Chronology (nenpu)*: when Tōju was a young man first dedicating himself to the pursuit of Chu Hsi's teaching, someone on seeing him approach said, "Here comes Confucius himself," mockingly referring to the very solemn bearing and strict manner exhibited by those cultivating the "seriousness" of that school.[55] Tōju too later reacted against this stern discipline and was attracted to the freer life style of Wang Chi and Wang Yang-ming.

In his mature thought (much of which is preserved in the writings of his son Tōgai),[bd] Jinsai scrutinized Sung concepts and practices in the light of the original teachings of Confucius and Mencius. In developing the contrast, Jinsai saw the reverence or seriousness of the Sung school not as a state of composure or serenity preserved in the midst of everyday affairs, but more narrowly as an introspective practice in the manner of Li T'ung, which to Jinsai compounded all the evils of Buddhist and Taoist quietism—the suppression of natural desires and the immobilizing of the will in the process of achieving a single-minded concentration on the original nature.[56] Like Sokō, Jinsai equated this view with Zen's "directly pointing to the mind's nature," and he saw as Zen-like too the experience of sudden enlightenment which Chu Hsi had described as "a sudden and total penetration" (*katsuzen kantsū*)[s] of the unitary principle.[57]

According to Jinsai, it was the subtle and pervasive influence of Buddhism which led to the belief in sudden enlightenment as the culminating experience of sagehood. The Sung was a time, he says, when all educated persons of all classes, ages and sexes were immersed in Zen and they read into the Confucian classics Buddhist meanings that were not really there.[58] Jinsai's principal written work, *The Meaning of Terms in the*

Analects and Mencius (Gomō jigi),[be 59] is a critical analysis of key terms in the Neo-Confucian lexicon (and especially those appearing in *Reflections on Things at Hand [Chin-ssu lu]*), intended to show that their original meanings had been corrupted by Taoism and Buddhism. Probably the most crucial misconception arose from the identification of man's essential nature with "principle." Principle to him was a "dead term." By this he meant that it applied to fixed norms or to the structure of inanimate objects. Principle was static and morally inert, whereas human nature was a living, dynamic value.

In Chuang Tzu, who talked most about principle (*li*) in classical times, and in Buddhism also, Jinsai saw both principle and nature as referring to an unconditioned, disembodied, transcendent state, implying a distinction between substance and phenomena, or between a quiescent inner nature and outward activity.[60] When translated into Sung doctrine this equation of man's nature with principle produced the fatal distinction between the manifest and unmanifest (*i-fa wei-fa*)[bf] states of nature, which for Jinsai completely undermined any claimed distinction between the Confucian view of man's nature as moral and the amoral view of Buddhism and Taoism. Man's moral nature, his humaneness, then came to be seen as a static principle to be perceived in a quiescent, desireless state, through an inexpressible mystical experience transcending the moral sphere.[61] Sung thinkers, he says, equated Heaven with principle, and "sought to contemplate Heaven through 'having no mind' [of one's own], thus falling into empty nothingness."[62]

By contrast, Jinsai insists, Confucius and Mencius had seen man's nature as fulfilled in outward activity benefitting mankind. Now, instead of man's "humaneness uniting him with Heaven and earth and all things" through ethical conduct, the impulse to engage in conscientious action has been deliberately stultified in the practice of a false reverence, and instead of practicability serving as the test of reality, practice has been relegated to the realm of the phenomenal and illusory.[63]

According to Jinsai, as Mencius had conceived of the goodness of human nature, it consisted in the impulse to action found in the four seeds or sprouts which, if exercised and cultivated, would lead to the fullness of virtue. It was not until Ch'eng I that this became distorted, and for the first time the virtues of humaneness, righteousness, decorum and wisdom were called "the nature," while the nature was identified with principle. Then instead of exerting themselves in the active exercise

of virtue, scholars adopted special practices of self-cultivation for the realization of the nature or principle, such as "sustained reverence" (*jikei*),[an]
"mastering quiescence" (*shusei*)[bg] and the "practicing of innate knowledge" (*chi ryōchi*).[bh] Thus, contemplative practice was substituted for
social action, and mind-cultivation replaced the active pursuit of the
Kingly Way for the benefit of mankind.[64]

To Jinsai, the significance of humaneness could not be understood
apart from the complementary virtues of reciprocity (mutuality) and righteousness or duty. Humaneness is given practical definition only through
a loving sense of identification with others and through actions which
respond to their needs in a fitting manner. In other words, humaneness is
expressed in the total context of a Way which extends beyond the individual and his self-centered experience. Jinsai says:

The sage perceives the Way in relation to all-under-Heaven; the Buddha and Lao
Tzu pursue the Way in relation to oneself. He who seeks the Way in relation to
himself will not concern himself with the service of others, but will seek to
achieve his own peace of mind through the practice of a pure desirelessness. In
the end this will lead to the abandonment of human relations and the discarding
of all decorum and good taste. This is the way of deviation and heterodoxy.[65]

If Jinsai refutes the Sung view of man's nature as essentially self-centered and self-absorbed, his concern is not simply to remedy the quietism
associated with its method of praxis. He is not unaware of that "orthodox"
Ch'eng-Chu school in which a strenuous moralism and activism belie
any taint of Buddhist quietism. In the Kyoto of his day, this rigoristic
Neo-Confucianism was vigorously championed by Yamazaki Ansai. To
Jinsai, it represented the opposite extreme from contemplative passivity,
but was nonetheless dangerous for its simultaneous denial of sense desires
and its assertion of the rightness of its own moral claims with the most
dogmatic fervor.[66]

The dangers of Sung subjectivism, however, were not to be found
solely in the extremes of passive quietism or self-righteous activism. A
failure to recognize the legitimacy of man's irrepressible physical desires,
according to Jinsai, could also lead to a default in the necessary disciplining and socializing of those desires, while an optimistic faith in the original goodness of man's nature could leave the way open to uninhibited
self-expression and total lack of restraint. To speak as the Sung scholars
did of "nurturing the nature" or of preserving the mind as "a clear mirror
or still water," without also speaking of the need to nurture and train the

feelings, "assumes that the feelings will naturally and spontaneously be in accord with what is right. This leaves one without a definite method for disciplining them."[67] Hence, the supposed "naturalness" and "spontaneity" which were meant to follow from the subjective realization of an innately good nature could be destructive to any established values or social morality.

In this respect, Jinsai shared with Yamaga Sokō a deep distrust of the individualistic subjectivism which had emerged as one powerful current in the mainstream of Neo-Confucianism—one which stressed the autonomous individual and his liberated consciousness as a dynamic force for historical change. Yet, at the same time, he sets limits on the pursuit of the objective investigation of things. In Chu Hsi's "broad learning" he saw a danger to man's proper self-cultivation, for the study of "dead" principles—value-free and morally inert—could be a distraction from man's humane concerns. Though capable of critical textual studies himself, this implied on Jinsai's part no wide-ranging scholarly inquiry or scientific interest. Thus he cites the diversity of studies spawned and proliferated by the Ch'eng-Chu school's "investigation of things," which were ungoverned by any sense of human priorities or moral relevance, and he anathematizes, besides a long list of sciences—natural, practical, and occult—the often-quoted precept of Chu Hsi concerning the study of principle even in a tree or blade of grass.[68] Clearly, Jinsai sees in Ch'eng-Chu learning, just as Wang Yang-ming did, the potential for a relatively value-free intellectuality, and he engages in a rather typical Neo-Confucian effort to restore the balance, and thereby to preserve the integrity and centrality of the sagely ideal. In this, he (like Sokō) took up certain options available in the Neo-Confucian synthesis and developed them at the expense of others.

Underlying these issues on which Jinsai challenged the Sung school is the central question of sagehood itself. Many of Jinsai's conclusions, such as: his view of principle as static; his refusal to identify man's nature with "dead" principle or see it as constant and unchanging; his rejection of the conception of a quiescent inner nature or state of desirelessness, to be attained in a transcendent experience of sagehood, as well as his strictures against "broad learning" and the unlimited objective investigation of things, suggest a disillusionment with the Sung ideal of sagehood as a state of lofty serenity and self-mastery which any one might aspire to through rigorous self-discipline, unremitting study and a culminating experience of enlightenment.

For his own part, Jinsai humanizes the sage in important respects. He argues that the sages did not know everything, were far from infallible, and were not without desires or faults. Confucius, the sage par excellence, was very much a feeling human being and not an impassive Buddha. But it is also true that for Jinsai Confucius stood out as a qualitatively superior human being. Jinsai refutes Wang Yang-ming's doctrine of the moral equality of the sages, based on their common fulfillment of a constant human nature—all pure gold, so to speak, despite differences in individual capacity. And in the end, Jinsai elevates the humanized sage, Confucius, to a level of attainment out of reach for most humans. Indeed, he reintroduces hierarchy among the sages, and endows the *Analects* with the same perfection and preeminence he attributes to Confucius. Thus, even though it may be said that for Jinsai, "To regard the *Analects* as the supreme book in the world and study it does not mean to follow Confucius blindly as the perfect model," [69] still there is an ambiguity that attaches to this, which can, insofar as it is meant to contrast with Wang Yang-ming's view, detract from the imitability of Confucius. Hence, Jinsai's denial of the homogeneity of sagehood, along with his stripping it of the egalitarian Sung-Ming emphasis on its universal accessibility, could well have discouraged the thought that there was an assured and practicable method for its attainment in the present.

The full implications of this view emerge in the next stage of Kogaku thought, with Ogyū Sorai's direct attack on the Sung-Ming belief that sagehood can be learned. We should not fail to observe, however, that Jinsai had already taken a significant step in this direction by stressing the unique superiority of Confucius and the *Analects*, by conceiving of them more as a source of authority than as a direct model, and by turning attention away from reputed latter-day sages to the original—and only genuine—example of sagehood in the distant past.

To say this is not to remove Jinsai from the ranks of the Neo-Confucians, but only to show that he was involved in much the same processes of growth and adjustment in Neo-Confucian thought as were the Ming thinkers who rejected a puritanical and moralistic conception of man in favor of a more concrete, physical and affective one, and who similarly sought to curb subjective idealism and individualism by reassert-

ing the objective authority of the classics and the social character of the
Way.

OGYŪ SORAI; INDIVIDUALITY WITHOUT INDIVIDUALISM

Ogyū Sorai[bi] (1666–1728), the culminating figure of the movement
toward "Ancient Learning" is by almost any reckoning a key to the transition from the Neo-Confucian study of the past (kogaku) to the modernizing trends of the eighteenth century. A "Renaissance" man in the range
of his interests and the versatility of his powers, Sorai also represented for
his time the most advanced and sophisticated methods of historical and
linguistic scholarship by means of which objective inquiry into the past
might develop new values for the present.

As with the early Italian Renaissance humanists, Sorai's studies were
initially in literature and history. His crucial learning experiences involved him in issues which today seem esoteric and recherché—the intricacies of Sung and Ming poetic theory and literary controversies already passé in China by the time he discovered their significance for
contemporary Japan. Only in his early fifties did his convictions mature
to the point where he felt prepared to meet the same obligation Confucius had felt at age fifty—to fulfill "the mission entrusted to him by
Heaven,"—by addressing the larger intellectual and social issues of his
time.[70] At that point he began his major works which he continued to
revise until his death in 1728.

His manifesto, the Bendō[bj] (1717), which expounds his interpretation
of the Confucian Way in its broadest terms, opens with a sweeping critique of previous Confucian thought. It leaves no doubt as to his basic intellectual orientation toward the Confucian tradition or the unprecedented role he says Heaven entrusted to him as the rediscoverer of its
true significance after the Way had been obscured for over a thousand
years.[71] If the discharge of this mission carries Sorai to the extreme fron-
tier of Confucian thought in his time—and in the eyes of some critics well
beyond its bounds—the Bendō makes it quite clear that he considered himself to be fulfilling the Confucian teaching, not breaking with it.

The issues taken up by Sorai in the Bendō are those shaped by the
Neo-Confucians and later redefined by Jinsai. He joins Jinsai in rejecting
the Ch'eng-Chu theory of human nature, sharing with both Sokō and

Jinsai the view that in deprecating the physical nature the Sung school had allowed Buddhist and Taoist influences to distort the original Confucian teaching. Like Sokō and Jinsai, too, Sorai goes over the heads of the Sung masters and invokes the original teaching of the Confucian classics as the test of Ch'eng-Chu orthodoxy. It is for this that the three have been classed together as advocates of the "Ancient Learning," though this represented no single school.

Where Sorai takes issue with Jinsai, however, is indicative also of the crucial issue between him and his Neo-Confucian predecessors. For Sorai considered Jinsai still unconsciously subject to Sung influence in his conception of human nature. This, said Sorai, predisposed Jinsai to look in only certain of the classics for confirmation of what he already believed, rather than to accept what an objective reading of the entire body of classical texts would reveal. Sorai had devoted nearly a life-time to developing the criteria for such an objective reading, by establishing the historical and linguistic context in which alone one could define the total configuration of the Way, and give precise meanings to the terms in which it was expressed. Jinsai, he believed, had limited his view of the relevant evidence essentially to the *Analects* and *Mencius* because these texts tended to confirm his own idealistic preconceptions concerning the Way and human nature,. part of the Sung system from which Jinsai had not liberated himself. Ancient Learning (*kogaku*) for Jinsai meant *kogigaku*, bk the study of the original meaning or significance of Confucian texts, but this Ancient Learning was carried on in terms which Sorai considered to be still unconsciously influenced by conceptions of human relevance current in the Sung. Thus Jinsai engaged in philosophical interpretation of texts in the same way Sung scholars had done when they derived from their classical inheritance meanings and values actually permeated by the contemporary climate of thought.[72] Sorai, however, like the Ming inheritors of Sung teachings, had reached the inevitable next stage in this process, which required an evidential basis for evaluating alternative philosophical derivations from the same texts. Plausibility or significance in contemporary terms would not suffice as a test when new generations of Neo-Confucians—among them Wang Yang-ming—found in the same old texts and terms new significance and different meanings suited to their own experience.

This dilemma inherent in the "study of ancient meanings" was resolved by Sorai through the "study of ancient terms" in their original contents (*kobunji gaku*),[bl] rather than on the basis of their contemporary relevance or generalized human significance. For this procedure Sorai invoked the authority of the Ming scholars, Li P'an-lung[bm] (1514–1570) and Wang Shih-chen[bn] (1526–1590). While they, as literary critics, had played no great role in Ming philosophy, for Sorai they served a major oracular function. As the dispenser of this new higher criticism, Sorai could put down Jinsai as clumsy and backward, while claiming himself to speak for the latest in sinological sophistication.

Beyond the immediate tactical advantages thus gained by Sorai, the uses to which he put his Ming mentors reflect also the manner in which Tokugawa Neo-Confucianism evolved along Ming lines. Rather than breaking with tradition Sorai was living it out, following an inner logic as inescapable for him as it had been for Li and Wang in the Ming, though they were known as champions of orthodoxy. It was Jinsai who had raised the question of the Sung school's fidelity to Confucian teaching, and Sorai, who in defense of tradition, conducted the objective investigation which found both Jinsai and the Sung school guilty on the same score of subjective idealism. Though he subscribed to Jinsai's dynamic physical conception of human nature, as opposed to the Ch'eng-Chu identification of the nature with an unchanging moral norm or transcendent principle, Sorai could not follow Jinsai further in adopting Mencius' definition of man's nature in terms of the mind's inner moral sensitivities, or Mencius' belief in the perfectability of that nature by the cultivation of man's moral growth from within. Sorai found this approach dangerously introverted, further intensifying the Neo-Confucian preoccupation with the mind at the expense of society, and rendering Jinsai's humaneness indistinguishable from Buddhist compassion as a subjective principle.[73] At one extreme it threatened a repression of the individual in conformity with an abstract ideal or moral norm; and at the other it encouraged either an uninhibited self-assertion or a subjective dogmatism of the rigoristic Neo-Confucian variety. Mencius was no one to restrain Yamazaki Ansai.

The crux of the matter, however, lay with the Ch'eng-Chu school, and its central doctrine of sagehood as the final goal of self-cultivation. For if there were any ground on which one might exclude Sorai from the Neo-Confucian fold it would be that he repudiated this goal in the very same terms that others before him had embraced it. Innumerable Neo-Confucian converts, earlier, persuaded by the idea that sagehood could be acquired through study and self-discipline, had committed themselves to attaining it. Sorai, however, just as decisively, rejected it. Thus the dimensions of the problem for Sorai (and the baffling problem *of* Sorai for his interpreters) are to be seen, on the one hand, in his insistence upon the absolute value and importance of sagehood, and on the other in his denial that it is still attainable.

Early in the *Bendō*, Sorai attacks the "fatuous idea that sagehood could be attained through studying it and that one could become a sage all by oneself."[74] Here Sorai not only repudiated the words of Chu Hsi in his commentaries on the *Analects* and *Mencius*, and also the essential message of the *Reflections on Things at Hand*, but he further attributed this prevalent fallacy to the Taoist notion of "sageliness within and kingliness without." For Sorai, true sageliness and kingliness were inseparable. The true sages were not those who claimed to have subjectively realized their ideal human nature within, but the Early Kings who manifested their virtue outwardly through the construction of a total social and political order.

In part, Sorai's rejection of the Sung model for sagehood can be seen as a defense of man's physical nature against the excessive demands of a moral ideal which spoke of achieving "complete unity with Heavenly principle without a trace of selfish desire."[75] Against this Sorai quotes both Confucius and Tzu Szu to the effect that even the early sages had their human limitations and Confucius himself was not without human desires. Moreover, when Chu Hsi in his commentary on the *Great Learning*, speaks of the sage as "plumbing the ultimate of Heavenly principle and being without so much as one iota of selfish human desire,"[76] this, for Sorai, involves a lack of realism in three basic respects.

First, individual natures differ and cannot be brought into conformity to a single ideal. To set up such a goal for human cultivation is to do violence to individual natures. The more a man becomes aware of the discrepancy between himself and the norm, and the more conscious he is of his own shortcomings, the more dissatisfied he becomes with himself and the further he is from achieving a sense of fulfillment. "To force upon the common man a standard which he is not capable of achieving, is to make men lose all hope in goodness."[77]

Second, Sorai insists that the psycho-physical nature of man cannot be changed and to attempt to curb fundamental human desires leads only to frustration and resentment.

The physical nature is the Heavenly nature. To try to use the force of man to overcome Heaven and thwart nature is not possible.[78]

The scholars of later times, ignorant of the Way of the Early Kings, have put forward their own superior wisdom, thinking to promote the doing of good and avoiding of evil, and to enlarge [the effective domain of] heavenly principle while restricting human desires. Once such a view is adopted, however, it becomes evident to all that their rulers are not Yaos or Shuns, that men are not sages, and that evil inevitably abounds while good is scarcely to be seen. Accordingly a deadly spirit of fault-finding pervades the world. Thus when [Chu Hsi's version of] the *General Mirror* is followed in government and the [*Great Compendium on*] *Human Nature and Principle* is the guide to moral discipline, no one can endure their rigors and everyone ends up thinking that the Confucians take delight in oppressing people.[79]

Third, given the differences in men's natures, as well as the extent of their common needs, it is apparent that only a total approach to the human economy will allow for individual differentiation while providing for the needs of all. To try to deal with the governance of men through self-cultivation and the practice of reverence—i.e., through self-examination and mind control to root out unworthy desires—is fatally to misconceive the nature of the problem. Minute attention to one's own motivations, on the theory that a small error at the point of inception can lead to major mistakes and serious consequences later, is incommensurate with the magnitude of the real problem: meeting the needs of human society as a whole. On the contrary, the Early Sage Kings dealt with the larger needs of the state and society, leaving the finer points of individual cultivation to be taken care of in the natural course of events. Action to meet the needs of mankind could not await the ruler's attainment of a lofty frame of mind. Similarly, for men in later ages, the task was to study and follow the pattern established by the Early Kings, not to engage in quiet-sitting, "sustained reverence" or the other disciplines of Neo-Confucian mind-control.[80]

If Sorai sees the Ch'eng-Chu school as fussily, even morbidly, preoccupied with mind-control and the cultivation of sagehood, in the end his own thinking seems greatly preoccupied with this issue, and there is more to it than just his concern over the repression of human desires or the neglect of the larger interests of society. His insistence that man's psychophysical disposition cannot be changed and that sagehood is unattainable, also reflects his distrust of the Neo-Confucian claim to the achievement of self-mastery and self-fulfillment for the individual. What he acknowledges indirectly is that the Ch'eng-Chu teaching had indeed addressed itself to the individual, and its appeal as a call to spiritual discipline was most powerful. As we have seen, it had been a crucial experience for the Ming Confucian Wu Yü-pi when he became convinced that by diligent effort he could transform his psycho-physical nature and achieve the self-mastery of the sage. The example of Chu Hsi's teacher, Li T'ung, had been particularly impressive to Wu, as it was later to Fujiwara Seika. Likewise Wu's own exemplary character—his purity, integrity, independence, and loftiness of mind, became an inspiration to later Ming Neo-Confucians who aspired to sagehood. Nor is there any doubt that Japanese scholars found this ideal equally compelling. To many of them it offered the promise of personal fulfillment based on the idea that one's own humanity could become complete in an experience of oneness with Heaven-and-earth and all things. To those capable of it this experience entailed no loss of individuality or selfhood. On the contrary, it was an experience of personal integration and self-realization which enabled them to be fully themselves and active participants in the affairs of men.

If then Sorai challenges this ideal, what does he offer in its stead? This is a question worth pondering in connection with Sorai's emphasis elsewhere upon freeing the individual from the moralistic straitjacket of the Chu Hsi system. Though a defender of human individuality and protective of the individual against the excessive moral demands of Ch'eng-Chu idealism, Sorai is no less protective of society against the dangers of individualism he sees in the inspirational message of the sagely ideal and the independent convictions of its proponents.

Here Sorai betrays a basic ambiguity concerning the autonomy of the individual and his independent role in society. On the one hand he takes a radical stand on the fundamental individuality of each man's nature:

The inborn nature differs with each individual and virtue for him varies according to his nature. There is no single way for men to achieve fulfillment or for their talents to be perfected.[81]

Heaven's decree is not the same for all . . . . the gentleman understands this and does not try to force it (i.e., conformity to a specific norm or model). And as regards the perfecting of their own talents, even the sages did not achieve complete success and therefore they did not try to force it on others. Consequently the idea that all men can achieve sagehood is false, and so is the idea that men's natures can be changed.[82]

Among Ming Neo-Confucians, and especially Wang Yang-ming, allowance for individual differences had not entailed the abandonment of
the concept of a common human nature, but had led rather to a redefinition of it and of sagehood. Sorai, however, resisted any solution of the
problem which would enhance further the status of the subjective self or
assert a single principle on the basis of which anyone could achieve
sagehood. In his view, if it was not possible by studying the principles of
things one by one eventually to achieve a personal integration of them (à
la Chu Hsi), neither was it possible to assert an a priori principle as the
ground on which one could achieve an experience of unity with Heaven-
and-earth and all things (à la Wang Yang-ming).[83]

Sorai, a man of broad learning himself, nevertheless believed, as Wang
Yang-ming had, that neither comprehensive knowledge nor an exhaustive objective investigation of things could be made a condition for one's
self-fulfillment. How conscious he actually was of the enormous growth
of knowledge in his time (i.e., conscious of it as growth) we cannot say,
but there is no doubt that he was keenly aware of how much there was to
be known, and how much more it was than could be comprehended by
the finite mind. Himself a product of Neo-Confucian critical rationalism,
he recognized man's fallibility and the difficulty man had in achieving accurate and reliable knowledge.[84]

As a man of urbanity and culture, too, aesthetically sensitive and lit-
erarily sophisticated, he resented what he considered to be the crude and
boorish dogmatism of those like Ansai, whose intensely subjective
method of self-cultivation enabled them to acquire strong convictions
about moral principles, to the extent that their religious "seriousness" and
zealotry became quite overbearing.[85] Says Sorai,

Principle is formless; therefore it provides no definite standard. To think that
the Mean can serve as the principle of proper conduct is to leave it to each man's
view of it and each man's view of it is different. Then everyone takes his own
mind as the judge of what is the Mean and what is proper conduct. . . . It is like
the people of two villages disputing the boundary between them, without any
magistrate to hear and judge the merits of the case.[86]

Here Sorai is clearly not arguing the case for a more plastic (modern)
view of human nature as opposed to the more rationalistic, rigid and confining one of Chu Hsi. Rather his concern is with the question of objective, public authority. For Sorai, there could be only one ultimate standard and it was not the Supreme Norm in the mind which the Sung

school had spoken of as unlimited or open-ended (*wu-chi*); it had to be something more objectively defined. For him this was the rites of the Early Kings.

The norm established by the Early Kings was the rites. . . . . Such concepts as the Supreme Ultimate of the normative principles of things, or the transforming of the physical nature, or studying to be a sage, have no basis in the original teaching of the Early Kings and Confucius. . . . In our times Itō Jinsai understood that this was so, and yet he went on to set up filiality, fraternity, humaneness and duty as normative standards for all. But how could this be? Everyone would have his own idea of filiality, fraternity, humaneness and duty, and what would provide the standard among them?[87]

"Man's mind is the people's mind," Sorai said, alluding to the *Book of Documents'* characterization of the people's mind as unstable and prone to excess.[88] "It is like driving a chariot with rotten reins. Therefore it [man's mind] is called 'precarious [and prone to err]'.[89] The mind of Tao is the mind which leads (*tao*) the people, and its workings are extremely subtle."[90]

There was indeed such a thing as sagely wisdom of the kind needed to lead the people, but it existed only in the past: "Sages existed in the past, but not in the present. Therefore study today must be addressed to the past."[91] Toward the sages of the past Sorai holds a most worshipful attitude as compared to the would-be sages of the present:

The sages' extraordinary intelligence and wisdom were powers received from Heaven; how could one expect to acquire them now through study? The spiritual luminosity of their virtue was beyond all calculation; how could it be searched out and fathomed? Thus even in ancient times there were only King T'ang, King Wu and Confucius who attempted to learn what it was to be a sage.[92]

The early sages were kings whose achievement lay in unifying the world and constructing a whole social order. This could only be a rare ambition in the present and would have to be matched by a natural endowment of extraordinary proportions. Certainly it could not be achieved by intuiting and following a natural principle within the mind, as the Ch'eng-Chu school would have it.[93] The mind, like the ultimate "principle"—understood ambivalently in the Ch'eng-Chu school as both definable (*t'ai-chi*) and indefinable (*wu-chi*)—was elusive and undependable, not fixed and certain:

The mind is formless and there is no way of controlling it. Therefore the Way of the Early Kings used rites to control the mind. For anyone to speak of governing the mind except through rites is to make things up out of one's own imagination. Why? If it is the mind that is to govern and the mind which is to be governed, this means my mind trying to govern itself—like a madman governing his own madness. How can there be any governing that way?[94]

Nevertheless, difficulties attached also to the study of the rites of the Early Kings, including difficulties of scholarly method which Sorai dealt with through his own philological, textual, and historical studies.[95] Reliable though that method might be as an objective, evidential approach, it would in the end yield only a painstaking, time-consuming procedure for arriving at an incomplete knowledge of the ancient rites, and even that could not serve as an exact model for the present, since times and circumstances had changed. In each age a system had to be devised which was suited to its own circumstances. Once established it ought to be followed and upheld, for it was essential that there be a uniform system and that the rulers enforce it, but once it was allowed to lapse, a new one had to be created appropriate to new times. Thus Sorai recognized the failure of the reformers' efforts to "revive the ancient order" in eleventh-century Sung China as being due to the unsuitability of the feudal institutions of the Chou to the centralized dynastic system of later times;[96] here the reformers had been carried away by their own ideals, "reading" their own hopes and dreams into both the ancient texts and their own situation.[97] In Japan, the Tokugawa would likewise need to devise a system appropriate to their own times. The general model would come from the Early Kings; the specific institutions would accord with the realities of Tokugawa Japan.

Sorai's other major works, the *Seidan* [bo] (c. 1727) and the *Taiheisaku* [bp] (c. 1721), contain his recommendations for his own times. In the *Bendō*, which explains the guiding principles of the Way, we learn more of the implications of this Way for the individual than we do of institutional reform. Here the real significance of Sorai's views cannot be understood simply in terms of "individualism," whether of the "bourgeois" or any other variety.[98] We are forced to make a distinction, I believe, between individuality or individuation, on the one hand, and individualism on the other. The distinction lies in a recognition of individual differentiation and a realistic acceptance of it as a social fact, in the first instance, and, in the second, a conscious advocacy of an enlarged role for the individual, a wider scope for his autonomous choices and in general a greater measure of what we call individual freedom in a social sense. I have discussed certain aspects of this problem in "Individualism and Humanitarianism in Late Ming Thought," where a recognition of the fact of individuality or individuation did not necessarily imply an advocacy of individualism.[99] Our discussion of Sokō and Jinsai has already raised similar questions.

On the first point, there can be no doubt that Sorai was highly conscious of human individuality or individuation in the sense of psychological and social differentiation; he clearly believed in the importance of the individual's being given scope for satisfying his own needs and talents. By stressing man's physical nature *as* his Heavenly nature, Sorai was affirming the inherent value of individual qualities, since the physical nature in Ch'eng-Chu thought represented the principle of individual differentiation. The early sages recognized this diversity among men, Sorai says, and their Way allowed for it.

For the scholar/samurai who wishes to study the Way of the Early Kings in order to achieve the fulfillment of virtue in himself, this Way must be recognized as manifold and multiform, and men's natures as also diverse. If one can recognize that the Way of the Early Kings comes down to providing peace and security for the world and on this basis one can exert oneself for the sake of humanity, then each man should follow what is closest to his own nature in order to achieve his potentiality of the Way. [As with Confucius' disciples] Tzu-lu's personal courage, Tzu-kung's penetrating intelligence, and Ch'iu's handiness, each of them was able to fulfill one talent.[100]

Sorai realized that in arguing for personal fulfillment on the basis of individual talents he was exposing himself to criticism for sacrificing a man's essential humanity to his functional utility, i.e., for treating him as a mere "utensil" (*ki*). Thus he tried to explain:

Confucius' teaching of his disciples can be seen as adapted in each case to their individual talents so as to perfect them. His saying that "the noble man is not a utensil," (*Analects* II: 12) refers to the humane man and to the instruments made use of by the ruler and his ministers, just like the [tools of the] craftsman and [the medicine of] the physician. Those who say that Confucius refers to [and rules out functional specialization like that of] the ship sailing on the sea and the cart traveling by land [but not vice versa], have no reason whatever for this view. "Relying on virtue and depending on humanity" each man can follow what is closest to his own nature and thus fulfill his virtue. If each can develop his own strengths, altogether they will suffice to be called humane men. This is what "not being a utensil" means.[101]

It is unclear whether this passage serves to identify Sorai as a full-fledged utilitarian, or whether his functional differentiation represents an amoral utilitarianism. On the one hand, Sorai argues that Confucius' pronouncement about "not being a utensil" does not rule out functional specialization, while on the other hand, he asserts that such functionality not only serves humane ends but is a moral value in itself.[102] What does emerge clearly, however, is that his affirmation of the value of the individual in no way enhances the status of the autonomous self. Man's "humanity" exists only as a part of the collectivity, and is fulfilled only in a total polity or cooperative community. Sorai states that:

The Way of the Early Kings is the way of bringing peace and contentment to the world. Though it takes manifold forms, they all must conform to this end of bringing peace and contentment to the world. . . . Thus the Way cannot be spoken of in terms of one man but only in terms of millions of men collectively.

If we look at the world as it is, who can stand by himself and not associate with some collectivity? Scholars and samurai, peasants, artisans and merchants together assist and nourish each other. They cannot survive otherwise. . . .

Even if a man relies on hs own virtue, he must necessarily conform to the Early King's Way of bringing peace and contentment to the world and he does not dare act contrary to it. Only thus is each man able to perfect his own virtue. In general, according to the Way of the Early Kings and Confucius, everyone had his own function to perform and his own purpose to serve, and the essential thing was to nurture and fulfill that capability. However, later men with a more dogmatic view insisted on "humaneness" as a comprehensive virtue and they could not help but leap upon it as one all-encompassing principle. In the end, however, it comes down to no more than the Buddhist doctrine of the law-body (dharmakāya) as the ultimate principle embracing all things.[103]

Since Sorai believed that individual fulfillment would only be achieved in the collectivity and through action in behalf of the social order, he resisted any idea that man possessed a unitary nature or uniform "humanity" which could serve as the basis for an experience of unity with all things. His disagreement with Jinsai concerned this basic point. For Jinsai, like Sorai, rejected the Sung notion of the nature as a static principle, but he held to the belief that man could achieve sagehood through the perfecting of his essential humanity. Sorai, on the other hand, saw any such conception of an inborn humanity, deriving from man's innate sense of commiseration with others, as leading to a mystical view of man's oneness with the universe which was no better than the Buddhist doctrine of undifferentiated compassion. As he put it: "Those who proclaim this teaching end up saying that Buddhism has [the concept of] humaneness but only lacks [the concept of] ethical duty. Buddhism, however, has no way of bringing peace and contentment to the world, so how can it be thought to have the concept of humaneness?"[104]

Among those who tended to equate Buddhist compassion with Confucian humaneness or love was not only Jinsai, whose Dōjimon [bq] Sorai may have in mind here,[105] but also Li T'ung, whose discussion of this issue served as the background for the doctrine of "the oneness of principle and its diverse particularizations" (li-i fen-shu).[o] Li T'ung had tended to concede the Buddhists' possession of a concept of "oneness in principle" based on their doctrine of compassion, but faulted them for having no corresponding sense of duty or binding obligation.[106] Sorai, for his part, would have none of this, since he rejected any notion of human self-fulfillment based on a subjective experience of all-encompassing unity. Such an experience was, however, an important, if not essential, element in the Neo-Confucian ethical mysticism expressed in terms of "the humaneness which forms one body with Heaven-and-earth and all things." This conception in turn underlay the doctrine that sagehood was achievable by any man, and had become a major inspiration for Ming Neo-Confucians, especially Wang Yang-ming and his followers, who gave much impetus to the individualistic and egalitarian thought of the late Ming. If Sorai cites Wang Yang-ming's "innate knowledge" as one of the simplistic, single principles which so mislead people, it reflects a profound difference in philosophical outlook between them. Wang encouraged individual self-expression as a good in itself, but Sorai, while witnessing the effects upon the individual of increasing economic and social change and especially technological development and differentiation, was unprepared to let these changes undermine, or work to liberalize, a highly structured, authoritarian society.

As the nineteenth-century Japanese Confucian scholar, Hirose Tansō,[br] observed: "The Confucian scholars of the Sung dynasty . . . identified Heaven with principle. . . . The duty of revering Heaven was thus extended to all [men and not just the ruler]. . . . This was the merit of the Sung Confucianists."[107]

That this egalitarian religiosity emerging from the Sung school was a concern of Sorai's is revealed in his sensitivity to the Sung school's concept and practice of "reverence" or "seriousness" (kei).[ba] What is significant here is not that he ridiculed the sober conscientiousness of the Ch'eng-Chu schoolmen in their fastidious attention to the moral implications of every action in life, or that he often deprecated their petty-minded preoccupation with the minute distinctions and infinitesimal details of their spiritual life.[108] Already in the Ming these preoccupations had been mocked as fussy, pretentious, and pompous by writers of a more liberal persuasion than Sorai.[109] But the latter is more concerned with the mystical aspect of this view of reverence—that is, with its inspirational power rather than with its obsessive ritualism. It seems to confer an absolute authority on the subjective convictions of the individual, to allow them an unlimited scope, and to breed an attitude of disrespect for established social conventions and ritual, which should provide objective standards and a higher authority for the governance of the individual.

The Confucians of later times have exalted knowledge and exerted themselves to "plumb principle" (kyūri)[bs] [as a single all-inclusive principle realized in the mind] and this has brought the destruction of the Way of the Early Kings and Confucius. The evil of "plumbing principle" is that Heaven and the gods and spirits need not then be held in awe, while the self is made arrogantly to stand between Heaven and earth. This being the pervasive defect of the later Confucians, how does it differ from the [Buddha's] saying: "In heaven above and earth beneath it is I alone who am to be revered"?[110]

How can one hope to plumb the limits of this vast universe? How can one plumb principle and exhaust it? He who says "I can know it exhaustively" is deluding himself. Therefore what they say outwardly shows respect to the Early Kings and Confucius, but inwardly opposes them. Their idea is that they themselves can discover and reveal what the ancient sages did not, without realizing that this means seeking to outdo the Early Kings and Confucius and surpass them.

Now the teaching of the sages represents perfection. How can one outdo and surpass them? What the sages left unsaid generally does not need to be said. If it needed to be said the Early Kings and Confucius would already have said it. How could there be anything left for later men to discover and reveal? It is simply unthinkable.[111]

It is perfectly clear from this how great a threat to order and authority Sorai sees in the central doctrines of the Sung school, and especially the link which he sees between its "plumbing of principle," (kyūri), the type of religiosity associated with its practice of "reverence" or "seriousness," and the dangers of private inspiration and individualistic self-assertion engendered by its subjective idealism. It is also quite clear what limits Sorai sets on the operation of individual intelligence, creativity, or self-expression.

In previous interpretations of Sorai there has been a tendency to emphasize his critical and empirical rationalism as an opponent of Neo-Confucianism and to see him as a key transitional figure in the growth of a "modern" value-free objectivity, which is contrasted to the moralistic and metaphysical view of the Neo-Confucians. There is an element of truth in this: the trend toward a more objective view of principle and an empirical approach to its study radically altered the context in which Sorai understood "the plumbing of principle." But what critics often fail to recognize is that Sorai, as a product of the Neo-Confucian tradition himself, is exercising certain options among the polar tendencies which coexist, often uneasily and in an unstable balance, within the Neo-Confucian synthesis. These, as we have seen, afford him a critical rationalism and empirical scholarship, which he here employs against another tendency in Neo-Confucianism—to him, dogmatic, arbitrary, self-assertive—that can be characterized in less pejorative terms as an inspirational, ethical mysticism and idealistic reformism deriving from Mencius. If this appears menacing to Sorai because of its proclivity toward individual freedom and even radical activism, one can well imagine how dogmatic and reactionary, how "feudal" and "medieval" Sorai's unyielding faith in the Way of the Early Kings might appear to others.

Sorai is not, of course, always so doctrinaire or dogmatic as he seems. There are, as we have already shown, two significant limits which he sets on the effective authority of the Early Kings: first, that their Way can only be followed in general terms, rather than as a precise model for later times; and second, that this Way can only be known through the most exacting contextual study and is not immediately knowable for direct application. Thus Sorai is skeptical in regard to present-day pundits and would-be sages because they fail to meet the very demanding requirements of his critical scholarship and objective, evidential inquiry. But belief in the Early Kings does not need to meet the same test. On the contrary, it is the inherent limits of human knowledge which render the achievements of the sages, not credible in rational terms, but compelling in their extraordinariness. To believe in the sage, man must make a leap of faith, and to do so is reasonable enough when he recognizes that his own rational powers fail to produce certain knowledge. Thus Sorai is skeptical toward man, not the divine, and his faith in the sages sustains him while he engages in the scholar's critical task.

The Sages' extraordinary intelligence and wisdom were powers received from Heaven. How could one expect to acquire them through study? The spiritual luminosity of their virtue was beyond all calculation. How could it be searched out and fathomed?[112]

For those who have heralded Sorai as a "modern" skeptical utilitarian, his own manifest religious faith has been an embarrassment, awkward to explain in so liberated an intelligence and so doughty a rationalist. To this question I shall return after first making clear that Sorai's own Neo-Confucian religiosity cannot be dismissed as a mere aberration but is integral to his position in regard to the Neo-Confucian tradition as a whole, and specifically to the Ch'eng-Chu school's practice of "reverence."

In the following passages Sorai diagnoses the disorders of subjectivity which had arisen with the Sung school's internalization of "reverence." In the *Bendō* he says:

The concept of reverence is based on reverence and respect toward Heaven. It is found thus in respect for the ruler, respect for the people, respect for oneself. How can one speak emptily of "sustaining reverence" [as an undifferentiated state of mind without any object of reverence]?

The Sung scholars extended great respect to Mencius and Tzu Ssu, and traced their ideas back to Tseng Tzu. Thus they set up their theory of the orthodox succession. But what could be more groundless? Either they spoke of it in terms of one principle, or one mind or of [the one ultimate spiritual and moral reality of] sincerity. If they spoke of it in terms of one principle, it was the same in Heaven, earth and man—which is simply the Buddhist view of the Law Body (*dharmakā-ya*) immanent in all things. If they spoke of it as "one mind" or as "sincerity," they attributed a basic value to the inner virtue of the sage but none to the [objective] Way of the Early Kings. . . . The School of Principle had no notion of practical affairs or effective action, and sought only a way to achieve the instant realization of principle [in themselves]. Thus for them loyalty and reciprocity served as empty idealizations of principle.[113]

The final point is a revealing one in relation to the widely-held view that Chu Hsi rationalism provided a clear rationalization and sanction for a hierarchical structure of authority. In fact, as stated earlier and as Sorai confirms, in this area it was essentially noncommital. Sorai is aware that the Ch'eng-Chu "plumbing of principle" (*kyūri*), as understood in the context of other key doctrines and practices, such as "dwelling in reverence" (*kyokei*), "sustaining reverence" (*jikei*), and "quiescence" (*sei*) or "quiet-sitting" (*seiza*),[bt] focused centrally on an experience of principle as "the nature" (*sei*) or as one's "humanity" (*jin*). It had, as he says, no particular object of reverence or respect, but was intended to overcome the subject-object dichotomy in an experience of oneness with Heaven-and-earth and all things. The individual was free, to a considerable degree, to interpret the significance of that experience as he chose or as he was disposed. Ch'eng I and Chu Hsi tended to be agnostic with respect to a personal god, but left it an open question. Sorai, however, could not tolerate the tendency to deny "objective" theistic worship, or the application of "reverence" to external ritual as objective standards of conduct. Even more to be warned against, however, was the free-thinking, libertarian individualism which emerged from this doctrine in Ming Neo-Confucianism.

Sorai's strong distaste for Wang Yang-ming's doctrine of innate knowledge suggests that, for him, Wang's intuitionism is a predictable consequence of the Ch'eng-Chu internalization of principle. He had unexceptionable authority for this in the views of Fujiwara Seika himself, who as a patriarch of Neo-Confucianism in Tokugawa Japan, recapitulated these developments from Sung to Ming in his own thought and saw thinkers like Ch'en Hsien-chang and Wang Yang-ming as legitimate heirs of Chu Hsi.[114] Ch'en Hsien-chang (1428–1500), a student of the Ch'eng-Chu schoolman Wu Yü-pi, had been an early exponent of this "subjectivist" tendency, and Sorai's critique of Neo-Confucian internalization of principle through the doctrine and practice of reverence, echoes Lo Ch'inshun's criticism of Ch'en on the same score.[115] Ming thought in general is greatly preoccupied with the Ch'eng-Chu problem of finding virtue within the self (*tzu-te*),[aw] (as Mencius did, rather than seeing it as something external) and yet not in the process abandoning all objective norms of morality.[116]

Wang Shih-chen, whom Sorai admired as an authority in literary matters, was, as a statesman and historian, one who upheld objective models and standards in social morality as well as in poetry. Though Sorai pays tribute to him primarily as an authority on classical literature, it is not unlikely that he would have been familiar with Wang's conservative views in regard to the egalitarian and libertarian thought of the sixteenth century as represented by Yen Chün,[bu] Ho Hsin-yin,[bv] Li Chih[bw] and other individualists of the T'ai-chou branch of the left-wing of the Wang Yang-ming school.[117] We know him to have been acquainted with the thinking of Wang Shih-chen's contemporary, Kuei Yu-kuang[bx] (1507–1571), who took a dim view of Neo-Confucian doctrines based on Mencius' conception of human nature as good.[118]

While comparatively well-versed in Ming literature and thought, Sorai did not usually acknowledge his indebtedness to Chinese writers.[119] There is reason to believe that his own thinking on the importance of social institutions as compared to the role of individuals, may have been influenced by Ch'en Liang[by] and the Yung-k'ang[bz] school of the Sung.[120] Nor would it be surprising to learn that Sorai had some familiarity with a similar line of thinking in the late Ming, from Chang Chü-cheng[ca] and Li Chih to the seventeenth-century masters, Huang Tsung-hsi,[cb] Wang Fu-chih[cc] and Ku Yen-wu.[cd][121] But there is no direct evidence of this, and for our purposes it will suffice to note that Huang Tsung-hsi held views similar to Sorai's without thereby yielding up his credentials as a philosopher of either the li-hsüeh (study of principle) or hsin-hsüeh (study of mind). There are probably no grounds for viewing Sorai as more "modern" in his method or less Neo-Confucian than Huang, while there are many for seeing his social philosophy as more conservative and authoritarian—so great was his antipathy to the subjective individualism of the Sung school and so concerned was he to subordinate the individual to social discipline and religious tradition. To him:

The whole Way of the Early Kings rests on a proper reverence for Heaven. It is on this basis that rulers and parents are also reverenced as its surrogates. Those who wish to reverence Heaven and carry out the Way of the Early Kings will do so by fulfilling their own Heavenly-assigned functions in the society.[122] The Sung school, however, ignores what the classics have to say about reverence and looks for the object of reverence in one's own mind. This is how "sustaining reverence" arose, and as supreme importance was attached to principle and knowledge, the gods and spirits ceased to be believed in and Heaven was not reverenced. Heaven was thought of as principle, and the gods and spirits as spiritual manifestations of yin and yang. Principle resided in the self. If one could exhaust principle, Heaven would be revealed in the self.[123]

Even Itō Jinsai with his prodigious talents, says Sorai, did not comprehend the teaching of the classics in regard to reverence, and being unable to free himself entirely from the Sung school's influence, "he spoke of reverence as simply serving the people."[124]

From this one can see that Sorai, far from being content with the rationalistic and utilitarian view of Jinsai on this point, feels obliged to condemn the latter as permeated by Buddhistic and Taoistic notions of "emptiness," "nothingness" and "having no mind," whence have arisen the doctrines of "abiding in reverence," "mastering quiescence" and "extending innate knowledge"—all notions which take the place of a deep faith in the teaching of the Sages.[125]

Nor can this be regarded as simply another convenient way for Sorai to belittle Jinsai as deficient in his knowledge of the classics. By far the longest section of Sorai's *Benmei*[ce] is that devoted to affirming the existence of gods and spirits. He says:

The existence of gods and spirits is attested to by the sages. How then can one doubt it? Those who say that gods and spirits do not exist do not believe in the sages, and their reason for not believing is that they have never seen them. But if their reason for disbelief in the spirits is that they have not seen them, why should they disbelieve only in the spirits? The same is true of Heaven and its mandate. Consequently the student of the Way must take belief in the sages as his fundamental basis. If he does not believe in the sages and relies solely on his own knowledge, there is nothing he will not do.[126]

Whether Sorai's religious standpoint qualifies or disqualifies him as a Neo-Confucian is a question of significance for our understanding of Neo-Confucianism no less than of Sorai. Those who think of the former as a "medieval religion" will have no difficulty accepting Sorai as both medieval and Neo-Confucian, but then they must deal with his rejection of much that has been thought central to Neo-Confucian religiosity. Those who have considered Sorai as "modern" in his rationalistic and critical method, and thus liberated from Neo-Confucianism, must deal with a fideism that is pervasive and profound in his thinking. Indeed for all of Sorai's differences with Chu Hsi—and here especially his attack on Chu as excessively rationalistic in his naturalistic view of "ghosts and spirits"—in a more fundamental sense Sorai is engaged in probing more deeply and redefining the dominant tendencies in Chu Hsi's thought which he summed up in terms of "plumbing principle and abiding in reverence."

The standpoint of this study has been to recognize in Neo-Confucianism an ambitious effort at synthesis of man's rational powers with his capacity for both moral commitment and spiritual self-transcendence. Its central concepts of "mind" and "principle," its pursuit of rational inquiry and the practice of reverence, combined these elements in differing degrees. Sorai's faith in the ancient sages reasserts and reformulates an essential and indeed dynamic element in the original Confucian revival in the Sung. Moreover, his belief in gods and spirits is an option availed of by the majority of Japanese Neo-Confucians, who from the start recognized in Shinto a powerful religious ally. The most significant cases are those who, following Hayashi Razan, pursued scholarly studies of an empirical and rationalistic sort, while accepting Shinto as a religion with neither a philosophy nor a theology to get in the way. They include, of course, all of the Kogaku thinkers as well as Kaibara Ekken. Sorai's synthesis of religious sympathy and literary/philological study enabled others to draw upon him for basic ingredients of the Neo-Shinto revival. The significance of the prefix "Neo" here lies in precisely the new elements contributed by Neo-Confucianism, and most directly by Sorai, to the revival. Hence Sorai's non-rational faith, rather than being a vestigial, atrophying appendage to his "modern" thought, actually complemented his critical rationalism and proved all the more conducive to new developments which outlasted him.[127]

What is even more significant in Sorai, however, is his redefinition of sagehood—the integrating element in the synthesis. This he eliminated almost entirely as a model of personal self-cultivation, and made of it a remote, though nonetheless commanding, symbol of external authority. To say that Sorai thereby disposed of the individual as an active moral agent, and relegated him to the role of simply another working part of the social system, would be going too far. Still there can be no mistaking his deep distrust of the Neo-Confucian idealism and individualism which drew so powerfully upon the moral egalitarianism and ethical mysticism of Mencius, or his fearful reaction to the liberal humanism of the Sung and Ming. Sorai's own fideism could serve as a check on the contagious enthusiasm which proclaimed every man a sage, while still meeting the Neo-Confucian need—a need even of a rationalist and skeptic like Sorai—for self-transcendence as a condition of thorough-going objectivity.

CONCLUSION

The starting point of this inquiry into the significance of sagehood in the "real" or "practical" learning of Neo-Confucianism was its multidimensional exemplification of a new humanism and secularism in contrast to the "medieval" outlook of Buddhism. For the Neo-Confucian, "reality" attached to basic human relationships and the secular tasks in the midst of which he could find his fulfillment as a person. It did not, as we have seen, mean a denial of religion or an end to spirituality. On the contrary, the Ch'eng-Chu school sought to reconcile the religious and secular, the metaphysical and physical, and the ideal and practical orders. Thus Chu Hsi said of the Ch'eng brothers that their great contribution was to unite the two spheres sundered by Buddhism, affirming the reality of human affairs and the phenomenal order (which Buddhism questioned) while providing a method of spirituality and mental discipline which Confucianism had previously failed to develop. Chu Hsi spoke of this synthesis in terms of a method for dealing with both subjective consciousness ("the ground of the mind") and external things.[128]

Since Buddhism had not in fact been totally unconcerned with secular matters or unwilling to grant some status in reality to the physical world, the essential significance of the Neo-Confucian view lay in its stress on moral and social realities. But if Neo-Confucians claimed a greater realism for their Way, their special insistence on the facts of man's physical being and affective nature was no small part of it. As a later Confucian summed it up:

Buddhism sets aside things and affairs, and thus deals with empty principles. . . . The Way to become one with and to establish the principle of Heaven lies in not renouncing the flesh. The sages and worthies of the past taught men the Way to keep the principle of Heaven in the flesh, without contorting the flesh. Therefore we say that the Way of Confucius is real (jitsu).[129]

But above all Neo-Confucianism professed the optimistic belief that man's self-perfection could be achieved through a process of involvement with concrete realities, with "things and affairs," which was at the same time an experience of self-transcendence. "Reality" for the Neo-Confucian was not already given as a completely unified structure of principle and things. Real or practical learning was a process of self-realization through an active effort to integrate the internal and external, the ideal and the actual, principle in man and in things.

Professor Ishida has said,

Tokugawa Chu Hsi-Confucian scholars . . . rejected Buddhism on the grounds that it was unrealistic. Confucianism, they said, was real. It is indeed usual to explain that Chu-Hsi-Confucianism marks the birth of the modern spirit in Japan. This is because Chu Hsi-Confucianism was realistic in its recognition of life in this world, its affirmation of human desire, and its rejection of medieval Buddhist transcendentalism.[130]

If these last three points may be considered to represent the "modern" spirit of Neo-Confucianism, it is fair to say, after reviewing the leading figures in the Ancient Learning (*Kogaku*) movement, that they too exhibited the same "realistic" and "modern" tendencies. The Ancient Learning is thus a further stage in their development, not a new departure. Moreover, if we look to the attitudes which characterized the later development of Neo-Confucianism in Ming and early Ch'ing China, almost all of them are also applicable to the Ancient Learning in late sixteenth- and early seventeenth-century Japan despite the considerable historical and cultural differences between the two situations. In other words, there is a notable continuity in the development of later Neo-Confucian thought into the Ancient Learning, a continuity shown not only in the drawing upon a common fund of ideas by successive generations of thinkers and teachers, but also in a pattern of inner growth emerging from similar conflicts and struggles within the tradition.

There is further support for this conclusion in that even the personal experiences of Kogaku thinkers have close parallels in Chinese Neo-Confucians of the sixteenth and seventeenth centuries. There are striking resemblances, for instance, between Yamaga Sokō (1622–1685) and Yen Yüan (1635–1704) in their reaction to the spiritual disciplines, ritual requirements and bookishness of Ch'eng-Chu orthodoxy as each of them had been schooled in it; and in a similar affirmation of man's physical nature, human desires and the need for practical learning. In each of them, too, we find a like resistance to the growing preoccupation with book-learning which followed from the Neo-Confucians' pursuit of "broad learning" and critical scholarship.

The second noteworthy point in Professor Ishida's characterization has to do with the Neo-Confucian's "rejection of medieval Buddhist transcendentalism." This attitude is found also in the Ancient Learning insofar as its leading spokesmen all reject the *kind* of transcendentalism represented by Buddhism—i.e., as they see it, a life-denying and otherworldly transcendentalism. It is an attitude still more characteristic of the Kogaku scholars, who carried it a step further in their attempt to purge the Ch'eng-Chu school itself of a lingering infection from this type of

Buddhist transcendentalism. Yet in no case does the rejection of Buddhism imply a total antipathy to religion or a denial of man's need for spiritual transcendence. On the contrary, even the most skeptical-minded of them, Ogyū Sorai, undertakes an extended defense of traditional religion, and makes a point of specifically affirming the reality of intangible spiritual and moral values (e.g., the mandate of Heaven) against those who might apply to them the test of mere sensory perception. The point is all the more tellingly made by one known, like Sorai, as an empiricist and utilitarian.

Thus the Ancient Learning stands as a further extension of the original Neo-Confucian trend away from Buddhism, and yet not away from religion itself but rather toward the development of new forms of a life-affirming religious humanism. In the case of Itō Jinsai this takes the form of a mysticism of the human order still closely akin to Mencius. In the case of Sorai, who still detects surreptitious Buddhist influences in the Mencian Jinsai, it is found as a religious conception more strongly oriented toward the human community in both its social and historical dimensions.

The religious aspect of the Kogaku, and especially of Sorai, has been seen by some as a vestige of the medieval past, contrasting with the "modern" character of its empiricism, utilitarianism and "individualism."[131] To take this view, however, is to set a preconceived limitation on modern man's experience in the religious sphere. One can more readily accede to Professor Imanaka Kanshi's judgment on Sorai, which is in accord with Professsor Needham's observations on "Taoist" empiricism in China, that a simple empiricism, stripped of any capacity for a high order of theoretical conceptualization, would represent a more serious disability in accommodating modern scientific thought.[132]

In this respect, Chu Hsi's original synthesis may well have been, as Professor Needham has suggested,[133] better adapted to the larger requirements of modern scientific thought. By contrast, one can readily discern the conceptual limitations implicit in such a statement of Sorai's as "the sages taught on the basis of facts, not principles. They dealt with human affairs, not words."[134] At the same time, the subjective idealism which Sorai sees as departing from this Way, and which was so vehemently scored by the Kogaku as a whole, survived these attacks, proving to be a persistent and potent force in the early stages of the modernization process at the end of the Tokugawa period. On the more popular level this disciplined idealism is seen in the Shingaku movement of Ishida Baigan.[cf135] Its effects on the ideological dynamics and political leadership of the late Tokugawa are found also in the puritan ethic and religious nationalism of the later Kimon school deriving from Yamazaki Ansai, as well as in the attempts of the late Tokugawa followers of Wang Yang-ming, like the Tung-lin at the end of the Ming, to reconstitute the Neo-Confucian synthesis as a spiritual and moral basis for political action. Thus even this seemingly doctrinaire or mystical idealism may have been less handicapped in facing the future than an empirical or practical attitude too greatly preoccupied with immediate secular concerns.

In its own way, however, the Ancient Learning was indeed a progressive intellectual force, carrying forward tendencies already visible in the more extroverted form of Neo-Confucianism espoused by Hayashi Razan and Kaibara Ekken. Its attention to man's biological needs, his external environment, and the social context of his existence, is accompanied by a like attention to the objective, evidential studies required to deal with the concrete problems and particularities of the Kogaku thinkers' own time. In this way they sought to ground ethics and intellectuality in the social process and natural world, while turning away from the more introverted forms of Neo-Confucian cultivation. As social experience took precedence for them over personal or private experience, they not only shed the spiritual disciplines developed within the Ch'eng-Chu school, but sought to purify themselves from any taint or odor of an inhuman sanctity.

In this process all three of the major Kogaku thinkers broke away from the particular model of sagehood that had attracted generations of Chinese and Japanese earlier, but without themselves becoming avowed iconoclasts or heretics. For them the very ideal which had appealed so powerfully to an earlier generation, moving from a medieval atmosphere of pessmism and austerity to a new and optimistic sense of the human potential, had become an anachronism. The context in which Chu Hsi had developed a method for integrating subjective consciousness and objective learning had changed, and the disciplines which had galvanized the moral and intellectual energies of Seika, Razan and their early followers, now seemed too Buddhistic and life-denying. If this was so, however, it was in part because the latter had been most effective as scholars and teachers in bringing the country to a new threshold of political, social and cultural life, just as the Neo-Confucians of the early Ming had contributed to the same process in the life of that dynasty. Social and cultural change brought new objective requirements to the old synthesis of inner and outer. Affluence encouraged new forms of creativity, loosened old inhibitions, and brought new tensions. Different needs drew variously on the resources of a rich and varied tradition, enhancing the appeal of certain features of the sagely ideal while detracting from others.

In the Ancient Learning we found a notable sense that historical change demands a new attention to the social and cultural contexts of "real learning," and to the compelling need for dealing with political and economic problems that were not susceptible of moralistic and spiritualistic solutions. Awareness of this need, common to late Ming and mid-Tokugawa thinkers, served also as a reminder that the Ch'eng-Chu school had neglected, relatively speaking, the study of governmental institutions and political economy. Nevertheless, the first sign that something was wrong in the consciousness of the new generation was a perception of failure—not so much in the concept of the sage as ruler, as in the notion of the sage as a model for the conduct of human life generally. As their experience of life changed in its manifold particularities and functions, so did their sense of a plausible synthesis of that experience and of a lifestyle in accord with actual circumstances.

What I have said in *The Unfolding of Neo-Confucianism* concerning Ming Neo-Confucianism applies equally well to the Tokugawa development:

As the Neo-Confucian became a better scholar he also became less of an aspirant to sagehood. As his secular preoccupations grew—the natural outgrowth of the original commitment to this world as opposed to Buddhism's renunciation of it—and as his learning produced an ever more complex culture, it became more difficult for the Confucian to sustain the all-embracing ideal of sagehood. . . . The secularization of Chinese thought, begun anew in the Sung, had moved on to yet another stage in the seventeenth century. Thus was advanced still further one of the elements of "modernity" which had manifested itself before the modern period. Sagehood as a goal of spiritual attainment had become almost as rare as had sainthood in the twentieth-century West.

In saying this I was referring to the Sung-Ming belief in the attainability of sagehood and to the disciplined path of self-cultivation which, by the turn of the seventeenth to the eighteenth century in Tokugawa Japan, had largely ceased to serve as a practicable method or model for emulation by the leaders of the educated class. The decline in this dominant ideal did not, however, totally remove sagehood from among the archetypal forms of the Confucian tradition. Whatever the altered perceptions of reality or the new demands of practicality in the seventeenth and eighteenth century, the validity of the traditional ideal, if not the worthiness of its vessels, came back in the end to its power of integration and reintegration. In Chu Hsi's case, the integration of the subconscious mind (*wei-fa*) and the several consciousnesses represented by the *i-fa* (the intellectual, moral, and aesthetic) had been his answer to the increasingly divided consciousness of the Confucian in the early modern era. And it remained the central concern of Wang Yang-ming in his effort to unify knowledge and action and avert the splitting or fragmenting of the mind as the Confucian performed his several roles in changing social and cultural contexts. If, from the standpoint of the Ancient Learning in Japan, both Chu and Wang had asserted too great an autonomy for the individual consciousness and made insufficient allowance for the claims of society and culture upon the individual, this criticism, whether as a philosophical judgment or as an historical commentary on the great Neo-Confucians, could not, in any case, be the last word.

In relation to the dominant aims of the Ch'eng-Chu school, "plumbing principle" and "abiding in reverence," the range and variety of principles to be explored had expanded markedly in the seventeenth century. With the assimilation of Chinese learning came an extensive store of literature and more intensive methods for its critical study. In the humane and natural sciences the growth of empirical scholarship brought further refinement and specialization, revealing an ever wider and finer network of principles to be explored, while in the social order increasing differentiation of economic and political functions produced still greater specialization in the social roles of the individual. For the Neo-Confucian, who recognized the claims made upon him by principle in all its forms, this growing differentiation of learning and social action could not but complicate any system of personal cultivation or integration which took sagehood or self-mastery as its goal.

Many of the processes of social and cultural differentiation in late seventeenth- and eighteenth-century Japan were similar to those at work in China. In both cases, specialized competence or expertise represented for the Confucian an undeniable value as well as an inescapable challenge. Confucius himself had spoken of true knowledge as "knowing what you do know and knowing what you don't know," thus allowing for the possibility of areas of ignorance and expertise, while also asserting the need for self-knowledge as a basis for self-mastery.

Practically speaking, however, as the Confucian saw himself becoming more of a specialist in scholarship or a technician in government, his involvement in new social and cultural technologies (including, for example, such different fields as hydraulic engineering and the new critical methodologies for classical studies), raised questions as to how all this complexity could be managed and, in the midst of it, that degree of self-awareness attained which alone could assure his essential freedom and self-mastery. To put it another way, as the need arose for greater objectivity and empirical study, how could one continue to nurture that deeper subjectivity which, as self-transcending detachment, preserved the essential Neo-Confucian equation between reverence and rational inquiry? Again, in Neo-Confucian terms, with "things and affairs" grown so much more complex, would this not alter one's understanding of the "humaneness" by which the sage entered into communion with Heaven-and-earth and all things? Or, in more modern terms, with the growing differentiation of functions accelerating the process of socially-determined individuation, how was it possible to nurture and preserve the sense of wholeness or integrity which gave that "humaneness" creative expression as genuine autonomy and individual freedom?

In the final analysis, for those who owed their intellectual and spiritual formation to the Neo-Confucian tradition, the conception of sagehood was not reducible to its several parts, nor could it be wholly invalidated by changes in the social and cultural conditions which helped to shape it from age to age. Intellectual styles and social mores might come and go, but the burden on the conscience of the Confucian would not grow lighter as he was called upon to serve more varied and specialized functions. The sitting sage, the learned savant, the literateur or the man of action might be more or less plausible as a model for emulation in peace or war, crisis or calm, prosperity or decline, but none of these roles could be meaningfully served except in the light of the total synthesis embodied in the conception of sagehood.

Even when, as in Sorai's case, sagehood became only an ultimate source of authority far removed from the field of direct, current engagement in human affairs, it remained a pole star and paradigm—or if dissolved perhaps in the distance, an emptiness to be filled. Whatever the mode of intellectuality, moral endeavor, social engagement or religious practice which prevailed in a given period—though each of these may have for us historical or biographical significance—for the Neo-Confucian the conception of the sage remained crucial as the expression of man in his fullness, embracing as wide a range of human experience as possible, and actively integrating it into a holistic view of life at one with the Way. This for the Neo-Confucian provided the larger context and ultimate criterion for real or practical learning.

And if, with the accelerated changes propelling Japan into an uncertain "modern" future, a simple return to earlier syntheses and conceptions of sagehood was no longer feasible, still, past experience remained a relevant gauge for measuring the new dimensions of man's humanity. These might go beyond the Neo-Confucian conception of sagehood, but man himself would be diminished if they fell short of it.

NOTES

1. Chu Hsi himself did not recommend it unreservedly and had doubts about its suitability in certain cases. Cf. Ch'ien Mu, *Chu Tzu hsin hsüeh-an*[cg] (Taipei: San-min shu-chü, 1971), 2:277 ff.

2. See my introduction to *The Unfolding of Neo-Confucianism* (New York: Columbia University Press, 1975), esp. pp. 14–15, 34.

3. Li Ching-te, ed., *Chu Tzu yü-lei,* Cheng-chung Book Co.[ch] reprint, 7:113/4364–5; Ch'ien Mu, *Chu Tzu hsin hsüeh-an*, p. 278.

4. Cf. Abe Yoshio, *Nihon Shushigaku to Chōsen*[ci] (Tokyo: Tokyo University Press, 1965), part 1; Ishida Ichirō and Kanaya Osamu, *Fujiwara Seika, Hayashi Razan,*[cj] *Nihon shisō taikei* (NST ed.), 28:411–89.

5. *Fujiwara Seika shū*[ck] (Tokyo: Kokumin seishin bunka kenkyū-jo, 1938–39), 2:395; Hayashi Razan, *Hayashi Razan bunshū*[cl] (Tokyo: Kōbun-sha, 1930), p. 349.

6. Wajima Yoshio, *Nihon Sōgakushi no kenkyū*[cm] (Tokyo: Yoshikawa kōbunkan, 1962), p. 294.

7. Okada Takehiko, "Shushi no chichi to shi,"[cn] part 2, *Seinan gakuin daigaku bunri ronshū,* 14(2):72–77; Abe, *Shushigaku to Chōsen,* pp. 105–6.

8. Cf. Chu Hsi, *Yen-p'ing ta-wen*[co] (*Chu Tzu i-shu* ed., I-wen yin-shu-kuan reprint of K'ang-hsi ed.), 1:23a–24b, 26b–28a. Okada, "Shushi no . . . shi," pp. 82–86; Abe, *Shushigaku to Chōsen,* pp. 97, 106; Tomoeda Ryūtarō, *Shushi no shisō keisei*[cp] (Tokyo: Shunjū-sha, 1969), pp. 51–60.

9. Chu Hsi, *Yen-p'ing ta-wen,* 1:17a; *Ta-hsüeh chang-chü,*[cq] commentary on *ko-wu.* ST 7:359(444).

10. Tomoeda, *Shushi no shisō,* pp. 57–59; Wajima, *Sōgakushi,* p. 296; Kanaya, *Fujiwara Seika, Hayashi Razan,* pp. 465–68.

11. *Ibid.* I did not appreciate this fully when I prepared the material on Seika some years ago for Tsunoda, de Bary, and Keene, eds., *Sources of Japanese Tradition* (New York: Columbia University Press, 1958), ch. 16.

12. Cf. Abe, *Shushigaku to Chōsen,* p. 104.

13. Cf. Kanaya Osamu, "On the Confucianism of Fujiwara Seika," paper delivered to the Regional Seminar in Neo-Confucian Studies, Columbia University, March 28, 1975.

14. Cf. Tomoeda, *Shushi no shisō,* p. 56.

15. See the background essays of Professor Ishida Ichirō and Kanaya Osamu in the above cited *Fujiwara Seika, Hayashi Razan,* esp. pp. 437–48, 461–63.

16. See de Bary, "Neo-Confucian Cultivation and the Seventeenth-Century 'Enlightenment,' " in de Bary, *Unfolding,* pp. 201–2, 205.

17. T'ang Chün-i, "Liu Tsung-chou's Doctrine of Moral Mind and Practice and His Critique of Wang Yang-ming," in de Bary, *Unfolding,* p. 323.

18. See Wajima, *Sōgakushi,* pp. 301, 305–6.

19. Abe, *Shushigaku to Chōsen,* pp. 520–28.

20. Cf. Ishida, *Fujiwara, Seika, Hayashi Razan,* pp. 419–25, 440–44, 476–79.

21. Ishida, "Tokugawa hōken shakai to Shushigakuha no shisō,"[cr] *Tōhoku daigaku bungakubu kenkyū nempō*, 13B:72–138, English preface, p. 4; also "Tokugawa Feudal Society and Neo-Confucian Thought," in *Philosophical Studies of Japan* (1964), 5:17–24.

22. *Ibid.*, p. 17.

23. *Ibid.*, p. 32.

24. *Ibid.*, p. 31.

25. *Ibid.*, p. 31.

26. *Hayashi Razan bunshū*, 34:384–99.

27. Abe, *Shushigaku to Chōsen*, pp. 520–23.

28. "The influence of Lo Ch'in-shun's *K'un chih chi* in the early Edo period," conference draft, p. 5. Professor Ishida, on the other hand, has been at some pains to establish that in his later years, after Seika's death, Razan had turned toward a view of principle closer to Chu Hsi's. It is a matter of some complexity; for our purposes here it may suffice to say that Razan's view of the objective reality of principle was consistent with a philosophy of principle *and* ether as opposed to 1) a dualism or 2) a monism of either principle or ether. He neither denied principle in favor of a monism of ether, nor abandoned his view of the objective reality of principle.

    Cf. Ishida, *Fujiwara Seika, Hayashi Razan*, pp. 419–25, 442–45.

29. Ishida, "Tokugawa Feudal Society," p. 3. The point is reemphasized in his more recent essay on "The Ideology of the Early Bakuhan System and the Thought of the Chu Hsi School," in *Fujiwara Seika, Hayashi Razan*, pp. 411 ff.

30. Yamaga Sokō, *Haisho zanpitsu*[cs] (NST ed.), 32:33–34; Tsunoda, de Bary, and Keene, *Sources of Japanese Tradition*, pp. 406–10.

31. *Seikyō yōroku*[ct] (NST ed.) (Tokyo: 1970), pp. 11–28, 341–46.

32. *Ibid.*, p. 11 (341).

33. *Ibid.*, pp. 12–14, 21.

34. See de Bary, *Unfolding*, pp. 155–56.

35. *Analects*, I: 6; *Seikyō yōroku*, p. 14.

36. *Seikyō yōroku*, pp. 21, 24–25; *Haisho zanpitsu*, 334; *Yamaga gorui*,[cu] 33:233.

37. *Seikyō yōroku* C, pp. 24–26; *Yamaga gorui*, 33:185–200.

38. *Yamaga gorui*, 41:265–72, 296–97.

39. *Ibid.*, pp. 292–93. Cf. also Tahara Tsuguo, "Yamaga Sokō ni okeru shisō no kihonteki kōsei,"[cv] in *Yamaga Sokō* (NST ed.), pp. 455–57.

40. Cf. Ishida, "Tokugawa Feudal Society," p. 9.

41. *Ibid.*, p. 10.

42. Cf. Abe, *Shushigaku to Chōsen*, pp. 201 ff.

43. Cf. Wm. Theodore de Bary et al., *Self and Society in Ming Thought* (New York: Columbia University Press, 1970), pp. 93–97.

44. Cf. Tahara, "Yamaga Sokō," p. 470.

45. Cf. de Bary, *Self and Society*, pp. 81–85, 162–203.

46. *Yamaga gorui*, 33:188–97, 355–56.

47. *Ibid.*, 41:158; Tahara, "Yamaga Sokō," p. 490.
48. *Seikyō yōroku*, pp. 21–22.
49. J. J. Spae, *Itō Jinsai* (Peiping: Catholic University of Peking, 1948), p. 85.
50. Yoshikawa Kōjirō, "Jinsai Tōgai gakuan,"[ew] *Itō Jinsai, Itō Tōgai*, NST, 33:600.
51. Okada Takehiko, *Ō Yōmei to Minmatsu no jugaku*[ex] (Tokyo: Meitoku shuppansha, 1970), pp. 320–21.
52. Itō Jinsai, *Dōjimon 25, Nihon rinri ihen*[cy] (NRI), p. 549.
53. *Gomō jigi, Kei* (NST ed.), p. 71; Itō Tōgai, *Kokon gakuhen,*[cz] *Shushi no gaku o ronzu* (NST ed.), p. 432.
54. *Ibid.*, pp. 432–33.
55. See *Tōju Sensei nenpu,*[da] in *Tōju Sensei zenshū* (Tokyo: Tōju shoin, 1940), 5:36.
56. Itō Tōgai, *Sō no Shu-Tei-Chō-Ri no gaku o ronzu*, NST, 33:423–26.
57. *Ibid.*, *Shushi no gaku o ronzu*, pp. 433–35.
58. *Gomō jigi, Ri* 4, p. 34.
59. First draft completed 1683, final draft 1704.
60. *Ibid.*, p. 33.
61. *Ibid.*, *Jin-gi-rei-chi*, p. 46.
62. *Ibid.*, *Tendō*, p. 19.
63. *Ibid.*, *Ri*, pp. 33–34.
64. *Ibid.*, *Jin-gi-rei-chi*, pp. 40–41.
65. Jinsai, *Dōjimon*, B, p. 13.
66. *Gomō jigi* (*Nihon no shisō* ed.), p. 109, note 1.
67. *Gomō jigi, Shin*, p. 47; *Sei* 4, pp. 51–52.
68. Chu Hsi and Lü Tsu-ch'ien, *Reflections on Things at Hand*, tr. by Wing-tsit Chan (New York: Columbia University Press, 1967), pp. 93–94 citing *Chu Tzu yü-lei*, 15:13b–14a.
69. Yoshikawa, "Jinsai Tōgai gakuan," NST, 33:613; also "Itō Jinsai" in *Acta Asiatica* 25:50.
70. Yoshikawa Kōjirō, "Sorai gakuan," *Ogyū Sorai*, NST (Tokyo: 1973) 36:716–17.
71. Olof G. Lidin, Ogyū Sorai's *Distinguishing the Way* (Tokyo: Sophia University Press, 1970), pp. xi, xii.
72. *Bendō* 1 (NST ed.), pp. 10–12 (Nishida Taichirō, ed.; Tokyo: 1973); original text p. 200; Lidin, *Distinguishing the Way*, pp. 6–12. Citations of this text hereafter will first give the original section number in roman numerals, follow it with the page reference to the text of the NST edition as annotated and rendered by Nishida, then in parentheses give the page reference to the original text in the same edition. Though my translations most often differ from Lidin's, I cite the corresponding page in his translation for easy reference.
73. *Benmei, Jin*, NST ed. p. 56 (213).
74. *Bendō* II, NST ed. p. 12 (200); Lidin, p. 12.
75. *Bendō* XI, NST ed. p. 22 (204); Lidin, pp. 62–64.

76. Chu Hsi, *Ta-hsüeh chang-chü*, commentary on chapter 1. ST, 7:351(443).
77. *Bendō* VI, NST ed. p. 17 (202); Lidin, p. 34.
78. *Bendō* XIV, NST ed. p. 24 (204); Lidin, p. 76.
79. *Bendō* IX, NST ed. p. 21 (203); Lidin, pp. 54–56.
80. *Bendō* X, XI, XII, NST ed. pp. 21–23 (203–4); Lidin, pp. 58–70.
81. *Gakusoku*, VII, NST ed. p. 196 (258).
82. *Ibid.*, NST ed. p. 196 (258).
83. Yoshikawa, "Sorai gakuan," NST, 36:730 ff.
84. *Bendō* I, NST ed. pp. 10–11 (200); XXV, pp. 25–26 (208).
85. Imanaka Kanshi, *Sorai-gaku no kisoteki kenkyū*[db] (Tokyo: Yoshikawa kōbun-kan, 1966), p. 485; Kanaya Osamu, ed., *Ogyū Sorai shu*, in *Nihon no shisō* (Tokyo: Kawade shobō, 1970), 12:14.
86. *Bendō* XIX, NST ed. p. 28 (205–6); Lidin, pp. 88–89.
87. *Bendō* VI, NST ed. p. 17 (202); Lidin, p. 36.
88. *Shu-ching*, V, 25/4.
89. *Ibid.*, XI, 2/15.
90. *Bendō* XXIV, NST ed. p. 34 (208); Lidin, p. 118.
91. *Gakusoku*[dc] 4, *Ogyū Sorai zenshū* (Tokyo: 1973), 1:10, 76.
92. *Benmei* A5, NST ed. p. 68 (218).
93. *Bendō* IV, V, NST ed. pp. 14–15 (201–2).
94. *Bendō* XVIII, NST ed. pp. 27–28 (205); Lidin, p. 88.
95. *Bendō* XXV, NST ed. pp. 35–36 (208).
96. Imanaka, *Sorai-gaku no kisoteki kenkyū*, pp. 187–99, 483.
97. Imanaka, *Sorai-gaku no kisoteki kenkyū*, p. 483.
98. For a discussion of Sorai as a spokesman for individualism see Kanaya, *Ogyū Sorai shu*, in *Nihon no shisō*[dd] 12:15–18.
99. Cf. de Bary, *Self and Society*, pp. 146–47, 213–14.
100. *Bendō* VII, NST ed. p. 18 (202); Lidin, p. 40.
101. *Bendō* XIV, NST ed. p. 24 (204); Lidin, pp. 76–78.
102. *Ibid.*, and p. 544n. Cf. also *Gakusoku*, VII, NST ed. p. 196 (258).
103. *Bendō* VII, NST ed. pp. 17–20 (203); Lidin, pp. 39–40, 48.
104. *Bendō* VII, NST ed. p. 18 (201–2); Lidin, p. 44; cf. also *Benmei, Jin* 1, NST ed. p. 56 (213–14).
105. Jinsai, *Dōjimon*, C27, NRI ed., v, 151.
106. See above, pp. 131–32.
107. Hirose Tansō, *Yakugen wakumon*[dc] (Tokyo: Iwanami, 1940), p. 68, cited by Ishida Ichirō in "Tokugawa Feudal Society and Neo-Confucian Thought," p. 27.
108. *Bendō* XI, XII, NST ed. pp. 22–23 (204); XVI, NST ed. p. 26 (205).
109. Cf. de Bary, *Self and Society*, pp. 204–5.
110. This expression (or slight variants of it) is attributed to the Buddha at birth in a variety of scriptural sources and popular literature. The precise language quoted by Sorai appears in the *Journey to the West* (*Hsi yu chi*,[df] *chüan* 6) and in Lo Ch'in-shun's *K'un-chih chi* (1622 ed.) 2:20b, where Lo attacks Ch'en Hsien-chang for saying "I am the Way." Sorai shared Lo's

view of Ch'en, and though the point he makes here is a slightly different one, in Sorai's mind the limits of both subjective conviction and objective investigation militated against the claim of sagehood for the ordinary individual. In this, Sorai has a basic sympathy with Lo, drawing upon and extending his empirical thought further. Cf. Irene Bloom, "Notes on Knowledge Painfully Acquired: A Translation and Analysis of the K'un-chih-chi by Lo Ch'in-shun," Columbia University Ph.D. dissertation (Ann Arbor: University Microfilms, 1976). For the contrasting view of Ch'en Hsien-chang, see Jen Yu-wen, "Ch'en Hsien-chang's Philosophy of the Natural," in de Bary, Self and Society, pp. 81–86.

111. Bendō XXI, NST ed. pp. 29–30 (206); Lidin, 96–98.
112. Benmei A, Sei 3, NST ed. p. 68 (218).
113. Bendō XXIV, NST ed. p. 35 (208); Lidin, p. 124.
114. Cf. Kanaya Osamu, Fujiwara Seika, Hayashi Razan, NST ed. p. 463.
115. See note 110 above.
116. Cf. Araki Kengo, "Confucianism and Buddhism in the Late Ming," in de Bary, Unfolding, pp. 41–46, 61.
117. Cf. de Bary, Self and Society, p. 178.
118. Imanaka, Sorai-gaku no kisoteki kenkyū, p. 183.
119. Ibid., pp. 165, 200–3.
120. Ibid., pp. 148–50.
121. Cf. Robert Crawford, "Chang Chü-cheng's Confucian Legalism," in de Bary, Self and Society; and Wm. Theodore de Bary, "Individualism and Humanitarianism in Late Ming Thought," in de Bary, Self and Society, pp. 201–3.
122. Benmei A, Kō-kei-sō-shindoku 2, NST ed. p. 96 (227); Gakusoku VII, NST ed. p. 197 (258).
123. Benmei A, II Kō-kei-sō-shindoku 2, NST ed. p. 97 (227). Sorai here takes issue with the "naturalistic" view expressed in Chu Hsi's Chin-ssu lu (Chu Tzu i-shu, I-wen yin-shu kuan reprint of K'ang-hsi edition). 1/2a, 7a; Wing-tsit Chan, tr., Reflections on Things at Hand, pp. 9–10, 32.
124. Benmei A, II, NST ed. p. 97 (227).
125. Benmei B, Ten-mei-tei-ki-shin 5, NST ed. p. 125 (236); Shin-shi-i 5, p. 147 (243); Gaku 7, p. 179 (250).
126. Benmei B, Ten-mei-tei-ki-shin 11, NST ed. pp. 128–29 (237).
127. The implications of this development for the larger processes of intellectual change are extensively discussed by Maruyama in Studies in the Intellectual History of Tokugawa Japan (Princeton: Princeton University Press, 1974), pp. 92–102, 135–71.
128. Ch'ien Mu, Chu Tzu hsin hsüeh-an, 1:99; p. 301, citing Chu Tzu yü-lei 12.
129. Ishida, "Tokugawa hōken shakai to Shushigakuha no shisō," pp. 126–27, quoting Satō Naokata, Unzōroku.[dg] The English translation in "Tokugawa Feudal Society" is abridged at this point.
130. Ishida, "Tokugawa Feudal Society," p. 26.
131. Kanaya, Ogyū Sorai shū, pp. 17–18.

132. Imanaka, *Ogyū Sorai*, p. 132; Joseph Needham, *Science and Civilisation in China* (Cambridge: Cambridge University Press, 1956), 2:161–63.
133. Needham, pp. 493–94. Cf. also de Bary, "Neo-Confucian Cultivation," in de Bary *Unfolding*, pp. 186–87.
134. *Bendō* XVI, NST ed. p. 26 (205).
135. Cf. Robert N. Bellah, *Tokugawa Religion: The Values of Pre-Industrial Japan* (Glencoe, Ill.: Free Press, 1957), and de Bary, "Neo-Confucian Cultivation," pp. 149–53.

GLOSSARY

a	吳與弼	am	配所殘筆	by	陳亮
b	李侗	an	持敬	bz	永康
c	太極	ao	聖教要錄	ca	張居正
d	無極	ap	性理大全	cb	黃宗羲
e	仁	aq	無極而太極	cc	王夫之
f	陳第	ar	太虛	cd	顧炎武
g	古学	as	未發之中	ce	辨明
h	藤原惺窩	at	人情	cf	石田梅岩
i	理学	au	義理	cg	錢穆，朱子新学案
j	李退溪	av	山崎闇斎	ch	黎靖德，朱子語類，
k	羅欽順	aw	自得		正中書局
l	林兆恩	ax	陳獻章	ci	阿部吉雄，日本朱子学
m	氣	ay	誠		と朝鮮
n	堀杏庵	az	伊藤仁斎	cj	石田一郎，金谷治：藤原惺
o	理一分殊	ba	敬		窩，林羅山，日本思想太系
p	延平答問	bb	胡居仁	ck	藤原惺窩集
q	體認	bc	吳庭翰	cl	林羅山文集
r	渾然一體	bd	東涯	cm	和島芳男，日本宋学史
s	豁然貫通	be	語孟字義		の研究
t	工夫	bf	已發未發	cn	岡田武彦，朱子の父と師，西
u	洒落	bg	主靜		南学院大学文理論集
v	居敬窮理	bh	致良知	co	朱熹，延平答問，朱子遺書
w	七情	bi	荻生徂徠	cp	友枝龍太郎，朱子の思想形成
x	氣質	bj	辨道	cq	大学章句
y	金谷治	bk	古義学	cr	石田一郎，德川封建制度と
z	中江藤樹	bl	古文辭学		朱子学派の思想，東北大学
aa	熊澤蕃山	bm	李攀龍		文学部研究年報
ab	四端七情	bn	王世貞	cs	山鹿素行，配所殘筆
ac	明心宝鑑	bo	政談	ct	聖教要錄
ad	困知記	bp	太平策	cu	山鹿語類
ae	博学	bq	童子問	cv	田原嗣郎，山鹿素行に於け
af	心学	br	廣瀬淡窓		る思想の基本的構成
ag	艮背	bs	窮理	cw	吉川幸次郎，仁斎東涯学案
ah	石田一郎	bt	靜坐	cx	岡田武彦，王陽明と明末の
ai	朱元璋	bu	顔鈞		儒学
aj	近思錄	bv	何心隱	cy	童子問，日本倫理彙編
ak	貝原益軒	bw	李贄	cz	伊藤東涯，古今学変
al	山鹿素行	bx	歸有光	da	藤樹先生年譜

db 今中寛司，徂徠学の基礎的
研究
dc 学則，荻生徂徠全集
dd 金谷治，荻生徂徠集，
日本の思想
de 廣瀬淡窓，約言或問
df 西遊記
dg 佐藤直方，蘊藏錄

Julia Ching

The Practical Learning of Chu Shun-shui (1600-1682)

During the past hundred years many Chinese scholars and statesmen have visited, lived, and studied in Japan. Sometimes they did so because of political difficulties in their home country. The names that come to mind at once are those of K'ang Yu-wei,[a] Liang Ch'i-ch'ao,[b] and Sun Yat-sen.[c] These men both learned from and contributed in some measure to the cultural and political interchange between China and Japan. Of the handful of Chinese refugee scholars in Tokugawa Japan, Chu Shun-shui[d] may be singled out as the one best remembered and most influential in terms of his contribution to Japanese education and intellectual history.[1]

HIS LIFE

Chu Chih-yü[e] (*tzu* Lu-yü),[f] better known by his other name, Shun-shui, lived during the very difficult times which saw the fall of the Ming dynasty and the conquest of China by the Manchus. Had the times been more peaceful, his life would have been very different, and he would no doubt have served the government as a scholar-official, as was expected of a man of his background. Instead, Chu, never an official in China, was destined to become the teacher of the Lord of Mito, Tokugawa Mitsu-

189

kuni (1628–1700) in Japan. He spent the most productive years of his life in that country—from age fifty-nine to eighty-two—and left an important imprint on Japanese intellectual history.[2] He was much less known in China until his rediscovery by a later generation of Chinese patriots, K'ang Yu-wei and Liang Ch'i-ch'ao, who themselves fled to Japan from their Manchu pursuers after the doomed Hundred Days Reform in 1898.[3]

Chu Chih-yü was a native of Yü-yao (Chekiang) and a fellow countryman of the philosopher Wang Yang-ming[g] (1472–1529). By his own account, his ancestors were related to the Ming imperial clan, but refused to enter government service, having changed their surname to a different character, Chu,[h] and reverted to their former name only in the year of Chih-yü's birth. However, his grandfather and father were both Ming officials. The youngest of three sons, Chih-yü lost his father at an early age, in 1607. His eldest brother, Chu Ch'i-ming,[i] also called Chu Chih-ch'i,[j] was a *chin-shih* of 1625 and served the government as a regional commander in Nanking, but lost the position after having offended the eunuchs in power, either Wei Chung-hsien[k] or his underlings. After the accession of Emperor Ssu-tsung[l] his honor was vindicated and he was promoted to be supreme commander; he never reached his post, however, as the Ming dynasty fell at the hands of peasant rebels. He refused to serve in the Manchu government and died in retirement. The second brother, Chu Chih-chin,[m] died as a young student.

Little is known of Chu Shun-shui's early life. He married young, becoming father to a boy at the age of eighteen. He later had another son by his first wife and a daughter by a second wife.[4] Discouraged by the political corruption of the time, he showed a disinclination for civil examinations and an official career. He explained to his wife that, while he could rise rather high on the official ladder if he chose to do so, he feared that the kind of advice he would be obliged to give as a civil official—particularly as a Censor—would be offensive to those in power, and so endanger himself and his family.[5] But if his wife was amenable to his preference for a life in retirement, his other relatives still expected him to prepare for government service. Chu continued to pursue his studies as a Confucian student at Sung-chiang fu.[n] He regarded examinations as "games," but won the attention of the Education Intendant Circuit which in 1638 recommended him to the Ministry of Rites as "excelling in both martial and literary arts."

However, the turbulent times in which he lived precluded his entering the peaceful service of the government or leading a life of retirement as a private scholar. He was destined to travel widely, as a political refugee and a patriot, and to attain renown overseas. Indeed, it is his fame in Japan, as a loyal Ming refugee, scholar, and a man of many gifts, which brought him the later attention of his own fellow countrymen, particularly toward the end of the Ch'ing dynasty with the emergence of a new wave of anti-Manchu patriotism.

Chu Shun-shui's life may be said to fall into two parts: before and after his final trip to Japan in 1659, when he received permission to reside there permanently. He was both a scholar and a man of action—with his action offering proof of the very "practical" understanding that he had of himself as a scholar living in a difficult time of war and invasion. Until late in 1659, his action took the form of wandering between China (Chusan or Amoy), Japan (Nagasaki) and Annam (Faifo). Nowhere did Chu himself clearly explain the reasons for his frequent trips to Japan (seven times) and Annam (four times). It is usually suggested that he was seeking some kind of foreign aid on behalf of the Ming pretenders against the Manchus.[6] Here and there in his writings, Chu himself lends support to this interpretation.[7] And when such foreign aid appeared impossible to obtain—as he must eventually have come to realize—he desired to live at least somewhere outside of Manchu control and remain loyal to the memory of the Ming dynasty as well as to China by continuing to wear his hairstyle and his robes according to Ming customs, *not* as a loyalist minister (*i-ch'en*)[o] since he never held an official position, but as a faithful commoner (*i-min*).[p] Such motivations, even more than any desire to spread Confucian learning, influenced his final decision to settle in Japan, and helped to intensify the impression of his personal integrity among the many Japanese who came into contact with him.

Chu Shun-shui's real or practical learning (*shih-hsüeh*)[q] is thus inseparable from his life, his experiences and his actions. His knowledge and experience went beyond the prescribed scope of his Confucian studies. He read widely, not only in the Confucian classics and Chinese history, but also in Japanese history. He had a good knowledge of the ancient ritual institutions, while being fully conversant with matters of government, law and music. He also knew farming, and was, in his own way, an architect and a craftsman. As his most distinguished disciple, Tokugawa Mitsukuni, remarked:

[Master Chu] is an expert in the practical realm. Should he have to live in the wilderness, he could combine in himself the roles of scholar, farmer, artisan and trader. He is also familiar with important subjects, such as ritual, music, penal institutions, and government, and also gardening, farming, cooking, wine-making, and the making of salt and sauce.[8]

Indeed, Chu was above all, a man who knew how to adapt himself to circumstances in order to survive honorably and be of use to others. He was a Confucian scholar, not in a specialist sense as a classicist or a philosopher, but rather as a "universalist." His learning had a situational character, and his life became a proof of these words from the *Mean*, XIV:

The gentleman does what is proper to his situation without wishing for what is not. In wealth and honor, he does what is proper to [such a situation]. In poverty and loneliness, he does what is proper to [such a situation]. . . . The gentleman can find himself in no situation in which he is not himself.[9]

The Wandering Patriot: 1645–1659

Chu was not invited to join Ming government service until after the fall of Peking in 1644. He received in the course of fifteen years a total of thirteen offers. These came from the Ming pretenders in southern China, Prince Fu (Chu Yu-sung,[r] r. 1644–1645) and his supporters, as well as Prince Lu (Chu I-hai,[s] d. 1662), the "administrator of the realm" and his supporters. One of the early offers—to be provincial surveillance vice-commissioner in Kiangsi and director of the bureau of operations, Ministry of War, with the task of inspecting the forces of Fang Kuo-an,[t] the duke of Ching-kuo[u]—came to him through Fang himself and Ma Shih-ying,[v] Prince Fu's right-hand man. Chu explained in later years his unwillingness to serve under such men, comparing his situation to that of the early Ming thinker, Wu Yü-pi[w] (1392–1469), who was also offered a position in the government.[10]

But his refusal was interpreted by the authorities as disrespect and Chu had to flee, probably to Chusan on the south China coast. There he heard of the fall of Nanking, the southern capital. Both Fang Kuo-an and Ma Shih-ying were killed after having surrendered to the Manchus. Chu sailed to Japan for the first time in 1645,[11] as Prince T'ang (Chu Yü-chien,[x] d. 1646) ascended the throne in Foochow, only to be captured and killed by the Manchus late the following year. Prince Kuei (Chu Yulang,[y] d. 1662) then proclaimed himself emperor in Chao-ch'ing (Kwangtung).

In 1646, Chu Shun-shui left Japan, having failed to obtain permission to reside there, and went for the first time to Annam. He soon returned to China, probably to Chusan, where the general in charge, Huang Pin-ch'ing,[z] several times offered him official positions, all of which he declined.[12] Yet this does not mean that Chu was uninterested in the Ming cause. He probably desired freedom of action, as his sense of reality convinced him of the futility of serving in any official capacity under the weak and incompetent pretenders and their contentious ministers. It was probably through Chu's advice that Huang Pin-ch'ing sent the Censor, Feng Ching-ti,[aa] on a mission to Japan in the name of Prince Lu to request military and financial help for the tottering Ming house;[13] it is possible that Chu accompanied this mission.[14] The Tokugawa government apparently made no official response, although the daimyo of Satsuma was ready to allot three thousand convicted men and several hundred thousand coins of the Wan-li period (1573–1619) to the Ming forces. As far as is known, the Japanese convicts did not set out for China.[15] However, in spite of the failure of this mission, Chu seems to have continued to work toward obtaining outside help for the Ming cause. This is the usual interpretation of the motives for his travels to both Annam and Japan; this also appears to be his own explanation to Prince Lu in 1657.[16]

In 1649, the Manchus chased Prince Lu from Amoy to Chusan, where he continued to provide a focus for sentiments of dynastic and national loyalty, appointing to high office several of Chu's best friends, including Wu Chung-luan,[ab] Chu Yung-yu,[ac] and Wang I.[ad] Chu himself was recommended to the government, but he declined the offers, apparently spending some time in the Ssu-ming mountains,[ae] with Wang I's "guerrilla forces."[17] Wang was to die the following year when the Manchus overran his mountain hide-out. By then, Chu was back in Chusan only to leave again for Annam and Japan. Chusan itself fell into Manchu hands in 1651, and both Wu Chung-luan and Chu Yung-yu died in its defense.[18] But by that time, Chu was once more overseas, traveling to Annam and Japan on one of the ships which made those frequent crossings in the middle of the seventeenth-century.[19]

In 1651, Chu wrote to ask the commander of Nagasaki for permission to stay in Japan. He lamented the misfortunes of the Ming dynasty, which, through the corruption of its high officials, had opened itself to peasant rebellions and the Manchu invasion. He said of himself:

I do not [wish to serve under the Manchus] because my grandfather, father, and elder brother, each in his turn, had passed civil examinations and received imperial favors. How could I bear to wear my hair in a queue, shave my forehead, and serve the enemies? I also have not died [for the Ming dynasty] although I have passed [certain] examinations . . . and thrice received imperial offers to serve the government. For I have seen the disorder of the world and the decline of the way of gentlemen . . . Besides, I have yet family affairs to settle, and am not free to commit my life to my prince.

But I hear that in your honorable country, the [Classics of] *Poetry* and *History* are honored and [the virtues of] propriety and righteousness are valued. Thus I have come here, without consulting my relatives . . . *I* can no longer go back; the three men who were my teachers and friends have all died . . . I therefore submit this letter . . . asking Your Excellency to pass it to higher authorities . . . so that I may be allowed to remain for a time in Nagasaki . . . Otherwise, I shall leave by boat to Tongking and Cochin and await further news there.[20]

Chu failed to obtain permission to remain in Japan. As on previous occasions, he probably was allowed to stay only during the winter and was obliged to leave with the ship again in spring.[21] He went to Annam, where he fell seriously ill in 1652. He sailed back to Japan that autumn, returned to Annam early the following year, and went again to Japan six months later. He also remained in touch with events in China, exchanging letters with Cheng Ch'eng-kung (*alias* Coxinga,[af] 1624–1662),[22] who was then planning from Amoy the recovery of Chusan. However, Chu went once more to Annam in 1654, to remain there this time for over four years, staying most of the time in Hui-an[ag] (Faifo), which is situated in the south. In 1656, he attempted to sail back to China, but without success. Then on February 14, 1657, a ship arrived, carrying with it an edict from Prince Lu, then based in Quemoy, summoning him to return to China and assist in the task of recovering the country from the Manchus.[23] This document had taken nearly two years to arrive. Chu was then preparing to leave for Siam, but on receiving the edict, he decided to wait in Annam and return to Amoy by ship. But again he was delayed by the Annamese authorities.

Nominally, the Lê[ah] dynasty was then ruling Annam from its capital, Thăng Long[ai] (Hanoi). In fact, the country was politically disunited. In the north, the power of the Lê government was in the hands, not of the king, Lê Duy Kỳ,[aj] but of the powerful Trịnh[ak] family. In the south, the Nguyên[al] family, based normally in Hué, was in control. The Nguyêns had previously aided the Lês in regaining the north from the Mạc[am] usurpers, whose influence had not been totally eliminated.[24] Chu's account of his experiences in Annam gives no indication of the names of the kings who were then ruling. From his sojourn at Faifo[25] in the south, however, one must infer that he lived in the territory governed by the Nguyêns, and that the accounts by Liang Ch'i-ch'ao and certain Japanese writers are incorrect in supposing that Chu had to deal with the Lê monarch who was allegedly struggling with the Mạcs.[26] In mid-1656, the Nguyêns had a military setback, but moved their base to Quáng-bình further north from Hué. The following year, Trịnh Cǎn[an] was in the command of the northern forces, many of whom surrendered to the Nguyêns. It was against such a political and military background that Chu's confrontation with the Annamese authorities of the South should be viewed.[27]

It appears that the Nguyên government was then anxious to enlist the help of Chinese scholars in drafting documents, probably in order to mobilize the population against the enemy. Chu's name was submitted by a local official, and he was immediately summoned and taken to the presence of the "king," Nguyên Phúc Tân,[ao] then stationed with his forces at a place not far from Hué. Chu had difficulty in regard to the prescribed prostration before the king. He presented his name with the title, "Tribute Student by Grace, favored by Imperial summons [from China]," explaining that it was not proper for him to perform the prostration. This aroused the anger of Nguyên's court and the population alike, and Chu found himself in prison, facing possible death. When pressed to enter the service of the Nyugên government, he continued to decline. But the king's personal kindness prompted Chu to write a letter to him directly, explaining his situation. He also performed certain services, apparently including the drafting of a document mobilizing the population against the king's enemies. We do not know how well Chu understood the political situation of Annam and the relative merits of the contending parties. He presumed that the king's cause was a just one. Eventually he returned to Faifo, only to find himself penniless, as his inn had been burglarized. In the summer of 1658, he managed to leave Annam for good, heading again for Japan, but with the intention of joining the followers of Prince Lu.[28]

It is interesting to speculate upon Chu's reasons for responding to Prince Lu's invitation after having declined the twelve offers which had come to him from many sources during the preceding years urging him to take an official position. This is all the more curious as Prince Lu was not emperor but only "guardian" or "administrator" of the "realm." Indeed, it could be noted here that the invitation itself was issued at a time when the Prince had voluntarily renounced even this title because his protector, Coxinga, paid no heed to it.[29] But Chu had been away and might not have been aware of all the nuances of this situation—unless these nuances themselves helped to move his heart. Certainly, he was touched by the fact that Prince Lu himself had written to him, as well as by the earnest tone of the letter itself and the news of recent victories it reported. Perhaps the fact that Prince Lu had been based in Chekiang and had many supporters in that area, including scholars like Wu Chung-luan and even Huang Tsung-hsi, also figured in Chu's response this time. Out of modesty, Chu never showed the letter to anyone in Japan during his later life, although it was discovered in his possession after his death.[30] He must have suspected the impossibility of Prince Lu's position, and yet he was ready to survey the situation in China before making any final decision.

Chu was apparently hoping to reach Amoy and join Prince Lu and his supporters. He was probably on his way when he heard of the fall of Chusan and the death of his close friends, Chu Yung-yu and Wu Chung-luan. Prince Lu, himself being under the protection of Coxinga, was not in active command of the situation.[31] In any case, it was during this visit to Nagasaki that Chu received letters from Andō Shuyaku (Seian)[ap] (1622–1701) and another Japanese, both of whom desired to become his disciples. He also received an invitation from Coxinga, who was then based in Amoy and preparing a full-scale invasion of Manchu-occupied territories. With some financial help from Andō Seian and a Chinese Buddhist monk, Chu left Nagasaki for Amoy in November, 1658. But what he found there greatly disappointed him and he never saw Coxinga. A letter he sent from there to Andō Seian revealed his interest in going back to Japan to spread Confucian learning.[32] However, Chu followed Coxinga's forces during their northern expedition. Both in his letter to Andō Seian and in his later work, *Yang-chiu shu-lüeh*,[aq] Chu pointed out the lack of discipline and firm command which he found among Coxinga's forces, whose eventual defeat near Nanking he foresaw.

He also suffered the loss of his second son, Chu Ta-hsien,[ar] who had come to visit him in Amoy, and followed the expedition with him only to die of sudden sickness in 1659.[33]

That winter, Chu returned to Japan and acquired, through the help of Andō Seian, special permission to reside in Nagasaki.[34] This time, he would make Japan his permanent home.

The Confucian Teacher in Nagasaki: 1660–1665

After obtaining permission to reside there, Chu rented a house in Nagasaki. He was in contact with visiting Chinese traders and with a few Japanese scholars and intellectuals, including some Buddhist monks. He was obliged to live frugally, sometimes borrowing from friends. Andō Seian came to see him from Yanagawa regularly twice a year, and offered him half of his own meagre annual stipend of forty koku[as] of rice.[35] Chu accepted with some reluctance, touched by the token of sincere friendship. When advised by a Buddhist monk to take the monk's habit—one way of finding a living, as had Ch'en Yüan-pin,[at] another Chinese refugee in Japan—Chu refused quite firmly, insisting upon the importance of keeping his hair intact, out of filial piety.[36] But he did not attack Buddhism itself; he answered another Buddhist who questioned him concerning his Confucian mission by saying, "Before Confucianism has become clear, Buddhism should not be attacked; once Confucianism has become clear, Buddhism need no longer be attacked."[37]

At Andō Seian's request, Chu wrote a long anti-Manchu tract, *Yang-chiu shu-lüeh* in 1661, in which he explained the causes of the fall of the Ming. He greatly blamed the scholar-officials who wrote meaningless examination essays, paying more attention to form than to content and often resorting to plagiarism, in the interests of official advancement and self-aggrandizement. Chu narrated many of the evils of misgovernment in late Ming and the sufferings of the common people, who turned to their Manchu conquerors for promises of land reform and the lightening of taxes and *corvée*. He also described the Manchu onslaught from north to south, the incompetence of the southern Ming pretenders, and the disunity which prevailed among the ranks of their followers. Chu gave some vivid accounts of Manchu cruelty and went on to offer a plan for the recovery of China from alien hands. He emphasized the practice of the Confucian virtues of benevolence and righteousness, presumably by those in responsibility, and remarked on the lack of discipline and morale among Coxinga's followers, factors which doomed his northern expedition from the beginning.[38]

While Chu was still in Nagasaki, mourning the fall of Ming and dreaming of an eventual Chinese victory over the Manchus, the situation in China continued to deteriorate for the Ming cause. By 1661, Prince Kuei, recognized as emperor by his followers, had fled to Burma and would soon be delivered into the hands of Wu San-kuei,[au] the general who had let the Manchus into China. Prince Lu lived under Coxinga's protection and in his shadow and eventually died in Quemoy in 1662.[39] Coxinga himself died in Taiwan in 1663, discouraged by his military setbacks and unhappy with the private conduct of his son and heir, Cheng Ching.[av] Such news could hardly have rejoiced Chu, who lived on his moderate means in Nagasaki. In 1663, a fire burned his house, and he was obliged to seek temporary shelter in a Buddhist monastery.[40]

In 1664, Chu received a visitor who appealed to his desires to put into practice his Confucian learning. This was Oyake Seijun[aw] (1638–1674), a scholar in the service of Tokugawa Mitsukuni, daimyo of Mito.[41] Impressed with Chu's scholarship and character, Oyake invited him, in Mitsukuni's name, to go to Edo to further Confucian learning. This became the turning point in Chu's life in Japan. The later exchange of correspondence between Chu and Oyake reveals Chu's determination in life: to be the "kind of man whom riches and honors cannot corrupt, and poverty and lowliness cannot change."[42] It also provides some idea of the kind of knowledge and information he was imparting to the persons who came into contact with him. Chu answered Oyake's questions on general geographic knowledge regarding China, Taiwan, and Cochinchina. He also expressed his esteem for Japan and the Japanese, blaming the "Japanese pirate raids" (wa-k'ou)[ax] of the fifteenth and sixteenth centuries on private brigands, and pointing out the need of a literary education for the martial Japanese samurai. He also made it clear that while he was ready to go to Edo, he desired to have first a formal offer, made with due propriety.[43]

In the following year, Chu received the official invitation, extended by Mitsukuni after he had requested permission of the Shogunal government. Chu's disciples in Nagasaki encouraged him to accept this. So in July 1665, he abandoned his plan to buy land for farming in Nagasaki and left for Edo in the company of special escorts provided by the governor of Nagasaki. He was received in Edo with great respect by Mitsukuni himself, who refrained from addressing Chu by his first and second names (*ming* and *tzu*),[ay] and inquired about a studio name. For that reason, Chu gave himself a third name, taken from a river in his native place, Shun-shui. And so, at the age of sixty-five and with a new name, he began a new page in his life.[44]

The Daimyo's Teacher

Tokugawa Mitsukuni was a grandson of the first Tokugawa shogun, Ieyasu,[az] and head of the Three Houses (*Go-sanke*),[ba] established by Ieyasu as a support to the Shogunate itself. Although the lords of the other two houses—Owari and Kii—had higher court rank and social status, the daimyo of Mito enjoyed more power and frequently resided at Edo as advisor to the Shogun himself. Mitsukuni's virtue and merits acquired such legendary greatness after his death that it is difficult to separate myth from history. Yet there can be no doubt that he requested Chu Shun-shui to become his teacher and advisor, with all the honor and recompense due to such a position. The two men became close friends, with Chu remaining under Mitsukuni's protection for the last seventeen years of his life, often in the daimyo's personal company.

It is difficult to measure Chu Shun-shui's influence on his most famous disciple. Mitsukuni was already thirty-seven years old when he received Chu at Edo. He had long been interested in Chinese culture and Confucian ideals, and had so impressed Chu himself with his scholarship and sincerity that the Chinese scholar was to write to a friend:

His Excellency is a close senior relative of the [ruler] today. He is feudal lord of a large state, belonging to one of the Three Houses. He is eminent in virtue and courage, gifted in intelligence, and well cultivated. He does not hesitate to follow the advice of his subordinates.[45]

And then, praising both Japan and Mitsukuni, Chu continued:

People of the world always say that the ancients are superior to the moderns, that China is better than other countries. This is due to their myopia. . . . Should such a lord be living in China and have the assistance of famous and worthy men, he would have no difficulty in bringing about a society of harmony and peace.[46]

As Mitsukuni's advisor and teacher, Chu discussed with him various political and intellectual questions, referring frequently to the classics and history for support in his arguments.[47] Mitsukuni was preoccupied with the task of achieving in Japan a society of perfect justice and peace, and Chu spoke to him of the Li-yün[bb] chapter in the Book of Rites, and the ideal society it describes—that of the Great Unity (ta-t'ung):[bc]

Whenever I read this passage, I used to sigh and ask myself, wondering whether I might one day see its realization, but [knowing] that this is not possible. Now that I am fortunate enough to enjoy your acquaintance and favors, I think that what is not possible in the China of recent ages, may be easily done in Japan, and what others in Japan may not be able to do, Your Excellency may do quite easily.[48]

Chu's letters to Mitsukuni provide an exposition of his own ideas on political ethics. He spoke above all of a government of jen[bd] (humaneness),[49] and the requirement that such a government educate and feed the people, urging Mitsukuni to pay special attention to procuring for the people the needs of their livelihood.[50] At Mitsukuni's request, he wrote a treatise on the proper rituals in the feudal lords' ancestral temples.[51] He also explained the Chinese system of civil examinations, giving an account of its evolution, and the advantages and disadvantages which came with certain changes.[52] In answer to Mitsukuni's questions, he also clarified his own background, the reasons for his having declined the numerous offers he had received from the Ming pretenders, as well as the meaning and ranks of the various Confucian official positions in the Ming government.[53]

As Mitsukuni's personal teacher and advisor, Chu was also invited to give public lectures, most likely with the help of Japanese interpreters. He mentioned with satisfaction the large crowds who came to listen to him, probably in 1667 during a visit to Mito, for he usually resided in Edo.[54] He also provided all the answers he could to questions asked of him, whether they concerned the meaning of technical terms or information related to weather, geography, human kinship, sicknesses, food and drink, animals and birds, grains and plants, and utensils. Such information is collected in a treatise, Chu-shih t'an-ch'i[be] (three chüan),[55] which also contains illustrations of letters and envelopes properly addressed, costumes for various occasions, coffin-making, the arrangement of tombs and tombstones, and miscellaneous other matters. It remains today as evidence of Chu's work as an untiring educator.

Through Mitsukuni, Chu came into contact with a host of Japanese scholars and was much sought after as a teacher and friend. Several of his disciples later had the responsibility of directing the compilation of the historical project, Dai Nihon shi. [bf] Others, both friends and disciples, were important figures in the development of the Chu Hsi school in Japan, or helped to initiate the intellectual movement known as Ancient Learning (Kogaku). [bg]

The Confucian Practitioner

Having accepted Mitsukuni's invitation to go to Edo and Mito, Chu became committed to the task of spreading Confucian education and cult in Tokugawa Japan. He first drew up a detailed plan of the Confucian temple and school compound, including all the dormitory buildings and passageways and even the roof decoration. Entitled Hsüeh-kung t'u-shuo, [bh] his plan, with its many diagrams, is included in the book, Chu-shih t'an-ch'i. He personally instructed the master carpenter, who made the model buildings according to his plan. This project took a complete year to finish. The Confucian temple of Mito with its adjacent buildings was completed in 1672. [56] The same plans would be used later, in 1799, in the rebuilding of the Confucian temple in Edo, so that today the Hall of Great Perfection (Taiseiden), [bi] of Yushima Seidō, [bj] still stands in modern Tokyo as a monument to Chu's careful planning. A statue of Confucius, brought to Japan by Chu is also enshrined there. [57]

Chu did his best to assure proper ritual at the Confucian temple. He wanted the best for the prescribed ceremonies and decided to make sacrificial vessels according to ancient specifications. The directions for making such vessels had long been lost in China itself, but certain extant pictures and diagrams helped Chu to rediscover the methods. He first made rulers and measuring containers according to ancient usage, and with these directed skilled artisans in the production of sacrificial vessels of the kind used during Chou times. [58]

Chu was also the author of the treatise, Shih-tien i-chu, [bk] which explains the officials and ceremonials of the Confucian cult. He begins this small work by modestly confessing his own inadequate knowledge of Japanese official institutions and customs and then goes on to explain the various duties of the sacrificial officials of the cult. He related the entire ceremonial involved, including: the sacrifices of oxen, sheep and pigs, their purification and offering, the music and dancing which accompany the rite, and all the bows and prostrations. He warns that reverence is required on such a solemn occasion and stresses the prohibition of laughter and noise, of quarrel, indulgence, and disorder during the ceremony.[59]

In 1672, Chu Shun-shui personally directed the Confucian students of Mito during the first celebration of the Confucian cult in the new temple. His instructions would later serve as direction for similar ceremonies held in Edo itself. Mitsukuni was present on one such occasion in 1675.[60] The daimyo also requested his teacher to design and make Ming costumes for all occasions. Probably owing to Chu's influence, he ordered the Confucian students of Mito to grow their hair long and wear scholars' robes.[61]

The Confucian's life is not solely one of social responsibilities and ritual expressions. There is also a time and a place for rejoicing, and for finding one's harmony with nature. Mitsukuni's father, Tokugawa Yorifusa,[bl] had laid out a garden in Edo on land given him by the Shogun in 1629. But it was Mitsukuni's task to complete the garden of sixty-three acres, and for this too he enlisted Chu's assistance.[62] The finished garden would include a lake with walks, stone lanterns, arched stone bridges and trees, all arranged skillfully in harmony with their surroundings. There were also miniature imitations of noted Japanese and Chinese scenic beauties, including the West Lake of Hangchow and Mount Lu of Kiangsi. A name was given to this beautiful garden: Kōrakuen,[bm] the characters being taken from the famous essay of Fan Chung-yen,[bn] the Sung statesman who said that the scholar should be the first to worry about the world's many cares and the last to enjoy its pleasures.[63] Chu was asked to write the three characters of the name. The garden still stands in today's Tokyo, although many of its fine structures were destroyed during the intervening years, especially in the 1923 earthquake and the 1945 air raids.

As early as 1670, Chu designed and ordered for himself a painted coffin in cypress wood, to have his body preserved for future removal to and final burial in China. This was envisaged for a time after the fall of the Manchus. He died in 1682, at the age of eighty-two, and was buried outside Mito, at the foot of Mount Zuiryū in Hitachi, according to Ming customs. He had lived frugally and saved a total of 3,000 gold ryō in the vain hope of contributing to the Ming cause. He left this sum on his

Chu Shun-shui

death to the lord of Mito. His grandson, Chu Yü-jen,[bo] had briefly visited Nagasaki in 1679 without seeing him and returned to Japan in 1684 to visit his grave.[64]

HIS PRACTICAL LEARNING

In his famous book, *Chung-kuo chin-san-pai-nien hsüeh-shu shih*[bp] (Intellectual Trends in China in the Past Three.Hundred Years), Liang Ch'i-ch'ao places Chu Shun-shui, together with Wang Fu-chih[bq] (1619–1692), as one of two *ch'i-ju*.[br] He uses this term in a laudatory sense, meaning unusual, outstanding, "strange," and independent Confucian scholars.[65] When we examine the writings of Chu and Wang we find a similar sense of patriotism and attachment to the Ming cause, a common concern for Confucian learning, and a shared conviction that the misinterpretation of classical Confucianism in more modern times had contributed to the social and political disorder and the intellectual abstruseness of late Ming times. Apart from these shared concerns, however, we find two very different personalities, reacting, each in his own way, to similar problems. Whereas Wang Fu-chih attempted to rebut the metaphysical "excesses" of the latter-day disciples of Chu Hsi[bs] (1130–1200), and especially of Wang Yang-ming,[66] on philosophical grounds, Chu Shun-shui devoted his attention to more pragmatic matters, refusing on principle to discuss *t'ai-chi* or *li* and *ch'i*,[bt] and committing himself to the task of spreading the Confucian cult and education in Tokugawa Japan. Although Chu cannot strictly be called a philosopher, he was not without philosophical views. He refused to integrate these into a system, preferring to find meaning through giving his own life and activities a special direction.

In terms of the conventional distinction between the two major Neo-Confucian schools, Chu Shun-shui has usually been considered—by Chinese and Japanese historians of ideas alike—a follower of the Chu Hsi tradition. Liang Ch'i-ch'ao favors this view; Chu Ch'ien-chih[bu] agrees with Inoue Tetsujirō[bv] in classifying Chu Shun-shui as a member of the Chu Hsi school in Japan.[67] Before accepting such a conclusion, however, let us examine Chu Shun-shui's own ideas on life and its meaning to decide whether he shared Chu Hsi's world-view and life-view.

The Return to Confucius

First of all, we cannot but be struck by Chu Shun-shui's emphatic op-position to metaphysical and cosmological discourse. When asked about the Supreme Ultimate (*t'ai-chi*) and yin and yang,^{bw} he replied:

In your honorable country many speak of the Supreme Ultimate . . . . But [Con-fucius] the master and sage did not speak of the Heavenly Way (*t'ien-tao*).^{bx} His disciple Tzu-kung,^{by} a famous and worthy man, said [too] that the Heavenly Way cannot be acquired [by learning].[68]

Chu Shun-shui was intent upon the imitation of Confucius rather than of Chu Hsi. He appealed to the Sage in order to defend his own anti-metaphysical position and to show clearly his adherence to the ear-lier tradition. He also returned to Confucius in his elucidations of sage-hood and the method of attaining it:

Of those called sages in the past and present, there is no one as esteemed as Con-fucius. There is also no one as intelligent and wise as [his disciple] Yen Yüan.^{bz} But when [Yen] asked about *jen*, Confucius could have adduced some subtle and mysterious explanation . . . and claimed it was a secret transmission passed on by the sages from mind to mind. Why should he only have replied: "Do not see what is contrary to propriety; do not hear what is contrary to propriety; . . . do not act in any way contrary to propriety"? . . . From this [we] know that the great Tao is to be found in these [words] and not elsewhere.[69]

DOCTRINE OF SAGEHOOD

Elsewhere Chu offered his own ideas of what a sage is. He first evoked those qualities of mind and heart which are emphasized in the *Mean* and other Confucian texts:

A sage is one who is sincere and has understanding. . . . A sage advances with propriety and retreats with righteousness. . . .[70]

And again:

A sage [does what is just right] without effort and [achieves understanding] with-out exercising thought.[71] A sage seeks to do good to the world when he is in a comfortable position, and to perfect himself alone when he is in poverty. A sage does not forget the swelling [disorder of the world].[72] He fears Heaven and has compassion for [his fellow] men. A sage is affable without being adulatory,[73] in-dependent and impartial. He corrects what is wrong in his sovereign's mind in order to allow the world to enjoy bliss.[74]

Chu was committed to the ideal of sagehood, but did not consider it easily attained. He took exception with those teachings that overemphasize the spontaneity of self-cultivation. In an essay discussing Confucian prescriptions on propriety, he wrote:

There is a way for acquiring sagehood. . . . . But [many in] this world who are learning [to become] sages . . . say that the way of sagehood is based on the natural (tzu-jan)[ea] and is quite without constraint. So their discussions tend to be abstract and general while their analysis of principle (li)[eb] becomes hair-splitting. And yet they are thousands of li[ec] away.[75]

In Chu Shun-shui's other writings, we find clear indications of Chu Hsi's influence on his thought and convictions. Evidently he accepted Chu Hsi's teachings on self-cultivation as a means for achieving sagehood. He regarded the Confucian virtue of sincerity in high esteem and spoke of inner reverence as that which leads to sincerity:

What is reverence? It is modesty and apprehension, reverence of the heart within and of our behavior without. . . . One should be the same in activity and in tranquillity, in the interior and the exterior life.[76]

Chu Shun-shui also had a good knowledge of rites and ceremonies, and considered these to be manifestations of Heavenly principle (t'ien-li).[ed] For him, the proper observance of ritual law was a sign of good government and prosperity, whereas its neglect showed the country's weakness and degeneration. On this point, he referred to his experience in Amoy, the military base of Coxinga. He observed that Coxinga's officers were billeted in the houses of wealthy people and appeared complacent and pleasure-loving, while neglecting propriety as a thing of the past: "From this I knew that he (Coxinga) would fail in his undertaking. Hence, although I travelled ten thousand li to get there, I returned without [visiting] him or leaving my name [card] at his place."[77]

Chu Shun-shui opposed excessive introspection and unwarranted preoccupation with the "preservation" (ts'un)[ee] of the mind, saying, "The great man is he who has not lost the mind of a child. Since he has not lost it, why should he need to preserve it?"[78] According to Chu, a Confucian must give first priority to self-cultivation. Once this is taken care of, he should also acquire "extensive learning" (po-hsüeh),[ef] in order to strengthen his character and give it "reality" (shih). After that, he also needs to acquire the art of literary expression in order to elucidate his thoughts.[79] Chu gave a low priority to the writing of poetry and the lowest to calligraphy.[80]

Chu Shun-shui and the Tung-lin School

In a long letter written to a Japanese friend, Chu concurred in the established opinion of the Sung thinkers, particularly Chu Hsi, regarding the loss of the real teaching of Confucius, the later dominance of Buddhism and Taoism, and the appearance of Chou Tun-i[cg] (1017–73) and others who revived the true Confucian Way.[81] Chu openly expressed admiration for Chou Tun-i's views on tranquillity and quiet contemplation and for his love of nature. He observed that contemplation is conducive to longevity.[82] But we have no clear evidence that Chu himself practiced meditation or quiet-sitting.

He definitely prefers Chu Hsi to his rival philosopher, Lu Chiu-yüan[ch] (1139–1193), but stresses that the way of virtue (tsun te-hsing)[ci] and that of knowledge (tao wen-hsüeh)[cj] [83] lead to the same goal, just as the sea route and the land route both lead the traveller from Nagasaki to Edo. Travel by the sea route depends on favorable winds: with them, one reaches the destination very quickly; without them, there can be no progress at all. Travel by the land route—apparently Chu Hsi's—is slower but surer.[84]

CRITICISMS OF WANG YANG-MING

Chu Shun-shui refrained from any direct criticism of Chu Hsi. However, he openly criticized Wang Yang-ming for his teaching of liang-chih,[ck] while praising Wang's practical accomplishments and military victories.[85] He repeated an anecdote about Wang Yang-ming involving a pun over Mencius' expression about the mind of a "child" (ch'ih-tzu:[cl] literally, a red baby).[86] He recounted how Yang-ming once answered a question regarding the "shape and color" of liang-chih by saying that it was "red"—being the mind of a "red baby"! Almost in the same breath, Chu added that he was merely joking and not expressing any approval of Yang-ming.[87] He attacked the "philosophical factionalism" of the late Ming as a legacy of Yang-ming's teaching, singling out for criticism Yang-ming's disciple Wang Chi[cm] (1498–1583), whose writings resemble "those of a Buddhist monk."[88] His criticisms, nevertheless, remained moderate in tone. And his own constant emphasis on practice, whether in virtue or in scholarship, shows an influence which derives from Yang-ming's teaching of the unity of knowledge and action.

INFLUENCE OF THE TUNG-LIN SCHOOL

In an article devoted to the relationship between Chu Shun-shui and the school of Ancient Learning in Japan, Fujisawa Makoto[cn] gives some importance to Chu's connection with the Tung-lin[co] school as evidence of his commitment to "real learning" (jitsugaku).[89] For Chu regarded himself as the disciple and friend of Wu Chung-luan,[90] Prince Lu's Minister of Rites. Wu was a student of Ku Hsien-ch'eng[cp] (1550–1612), one of the founders of the Tung-lin school, which took upon itself the task of correcting the more metaphysical tendencies of the followers of Wang Yang-ming, and of orienting thought and scholarship to practical use and service to society.[91] This same concern was even more obvious in Chu, who tended to blame the fall of the Ming on the state of its abstract learning and committed himself to more practical scholarship.

But it should be said here that Chu openly expressed disapproval of several important figures of the Tung-lin school for teaching a tao-hsüeh[cq] which was removed from common sense and human feelings (jen-ch'ing)[cr] and for promoting academic factionalism. He mentioned specifically the names of Tsou Yüan-piao,[cs] Kao P'an-lung[ct] and Liu Tsung-chou,[cu] saying that they cannot merit the title of "great scholars" (chü-ju).[cv] A great scholar, he added, is a man who devotes himself to "the direction of the country, the education of the people, and generosity [in the service of all] in the midst of difficulties."[92] In explaining what he meant by academic factionalism, Chu referred particularly to the conflicts between adherents of tao-hsüeh—Neo-Confucian metaphysics—and those who preferred wen-chang[cw]—the promotion of letters. He cited as an example the conflict between the Sung philosopher Ch'eng I[cx] (1033–1107), Chu Hsi's intellectual predecessor, and the great poet Su Shih[cy] (1037–1101), praising the latter for his sense of political responsibility and reality.[93]

And so, while accepting some possible connection between Chu Shun-shui and the Tung-lin movement, we must acknowledge his basic independence of mind regarding the whole tradition of Ch'eng I and Chu Hsi, of Sung as well as Ming. He differs from his Confucian predecessors, not as a rebel against a tradition, but as one committed to intellec-

tual honesty and convinced that the fall of the Ming was in part attributable to the protagonists of Neo-Confucian *tao-hsüeh*. In his own words:
"I have not rebelled against Chou [Tun-i], the Ch'eng [brothers], Chang
[Tsai][cz] and Chu [Hsi]. Even if I have criticized them for one thing or
another, I have not deviated from the right way. . . . The gentleman is
affable but not adulatory."[94]

Just what was Chu Shun-shui's position with regard to the intellectual
evolution of late Ming China? Did his views reflect those of his contemporary Chinese scholars, men like Huang Tsung-hsi[da] (1610–95), Ku
Yen-wu (1613–82),[db] and Wang Fu-chih, all of whom were Ming loyalists? In attempting to assess Chu's contributions to the whole movement
of thought which is known as real or practical learning, should we not
first regard him against the Chinese background of his own times and the
prevailing climate of opinion before going on to discuss his role in promoting the Japanese *jitsugaku*?

In examining Chu Shun-shui's friendships, we find that his closest
friends were loyal supporters of several southern Ming pretenders, especially of Prince Lu, but did not include any of the prominent names in
late Ming Confucian scholarship. As we have seen, he had some association with Tung-lin or post-Tung-lin circles, probably the Chi-she.[dc] But
there is no proof that he knew Huang Tsung-hsi personally, although
they came from the same native place, were both friends of Wu Chung-
luan and Wang I, lived in Chusan during the same year, and had trav-
eled at different times to Japan in the hope of getting aid for the Ming
cause.[95] Huang was more interested in metaphysical subjects, more committed to the Wang Yang-ming philosophy, and more provocative and
prolific as a scholar, while Chu was a more practical man who gave instruction to disciples according to their needs and desires. In his reaction
against abstract scholarship and his orientation to the practical he perhaps
had more in common with Ku Yen-wu and Wang Fu-chih.[96] He shared
Ku's attentiveness to detailed information concerning customs and institutions but lacked his thirst for knowledge for its own sake. He also shared
Wang Fu-chih's historical interests but not his philosophical concerns.
Yet Chu's criticisms of late Ming government and politics, of the examination system with its eight-legged essays, of the dangers and futility of an
abstract quest for sagehood, together with his undying loyalty to the Ming
cause, reveal a mentality basically similar to that of Huang, Ku and
Wang.

In an article on the subject of the school of "practical affairs" in the late Ming and early Ch'ing times, Yamanoi Yū^{dd} speaks of the Tung-lin school and its contribution to the growth of a *jitsugaku* which concentrated on *ching-shih chih-yung*^{de} or practical statesmanship.[97] He describes Huang Tsung-hsi, Ku Yen-wu and Wang Fu-chih as practical-minded historians, but speaks in particular of the *jissen-ha*,^{df} or men who gave special attention to the more "practical" realms of scholarship. These included Sun Ch'i-feng^{dg} (1585–1675), with his knowledge of warfare, who sought also to reconcile the thought of Chu Hsi and Wang Yang-ming; Li Yü^{dh} (1627–1705), with his special interest in history and government; Yen Yüan^{di} (1635–1704), conversant in agriculture and the art of war as well as ritual and music; and Lu Shih-i^{dj} (1611–1672), whose interests extended to astronomy, geography and irrigation. Chu Shun-shui is listed with these men. Bearing in mind Chu's more technical talents, it is possible to argue that he could also be placed in another category of late Ming scholars. These were men like Li Shih-chen (1518–93),^{dk} author of *Pen-ts'ao kang-mu*^{dl} (1593), a rich source of knowledge of herbal medicine; Hsü Kuang-ch'i^{dm} (1562–1633), friend of the Jesuit missionaries and author of several scientific works, including *Nung-cheng ch'üan-shu*^{dn} (1628), a work on agronomy; Sung Ying-hsing,^{do} author of *T'ien-kung k'ai-wu*^{dp} (1637), a detailed history of technology which became better known in Japan than in China itself;[98] and Fang I-chih^{dq} (1611–1671), author of *Wu-li hsiao-chih,*^{dr} an early work on natural science. But Chu never wrote on any specific subject except when requested to do so by his disciples for their edification. He was more an educator than a specialist. His pragmatic emphasis prefigured the directions in which Chinese scholarship would evolve during the Ch'ing dynasty. Chu both taught and practiced what Yen Yüan would so strongly advocate: the orientation of learning to the practical and useful in the name of the real Confucius and his true teaching.[99]

MITOGAKU^{ds} OR KOGAKU?

As the guest and advisor of Tokugawa Mitsukuni, Chu Shun-shui lived in both Edo and Mito, but his influence was naturally felt most in the circle of those scholars connected with Mitsukuni and his feudal domain. This group of men has been identified as the "early Mito school," classified as a group with special historical interest belonging generally to the philosophical school of Chu Hsi.[100] They were especially associated with

Mitsukuni's historical project, the writing of the *Dai Nihon shi*, a work in 397 chapters, which was formally begun in 1672 and completed only in 1906. It is, however, extremely difficult to assess Chu Shun-shui's role in the writing of this history. Mitsukuni had long been interested in Chinese scholarship and historiography, particularly in the *Spring and Autumn Annals* and in Chu Hsi's *T'ung-chien kang-mu*.[dt][101] Since 1661, he had been assembling a group of scholars who could help realize the writing of the new history as well as other works.

These persons came from different scholarly traditions within the Japanese Chu Hsi school (*Shushigaku*), which was, after all, the established orthodoxy.[102] Following Mitsukuni's example, many of them became Chu Shun-shui's close friends, and some acknowledged themselves to be his disciples. They included Yoshihiro Genjō (Keisai),[du] Itagaki Tsune (Sōtan),[dv] Hitomi Den (Bōsai),[dw] Imai Kōsai[dx] and Asaka Kaku (Tanpaku).[dy] Yoshihiro and Hitomi exchanged many letters with Chu, although Chu's correspondence with them dealt with general questions of scholarship rather than the preparatory work of the *Dai Nihon shi*.[103] Both Imai and Asaka became Chu's disciples very young. Asaka was to be made general editor of the *Dai Nihon shi* in 1693. In spite of an allusion made by Andō Seian, when Chu first went to Edo,[104] it must therefore be assumed that Chu did not personally participate in the writing itself. But, as a scholar familiar with Chinese history and historiography, he could have helped to assure its high quality as a work written in the same genre as many Chinese histories, particularly the *Tzu-chih t'ung-chien*[dz] and the *T'ung-chien kang-mu*. Above all, he provided a source of Confucian inspiration for the project, all the more so as a living example of Confucian virtues, particularly political loyalty, or patriotism.

TAIGI MEIBUN[ea] AND THE *DAI NIHON SHI*

It is therefore reasonable to assume that Chu Shun-shui strengthened and confirmed Mitsukuni's ideals of political virtue, and thus assisted in the eventual translation of these ideals into historical writing. Certainly the principal ethical inspiration flowing through the many chapters of the *Dai Nihon shi* is that of *taigi meibun*, an alliance of virtue and legitimacy and an expression of Confucius' doctrine of the "rectification of names," which had allegedly guided the sage's writing of the *Spring and Autumn Annals*. Given this moral perspective, the *Dai Nihon shi* came out in support of the legitimacy of the Southern house centered at Yoshino—

the base of Emperor Go-Daigo[eb] and his descendants during the turbulent period of the Northern and Southern dynasties (1318–92)—when their rule was continually challenged by the Ashikaga shogunate. It is interesting to note that Chu Shun-shui himself wrote two eulogies, one for Kusunoki Masashige[ec] (1294–1336), the faithful supporter of Emperor Go-Daigo, and the other for his son, Masatsura[ed] (1326–1348), who sought to continue his father's resistance to the Ashikaga shogunate, only to meet a similar death as a political martyr.[105]

In the Meiji era, Chu Shun-shui was frequently praised for his example as a political loyalist, for his eulogy of the Kusunokis, and for his inspiration to a spirit of patriotism and of reverence for the sovereign. In the words of one Meiji statesman:

[Chu's] spirit of pure loyalty and reverence for the prince (sonnō)[ee] . . . fermented in silence and obscurity for about two hundred years before inspiring the patriots (shishi)[ef] to urge all to rally to the prince (i.e., emperor), change to a policy of princely rule according to antiquity, and thus accomplish the great task of renewal (ishin),[eg] which has led to the prosperity of our nation today. We have indeed received much from [Chu] Chih-yü.[106]

The early Mito school was also noted for its intellectual tolerance regarding the various schools of Confucianism, Shinto and Buddhism. Mitsukuni himself wrote on Shinto themes and sponsored the work of editing and commenting on the eighth-century Japanese anthology, the Manyō shū.[eh] He also built an important Sōtō Zen temple in Mito and invited there—after Chu Shun-shui's death—the Chinese monk from Hangchow, Hsin-yüeh (Shinetsu,[ei] 1639–1695).[107] Chu also showed a similar broad–mindedness. He always emphasized the beneficial effects of Confucianism but never attacked Buddhism directly, and appeared tolerant enough of Shinto beliefs. His advocacy of the union of literary and classical knowledge (wen)[ej] and martial spirit and skill (wu)[ek] must have been especially appealing to the Japanese samurai class.[108]

Chu Shun-shui and the Ancient Learning (Kogaku)

What was Chu's relationship with the broader philosophical movements in Tokugawa Japan, in particular with Shushigaku,[el] Yōmeigaku,[em] and Kogaku (the school of Ancient Learning)? Was he in contact with the philosophical and scholarly leaders of Japanese Confucianism, with the Hayashi family of Edo and with his contemporaries, Kumazawa

Banzan[en] (1619–1691), Yamaga Sokō[eo] (1622–1685), and Itō Jinsai[ep] (1627–1705)? What influence was he able to exert on the evolution of Japanese Neo-Confucianism?

When Inoue Tetsujirō described Chu Shun-shui as a follower of Chu Hsi rather than of Wang Yang-ming, he also added that Chu's learning showed some resemblance to that of the school of Ancient Learning, which emerged in seventeenth- and eighteenth-century Japan with the rise of several great scholars, in particular Yamaga Sokō, Itō Jinsai, and Ogyū Sorai (1666–1728).[eq] Inoue's point was that Chu's learning gave emphasis to the notion that knowledge should be of use to society and focused on ritual matters and history.[109]

Without a doubt, Chu Shun-shui was on friendly terms with the Hayashi family of Edo. He knew Hayashi Razan's[er] (1583–1657) son, Shunsai (Gahō,[es] 1618–1680), and grandson Hōkō[et] (1644–1732), the official Head of the State University, but was particularly friendly with Hōkō's eldest brother, Harunobu[eu] (1643–1666). Several of Chu's important letters were written to Harunobu, answering his many questions about Confucian learning. Chu also mourned Harunobu's early death, and wrote a memorial essay in the young man's honor.[110] Even more important, Chu exchanged numerous letters with Kinoshita Jun'an[ev] (1621–1699), the Shushigaku scholar noted for his devotion to education and hailed by Ogyū Sorai as an early founder of Kogaku. Kinoshita is usually regarded as a follower of Hayashi Razan, but he also sought counsel and advice from Chu for a period of fourteen years.[11]

Chu Shun-shui does not appear to have had any contact with the Wang Yang-ming school (Yōmeigaku) in Japan. He does not seem to have known Kumazawa Banzan.[112] His contacts extended to friends and disciples in Kyushu, met during his Nagasaki sojourns, as well as to those persons he met in Edo and Mito, but not beyond those circles.

Chu Shun-shui's first disciple and life-long friend, Andō Seian, is known as a Shushigaku scholar.[113] Seian was a modest man and ascribed his own knowledge of the Sung philosophers, the Ch'eng brothers and Chu Hsi, to Chu's teaching. But his interest in Sung and Ming philosophy predated his meeting with Chu, who did not share his predilection for Lo Ch'in-shun's[ew] (1465–1547) metaphysics of li and ch'i. Seian was in contact with other scholars of the time, including Kaibara Ekken[ex] (1630–1714), who in turn was in contact with scholars in Mitsukuni's service, but apparently never met Chu. Seian was particularly eager to introduce to Chu, Itō Jinsai, the classicist and philologist. But Chu declined meeting the younger Japanese scholar on the ground of an important difference between his own approach to learning and that of Itō:

Itō Seishū[ey] is truly an outstanding scholar of your honorable country . . . His [literary] workmanship (kung)[ez] is sophisticated, but quite useless to the service of the world. What he (Itō) considers to be the Way, is not my Way. When my Way is not used, I fold it up and hide it away. Should it ever be used, it can certainly make sons filial, ministers loyal, the times harmonious, the years fruitful, and government return to order.[114]

And then, comparing himself modestly with Itō Jinsai, but placing emphasis upon the *practical* nature of his own concerns, he added:

My learning is only [about] wooden utensils, earthen lamps, cloth and silk, beans and grain. Itō's learning is [like] engraving designs and embroidering on silk.[115]

Although Chu Shun-shui never met Itō Jinsai, he was personally acquainted with Yamaga Sokō, the teacher of Bushido[fa] and an important figure in the development of Ancient Learning. Chu wrote an essay for Yamaga on the subject of reverence which was an exhortation to self-cultivation.[116] But there is no evidence that Chu exerted any influence on Yamaga's intellectual development.

In his article on Chu Shun-shui, Fujisawa Makoto refers to Chu's comments on Itō Jinsai and the difference between the two men's understanding of learning and scholarship, but suggests also that Chu's praise of Itō's Chinese prose could have been a real encouragement to the latter. He attaches little importance to Chu's relationship with Yamaga Sokō, but points out the important exchange of letters between Ogyū Sorai, the great Kogaku scholar, and Chu's disciple Asaka Tanpaku.[117] It appears that Sorai had originally regarded Chu as purely a follower of the Sung school of Ch'eng I and Chu Hsi. He mentioned this to Asaka Tanpaku, saying that Asaka would probably consider him (Sorai) to be a heretic for his criticisms of the Sung thinkers.[118] In reply, Asaka refered to his own devotion to the Sung philosophers as having begun only in his middle age, but described his former teacher clearly and unequivocally as a lover of Ancient Learning:

[Chu-Shun-shui] was intent on Ancient Learning and did not so much respect and believe in the Sung scholars. His Collected Writings provide evidence of the differences of views between himself and [the Sung masters]. [I still consider it] regrettable that I was then a young child and did not know what he meant then by Ancient Learning.[119]

However, on the basis of this study, it is quite clear that Chu Shun-shui could only be called a lover of Ancient Learning in a special sense, that of learning from the past all that is of service to the present. He learned from the Confucian texts and taught to others the importance of the good life, a life given to the practice of virtue, and to the service of state and society. He belonged to a broader tradition than that of the more orthodox Chu Hsi or Wang Yang-ming or even the Tung-lin school. He profited from Chu Hsi's teachings on self-cultivation, but praised also those Confucian scholars of the Sung period who argued for a political philosophy with a stronger emphasis on "enriching the country and strengthening the army," especially Ch'en Liang[fb] (1143–1194):

I say that the official in charge of governing the people [has a task] very different from that of the student of the classics. Whatever good he does will result in the people receiving some benefit, and the court benefitting from his service. [Such work] does not merely consist in the exhaustive investigation of the philosophy of principle (li-hsüeh).[fc] I fear that Hui-an's[fd] (Chu Hsi's) criticism of Ch'en T'ung-fu[fe] (Ch'en Liang) as a heretic (i-tuan)[ff] was too severe.[120]

Indeed, Chu Shun-shui's learning is firmly rooted in the Chinese Confucian tradition and yet quite free from the kind of philosophical and academic "factionalism" which he personally dreaded. His learning was real and practical, but without the later more narrow and almost sectarian meaning of *jitsugaku* as an exclusive interest in science and technology. Chu did not claim to be a great philosopher or a specialized philologist. He could not help Itō Jinsai or Ogyū Sorai in their quest for a genuine and clear understanding of early Confucian texts or detailed historical knowledge. But his example for the Japanese was one which helped to orient Japanese Confucianism to the real, the human, the objective, and the practical, which for them were stepping stones toward the encounter with Western science and technology.

Chu Shun-shui and "Real Learning"

The Chinese word "learning" (hsüeh),[fg] like its correlate "knowledge" (chih),[fh] has a certain ambivalence of meaning. "Learning" may refer to intellectual pursuit, which, in premodern China, meant classical studies. This usually signifies the preparation of scholars for an official career. Here, the notion of service and practicality enters, for education was sponsored by the state and encouraged by families for the production of statesmen, bureaucrats, and teachers. And "learning" may also connote "learning to be a sage," the pursuit of transcendental greatness through the conscious cultivation of one's moral character. Here too, a note of practicality can be discerned, all the more so as the potential Confucian sage is expected to give himself to the service of state and society through some form of activity which is to be united to his contemplation of metaphysical reality, should he be philosophically inclined.

In spite of the implicit acknowledgment that learning must be somehow oriented to the realm of the practical, Confucians have debated among themselves as to the "reality" of such practicality, or rather, the "reality" of their learning. After all, the other Chinese word, shih[fi] connotes directly and immediately the real, or the solid, rather than the practical, even if shih-hsüeh (real learning), took on historically the meaning of "practical learning." Real learning is, of course, real knowledge. And since the Chinese word "knowledge" (chih) refers both to the knowledge of information as well as wisdom, real knowledge is preeminently the science and art of wisdom.

In his book, Jitsugaku to Kyogaku,[fj] Professor Minamoto Ryōen[fk] defines jitsugaku (shih-hsüeh) by opposing it to kyogaku (hsü-hsüeh). He explains that the term originated with Chu Hsi, for whom the study and cultivation of Confucian social virtues constituted real learning, in contradistinction to the purely metaphysical interests of philosophical Buddhism, with its talk of śūnyatā (emptiness) and its more negative attitude toward human society. He also speaks of the later evolution of the meaning of this term, as the emphasis moved from a more "realistic" attitude toward metaphysical, ethical and social questions to a more practical or "pragmatic" approach to knowledge itself, without neglecting the importance of founding knowledge on "reality," i.e., on real proofs or documentary evidence.[121] In the realm of thought, this meant that Shushigaku came gradually to be viewed as "empty learning" because its more theoretical and academic approach to the quest of sagehood as well as to social problems was found inadequate. The much more practically oriented Yōmeigaku rose to prominence, widening the concept of sagehood by stressing the universal possibility of its attainment, with or without intellectual pursuit. The emergence of the Ancient Learning represents a further step in the direction of the "real" and "practical," even if that be in the name of a revival of antiquity. The claim was made for a return to the "real" Confucius and Confucianism of the sixth century B.C., rather than to his interpreters of the eleventh or twelfth century A.D. The adherents of this school also espoused the view that the whole human nature was good and insisted that the "real" human nature included the human emotions, which should not be disparaged, as had some followers of the Ch'eng-Chu school of Confucianism.[122] Seen in this light, the efforts of Japanese Confucians to integrate Confucian ethics with the "real" Japanese spirit—such as the samurai spirit and, generally speaking, Shinto—become more comprehensible.

With this interpretation in mind, let us return to Chu Shun-shui and his "real learning." In him, we find *all* the meanings of *shih-hsüeh* or *jitsugaku* realized. He was careful in cultivating Confucian social virtues and taught others to do the same. He manifested a preference for ancient traditions, while being able to find uses for them in the present. He had a practical, even pragmatic approach to knowledge, devoting himself to the concrete forms for manifesting the Confucian way of life. For him, the investigation of things (*ko-wu*)[n] referred less to the metaphysical understanding of principle and material force, as it had for Chu Hsi, or to the realization of the mind and heart, as Wang Yang-ming had urged, and more to coping with concrete situations. At the same time, the extension of knowledge (*chih-chih*)[m] applied not only to knowledge of the Confucian classics, but also to all that is useful in life. In his own way, Chu Shun-shui followed in the footsteps of *both* Chu Hsi and Wang Yang-ming, by adhering faithfully to basic Confucian ethical and social ideals, but independently adapting them to the unusual circumstances in which he found himself. He was a "transitional" figure, representing the seventeenth century in both China and Japan, and transmitting certain philosophical views of the Sung and Ming thinkers while signalizing the emergence of a new generation of more pragmatically oriented scholars in both countries.

Chu Shun-shui's "real learning" signified a conscious return to, and imitation of, Confucius himself. Like Confucius, Chu was basically concerned with practical morality, with ritual practices and with the service of state and society. Like Confucius also, Chu travelled from state to state, but rather than a ruler to use his services, he sought the restoration of the Ming cause. More fortunate than Confucius, he found that which he did not seek—a political patron very eager for his advice and counsel. Once more, like Confucius, Chu became renowned above all as a teacher.

Asaka Tanpaku left behind this fitting eulogy to the teacher of his youth:

The Master was a highly gifted and independent person, who considered as learning not the dutiful course of academic studies but rather the invention of things, the accomplishment of practical affairs, and the service of state and society, and such important matters as the details of ritual, music, penal institutions and government, as well as such lesser concerns as the making of things and objects. In his teaching of disciples he did not speak on the exalted subjects of the nature and destiny, or give empty discourses in a vacuum. Rather, he exhorted the practice of filial piety and fraternal love and preferred to speak only of what is useful to the daily life of the people and their ethical relationships. He based [his teachings] on sincerity and placed emphasis on reverence. He proved by his behavior that to which he gave expression in words. He was earnest and untiring in the work of education, for the purpose of forming useful persons who could serve the country.[123]

Chu Shun-shui was indeed an unusually independent-minded scholar. For him, the principal characteristic of Confucian teaching was its moral relevance and usefulness to human life and society. This was the consistent norm by which he judged the value of the thought and scholarship of the past. This was the essence of his own understanding of learning and scholarship. He did not denigrate intellectual pursuits as a whole. He insisted upon the study of the Four Books and the Six Classics, of philosophy, history, and ancient literature. But such learning was not pursued for its own sake. It should lead first and foremost to the practice of virtue. Making reference time and again to Confucius' favorite disciple, Yen Yüan, he said:

The way of learning (hsüeh-wen)[fn] lies especially in real practice (shih-hsing).[fo] Yen Tzu learned ten things from [every] one thing he heard. [But] he was classed as outstanding in virtuous behavior. This shows what [learning is all about].[124]

And again:

Confucius said: "I have a disciple called Yen Hui[fp] who is fond of learning. He does not transfer his anger and does not make the same mistake twice." Does this not show how the learning of the sages and worthies lies in practice (chien-lü)?[fq] [125]

The real learning of Chu Shun-shui was the practical wisdom of a competent and dedicated teacher, a popularizer of the Confucian cult, and a living example of the Confucian virtues which he taught others. It was the learning of a *chün-tzu*, [fr] the Confucian gentleman, who always "does what is proper to his situation without wishing for what is not," and who "can find himself in no situation in which he is not himself." [126] Chu's presence and activities in Nagasaki, Edo, and Mito enriched the intellectual and moral life of those who came into contact with him and left a lasting impact on Japanese Confucianism.

NOTES

1. There are several collections of Chu Shun-shui's extant writings. These include: *Ming Chu Cheng-chün chi*[fs] (*Min Shu Chō-kun shū*), 10 ch., comp. by Isokawa Gōhaku,[ft] known as the Kaga ed. (1684); *Chu Shun-shui hsien-sheng wen-chi*[fu] (*Shu Shunsui sensei bunshū*), 28 ch., comp. by Tokugawa Mitsukuni, known as the Mito ed. (1715); *Chu Shun-shui ch'üan-chi*[fv] (*Shu Shunsui zenshū*), 86 ch. plus supplements, comp. by Inaba Iwakichi[fw] (Tokyo: 1912); *Shun-shui i-shu,*[fx] 25 + 4 ch., Preface of T'ang Shou-ch'ien[fy] (1913), ed. by Ma Fou[fz] (Taipei reprint: 1969).

   Of these collections, the most comprehensive is that of Inaba, which includes principally the contents of the Mito ed., while adding to it those parts of the Kaga edition which have not previously been included. Besides, the supplements include also letters and essays by many of Shun-shui's important disciples, such as Asaka Kaku, Tokugawa Mitsukuni, and Kinoshita Teikan, which are not in the other editions. The Chinese edition (1913/1969), although the latest, is not as complete.

   For more information concerning Shun-shui's writings and the various editions, including the history of these editions, and how they were made to include Shun-shui's scattered writings, see an article by Yamamoto Takeo,[ga] "Shu Shunsui bunshū no seiritsu o megutte,"[gb] in *Kokiroku no kenkyū*[gc] ed. by Takahashi Ryūzō Sensei kiju kinen ronshū kankōkai[gd] (Tokyo: 1970), pp. 821–34. Here a word of thanks should be noted by this writer, who has received help from Professor Yamamoto of the Institute of Historiography, Tokyo University. For the purposes of this paper, I have relied principally on the Chinese edition, although I have at my disposal the Supplements from the Inaba edition, as well as other selections.

2. The Chinese sources for Chu's life include a few short biographical notices, notably Shao T'ing-ts'ai,[ge] *Ming i-min so-chih chuan,*[gf] in *Ssu-fu-t'ang wen-chi,*[gg] ch. 3; Weng-chou-lao-min,[gh] *Hai-tung i-shih,*[gi] ch. 18, included in *Shun-shui i-shu,* Supplements; Wen Jui-lin[gj] (fl. 1705), *Nan-chiang i-shih*[gk] (Shanghai ed.: Hong Kong reprint, 1971), I, 335; Chao Erh-sun[gl] et al., *Ch'ing-shih kao*[gm] (Preface, 1927) (Peking: 1927), 504:13a–14a; Min Erh-ch'ang,[gn] *Pei-chuan chi-pu*[go] (Peking: 1931), 35:2b–7b. Some of these contain factual errors.

   Chu Shun-shui's own writings and the records of his Japanese disciples form the best source for a knowledge of his life. A chronological biography compiled by Liang Ch'i-ch'ao, *Chu Shun-shui hsien-sheng nien-p'u*[gp] (1936), in *Yin-ping shih ho-chi, chuan-chi,*[gq] 97, is an indispensable help, especially as Liang has carefully sifted various accounts concerning Chu's activities, particularly those which took place before he finally settled down in Japan. However, it still contains a few errors, for example, in connection with Chu's sojourn in Annam, as will be pointed out in this paper.

The best modern biography in Japanese is by Ishihara Michihiro,[gr] *Shu Shunsui* (Tokyo: Yoshikawa kōbunkan, 1961). It is brief, but gives good references.

There is also a short biography in English by Shunzō Sakamaki, given in A. Hummel, ed., *Eminent Chinese of the Ch'ing Period*, Washington, D.C.: Government Printing Office, 1943) 1:179–80.

There is also an article in German on Chu Shun-shui: Heinz Friese, "Chu Shun-shui (1600–1682) und Japan," *Nachrichten* (Gesellschaft für Natur- und Völkerkunde Ostasiens, Hamburg) (June 1966), 99:35–36.

3. Both K'ang and Liang fled to Japan following the unsuccessful Hundred Days Reform (1898). See K'ang's five poems in honor of Chu in *K'ang Nan-hai wen-chi*[gs] (Shanghai: 1914), 12:9b. See also Ishihara Michihiro, "Shu Shunsui to Kō Nankai,"[gt] in *Rekishi Kyōiku*[gu] (1960), 8:60–62.

4. See the biographical account of Chu by two of his Japanese disciples, Imai Kōsai and Asaka Kaku, in *Shun-shui i-shu*, supplements, 6a.

5. *Ibid.*, 1b.

6. *Ibid.*, 2a. Chu Shun-shui mentioned having studied under Chu Yung-yu, a native of Sung-chiang. Possibly Chu Yung-yu was a teacher in that particular Confucian school.

7. *Ibid.*, 2a–b.

8. Quoted in Takasu Yoshijirō,[gv] *Mitogaku taikei*,[gw] vol. 5: *Mito gikō rekkō shū*[gx] (Tokyo: 1943), Introduction, pp. 2–3.

9. English translation adapted from James Legge, tr., *The Chinese Classics* (Oxford: 1892), 1:395.

10. See his answer to Andō Seian, *Shun-shui i-shu* 14:2b. See also Liang Ch'i-ch'ao, *Chu Shun-shui hsien-sheng nien-p'u*, pp. 9–10. For Wu Yü-pi, see Huang Tsung-hsi, *Ming-ju hsüeh-an*[gy] (MJHA) (SPPY ed.), 1:1a–2b.

11. Liang Ch'i-ch'ao, *Nien-p'u*, p. 10. For Prince Fu's brief reign, see T'an Ch'ien,[gz] *Kuo-chüeh*[ha] (1621 preface, Peking ed., 1958), pp. 6173–217; Chi Liu-ch'i,[hb] *Ming-chi nan-lüeh*[hc] (Changsha: 1938), *chüan* 1–9. For Prince T'ang, see pp. 241–49.

12. Liang Ch'i-ch'ao, *Nien-p'u*, p. 10.

13. Hsü Nai,[hd] *Hsiao-tien chi-nien fu-k'ao*[he] (1861 preface, Peking ed., 1957).

14. Liang Ch'i-ch'ao, *Nien-p'u*, pp. 11–12.

15. There had been several unsuccessful requests for Japanese aid. See Huang Tsung-hsi, "Jih-pen ch'i-shih chi,"[hf] in *Li-chou i-chu hui-k'an*[hg] (Shanghai: 1910), 2 pages. See also Liang Ch'i-ch'ao, "Huang Li-chou Chu Shun-shui ch'i-shih Jih-pen pien,"[hh] in *Tung-fang tsa-chih*[hi] (1923), 20(6):54–56.

16. See his letter to Prince Lu, *Shun-shui i-shu*, 3:2a–b.

17. For Wang I, see Hsü Nai, *Hsiao-tien chi-nien fu-k'ao*, pp. 581–89. See also Huang Tsung-hsi, "Ssu-ming shan-chai chi,"[hj] in *Li-chou i-chu hui-k'an*, 3 pages. According to Imai and Asaka, Chu had planned to get foreign aid for Wang I in the hope of serving the Ming cause. See their biographical account, 2b–3a.

18. For the fall of Chusan, see Hsü Nai, *Hsiao-tien chi-nien fu-k'ao*, pp. 665–71, and *Shun-shui i-shu*, 4:5a–b, 6b–7a. See also Huang Tsung-hsi, "Chou-shan hsing-fei,"[hk] *Li-chou i-chu hui-k'an*, 3 pages.

19. For the sea voyage between China, Japan, and Annam during that period, see Ch'en Ching-ho,[hl] "Ch'ing-ch'u Hua-p'o chih Ch'ang-ch'i mao-i chi Jih-Nan hang-yün,"[hm] (The Role of Chinese Junks in Nagasaki-South Trade and Navigation during Early Ch'ing), in *Nan-yang hsüeh-pao*,[hn] (Journal of the South Seas Society) (1957) 13(1):1–53.

20. *Shun-shui i-shu* 3:4a.

21. Liang Ch'i-ch'ao, *Nien-p'u*, p. 28.

22. *Ibid.*, p. 16. For Coxinga's activities, see Hsü Nai, *Hsiao-tien chi-nien fu-k'ao*, p. 674; see also his biography under the name of Cheng Ch'eng-kung by Earl Swisher, *Eminent Chinese*, 1:108–10. Chu Shun-shui leaves his account of the experiences in *An-nan kung-i chi-shih*,[ho] given in *Shun-shui i-shu*.

23. See *Shun-shui i-shu*, 3:1b.

24. For the history of Annam, see *Kham-dinh Viêt-su thong giam cu'o'ng-muc*,[hp] (1884; Taipei reprint, 1969), 32:3b–4a, 8a–b, 14a.

25. See *An-nan kung-i chi-shih*, 5a. See also G. Devéria, *Histoire des Relations de la Chine Avec l'Annam-Viêtnam du 16e au 19e siècle* (Paris: 1880), which includes a map (1579) of routes between the two countries. For more information on Faifo and the Chinese community there, see also a seventeenth-century work by the Buddhist monk Ta-shan,[hq] *Hai-wai chi-shih*[hr] (1696), given in Ch'en Ching-ho, *Shih-ch'i shih-chi kuang-nan chih hsin shih-liao*[hs] (Taipei: 1960), 4:9a–b.

26. See Iwamura Shigemitsu,[ht] *Annan tsūshi*[hu] (Tokyo: 1941), pp. 179–81.

27. *Ibid.*, pp. 254–57.

28. *An-nan kung-i chi-shih*, 1b–12a.

29. See the biography of Chu I-hai (Prince Lu) in *Eminent Chinese*, 1:180–81.

30. *Shun-shui i-shu*, 3:1b–2a.

31. Hsü Nai, *Hsiao-tien chi-nien fu k'ao*, pp. 689–90.

32. *Shun-Shui i-shu*, 9:8a–10b; Liang, *Nien-p'u*, pp. 23–24.

33. *Yang-chiu shu-lüeh* (given in *Shun-shui i-shu*), 9a. See also his letter to a friend in *Shun-shui i-shu*, 4:2a–b.

34. Hsü Nai, *Hsiao-tien chi-nien fu k'ao*, pp. 744–752. See also James Murdoch, *A History of Japan* (London: Kegan Paul, Trübner, 1926), 3:148.

35. See Chu's letter to Andō Seian, *Shun-shui i-shu*, 9:13a, and also Chu's letter to his grandson, *Shun-shui i-shu*, 4:5a–6a. See also Andō Seian's letter to Chu, given in *Chu Shun-shui ch'üan-chi*, supplements, p. 731. In later life, Chu frequently sent presents to Andō who accepted the small gifts but returned the more costly ones. *Shun-shui ch'üan-chi*, supplements, p. 737.

36. *Shun-shui i-shu*, 4:8a–b. Ch'en Yüan-pin (d. 1671) stayed some time in Nagasaki before being invited by the Lord of Owari to go up north. He contributed to the Japanese knowledge of *jujutsu*.[hv] Chu Shun-shui knew him and corresponded with him. *Shun-shui i-shu*, 12:8b, 12a. See also Tsuji

Zennosuke,[hw] *Kaigai kōtsū shiwa*[hx] (Tōadō shobō: 1930), pp. 660–68, for more information on him and other Chinese refugees, including a physician in Edo and the founder in 1659 of the Ōbaku monastery in Uji.

37. *Shun-shui i-shu*, 4:9a. Chu exchanged letters with many Buddhist monks, regarding them as friends, although he lamented the dominant position of Buddhism in Japan and the relative ignorance regarding Confucianism. *Shun-shui i-shu*, 8:5a.

38. *Yang-chiu shu-lüeh*, 9 pages.

39. See the biography of Prince Lu (Chu I-hai) by J. C. Yang, in *Eminent Chinese*, 1:180–81. See also Ishihara Michihiro, *Shu Shunsui*, pp. 110–11.

40. Imai and Asaka, *Shun-shui i-shu*, supplements, 4b.

41. For the conversations, conducted in writing between Chu and Oyake, see *Shun-shui i-shu*, 15:8b–17b. Evidently Oyake stayed in the Nagasaki area for about two months.

42. *Shun-shui i-shu*, 8:6a–8b. The reference is to *Mencius*, 3B:2; see Legge, *The Chinese Classics*, 2:265. The English translation here is my own.

43. *Shun-shui i-shu*, 8:6a–8b, 15:8b–17b.

44. *Shun-shui i-shu*, 9:6a–b; Liang, *Nien-p'u*, p. 41.

45. *Shun-shui i-shu*, 4:3a–b.

46. *Ibid.* See also Ishihara Michihiro, "Mindai Chūgokujin no Nihonkan,"[hy] *Rekishi Kyōiku* (1960), 8:44–51, for the evolution of Ming Chinese views of Japan.

47. See Imai and Asaka, *Shun-shui i-shu*, supplements, 5a.

48. *Shun-shui i-shu*, 7:1a.

49. *Ibid.*, 7:1b.

50. *Ibid.*, 7:2b.

51. *Ibid.*, 7:10 a–b, 12a–b; Imai and Asaka, *Shun-shui i-shu*, supplements, 5b.

52. *Ibid.*, 13:1a–3b.

53. *Ibid.*, 13:4a–5b, 6a–8a.

54. *Ibid.*, 12:34b. Mitsukuni paid special attention to the task of popularizing Confucian education through public lectures which he sponsored both in Edo and Mito. See Yoshida Kazunori,[hz] *Dai Nihon shi ki den shi hyō senja kō*[ia] (Tokyo: Kazama shobō, 1965), pp. 472–91.

55. *Chu-shih t'an-ch'i* (1707 preface).

56. Imai and Asaka, *Shun-shui i-shu*, supplements, 6a–b; Liang, *Nien-p'u*, pp. 49–50. See also Iida Sugashi,[ib] "Kōto-jidai no Kōshibyō kenchiku,"[ic] in Fukushima Kanezō,[id] ed., *Kinsei Nihon no Jugaku*[ie] (Tokyo: Iwanami shoten, 1939), pp. 948–51, 957–59. Iida Sugashi includes a diagram of Chu Shun-shui's general ground-plan for the Confucian temple and adjunct buildings, as well as a photograph of the wooden model of the Taiseiden. See pp. 1004–5.

57. See Suzuki Miyao,[if] "Shu Shunsui no tazusae kitatta Kōshizō ni tsuite,"[ig] *Shibun*[ih] (1972), 68:16–19, for a history of that statue which Chu originally gave to Andō Seian.

58. Imai and Asaka, *Shun-shui i-shu*, supplements, 6a.

59. This treatise is given in *Shun-shui i-shu*, following ch. 25. See 1a–7a.
60. Imai and Asaka, *Shun-shui i-shu*, supplements, 6a.
61. This was probably intended to separate the Confucian class visibly from the Buddhist monks.
62. Imai and Asaka, *Shun-shui i-shu*, supplements 6a. See especially Koishikawa Kuyakusho, ed. *Koishikawa-ku shi*[ii] (Tokyo: 1935), pp. 867–69.
63. Fan Chung-yen, "Yüeh-yang-lou chi,"[ij] *Fan Wen-cheng kung wen-chi*[ik] (TSCC ed.), 1st ser., 3:19.
64. Imai and Asaka, *Shun-shui i-shu*, supplements, 5b–6a. See also *Shun-shui i-shu*, 13:13b–14a for Chu's instructions on the making of coffins.
65. See Liang Ch'i-ch'ao, *Chung-kuo chin-san-pai-nien hsüeh-shu shih* (1936; Taipei reprint, 1970), pp. 81–84.
66. *Ibid.*, pp. 74–81.
67. Chu Ch'ien-chih, *Jih-pen te Chu-tzu hsüeh*,[il] Inoue Tetsujirō, *Nihon Shu-shigakuha no tetsugaku*[im] (Tokyo: 1945), pp. 809–20.
68. *Shun-shui i-shu*, 15:1a–b.
69. *Ibid.*, 18:1b. Allusion is to *Analects*, XII: 1; see Legge, *The Chinese Classics*, 1:250.
70. *Shun-shui i-shu*, 25:8a.
71. Allusion to the *Mean*, XX: 18; see Legge, *The Chinese Classics*, 1:413.
72. Allusion to *Analects*, XVIII: 6; see Legge, *The Chinese Classics*, 1:334.
73. Allusion to *Analects*, XIII: 23; see Legge, *The Chinese Classics*, 1:273.
74. *Shun-shui i-shu*, 18:1a.
75. *Ibid.*, 18:1a–b.
76. *Ibid.*, 20:3b.
77. *Ibid.*, 6:6a.
78. *Ibid.*, 15:1b.
79. *Ibid.*, 14:5b–6a.
80. *Ibid.*, 9:19a.
81. *Ibid.*, 5:1a–2b.
82. *Ibid.*, 25:12b.
83. The *Mean*, XXVII; see Legge, *The Chinese Classics*, 1:422.
84. *Shun-shui i-shu*, 14:6b.
85. *Ibid.*, 14:7a.
86. Allusion to *Mencius*, IVB:12; see Legge, *The Chinese Classics*, 2:322.
87. *Shun-shui i-shu*, 15:1b.
88. *Ibid.*, 14:7a.
89. Fujisawa Makoto, "Shu Shunsui no Kogaku shisō to waga Kogakuha to no kankei,"[in] *Tōkyō Shinagakuhō*[jo] (1966), 12:28–29.
   sics, 1:273.
90. For Wu Chung-luan, see MJHA, ch. 61.
91. For the Tung-lin school, see MJHA, chs. 58–61.
92. *Shun-shui i-shu*, 15:2a.
93. *Ibid.*, 15:2a.
94. *Ibid.*, 6:10b. Allusion is to *Analects*, XIII:23; see Legge, *The Chinese Classics*, 1:273.

95. For Huang Tsung-hsi, see Liang Ch'i-ch'ao, *Chung-kuo chin-san-pai-nien hsüeh-shu shih*, pp. 43–52.
96. For Ku Yen-wu, see Liang Ch'i-ch'ao, *ibid.*, pp. 53–65. For Wang Fu-chih, see pp. 74–81.
97. Yamanoi Yū, "Minmatsu Shinsho ni okeru keisei shiyō no gaku,"[ip] in *Tōhōgaku Ronshū*,[iq] (February 1954) (1):140–43.
98. The first known Japanese edition appeared in 1771. See Yabuuchi Kiyoshi,[ir] et al., *Tenkō kaibutsu kenkyū ronbun shū*,[is] tr. into Chinese by Chang Hsiung[it] and Wu Chieh[iu] (Peking: 1959). In his introductory chapter, he emphasizes the importance of regarding Wang Yang-ming's thought as stimulating such practical works. This is also brought out by Sugimoto Kaoru[iv] in his work, *Kinsei jitsugaku shi no kenkyū*[iw] (Tokyo: Yoshikawa Kōbunkan 1962), p. 10.
99. See Liang Ch'i-ch'ao, *Chung-kuo chin-san-pai-nien hsüeh-shu shih*, pp. 105–34.
100. For the early Mito school, see the collected writings assembled by Takasu Yoshijirō in *Mitogaku taikei*, especially vols. 2, 3, 5, 6, 7. See also Nagoya Tokimasa,[ix] *Mitogaku no dōtō*[iy] (Mito: 1972). See also Herschel F. Webb, "The Thought and Work of the Early Mito School" (Ph.D. dissertation, Columbia University, 1958).
101. Imai and Asaka, *Shun-shui i-shu*, supplements 8a–b; Liang, *Nien-p'u*, pp. 53, 57.
102. See Yoshida Kazunori, *Dai Nihon shi kiden shihyō senja kō*, pp. 472–91. For a discussion of the *Dai Nihon shi* itself, see Herschel Webb, "What is the *Dai Nihon shi?*" *Journal of Asian Studies* (1960), 19:135–49.
103. Chu wrote numerous letters to Hitomi. See especially *Shun-shui i-shu*, ch. 5. For his letters to Yoshihiro, see 8:14a, 13a–14a, 10:22a, 12:29a–31a.
104. *Shun-shui ch'üan-chi*, supplements, p. 741.
105. *Shun-shui i-shu*, 20:1b–2a.
106. Gotō Shimpei's[iz] words in his preface to Inaba's edition of *Shun-shui ch'üan-chi*, quoted also in Liang Jung-jo,[ja] "Chu Shun-shui yü Jih-pen wen-hua,"[jb] *Ta-lu tsa-chih*,[jc] (1954), 8(4):105.
107. Tsuji Zennosuke,[jd] *Nihon bunka shi*[je] (Tokyo: Shunjū-sha, 1950), 5:112–28.
108. See Chu's essay, "Shu-chien-t'ang shuo,"[jf] *Shun-shui i-shu*, 19:4a–b.
109. Inoue Tetsujirō, *Nihon Shushigakuha no tetsugaku*, pp. 809–20.
110. *Shun-shui i-shu*, 12:10b, 21:1a–4a.
111. See *Shun-shui i-shu*, 5:7a–10a for Chu's letters to Kinoshita and *Shun-shui ch'üan-chi*, supplements, pp. 774–75, for Kinoshita's replies. Kinoshita's disciples Okumura Yōrei[jg] and Isokawa Gōhaku are sometimes regarded as Chu's disciples.
112. For Kumazawa Banzan, see Gotō Yoichi[jh] et al., *Nihon shisō taikei*[ji] (NST), (Tokyo: Iwanami shoten, 1971), 30:467–534.
113. For Andō Seian, see Inoue Tetsujirō, *Nihon Shushigakuha no tetsugaku*, p. 149.
114. *Shun-shui i-shu*, 9:5a. For Itō Jinsai, see Yoshikawa Kōjirō[jj] et al., *Itō Jin-*

sai, NST (Tokyo: 1971), 33: especially pp. 565–618. Seishū was another name for Jinsai.

115. *Shun-shui i-shu,* 9:7a.

116. *Shun-shui ch'üan-chi,* ch. 16, p. 334. For Yamaga Sokō, see the volume compiled by Tahara Tsuguo[jk] et al., NST, vol. 32 (Tokyo: Iwanami shoten, 1979).

117. Fujisawa Makoto, "Shu shunsui no Kogaku shisō to waga Kogakuha to no kankei," pp. 39–42.

118. See *Sorai-shu,*[jl] ch. 28, in Yoshikawa Kōjirō et al., *Ogyū Sorai,* NST (Tokyo: Iwanami shoten, 1973), 36:537–38.

119. See Asaka's reply to Ogyū Sorai in *Shun-shui ch'üan-chi,* supplements, pp. 763–64.

120. *Shun-shui i-shu,* 15:4a.

121. Minamoto Ryōen, *Jitsugaku to kyogaku* (Toyama: 1971), pp. 36–37.

122. *Ibid.,* pp. 40–41. See also his more recent book, *Tokugawa shisō shōshi*[jm] (Tokyo: Chūō Kōron-sha, 1973), pp. 26–90.

123. See Asaka's epilogue to the Collected Writings of Chu Shun-shui given in *Shun-shui i-shu,* supplements, 15b.

124. *Shun-shui i-shu,* 14:1b. The allusion is to *Analects,* V: 8. See Legge, *The Chinese Classics,* 1:176.

125. *Shun-shui i-shu,* 14:1b. The allusion is to *Analects,* VI: 2. See Legge, *The Chinese Classics,* 1:185.

126. *Mean,* XIV; English translation adapted from Legge, *The Chinese Classics,* 1:395.

GLOSSARY

a	康有爲	am	莫	by	子貢	
b	梁啟超	an	鄭根	bz	顏淵	
c	孫逸仙	ao	阮福瀕	ca	自然	
d	朱舜水	ap	安東守約（省庵）	cb	理	
e	朱之瑜	aq	陽九逑略	cc	里	
f	魯嶼	ar	朱大咸	cd	天理	
g	王陽明	as	石	ce	存	
h	諸	at	陳元贇	cf	博學	
i	朱敿明	au	吳三桂	cg	周敦頤	
j	之琦	av	鄭經	ch	陸九淵	
k	魏忠賢	aw	小宅生順	ci	尊德性	
l	思宗	ax	倭寇	cj	道問學	
m	之瑾	ay	名、字	ck	良知	
n	松江府	az	德川家康	cl	赤子	
o	遺臣	ba	御三家	cm	王畿	
p	遺民	bb	禮運	cn	藤澤誠	
q	實學	bc	大同	co	東林	
r	福王（朱由崧）	bd	仁	cp	顧憲成	
s	魯王（朱以海）	be	朱氏談綺	cq	道學	
t	方國安	bf	大日本史	cr	人情	
u	荊國	bg	古學	cs	鄒元標	
v	馬士英	bh	學宮圖說	ct	高攀龍	
w	吳與弼	bi	大成殿	cu	劉宗周	
x	唐王（朱聿鍵）	bj	湯島聖堂	cv	巨儒	
y	桂王（朱由榔）	bk	釋典儀注	cw	文章	
z	黃斌卿	bl	德川賴房	cx	程頤	
aa	馮京第	bm	後樂園	cy	蘇軾	
ab	吳鍾巒	bn	范仲淹	cz	張載	
ac	朱永佑	bo	朱毓仁	da	黃宗羲	
ad	王翊	bp	中國近三百年學術史	db	顧炎武	
ae	四明山	bq	王夫之	dc	幾社	
af	鄭成功（國姓爺）	br	畸儒	dd	山井湧	
ag	會安	bs	朱熹	de	經世致用	
ah	黎	bt	太極、理、氣	df	實踐派	
ai	昇龍	bu	朱謙之	dg	孫奇逢	
aj	黎維禔	bv	井上哲次郎	dh	李顒	
ak	鄭	bw	陰陽	di	顏元	
al	阮	bx	天道	dj	陸世儀	

dk 李時珍
dl 本草綱目
dm 徐光啟
dn 農政全書
do 宋應星
dp 天工開物
dq 方以智
dr 物理小識
ds 水戶學
dt 通鑑綱目
du 吉弘元常（磬齋）
dv 板垣矩（宗澹）
dw 人見傳（懋齋）
dx 今井弘濟
dy 安積覺（澹泊）
dz 資治通鑑
ea 大義名分
eb 後醍醐
ec 楠木正成
ed 楠木正行
ee 尊王
ef 志士
eg 維新
eh 萬葉集
ei 心越
ej 文
ek 武
el 朱子學
em 陽明學
en 熊澤蕃山
eo 山鹿素行
ep 伊藤仁齋
eq 荻生徂徠
er 林羅山
es 春齋（鵞峯）
et 鳳岡
eu 春信
ev 木下順庵
ew 羅欽順
ex 貝原益軒
ey 伊藤誠修

ez 工
fa 武士道
fb 陳亮
fc 理學
fd 晦庵
fe 陳同甫
ff 異端
fg 學
fh 知
fi 實
fj 實學と虛學
fk 源了圓
fl 格物
fm 致知
fn 學問
fo 實行
fp 顏回
fq 踐履
fr 君子
fs 明朱徵君集
ft 五十川剛伯
fu 朱舜水先生文集
fv 朱舜水全集
fw 稻葉岩吉
fx 舜水遺書
fy 湯壽潛
fz 馬浮
ga 山本武夫
gb 朱舜水文集の成立をめぐって
gc 古紀錄の研究
gd 高橋隆三先生喜壽紀念論集
　　刊行會
ge 邵廷采
gf 明遺民所知傳
gg 思復堂文集
gh 翁洲老民
gi 海東逸史
gj 溫睿臨
gk 南疆佚史
gl 趙爾巽
gm 清史稿

gn 閔爾昌
go 碑傳集補
gp 朱舜水先生年譜
gq 飲冰室合集、專集
gr 石原道博
gs 康南海文集
gt 朱舜水と康南海
gu 歷史教育
gv 高須芳次郎
gw 水戸学大系
gx 水戸義公烈公集
gy 明儒學案
gz 談遷
ha 國権
hb 計六奇
hc 明季南略
hd 徐鼐
he 小腆紀年附考
hf 日本乞師記
hg 梨洲遺著彙刊
hh 黃梨洲朱舜水乞師日本弁
hi 東方雜誌
hj 四明山寨記
hk 舟山興廢
hl 陳荊和
hm 清初華舶之長崎貿易及日南航運
hn 南洋學報
ho 安南供役紀事
hp 欽定越史通鑑綱目
hq 大汕
hr 海外紀事
hs 十七世紀廣南之新史料
ht 岩村成允
hu 安南通史
hv 柔術
hw 辻善之助
hx 海外交通史話
hy 明代中國人の日本觀
hz 吉田一德
ia 大日本史紀傳志表撰者考

ib 飯田須賀斯
ic 江戸時代の孔子廟建築
id 福島甲子三
ie 近世日本の儒学
if 鈴木三八男
ig 朱舜水の携え來っ太孔子像について
ih 斯文
ii 小石川區史
ij 岳陽樓記
ik 范文正公文集
il 日本的朱子學
im 日本朱子學派の哲學
in 朱舜水の古學思想と我が古學派上の關係
io 東京支那學報
ip 明末清初に於ける經世致用の学
iq 東方学會集
ir 藪內清
is 天工開物研究論文集
it 章熊
iu 吳傑
iv 杉本勳
iw 近世實學史の研究
ix 名越時正
iy 水戸學の道統
iz 後藤新平
ja 梁容若
jb 朱舜水與日本文化
jc 大陸雜誌
jd 辻善之助
je 日本文化史
jf 書劍堂說
jg 奥村庸禮
jh 後藤陽一
ji 日本思想大系
jj 吉川幸次郎
jk 田原嗣郎
jl 徂徠集
jm 德川思想小史

Okada Takehiko

Practical Learning in the Chu Hsi School: Yamazaki Ansai and Kaibara Ekken

PRACTICAL LEARNING AND EMPTY LEARNING

Shih-hsüeh or *jitsugaku* [a] was the expression used by Sung philosophers in order to convey the distinctive character of their thought in contrast both to the textual exegesis and commentary of the Han and T'ang scholars and to the negativism and quietism of the Buddhists and Taoists. For them it was the pursuit of the Way which actually served a purpose in the common life of mankind. In other words, it was learning that was useful and practical. It goes without saying that, as a Confucian philosophy, this teaching was primarily ethical, but the Sung scholars who developed Neo-Confucianism stressed its practicality as an antidote to heterodoxy and heresy. Ch'eng I (1033–1107) said, "The study of the Confucian classics is itself practical learning (*shih-hsüeh*)."[1] He used the *Mean* as evidence for the fact that the study of the Confucian classics was not vain and useless like Han and T'ang exegetics or the "emptiness" of Buddhism and the "nothingness" of Taoism. At the beginning of his *Chung-yung chang-chü* [b] (Commentary on the Words and Phrases of the *Mean*), Chu Hsi (1130–1200) quoted the words of Ch'eng I, explaining that the *Mean* was a book on practical learning which explicated the profound meaning of the truth of "clarifying the essence and effectively applying it" (*ming-t'i shih-yung*).[c] Chu Hsi's contemporary, Lu Hsiang-

231

shan (1139–1193), also used the term *shih-hsüeh* and emphasized the
necessity of practical application in discussing substance and function,
knowledge and action and the active pursuit of learning.[2] *Shih-hsüeh* was
a very popular phrase at that time, and many contemporaries of Chu Hsi
used this term in discussing the importance of the practical application of
learning.

The meaning of *shih* and *hsü* differed from school to school, and in a
sense the distinctions among schools arose from the difference in their
views on *shih-hsüeh*. From the standpoint of Chu Hsi's School of Principle, Lu Hsiang-shan's School of Mind came close to the "empty" learning *(hsü-hsüeh)*[d] of Buddhism and Taoism. From the standpoint of Lu
Hsiang-shan's School of Mind, Chu Hsi's School of Principle came close
to the "empty" learning of Han and T'ang classical exegesis. From the
standpoint of the evidential research of the Han Learning *(Han-hsüeh)*[e] of
the Ch'ing period, which sought factual accuracy, both the Sung and
Ming Schools of Principle and Mind came close to the "empty" learning
of Buddhism and Taoism. For the Confucians who embraced the Sung
and Ming Schools of Principle and Mind, the evidential research of the
scholars of Han Learning was of no practical use to society and consequently it was "empty" learning.[3] A similar situation existed among the
different schools of Confucianism in the Tokugawa period, i.e., among
the Chu Hsi school,[f] the Wang Yang-ming school,[g] the Ancient Learning school *(Kogaku)*,[h] and the Ancient Textual Studies school *(Kobunjigaku)*.[i] In the early Meiji period, Fukuzawa Yukichi[j] (1835–1901) defined *jitsugaku* in terms of Western scientific and industrial technologies
that had a direct impact on the daily lives of men. For him, *jitsugaku*
was different from and independent of Confucianism. In his view, Confucianism was "empty" learning. With Fukuzawa, the "practical" or
"real" learning advocated by the Sung Confucians was completely different in its nature. The "practical learning" of Fukuzawa's definition
came to be commonly accepted by modern Japanese. Since then Japanese historians have regarded *jitsugaku* as a study of Western scientific
and industrial technologies that was totally separate from ethics and the
philosophy of life.

Since the beginning of the Tokugawa period, however, Confucians
had also been interested, in varying degrees, in *jitsugaku* as the study of
scientific and industrial technologies. In this chapter, "practical learning"
is used in this inclusive sense. The practical learning of Yamazaki Ansai
was not an exception.

Chu Hsi, having rejected Buddhism and Taoism, brought the School of Principle to its highest point of development by synthesizing the Confucian thought of the Northern Sung. He constructed a comprehensive philosophical system that included the study of ethics, society, and natural science based on a Confucian world view. Moral philosophy was his primary concern, as may be clearly discerned in his doctrine of "total substance and great functioning" (ch'üan-t'i ta-yung).[k] But his interests extended to the natural sciences and technology, which were not, to him, separate from and independent of ethics, but bound up integrally with them. Chu Hsi believed that Confucianism was "practical learning" because it comprised not only moral philosophy but the natural sciences and technology as well.

There were three schools of Chu Hsi tradition in the early Tokugawa period: the school of the Hayashi family,[1] the Bokumon[m] school led by Kinoshita Jun'an[n] (1621–1699), and the Kimon[o] school founded by Yamazaki Ansai[p] (1611–1682). Of the three, the school that flourished most was the Kimon. The Sentetsu sōdan[q] (Biographies of Leading Philosophers) states that more than six thousand students were enrolled in the school.[4] This school excelled in its adherence to and practice of Chu Hsi's teaching. Indeed, the members of this school followed the Master's teaching with religious dedication and enthusiasm. They transmitted the tradition of the school without a break, passing it on in much the same spirit as the Buddhists' "transmission of the lamp." Altogether there are about one hundred and eighty scholars listed in the legitimate succession of this school in the Nihon Dōgaku engen roku[r] (Origin of Japanese Neo-Confucianism) by Ōtsuka Kanran[s] (1761–1825), the Nihon Dōgaku engen zokuroku[t] (Sequel to the Origin of Japanese Neo-Confucianism) by Senju Kyokuzan[u] (1785–1859), and the Nihon Dōgaku engen zokuroku zōho[v] (Supplement to the Sequel to the Origin of Japanese Neo-Confucianism) by Kusumoto Sekisui[w] (1832–1916). The popularity of this school is well attested by these books.

Translated by Hiroshi Miyaji

YAMAZAKI ANSAI: PRACTICAL LEARNING AS PERSONAL EXPERIENCE OF TRUTH

By Ansai's time the Tokugawa government had firmly established itself. Industrial and technological studies had developed rapidly in response to the needs of the time, and a number of famous *jitsugaku* scholars such as Kaibara Ekken[x] (1630–1714) had emerged. Yasui Shunkai[y] (or Shibukawa Shunkai,[z] 1639–1715), the creator of his own celestial globe based on Chinese principles and an expert on the calendar, was a student of Yamazaki Ansai. Ansai was impressed with the *Yamato shichiyō reki*[aa] (Seven-day Calendar of Japan), a work written by Yasui, and said that he learned something from this book which had been unknown to Chu Hsi.[5] Ansai's interest in calendrical studies is also shown in his *Bunkai hitsuroku*[ab] (Reading Notes),[6] which contains passages from Chang Kuo's[ac] *Hsing-tsung*[ad] (The Company of the Stars, A.D. 732), Kuo Shou-ching's[ae] *Shou-shih li*[af](Shou-shih Calendar, 1281), Huang Ting's[ag] *T'ien-wen ta-ch'eng kuan-k'uei chi-yao*[ah] (Essentials of Observations of Celestial Bodies through the Sighting Tube), Wang Hsi-shan's[ai] (1628–1682) *Ta-t'ung-li hsi-li ch'i-meng,*[aj] and Ch'iu Chün's[ak] (1420–1495) *Ta-hsüeh yen-i pu*[al] (Supplement to the *Great Learning, Elaborated*). Ansai wrote the *Honchō kaigen kō*[am] (On the Change of Period Names in Japan) and the *Koshinkō.*[an] He contributed prefaces to the *Gyō reki*[ao] (Yao Calendar) by Lord Inoue Masatoshi[ap] and the *Azuma kagami rekisan kaiho*[aq] (Revision of Dating in the *Azuma kagami*) by Andō Yūeki[ar] (1624–1708), who was an expert on mathematics in Aizu. Ansai wrote the *Yamato kagami,*[as] in which he attempted to investigate on the basis of sources other than the dynastic histories, data on the zodiac, lunar intercalation, and solar and lunar eclipses.[7] He was also interested in mathematics and read the *Chou pei suan-ching*[at] (Arithmetical Classic of the Gnomon and the Circular Paths of Heaven) with its commentary by Li Ch'un-feng.[au] Ansai edited and published the *Shueki engi*[av] and the *Kōhan zenshū,*[aw] which reflect some competence of his own in mathematics. He is said to have edited the *Aizu fudoki*[ax] (Topography of Aizu), published by Hoshina Masayuki,[ay] which shows that he was not without some interest in topography. At that time there were Confucian scholars conversant with medical science called "Confucian physicians" (*jui*).[az] Ansai too seems to have shared this interest. He read the *Huang-ti nei-ching su-wen*[ba] (Yellow Emperor's Classic of Internal Medicine) and the *Ku-chin i-t'ung*[bb] and other books on medicine and discussed the dating of the *Huang-ti nei-ching su-wen.*

Ansai revered Chu Hsi and had little use for the views of Yüan and Ming Confucians. Nevertheless, he familiarized himself with the views of later Neo-Confucians such as Huang Kan[bc] (1152–1221), Ts'ai Yüan-ting[bd] (1135–1198) and his son, Ts'ai Shen[be] (1167–1230), and Chen Te-hsiu[bf] (1178–1235); the Ming scholars, Ch'iu Chün, Hsüeh Hsüan[bg] (1389–1464), and Hu Chü-jen[bh] (1434–1484); and the Korean Neo-Confucian, Yi T'oegye[bi] (1501–1570). Among these scholars, Huang Kan, Ts'ai Yüan-ting, Ts'ai Shen, and Ch'iu Chün had inherited and expanded Chu Hsi's doctrine of "total substance and great functioning." Huang Kan wrote the sequel to the *I-li ching-ch'uan t'ung-chieh*[bj] and Ts'ai Shen succeeded his father, Ts'ai Yüan-ting, an expert on the pitch-pipes and numerology,[bk] and published the *Huang-chi nei-p'ien*,[bl] with which he further developed the mathematical theories of Shao Yung[bm] (1011–1077). Chen Te-hsiu published the *Ta-hsüeh yen-i*[bn] (The *Great Learning*, Elaborated) and discussed "total substance and great functioning." Ch'iu Chün wrote the *Ta-hsüeh yen-i pu* and fostered practical learning by asserting the importance of the study of the principles of external things (*wu-li*)[bo] along with the study of the principles of human nature (*hsing-li*).[bp][8]

It was natural that Ansai, familiar as he was with the views of these scholars, should have become interested in the study of Chu Hsi's "total substance and great functioning." Furthermore, it was reasonable that Ansai should also have attached importance to Chu Hsi's grain storage system (*she-ts'ang fa*),[bq] the best exemplification of Chu Hsi's idea of "total substance and great functioning." During the Heian period, the famine relief measures of the "ever-normal granaries" of the Han dynasty and the "relief granaries" (*i-ts'ang*)[br] of the Sui and T'ang dynasties had been formally adopted in Japan, but they had subsequently been abandoned. During the Tokugawa period, Chu Hsi's grain storage system was put into effect. Ansai was the first scholar to introduce this system with his publication of the *Chu Tzu she-ts'ang fa*.[bs] This book contributed greatly to the famine relief activities of various fiefdoms. It begins with Chu Hsi's writings concerning the grain storage system as recorded in the *Tzu-chih t'ung-chien kang-mu*[bt] and then quotes Chu Hsi's history of famine relief in the districts of Ch'ung-an, Chin-hua, Chien-yang, Kuang-tse, I-hsing, Nan-ch'eng, and P'u-ch'eng. The book ends with Ansai's comments.[9]

Ansai's works deal either with Confucianism or Shinto. His major works have been published in the *Yamazaki Ansai zenshū*[bu] (Complete Works of Yamazaki Ansai, two volumes) and the *Zoku Yamazaki Ansai zenshū*[bv] (Sequel to the Complete Works of Yamazaki Ansai, three volumes).[10] The works on Confucianism that are not included in these collections are brief anthologies of Chou Tun-i (*Shū sho shōryaku*),[bw] Chang Tsai (*Chō sho shōryaku*),[bx] the Ch'eng brothers (*Tei sho shōryaku*),[by] and Chu Hsi (*Shu sho shōryaku*).[bz] Among the works attributed to Ansai, some are of dubious authenticity, and some are definitely spurious writings. The most important work of Ansai is the *Bunkai hitsuroku* (Reading Notes, 20 books). Chu Hsi said, "Read the *Chin-ssu lu*[ca] (Reflections on Things at Hand) carefully. The Four Books are the best introduction to the Six Classics. The *Chin-ssu lu* is the best introduction to the Four Books."[11] Ansai's *Bunkai hitsuroku* may in turn be the best introduction to Chu Hsi's thought.

When one reads the *Bunkai hitsuroku* one recognizes that Ansai had a thorough, deep and precise knowledge of Chu Hsi's philosophy. It was not without reason that Ansai's followers considered him superior to anyone who came after Chu Hsi and that his school attracted far more students than any of the other schools of Confucianism in Japan. Inaba Mokusai[cb] (1732–1799) of the Kimon school wrote:

Bunkai hitsuroku appears exceedingly broad and diffuse in its contents. Actually, it is highly condensed and reduced to the very essentials. Those who read the works of Chu Hsi without being guided by this book will fail to reach real comprehension of the essence of Chu Hsi's thought and to understand its principles. The book is exceedingly precise in its handling of factual matters, but, more than this, it helps one to read between the lines and get at the hidden meaning.[12]

Bunkai hitsuroku represents Ansai's compilation of materials related to Chu Hsi's philosophy, his school and other source materials related to the Chu Hsi school. It also includes Ansai's brief critical comments and interpretations. The book reveals Ansai's outstanding scholarly qualities. It is evidence of Ansai's endeavor to make known to the world the value of Chu Hsi's thought by a systematic and accurate presentation of essential materials assembled and arranged through thorough research. Ansai revered Chu Hsi's thought with a passionate religious devotion, but this does not mean that he blindly believed in it. He became convinced of its worth only after clarifying for himself the truth of Chu Hsi's views by means of logical and empirical methods. The nature and quality of his method are immediately noticeable in the *Bunkai hitsuroku*. For example, in the book he identifies those points in the *Chu Tzu wen-chi*[cc] (Collection of Literary Works by Chu Hsi) and the *Chu Tzu yü-lei*[cd] (Classified Conversations of Chu Hsi) on which Chu Hsi had not yet reached definitive conclusions. He also identifies spurious records and typographical errors and clarifies the meaning of colloquial expressions used in the *Chu Tzu yü-lei*.

As we can conjecture from Ansai's statement that, "Chu Hsi's commentaries [on the Four Books] can hardly be improved upon," he assigned the highest value to these among Chu Hsi's works. This was because Ansai considered the *Ssu-shu chang-chü chi-chu*[ce] (Collected Commentaries on the Words and Phrases of the Four Books) to be essential for the clear understanding of Chu Hsi's commentaries on the Five Classics and his other views, stated in different connections, which are found in the *Chu Tzu wen-chi* and *Chu Tzu yü-lei*.[13] Ansai carefully examined the opinions of various Yüan and Ming scholars on Chu Hsi's commentaries and found them wanting. Their interpretations would lead to a misunderstanding of Chu Hsi's thought and one would be worse off than with Chu Hsi's commentaries alone. However, some scholars of Chu Hsi in later periods have been critical of Ansai's attitude. For example, Namiki Rissui[cf] (1829–1914) said that Ansai was often careless because he ignored the views of later and lesser Confucians.[14]

Among the scholars of the Chu Hsi school, Ansai respected Huang Kan and Ts'ai Yüan-ting, but he was critical of Ch'en Ch'un[cg] (1159–1223). This fact is important for the understanding of Ansai's thought. The *Pei-hsi hsien-sheng tzu-i hsiang-chiang*[ch] written by Ch'en Ch'un was spoken of as the indispensable introduction to Chu Hsi's thought. In this book, Ch'en Ch'un clearly explained the basic concepts of Chu Hsi's philosophy. Further, Ch'en Ch'un distinguished himself by his refutation of the views held by the Lu school. Ansai, however, criticized Ch'en Ch'un's book saying, "This book is of no real interest," and even, "This book suffers from the defect of shallowness."[15] It was natural that Ansai, who emphasized the importance of a thoroughgoing personal experience of truth and the constant cultivation of it, should have been critical of Ch'en Ch'un. Ansai esteemed the views of Hsüeh Hsüan and Hu Chü-jen, Chu Hsi scholars of the early Ming period, because they emphasized maintaining and developing reverence or seriousness (*ching; kei*).[ci] It seems, however, that Ansai was not entirely satisfied with their views either. According to the *Yamazaki sensei goroku*[cj] (Recorded Sayings of Master Yamazaki Ansai), an unpublished manuscript, Ansai stated that, for those who were pursuing the study of principle (*ri*)[ck] a reading of the *Tu-shu lu*[cl] (Record of My Reading) by Hsüeh Hsüan would serve no useful purpose. About the *Chü-yeh lu*[cm] (Record of Occupying One's Sphere of Activity), by Hu Chü-jen, Ansai said:

The teaching of Hu Chü-jen does not depart from the truth. But his knowledge is not as broad as Ch'iu Chün's, and his vision does not extend as far as Hsüeh

Hsüan's. Often both the thought of the *Chü-yeh lu* and its manner of expression are somewhat overdone.[16]

As for Ch'iu Chün, Ansai was willing to recognize his extensive knowledge and scholarship in practical learning as "the study of the principles of things" (*wu-li chih hsüeh; butsuri no gaku*).[cn] But in the clear understanding of the nature of mind, Ch'iu did not reach the level of Hsüeh Hsüan. Ansai is said to have been dissatisfied with Ch'iu's *Ch'iung-t'ai hui-kao.*[co][17]

The scholar of Chu Hsi's philosophy whom Ansai most respected was Yi T'oegye. Ansai declared that T'oegye truly understood the meaning of Chu Hsi's extension of knowledge through the investigation of things.[18] He recommended T'oegye's *Chujasŏ chŏryo*[cp] (Essentials of Chu Hsi's Writings) and said: "T'oegye's finest efforts are all contained in this book."[19] Ansai's understanding of the basic significance of the books edited and compiled by Chu Hsi is probably attributable to T'oegye. Ansai was the first person to have introduced T'oegye to Japan, and the scholars of his school carried on the study of T'oegye's writings thereafter. Ansai was, however, quite objective in his evaluation of T'oegye's views and did not hesitate to say when he thought them in error.

In order to understand the characteristics of Ansai's thought, we must pay close attention to the special character of his publications. The majority of these are compilations and publications of Chu Hsi's own works, so that we learn Ansai's views mostly through his prefaces and postscripts to these books. These publications can be classified as follows: 1) the publication of his edition of the original works of Chu Hsi; 2) the restoration of Chu Hsi's missing works and the compilation of selected passages in order to elucidate Chu Hsi's view on particular issues; 3) the publication of anthologies of quotations from Chou Tun-i, Chang Tsai, the Ch'eng brothers and Chu Hsi; 4) the publication of Chu Hsi's important sayings, poems, and essays.

In his labors to republish Chu Hsi's books, Ansai selected those writings that, in his judgment, represented the essence of Chu Hsi's thought from the *Chu Tzu wen-chi* and the *Chu Tzu yü-lei*. Ansai occasionally wrote in his own brief comments, but the majority of his publications followed the format of first introducing the views of Chu Hsi himself and then supplementing them with the best interpretations of these views offered by later scholars, for further clarification. This was, according to Hayashi

Jo,[eq] (Hayashi Gahō, 1618–1680), "Letting the words of Chu Hsi speak for themselves."[20] There is probably no better way to approach Chu Hsi's thought. Hayashi Jo pointed out that, though Ch'en Ch'un claimed that the interpretations in his *Pei-hsi hsien-sheng tzu-i hsiang-chiang* of the basic concepts of Chu Hsi's philosophy derived from Chu Hsi's views themselves, he sometimes failed to keep from intruding his own opinions.[21] Ansai's publications are free from this shortcoming. Ansai called Chu Hsi back to this world and had him lecture directly to his readers. In this way, Ansai succeeded in accomplishing the task of resurrecting Chu Hsi's thought and bringing it back to life.

For Ansai, any disagreement with Chu Hsi's views indicated a lack of real understanding of Chu's views. Kume Teisai[cr] (1699–1784), of the Kimon school, once stated that when Yüan and Ming scholars dissented from Chu Hsi's views, it was because they failed to comprehend them.[22] If Ansai's publications reveal his profound understanding of the spirit of Chu Hsi's thought, it is because he truly possessed extraordinary insight into Chu Hsi's mind. Ansai revered Chu Hsi with religious devotion, saying, "Our teacher is the only philosopher since Confucius."[23] For Ansai to differ from Chu Hsi's teaching was like committing "a crime of willful irrationality."[24] For him, Chu Hsi was the leading successor to Confucius, who synthesized the Way of the Sages and compiled the classics.[25] Confucius said of himself in regard to the teachings of the sages that he was "a transmitter and not a creator, believing in and loving the ancients."[26] This was Ansai's attitude toward Chu Hsi. He said:

I think the basic doctrine of Chu Hsi is "abiding in reverence and plumbing principle" (*chü-ching ch'iung-li*).[cs] Chu Hsi propagated the Confucian teachings and never differed from them. If I am wrong in studying Chu Hsi's thought, both he and I would be in error together. What should I have to regret? This is the reason why I believe in Chu Hsi and propagate his thought and do not create my own.[27]

Ansai was different from other teachers of Confucianism. He warned his students against taking pride in formulating their own views. In the *Yamazaki sensei goroku* we find the following passage:

Our teacher, when he met someone who was inclined to express original views, would ask, "In which book did you find such an interesting view?" When one answered that he had conceived the idea on his own, our teacher would say, "Don't be proud of your originality. The books written by the Sages never left anything out, though you might think it is your own original idea."

"A transmitter and not a creator," was the basic rule of the Kimon school. Asami Keisai[ct] (1652–1711) adhered to this rule and stated: "My study is no more than succeeding to Mr. Kaemon [Ansai] and trying not to lose the teachings that he left for us."[28]

According to Ansai's own account, he first read the Four Books when he was quite young. Then while still in his youth he became a Buddhist monk. Around the age of twenty-two or twenty-three he followed the teaching of the Ch'an master K'ung-ku Ching-lung[cu] (1392–1443+) and accepted the theory of the unity of the Three Teachings. At the age of twenty-five, however, he read Chu Hsi's books for the first time, and becoming convinced of the wrongness of Buddhism, he converted to Confucianism. At about the age of thirty, while deploring his own slow progress in learning, he wrote the Heki i[cv] (Refutation of Heresies) out of concern over the way people were deluded by heresies.[29] Against those contemporaries who insisted that one could not discern the fallacies of Buddhism unless one had studied and practiced it, he proclaimed:

The Way is the three fundamental principles in human relations and the five cardinal virtues. Since the Buddha abandoned these, his teaching cannot be the Way. This is obvious without even studying his teaching.[30]

Ansai, like other scholars, distinguished between Confucianism and Buddhism on the basis of their affirmation or negation of moral principles, and he accused the Buddha of renouncing these principles.[31] He attacked Ta-hui Tsung-kao[cw] (1089–1163), the greatest monk of the Lin-chi[cx] sect of the Sung dynasty, and called him "an offender against morality."[32]

The difference between Confucianism and Buddhism lies in how the substance of the Way is conceived. The error of Buddhism lies in its method of nurturing and developing the mind. It is not that Buddhism lacks an approach to human affairs.[33]

Neither Chu Hsi nor Ansai established the distinction between Confucianism and Buddhism merely on the basis of whether they had a concern for practical affairs. From the biography of Kuei-shan Ling-yu[cy] (771–853) in the Ching-te ch'uan-teng lu[cz] (Record of the Transmission of the Lamp), Chu Hsi quoted the passage, "The followers of Buddhism do not ignore even a single matter," and said that even Buddhism dealt with human affairs. Therefore, Buddhists would not be convinced of the superiority of Confucianism by the argument that it possessed a way of dealing with human affairs whereas Buddhism did not.[34] For Ansai, the ground for the rejection of Buddhism was its lack of a clear affirmation of the immutability of moral principles, that is, of there being fixed principles. It goes without saying that Ansai emphasized the sincere personal experience and self-realization (*t'i-jen, tzu-te; tainin, jitoku*)[da] of these moral principles.

Chuang Tzu had defined a child's love of his parents as "destiny" and a subject's service of his ruler as "duty."[35] But Ansai was unhappy with this formulation and preferred Master Ch'eng's view of love and duty as fixed principles.[36] These were, of course, the principles of reality. The Ch'eng-Chu school applied the criterion of the reality of principle to distinguish authentic Confucianism from heterodoxy. Ansai criticized the Buddhist concept of the mind as vacuous spirituality (*hsü-ling*),[db] Lieh Tzu's reference to the mind as "a place of an inch square" (*fang-ts'un*),[dc] and Chuang Tzu's image of the mind as a "spirit tower" (*ling-t'ai*).[dd] He said that these people did not realize that the mind contained all principles. He refuted heterodoxy by quoting the words of Chu Hsi, "Ch'an Buddhists take an empty and mysterious mind as the nature and do not refer to the mind's possession of principles."[37] Despite this, according to Ansai, Confucians are often dazzled by Buddhism because their own learning is limited to the memorization and recitation of a vast number of dicta of the sages, and though they can read passages and explicate the Way, their main interest is in literary style or philological research.[38]

Ansai also severely criticized those Confucians who were only nominally Confucian and covertly Buddhist. Thus he criticized Chang Chiu-ch'eng[de] (1092–1159) and the Lu school, and discussions of differences and similarities between Chu and Lu on the part of Wu Ch'eng[df] (1249–1333), Chao Fang[dg] (1319–1369), Ch'eng Min-cheng[dh] (1445–1499+), and Wang Yang-ming[di] (1472–1529). Ch'en Chien[dj] (1497–1567), of the late Ming, in his *Hsüeh-pu t'ung-pien*[dk] (General Critique of Obscurations of Learning) and Feng K'o,[dl] in his *Ch'iu-shih pien*[dm] (Search for the Right), had sharply attacked the views of the Lu school and rejected the comparison between Lu Hsiang-shan and Chu Hsi. Ansai, however, was dissatisfied with their arguments, asserting that, "They have not yet reached the innermost chamber of Chu Hsi's philosophy. [Their attempt is like trying] to extinguish a fire on Mt. K'un with one scoop of water."[39] For Ansai, none of these excelled Chu Hsi's own refutation of Lu Hsiang-shan, and consequently he compiled Chu Hsi's criticisms of Lu and published the *Taika shōryōshū*[dn] (Collection of Chu Hsi's Considered Judgments).

The leading Confucian of the Yüan dynasty, Wu Ch'eng, held to a Chu-Lu eclecticism. Ansai pointed out that past scholars had already established that Wu Ch'eng was a follower of Lu's philosophy and said, "You cannot trust the man simply on the basis of what he said."[40] Ansai called Fujiwara Seika[do] (1561–1619) a follower of Wu Ch'eng because, despite Seika's paying homage to Chu Hsi as his teacher, in many points he followed Lu.[41]

Ansai made an extremely fierce attack on the Lu school. He insisted that the refutation of Lu's philosophy be made on common ground, as a public issue and not as a partisan matter of one school versus another. Moreover, he cautioned his students that unless one held a positive hatred for evil and an active contempt for Lu's philosophy, one could easily be seduced by Lu's theory of the unity of Confucianism, Buddhism, and Taoism.[42] The utimate motive of Ansai's attack against Lu was his adherence to Chu Hsi's doctrine of personal experience and self-realization. He did not, however, publish his own refutation. Instead, he compiled the *Taika shōryōshū* and made Chu Hsi's position public. Asami Keisai recorded Ansai's own explanation in his *Taika shōryōshū kōgi*[dp] (Exposition of the Collection of Chu Hsi's Considered Judgments) and said:

Lu Hsiang-shan was a contemporary of Chu Hsi. Chu Hsi's disproof of Lu is distinctly expressed in his writings. Chu Hsi's direct retort against Lu in the *Chu Tzu wen-chi* and the *Chu Tzu yü-lei* is so clear that there is no need for further discussion. Now you understand why I compiled Chu Hsi's direct references to Lu in the *Wen-chi* and the *Yü-lei* and compiled a two-volume book.[43]

As has already been observed, the basic criticism of Buddhism made by the Ch'eng-Chu school was that it abandoned the moral constants bound up in key human relationships. Thus Ansai stressed a clear understanding of these moral constants as the essence of Confucian orthodoxy and the only guarantee against a lapse into heterodoxy, stating, "There has never been anyone who, lacking a firm grasp of the Way of the Constant Relations, was not susceptible to Buddhism."[44]

The most important expression of the moral nature of man is the Five Relations. Chu Hsi emphasized the necessity of manifesting these principles among the first of the school regulations listed in his Precepts of the White Deer Grotto Academy (*Po-lu-tung shu-yüan chieh-shih*).[dq] Ansai extracted these standards from the *Chu Tzu wen-chi* and published them with his own commentary. For Ansai, too, these moral relations were the basis of education, and self-respect (*keishin*)[dr] was the basis of moral relations.[45] Ansai feared lest talk of "manifesting moral relations" should become mere empty verbiage. Instead he sought for a concrete method by which to put it into practice. It is difficult to know in detail how Ansai conceived of what was essential to its practice, but we may be able to reconstruct Ansai's view from the discussion included in Asami Keisai's *Hakurokudō-shoin keiji kōgi*[ds] (Exposition of the Precepts of the White Deer Grotto Academy).

The Precepts of Chu Hsi begin with the lines:

Between father and son, there is intimacy;
Between lord and vassal, there is duty;
Between husband and wife, there is differentiation;
Between elder and younger, there is precedence;
Between friends, there is trust.

Asami Keisai interprets "there is" in each line as follows: "The meaning of 'there is' here is that one carries out in action what one possesses at birth." According to Keisai, the Five Relations are what men are "naturally born with" and are "the innate Way."[46] Thus he says, "The goal of learning is nothing strange or novel,"[47] and the Ch'eng-Chu doctrine of abiding in reverence or seriousness does not represent an empty method of mind cultivation such as mere concentration or one-pointedness. It is putting into common and daily practice the ordinary rules of human relationship. Chu Hsi's "plumbing of principle" (*ch'iung-li*), Keisai explains, is not an abstract theory but an inquiry into the nature of human morality as real principles applicable to daily life.[48]

Morality is a priori; consequently, the manifestation of moral principles must be an autonomous act. This was the reason Chu Hsi employed the word "precepts" instead of "school regulations." Keisai explained Chu Hsi's intention. He criticized Fang Hsiao-ju[dt] (1357–1402) and Ch'iu Chün for their use of the term "school regulations" (*hsüeh-kuei*)[du] and said that "precepts"[dv] was preferable because school regulations could not really guide the mind to righteousness, and one could only state the intentions to which one was asked to subscribe.[49] Keisai faithfully conveyed Ansai's thought.

Ansai placed great value on the sense of duty between lord and vassal and strictly upheld this principle. From his youth, Ansai posted the Precepts in his study and contemplated them, seeking to penetrate their meaning.[50] The Precepts contain the following words of Tung Chung-shu[dw] (179?–104? B.C.):

Not to seek out selfish gain, but to rectify one's sense of duty; Not to cherish thoughts of personal achievement, but to magnify the Way.

In the Sung and Ming the School of Principle often cited these words and urged the importance of a clear distinction between duty and personal gain. Ansai followed them and stressed the same distinction. Chu Hsi asserted humaneness as the primary principle among the five virtues and elucidated its essence in the *Jen-shuo*[dx][51] (Treatise on Humaneness) and the *Yü-shan chiang-i* [dy][52] (Lecture at Yü-shan). Ansai selected these two works from the *Chu Tzu wen-chi* and published them.

To do this was only natural in one who so devotedly served Chu Hsi's teaching in all respects. Nevertheless, in his own teaching Ansai placed more emphasis on duty than on humaneness. Thus, the emphasis on duty became a tradition of the Kimon school and its scholars were different from those of other schools in the stern rigidity with which they held to one's course of action and the strictness in fulfilling one's duty. Ansai must have known well that for Chu Hsi humaneness was the highest virtue. Why did he emphasize duty so much more strongly? Humaneness and duty are alike in being virtues of the nature endowed by Heaven, but they differ in the relative ease or difficulty of their cultivation. It can be easily understood that humaneness and love between father and son are natural human sentiments. But it requires some intellectual effort to comprehend that duty between ruler and subject is also based on natural human sentiments. It is extremely difficult to attain true humaneness, but in the case of duty there is a direct method for its exercise, and, through employing this method, one may come to an understanding of the genuine and profound meaning of humaneness. Thus, fulfillment of specific duties may lead to the perfecting of humaneness. On this ground Ansai taught the importance of duty. It was Asami Keisai who skillfully elucidated Ansai's idea. Keisai said:

Among the human relationships, those between lord and vassal and father and son are the most important to examine because they are the basis of humaneness and duty.[53]

Since father and son are of the same flesh and blood, they somehow feel close. But ruler and subject are originally unrelated. The principle of duty, therefore, is only established in natural feeling by way of reasoning. This is why this principle has often been subject to destruction from of old. For to establish it on a rational basis alone does not suffice for its full realization.[54]

Keisai further argued that the love of a son toward his father and the love of a vassal toward his lord are essentially the same because love here is not selfish love but the ultimate sentiment of which human nature is capable.[55] It is important to recognize that Keisai found the real meaning of duty here to lie in the heart and mind rather than in discursive reasoning. For it is in this that we can discern the true spirit of the *jitsugaku* of the Kimon school.

Ansai taught the duty between lord and vassal in order to stress the importance of fulfilling one's fixed obligations (*meibun*)[dz] in life. For this purpose he published the *Chü-yu ts'ao*[ea] of Han Yü[eb] (768–824), introducing it for the first time to the Japanese. His edition of it begins with the entire original text, followed by selections from the comments on it in the *Ch'eng Tzu i-shu*[ec] (Literary Remains of the Two Ch'engs) and the *Chu Tzu yü-lei*, and ending with a postscript by Ansai. Following its publication many scholars of the Kimon school discussed the *Chü-yu ts'ao*. Asami Keisai wrote a supplement to Ansai's edition and further elucidated its significance. Keisai's *Seiken igen*,[ed] which exerted a profound influence on loyalist thought at the end of the Tokugawa period, was inspired by Ansai's edition of the *Chü-yu ts'ao*. Satō Naokata[ee] (1650–1719), one of the most outstanding disciples of Ansai, also wrote a critique of the *Chü-yu ts'ao*. His arguments were cogent and, in some respects advanced the understanding of the work beyond that of Ansai and Keisai.[56]

From the *Chü-yu ts'ao*, Ansai learned of the supreme virtue of King Wen and the necessity for a dutiful relationship between a lord and vassal. He keenly felt the importance of fulfilling fixed moral obligations (*meibun*) when he became aware of the steadfast adherence to moral principles by Po-i, Shu-ch'i and T'ai-po. Consequently, Ansai became critical of the rebellions of Kings T'ang and Wu and of other rebellions in Chinese history, Ansai wrote the *Tō Bu kakumei ron*,[ef] in which he argued—reviewing different perspectives on Kings T'ang and Wu—that King Wen's submission to Yin when the mandate of Heaven was about to change was in accord with "the great norm of Heaven and earth,"

whereas the rebellions of T'ang and Wu were "great historical adaptations, bending to a change in the mandate of Heaven and responding to
the people." Thus Ansai expressed the difference between King Wen and
Kings T'ang and Wu through the terms "norm" (kei)[eg] and "adaptation"
(ken),[eh] concluding that T'ang and Wu "did not reach the highest
good."[57] Asami Keisai intensified Ansai's criticism of the rebellions of
T'ang and Wu. Satō Naokata, however, held a different view and was
rather critical of Keisai. For Naokata, although there is a difference between "norm" and "adaptation," as exemplified by the sense of duty
displayed by King Wen and that shown by T'ang and Wu, the Way is
one. Yao and Shun had not made the universe their private possession,
nor had T'ang and Wu, who merely responded to the will of Heaven and
the people.[58]

Ansai had attacked the view of earlier scholars who had praised the behavior of Yen Tzu-ling[ei] in stepping on the abdomen of Emperor
Kuang-wu. For Ansai, this action violated the great principle of duty to
one's lord. Ansai also criticized Hsü Heng[ej] (1209–1281), a great Neo-
Confucian scholar who served the court of the barbarian Yüan dynasty.
These criticisms were the natural reflection of Ansai's high sense of moral
obligation. Ansai said that "not to live under the same sky with the
enemy of one's master" is a universal and constant duty for all, regardless
of social status. Yet Yen Tzu-ling, at the time of the rebellion of Wang
Mang (A.D. 9–23), was haughty and indifferent, and he failed to rise to
defend his dynasty in fulfillment of his duty. He also violated the proprie-
ties for a vassal when he later served Emperor Kuang-wu. These acts offended against the great principle of duty to one's lord.[59]

Ansai's view of the conduct of Hsü Heng is discernible in his book
Rozaikō[ek] in two chapters. The first chapter is composed of Ch'iu
Chün's criticism of Hsü Heng, and the second of an encomium by
Hsüeh Hsüan.[60] Ch'iu believed that Hsü's having served a foreign master
who had overthrown a native Chinese dynasty was in violation of the
canonical norm of the Spring and Autumn Annals, which distinguished
between native and foreign rule. Hsüeh believed that Hsü's service to the
court was in conformity with the Way of the Sages, that his teaching and
practice were faithful to the Ch'eng-Chu tradition and that they were
beneficial both in terms of secular needs and popular wishes. Though
Ansai did not in the Rozaikō express a preference for either view, his own
judgment would seem to be revealed in the fact that Ch'iu's criticism was
given precedence and in the fact that in the Bunkai hitsuroku Ch'iu's

argument earned Ansai's praise. Among Ansai's disciples, Satō Naokata and Miyake Shōsai[el] (1662–1741) accepted Ch'iu Chün's view and criticized Hsü Heng.[61]

Mere theoretical discussion of moral obligation has little to recommend it over rote learning. Hence, in contrast to other schools, the scholars of the Kimon school endeavored to achieve real mastery and to exemplify in practice the doctrine of moral obligation. The conduct of Kusumoto Sekisui of the Hirado han, the last great scholar of the Kimon, affords an illustration of the spirit of the school. For him to receive a stipend fief from his master was to receive it from the shogunate, in violation of the great principle of duty to one's sovereign. Sekisui returned his stipend to his master, proclaiming, "The basic meaning of loyalty is not to serve the military government." Sekisui, out of his sense of moral obligation, resumed his family name of Kusumoto, and discarded the family name of Sassa,[em] the vassal household into which he had been adopted.[62]

In Ansai, along with his dedication to Confucianism, we find a deep-rooted conviction about the Japanese polity.

Emperor T'ai-tsung of the Sung dynasty talked about the rebellion toward the end of the T'ang dynasty in China. This kind of turmoil was not limited to the end of the T'ang dynasty. It had been the same since the Ch'in and Han dynasties. If we infer from this and look further back into Chinese history, we find that, when Fu-hsi died, Shen-nung arose, when Shen-nung passed away, Huang-ti, Yao and Shun appeared, and T'ang and Wu responded to the change in the mandate of Heaven. In our country the Divine Edict on the eternity of the throne is indisputable throughout our history. People have never read nor heard of such a polity in any other written or oral tradition in the whole world.[63]

When this conviction was reinforced by Ansai's strong sense of moral obligation, he was led naturally toward nationalism. Duty between lord and vassal was interpreted as the bond between the emperor and the people. Ansai is said to have declared that if a Chinese force invaded Japan, led by Confucius as the commander and Mencius as the vice-commander, he would rise up in arms, fight against the enemy, and capture Confucius and Mencius. According to him, this was the way to repay his debt of gratitude to the nation and to fulfill the Way of Confucius and Mencius.[64]

Ansai's interest in Japanese tradition and his increasing devotion to Shinto was the natural course of this line of thought. It is well known that he formulated Suika Shinto[en] and called himself "Old Man Suika" (*Suika Ō*).[eo] Suika Shinto is an interpretation of Shinto according to the Confucian world view. Ansai said:

Since principle is one throughout the universe, despite the differences between Japan, the country of the east where the sun rises and divine men were born, and China, the country of the west where the sun sets and the sages were born, the two coexist in mysterious agreement. This is something wondrous that we must contemplate with awe.[65]

In this way, Ansai discussed the unity of Shinto and Confucianism. He claimed that the unity of Heaven and man, the Way of Confucianism, and the oneness of the *kami*[ep] and man, the Way of Shinto, originally represented the same principle. In due course, however, they became differentiated. Atobe Ryōken[eq] stated:

The words of the divine doctrine are easy and clear and have profound meaning. The oral transmission and divine words of Shinto are unfathomable and mysterious. The Shinto doctrine teaches many things that were never conceived by the Chinese sages. The Way of worshipping the *kami*, cultivating the self, and governing the people is explicit and self-evident without any help from Confucianism. Shinto is the only Way in the universe. Confucianism assists Shinto when its principles are consistent with Shinto. Our teacher [Ansai] fully stated this truth and left his teaching to posterity. There are those who assert that our teacher is wrong and mock him. They do not possess the spirit of true scholarship (*jitsugaku*) and it is no use trying to argue with them.[66]

Ryōken, however, stated that Ansai's teaching was such that, in his view, exclusive adherence to either teaching was wrong.[67] According to the *Kyōsai sensei zatsuwa hikki*[er] (Notes on Casual Talks by Master Kyōsai), by Wakabayashi Kyōsai[es] (1679–1732), Ansai proposed to accept intact unsophisticated ancient accounts of Shinto beliefs because Shinto would lose its basic meaning if one tried to rationalize the ancient accounts. Kyōsai reported that Ansai had said, "The essential thing is to use the language of children."[68] Ansai seems to have thought that only when a person read Shinto accounts with a simple and sincere mind would he achieve a mysterious resonance with the divine.

Ansai's Shinto views might be thought to turn away from the realities of Confucianism to something less substantial. Namiki Rissui declared that Ansai's teaching had been emptied of real substance once he started to preach Shinto.[69] It is understandable that all three of the great scholars of the Kimon—Asami Keisai, Satō Naokata, and Miyake Shōsai—

became highly critical of their teacher's involvement in Shinto, and not without some reason. At the same time, Ansai's involvement with Shinto can be seen as a natural outcome of the thoroughgoing manner in which he pursued the substance of Chu Hsi's teaching, which inevitably led him back to traditional Japanese thought itself. The religious intensity with which he had committed himself to Chu Hsi was already one manifestation of this.

In moral relations Ansai gave primary importance to duty, and in praxis he stressed reverence. As we can infer from his use of the alias Keigi,[et] "reverence and duty" (keigi) were the overriding concerns of his teaching. For him, the essentials of Confucian praxis could be summarized in the injunction of Ch'eng I to "hold fast to both reverence and duty" (ching-i chia-ch'ih; keigi kyōji)[eu] and in the phrase of the Wen-yen[ev] commentary to the k'un[ew] hexagram of the Book of Changes, "reverence and duty for inner and outer" (ching-i nei-wai).[ex] According to Ansai, reverence and duty constitute the Way which underlies and unites the teachings of the Analects, the Great Learning, and the Mean. The applications are limitless.

According to the Book of Changes, reverence and duty are the Way for both inner and outer dimensions of personal cultivation. Ansai, following Ch'eng I, taught the unity of inner and outer. He defined "inner" as self and "outer" as family, country and world. But some of Ansai's students defined "inner" as mind and "outer" as bodily self. Consequently, a dispute developed between Ansai and his disciples. Asami Keisai and Satō Naokata opposed most strongly their teacher's view. Each advanced his own view of it, Keisai in his Keigi naigai setsu[ey] (Theory of Reverence and Duty for Inner and Outer [Cultivation]) and Naokata in his Keigi naigai kō[ez] (Study of Reverence and Duty for Inner and Outer [Cultivation]).[70] This dispute resulted in the expulsion of the two from the school.

According to Ansai, the phrase in the Book of Changes, "to correct the inner life through reverence," (ching i chih nei)[fa] is the Way related to both mind and self, and it is the essential message of the Book of Changes. The views expressed in the Analects, Mencius, Great Learning and Mean are all based on this. The Ch'eng brothers and Chu Hsi also followed it.[71] Ch'eng and Chu, however, sometimes took this expression to represent the way of cultivating the mind and thus defined "inner" as mind. There was indeed much discussion of the nature of mind in the

Mean and the *Mencius*. Ansai argued, however, that this focusing on the mind came in response to certain special challenges at that time and should not be taken as typical of their overall view. If we fail to recognize this circumstance and assume that the Ch'eng brothers and Chu Hsi had defined "inner" as mind without ascertaining their true views, we fall into heterodoxy. [72]

Ansai thought that if "inner" were defined as mind, then one would rely upon the simple method of arousing and shocking the mind as the way of "preserving the mind." One would never exert one's effort in actual practice because he would be directly concerned only with mind and would neglect the whole self. For Ansai, this would be heretical. [73] In this view he followed Chu Hsi, who had said:

Nowadays when people discuss human nature, they only discuss principles and not affairs. They elucidate mind but not body. Their views sound quite lofty, but they are actually flighty and careless. They fall into the emptiness of Buddhism and Taoism. [74]

Ansai followed Chu Hsi's view and intended to adhere strictly to the substantiality (*jitsu*) of Confucianism against the emptiness (*kyo*) of Buddhism and Taoism.

Ansai defined learning as both knowledge and practice. In knowledge he emphasized true breadth, in contradistinction to being indiscriminate, and precision, in contradistinction to nit-picking. In practice he rejected ambiguity (*ni*)[fb] and superficiality (*haku*),[fc] while expounding singleness of purpose (*i*)[fd] and dedication (*toku*).[fe] He asserted that by advancing simultaneously in knowledge and practice one could make upward progress. For Ansai these were the teachings of Chu Hsi which distinguished him from vulgar Confucians and from Lu Hsiang-shan. [75]

Ansai, who earnestly sought the actual practice of learning, considered the preservation of one's mind and the nourishment of one's nature (*sonyō*)[ff] to be the consistent principle which integrates knowledge and practice. Ansai said that in the Han and T'ang there had been many who excelled in either knowledge or practice but who had failed to attain sagehood because they were ignorant of the means by which one could develop these together. [76] Ansai's principle of preservation of the mind and nourishment of the nature differed in no way from what the Ch'eng brothers and Chu Hsi referred to as reverence or seriousness. Reverence, according to Ansai, was "the method of cultivation of mind transmitted from the sages,"[77] and the Way revealed by the Six Classics, the *Analects*, the *Mencius*, the *Great Learning*, the *Mean*, and the *Hsiao-hsüeh* [fg] (Elementary Learning).[78] He asserted that both the investigation of principle and personal practice could only be realized on the basis of reverence.

If reverence were no more than a method of cultivating the mind to achieve enlightenment, it might lead one into the emptiness of Buddhism and Taoism. Ansai, therefore, advocated "self-respect" (*keishin*)[dr] and "self-cultivation" (*shūshin*).[fh] In one of his poems he wrote, "The Way exists in the illumination of moral bonds; it is grounded in self-respect."[79] He asserted that the basic teaching of the Four Books was self-cultivation,[80] and the eight items of the *Great Learning* were also based on self-cultivation. He emphasized that this was all quite plain and practical, not lofty and impractical (empty).[81] Even if one employs self-respect and self-cultivation as the means to nurture his mind, if his practice is superficial, he will only attain inferior knowledge and fail to reach superior attainment. Therefore, Ansai taught the nourishment of mind by quiet-sitting, as Chou Tun-i, the Ch'eng brothers, Lo Ts'ung-yen[fi] (1072–1135) and Li T'ung[fj] (1093–1163) had recommended. He regretted that some contemporary Confucians did not emphasize quiet-sitting and some even regarded it as an heretical method.[82] Of course, Ansai warned that if one did not grasp the true significance of quiet-sitting as Chu Hsi had done, one would fall into the heterodox "sitting in meditation" of Ch'an Buddhism.[83]

Within the Kimon school, Satō Naokata and his followers particularly emphasized quiet-sitting. Yanagawa Gōgi[fk] wrote the *Shushi seiza shūsetsu*[fl] (Collection of Chu Hsi's Sayings on Quiet-Sitting), to which Naokata contributed the preface. In the postscript, Gōgi stated that the reason for the lack of integration and seriousness in the scholarship of recent Confucians was their neglect of quiet-sitting. He compared the situation to a boat without its rudder. The one who devoted the most attention to quiet-sitting was Atobe Ryōken. Kusumoto Tanzan[fm] (1828–1883) was experienced in Ryōken's method of quiet-sitting and also mastered the methods of Lo Hung-hsien[fn] (1504–1564) of the quietist branch of the Wang Yang-ming school, of Kao P'an-lung[fo] (1562–1626) of the neo-orthodox Tung-lin[fp] school of the late Ming, and the quiet-sitting of Li T'ung based on Chou Tun-i's doctrine of "regarding tranquillity as fundamental." Asami Keisai did not necessarily support this view of Naokata and others, claiming that quiet-sitting was just one aspect of the preservation of mind.[84] In my judgment, however, it was through the contribution of quiet-sitting that the teaching of the Kimon school acquired profundity, precision and clarity.

A point emphasized only by the Kimon school and not noticed by any other school of Yüan and Ming China or Tokugawa Japan was the theory of the "store of knowledge" (chih-tsang; chizō).[fq] In the introduction to his edition of the Chin-ssu lu, Ansai wrote:

Our teacher [Chu Hsi] took great pains to expound the significance of humaneness and love and to show that the store of knowledge has no perceptible trace.[85]

Ansai brought to light Chu Hsi's theory on the store of knowledge. He praised Lord Hoshina Masayuki of Aizu, whom he once served, and wrote for the monument in the Lord's memory:

[Lord Hoshina Masayuki said,] "Knowledge is hidden and shows no perceptible trace, One should discuss the essence of the Way and the soul only after learning the nature of knowledge.

The interaction of humaneness and knowledge is the basis for the myriad transformations. It is the Way that brings Heaven and man into communion."

These words of the Lord express the very essence of Chu Hsi's thought. There has been no one else who perceived this essence after Ts'ai Yüan-ting, Ts'ai Shen and Chen Te-hsiu.

In the biography of Masayuki, Ansai said:

Humaneness is love not yet manifested. Knowledge is the store that has no perceptible trace. Humaneness and knowledge interact. [Lord Hoshina was the one] beside Ts'ai Yüan-ting and Ts'ai Shen of the Chu Hsi school who perceived these points on his own and in the silence of his own mind.[86]

Actually, Ansai was the scholar who independently recognized Chu Hsi's theory of the store of knowledge and imparted it to Masayuki. In the first half of the supplement to Chu Hsi's Yü-shan chiang-i (Gyokuzan kōgi) published by Masayuki, Ansai compiled about twenty passages on the store of knowledge from the Chu Tzu wen-chi, the Chu Wen-kung hsü-chi[fr] (Sequel to the Collection of Literary Works of Chu Hsi) and the Chu Tzu yü-lei. Obviously Masayuki was repeating his teacher's view.

The three main points to observe here are: First, the definition of humaneness as love not yet manifested which is essential to an understanding of Chu Hsi's discussion of humaneness in his *Jen-shuo t'u;*[fs] second, the view of knowledge as hidden and without perceptible trace; and third, the view of the interaction of humaneness and knowledge as the basis for the myriad transformations.

According to Chu Hsi, the three virtues (*san-te*),[ft] humaneness, duty, and decorum, are manifested as three beginnings of virtue (*san-tuan*):[fu] commiseration (*ts'e-yin*),[fv] shame and aversion (*hsiu-o*),[fw] and deference and respect (*kung-ching*).[fx] These virtues have important applications and produce concrete effects in the conduct of affairs. In the case of knowledge, there is a distinction of right and wrong, but though we can perceive the activities of intellect, there are no observable operations or concrete effects. Knowledge is completely hidden within a man.[87]

As to the four virtues (*ssu-te*)[fy] or four beginnings (*ssu-tuan*),[fz] when viewed in terms of their significance for the development of life, humaneness is the creativity of life, decorum is the growth of life, duty is the gathering in of life, and knowledge is the storing of life.[88] Knowledge is "where the primal *ch'i* resides."[89] It is winter, the point when the quiescence of yin is at its limit, and the hour of the rat (midnight). In the store of knowledge everything is gathered in and hidden and not a trace of it can be found.[90] Chu Hsi therefore said, "Knowledge is concealed and unfathomable principle."[91] The greater the store of knowledge, the more profound wisdom will be.[92] Knowledge differs from duty and decorum and is equal to humaneness in its capacity to include the other virtues. As an integrating virtue it is on a par with humaneness.

Therefore Chu Hsi said, "Knowledge is originally the store of humaneness, duty and decorum. These are stored and contained within knowledge."[93] Consequently, he also said that, for Mencius, among the four beginnings, humaneness and knowledge are most important.[94]

Among the four beginnings, humaneness is listed first and knowledge last by Mencius. Chu Hsi, who saw humaneness and knowledge as including and integrating the other virtues, spoke of the four virtues as cyclic.[95] Thus he said: "Without correctness and firmness, origination will not take place. Without knowledge, how can humaneness exist?"[96]

As firm correctness (*chen*)[ga] is the starting point of origination (*yüan*)[gb] in the cycle of Heavenly virtues, knowledge is the starting point of humaneness. Thus Chu Hsi asserted that the interaction of humaneness and knowledge is the pivotal factor in self-transformation. This was the reason for Chu Hsi's finding in knowledge the significance not only of "store" but also of "beginning and end."[97] Chu Hsi recognized the idea of the "store of knowledge" in the image of the hexagram of return (fu-kua)[gc] in the Book of Changes and said:

> In winter the old is harvested and stored in order greatly to illumine beginnings and endings. If there were no endings, how could there be beginnings? Therefore it says in the Book of Changes:

> "The kings of antiquity closed the passes
> At the time of the solstice.
> Merchants and strangers did not go about,
> And the ruler
> Did not travel through the provinces."[98]

The implication of the passage is that, for everything, there is benefit in restful nurturing during the period when the sun is at its weakest.

Ansai also identified the source of the "store of knowledge" in the Book of Changes in the phrase from the Shuo-kua[gd] (Discussion of the Hexagrams), "k'un provides the store."[99] The Ch'eng brothers and Chang Tsai, acording to Ansai, showed that the store of knowledge had no external trace, and finally Chu Hsi discussed it thoroughly and in detail. The store of knowledge was, for him, the secret principle of the ancient sages.[100]

Ansai was deeply impressed by Chu Hsi's painstaking study of the store of knowledge and spared no effort in seeking its further elucidation. Ansai's view on the store of knowledge was inherited by his students; Miyake Shōsai particularly discussed the issue and wrote the Chizō setsu[ge] (Theory of the Store of Knowledge).[101] In the book Shōsai asserted that the store of knowledge was the substance of the Way and that humaneness and knowledge were the same in substance and inclusive of the other virtues. Further, he argued the unity of principle and knowledge, saying, "Knowledge is the living principle. Principle as it is is knowledge."[102]

The scholar who best set forth and explained the theory of the store of knowledge of Ansai and Shōsai was perhaps Kusumoto Tanzan. Tanzan gave an expanded interpretation of the theory, claiming that it is implicit in the concepts of the Supreme Ultimate (t'ai-chi)[gf] and of "storing up the past and knowing the future" (ts'ang-wang chih-lai)[gg] in the Book of Changes, in the nature as Heaven's decree[gh] and the centrality of the unmanifest state[gi] in the *Mean;* in the reality of the Infinite (*wu-chi chih chen*),[gj] "regarding tranquillity as fundamental" (*chu-ching*)[gk] and "establishing oneself as the ultimate standard for man" (*li-chi*)[gl] in Chou Tun-i's *T'ai-chi-t'u shuo*[gm] (Diagram of the Supreme Ultimate, Explained); in the concept of the Infinite (*wu-chi*)[gn] of Shao Yung, in the "emptiness and tranquillity without any sign" (*ch'ung-mo wu-chen*)[go] of Master Ch'eng; and finally, in the "as yet unmanifested disposition" (*weifa chih ch'i-hsiang*)[gp] of Li T'ung. All these ideas presuppose the store of knowledge. Tanzan had sought personal experience of truth through the quiet-sitting of Li T'ung and had grasped the secret key to substance and function. To him it was significant that Chu Hsi had followed the *Mean* in his theory of knowledge, since the *Mean* was the most subtle and metaphysical of the Four Books. He was deeply impressed with Ansai's keen appreciation of Chu Hsi on this point and declared:

It is the kind of insight that comes once in a thousand years and has a profound significance for all ages. There were few among the Confucians of the Yüan and Ming dynasties who perceived it.[103]

The store of knowledge has no external trace. Like the extreme desolation of winter, it is the total substance imperceptible to the senses, but also the ground of all life and activity.[104]

These words of Tanzan were explained by his grandson, Dr. Kusumoto Masatsugu,[gq] as follows:

The most profound human knowledge does not show any externally recognizable trace. It is like winter when everything is stored away, motionless and quiet. This is the original nature of man's mind that does not issue forth in any sound or scent. It is the absolute nature of the universe and the mind of creation. In its very stillness there is the potential for infinite activity. The inner world of mind becomes the external world. Conversely, the true meaning of the active external world can be perceived only by attaining an unagitated state of mind. Then the sense of community in life arises and men's minds return to thoughts of creation. This is the cultivation of profound knowledge through quiet-sitting.

This statement by Dr. Kusumoto conveys well the meaning of the theory of the store of knowledge held by Ansai and his followers.

Yamazaki Ansai's *jitsugaku* differs radically from Kaibara Ekken's. Ekken started with the study of Chu Hsi's concept of total substance and great functioning and became interested in natural scientific inquiry. He contributed a great deal to the advancement of the natural sciences in

Japan. Ansai concentrated on intimate personal experience and self-realization (*tainin; jitoku*) of truth as a basis for moral relations and laid great stress on actual experience in practice. He too accomplished much by opening up these aspects of Chu Hsi's practical learning. In this area the profundity of Ansai's *jitsugaku* was unrivaled. Kusumoto Tanzan, who sought to reconcile the divergent streams of Neo-Confucianism at the end of the Tokugawa period, praised the school and said:

The Kimon school succeeded to the orthodox tradition of Confucius and Chu Hsi. Its heritage is authentic. Its thought is profound and subtle. Ordinary scholars who follow the Sung Learning have attained only a superficial comprehension of one or another aspect of Chu Hsi's philosophy. They can hardly lay claim to the full orthodox inheritance. [105]

Ansai never put forward his own views but only publicized Chu Hsi's. Even when he expressed himself it was in the form of simple and short analyses of the main points in Chu Hsi's thought. He never discussed any issue in detail. This was because of his emphasis on personal experience and self-realization of the essence of Chu Hsi's thought, to the total exclusion of rote learning and mere lip service. Wang Yang-ming said:

The method of learning has to be simple and direct. The more direct to the issue the method is, the simpler it will be. The simpler the method is, the more direct it will be. [106]

In a certain sense, these words are applicable to the Kimon school.

Ansai's fervent effort personally to realize and fulfill Chu Hsi's practical learning led him to create his own unique system of thought that was inseparable from his own experience and personality. Despite his unbending demand that his students adhere to his teaching and strict training, he attracted many pupils. And they in turn, despite the seemingly rigid and authoritarian character of Ansai's teaching, developed strong personalities of their own and a way of thought that was thoroughly integrated with their own character. No doubt this too was a reflection of the nature of Ansai's thought.

Ansai's characteristic devotion to Chu Hsi's thought was exemplary: his own disciples also esteemed Ansai's views and endeavored intently to master them. Just as Ansai had rejected all mechanical and rote learning and insisted on the practical integration of Chu Hsi's teaching into his own life and person, so too did his students take Ansai's teaching as something to be followed intently and mastered in concrete detail. Thus, they were careful to take notes on his lectures, which they were willing to share only with persons of similar commitment.

Those who have criticized the thought of the Kimon school have often asserted that it blindly followed Chu Hsi and hence became rigid and intolerant. There is a certain validity to this, but, even so, it is merely a superficial observation which does not penetrate to the real depths of its spirit and substance. The fundamental spirit of Chu Hsi's teaching was not simply moralistic, even though it centered on the fulfillment of moral relations. It was more truly the spirit of personal experience and self-realization of truth. If this is recognized, then the Kimon school surpassed all others in its dynamic spirituality, which, for the Japanese, necessarily involved an adaptation to their native traditions and the full incorporation of these into their own practice of Chu Hsi's practical learning.

Translated by Hiroshi Miyaji

KAIBARA EKKEN'S EXPLORATION OF PRINCIPLE IN NATURE

Kaibara Ekken was an outstanding Confucian scholar of the early Tokugawa period as well as a pioneer in *jitsugaku* and natural science. He was a prolific writer who authored more than one hundred and ten works, including the first Japanese commentary on the *Chin-ssu lu,* the *Kinshiroku bikō*[gr] (Notes on *Reflections on Things at Hand*), a work of sufficient depth to evoke the wonder and admiration of Chinese Confucian scholars. One of his most important and well-known works is the *Taigiroku*[gs] (Record of Grave Doubts), which became a standard for later criticism of Chu Hsi's thought. This work was by no means an attack, for Ekken remained a devoted admirer of Chu Hsi. Nonetheless, he intensively scrutinized that which he felt should be doubted, maintaining his own independent position while giving voice to views similar to those of the Ancient Learning school. He also wrote a number of works devoted to education and moral instruction (*kunmono*),[gt] such as *Yōjōkun*[gu] (Precepts for Healthy Living) and *Onna daigaku*[gv] (The Great Learning for Women), which are still quite popular today. He absorbed, modified, and surpassed the traditional Chinese herbological studies, applying the principle with creative insight to the Japanese context in his *Yamato honzō*[gw] (Herbs of Japan), which had an enormous influence on the development of later pharmacological, botanical, and zoological research in Japan. The breadth of his scholarship is further demonstrated by another work, still fondly perused by experts in the field, *Chikuzen no kuni zokufudoki*[gx] (A Supplementary Guide to the Topography of Chikuzen). Ekken was a forerunner of *jitsugaku* scholarship in his time, with his interests encompassing such varied fields as medicine, botany, agriculture, physics, food sanitation, astronomy, geography, and mathematics. That Ekken was able to achieve such an amazing breadth and depth of scholarship is attributable to a number of factors including his native genius, the demands of the age in which he lived, his environment and, particularly, his relationship to friends and colleagues. However, over and above these there is the fact that Ekken felt he had a mission to fulfill as a Confucian scholar, and thus his *jitsugaku* is inextricably bound up with his Confucian thought. Let us begin with a general consideration of the role of Confucian thought in the life of Ekken.

Ekken established his position as a Confucian scholar when, at the age of twenty-eight, he went to Kyoto to study and came to know some of the most famous Confucian scholars of the Chu Hsi school at that time. During this period, he immersed himself in the philosophy of Chu Hsi[107] and his attitude towards Chu Hsi's thought was similar to that of two other prominent scholars, Kinoshita Jun'an and Nakamura Tekisai[gy] (1629–1702). Jun'an, while a student of Matsunaga Sekigo[gz] (1592–1657), was not content with adopting a narrow "school view" but took a much more comprehensive stand and consequently became interested in *jitsugaku*. Tekisai, although quite conservative in his defense of Chu Hsi's thought in all its purity, nonetheless made quite a name for himself as a *jitsugakusha* or scholar of practical learning. Ekken studied with Jun'an and gradually cemented a long-lasting friendship with him, and also engaged in lively discussions with Tekisai, in which they mutually improved their grasp of the intricacies of philosophical problems.[108] Ekken also attended lectures given by Yamazaki Ansai, but found very little to excite his enthusiasm, and thus there was very little in the way of positive interaction between the two. On the contrary, throughout his entire life Ekken was quite critical of Ansai's Shushigaku.[109] Why should this have been the case?

One reason is that Ekken's basic disposition contrasted markedly with that of the more austere Ansai. Ekken rhapsodizes on the peaceful state of the world in which he lived, saying, "Through the beneficence of the Emperor (Ōgimi)[ha] I was born into a peaceful world with a truly moral government and I have reached a ripe age without ever having had to go to war. This has been great happiness (dainaru tanoshimi)."[hb][110] He could also say that:

On the whole men's minds have the great peaceful energy which is granted by Nature (tenchi),[hc] and this is the principle which governs men's lives. Just as plants and trees continue to sprout without ceasing, so too the "life force" thrives within us and the heart is made eternally glad—this is happiness (tanoshimi).[111]

"Happiness," as understood by Ekken, is an a priori principle of life.[112] The essence of pure happiness is, "To have some leisure time, the body rested, and not to worry about whether one is rich or poor."[113] This was the "natural inheritance, the proper state of the human mind and the unceasing principle of life"[114] as well as the locus of the joy to be found in the "association with other human beings."[115]

Ekken, who held this optimistic world view, evinced a keen interest in jitsugaku quite early in life, as can be seen from the fact that he had consumed over sixty multi-volume Chinese and Japanese treatises in the field by the age of thirty-five. With this optimistic attitude and this interest in jitsugaku it is quite natural that he should have been basically incompatible with Ansai. For Ansai consistently maintained a purely idealistic standpoint and advocated a pure and profound Tao which strictly governed the things of the world. In pursuit of this goal, he engaged in detailed and assiduous practices to nourish a deep understanding of the Tao through personal experience (tainin). Furthermore, Ansai tended to be quite dogmatic and narrowly sectarian in his views. It would be difficult to imagine a more pronounced contrast.

As was mentioned above, Ekken became quite fond of Chu Hsi's thought early in life, but it was not until 1660, when he was thirty-six years of age, that he was fully converted. Up until that time he had been inclined toward the thought of Lu Hsiang-shan and Wang Yang-ming. According to the Ganko mokuroku,[hd] a catalogue of books Ekken read, Ekken had by the age of thirty-five done extensive reading in works devoted to Lu and Wang as well as to the Existential Realization school (Genseiha)[he] of Wang's followers. Although he was apparently not overly interested in or sympathetic to the Existential Realization school, he did have a very keen interest in Wang's *Ch'uan-hsi lu*[hf] (Instructions for Practical Living) which, it is recorded, he read through twelve times.[116] When he was thirty-six, he read Ch'en Chien's *Hsüeh-pu t'ung-pien*.[117] Ch'en had rejected Buddhism from a nationalistic standpoint. He argued that since Lu, Wang and their followers all emphasized the path of nourishing one's spirit (*yōjin no ichiro*),[hg] their teachings were nothing more than Buddhism in disguise. Thus, he attempted to distinguish their teachings from those of Ch'eng I and Chu Hsi and to launch a devastating attack on the entire Lu-Wang tradition. It was only after reading Ch'en Chien's work that Ekken rejected the Lu-Wang tradition in favor of the Ch'eng-Chu philosophy.[118] The primary reason for his rejecting the Lu-Wang tradition was that he felt deeply anguished over the excesses of the radical followers of the Wang school. Their School of the Mind emphasized direct and immediate enlightenment, and they insisted that there were shortcuts to wisdom. This brought confusion to the minds of the people and obscured the true teachings of Confucianism.[119] Ekken was also influenced by his reading of Feng K'o's *Ch'iu-shih pien*, another late Ming attack on the Lu-Wang tradition.[120]

As indicated above, Ekken was a scholar of broad knowledge and experience and one whose pursuit of practical learning extended to a wide variety of fields. This fact emerges clearly upon examination of the titles of the books he had worked his way through by the age of forty. According to the *Ganko mokuroku*, Ekken had by then consumed over three hundred and twenty treatises, two hundred and fifty in Chinese, seventy in Japanese. The works written in Chinese naturally included the classics, histories, and literary compilations, but a substantial number were works relating to the Neo-Confucianism of Chu Hsi. These included not only works of the Sung, Yüan and Ming periods, but also the collected writings of Fujiwara Seika and Hayashi Razan as well as the *Chuja haengjangju*[hh] (Commentary on Chu Hsi's Life), *Chasŏngnok*[hi] (Record of Self-Examination) and the *Chujasŏ chŏryo* by Yi T'oegye.

It is significant that the Ming texts included not only the *Hsüeh-pu t'ung-pien* and the *Ch'iu-shih pien*, mentioned above, among the works critical of the Lu-Wang school, but also a number of commentaries on the Four Books written from the standpoint of a reformed Chu Hsi philosophy, and various works written with the object of revising the Chu Hsi philosophy in such a way that the metaphysical dualism of the Ch'eng-Chu school would be amended in favor of a monism based either on principle (li) or material force (ch'i). Works in the latter category included the *Tu-shu lu* by Hsüeh Hsüan, the *Chü-yeh lu* by Hu Chü-jen, and the *K'un-chih chi*ʰʲ (Notes on Knowledge Painfully Acquired) by Lo Ch'in-shunʰᵏ (1465–1547). These works are important because of their intimate connection with the critique of Chu Hsi developed by Ekken in his later years, and we will have occasion later to recur to the influence of the *K'un-chih chi* on Ekken's thought and scholarly method. Among the works read by Ekken by the time he was forty, many were *jitsugaku* works which dealt with subjects of immediate importance to daily living, such as botany, medicine, geography, linguistics, and lexicography. Among these, works on botany and medicine were most numerous, with the largest number of all having been devoted to medicine.

During this period, Ekken became increasingly fervent in promoting the teaching of Chu Hsi. In order to aid those people incapable of reading the complete text of Chu Hsi's collected works by themselves, he compiled a selection of the most essential passages and provided punctuation and directive marks (*kunten*)ʰˡ so that they could be read in Japanese. He published it under the title *Shushi bunpan*ʰᵐ (A Selection of Chu Hsi's Writings). He also published *Kinshiroku bikō* (Notes on *Reflections on Things at Hand*) and *Shōgaku kutō bikō*ʰⁿ (Notes on Philology and Punctuation).[121] Ekken's Shushigaku resembled that of the careful, reliable, and versatile Confucian scholar Nakamura Tekisai, but, as Tekisai remarked, there were certain respects in which Ekken's "broad learning" was "indiscriminate." Tekisai's criticism of Ekken as indiscriminate was made when the latter was seventy years of age,[122] but the tendency he referred to can already be discerned in his *Kinshiroku bikō* where, for example, Chu Hsi's theory of *li* and *ch'i* and the interpretations of later scholars seeking to revise that theory are cited side by side.[123]

As Ekken grew older, he began to harbor doubts about Chu Hsi's theories, and as a result published the *Taigiroku* (Record of Grave Doubts) in which he presented those theories of Chu Hsi and other Sung Confucians which he could not accept, adding his own criticisms in each case.[124] The reason he harbored these "grave doubts" was that he saw these theories as having been grounded in Buddhism and Taoism. Ekken, who from the outset adopted a critical attitude toward Buddhism and Taoism, in his later years came to have much greater familiarity with Buddhist texts, which may explain why he became still more keenly aware of Buddhist influence on the Sung writers. Such an observation

has already been made by Mori Rantaku[ho] (1722–1777), a disciple of
Dazai Shundai[hp] (1680–1747) and the author of *Zoku Benmei*[hq] (A Further Examination of Chu Hsi's Concepts).[125] Ekken wrote, "In that the
Sung Confucian scholars . . . were quite close to the teachings of the
Buddhists and Taoists, there is much that is dubious in their work."[126]
He then cited eight theories of Sung Confucianism and presented his
criticism of each. The essential elements in Ekken's critique of Buddhism
and Taoism can be seen in the section entitled "A Discussion of Buddhism"[hr] in his *Shinshi zokuroku*[hs] (Further Notes on Thoughtful Reflection), a work still preserved in manuscript form. This aversion to Buddhism and Taoism was, no doubt, quite natural in a man who was at
once a Confucian scholar and a student of *jitsugaku*. However, while
Ekken was quite critical of Buddhism and Taoism, the same was not true
of his attitude toward Shinto. He espoused the theory that Shinto and
Confucianism formed a unity (*shinju ittai setsu*)[ht][127] and was critical
both of those who supported Shinto and attacked Confucianism and of
those who supported Confucianism and rejected Shinto. It was on the
basis of the theory that "Shinto and Confucianism form a unity" that he
attacked the *honji suijaku*[hu] doctrine that the Shinto deities are manifestations of Buddhas and bodhisattvas.

There are three particularly important points to be made in connection
with Ekken's later writings. The first is that he wrote quite a number of
works intended primarily for the education and enlightenment of the
masses. These were the so-called *kunmono*, written not in Chinese but in
relatively simple Japanese. The second point is that it was during these
years that he wrote most of his *jitsugaku* works. The final point is that by
the time he wrote the *Taigiroku* he had come to espouse a position very
similar to that of the Ancient Learning school in terms of its critique of
Chu Hsi philosophy.

When one views all of Ekken's pedagogical works and not merely the
ones written in simple Japanese, it is apparent that Ekken's view of Chu
Hsi and Sung Confucianism was not narrow or distorted, but displayed a
well balanced understanding of the entire system. Yet one may feel a certain disappointment over the fact that he was not sufficiently intense in
his effort to probe deeply into the philosophical ground to discover the
living root which was the ultimate source of the flowering of this remarkable plant. Even though he discussed what Chu Hsi referred to as "the
store of knowledge" (*chih-tsang*),[fq] Ekken was apparently not fully mind-

ful of the kind of effort (*kufū*) that was so characteristic of Chu Hsi's endeavor to attain the qualities of depth and purity.[128] At the same time, it was altogether natural that Ekken, who poured his energies into *jitsugaku*, should have harbored doubts about the intense predilection for interiority which characterized Chu Hsi's efforts in personal cultivation, the quietistic orientation involved in his tendency to associate "abiding in tranquillity" (*chü-ching*) with "personal experience" (*t'i-jen*), and his commitment to a metaphysical dualism which accorded priority to *li* or principle.

Although the *Taigiroku* was the product of his latter years, Ekken was loathe to make it public primarily because he feared it would be said that he had turned his back on Chu Hsi and was now propagating heretical views. His disciples understood his reluctance and preserved the secrecy of the work during his lifetime. However, it does seem that Ekken's most talented disciple, Takeda Shun'an,[hv] showed the work to Ogyū Sorai[hw] some three years after Ekken's death. Sorai commented "This is the first chance I have had to read the *Taigiroku*. It gives me great pleasure to find that there is a scholar in a faraway place who has anticipated my own thoughts."[129]

Fifty years later this treatise was published by Ōno Hokkai,[hx] one of Sorai's followers. Why was it that Ekken's own disciples kept the work secret rather than having published it? According to Mori Rantaku, a member of the Ancient Learning school, they were apprehensive that this book would vitiate in the minds of the public all of Ekken's remarkably deep and penetrating insights, and they could not bear the thought of his disgrace. Rantaku regarded the behavior of the disciples as comparable to the overly protective and timid instincts of women and children. He himself praised the *Taigiroku* saying:

The one volume of the *Taigiroku* is superlative, a comprehensive treatise which is the result of extensive scholarship and deep dedication. Furthermore he completed the work on his own without having borrowed the assistance of Emperor Wen. This book alone sufficiently displays Ekken's greatness as a master. It is an ever-shining beacon of scholarship.[130]

Both the published version and a handwritten copy of the *Taigiroku* have been preserved. Although there are some differences in chapter divisions and phraseology, the divergence is not great. The handwritten copy was made by Takeda Shun'an and contains 113 sections more than the published version. There are some differences in phrasing but the meaning is almost identical, and, since the arguments are developed in greater detail in the handwritten copy, it is worth consulting for reference. Ekken's own preface to the *Taigiroku* was written in 1713, when he was eighty-four, but since Shun'an's copy seems to have been made in 1711, the handwritten copy is obviously earlier than the published version. Moreover, there is a volume entitled the *Shinshi betsuroku*[hy] (More Notes on Thoughtful Reflections), and in a letter to Shun'an, Ekken states, "I am sending you a copy of *Shinshi betsuroku* for your perusal. I believe it will make all of my deliberations evident. . . . I have not shown this to others for fear that it would be misinterpreted as heretical."[131] Since this letter was written in 1701 or 1702, when Ekken was seventy-three or -four, it clearly predated the manuscript.[132] The *Betsuroku* seems to record the criticism of Chu Hsi's thought which he did not wish to make public when he wrote the *Shinshiroku*. The argument of the *Betsuroku* has various similarities with both the manuscript and the published version of the *Taigiroku*, but contains only fifty-six sections, some twenty sections fewer than the published text.

With respect to the time when he began to harbor doubts about Chu Hsi's thought, Ekken remarks in the *Taigiroku*,

> From my early years I assiduously read Chu Hsi, respected his way, and submitted to his teachings. However there were some points which I could not understand. I came to have definite doubts and, although I was fond of him, I could not be so obsequious as to blind myself to these doubts. I could only wait, hoping that one day everything would become clear to me.[133]

It thus seems that his doubts about aspects of Chu Hsi's thought arose quite early, and in a letter to his friend and fellow scholar, Tani Issai[hz] (1625–1695), an adherent of the Chu Hsi school, Ekken, who was then about forty-six, referred to certain dissatisfactions with Ch'eng-Chu teachings.[134] In response, Issai charged that Ekken's views resembled those of Itō Jinsai[ia] (1627–1705), and he added a rejoinder by way of criticism of Ekken's stand.[135] Nevertheless, according to the preface to *Taigiroku*, Ekken was over fifty before he came to the painful realization that his perplexities with respect to Chu Hsi's teachings might be irresolvable. In a letter written to Shun'an when he was about fifty-six Ekken declared, "There are a number of things I cannot accept in the writings of Confucian scholars of the past."[136] According to the *Ganko mokuroku*, it was at this same age that he read Wu T'ing-han's[ib] critique of Chu Hsi, *Chi-chai man-lu*[ic] (The Jottings of Chi-chai),[137] and at the age of seventy that he read Ho Ching's (Ho Ching-shan,[id] 1558–1639) *Shih-hsi hsin-chih*[ie] (New Insights Acquired Through Constant Study). His reading of these and other works gradually confirmed the validity of the reservations he already had. It may be for this reason that, although he did not go into detail, he wrote his good friend Tekisai of his doubts about Chu Hsi's teachings.[138]

As Tani Issai rightly pointed out, the arguments of *Taigiroku* resemble those of Itō Jinsai, a strong advocate of Ancient Learning. Was there any direct scholarly interchange between Ekken and Jinsai? It is a matter of record that Ekken made frequent trips to Kyoto for academic purposes, mingling with many of the famous scholars of the time.[139] According to *Kanbun nikki*[if] (A Diary of the Kanbun Period), Ekken visited the residence of an important personage in the company of Jinsai and Yonekawa Sōken[ig] (1625–1676), a disciple of Jun'an, in 1668, when he was thirty-nine. It seems that in the ensuing discussion he disagreed with the views expounded by Jinsai.[140] This is understandable since Ekken was at that time a stalwart adherent of Shushigaku, whereas Jinsai had already begun to espouse Kogaku views. There is no evidence that the two had any direct contact afterward. At that time there was a scholar by the name of Andō Seian[ih] (1622–1701), whom Ekken greatly respected and who carried on a cordial and lively correspondence with Jinsai. Thus, while Ekken had no direct interchange with Jinsai, he was probably well-informed concerning his scholarship and his views. According to an account by Jinsai's son, Tōgai[ii] (1670–1736), Katsuki Gyūzan[ij] (1668–1740), a Confucian scholar who was a fellow countryman and close friend of Ekken, would occasionally come to Kyoto and visit Jinsai, making the rounds as it were by staying with Seian, Jinsai, and Ekken.[141] That Ekken's views were quite similar to Jinsai's has been pointed out a number of times, but an example might help to show this similarity. When Ekken argues in the *Taigiroku* that the phrase "the Infinite and also the Supreme Ultimate" (*wu-chi erh t'ai-chi*)[ik] derived from the *Hua-yen fa-chieh kuan*[il] (The Hua-yen View of the Realm of the Dharmas),[142] he seems to be basing his criticisms on arguments found in the *Shang-chih pien*[im] (1440) by K'ung-ku Ching-lung, which were also set forth in Jinsai's *Gomō jigi*.[in] Or it may have been that Ekken simply took them directly from Jinsai. Even though his interpretations grew more and more similar to those of the Kogaku school, he, unlike Seian, remained severely critical of Jinsai's position to the end.[143] An example of this may be found in the dissatisfaction he felt when, at the age of seventy-nine, he read a critique of Jinsai by Yamamoto Kanzan[io] of Echizen, a disciple of Kumazawa Banzan[ip] (1619–1691) who had once leaned toward Jinsai's position. Kanzan had later come to criticize Jinsai, but Ekken regretted that his critique was not as thoroughgoing and complete as it might have been.[144]

The essence of Ekken's critique of Jinsai can be gleaned from his *Dōjimon higo*[iq] (A Critique of *Boy's Questions*).[145] It is not possible here to examine the content of that work, but it is both significant and surprising that Ekken, who had developed a critique of Chu Hsi in his *Taigiroku*, should in this work have staunchly defended Chu Hsi's position and used it as a basis for criticizing Jinsai. Ho Ching's *Shih-hsi hsin-chih* was a work that went even further than the *Chi-chai man-lu* in espousing a philosophy of *ch'i*, criticizing the Sung thinkers' philosophy of *li*, and advocating a return to the ancient learning. As the following quotation indicates, Ekken scored the theories put forward by Jinsai in *Dōjimon*[ir] (Boy's Questions) for having been based on the *Shih-hsi hsin-chih*:

Jinsai's position is essentially based on the views of Ho Ching-shan (Ho Ching) and others like him. Quite often the points he makes are identical with those made in *Shih-hsi hsin-chih*. . . . At first I had no idea what the origin of Jinsai's views were. But now after having read Ho Ching-shan's *Shih-hsi hsin-chih* I realize that it forms the foundation for Jinsai's position. What Jinsai expounds is precisely what Ho did. They fit together like two halves of a tally puzzle.[146]

Ekken, who thought it "most proper that the distinction of Confucianism and heresy be made from the standpoint of *dōgaku*[is] (the Neo-Confucian philosophy of the Way)," could not forgive Jinsai's maligning that position.[147] In explaining his motives for writing *Dōjimon higo*, Ekken wrote:

In the summer of 1702 I had the occasion to read over Itō Jinsai's *Dōjimon*. Quite often the text would make light of the scholarship of Chu Hsi and vilify his doctrines. I could not approve of this. . . . In this work I have cited a number of examples of Jinsai's misleading interpretations and have tried to demonstrate that Chu Hsi is not guilty of the errors imputed to him by Jinsai and in so doing to clear Chu Hsi's name.[148]

While Ekken entertained doubts about Sung learning, he was temperamentally unable to break out of its confines, and in the end did no more than modify Sung thought, believing that this was the way of a good and faithful servant of the Sung Confucians. In the end, he was a follower of the Sung Confucians, and yet at the same time he doubted them. Thus Dazai Shundai said of him, "He is truly a strange one. His doubts are just that, doubts; he was not yet able to reject them."[149] Jinsai too came to harbor doubts about Sung Confucianism but, unlike Ekken, he came to overthrow and reject them in the end.

The doubts harbored by Ekken in respect to the Sung learning were such that he was prompted to take up the fight that Ch'en Chien had waged against Lu Hsiang-shan and Wang Yang-ming in his *Hsüeh-pu t'ung-pien* and to carry it into the halls of Sung learning, in an effort to dispel the dark and gloomy shadows of Buddhism and Taoism which, in Ekken's view, still lingered there like an oppressive and obfuscating fog. This was his only object. Why, despite his doubts, was he unable to break free of the Sung learning? It was because he felt deep respect and gratitude toward the Sung Confucians just as he did toward the various gods of Heaven-and-earth. In fact, this tender feeling and sensitivity to nature were nurtured by his reading of Sung philosophy. This awareness of nature became the motivating force behind his study of *jitsugaku* and his authorship of so many works designed to enhance man's understanding of the natural and social world in which he lived.

It was some time after Ekken's death before *jitsugaku* came to be regarded as having as its primary object the scientific skills directly or indirectly necessary to the maintenance of human life. Although Japanese intellectual historians frequently identify the history of *jitsugaku* with the history of natural science, it is important to note that such a simple identification will not be adequate in Ekken's case. Ekken's *jitsugaku* was quite extensive in scope; it included the humanities, society and nature, but always had the study of morals (moral life) as its central focus. Morality (*dōtokugaku*)[it] inevitably took precedence over the other fields of investigation. Thus even if one were to interpret *jitsugaku* in the narrow sense to mean science and technology (*kagaku gijutsu*),[iu] it should not be forgotten that Ekken's *jitsugaku* always remained within the bounds of Confucian studies, and as such had a moral dimension which seems to be lacking in the modern concept of science. Thus, during Ekken's time, *jitsugaku*, even in this narrow sense, was not independent of Confucian scholarship. At that time, Confucians constituted the core of the intellectual class, and they all, to a greater or lesser extent, studied *jitsugaku*, many having been particularly interested in medicine. The importance of medicine is that it is crucial to sustaining human life. Thus we find that there were many Confucian scholars in this period who were also physicians. It was this phenomenon which, incidentally, gave rise to the term *jui*, or Confucian physician, which enjoyed wide currency. Ekken remarked:

In the various arts there are many things completely useless to everyday life. Medicine is an outstanding exception. Even if one does not intend to be a physician he should study this subject. A Confucian scholar should attempt to be familiar with all phenomena. For this reason medicine, since ancient times, has been one of the fields of Confucian scholarship.[150]

Many of the Confucian scholars with whom Ekken was acquainted were physicians. His father, Kansai[iv] (1597–1665), was well versed in medicine. Ekken himself had from birth had a weak constitution, thus providing a deep personal reason for his interest in medicine from his early years. At one point he had decided to make his living as a physician.[151]

The scope of Ekken's *jitsugaku* was truly amazing, covering everything from the experience and practice of ethics to manners, institutions, linguistics, medicine, botany, zoology, agriculture, production, taxonomy, food sanitation, law, mathematics (computation), music, and military tactics. That he should have become famous as the most widely accomplished *jitsugaku* scholar of his time was due, of course, to his awesome talent and diligence. However, it must be remembered that he was helped by associating and cooperating with many famous *jitsugaku* scholars. He was, of course, familiar with the results of traditional Japanese and Chinese *jitsugaku* research, but he was also familiar with a few Western treatises. Interest in *jitsugaku* brought Ekken in close contact with many scholars who influenced the creative development of his study of herbology (*honzōgaku*).[iw] Some of these scholars were: the famous Confucian and author of *Kunmō zui*,[ix] Nakamura Tekisai; Mukai Genshō[iy] (1609–1677), the author of the *Hōchū biyō Yamato honzō*[iz] (Medicinal Herbs in the Home), who founded the Seidō[ja] (Sage's Hall) in Nagasaki and also, in addition to being a Confucian scholar, was interested in astronomy, herbology, and medicine; the physician and herbologist who authored *Shobutsu ruisan*[jb] (A Classification of Common Herbs), Inao Jakusui[jc] (1655–1715); as well as the disciple who helped complete the work, Matsuoka Jo'an[jd] (1668–1746). In addition, there was Miyazaki Yasusada[je] (1623–1697), the author of Nōgyō zensho[jf] (Agricultural Compendium), whose correspondence with Ekken helped him to do pioneering work in the field of agriculture. He was also close to scholars such as Kurokawa Dōyū[jg] (d. 1691), a Confucian physician who wrote Honchō igaku kō[jh] (A Study on Japanese Medicine) as well as a geographical treatise entitled Yōshū-fu shi[ji] (Geographic Annals of Yamashiro), and Katsuki Gyūzan, one of Ekken's brightest students, who particularly distinguished himself in the field of medicine as a member of the Gosei-ha.[jj] Ekken also seems to have had indirect contact with Nagoya Gen'i,[jk] the founder of Ko-ihō[jl] (Ancient Medical Method) and author of Tansuishi.[jm] Moreover, he lent his assistance to the astronomical research group of scholars in the Kuroda domain led by Yasui Shunkai, who used Chinese astronomical instruments to develop his own original theories. Ekken was also a close friend of the astronomer Hoshino Sanenobu,[jn] the author of Kokōgenshō[jo] (A Mathematical Treatise), Unki rokujūnen zu[jp] (A Sixty Year Astrological Chart), and Konyo bōtsūgi zusetsu[jq] (A Complete Atlas of the World).[152] All of these jitsugaku scholars became prominent around the Genroku era, and while they were familiar with Chinese treatises on jitsugaku they endeavored to break new ground in Japan. Ekken was nurtured in this fertile environment and he responded by establishing his own creative and productive field of study, thereby making a truly magnificent contribution to the later development of jitsugaku.

Ekken was able to accomplish what he did and publish a great number of jitsugaku works partly because he was favored with excellent colleagues such as his nephew, Kaibara Chiken[jr] (1664–1700), and his disciple, Takeda Shun'an, who was both a talented jitsugakusha and a great Confucian scholar. It may well be that Ekken could not have made his momentous contributions without Shun'an's assistance. It is well known that Ekken's wife, Tōken[js] (1652–1713), was also of great help to him.

For Ekken, as we have seen, all true Confucian scholarship was jitsugaku. Science and technology were a part of it and Ekken displayed an originality and creativeness in this area equal to that which he displayed in traditional Confucian scholarship. However, for the moment let us use the term jitsugaku to refer to Ekken's scientific and technological interests alone, and to distinguish this area from Confucian studies in the broader sense. The distinction is not absolute but it will be useful for our understanding. In doing so, we will turn our attention first to the characteristic features of Ekken's *jitsugaku* research methodology and its relationship to his Confucian thought.

The fact that Ekken's *jitsugaku* research was fundamentally rooted in the Ch'eng-Chu tradition of *ko-wu ch'iung-li*[it] (the investigation of things and exploration of principle) need not be belabored, but it is instructive to see what he says in the introduction to *Yamato honzō* about the general outlines of his methodology:

One should not blindly regard all one has heard as true and reject what others say merely because they disagree, nor be stubborn and refuse to admit mistakes. To have inadequate information, to be overly credulous about what one has seen and heard, to adhere rigidly to one's own interpretation, or to make a determination in a precipitate manner—all these four modes of thinking are erroneous.[153]

Thus Ekken gives four basic categories of unacceptable or erroneous thought: 1) relying on inadequate information; 2) being overly credulous about what one sees or hears; 3) remaining stubbornly attached to one's own point of view; and 4) forming precipitate judgments. In contrast, he proposes four characteristics of proper methodology: 1) valuing broad learning and wide experience; 2) not being overly credulous but remaining skeptical in regard to doubtful cases; 3) being fair and objective in one's judgments; and 4) investigating thoroughly and reflecting carefully before making a judgment.

Why did Ekken insist on the broadest possible knowledge? As he put it, "The ancients said that all things under the sun are their province, and I too must become a man to whom the principles governing all things in the wide world are known."[154] In making this statement, Ekken was thinking of something along the lines of Lu Hsiang-shan's statement that, "All things within the universe are in my province."[155] In Ekken's view, the products of the world are abundant, almost limitlessly so, and, accordingly, the possible benefits to the inhabitants of the world are similarly infinite. In order to realize this possibility, it is necessary for one to understand the principles of all things (*mono no ri*).[ju] If one does not, one will not be able to fulfill the Confucian mission to govern the world (*ching-shih chih-yung; keisei chiyō*).[jv] [156] Elsewhere Ekken observed,

The Way (*dōtai*)[jw] is extensive and the principles of righteousness (*giri*)[jx] subtle, permeating all things between Heaven and earth from time immemorial. Thus it is no easy matter to explore and comprehend them fully. If one were a true sage things might be different, but even scholars as brilliant and profound as the Ch'eng brothers and Chu Hsi were not able to do so on the basis of their own individual talents.[157]

It goes almost without saying that "broad learning"[jy] for Ekken involved reading both Japanese and Chinese books, ancient and modern, including the classics, histories, and literary compilations, but it also extended to the principles of things (*mono no ri*) applying over the broadest possible range—in other words, to science and technology. But, perhaps more significantly, his desire to become conversant with whatever might be of some value to the everyday life of the people led him to consult esoteric works and ancient tales as well as works pertaining to areas which, in the eyes of many Confucians, might have been considered trivial and demeaning, or not worth the name of scholarship, such as proverbs, farming, horticulture, and arithmetical computation. As he put it,

I followed up on what the townspeople spoke of, salvaged what I could prove out of even the most insane utterances, and made inquiries of people of the most lowly station. I was always willing to inquire into the most mundane and everyday matters and give consideration to all opinions. Forgetting about myself, I listened to others.[158]

Ekken was convinced that without broad learning and extensive experience (*hakugaku gōbun*)[jz] it was impossible to make a proper assessment of matters. One would lose detachment and fall into dogmatism. In other words, one would be incapable of making judgments on a rational and objective basis. Thus, emphasis on rationality and objectivity is a distinguishing characteristic of Ekken's thought. Ekken was quite strict here, as may be gleaned from the praise of Western medicine in his preface to *Kōi geka sōden*[ka] (Western Surgical Techniques) by the Nagasaki physician, Narabayashi Chinzan,[kb] founder of the Narabayashi School of Surgery. His impartiality and rationality can also be seen in his recognition in his own *Fusō kishō*[ke] (Famous Places of Japan) of the moral sense of Europeans. This strongly contrasts with the position taken by his friend, Mukai Genshō. Mukai applauded the results of European astronomy, but vehemently rejected the theoretical and moral outlook which formed the basis of Western science.[159]

As Ekken's commitment to "broad learning and extensive experience" led him to read widely both in Chinese and Japanese works, his pursuit of rationality (gōrisei)[kd] and objectivity prompted him to reject glib theorizing, blind speculation and abstruse discussion.[160] For him, the object of learning was not the acquisition of unrelated information or random knowledge but was, essentially, the rational and objective exploration of principle (kyūri).[ke] He believed that if the various phenomena were not comprehended in terms of rational principle, knowledge would lack a solid foundation.[161] He said that, since all phenomena are based on principle, "True scholarship attempts to explain the principles behind phenomena, thus deriving an understanding of them. Without this explanation, the inquiry, no matter how far-reaching and detailed, will be worthless."[162] It was necessary to attain an understanding of principle through careful reflection, thorough deliberation, and the examination of alternatives. Evidently, Ekken had fully comprehended Chu Hsi's doctrine that the exploration of principle extended both to the reasons for "things beings as they are" (suo i jan)[kf] and to the norms governing "things as they should be" (suo tang jan),[kg] while he himself sought to be absolutely thoroughgoing in the rationality and objectivity that he brought to bear in the exploration of principle. This may explain his conclusion, following an inquiry into the reasons for vines twisting to the left, that the answer lay in the general character of Nature (tendō)[kh] to twist to the left.

A good illustration of Ekken's rationality is found in his view of life and death.[163] According to Ekken, the spirit (tamashii)[ki] is what imparts life to material force. Thus when human beings die, material force is destroyed, and with it, the living spirit. This "naturalistic" interpretation is in direct opposition to the doctrine of the immortality of the soul (seikon fumetsu)[kj] of Chang Tsai[kk] and to the notion that principle has no birth or death. Ekken dismissed both of these views as mere carry-overs from the Buddhist doctrine of transmigration and developed his own theory of li and ch'i as one substance (ri ki ittai).[kl] This was a view consonant with that of Lo Ch'in-shun, who had criticized Chang Tsai from the same standpoint and had elaborated a similar argument on li and ch'i. Thus, it was natural that Ekken should have regarded Lo's theory as one that served to combat the mistaken view of heretics and to resolve the doubts of scholars.[164]

It was also as a consequence of his concern for the rational and objective "exploration of principle" that Ekken expounded his theory of the "constancy and transformation of principle" (*ri no jōhen*).[km 165] According to Ekken, principle is characterized by both constancy and transformation. Since even transformation itself is an aspect of principle, there is nothing in the world that is outside the sphere of principle (*tenka ni wa rigai no mono wa nai*);[kn] to argue, to the contrary, that there are many things in the world that are outside the sphere of principle merely indicates a lack of precision and rigor in the exploration of principle. Without an understanding of the transformation of principle, one cannot fully understand the principles governing the objects and events of the world.

According to Ekken's theory on the cultivation of life (*yōjō setsu*),[ko] moderation of the desires and the preservation of life were taken as constants, while sacrificing one's life for the sake of righteousness represented an instance of the transformation of principle.[166] Ekken, like Lo Ch'in-shun, opposed the dualistic view of *li* and *ch'i* of the Sung Confucians and considered that, since principle was the principle of material force, principle and material force could not be separated, but were one reality.[167] Ekken also opposed the Sung Confucian view that there were two natures, the nature of Heaven-and-earth and the physical nature. He thought that there was one nature and that the original reality of the physical being (*kishitsu no honzen*)[kp] was the nature of Heaven-and-earth (*tenchi no sei*).[kq] Therefore, he also approved of Lo Ch'in-shun's theory that the nature of Heaven-and-earth was the original reality of the physical being.[168] In Ekken's case, this led to the attempt to find principle directly in the flow and transformation of material force, with specific reference, for example, to the time, place, land and people that were involved.[169] This is the explanation for Ekken's discussions of the appropriateness of time (*jūgi ron*) and place (*dogi ron*)[kr] and his theory of the "tendency of the times" (*kiun kaika*).[ks 170] In turn, his notion that principle was to be discovered in direct relation to material force would seem to have been derived from the doctrine of the unity of principle and the diversity of its particularizations (*ri ichi bunshu*),[kt] a doctrine which he concretized on the basis of his theory of *li* and *ch'i* as one substance. Ekken thus emphasized material force, paying particular attention to the individual forms that it took. But a distinction must be made between his view and that of the Ming Confucian, Wu T'ing-han, in whose monism of *ch'i*, *li* was associated not with the quality of *ch'i*, but with its quantity. The theory of the unity of principle and the diversity of its particularizations had had currency from Northern Sung times on and had been further developed by Lo Ch'in-shun from the point of view of material force. Ekken's view in this was consistent with Lo's.

If one examines his *jitsugaku* writings, it will be immediately apparent that Ekken's *jitsugaku* was most directly and integrally related to the theory of the unity of principle and the diversity of its particularizations. The point is well illustrated in the introduction to *Yamato honzō*, one of his most representative works. Here Ekken says:

The things of the world are constantly in a state of flux. Thus many things which did not exist before are present now. There are so many things which we now know that we were ignorant of previously that it is nearly impossible to record all this knowledge. We cannot afford to waste anything which may be of use. The Middle Kingdom and the Western barbarians are each quite different, and both north and south have their admirable features as well as their defects. Thus the task of recording the principles of things has always changed with the development of the times and the gradual expansion of knowledge. This is as it should be.[171]

Ekken argues that in medicine especially it is good practice to make adjustments in accordance with changing times so that the practice will be appropriate to the time.[172] This is a view which can be considered to derive from his position on the unity of principle and the diversity of its particularizations.

Since Ekken placed such emphasis on the importance of the flow and transformation of material force, it is understandable that he thought that the yin-yang theory[ku] and the doctrine of the permutation of the five phases or five agents (*wu-hsing*)[kv] of the *Book of Changes* were indispensable to *jitsugaku* research, especially in medicine.[173] From this point of view, it is evident that Ekken's *jitsugaku* research is closely connected to traditional Confucian thought. Whether this was ultimately conducive or inimical to the development of rational and objective scientific inquiry is a question which is not susceptible to simple resolution. Yet, in either case, it must be admitted that Ekken's attitude toward rational and objective inquiry had a profound bearing on the development of the methodology of *jitsugaku* investigation in later generations.

Ekken's *jitsugaku* was broad in scope, rigorous, and detailed. Equally important, he was able to remain constantly sensitive to changing times and attentive to particular conditions in Japan and to carry out rational and objective research on this basis, never falling victim to adulation of the past or to slavish imitation of the Chinese. This was largely the result of his espousal of the Confucian theory of the unity of principle and the diversity of its particularizations, which was in turn based on his view of principle and material force as one substance. In the second part of his *Jigoshū* [kw] (Essay Written to Amuse Myself), Ekken gives an exposition of this theory in which he discusses such matters as human nature and social relationships and the nature of other living things from this standpoint.

If one embarks on the path of thoroughgoing rationalism one must always be wary of clinging to subjective opinion and losing objectivity. This is the reason that Ekken declares that one should suspend judgment on anything about which he has even the slightest doubt. In medicine, for example, both blindly adhering to a particular view and making judgments without proper evidence have always been unacceptable. He cites a famous enjoinder from *Analects* 2:11 to "review the old so as to discover the new," in support of his contention that inquiry must be flexible and open. [174]

Moreover, the pursuit of rationalism and objectivity leads to the adoption of positivism and empiricism. Accordingly, Ekken writes:

Even the ancients talked about comprehensive knowledge but often made empty pronouncements since they were unaccustomed to testing things themselves, and thus a great number of mistaken views have been perpetuated. If a man speaks nonsense and what he says is passed on by the multitude of men, it will eventually be taken to be fact. Mencius says that it would be better to be without the *Book of History* than to believe it in its entirety. How true this is! [175]

By performing actual experiments, Ekken demonstrated the untenability of the theory of Li Shih-chen [kx] (1518–1593), that honey came from non-poisonous flowers fermented by the bees' feces, and of the theory of T'ao Hung-ching [ky] (452–536), that bee urine was the fermenting agent. [176] Ekken's *Chikuzen no kuni zokufudoki* (A Supplementary Guide to the Topography of Chikuzen) was not merely a collection of hearsay information, but was completed only after he had personally travelled to all hamlets, mountains and valleys in the area. This gives further evidence of the importance he attached to empirical investigation. Nonetheless, even though one speaks of empiricism or positivism in such cases, if *jitsugaku* is not integrated into existing theory and knowledge, there is danger that it will lack objectivity and rationality. It might be said that Miyazaki Yasusada, in his famous *Nōgyō zensho* (Agricultural Compendium), provided the experimental verification for Ekken's theories about agronomy. One could, with equal justification, say that the publication of this work was a direct application of the *jitsugaku* methodology for which Ekken argued, i.e., its results were due to the cooperative efforts of both men.[177]

Ekken was both a Confucian and a follower of the Neo-Confucian School of the Way (*tao-hsüeh; dōgaku*), and he did not think that one could truly be said to be either if he were to forget about human ethical concerns (*giri no gaku*)[kz] or practical techniques for dealing with human affairs, no matter how extensive his learning might be otherwise. *Dōgaku*, for Ekken, involved careful reflection and intense contemplation as prerequisites for genuine understanding and effective practice, for, without this depth, one might slip into routine textual exegesis and philological exercises, or into the most superficial kind of learning. On the other hand, merely to fixate on the Way and virtue or on the nature and destiny without appropriate attention to matters of government service and political action (*ching-shih chih-yung; keisei chiyō*) or to be oblivious to changes in the times or to conditions prevailing in a particular locality would cause one to lapse into narrow-mindedness and inflexibility. Either way one would be scorned by one's contemporaries as ignorant and useless. For Ekken such learning would be *dōgaku* (*tao-hsüeh*) in name only; the essence would be completely lost.[178] It follows that Ekken would thoroughly reject the empty sudden enlightenment of the Taoists and Buddhists, which was basically asocial if not anti-social, as well as the opposing extreme of utilitarianism.

Although Ekken was doubtful about the static quality of Chu Hsi's metaphysics and his emphasis on principle, he could well appreciate the Sung philosopher's attacks on the teachings of Lu Hsiang-shan and Ch'an and also on the *shih-kung*,[la] or utilitarian, school, in what are referred to as "Chu Hsi's two great disputes." Thus he thought that to forget about the cultivation of the moral sense (*giri*) within one's own heart and to seek after worldly success was the way of a specialist,[lb] and that to attempt to discover techniques to penetrate into the principle underlying all things was the work of the technician.[lc] Neither was the work of the Confucian scholar. There was, in Ekken's view, a fundamental hierarchical distinction between *dōgaku* and technology (*gigei*)[ld] which is reflected in the statement "the three ancient dynasties regarded the arts as being of the lowest priority." He strongly cautioned against confusing the two,[179] saying that a scholar who attached more importance to technology than to *dōgaku*, did not understand principle and had the fundamental priorities reversed. In other words, for Ekken, Confucian learning (*jugaku*)[le] was the base on which *jitsugaku* rested. This is the reason he took the position that "Ethical relationships must be taught first."[180]

However, even in the realm of ethical relationships one's concern had to extend beyond the cultivation of one's own mind and body and be applied to the life of society as a whole or one would be hard put to fulfill one's ideals as a Confucian. And further, this application would be impossible without the skills and techniques to operate in accordance with the principles governing all things. Even in the most trivial of arts one could not perform successfully if one did not learn technique. Thus he argued that the actualization of the Confucian ideal required not only learning the traditional Confucian teaching concerning basic human relationships, but also learning a wide assortment of skills which were necessary to human existence. This was especially true for medicine and agriculture which were directly bound up with the people's life and death. If these techniques could be used to alleviate the distress of the people then one might possibly attain the Confucian ideal of assisting in the great enterprise of the universe—what the *Mean* spoke of as bringing harmonious order to Heaven-and-earth and nurturing all living things.

Thus Ekken contended that a physician must be proficient in the practice or the art of humaneness (*jinjutsu*).[lf181] By forgetting the importance either of the techniques of "nourishing life" (*yōjō no jutsu*)[lg] or of moral obligation (*giri*),[lx] one would become like the Chinese Taoist seekers of immortality.[182] And to study horticultural techniques and cultivate flowering plants solely out of love for their beauty and color and without regard for "the proclivity of nature to give birth to living things," would amount to "trifling with things and losing one's sense of purpose."[lh183] Yet Ekken, for all that he said about the importance of morality, could not help but emphasize the importance of science and technology—in other words, of *jitsugaku*—and to apply his energies with greatest intensity to research and publication in this area. This attitude set him apart from Itō Jinsai, who concentrated his efforts solely on moral cultivation and was almost entirely uninterested in *jitsugaku*. It was Jinsai's view that, "The ancients regarded learning as confined to the moral cultivation of the self and the governing of people. Discovering the principle underlying the behavior of things was thought to be superfluous, and thus they did not expend their energies in this direction . . ."[184] That this attitude of Jinsai's was more representative of the majority of Confucian scholars of the period than was Ekken's may be inferred from an event which occurred in connection with the publication by Miyazaki Yasusada of his Nōgyō zensho. When, having completed the draft of the work, Yasusada requested Ekken's older brother, Rakuken[li] (1625–1702), to edit it and check for errors, the latter declined on the grounds that it was an unimportant and trivial subject. Yasusada then renewed his request with the suggestion that his work might yet provide a modicum of assistance to the fulfillment of the great Way in nature, and on this basis he secured Rakuken's consent.[185] Ekken, however, shared Yasusada's view of the nature and function of jitsugaku. He wrote the introduction to Nōgyō zensho and in it said, "The duties of a sage lie only in the education and nourishment of the people." He quoted the teachings of Mencius and Kuan Tzu concerning the moral responsibility of government for the people's livelihood,[lj] saying that agricultural research is indispensable for the life of the people.[186]

As Ekken grew older, he put more and more of his effort into jitsugaku research and exposition. The importance he attached to jitsugaku may be seen from the following quotation from the introduction to his Saifu[lk] (Vegetable Encyclopedia).

Once there was a disciple of Confucius who wanted to learn the art of husbandry and gardening. . . . Now, although this lowly occupation was something which deserved to be investigated, the gentleman (kunshi),[ll] fearing that he might become soiled by it, did not take up its study. Not only do I lack great virtue, but I am without the ability to perform great deeds or to utter profound words. If I eat my fill without tending the rice field, wear warm clothes but do no weaving, and squander the riches of the world, I become a nuisance to society. If one lives in the world without having anything to do, one lives a life like that of the birds and animals; one withers together with the vegetation. Since this would be unbearably frustrating . . . I thought I could at least attempt to do what is within my power and thus I have written this trifling work. My only hope is that I might possibly be able to aid the teaching of the old gardener [referred to by Confucius] and to be of some assistance to the livelihood of the people. On this point I am not at all ashamed to face the deprecations of the gentlemen of the School of the Way (dōgaku).[187]

Ekken plunged into jitsugaku research with passionate fervor, quite aware that he might be the object of derisive laughter from the followers of dōgaku, who regarded such studies as trivial and demeaning. It was precisely because he had this passion that he was able to accomplish so enormous an undertaking in the sphere of *jitsugaku*. One may well feel that a statement such as the one quoted here reveals Ekken as much as a pure Confucian in his inspiration and motivation as a proponent of *jitsugaku*.

When Ekken used the term *jitsugaku* he meant scholarship for the purpose of self-cultivation (*shūshin*),[fh] or, in the words of *Analects* XIV: 25, "learning with a view to one's own improvement," in contrast to scholarship which is solely concerned with reputation, i.e., "learning with a view to the approbation of others."[188] Perhaps it would be best to characterize his notion of *jitsugaku* as being that of "useful learning" (*yūyō no gaku*).[lm] Since Ekken rejected crass utilitarianism, what did "useful learning" mean for him concretely? It referred to study which would benefit oneself in the sense of improving oneself morally. This concept of learning which "was to improve oneself" was the sort of thing earnestly discussed by the Ch'eng brothers, Chu Hsi and Chang Shih[ln] (Chang Nan-hsien,[lo] 1133–1180), who abjured the moribund memorization and textual criticism of the Han and T'ang periods. Accordingly, Ekken repudiated both "utilitarian learning" (*jikō no gaku*),[lp] which he saw as vulgar learning concerned with reputation and self-aggrandizement, as well as the sciolistic learning that consisted in mere talking and listening and which made much of "broad learning" but often amounted to no more than repeating or regurgitating what others had said without subjecting it to any analysis. Consequently, he concerned himself with a tradition oriented to the whole man in which what was learned would be "preserved in the heart and carried out in action" (*juyō no gaku*).[lq] This he considered to be truly "useful learning"[189] because its subject matter is the moral obligation entailed in human relationships (*jinrin dōgi*)[lr] which form the pillars supporting men's communal existence.

To borrow Ekken's words, *jitsugaku* was learning that would "benefit both oneself and others," which meant that it would "seek to realize the essence of humanity and righteousness, foster the ideal moral relationships, bring about good, and seek whatever would benefit man."[190] This passage reveals Ekken's basic orientation with respect to the essence of scholarship and the meaning of extensive learning. What Ekken meant by "useful knowledge" (*yūyō no gaku*) was learning that seeks to benefit society as a whole and is based on personal experience of the core of human moral relationships (*jinrin dōtoku*).[ls] This is precisely what Chu

Hsi called *jitsugaku* in the opening section of his commentary on the *Mean* (*Chung-yung chang-chü*). Chu Hsi considered everything expounded in the *Mean* to be *jitsugaku* because the Way which it expounded involved both ethics and metaphysics and practical statecraft; in other words, it encompassed both internal and external reality, mind and matter, and linked the philosophy of the moral mind with a concern for practical benefits in the life of society. At the same time a clear distinction was made between what was considered primary and what was secondary, between matters of urgent importance and those of less immediate concern. The same was true of Ekken.

But, although Ekken too used the terms *jitsugaku* and "useful knowledge," the content with which he invested them was different in a number of respects. One difference was that Ekken's *jitsugaku* took as its subject anything, no matter how mean or humble, which would be of practical usefulness to the daily life of ordinary people. He took as his object whatever might be regarded as having practical utility, and his concern was such as to admit no distinction between specialized research and popular education. It was even extended to include scientific techniques. Modern scholars have particularly emphasized this latter aspect of *jitsugaku*, but where the *jitsugaku* of Ekken is concerned, it is inappropriate to apply the term in this narrow sense. As indicated in the preceding discussion, Ekken's *jitsugaku* is properly understood in a broader sense, a point which deserves most careful attention in light of the contemporary significance of such problems as the relation between "the natural and the human" and between "natural science and humane values." With this in mind, we should try to go on to examine Ekken's *jitsugaku* in the original broad sense.

Although Ekken constantly spoke about "useful knowledge," he was careful to establish a hierarchy of priorities, and thus in the *Jigoshū* he outlined the view that "Ethical relationships must be taught first and are of primary importance." However, no matter how much one establishes oneself in the moral life and remains steadfast personally, this is not sufficient. For if this is not directly connected to wider social relations, i.e., if it is not concretely realized in action, then this *jitsugaku*, this "useful learning," becomes mere "substance without function."[lt] Sung Confucians realized this and that is why Hu Yüan[lu] (Hu An-ting,[lv] 993–1059) propounded the doctrine of "clarifying the essence and effectively applying it"(*ming-t'i shih-yung*),[c] Ch'eng I, the doctrines of "unity of substance and function" (*t'i-yung i-yüan*)^{lw} and "the ultimate inseparability of the apparent (phenomena) and the hidden (underlying reality)" (*hsien-wei wu-chien*),^{lx} while Chu Hsi referred to "total substance and great functioning" (*ch'üan-t'i ta-yung*).

This doctrine of "total substance and great functioning" is partly a legacy of his repudiation of the doctrines of the Buddhists and Taoists and the utilitarians. In the end, however, it represents a fusion and integration of the thought of Chou Tun-i with the theories of substance and function developed by Hu Yüan and Ch'eng I. For Chu Hsi, all of ethics and morality were founded in the nature of the mind and it was only when its subtlety was fully comprehended that the ideal Confucian state could be realized. But without exploring the principles of all things individually, it would be difficult to attain a complete understanding of the total substance of the mind, and thus one could not readily expect to achieve its "great functioning." Thus he wrote, "Without penetrating into the essence of all things, their manifest character and hidden nature as well, the total substance and great functioning of our minds will not become clear."[191] It is only when one thoroughly understands the principles governing all the things in this world that one's understanding will be able to penetrate the mind's "total substance." Here "total substance" means that the essence of mind is formless and embraces the principles governing all things, while "great functioning" means that the mind is lively and active and moves in accord with all things. Of course the principle of humaneness (*jen*)^{ly} is central to what Chu Hsi called "the total substance of mind, and the feeling of love which responds to all things is the core of its great functioning." This attitude found concrete form in his economic policy of maintaining granaries to provide for the livelihood of the people (*she-ts'ang fa*). The importance of this concept was recognized by those later students of Chu Hsi who had a good understanding of his teachings, and their efforts resulted in its development and elaboration.[192]

The concept of "total substance and great functioning" also had a profound impact on Ekken's *jitsugaku*. Ekken considered it essential both to "reflect on what is inherent in one's own being and to investigate the principles of all things." Furthermore, he distinguished these activities in terms of their relative importance and established a unified hierarchy into which they fit.[193] Without an investigation of all things one could not attain a detailed and comprehensive understanding of the principle of righteousness, or duty (giri)[jx] inherent in one's own being. At the same time, he emphasized a knowledge of techniques saying, "In all things there is a technique which must be mastered. If that technique is not known then it will not be possible to do that particular task."[194] The importance that Ekken attached to the concept of total substance and great functioning is further suggested by the fact that he carefully read and annotated works by certain later disciples of Chu Hsi, who may be considered to have been most influential in carrying on the legacy of that idea. These included: the Hsin-ching[lz] (Classic on the Mind) and the Ta-hsüeh yen-i (The Great Learning, Elaborated) by Chen Te-hsiu (1178–1235), and the Hsin-ching fu-chu[ma] (Commentary on the Classic on the Mind) by the Ming writer Ch'eng Huang-tun[mb] and the Ta-hsüeh yen-i pu (Supplement to The Great Learning, Elaborated) by Ch'iu Chün.[195] But the concept of total substance and great functioning as it has been developed in the Chu Hsi school tended to be bound up with the issues of government, society, and economy, while Ekken's contribution involved his pioneering in an independent course and placing new emphasis on scientific techniques (jitsugaku in the narrow sense). He also differed from most Confucians whose thinking was basically oriented toward government and reflected their personal experience in political administration. Ekken was far more concerned with the plight of the common people, for he was able to empathize with them and to look at things from their point of view. Consequently, he stressed the study of those things which would be of use to them in their daily lives. This meant that he not only concerned himself with the moral relations inherent in their day-to-day existence, but also felt the need to investigate and comprehend all sorts of other matters which were essential to their well-being. As a result, he authored a large number of books in simple Japanese which were basically concerned with practical matters, considering this to be his mission as a Confucian scholar.

Although Ekken was a scholar of the Kuroda han, he often travelled to Kyoto and Edo and had extensive contact with prominent Confucians of the period, lecturing and attending lectures, and publishing a number of distinguished works on specialized areas of Confucian thought. Why then, despite the fame and honor accorded him in the orthodox world of scholarship, did he devote his energies to jitsugaku studies designed to benefit the common people? One may attribute it to the times, but the only adequate explanation lies in his deep and abiding affection for the common people and concern for their lives, a concern which was rooted in his concept of "forming one body with all things" (*banbutsu ittai*).[mc] This concept had its origins in the idea of *jen*, or humaneness, which had been of such importance in the Neo-Confucianism of Sung and Ming China and in the Sung and Ming concept of "forming one body with all things." But it must not be forgotten that it was Ekken's Japanese sensibility, his love for and understanding of the land and people of Japan, which quickened and vivified these concepts and made them figure so centrally in his philosophy. Recent research on Ekken has tended to put great emphasis on *Taigiroku* and on his popular educational works, and particularly those writings which have a bearing on science and technology, while, unfortunately, neglecting the conceptual basis for these ideas, which is to be found in the noble and moving ideals of humaneness and forming one body with all things.

Ekken comments innumerable times in his works on the notion of humaneness and forming one body with all things, but since his favorite and best qualified student, Takeda Shun'an, quotes the most explicit and concise statement of Ekken's view in the introduction to Ekken's *Bunkun*[md] (Literary Style) let it suffice for our explanation of his views:

Nature gives birth to all and supplies each person with the means to perform his function. From the highest governmental officer to the lowliest workman, each is accorded the ability to benefit society in his own measure. Great Heaven gives birth to us all and we are deeply indebted to it. It has given us all the necessary means for obtaining the requisite food, clothing, shelter, and means for making a living. The debt we owe to Heaven is apparent in all aspects of our existence and is so great that we can never fully repay it. All we can do to repay even the most minute fraction of the debt is to act in accord with the will of Heaven and attempt to benefit man. It would be a dreadful affront to Heaven to spend one's life aimlessly, merely content with one's own relative comfort. I have no art of myself. Yet since I am fortunate enough to have the ability to read the works of the old masters and to write something which will help people to understand what I have read, I am duty bound to utilize this talent for the benefit of all men. We scholars of a later age cannot hope to equal the profound understanding of nature, destiny, the Way, and virtue which the sages of the past possessed. Since they have left detailed treatises on these subjects it is sufficient to read them. What need is there for writers of a decadent age to add redundant words? All that I have undertaken in my own humble writings has been the task of helping the young and the ordinary person to whatever extent I can.[196]

For Chu Hsi, the operation of the principle of the Supreme Ultimate, i.e., the reason why things are as they are (*suo i jan*),[kf] was natural and

was not to be understood in quantitative or mechanistic terms. It had the
sublime purpose of giving birth to the myriad things of the world and was
thus termed "the heart of Nature" (*tenchi no kokoro*).[me] This is also why
birth (*sei*)[mf] was regarded in the *Book of Changes* as the supreme virtue of
Nature. Origination (*yüan; gen*),[gb] the highest virtue in Nature, corresponds to humaneness (*jen; jin*) in man. Thus, both *yüan* and *jen* refer
to the underlying ground of all things, to the principle of things as they
are (*suo i jan*). The resulting identification of nature and man was expressed in terms of a perfection in which "nature and man form a unity"
(*t'ien-jen ho-i*).[mg] In accordance with this view, there arose the sense that
the morality of the family and state was the basis of the universe, and the
conviction that it was through preserving this morality that the great and
wondrous purposes of nature could be fulfilled. It was for this reason that
Chu Hsi placed so much emphasis on the *Hsi-ming*[mh] (Western Inscription) of Chang Tsai.[197]

At the heart of the "Western Inscription" is the sentiment of "forming
one body with all things," that is, the sentiment of brotherhood. Heaven
and earth are the father and mother of humanity, all living creatures are
brothers and sisters, and all living things are one in their life force(*ch'i*).
In the words of Professor Kusumoto Masatsugu, "It spoke of a moral path
centered on humane love in which the keynote was a religious feeling of
reverence and awe even more profound than belief in the gods."[198] In
this view the morality of the family, society and the state was suffused
with the sentiments of love and devotion felt for one's parents. The affection which one felt for one's parents was directed toward nature, while
the awe and respect which one accorded nature were carried over to one's
feelings for the family, the society and the state. It referred to that area of
human feeling where love and trust predominated and where man and
nature were one.

It is clear that Ekken was greatly indebted to Chu Hsi's interpretation
of humaneness and Chang Tsai's notion of brotherly love. He made this
clear in his exposition of the doctrine of the identity of humaneness and
filiality(*jen-hsiao i-li; jinkō ichiri*)[mi][199] and in his wholehearted appreciation of the "Western Inscription" with its notion of all things forming
one body.[200] How well Ekken understood the meaning and import of the
"Western Inscription" will be apparent if one examines the chapter by
that title in the second volume of his *Shogaku chiyō*[mj] (Essentials of the
Elementary Learning).[201] But Ekken's notion of the unity of all things

was probably imbued with even more fervent religious and moral feeling than was Chang's. For Ekken's concept was permeated with a poignant sense of respect, awe, gratitude, and obligation to Nature and patron deities, ruler and father, sages, teachers, the extended family, and farmers, among others.[202] Thus he felt that one who did not have a deep respect for the awesomeness of nature and a desire to make some recompense for benefits received was to be regarded as a profligate and an ingrate. Such a person did not deserve to be placed in positions of authority and would surely incur the wrath of Heaven.[203] The presence or absence of this feeling of gratitude provided Ekken with a criterion for distinguishing between the superior man and the small man.[204] Moreover, since humaneness represents oneness with all things, service to man and society through its complete and utter application is, according to Ekken, the lifelong vocation of the Confucian scholar.[205] When one reflects on the centrality of the concept of humaneness in his thought and his identification of humaneness with filiality, one finds some evidence that, although Ekken outwardly rejected the doctrine of the mind associated with the Lu-Wang tradition, he may nonetheless have been inwardly receptive to its emphasis on filial piety and incorporated it into his own thought.

The passage which has just been cited from Ekken's writings reveals another facet of his thought which must be given careful consideration. Ekken's words display a concrete application of Ch'eng I's admonition to "know what is sufficient and be content with your lot"[206] and a sentiment identical to that of Wang Yang-ming, who felt that in "completely fulfilling the duties of one's post"[207] one possessed the humaneness through which one formed one body with all things. The similarity is not coincidental, for this concept of the unity of all things played a crucial role in the formation of Ekken's philosophical perspective. Ekken thought that rich and poor, the great and the lowly, each had their delimited sphere; each of the four classes, samurai, peasant, artisan, and merchant, could fulfill their obligation (hōon)[mk] to nature by doing their respective tasks with all the skill at their disposal.[208] Ekken discloses what he regarded as his "Heaven appointed" task in the introductory remarks to the Yamato honzō.[209] With great humility, he says that he has neither erudition which can be effectively put to use nor the power or position to relieve the distress of the people. Moreover, if he attempted to interpret the meaning of classical texts, he could do no more than mimic earlier scholars who had done the job far better than he could. Nor did he have the talent and virtue which were requisite to fulfilling the ideals of the Sung philosophers. All he could do was to write books in simple Japanese for the unlettered of his native place in the hope that such works might prove to have some educational value. If through this he could be of some slight assistance to the common people in their everyday life, he might avoid being a burden on society and escape being guilty of ingratitude to Heaven.[210]

In this one may recognize the motive, the purpose, and the spirit behind Ekken's *jitsugaku*. While he was committed to the view that all things form one body, he spoke of universal love for all things in terms of the unity of principle and of the actual differences among them in terms of its diverse particularizations.[211] Ekken was able to go the way of "forming one body with all things" and also the way of the unity of principle and the diversity of its particularizations. Universal love was the one principle, while differences in its mode of actualization among things provided the multiplicity of its manifestations.[212] Certainly he was one who had a profound understanding of the "Western Inscription."

Within the framework of the theory of generation and regeneration[ml] and the theory of original substance and conscious effort,[mm] Chu Hsi founded what came to be known as orthodox Neo-Confucianism (*tao-hsüeh; dōgaku*), adopting a dualistic perspective to treat such questions as the relation of *li* and *ch'i*, yin and yang and the Supreme Ultimate, Tao and concrete things, the nature and material force, the mind and the nature, the nature and the emotions, natural principle and human desire, the moral mind and the human mind (*tao-hsin, jen-hsin*),[mn] the yet unmanifest and the manifest (*wei-fa, i-fa*),[mo] substance and function, movement and quiescence, and the original nature (*pen-jan chih hsing*)[mp] and the physical nature (*ch'i-chih chih hsing*).[mq] This dualistic position was forced on him because his object was to restore Confucian idealism to its rightful place by eliminating both the nihilistic teachings of Buddhism and Taoism, which were philosophically pure and metaphysically comprehensive but lacking in social relevance and realism, and the teachings of the utilitarian school, which had precisely the opposite strengths and weaknesses.

Ekken had the greatest respect for the teachings of Chu Hsi. But since he placed such emphasis on social relevance and realism, he condemned the uselessness of Buddhism and Taoism and espoused the doctrine of useful learning. He could not help feeling that a lingering taint of uselessness and nihilism associated with Buddhism and Taoism hung on in the Sung learning in its inclination toward quietism and its commitment to a metaphysical dualism in which priority was accorded to *li*. This is why he came to the point of harboring "grave doubts" about Shushigaku and the Sung Confucianism from which it sprang, and criticizing those of its doctrines which, in his view, derived from Buddhism and Taoism and departed from the Way of Confucius and Mencius. These included: the doctrine of the Supreme Ultimate and the Infinite (*t'ai-chi wu-chi; taikyoku mukyoku*), the doctrine of abiding in tranquillity, the doctrine of quiet-sitting, the identification of nature with principle, the distinction between an original nature and a physical nature, the dualism of principle and material force, the idea of the indestructibility of principle and the nature,[mr] the idea of clear virtue as tranquil and unobscured,[ms] the idea of the Principle of Nature as empty, tranquil and without any sign,[go] the idea of one source for substance and function, and the idea of the identity of the manifest and the hidden.[213]

According to Ekken, Chou Tun-i's "the Infinite and the Supreme Ultimate," was taken from the T'ang dynasty *Hua-yen fa-chieh kuan* by Tu-shun[mt] (557–640), while Ch'eng I's "one source for substance and function" and "identity of the manifest and the hidden" were derived from the *Hua-yen-ching shu*[mu] of Ch'eng-kuan.[mv] These formulations were rejected by Ekken as the language of Buddhism.[214] He also rejected the doctrine of the indestructibility of principle and the nature, which was based on Chang Tsai's notion of the indestructibility of *ch'i*, as being nothing more than the Buddhist doctrine of transmigration in disguise.[215]

Small wonder that Ekken paid such careful attention to the revisionists of the Ch'eng-Chu school in the early Ming period, especially to the writings of Lo Ch'in-shun, who staunchly preserved the spirit of Chu Hsi's philosophy. True, Ekken was dissatisfied with Lo's dualistic position on the theory of substance and function, the dichotomy of the moral mind and the human mind, and the distinction of the yet unmanifest and the manifest. However, he naturally applauded Lo's opposition to the idealism of Ch'an and to idealistic elements in the Lu-Wang tradition, as well as his criticism of dualistic features of the orthodox rationalistic school. Especially appealing to Ekken were Lo's views on the relation of *li* and *ch'i*. Lo advocated the view that principle (*li*) and material force (*ch'i*) were one substance, saying, "Principle is only the principle of material force." This was in marked contrast with the Ch'eng-Chu view that there is a fundamental metaphysical distinction between *li* and *ch'i*, original nature and physical nature. On this important point, he argued for a monism based on the doctrine that principle is one but its particularizations are many, saying that the original nature is to be found in the physical nature. Further, Ekken lauded Lo's ability to avoid an obsequious and slavish attitude toward the Sung Confucians, as well as his courage in revising what he conceived to be errors. Ekken summarized his assessment in these words:

Only Master Lo honored the Ch'eng brothers and Chu Hsi as his teachers without subscribing uncritically to their views. His opinions should be considered most correct and appropriate. There is no Confucian scholar to compare with him in the Yüan and Ming periods. He must be regarded as a truly distinguished scholar. Hsüeh Hsüan and Hu Chü-jen are said to be the two beacons of Ming Confucianism, but they are greatly inferior to him in the depth of their understanding. [216]

From this it is quite clear that Ekken's basic stance was quite similar to Lo's, that is, he was a revisionist follower of Chu Hsi.

Viewed purely in terms of their criticism of Sung Neo-Confucianism, the scholar closest to Ekken, apart from Lo, is the author of the *Chi-chai man-lu* (The Jottings of Chi-chai), Wu T'ing-han. But Wu, while he did not completely reject Chu Hsi's views, was strongly inclined to accord a position of centrality to material force (*ch'i*), saying, for example, "I venture to assert that material force (*ch'i*) is principle (*li*)." In the end, Wu must be considered a critic of Chu Hsi, and in this sense he differs from Ekken, who, despite his criticisms of Chu Hsi, may yet be regarded as one who maintained a deep respect for and confidence in him. [217] It cannot be denied that there are points of similarity between Ekken's criticisms of Chu Hsi and those found in such works as Ho Ching's *Shih-hsi hsin-chih*, as well as in the writings of several of Ekken's Japanese contemporaries. One might consider, for example, the arguments advanced in works such as *Chūyō hakki*[mw] (Elucidation of the *Mean*), *Ronmō kogi*[mx] (The Original Meaning of the *Mencius*), *Gomō jigi* (The Meaning of Terms in the *Analects* and *Mencius*) and *Dōjimon* by Itō Jinsai, as well as the *Seikyō yōroku*[my] (The Essence of the Sage's Teaching) and the *Haisho zanpitsu*[mz] (Autobiography in Exile) by Yamaga Sokō[na] (1622–1685). Yet, even in respect to their criticisms of Chu Hsi, there are differences as well as similarities among them. A detailed discussion of this crucial subject would be beyond the scope of the present essay, and I should only like to point out here that there are connections, both direct and indirect, between Ekken's critique of Chu Hsi and the views of these other Confucian scholars.

However, to consider only Ekken's criticisms of Chu Hsi and consequently to represent him as an adherent of the Ancient Learning (Kogaku) school would doubtless not be valid. It is necessary to examine carefully his thought and scholarship as a whole and to have a clear understanding of the spirit that informs the Taigiroku. This is essential because Ekken was by temperament a follower of Chu Hsi. Although there may be differences of opinion as to the degree of his commitment to, and the depth of his understanding of, its fundamental spirit, my belief is that not only was he heir to the lofty idealistic spirit of the Chu Hsi school, but that it was this very spirit which nurtured his splendid jitsugaku research. In other words, his jitsugaku was the outgrowth of Chu Hsi's notion of the exhaustive exploration of principle.

From the standpoint of original substance (pen-t'i), Chu Hsi regarded principle as primary and material force as secondary, while from the standpoint of the human endowment, the relation was reversed. He thus came to the conclusion that there was no principle without material force and vice versa. Nonetheless, he argued that to regard the two as interfused was a serious error and that a distinction must be made between them in terms of their value. If one does not firmly maintain that principle is absolutely pure, perfect, and good, it becomes a mixture of various characteristics—purity and impurity, good and evil. Such a principle could not possibly maintain directive power over material force. This is the reason that Chu Hsi advanced a metaphysical dualism in which priority was accorded to principle.

Yet, if one understands Chu Hsi's actual conception of principle as a directing agent, one will understand why he was at the same time forced to maintain the inseparability of li and ch'i. If these were not inseparable, principle would lose its character as a principle of actuality (jitsuri) and would degenerate into a principle of emptiness. This implied a lapse into the nihilistic quiescence of the Buddhists and Taoists, in which case principle would lose its relevance for society and the actual world and forfeit its directive power with respect to material force, which would have been an untenable position. Thus, although in his metaphysics Chu Hsi accorded priority to principle, he also made a detailed and thorough investigation of the different forms that material force assumed in the physical world. This was the reason he took the interest he did in Shao Yung's interpretation of the hexagrams of the *Book of Changes* and in Chang Tsai's theory of material force. He not only discussed the need for careful discipline in preserving the mind and the nature and for greater understanding and more practical effort in human relations and morality, but, in addition, he carried out the investigation of things and exploration of principle in a wide range of fields covering the natural and social sciences as well as the humanities. These included ceremonial rites, government, surveying, famine relief, astronomy and geography.[218]

Ekken assumed the practice of *jitsugaku* as his mission in life. In this, he independently opened a whole new field, and yet, as I have indicated, he began with Chu Hsi's doctrine of the exhaustive exploration of principle and went on to develop and refine this one aspect of his philosophy to the fullest possible extent. His research methodology is also of the greatest interest, though, as I have suggested, it may be that this too derived from the rationalistic spirit which existed at the core of the doctrine of the exploration of principle. In his later years, Ekken harbored "grave doubts" with respect to Chu Hsi's metaphysics, but, even so, he may be said to have been following through on the rationalism inherent in Chu Hsi's philosophy. Thus we may appreciate the degree to which Ekken, in his Confucianism and his *jitsugaku* alike, was indebted to Chu Hsi.

Ekken himself felt such limitless gratitude to Chu Hsi that he wrote, "I respect him as if he were a god, and I believe him as one might believe the oracle bones."[219] He believed what was worthy of belief and doubted what warranted doubt, feeling that not bending his principles out of a false sense of loyalty to his teacher was the best way to repay the debt that he owed him. His doubt was itself a tribute to his belief, for he felt that it was through a just and unselfish attitude that he could become a loyal disciple of Chu Hsi. He felt the utmost distaste for the unorthodox thinkers of the late Ming and early Ch'ing who, as he thought, had forgotten their obligation to Chu Hsi and "entered the room with spear in hand," prepared for combat rather than debate.[220] Is it not appropriate to call Ekken a Confucian who founded a new branch of the Chu Hsi school, a Confucian who established a reformed Shushigaku?

Translated by Robert Wargo

NOTES

1. *Erh-Ch'eng ch'üan-shu*,[nb] *chüan* 1.

2. See Lu Hsiang-shan's three letters to Chan Tzu-nan[nc] in *Hsiang-shan ch'üan-chi*,[nd] *chüan* 7; his letter to Pao Hsiang-tao[ne] in *chüan* 14; and the *Yü-lu*,[nf] sections 1 and 2 in *chüan* 34–35.

3. *Han-hsüeh shang-tui*,[ng] 2:1 and 2:2.

4. *Sentetsu sōdan, kan* 3.

5. *Bunkai hitsuroku*, 8:1 in *Yamazaki Ansai zenshū* (Tokyo: comp., Nihon koten gakkai, 1936–37), 1:374.

6. *Ibid.*

7. The *Yamato kagami* has been lost except for its table of contents, which is included in *Yamazaki Ansai zenshū*, 2:686–88. It is not known whether or not Ansai completed the work.

8. In the *Bunkai hitsuroku*, ch. 20 in *Yamazaki Ansai zenshū*, 2:618, Ansai quotes Ch'iu Chün's phrase, "the study of the principles of things," (*wu-li chih hsüeh*) from the *Ch'iung-t'ai hui-kao*.

9. The *Gaitetsuron*,[nh] transmitted in manuscript, is said to have been written by Ansai, though it is probably a forgery. Nonetheless, the account in the work of Ansai's successful effort to salvage the serious financial crisis of a certain fiefdom is in all likelihood not unfounded.

10. *Zoku Yamazaki Ansai zenshū* (Tokyo: comp. Nihon koten gakkai, 1937).

11. *Chu Tzu yü-lei, chüan* 105.

12. Quoted by Ikegami Kōjirō,[ni] from Inaba Mokusai's *Bunkai hitsuroku o yomu*,[nj] in *Zoku Yamazaki Ansai zenshū*, 3:387.

13. *Shisho matsuso ben*,[nk] in *Yamazaki Ansai zenshū*, 2:812–13.

14. Okada Takehiko,[nl] ed., *Bakumatsu ishin Shushigakusha shokan shū*[nm] (Correspondence among Scholars of the Chu Hsi School at the End of the Tokugawa and the Beginning of the Meiji Period), ST (Tokyo: Meitoku shuppansha, 1975), 14:140.

15. *Bunkai hitsuroku, kan* 3 in *Yamazaki Ansai zenshū*, 1:167.

16. *Shueki engi, kan* 2, in *Zoku Yamazaki Ansai zenshū*, 2:211.

17. Wakabayashi Kyōsai, *Kyōsai sensei zatsuwa hikki*, pp. 11–12.

18. *Bunkai hitsuroku, kan* 3 in *Yamazaki Ansai zenshū*, 1:174.

19. *Ibid., kan* 20 in *Yamazaki Ansai zenshū*, 2:638.

20. *Gyokuzan kōgi furoku batsu.*[nn]

21. *Ibid.*

22. Quoted in *Yamazaki Ansai to sono monryū*[no] (Tokyo: comp. Denki gakkai, 1943), p. 229.

23. *Manabe Chūan ni kotafuru sho*[np] (Letter in Reply to Manabe Chūan) in *Yamazaki Ansai zenshū*, 2:683.

24. *Kinshiroku jo*[nq] (Preface to *Reflections on Things at Hand*) in *Yamazaki Ansai zenshū*, 1:76–77.

25. *Manabe Chūan ni kotafuru sho.*

26. *Analects*, VII:1.
27. Quoted by Inoue Tetsujirō[nr] in his *Nihon Shushi gakuha no tetsugaku*[ns] (Tokyo: Fuzanbō, 1905), p. 419.
28. *Kyōsai sensei zatsuwa hikki*, p. 18.
29. *Heki-i batsu*,[nt] in *Yamazaki Ansai zenshū*, 2:726–27.
30. *Ibid.*
31. *Ibid.*
32. *Bunkai hitsuroku, kan* 5, in *Yamazaki Ansai zenshū* 1:271.
33. *Yamazaki sensei goroku*, manuscript.
34. *Chu Tzu yü-lei, chüan* 126.
35. *Chuang Tzu, Jen-chien shih p'ien.*[nu]
36. *Bunkai hitsuroku, kan* 2, in *Yamazaki Ansai zenshū*, 1:146.
37. *Ibid., kan* 3, in *Yamazaki Ansai zenshū*, 1:170.
38. *Heki-i batsu*, in *Yamazaki Ansai zenshū*, 2:726–27.
39. *Manabe Chūan ni kotafuru sho.*
40. *Keisai shin bunchū furoku no nochi ni shosu*,[nv] in *Yamazaki Ansai zenshū*, 1:83.
41. *Manabe Chūan ni kotafuru sho.*
42. *Taika shōryōshū kōgi*, manuscript.
43. This work is available in manuscript form. It is probably the notes taken by Asami Keisai.
44. *Heki-i batsu*, in *Yamazaki Ansai zenshū*, 2:726–27.
45. *Hakurokudō gakki shūchū jo*,[nw] in *Yamazaki Ansai zenshū*, 1:66–67.
46. *Hakurokudō shoin keiji kōgi*, manuscript.
47. *Ibid.*
48. *Ibid.*
49. *Ibid.*
50. *Hakurokudō gakki shūchū jo*, in *Yamazaki Ansai zenshū*, 1:66–67.
51. *Chu Tzu wen-chi, chüan* 67.
52. *Ibid., chüan* 74.
53. *Kōyūsō shisetsu*,[nx] manuscript.
54. *Ibid.*
55. *Ibid.*
56. *Yamazaki Ansai to sono monryū*, p. 85. The original text of Han Yü's poem appears in *Han Ch'ang-li ch'uan-chi*,[ny] *chüan* 1 where it is part of a cycle of ten poems entitled *Ch'in-ts'ao.*[nz] Ansai's postscript to the work is found in *Yamazaki Ansai zenshū*, 1:85.
57. *Tō Bu kakumei ron*, in *Yamazaki Ansai zenshū*, 2:707. Ansai himself was critical of the rebellions of T'ang and Wu. Though he did not openly express his view, it is apparent in the funeral inscription for Hanitsu Reishin (Hoshina Masayuki) in *Yamazaki Ansai zenshū*, 2:717–20.
58. Miyake Shōsai, *Mokushikiroku*,[oa] p. 5.
59. *Gan Shiryō ron*,[ob] in *Yamazaki Ansai zenshū*, 1:63.
60. Ch'iu Chün criticized Hsü Heng, asserting that to serve a barbarian master who interrupted the succession of Chinese emperors was to violate the princi-

ple of the *Spring and Autumn Annals*. Hsüeh Hsüan, however, declared that Hsü Heng's act was in accordance with the Way of the sages. He praised Hsü Heng's morality and scholarship and argued that he contributed a great deal to society through his outstanding propagation of Ch'eng-Chu philosophy.

61. Satō Naokata, *Unzōroku*.[oc] Miyake Shōsai, *Mokushikiroku*, 3:13, 14, 16, 20.
62. *Sekisui sensei isho*,[od] *Sekisuiden*,[oe] *Katei yobun*.[of]
63. *Bunkai hitsuroku*, 8:2, in *Yamazaki Ansai zenshū*, 1:373–74.
64. *Sentetsu sōdan, kan* 3.
65. *Kōhan zensho jo*,[og] in *Yamazaki Ansai zenshū*, 1:73–74.
66. *Zoku Suika bunshū jo*,[oh] in *Yamazaki Ansai zenshū*, 2:765.
67. *Ibid*.
68. *Kyōsai sensei zatsuwa hikki*, 5:5.
69. *Bakumatsu ishin Shushigakusha shokan shū*, ST, 14:141.
70. In the *Unzōroku*.
71. *Yamazaki sensei hi Kuwana Shōun sho*,[oi] manuscript.
72. *Ibid*.
73. *Keigi naigai setsu*.
74. *Chu Tzu yü-lei, chüan* 120.
75. *Chūan ni atafuru sho*,[oj] in *Yamazaki Ansai zenshū*, 2:684–85.
76. *Kinshiroku jo*, in *Yamazaki Ansai zenshū*, 1:76–77.
77. *Bumei kōchū jo*,[ok] in *Yamazaki Ansai zenshū*, 1:72.
78. *Ibid*. See also *Mōyō keihatsu shū jo*,[ol] in *Yamazaki Ansai zenshū*, 1:75–76, and *Bunkai hitsuroku, kan* 3 in *Yamazaki Ansai zenshū*, 1:166.
79. *Hototogisu o kikite kan ari*,[om] in *Yamazaki Ansai zenshū*, 1:15.
80. *Bunkai hitsuroku, kan* 3 in *Yamazaki Ansai zenshū*, 1:172.
81. *Ibid*.
82. *Sanshiden shinroku no nochi ni batsu su*,[on] in *Yamazaki Ansai zenshū*, 1:87.
83. *Bunkai hitsuroku, kan* 2 in *Yamazaki Ansai zenshū*, 1:152.
84. *Keisai Ō Atobe Ryōken no toi ni kotafuru sho*.[oo]
85. *Yamazaki Ansai zenshū*, 1:77.
86. *Hanitsu Reishin gyōjō*,[op] in *Yamazaki Ansai zenshū*, 2:768–71.
87. Ansai said that one could not understand Chu Hsi's *Jen-shuo t'u* unless one comprehended the fact that humaneness was as yet unmanifested love. See the *Jinsetsu mondō*,[oq] and the *Jinsetsu zusetsu*,[or] in *Zoku Yamazaki Ansai zenshū*, 3:46–58.
88. *Chu Tzu yü-lei, chüan* 9, 17, and 53; *Ta Li Hsiao-shu chi-shan wen-mu*,[os] in *Chu Wen-kung hsü-chi, chüan* 10; *Chu Tzu yü-lei, chüan* 6.
89. *Yüan-heng-li-chen shuo*,[ot] in *Chu Tzu wen-chi, chüan* 67; *Ta Li Hsiao-shu chi-shan wen-mu*, in *Chu Wen-kung hsü-chi, chüan* 10.
90. *Chu Tzu yü-lei, chüan* 15, 19.
91. *Ibid*., *chüan* 32; *Ta Ch'en Ch'i-chih wen Yü-shan chiang-i*,[ou] in *Chu Tzu wen-chi, chüan* 58; *Ta Li Hsiao-shu chi-shan wen-mu*, in *Chu Wen-kung hsü-chi, chüan* 10.
92. *Chu Tzu yü-lei, chüan* 32.

93. *Ibid.*, *chüan* 53.
94. *Ibid.*
95. *Ibid.*, *chüan* 60.
96. *Ibid.*, *chüan* 53.
97. *Ibid.*, *chüan* 60.
98. *Ibid.*, *chüan* 53, quoting *I-ching*, *fu-kua*.
99. *I-ching*, *Shuo-kua*.
100. *Bunkai hitsuroku*, *kan* 15 in *Yamazaki Ansai zenshū*, 2:539. Chu Hsi's views on the store of knowledge are found in the *Yü-shan chiang-i fu-lu*.[ov] The views of the Ch'eng brothers and Chang Tsai are said to be found in *Tei sho shōryaku* and *Chō sho shōryaku*, but I have been unable to consult these texts.
101. A manuscript of this text is extant. It is also called *Chizō setsu hikki*.[ow]
102. Shōsai's view is found in *Rōchiroku*,[ox] *kan* 1.
103. *Tanzan sensei isho*,[oy] *kan* 6. *Gakushūroku*,[oz] *kan* 2.
104. *Ibid.*
105. *Ibid.*
106. *Ch'i-an fu-chu t'ung-chih*,[pa] in *Wang Wen-ch'eng kung ch'üan-shu*,[pb] *chüan* 6.
107. *Ekken Nenpu*,[pc] in *Kaibara Ekken zenshū*[pd] (Tokyo: Ekken zenshū kankōbu, 1911), vol. 1.
108. *Ibid.*
109. Ekken's letters to Takeda Shun'an, in *Ekken shiryō*,[pe] *Kyūshū shiryō sōsho* (Fukuoka: Kyūshū shiryō kankōkai, 1959), 5:37, 104, 116.
110. *Rakukun*,[pf] *Kaibara Ekken zenshū*, 3:636.
111. *Yōjōkun*, *Kaibara Ekken zenshū*, 3:605.
112. *Ibid.*
113. *Rakukun*, *Kaibara Ekken zenshū*, 3:615; "Seifuku jūni kōsetsu,"[pg] in *Jigoshū*, *Kaibara Ekken zenshū*, vol. 2.
114. *Jigoshū*, *Kaibara Ekken zenshū*, 2:205.
115. *Rakukun*, *Kaibara Ekken zenshū*, 3:205.
116. *Ganko mokuroku*, *Ekken shiryō*, supplement.
117. See Okada Takehiko, *O Yōmei to Minmatsu no Jugaku*[ph] (Tokyo: Meitoku Press, 1970), ch. 8, section 3.
118. *Ekken Nenpu*.
119. Ekken's letter to Araki Tōzaemon,[pi] *Ekken shiryō*, 6:19–20.
120. Ekken's letter to Takeda Sadanao,[pj] *Ekken shiryō*, 5:48.
121. *Ekken Nenpu*.
122. Nakamura Tekisai's letter to Ekken, *Ekken shiryō*, 6:16.
123. *Kinshiroku bikō* 1, *Kaibara Ekken zenshū*, 2:637 (cites the theories of Hsüeh Hsüan in the *Tu-shu lu* [Record of My Reading] in which he revised Chu Hsi's theory of the priority of *li* over *ch'i*).
124. Hosono Yōsai[pk] of the Kimon school said that the *Taigiroku* was either a forgery or the work of Ekken's early years. The postface to the *Taigiroku* (manuscript).

125. *Ibid.*
126. *Taigiroku, Kaibara Ekken zenshū,* 2:161.
127. Ekken gives the main thrust of the view that Shinto and Confucianism form a unity in his "Shinju heikō shite ai motorazaru no ron."[pl] Also see *Shingikun*[pm] (On the Gods), *Kaibara Ekken zenshū* 3; *Jigoshū, Kaibara Ekken zenshū* 2, the "Honpō shichizen setsu"[pn] and "Kokuzokuron."[po] He also discusses it at other points in the *Shinshiroku.*
128. "First Letter to the Hunan Gentlemen on Equilibrium and Harmony," in *Chu Tzu wen-chi, chüan* 64.
129. Letter of Ogyū Sorai[hw] to Takeda Shun'an, *Ekken shiryō,* 6:69.
130. Postface to *Taigiroku* (manuscript).
131. *Ekken shiryō,* 4:97.
132. *Ibid.*
133. *Taigiroku, Kaibara Ekken zenshū,* 2:153.
134. *Ekken shiryō,* 6:42.
135. *Ibid.,* pp. 40–41.
136. *Ekken shiryō,* 4:69.
137. According to the *Ganko mokuroku,* Ekken read *Chi-chai man-lu* when he was fifty-seven. It was the same age that he read Wu T'ing-han's *Weng-chi*[pp] and *Tu-chi.*[pq]
138. *Ekken shiryō,* 6:16.
139. *Ekken shiryō,* 1:103.
140. *Shōjutsu sensei bunshū*[pr] 15, "Kaibara ō oyobi tsuma bō no jichō ni daisu"[ps] (Tokyo: 1955).
141. *Ibid.*
142. *Taigiroku, Kaibara Ekken zenshū,* 2:167.
143. *Kyoka nikki,*[pt] *Ekken shiryō,* 3:25–26.
144. *Ekken shiryō,* 4:110.
145. This work is preserved in manuscript form, and two copies are extant. One is in the Kaibara family library and the other in the Shidō Collection of Keiō University. The content of the *Dōjimon higo* is discussed in Inoue Tadashi's[pu] "Kaibara Ekken no *Dōjimon higo* ni tsuite"[pv] (Concerning Kaibara Ekken's *Dōjimon higo*), in *Kyūshū jugaku shisō no kenkyū*[pw] (Fukuoka: Research Center for the History of Chinese Philosophy, Kyushu University, 1957), and in Araki Kengo's[px] "Kaibara Ekken no shisō"[py] NST, vol. 34.
146. *Dōjimon higo.*
147. *Ibid.*
148. *Ibid.*
149. Dazai Shundai, "Shundai sensei Sonken sensei no *Taigiroku* o yomu,"[pz] in *Kaibara Ekken zenshū,* 2:148.
150. *Yōjōkun* 6, *Kaibara Ekken zenshū,* 3:560–61.
151. Inoue Tadashi, *Kaibara Ekken* (Tokyo: Yoshikawa kōbunkan, 1963), p. 22.
152. See Inoue Tadashi, *Kaibara Ekken.*
153. *Kaibara Ekken zenshū,* 6:2.
154. Introduction to *Chikuzen no kuni zokufudoki,*[gx] *Kaibara Ekken zenshū,* 4:1.

155. *Ibid.*

156. Introduction to *Yamato honzō*, *Kaibara Ekken zenshū*, 6:2.

157. Postface to *Kuroda kafu*, [qa] *Kaibara Ekken zenshū*, 5:464.

158. *Ibid.*; Postface to *Wakan kogen*, [qb] *Kaibara Ekken zenshū*, 1:436; *Shinshiroku* 6, *Kaibara Ekken zenshū*, 1:146; Introduction to *Saifu*, *Kaibara Ekken zenshū*, 1:209; *Bunkun* 4, *Kaibara Ekken zenshū*, 3:362.

159. Inoue Tadashi, *Kaibara Ekken*, pp. 18, 281–82.

160. Introductory remarks to *Nihon saijiki*, [qc] *Kaibara Ekken zenshū*, 1:438; Introductory remarks to *Chūka kotohajime*, [qd] *Kaibara Ekken zenshū*, 1:562; Introductory remarks to *Yamato honzō*, *Kaibara Ekken zenshū*, 6:11.

161. Preface to *Wajikai*, [qe] *Kaibara Ekken zenshū*, 1:108.

162. Introduction to *Wakan kotohajime*, [qf] *Kaibara Ekken zenshū*, 1:561.

163. *Taigiroku*, *Kaibara Ekken zenshū*, 2:173–174; *Yamato honzō* 1, *Kaibara Ekken zenshū*, 6:23.

164. *Jigoshū* 7, "Genki shōsoku setsu" [qg] (Dispersal of the Primal *Ch'i*), "Shisei setsu" [qh] (On Life and Death), "Jinki setsu" [qi] (On the Human Spirit), *Kaibara Ekken zenshū*, 7:316–18.

165. *Shinshiroku* 5, *Kaibara Ekken zenshū*, 2:111; *Yamato honzō* 1, *Kaibara Ekken zenshū*, 6:25.

166. Ekken's postface to *Isei shūyō*, [qj] *Kaibara Ekken zenshū*, 7:753.

167. *Taigiroku*, *Kaibara Ekken zenshū*, 2:172–73.

168. *Shinshiroku* 1, *Kaibara Ekken zenshū*, 2:21.

169. *Yōjōkun* 6, *Kaibara Ekken zenshū*, 3:560.

170. *Shogaku chiyō* [mj] 3, *Kaibara Ekken zenshū*, 2:414–16, 424–25; *Shinshiroku* 6, *Kaibara Ekken zenshū*, 2:140–41; *Jigoshū* 2, *Kaibara Ekken zenshū*, 2:216–17.

171. *Kaibara Ekken zenshū*, 6:2.

172. *Shinshiroku* 6, *Kaibara Ekken zenshū*, 2:142.

173. *Yōjōkun* 3, *Kaibara Ekken zenshū*, 3:506–7; *Yōjōkun* 6, *Kaibara Ekken zenshū*, 3:555–61.

174. *Ibid.*, p. 560.

175. *Yamato honzō* 14, *Kaibara Ekken zenshū*, 6:362.

176. *Ibid.*, pp. 361–62.

177. Inoue Tadashi, *Kaibara Ekken*, pp. 41–42.

178. *Shinshiroku* 4, *Kaibara Ekken zenshū*, 2:91; *Kunshikun* [qk] 1, *Kaibara Ekken zenshū*, 3:393; *Taigiroku* (first manuscript), *Ekken shiryō*, 6:124–25; *Bunkun*, *Kaibara Ekken zenshū*, 3:344, 355, 358; *Gojōkun* [ql] 5, *Kaibara Ekken zenshū*, 3:304.

179. *Jigoshū* 1, *Kaibara Ekken zenshū*, 2:187.

180. *Shogaku chiyō* 1, *Kaibara Ekken zenshū*, 2:384.

181. *Yōjōkun* 1, *Kaibara Ekken zenshū*, 3:486.

182. *Isei shūyō*, Ekken's introduction, *Kaibara Ekken zenshū*, 7:753.

183. Introduction to *Kafu*, [qm] *Kaibara Ekken zenshū*, 1:120.

184. *Dōjimon.*

185. Introduction to *Nōgyō zensho*, *Kaibara Ekken zenshū*, 8:560.

186. *Ibid.*, Ekken's preface, p. 557.
187. *Kaibara Ekken zenshū*, 1:209.
188. *Yamato zokukun*^{an} 1, *Kaibara Ekken zenshū*, 3:59.
189. *Ibid.*, p. 60.
190. *Ibid.*, 2:71.
191. *Ta-hsüeh chang-chü pu-chuan.*^{ao}
192. For a discussion of Chu Hsi's concept of "total substance and great functioning," see Okada Takehiko, "Sō-Min no Shushigaku,"^{ap} in ST (Tokyo: Meitoku Press, 1974), 1:93. For more detail, see Kusumoto Masatsugu, "Zentai taiyō shisō,"^{aq} *Nihon Chūgoku gakkai hō*, no. 4, 1953.
193. *Shinshiroku* 1, *Kaibara Ekken zenshū*, 2:7.
194. *Yōjōkun* 7, *Kaibara Ekken zenshū*, 4:86.
195. *Ganko mokuroku.*
196. *Kaibara Ekken zenshū*, 3:319–20.
197. Okada Takehiko, "Sō-Min no Shushigaku," in ST, 1:85–86.
198. Kusumoto Masatsugu, *Sō-Min jidai Jugaku shisō kenkyū* (Tokyo: Hiroike Gakuen Press, 1962), p. 80.
199. *Shogaku chiyō* 2, *Kaibara Ekken zenshū*, 2:392; *Shogakukun* 1, *Kaibara Ekken zenshū* 3:2.
200. *Shinshiroku* 5, *Kaibara Ekken zenshū*, 2:93, 113; see also *Jigoshū*, *Shogaku chiyō*, *Kunmono*.
201. *Shogaku chiyō* 2, *Kaibara Ekken zenshū*, 2:392–93.
202. *Yōjōkun* 4, *Kaibara Ekken zenshū*, 3:539.
203. *Shinshiroku* 2, *Kaibara Ekken zenshū*, 2:45.
204. *Ibid.*
205. *Shogaku chiyō* 2, *Kaibara Ekken zenshū*, 2:392.
206. *I-ch'uan I-chuan,*^{ar} commentary on the *lü* hexagram.^{as}
207. Okada Takehiko, *Ō Yōmei to Minmatsu no Jugaku*, pp. 78–80.
208. *Shinshiroku* 5, *Kaibara Ekken zenshū*, 2:106; *Kafu* 3, *Kaibara Ekken zenshū*, 1:208.
209. *Kaibara Ekken zenshū*, 6:14.
210. Introduction to *Saifu*, *Kaibara Ekken zenshū*, 1:209. See also Introduction to *Nihon saijiki*, *Kaibara Ekken zenshū*, 1:437.
211. *Gojōkun* 4, *Kaibara Ekken zenshū*, 3:278.
212. See *I-ch'uan wen-chi*^{at} 5 in *Erh-Ch'eng ch'üan-shu*, "Ta Yang Shih lun Hsi-ming shu."^{au} *Yang Kuei-shan wen-chi,*^{av} *chüan* 11, *Yü-lu,*^{aw} and *chüan* 16, "Ch'i I-ch'uan hsien-sheng,"^{ax} and "Fu I-ch'uan ta *Hsi-ming* lun."^{ay} See also *Chu Tzu Hsi-ming chieh.*^{az}
213. Okada Takehiko, "Sō-Min no Shushigaku," in ST, 1:89, 102–5; *Taigiroku*, *Kaibara Ekken zenshū*, 2:294; *Shinshiroku* 6, *Kaibara Ekken zenshū*, 2:133, 138.
214. *Taigiroku*, *Kaibara Ekken zenshū*, 2:164.
215. *Jigoshū* 7, *Kaibara Ekken zenshū*, 2:316–18.
216. *Taigiroku*, *Kaibara Ekken zenshū* 2:162.
217. In *Chi-chai man-lu*, Wu T'ing-han approves of Chou Tun-i's theory of "the

Infinite and the Supreme Ultimate," as well as his view of "abiding in tranquillity," arguing that they have much in common with the thought of Ch'eng Hao. Ekken, however, regarded Chou's views to have been founded on Buddhist and Taoist thought and was thus critical of their influence on Chu Hsi. For details, see *Taigiroku* and Okada Takehiko, *Ō Yōmei to Minmatsu no Jugaku*, ch. 8, section 4.

218. Okada Takehiko, "Sō-Min no Shushigaku," in ST, 1:186.
219. *Taigiroku*, in *Kaibara Ekken zenshū*, 2:152.
220. *Ibid.*, pp. 159, 162; *Jigoshū*, in *Kaibara Ekken zenshū*, 2:227, 257.

GLOSSARY

a　實学
b　中庸章句
c　明體適用
d　虛学
e　漢学
f　朱子学
g　陽明学
h　古學
i　古文辭學
j　福澤諭吉
k　全體大用
l　林家
m　木門
n　木下順庵
o　崎門
p　山崎闇齋
q　先哲叢談
r　日本道學渊源錄
s　大塚觀瀾
t　日本道學渊源續錄
u　千手旭山
v　日本道學渊源續錄增補
w　楠本碩水
x　貝原益軒
y　保井春海
z　渋川春海
aa　大倭七曜曆
ab　文会筆錄
ac　張果
ad　星宗
ae　郭守敬
af　授時曆
ag　黄鼎
ah　天文大成管窺輯要
ai　王錫闡
aj　大統曆西曆啓蒙
ak　丘濬
al　大學衍義補

am　本朝改元考
an　庚申考
ao　堯曆
ap　井上正利
aq　東鑑曆算改補
ar　安藤有益
as　倭鑑
at　周牌算經
au　李淳風
av　朱易衍義
aw　洪範全書
ax　會津風士記
ay　保科正之
az　儒醫
ba　黄帝內經素問
bb　古今醫統
bc　黄榦
bd　蔡元定
be　蔡沈
bf　眞德秀
bg　薛瑄
bh　胡居仁
bi　李退溪
bj　儀禮經傳通解
bk　律呂象數
bl　皇極內篇
bm　邵雍
bn　大學衍義
bo　物理
bp　性理
bq　社倉法
br　義倉
bs　朱子社倉法
bt　資治通鑑綱目
bu　山崎闇齋先生全集
bv　續山崎闇齋先生全集
bw　周書抄略
bx　張書抄略

fc	薄	gr	近思錄備考
fd	一	gs	大疑錄
fe	篤	gt	訓もの
ff	存養	gu	養生訓
fg	小學	gv	女大學
fh	修身	gw	大和本草
fi	羅從彥	gx	筑前國續風土記
fj	李侗	gy	中村惕齋
fk	柳川剛義	gz	松永尺五
fl	朱子靜坐集說	ha	大君
fm	楠本端山	hb	大なる樂しみ
fn	羅洪先	hc	天地
fo	高攀龍	hd	玩古目錄
fp	東林	he	現成派
fq	智藏	hf	傳習錄
fr	朱文公續集	hg	養神一路
fs	仁說圖	hh	朱子行狀註
ft	三德	hi	自省錄
fu	三端	hj	困知記
fv	惻隱	hk	羅欽順
fw	羞惡	hl	訓點
fx	恭敬	hm	朱子文範
fy	四德	hn	小學句讀備考
fz	四端	ho	森蘭澤
ga	貞	hp	太宰春臺
gb	元	hq	續辨名
gc	復卦	hr	論仏篇
gd	說卦	hs	愼思續錄
ge	智藏說	ht	神儒一體說
gf	太極	hu	本地垂迹
gg	藏往知來	hv	竹田春庵
gh	天命之性	hw	荻生徂徠
gi	未發之中	hx	大野北海
gj	無極之眞	hy	愼思別錄
gk	主靜	hz	谷一齋
gl	立極	ia	伊藤仁齋
gm	太極圖說	ib	吳廷翰
gn	無極	ic	吉齋漫錄
go	沖漠無朕	id	郝敬，郝京山
gp	未發之氣象	ie	時習新知
gq	楠本正継	if	寬文日記

ig 米川操軒
ih 安東省庵
ii 東涯
ij 香月牛山
ik 無極而太極
il 華嚴法界觀
im 尚直編
in 語孟字義
io 山本簡山
ip 熊沢蕃山
iq 童子問批語
ir 童子問
is 道學
it 道德學
iu 科學技術
iv 寬齋
iw 本草學
ix 訓蒙圖彙
iy 向井元升
iz 庖厨備用大和本草
ja 聖堂
jb 庶物類纂
jc 稲生若水
jd 松岡恕庵
je 宮崎安貞
jf 農業全書
jg 黑川道祐
jh 本朝医學考
ji 雍州府志
jj 後世家
jk 名古屋玄医
jl 古医法
jm 丹水子
jn 星野實宣
jo 股勾弦鈔
jp 運気六十年圖
jq 坤輿旁通儀圖說
jr 貝原恥軒
js 東軒
jt 格物窮理
ju 物の理

jv 經世致用
jw 道體
jx 義理
jy 博學
jz 博學洽聞
ka 紅夷外科宗傳
kb 楢林鎮山
kc 扶桑記勝
kd 合理性
ke 窮理
kf 所以然
kg 所當然
kh 天道
ki 魂
kj 精魂不滅
kk 張載
kl 理氣一體
km 理の常変
kn 天下には理外のものはない
ko 養生說
kp 氣質の本然
kq 天地の性
kr 時宜論，土宜論
ks 氣運開化
kt 理一分殊
ku 陰陽論
kv 五行論
kw 自娛集
kx 李時珍
ky 陶弘景
kz 義理の學
la 事功
lb 伯者
lc 技術者
ld 技芸
le 儒學
lf 仁術
lg 養生の術
lh 玩物喪志
li 樂軒
lj 民生主義的德治

lk 菜譜
ll 君子
lm 有用の學
ln 張栻
lo 張南軒
lp 事功の學
lq 受用の學
lr 人倫道義
ls 人倫道德
lt 有體無用
lu 胡瑗
lv 胡安定
lw 體用一源
lx 顯微無間
ly 仁
lz 心經
ma 心經附註
mb 程篁墩
mc 萬物一體
md 文訓
me 天地の心
mf 生
mg 天人合一
mh 西銘
mi 仁孝一理
mj 初學知要
mk 報恩
ml 生成論
mm 本體工夫論
mn 道心，人心
mo 未發，已發
mp 本然之性
mq 氣質之性
mr 性理不滅說
ms 明德虛靈不昧說
mt 杜順
mu 華嚴經疏
mv 澄觀
mw 中庸發揮
mx 論孟古義
my 聖教要錄

mz 配所残筆
na 山鹿素行
nb 二程全書
nc 詹子南
nd 象山全集
ne 包詳道
nf 語錄
ng 漢學商兌
nh 盍徹論
ni 池上幸二郎
nj 讀文會筆錄
nk 四書末疏辨
nl 岡田武彦
nm 幕末維新朱子学者書簡集
nn 玉山講義付錄跋
no 山崎闇齋と其門流
np 答眞邊仲庵書
nq 近思錄序
nr 井上哲次郎
ns 日本朱子学派の哲学
nt 闢異跋
nu 莊子，人閒世篇
nv 敬齋箴分註付錄後
nw 白鹿洞学規集註序
nx 拘幽操師說
ny 韓昌黎全集
nz 琴操
oa 默識錄
ob 嚴子陵論
oc 韞藏錄
od 碩水先生遺書
oe 碩水伝
of 家庭餘聞
og 洪範全書序
oh 續垂加文集序
oi 山崎先生批桑名松雲書
oj 與仲庵書
ok 武銘考註序
ol 蒙養啓發集序
om 聞鵑有感
on 跋三子傳心錄後

qc 日本歳事記
qd 中華事始
qe 和字解
qf 和漢事始
qg 元氣消息說
qh 死生說
qi 人鬼說
qj 頤生輯要
qk 君子訓
ql 五常訓
qm 花譜
qn 大和俗訓
qo 大學章句補伝
qp 宋明の朱子學
qq 全体大用思想
qr 伊川易傳
qs 履卦傳
qt 伊川文集
qu 答楊時論西銘書
qv 楊龜山文集
qw 語錄
qx 寄伊川先生
qy 附伊川答西銘論
qz 朱子西銘解

Yamashita Ryūji

Nakae Tōju's Religious Thought and Its Relation to "Jitsugaku"

Nakae Tōju[a] (1608–1648), as an early student of Chu Hsi's philosophy who also assimilated much of the Ming dynasty thought of the Wang Yang-ming school, is an important transitional figure in the development of early Tokugawa Neo-Confucianism and its view of *jitsugaku*. His major work, *Okina mondō*[b] (Dialogues with an Old Man) reveals how the development of Tōju's religious thought affected his conception of "real" or practical learning.

THE BACKGROUND OF OKINA MONDŌ

Following the usual course of studies in his time, Tōju first read the *Great Learning* and then attended lectures on the *Analects* given by a priest of the Zen sect. He then purchased a copy of the *Ssu-shu ta-ch'üan*[c] (Great Compendium of Commentaries on the Four Books), in which he read through the *Ta-hsüeh ta-ch'üan*[d] (Great Compendium of Commentaries on the *Great Learning*) hundreds of times. Having mastered this material, he went on to read the *Lun-yü ta-ch'üan*[e] (Great Compendium of Commentaries on the *Analects*) and the *Meng-tzu ta-ch'üan*[f] (Great Compendium of Commentaries on the *Mencius*), gaining a thorough understanding of these works as well. These were the works, according to the *Tōju sensei nenpu*^g (Chronological Biography of Master Tōju) studied by Tōju up through his seventeenth year.[1]

The *Ssu-shu ta-ch'üan* had been completed by imperial order at the beginning of the Ming period. It was based on the commentaries of Chu Hsi and included also the views of other Sung Confucians. In China the work had become a required text for the civil service examinations. Chu Hsi had awarded priority to the *Great Learning* as an introductory text, and in the Ming the *Ssu-shu ta-ch'üan* was a work of considerable importance. Tōju as a youth was consequently completely steeped in the study of Chu Hsi philosophy.

The *Nenpu* for Tōju's twentieth year states:

Master Tōju was primarily devoted to the study of the philosophy of Chu Hsi, and he observed and practiced with great intensity the formal modes of conduct (*ko-t'ao; kakutō*)^h of the Chu Hsi school.[2]

In this year he began to discuss the *Great Learning* with many colleagues and gained the aspiration to take the sagely learning[i] as his own task.[3]

At the age of twenty-one, according to the *Nenpu*, he wrote his *Daigaku keimō*^j (Resolving Obscurities Concerning the *Great Learning*).[4] This work was a simplified version of the *Ssu-shu ta-ch'üan*. Tōju later destroyed it.

For Tōju's twenty-second year, the *Nenpu* records that:

There was a certain man named Araki, who, upon seeing Master Tōju approach, remarked, "Here comes Confucius!" In his heart Araki was critical of Master Tōju's way of learning.[5]

Tōju, it seems, had adopted an extremely solemn and strict attitude and had come to espouse the formalism of the Chu Hsi school.

At twenty-eight Tōju became proficient in the methods of divination found in the *Book of changes*. In this year he thoroughly digested Chu Hsi's *I-hsüeh ch'i-meng*^k (Resolving Obscurities Concerning the Study of the *Changes*).[6]

For his thirtieth year, the *Nenpu* records:

This year he married the daughter of a certain Takahashi. Master Tōju was still at this time under the influence of the formal prescriptions of conduct of the Chu Hsi school. Therefore he observed the principle of "marrying when one becomes thirty," as originally prescribed in the *Book of Rites*, where it says, "At thirty one takes a wife."[7]

While Tōju harbored some doubts about the Chu Hsi school, he was still unable to break with it completely.

At thirty-one,

In the summer he wrote two works, *Jikei zusetsu*[l] (The Diagram of Holding Fast to Reverence, Explained) and *Genjin*[m] (Inquiry into Man). Prior to this he had been primarily devoted to reading the Four Books and steadfastly observing the formal codes of conduct. Tōju thought that he had to observe each and every one of the regulations and ritual practices established by the sages. However, these prescribed modes of conduct were often out of harmony with the times and circumstances, and there were obstacles to their observance. He therefore thought, "If the Way of the sages is as difficult as this, it will be entirely unattainable by us in the present age." And so after he took up the Five Classics and studied them diligently, he was deeply moved by the enlightenment which he experienced.[8]

There is great significance in Tōju's conversion from the Four Books to the Five Classics. As can be seen from the compilation of the *Wu-ching cheng-i*[n] (The Correct Interpretation of the Five Classics) in the T'ang, the Confucian classics revered during the Han and T'ang were the Five Classics (the *Book of Changes*, the *Book of Odes*, the *Book of Documents*, the *Book of Rites*, and the *Spring and Autumn Annals*). The Four Books (the *Great Learning*, the *Mean*, the *Analects*, and the *Mencius*) became authoritative only in the Sung, and it was Chu Hsi who made them authoritative. That Tōju revered not the Four Books, the essential classics of the Chu Hsi school, but the Five Classics, may be called his "restorationism." Just as Wang Yang-ming had come forth with the *Ta-hsüeh ku-pen*[o] (The Ancient Text of the *Great Learning*), in which he rejected the emendation and revision done by Chu Hsi in his *Ta-hsüeh chang-chü*[p] (Commentary on the Words and Phrases of the *Great Learning*), Tōju's restorationism revealed a sentiment of negative criticism against the Chu Hsi school.

As the Four Books, in point of origin, are newer than the Five Classics, they lack some of the mystical coloration of the Five Classics. Moreover, when the Four Books are read through Chu Hsi's commentaries, their contents take on an even more rational cast, as may be seen, for example, in Chu Hsi's interpretation of the passage in *Analects* VI: 20, "Respect the ghosts and spirits, and keep them at a distance." Pao Hsien[q] of the Latter Han had interpreted the passage to mean, "One must respect the gods without profanation: one must keep one's distance so as not to commit a profanation by approaching the gods." In other words, since Confucius truly respected the gods, he taught that one should not approach them while defiled in mind and body. Huang K'an[r] of the Liang, Hsing Ping[s] (932–1010) of the Sung, and Liu Pao-nan[t] (1791–1855) of the Ch'ing all followed the interpretation of Pao Hsien, recognizing the existence of the ghosts and spirits as personal gods and regarding them as worthy of true belief and respect.[9] Chu Hsi, however, was apprehensive that men would be deluded by believing in the ghosts and spirits, and he therefore interpreted the text as follows: "Ghosts and spirits are to be respected, but one should keep one's distance from them without believing in them too much. This is called wisdom."[10] In other words, Chu Hsi was opposed to the interpretation of ghosts and spirits as personal gods and to a profound belief in such gods. He had adopted an atheistic reinterpretation of words of Confucius which had been based on the theism of antiquity. Chu also interpreted the reference to ghosts and spirits in the *Mean*, XVI to mean that the ghosts and spirits are "the yin and the yang, the two aspects of *ch'i*," conceiving them not as gods but as physical laws. His rationalism was atheistic.

Among the Four Books, the *Great Learning* is articulated in a more logical manner than the *Analects* and the *Mencius*. The *Great Learning* establishes a direct link between personal virtue and the government of the state and unifies the individual, the family, the state, and the world through the principle of "sincerity" (*ch'eng*).[u] This logical style accorded well with Chu Hsi's rationalistic mode of thinking, which is why he placed primary emphasis on this text.

By contrast, there are many passages in two of the Five Classics, the *Book of Odes* and the *Book of Documents*, which recognize the existence of, and indicate belief in, a Lord of Heaven (*t'ien-ti*),[v] or Lord on High (*shang-ti*),[w] as the one God of Heaven. There is evidence in the *Odes* and the *Documents* that the sage-kings Wen and Wu administered government while believing in, depending upon, and following the will of the gods. The Five Classics, characterized as they are by a more mystical coloration than the Four Books, also require a more reverential attitude on the part of man for the gods. Moreover, the *Book of Changes* is based on divination, and divination is the process of inquiring after the will of unseen gods. Chu Hsi attempted to investigate the laws of yin and yang through the *Book of Changes*. The *Book of Changes*, however, is a mystical and essentially theistic work.

Tōju's study of the *Book of Changes* and his absorption in the Five Classics reflect his recognition of the existence of the gods and the deepening of his interest in the mystical and the non-rational. In his *Genjin*, which he wrote after studying the Five Classics, he stated:

The August High Lord is "the Infinite and yet the Supreme Ultimate," perfect sincerity and yet perfect mystery. The material force (*ch'i*) of yin and yang and the Five Agents is the medium through which the August High Lord appears, and the principle (*li*) of the Infinite is the mind of the August High Lord.[11]

The phrases, "the Infinite and yet the Supreme Ultimate,"[x] and "the material force of yin and yang and the five agents,"[y] derive from Chou Tun-i's *T'ai-chi-t'u shuo*[z] (Diagram of the Supreme Ultimate, Explained). But the term "August High Lord" (*huang shang-ti*)[aa] does not appear in Chou Tun-i's work. Tōju directly linked the Chu Hsi school's doctrine of "the Infinite and yet the Supreme Ultimate"—which Chu Hsi had interpreted as principle (*li*)[ab]—and its doctrine of yin and yang and the five agents—which Chu had interpreted as material force (*ch'i*)[ac]—with God.

In the Sung school from Chou Tun-i to Chu Hsi, *li* and *ch'i* were interpreted as the two principles of the formation of the universe. The universe is created by these two principles. Accordingly, in the Sung Learning there had been no theory of the creation of the universe by the August High Lord, and conceptions of rule over the world by God are extremely rare in comparison with those that derive from the classical period of antiquity. From the atheism of the Chu Hsi school Tōju again returned to the theism of classical antiquity. In the *Genjin* he cites the verses of the *Book of Odes*, "The distant and vast Heaven is the father and mother of the people," and "The broad and great Lord on High is the ruler over the people below."[12] These citations reflect Tōju's belief in the August High Lord. And in his *Jikei zusetsu* he wrote:

Reverence (*ching*)[ad] means to fear the mandate of Heaven (*t'ien-ming*)[ae] and to honor the virtuous nature (*te-hsing*).[af] Ch'eng I taught that reverence means "concentrating on one thing without getting away from it (*chu-i wu-shih*).[ag][13]

In the Chu Hsi school, *ching* meant controlling the mind; it did not connote paying homage to the gods or to great men. Tōju, however, wrote of "fearing the mandate of Heaven," in other words, fearfully and reverentially receiving the command of the August High Lord of Heaven.

Ogyū Sorai[ah] later wrote:

Reverence takes respecting Heaven and respecting the ghosts and spirits as its foundation. There can be no reverence without an object of reverence. Chu Hsi originated the codes for cultivating reverence, but his was a reverence without an object to be reverenced.[14]

Sorai also taught deep faith in the gods, and his interpretation of Confucius' words, "Respect the ghosts and spirits, and keep them at a distance," differed from that of Chu Hsi and coincided with the commentaries of the Han and T'ang. It is noteworthy that both the Yōmeigaku (Wang Yang-ming) and Kogaku (Ancient Learning) schools of the Tokugawa period held theistic positions, in contradistinction to Chu Hsi.

Tōju wrote:

If one fears the mandate of Heaven and honors the virtuous nature, he will naturally concentrate on one thing without getting away from it and will naturally be careful and serious. . . . His mind will be naturally serene, and no evil from any exterior source will enter his mind.[15]

As seen in this passage, Tōju regarded the August High Lord as the one God and attached the highest significance to following God's commands. He therefore separated himself from the atheism of the Chu Hsi school. Since the Shushigaku teaching of reverence without its proper object and of holding fast to reverence (ch'ih-ching)[ai] to maintain seriousness was indeed formalistic, it was natural that Tōju should have come to have doubts about the Chu Hsi teaching.

Let us compare this with the course of development of Wang Yang-ming's thought. Wang Yang-ming also had Chu Hsi's thought as the point of departure for his learning. After passing the civil service examinations and becoming an official, he was exiled to Lung-ch'ang by the eunuch Liu Chin[aj] (d. 1510). At Lung-ch'ang, Yang-ming awoke to the realization that, "The Way of the sages already fully exists within our original nature. My former search for principle within things in accord with Chu Hsi's teaching was erroneous." He wrote his Wu-ching i-shuo[ak] (Opinions on the Five Classics) to demonstrate this in the phrases of the Five Classics. Since Shushigaku was a style of learning centering on the Four Books, Yang-ming went beyond Chu Hsi's thought by giving special attention to the Five Classics.

Tōju wrote his Tōju ki[al] at the age of thirty-two. It was modelled on Chu Hsi's Po-lu-tung shu-yüan chieh-shih[am] (Precepts of the White Deer Grotto Academy). He followed Chu Hsi in articulating the teaching of the Mean concerning broad learning,[an] extensive inquiry,[ao] reflective thought,[ap] clear discernment,[aq] and sincere practice,[ar] and referring to *Analects* XV: 5 with its appeal for "words that are honorable and careful."[as] In this work, however, Tōju spoke of "fearing the mandate of Heaven and honoring the virtuous nature," saying that this phrase is the foundation for making progress in one's cultivation. While absorbing Chu Hsi's thought, Tōju grounded it on the concept of "fearing the mandate of Heaven." Like Wang Yang-ming, he strongly advocated honoring one's own virtuous nature.

Since it is recorded in the *Nenpu* that, "From the summer to the winter of the following year he lectured on the *Hsiao-hsüeh*[at] (Elementary Learning), and his disciples practiced the formal modes of conduct,"[16] we may surmise that Tōju had not at this time entirely transcended the formalism of the Chu Hsi school. In the fall of his thirty-second year he read the *Hsiang-tang*[au] chapter of the *Analects* and was greatly moved by the enlightenment he experienced. This section is a record not of Confucius' words, but of his actions, and it contains a detailed description of Confucius' daily activities. It records that Confucius observed the funeral ceremonies with great dignity and also conducted himself with great dignity at the ancestral temple. In other words, this section provides a clear account of Confucius' religious behavior. What affected Tōju so greatly was the attitude of Confucius toward his daily activities. In reference to the description of Confucius which recorded, "His countenance was always transformed in violent thunder and storm winds," Tōju wrote in his *Rongo kyōtō keimō yokuden*[av] (Resolving Obscurities Concerning the *Hsiang-tang* Chapter of the *Analects*):

In this passage it is recorded how Confucius respected Heaven and how he conducted himself. According to it, Heaven is the great sage, and the sage is the small Heaven. . . . The violent thunder and storm winds signify the mystical functions of Heaven and earth and of the ghosts and spirits; they are the physical tranformations of the Supreme Vacuity (*t'ai-hsü*).[aw] Therefore the sage who becomes one with Heaven and earth and with the ghosts and spirits unconsciously follows the norms which the August High Lord reveals; his countenance is naturally transformed, and he becomes one with the physical transformations of the Supreme Vacuity. Transformation signifies that the reverential mind is expressed in his countenance.[17]

From this passage it is clear that Tōju was greatly affected by the description of the behavior of Confucius who possessed a mind which was so reverential toward Heaven and the August High Lord.

For Tōju's thirty-third year, the *Nenpu* records:

In the summer he read the *Classic of Filial Piety*[ax] and increasingly came to feel that its meaning was truly profound. From this time on he bowed before and recited the *Classic of Filial Piety* every morning. During this year he also read the *Hsing-li hui-t'ung.*[ay] He was moved by the new views found in this work, and on the first day of every month he purified his body and worshipped *T'ai-i shen,*[az] the great original god who created the myriad things. In ancient times the Son of Heaven worshipped Heaven and there were no ceremonies of worshipping Heaven for the literati or common people. But Tōju regarded this ceremony as the way the literati and common people could worship Heaven.[18]

The *Hsing-li hui-t'ung* (Comprehensive Anthology of Commentaries on the Nature and Principle), the work of Chung Jen-chieh[ba] of the late Ming, was published in 1634. This work added to the *Hsing-li ta-ch'üan*[bb] (Great Compendium of Commentaries on the Nature and Principle) the teachings of the Ming scholars. Compiled in it were the views of such thinkers as Wang Yang-ming, Wang Chi,[bc] (1498–1583), and Chou Ju-teng[bd] (1547–1629?) of the Yang-ming school, and of such philosophers as Lo Ch'in-shun[be] (1465–1547) and Wang T'ing-hsiang[bf] (1474–1544). Through this work Tōju became acquainted with the modes of thought developed in the latter half of the Ming period and was profoundly influenced by them.[19] Many scholars of the late Ming had been attracted to the teachings of Taoism and Ch'an Buddhism, and several adherents of the left wing of the Wang Yang-ming school—for example, Wang Chi, Lo Ju-fang[bg] (1515–1588), and Li Chih[bh] (1527–1602)—were drawn to the syncretic mode of thought which regarded the "three teachings" (Confucianism, Taoism, and Buddhism) as one in essence. The Kung-an[bi] literary school centering around Yüan Hung-tao[bj] (1568–1610) clearly exemplifies this tendency. These Kung-an writers repudiated Chu Hsi's philosophy of principle (*li*). Yüan Hung-tao's brother Yüan Chung-tao[bk] (1570–1624) affirmed the existence of ghosts and spirits, and his *Ching-hsi lei-shuo*[bl] indicates that he regarded thunder as the mystical function of the ghosts and spirits. In this attitude there was a faith similar to that of Confucius, who displayed a reverential attitude upon seeing the thunder as a function of God and Heaven. This kind of religious philosophy existed on a fairly broad front in the late Ming as a theistic mysticism or anti-rationalism which stood in opposition to the rationalism of the Chu Hsi school. For Tōju, the *Hsing-li hui-t'ung* was useful in supporting his critique of the Chu Hsi school. Not only was Tōju's thought closely related to that of Wang Yang-ming, but his belief in God and recognition of mystical powers were deeply influenced by the late Ming doctrine of the unity of the three teachings.[bm]

In antiquity, only the Son of Heaven had the authority to worship Heaven. The literati and common people were only allowed to worship their own ancestral gods. In the Chu Hsi school as well, there was no teaching that the literati and the common people could worship Heaven. Chu Hsi merely held that Heaven gave the people their "original nature," which was moral in character, and that the people should follow that nature. This teaching derived from Mencius' theory of the original good nature and from the doctrine of the mandate of Heaven (*t'ien-ming*) and the idea of "according with the nature" (*shuai-hsing*)[bn] found in the *Mean*. According to Mencius, Heaven invests the Son of Heaven with authority. Mencius taught that the will of Heaven is manifested in the will of the people, but Heaven's function ended with investing the Son of Heaven with authority; there was no obvious relation between Heaven and the common people. The Son of Heaven, by worshipping Heaven, was related to Heaven, but the literati and common people in general could not worship Heaven directly. The Chu Hsi school theoretically recognized a reciprocal relationship between Heaven and man, but this did not mean that it recognized the right of the people in general to worship Heaven as a religious activity.

It is noteworthy that Tōju went beyond this limitation of the Chu Hsi school, allowing that all the literati and common people could worship Heaven directly and, in his own case, carrying out this concept in actual practice. In other words, Tōju universalized the belief in Heaven; regardless of status, anyone could have a direct relationship with Heaven, and all men were equal before God. This concept, which resembles Wang Yang-ming's teaching that, "Every man on the street is a sage," recalls Wang's strong insistence that every person, transcending all forms of social stratification, possesses the same innate knowledge (*liang-chih*).[bo] Wang Yang-ming opposed the view that learning was the exclusive prerogative of the literati class, and liberated learning for persons of lower social rank as well. Tōju was able to liberate Heaven, the August High Lord, and *T'ai-i shen*, the god of creation, for all the people.

In the winter of his thirty-third year, Tōju came into possession of the *Wang Lung-hsi yü-lu*[bp] (Recorded Conversations of Wang Chi) and was greatly impressed with it. He came to think that the Way of the Supreme Vacuity permeates this world and that awakening to the Way of the

Supreme Vacuity constitutes the true learning. The Supreme Vacuity is the fountainhead of this universe; it produces the material force (ch'i) of yin and yang, it creates the myriad things. The ruler of this Supreme Vacuity is the August Supreme Lord. Chu Hsi had interpreted the Supreme Ultimate as principle, which meant that strict law became the foundation of everything. It was Chang Tsai who had espoused the idea of the Supreme Vacuity, and the Supreme Vacuity was material force. Ch'i produces the myriad things, as well as the mind of man, and the mind includes the emotions and desires. Tōju rejected Chu Hsi's teaching that the nature is principle (hsing chi li)[bq]—the view that the original moral nature of man is principle, while the emotions and desires belong to the category of material force. The idea of the Supreme Vacuity had been revived in the mid-Ming by Lo Ch'in-shun in the form of a philosophy of ch'i, and Wang Chi had also been involved in the transmission of his philosophy of ch'i. Tōju first became aware of the philosophy of ch'i and late Ming developments in the philosophy of innate knowledge through the Hsing-li hui-t'ung and then through the Wang Lung-hsi yü-lu. He completed his Okina Mondō in the following year, at the age of thirty-four.[20]

WANG CHI AND TŌJU'S OKINA MONDŌ

To transcend the formalism of the Chu Hsi school was Tōju's great aim; the philosophy which exerted a strong stimulus in this direction was that of Wang Chi. Passages frequently appear in the Wang Lung-hsi yü-lu which repudiate and eliminate the formalism (ko-t'ao) taught by the Chu Hsi school. For example, in Wang Chi's Wei-yang wu-yü,[br] there is the following assertion:

To deal with affairs according to detailed norms without regard to whether they accord well with the times and circumstances is to have one's mind adulterated by formalism (ko-t'ao) and is not the true innate knowledge.[21]

And in his Fu-chou Ni-hsien-t'ai hui-yü[bs] Wang Chi wrote:

When there is even the slightest thought of forming a clique, this is a thought which has arisen from formalism (ko-t'ao) and not from the true learning (shih-hsüeh) which learns for its own sake.[22]

The term *k'o-t'ao*,[bt] with the nuance of outer shell or husk, is also employed with the same meaning as *ko-t'ao*, and this too is repudiated. Tōju wrote:

Not understanding that the Way exists in their own minds, men recognize as the Way only the laws laid down by the sage kings of old or deeds carried out by the sages and excellent individuals; they define the good in terms of conventions (*ko-t'ao*) frequently observed in society; they affirm as true principle the modes of reasoning that are current in society. And since men exert themselves to correct their minds and cultivate their bodies according to these codes and conventions and reasonings, the original, active mind which can adapt spontaneously to circumstances is correspondingly diminished.[23]

Tōju did not regard the codes and conventions of society as passed down from antiquity to be good in themselves. Just as Wang Chi conceived the original mind as "being in accord with the times and circumstances," Tōju stressed "acting in accord with the time, place and rank." The "time" refers to the actions of a man being consonant with the trend of the times and with the historical age; the "place" refers to his actions being appropriate under the circumstances; and "rank" refers to his acting in a manner befitting his social rank and position. Tōju wrote:

To follow the course (*tao-li; dōri*)[bu] which is appropriate to the time, the place, and one's own lot—this is what is good.[24]

Again,

Those modes of conduct which are applicable in every age are very few. Since these modes of conduct change with the times, the circumstances, and the persons involved, even the Buddhists have repudiated the observance of fixed codes of behavior.[25]

At the base of this rejection of behavioral formalism (*ko-t'ao*) was the philosophy, shared by Wang Chi and Tōju, that all laws and customs change with the historical times.

Wang Chi had been the greatest disciple of Wang Yang-ming. Yang-ming himself had said:

The method by which the sages and worthies instructed the people was just like prescribing medicine to suit a particular illness. There is no one fixed method for curing all forms of illness.[26]

Wang Yang-ming did not hold that the good consisted in practicing the modes of proper conduct just as they were described in the ancient classics. The good necessarily requires an individual to act on the basis of the judgments of his own innate knowledge. Therefore, while Wang Yang-ming did not employ the term *"ko-t'ao,"* his teaching that one must never lose the dynamic spontaneous mind was altogether consistent with the views of Wang Chi and Tōju. The manifestation of innate know-ledge—in other words, the extension of innate knowledge (*chih liang-chih*)ᵇᵛ—means to respond in accord with time and place, which is the essence of *jitsugaku*.

Jitsugaku refers to pragmatic learning, learning useful in actual affairs; it is a learning that issues in positive achievement, a learning that results in action. Because of this pragmatic, positive character, it is necessary that one's response be fully efficacious; one must immediately react to the changes of circumstance. There can be no *jitsugaku* if one cannot re-spond because he adheres rigidly to a fixed pattern of thought. Tōju called this practical learning the "way of adaptation" (*ken no michi*).ᵇʷ He wrote:

> The metaphor of the balance refers to delicately balanced weights. . . . The sage is one with Heaven. . . . He is independent in his actions. He is spontaneous. Since the actions of the sage are always in perfect conformity with the way of Heaven, the metaphor of the balance which freely moves aptly symbolizes the ac-tivity of the sage.²⁷

Tōju maintained that since the sage alone attains this kind of freedom, ordinary men must observe the codes of conduct established by them. But since he took free activity to be the ideal, ordinary men could also at-tain some degree of freedom from fixed modes of conduct—in other words, from rigid psychological bonds.

Wang Chi had lived a free and somewhat dissolute life as a youth. The formalism of the Chu Hsi school ran contrary to his character. Thus, after he became a disciple of Wang Yang-ming, he stressed Wang's teaching that, "the learning of the sages is never rigid, never binds men." He took as his model Confucius' disciple Tseng Tien, who, according to the *Analects*, would take his place before Confucius and, while playing his lute, would listen to the discussion between Confucius and the older disciples. Tseng Tien's ideal was not to become a prime minister or a great general. In *Analects* XI: 25 he is recorded to have said, "Among the rain altars I would enjoy the cool breezes and return home singing." Tseng Tien was a person completely free of the bonds of *ko-t'ao*, and his free mind was attained in a holy place, such as among the rain altars, the

quiet groves where ceremonial dances were performed in dry weather. He
was at home in the holy places. We can even call this the serenity of
mind of one who is in the hands of God. It can be called a religious
mentality. Both Wang Chi, who took as his ideal the kind of leisurely,
free mind exemplified by Tseng Tien, and Tōju, who was influenced by
Wang Chi, repudiated formalism. Their freedom from it was, so to
speak, like liberation from the "law" of the Old Testament. Liberation
from the law means the attainment of a serenity of mind not by abandoning God, but by being held in God's embrace.

In the summer of his thirty-fourth year, the year after he came into
possession of Wang Chi's Yü-lu, Tōju made a pilgrimage to Ise. According to the Nenpu, he had prior to this time held the view that, "God is
the being of the highest dignity. A samurai of low status cannot approach
a person of high status, and he fears to insult a noble man. How much
less can he approach God." [28] Just as Chu Hsi had held that the ghosts
and spirits should be respected and held at a distance, so too had Tōju
kept his distance from the Ise shrine. But from this time forward his
thought underwent a transformation. In its account of the events of the
autumn of this year the Nenpu records:

In this year he realized for the first time that it is not correct to observe a formal
code of conduct (ko-t'ao). Prior to this, he had devoted himself to the commentaries of Chu Hsi, lecturing daily and teaching his disciples the rules of the Hsiao-
hsüeh (Elementary Learning). Because of this his disciples became obsessed with
these formal codes, adhering to them with ever greater rigidity, so that their spirits
became ever more oppressed. The personalities of some became so harsh that the
bonds of good fellowship were broken even among friends. Master Tōju instructed them: "For a long time I have acted according to the formal codes of
conduct. I have recently come to understand that such codes are wrong. Although it cannot be said that the motive of such behavior is the same as the desire
for fame and profit, they are similar in the sense that both cause one to lose one's
spontaneous original nature. Abandon the form of desire which causes you to
adhere to formal codes, have faith in your own essential mind, do not be attached
to mere convention!" His disciples were deeply moved, and their spirits became
healthy and bright again. [29]

Wang Chi wrote:

Persons of the kind described as "your good, careful people of the villages"
(hsiang-yüan)"[bx] are neither ardent (k'uang)[by] nor cautiously decided (chüan).[bz]
They at first strive to become sages, but they vainly learn only the outer forms of
sagehood and finally end up adhering to formal codes of conduct. [30]

Since Wang Chi, like Tseng Tien, had an "ardent" personality, he often praised the "man of ardor." Tōju also wrote on the same theme in a long passage found in the second part of *Okina mondō*. There is first "the sage," then "the man who acts according to the Mean (*chung-hsing*),"[ca] then "the man of ardor," then the man who is "cautiously decided." Tōju wrote, "As both the Buddha and Bodhidharma were excellent persons of ardent disposition, had they met a sage, they would certainly have awakened to the subtle Way of the *Mean* and attained to the level of the man who acts according to the Mean." Tōju also called Chuang Tzu a man of ardor. While severely criticizing the philosophies of Lao Tzu, Chuang Tzu, and the Buddhists, he recognized that even proponents of heterodox teachings had attained to the level of the "man of ardor."

Toju had no intention of setting up a Confucian school in opposition to Buddhism and other schools. Rather he endeavored to see all religions as one. His view was that the whole world under the August High Lord of the Supreme Vacuity is one:

The August High Lord of the Supreme Vacuity is the great ancestor of the human race. Seen from the heavenly principle of this truth, all men who dwell in the world—the sages and wise men, Sakyamuni and Bodhidharma, Confucians and Buddhists, myself and other men—are the descendants of the August High Lord.[31]

His teaching of the unity of the world coincided with that of Wang Yang-ming, who had written:

The great man regards Heaven, earth, and the myriad things as one body, He regards the world as one family and the country as one person.[32]

Uchimura Kanzō[cb] (1861–1930), the founder of the No-Church (*mukyōkai*)[cc] Christian movement in Meiji Japan, included a chapter on Nakae Tōju in his work, *Representative Men of Japan*.[33] In another work, *Chijinron*,[cd] Uchimura cites the words of Wang Yang-ming which are quoted above and went on to write, "I must be not only a Japanese but also a world-man (Weltmann)."[34] The religious view of the unity of the world—namely, that the whole world under one God is one—was a mode of thought which linked Nakae Tōju and Uchimura Kanzō. Wang Yang-ming regarded the world as one, not through a philosophy postulating one god, but through his conception that all men possess innate knowledge. Since the world is one, Confucianism, Buddhism, and Taoism must not be opposed. That the theory of the unity of the three teachings flourished in the latter part of the Ming period, after the time of Wang Chi, can be understood as a development which derived from Wang Yang-ming's doctrine of innate knowledge.

Tōju wrote that since Sakyamuni, Bodhidharma, and Chuang Tzu were all "men of ardor," it was possible for them to become sages. To effect a unification of the three teachings—and Shinto as well—Tōju expounded his teaching of the August High Lord of the Supreme Vacuity. Concerning "your good, careful people of the villages," Wang Chi had said:

Looking at their outward appearances and activities, they resemble the sages in trustworthiness, honesty, and integrity. . . . But these people only strive to be thought well of by others, and so feverishly devote themselves to putting on clever outward appearances.[35]

Compare this with Tōju's statement on the subject of the *hsiang-yüan* in *Okina mondō:*

"Your good, careful people of the villages" are very calculating, their knowledge is superior to most, and they are adept at dealing with any situation. While they seem to strive to be filial to their parents, respectful to their older brothers, loyal to their superiors, and trustworthy to their friends, and while they appear to be honest, without gross desires, and blameless in every respect, their intention is to gain the reputation of being praised by their contemporaries and the profit of advancing their careers as they gain the commendation of their lords. . . . Their honesty and lack of gross desires are mere appearance and not genuine.[36]

The resemblance between the two passages is remarkable.

Tōju often used the terms "the August High Lord of the Supreme Vacuity" and "the far-ranging vastness of the Supreme Vacuity" (*t'ai-hsü liao-kuo*).[ce] The myriad things proceed from this vast Supreme Vacuity. Wang Chi had written, "The Supreme Vacuity embraces every phenomenon,"[37] and had extolled the fact that no sooner do the winds, rain, clouds, and thunder appear than they disappear, while the Supreme Vacuity itself does not change in the least. He wrote, "There is no better method of cultivation than to stand the whole day through in the presence of the Lord on High."[38] And again, "Always standing in the presence of the Lord on High, there is no time to be idle, there is also no need to read books."[39] Wang Chi conceived innate knowledge as the Lord on High, and Tōju's religious philosophy of the August High Lord of the Supreme Vacuity was influenced by this aspect of Wang's thought.

That he was acquainted with Wang Chi's philosophy of the Lord on High even prior to knowing Wang Yang-ming's teaching of the extension of innate knowledge, was the reason Tōju's thought took on this religious or theistic dimension. Yet Tōju did not abandon worship of the ancestral Japanese kami. The August High Lord was both the ancestral kami and the God who creates the universe, and the many Japanese kami were gods subordinate to the August High Lord. Tōju's position can be called a synthesis of theism and polytheism.

As noted above, the philosophy of the Supreme Vacuity began with Chang Tsai. Chang Tsai had held that the material force (ch'i) of the yin and yang is born of the Supreme Vacuity, and as the yin and yang they function to produce the myriad things. Ultimately, the myriad things again become ch'i and return to the Supreme Vacuity. This theory explains the mechanism of the creation of the universe. Tōju conceived the essence of the Supreme Vacuity as the life force of the universe. Therefore he understood it as analogous to the process whereby human beings inherit the life force from their ancestors. Truly to live without losing the life force of the Supreme Vacuity, he regarded as filial piety. He broadened the scope of the concept from that of serving one's parents to preserving the life force of the Supreme Vacuity. And to worship the August High Lord who rules the Supreme Vacuity was also filial piety.

Tōju identified this filial piety with the concept of "illumined virtue" from the Great Learning, and then identified both with innate knowledge. As innate knowledge permeates the Supreme Vacuity, so too does filial piety. Wang Chi had written, "That which permeates Heaven and earth and the myriad things is material force, and innate knowledge is the soul of material force."[40] Wang Chi and Tōju shared the same mode of thought that illumined virtue, innate knowledge, and filial piety were intrinsic to the human mind and yet also transcend the mind and extend to the Supreme Vacuity and Heaven-and-earth. It is significant that terms which originally conveyed a moral sense were transformed so that they entailed religious meanings which were mystical in character.

From the above it is clear how great an influence Wang Chi's Yü-lu exerted on Nakae Tōju. Of course, Wang Yang-ming's influence on Tōju was considerable; but during the time Tōju was writing his Okina mondō it was Wang Chi who exerted the greater influence. And the Tōju school which later formed a religious organization called the Tōju kyō^{ef}

received greater influence from the religious thought of the late Ming than from Wang Yang-ming himself.

TŌJU AND JITSUGAKU

The word *jitsugaku* was not frequently used by Tōju. In one text, his *Rinshi teihatsu jui ben*,[cg] (On Master Hayashi's Taking the Tonsure and Being Accorded the Highest Priestly Rank) written when he was twenty-four, Tōju severely criticized Hayashi Razan[ch] for taking the tonsure and accepting the highest priestly rank of hōin,[ci] in the following words:

Everyone believes that the way of the Confucian scholar (*jusha*)[cj] is typified by someone like Hayashi Razan. There is no one who knows the *jitsugaku* of the phrase of the *Great Learning*: "to illumine clear virtue and cherish the people" (*ming-te ch'in-min*).[ck] Therefore even if men of later times should desire to know *jitsugaku*, they will not be able to learn it from anyone.[41]

Tōju used the term *jitsugaku* here in the sense of illumining one's virtuous nature and bringing good government to the people; it was the ancient Confucian sentiment of achieving good government for the people through the cultivation of the self (*hsiu-chi chih-jen*).[cl] Another instance is found in a reply which Tōju wrote at the age of thirty-five to a certain Ogawa; here Tōju used the phrase *moto o tsutomuru no jitsugaku*.[cm][42] *Moto o tsutomu* signifies that the important matter is to exert one's effort not in reading and memorizing the Confucian classics but in putting them into practice; this is what is fundamental. Tōju put a higher priority on "practice" than on "knowledge." His thought coincides with Wang Yang-ming's teaching of the unity of knowledge and action (*chih hsing ho-i*).[cn]

For Chu Hsi, knowledge had priority and action was to follow (*chih-hsien hsing-hou*).[co] Yet Chu also put great stress on practice and said that, "Book learning, for the student, is secondary in significance."[43] He himself did not give priority to memorizing the classics. Nevertheless, in the Ming dynasty when his teachings were studied for the official examinations, it became necessary first to read Chu Hsi's numerous commentaries on the Confucian classics, with the result that the priority was put on knowledge rather than on practice. It was against this trend that Wang Yang-ming advocated the doctrine of the unity of knowledge and action and insisted that true knowledge can only be obtained through practice. Chu Hsi had taught that one must know what should be done in order to do it, but it is not enough to have knowledge without practice. He taught that knowledge and action are equally necessary, but, as an ethical value, action has the higher significance.

Wang Yang-ming agreed with Chu Hsi in recognizing the ethical value of practice, but at the same time he went a step further in insisting that knowledge and action are inseparable. In other words, knowledge is included in action even in the epistemological domain. For example, we feel cold in winter. Our knowledge in this instance only becomes truly personal as we experience the wintry coldness. Wang Yang-ming wrote that filial piety, which is an ethical virtue, is similarly not something known through reading the classics, but only truly known when practiced. Taking the doctrine that knowledge is included in action to its ultimate conclusion, one can act even without reading the classics. Men are taught how to act not by the classics or the sages, but by the innate knowledge which each one possesses in his own mind. Therefore the doctrine of the unity of knowledge and action results in putting a low priority on reading the classics. Since Chu Hsi considered practice to be important but also placed a high value on reading the classics, he differed from Wang Yang-ming in this respect.

In the revision of his *Okina mondō*, Tōju wrote:

In the present age people consider those who read the Confucian classics to be Confucian scholars (*jusha*). They are mistaken. . . . Even an entirely illiterate man, if his humanity and righteousness are clear, is not an ordinary person. He is a Confucian scholar who does not read characters.[44]

Since the Way exists in the mind of every man, even if one does not read the classics, he can become a true Confucian scholar by following his own living mind or innate knowledge. This is entirely consistent with Wang Yang-ming's teaching of the unity of knowledge and action.

In contrast to the term "real" (*shih, jitsu*)[cp] there is the term "empty" (*hsü;kyo*),[cq] and the latter is employed in two senses. *Kyogen (hsü-yen)*[cr] means a lie, or a falsehood. *Kyosei (hsü-sheng)*[cs] means to live an unproductive, empty life. Both connotations are pejorative. On the other hand, *kyorei (hsü-ling)*[ct] refers to one who is unselfish, impartial, and spiritual. *Kyomei (hsü-ming)*[cu] indicates an impartial and open-minded person. Both of the latter phrases are positive in connotation. Tōju often employed the term *kyo* in these positive senses. For example, in his *Denshi o okuru*,[cv] written when he was thirty-five, we have the words, "In order to discipline one's mind, one must eliminate all self-conceit and thoroughly realize *kyo* [obliterate the self, eliminate egoistic attachment]."[45] In a letter written when he was thirty-nine, Tōju said, "The *kyomei* of the mind [the mind which is clear, without egoistic attachment] refers to modesty."[46]

The most significant instance of the term *kyo* in the positive sense occurs in Tōju's use of the term *taikyo* (*t'ai-hsü*), the Supreme Vacuity. As he explained it in one passage in *Okina mondō*:

Since our bodies are produced by our parents, and their bodies are produced by Heaven and earth, and Heaven and earth are produced by the Supreme Vacuity, in essence our bodies come into being as subtle transformations of a minute part of the mysterious and wonderful spiritual Supreme Vacuity.[47]

The Supreme Vacuity is the great "emptiness"; it is the origin of Heaven-and-earth and of man.

When Tōju used the term *jitsugaku* he did not deny this *kyo*. *Jitsu* signifies what is real. *Jitsugaku* means real learning, the true Confucian learning. The *jitsugaku* he expounded affirmed the Supreme Vacuity as the true existence; it signified his faith in the August High Lord who rules over the Supreme Vacuity. Since *jitsugaku* involves true awareness of the great "emptiness" (*kyo*), *jitsu* and *kyo* are not contradictory but complementary. Since it is the empty (*kyo*) which is actually real, Tōju's *jitsugaku* can, paradoxically, be called *kyogaku*.[cw] The atheistic, rationalistic advocates of Shushigaku would probably regard this kind of religious *kyogaku* as an irrationalism which was evil in the sense that it was destructive of both skill or technique (*gijutsu*)[ex] and of the ethical relations among human beings. Tōju, however, meant to deny neither skill nor ethical relations; rather, he was emphasizing their importance.

As proof of this, let me next take up Tōju's abiding interest in medicine and military tactics. When he was thirty, Tōju wrote for Ōno Ryōsa,[cy] a simple-minded disciple, a work entitled *Shōkei isen*.[cz] This book was a simplified compendium of the entirety of medical knowledge; Ōno was able to become a doctor after studying it. When he was thirty-six, Tōju wrote a medical work entitled *Shōi nanshin*;[da] at thirty-seven, he wrote another such work entitled *Shinpō kijutsu*.[db] So after coming to believe in the August High Lord and *T'ai-i shen*, Tōju devoted himself all the more to medicine. According to the commentary of Ryō Onjin,[dc] which appears in the fourth volume of the *Tōju sensei zenshū*, Tōju wrote these works after he had done extensive research in the medical books of ancient China and of the Sung, Yüan, and Ming dynasties. His description of the modern disease of syphilis he drew from his reading of Ming dynasty medical works and writings of the sixteenth-century Japanese scholar, Manase Dōsan[dd] (1507–1595). Considering that Tōju expounded the teachings of Manase Dōsan, who is called the father of Japanese medicine, Tōju's *kyogaku* can be understood as even more practical and empirical than that of the adherents of Shushigaku. Although it has become an established theory that practical, technical, scientific learning (*jitsugaku* can be used in these senses too) derived from the Chu Hsi school, a consideration of Tōju's medical learning helps us understand that a practical, technical, scientific *jitsugaku* came out of the Wang Yang-ming school as well.

In *Okina mondō* Tōju developed a detailed account of military tactics. He wrote:

Literary culture (*bun*)[de] unaccompanied by the military arts (*bu*)[df] is not true literary culture. The military arts without literary culture are not true military arts. Just as the yin principle becomes the source which produces the yang principle, and the yang principle becomes the source of the yin, so too are *bun* and *bu* each a source of the other.[48]

Tōju taught that even Confucius was well versed in the military arts. Since he was expounding this teaching for contemporary samurai, he placed this emphasis on the military arts. However, in that contemporary Confucian scholars placed their emphasis on the work of literary culture, namely on how to write characters and read books, Tōju's advocacy of the military arts was somewhat exceptional for his time. He recommended careful reading of such Chinese military classics as the *Sun-tzu*[dg] and *Wu-tzu*.[dh] And he taught that in military tactics one must be able to respond skillfully to times, places, and men. Military tactics are extremely rationalistic techniques (*gijutsu*) of vanquishing the enemy. These techniques were essential to the samurai. They had to stand him in good stead in actual battle. Naturally they had to be practical and scientific techniques. Moreover, Tōju advocated that military tactics would be of benefit to one who had the virtues of humanity and righteousness. Military tactics were of value in that they brought peace to human life. Tōju synthesized the *jitsugaku* of "illumining one's virtue and cherishing the people" and the *jitsugaku* of military tactics. He unified the *kyogaku* of his faith in the August High Lord with the technical skills of medicine and military tactics (*jitsugaku*). It is of paramount importance for scholars of Tōju's thought to understand this synthesis of *kyo* and *jitsu*.

Wang Yang-ming taught that one should develop his own innate knowledge (*liang-chih*) by striving skillfully to manage one's affairs in the midst of everyday living, rather than by quiet-sitting and writing commentaries on the classics. He also placed a high value on school education. He recommended that in schools the cultivation of virtue should be the foundation but that agricultural, handicraft, and commercial skills should also be taught according to the talents and capacities of the students.[49] He taught that the world would become one family through the farmers, artisans, and merchants each fulfilling their respective roles in society. Tōju wrote in a similar vein:

The farmers, artisans, and merchants must each strive diligently in their work, contribute to the production of goods, not wasting anything, being discreet in their behavior, respecting the government, and obeying its laws. That is the filial piety of the common people.[50]

In the Wang Yang-ming school, emphasis is placed on a practical *jitsugaku* that will benefit production techniques and daily living. Wang Yang-ming did not, as Tōju did, study medicine, but he often spoke of the methods of curing illnesses as an analogue of the methods of personal cultivation. And it is a fact that Wang Yang-ming was interested in medicine.

From his early youth, Wang Yang-ming was fond of studying military tactics; his many victories on the battlefield where he actually employed such tactics are well-known. The fundamental theme of the Wang Yang-ming school, namely to honor one's innate knowledge and act according to it, had the aim of unifying Heaven-and-earth and the myriad things as one body—in other words, of ensuring that all the people of the world would lead peaceful lives. The doctrine that Heaven-and-earth and the myriad things form one body is perhaps to be understood in terms of his *kyogaku*. However, in order to unify actual society, a technical, scientific *jitsugaku* becomes essential. Wang Yang-ming can also be thought to have united his *kyogaku* and his *jitsugaku*.

Tōju cited Yen Tzu, Tseng Tzu, Tzu-ssu, and Mencius as sages, and to this list he added Chu-ko Liang[di] and Wang Yang-ming.[51] It is noteworthy that he excluded Chu Hsi. He regarded adherents of the Chu Hsi school as persons who had only read the classics and performed no useful function. In order to realize the ideal of unifying Heaven-and-earth and the myriad things, and thereby allow all men to live peacefully, it was first necessary to have people acquire a perfectly communal consciousness. That which becomes most fundamental to this communal consciousness is what Wang Yang-ming called innate knowledge and Tōju called the August High Lord. Wang Yang-ming at first regarded innate knowledge as a power of ethical judgment. In later years, he came to teach that this *liang-chih* created Heaven-and-earth and the myriad things. Understanding *liang-chih* in this way as a creative power, it assumes almost the same significance as the Lord on High (*shang-ti*). Wang Chi often spoke of belief in the Lord on High. Like Wang Yang-ming, Wang Chi regarded *liang-chih* as the foundation, but he also expressed it as "vacuity" (*hsü*). He regarded the Supreme Vacuity (*t'ai-hsü*) as the origin of Heaven-and-earth. Wang Chi was the bridge linking Wang Yang-ming and Tōju. Wang Yang-ming regarded *liang-chih* as the origin of Heaven-and-earth; Wang Chi went a step further, equating *liang-chih* and the Lord on High. Tōju came to speak more frequently of *t'ai-hsü* than of *liang-chih* and developed the idea of the August High Lord of the Supreme Vacuity.

In the Japanese Wang Yang-ming school, this concept of the Supreme Vacuity was transmitted to Ōshio Heihachirō[dj] (1793–1837), who considered the Confucian concepts of "emptiness" (*k'ung; kū*)[dk] and "vacuity" to be the most significant ones. He wrote his *Jumon kūkyo shūgo*[dl] by compiling instances of the concept of *kyo* in the Confucian classics. In the preface to that work, Ōshio wrote: "The Supreme Vacuity is without form, spiritual, and bright; it embraces and permeates all principles and all existing things."[52]

Ōshio thought that men return at death to the Supreme Vacuity and would live forever in it. His philosophy was indeed a *kyogaku*. He was not particularly interested in medicine or military tactics, but he was an extremely capable *yoriki*[dm] (an office which combined police and juridical functions, next in rank to *machibugyō*,[dn] or mayor). He collected evidence in a rational manner and wrote legal briefs in an extremely logical form. He was truly capable in his actual work as a judge. Ōshio's *kyogaku* developed in the midst of his work of detecting and eliminating wrongdoing in society. It can be said that his non-rational *kyogaku* supported his rational *jitsugaku*.

A strain of practical, scientific *jitsugaku* can be seen in the development of the Wang Yang-ming school in China as well. Fang I-chih[do] (1611–1671) was the author of such works of natural science as *T'ung-ya*[dp] and *Wu-li hsiao-chih*.[dq] His great-grandfather, Fang Hsüeh-chien,[dr] was an adherent of the T'ai-chou[ds] school (branch of Wang Ken);[dt] his grandfather, Fang Ta-chen[du] (1558–1631), was also a follower of the Wang Yang-ming school. His father, Fang K'ung-chao[dv] (1591–1655), was a member of the Tung-lin[dw] school. Fang I-chih read the works of his great-grandfather, Fang Hsüeh-chien, on the Wang Yang-ming teaching. Sakade Yoshinobu[dx] has indicated that Fang I-chih attempted a synthesis of the standpoints of Chu Hsi and Wang Yang-ming.[53]

The Chɔ Hsi school explained the world rationally through the concepts of *li*, *ch'i*, yin and yang. Its explanation of all phenomena through a synthesis of the astronomical and mathematical knowledge of the Sung period and the teachings of such Confucian classics as the *Book of Changes* was a remarkable achievement. However, when Western concepts of natural science entered China in the late Ming, this rationalism of Chu Hsi produced a trend of thought which was essentially anti-scientific. Adherents of the Chu Hsi school, who were at odds with Christianity, extended their opposition to Western natural science as well. In that it differed from the rationalism that had developed in China up to that time, Western natural science was rejected as unintelligible. The Chu Hsi philosophy explained the Confucian classics in rationalistic terms, but its particular form of rationalism was one that unqualifiedly affirmed the conceptual framework of the *Book of Changes*, according to which the universe is established through the dual principles of yin and yang. Its rationalism was a compromise with the Confucian classics, and that compromise was in danger of being undermined by the reception of Western natural science. Its rationalism was one with the Confucian classics, whereas the acceptance of Western natural science required the courage to reject the contents of the Confucian classics.

The Wang Yang-ming school did negate Chu Hsi's rationalism and proclaimed that it was unnecessary even to read the Confucian classics. It negated the atheism of the Chu Hsi school by expounding the doctrine of innate knowledge and the Lord on High. It also recognized that truth exists outside the Confucian classics, in Buddhism and Taoism. These positions had the effect of destroying the rationalism of the Chu Hsi school. Only when the Chu Hsi rationalism was destroyed did the reception of the new Western rationalism become a possibility. The anti-rationalism apparent in the Wang Yang-ming school played the role of negating the rationalism of the Chu Hsi school. In my opinion, Fang I-chih's ability to accept Western natural scientific thought is traceable to the influence of the Wang Yang-ming school. In Japan, Yokoi Shōnan[dy] (1809–1869) was a proponent of *jitsugaku;* he represents a continuing influence of the Wang Yang-ming school. Shōnan's son, Yokoi Tokio,[dz] became a fervent Christian and labored for the propagation of the Christian faith. I think we can see from many such facts the development of a scientific *jitsugaku* from the so-called *kyogaku.* The religious sentiment energizes the social activities of men. It may result in discovering a practical, scientific *jitsugaku* to perfect human life. *Jitsugaku* could only be developed when supported by *kyogaku.* It was Nakae Tōju who exemplified this in his career.

Translated by David A. Dilworth

NOTES

1. *Tōju sensei nenpu*, in *Tōju sensei zenshū*[ea] (5 vols.; Tokyo Iwanami shoten, 1940), 5:12. All subsequent citations of Tōju's works are to this edition.

2. *Ko-t'ao* refers to such practices as methods of reading, detailed ritual prescriptions, codes of ethics, and methods of cultivation advocated by the Chu Hsi school. They were the standards and signified formally exact customs and rules of conduct.

3. *Tōju sensei nenpu* (Okada[eb] text), in *Tōju sensei zenshū*, 5:13.

4. *Ibid.*

5. *Ibid.*

6. *Ibid.*, p. 17.

7. *Ibid.*, p. 18.

8. *Ibid.*, p. 20.

9. Yamashita Ryūji,[ec] "Jukyō no shūkyōteki seikaku"[ed] (The Religious Character of Confucianism), in *Yōmeigaku no kenkyū*[ee] (Tokyo: Gendai jōhōsha, 1971), vol. 1, ch. 2, pp. 28–31.

10. Chu Hsi, *Lun-yü chi-chu, Yung-yeh p'ien,*[ef] section 20.

11. Nakae Tōju, *Genjin*, in *Tōju sensei zenshū*, 1:128.

12. *Ibid.*

13. Nakae Tōju, *Jikei zusetsu*, in *Tōju sensei zenshū*, 1:684.

14. Ogyū Sorai, *Rongo chō, Gakuji hen,*[eg] section 5, in *Shisho chūshaku zensho,*[eh] 7:13.

15. Nakae Tōju, *Jikei zusetsu*, in *Tōju sensei zenshū*, 1:687.

16. *Tōju sensei nenpu* (Okada text), in *Tōju sensei zenshū*, 5:21.

17. Nakae Tōju, *Rongo kyōtō keimō yokuden*, in *Tōju sensei zenshū*, 1:490.

18. *Tōju sensei nenpu* (Okada text), in *Tōju sensei zenshū*, 5:21.

19. The *Hsing-li hui-t'ung* contained the works of Lin Chao-en[ei] (1517–1598), who taught the doctrine of the unity of the three teachings, and T'ang Shu,[ej] who believed in the *T'ai-i shen*.

20. *Okina mondō kaisei hen*[ek] (revision of *Okina mondō*), preface in *Tōju sensei zenshū*, 3:277.

21. Wang Chi, *Wei-yang wu-yü*, in *Wang Lung-hsi ch'üan-chi*[el] (Ts'ung-shu hui-pien reprint of the Ch'ing Tao-kuang 2 [1822] ed.), 1:9a.

22. Wang Chi, *Fu-chou Ni-hsien-t'ai hui-yü*, in *Wang Lung-hsi ch'üan-chi* 1:21b–22a.

23. Nakae Tōju, *Okina mondō kaisei hen*, in *Tōju sensei zenshū*, 3:287.

24. Nakae Tōju, *Okina mondō*, ch. 1, in *Tōju sensei zenshū*, 3:133.

25. Nakae Tōju, *Okina mondō*, ch. 2, in *Tōju sensei zenshū*, 3:249.

26. Wang Yang-ming, *Ch'uan-hsi lu* (Instructions for Practical Living), Hsü Ai's preface.[em]

27. Nakae Tōju, *Okina mondō*, ch. 2, in *Tōju sensei zenshū*, 3:238–39.

28. *Tōju sensei nenpu* (Okada text), in *Tōju sensei zenshū*, 5:22.

29. *Tōju sensei nenpu* (Okada text), in *Tōju sensei zenshū*, 5:23.

30. Wang Chi, *Yü Mei Ch'un-fu wen-ta*,[en] in *Wang Lung-hsi ch'üan-chi*, 1:5b.
31. Nakae Tōju, *Okina mondō*, ch. 2, in *Tōju sensei zenshū*, 3:239.
32. Wang Yang-ming, *Ta-hsüeh wen*[eo] (Inquiry on the *Great Learning*), in *Wang Wen-ch'eng kung ch'üan-shu*,[ep] 26:1b. Translated by Wing-tsit Chan in *Instructions for Practical Living and Other Neo-Confucian Writings by Wang Yang-ming* (New York: Columbia University Press, 1963), p. 272.
33. Uchimura Kanzō, the religious leader and social critic, graduated from the Sapporo Agricultural School and studied in the United States. He developed his teaching of No-Church Christianity in opposition to institutional Christianity. Through his independent teaching, which harmonized with the spirit of Japanese *Bushidō*,[eq] he broadened the appeal of Christianity among intellectuals. Among his many followers were: Arishima Takeo[er] (1878–1923), the novelist, Osanai Kaoru [es] (1881–1928), founder of the New Theatre movement, Nanbara Shigeru[et] (1889–1974), president of Tokyo University, and Yanaihara Tadao[eu] (1893–1961), former president of Tokyo University. *Representative Men of Japan* (1908) was a revision of *Japan and the Japanese* (1894), written in English. It contains appreciations of Saigō Takamori[ev] (1828–1877), Uesugi Yōzan[ew] (1746–1822), Ninomiya Sontoku[ex] (1787–1856), Nakae Tōju, and Nichiren[ey] (1222–1282). Uchimura praised Wang Yang-ming most highly among the Chinese philosophers. He emphasized the theistic and religious character of Nakae Tōju's thought and pointed to many similarities with Christianity. In this way he clashed with Inoue Tetsujirō[ez] (1856–1944), who stressed the ethical, rather than the religious, character of Tōju's thought.
34. Uchimura's *Chijinron* (1894), published by Iwanami shoten in 1942, first appeared under the title *Chirigaku kō*[fa] (Geographical Studies), but this was changed to *Chijinron* in 1897. Uchimura gave it the English titles of *Spirit of Geography* and *Religion of Geography*.
35. Wang Chi, *Yü Mei Ch'un-fu wen-ta*, in *Wang Lung-hsi ch'üan-chi*, 1:5b.
36. Nakae Tōju, *Okina mondō*, ch. 2, in *Tōju sensei zenshū*, 3:236–37.
37. Wang Chi, *T'ien-shan ta-wen*,[fb] in *Lung-hsi hui-yü* (Inaba Iwakichi: 1932 reprint of the Ming Wan-li 4 [1576] ed.), 6:10a.
38. Wang Chi, *Fu-chou Ni hsien-t'ai hui-yü*, in *Wang Lung-hsi ch'üan-chi*, 1:20b.
39. *Ibid.*, 1:25b.
40. Wang Chi, *Ou-yang Nan-yeh wen-hsüan hsü*,[fc] in *Wang Lung-hsi ch'üan-chi*, 13:11a.
41. Nakae Tōju, *Rinshi teihatsu jui ben*,[fd] in *Tōju sensei zenshū*, 1:123.
42. Nakae Tōju, *Ogawa shi no gimon ni kotaeru*,[fe] in *Tōju sensei zenshū* 1:170.
43. *Chu Tzu yü-lei* (Taipei: 1970 reprint of the Ming Ch'eng-hua 9 [1473] ed.), 10:1a.
44. Nakae Tōju, *Okina mondō kaisei hen*, in *Tōju sensei zenshū*, 3:282.
45. Nakae Tōju, *Denshi o okuru*, in *Tōju sensei zenshū*, 1:182–84.
46. Nakae Tōju, *Morimura shi no maki ni shosu*,[ff] in *Tōju sensei zenshū*, 1:178.
47. Nakae Tōju, *Okina mondō*, ch. 1, in *Tōju sensei zenshū*, 3:67.

48. *Ibid.*, p. 115.
49. Wang Yang-ming, *Pa-pen sai-yüan lun*[fg] (Pulling up the Root and Stopping up the Source), *Ta Ku Tung-ch'iao shu*[fh] (Letter in Reply to Ku Tung-ch'iao), in *Ch'uan-hsi lu*, part 2.
50. Nakae Tōju, *Okina mondō*, ch. 1, in *Tōju sensei zenshū*, 3:73.
51. *Ibid.*, ch. 2, p. 189.
52. Ōshio Heihachirō, *Jumon kūkyo shūgo*, in NRI, 3:443.
53. Sakade Yoshinobu, "Ho Ichi no shisō,"[fi] in *Kyōto Daigaku Jinbun Kagaku Kenkyūjo kenkyū hōkoku,*[fj] *Min Shin jidai no kagaku gijutsu shi.*[fk]

GLOSSARY

a 中江藤樹
b 翁問答
c 四書大全
d 大学大全
e 論語大全
f 孟子大全
g 藤樹先生年譜
h 格套
i 聖学
j 大学啓蒙
k 易学啓蒙
l 持敬圖說
m 原人
n 五經正義
o 大学古本
p 大学章句
q 包咸
r 皇侃
s 邢昺
t 劉宝楠
u 誠
v 天帝
w 上帝
x 無極而太極
y 二五之氣
z 太極圖說
aa 皇上帝
ab 理
ac 氣
ad 敬
ae 天命
af 德性
ag 主一無適
ah 荻生徂徠
ai 持敬
aj 劉瑾
ak 五經臆說
al 藤樹規

am 白鹿洞書院揭示
an 博学
ao 審問
ap 愼思
aq 明辨
ar 篤行
as 言忠信，行篤敬
at 小学
au 鄉黨
av 論語鄉黨啓蒙翼伝
aw 太虛
ax 孝經
ay 性理会通
az 太乙神
ba 鍾人傑
bb 性理大全
bc 王畿
bd 周汝登
be 羅欽順
bf 王廷相
bg 羅汝芳
bh 李贄
bi 公安
bj 袁宏道
bk 袁中道
bl 青溪雷說
bm 三敎合一
bn 率性
bo 良知
bp 王龍溪語錄
bq 性即理
br 維揚晤語
bs 撫州擬峴臺會語
bt 殼套
bu 道理
bv 致良知
bw 權道
bx 鄉愿

by 狂
bz 狷
ca 中行
cb 內村鑑三
cc 無敎会
cd 地人論
ce 太虛廖廓
cf 藤樹敎
cg 林氏剃髮受位辨
ch 林羅山
ci 法印
cj 儒者
ck 明德親民
cl 修己治人
cm 務本之実学
cn 知行合一
co 知先行後
cp 實
cq 虛
cr 虛言
cs 虛生
ct 虛靈
cu 虛明
cv 送佃子
cw 虛学
cx 技術
cy 大野了佐
cz 捷徑医筌
da 小医南針
db 神方奇術
dc 廖溫仁
dd 曲直瀨道三
de 文
df 武
dg 孫子
dh 吳子
di 諸葛亮
dj 大塩平八郎

dk 空
dl 儒門空虛聚語
dm 與力
dn 町奉行
do 方以智
dp 通雅
dq 物理小識
dr 方學漸
ds 泰州
dt 王艮
du 方大鎮
dv 方孔炤
dw 東林
dx 坂出祥伸
dy 横井小楠
dz 横井時雄
ea 藤樹先生全集
eb 岡田
ec 山下龍二
ed 儒教の宗教的性格
ee 陽明学の研究
ef 論語集注，雍也篇
eg 論語徵，学而篇
eh 四書註釈全書
ei 林兆恩
ej 唐樞
ek 翁問答改正篇
el 王龍溪全集
em 傳習錄，徐愛序
en 與梅純甫問答
eo 大學問
ep 王文成公全書
eq 武士道
er 有鳥武郎
es 小山内薫
et 南原繁
eu 矢内原忠雄
ev 西郷隆盛
ew 上杉鷹山
ex 二宮尊德
ey 日蓮

ez 井上哲次郎
fa 地理学考
fb 天山答問
fc 歐陽南野文選序
fd 林氏剃髮受位辨
fe 答小川子疑問
ff 書森村子卷
fg 拔本塞源論
fh 答顧東橋書
fi 坂出祥伸，方以智の思想
fj 京都大学人文科学研究所研
　　究報告
fk 明清時代の科学技術史

Ian James McMullen

Kumazawa Banzan and "Jitsugaku": Toward Pragmatic Action

On the first day of the eighth month of 1686, Kumazawa Banzan[a] (1619–1691), then aged sixty-eight and living in exile in Yada,[b] near Nara,[c] wrote an agitated letter to his son-in-law Inaba Hikobei.[d]

I am uncertain of our fate even for the rest of this year. This concerns Japan itself. To keep silent about it would be wrong. . . . I think it likely that the Tartars[e] will come next year or the year after. If they come next year and if the authorities do not make preparations during the eighth, ninth or at latest the tenth month of this year, by the eleventh or twelfth month the situation will be beyond even a [Chu-ko] K'ung-ming[f] or a Chang Liang[g][1]. . . . The Tartars will come suddenly and without warning. There is not the slightest evidence of the necessary military preparedness.[2] (6:197)

Banzan had, he told Hikobei, considered making the journey to the Kantō[h] to discuss the problem with the Rōjū[i] Matsudaira Nobuyuki[j] (1631–1686), or at least writing to him, but he himself had been ill and Nobuyuki was now dead. He was, therefore, sending with this letter the table of contents of a projected memorial which would discuss the problem at greater length. If written out in full, it would cover "forty or fifty sheets." He suggested that Hikobei might show the table of contents to Kitami Shigemasa, the Governor of Wakasa,[k] a favorite of Tokugawa Tsunayoshi[l] (1646–1709).

The projected memorial mentioned in Banzan's letter is generally

337

identified with his *Daigaku wakumon*[m] (Questions on the *Great Learning*), probably complete by the autumn of the following year. It is also generally assumed that it was in the form of this work that Banzan's fears finally came to the attention of the Bakufu.[n] The latter, however, reacted with suspicion, and Banzan was ordered to the Kantō and put under house arrest in Koga[o] castle for the remaining four years of his life.

Daigaku wakumon contains a discussion of the strategic problems posed by a Manchu invasion and has passages describing with apocalyptic vividness the likely consequences of such an invasion. But the work was wider in scope than Banzan's letter to Hikobei might suggest. Banzan had long held a profoundly pessimistic view of the development of contemporary Japanese society. In *Daigaku wakumon* he finally overcame his Confucian inhibition over discussion of public policy and attempted to identify the causes of deterioration and to offer remedial proposals. The work is probably the most distinguished analysis of Japanese society and economy to come from seventeenth-century Japan. Banzan offered a detailed description of the effect on various social groups of the contemporary practice of exchanging rice for cash, and showed how the system, by concentrating rice in a few centers, would produce serious logistical difficulties in the event of a foreign invasion. The work also discussed questions relating to grain conservation, taxation, foreign trade, the resettlement of the samurai on the land, the resettlement of peasants from overcrowded villages, sericulture, forestry, riparian engineering, irrigation, religious policy, education, and the formulation of new codes of conduct. The aim of Banzan's proposals was to create by means of a humane or "benevolent" administration (*jinsei*)[p] a harmonious society of high morale and sufficient wealth to withstand any threat to its security.

Throughout the work Banzan's argument is strikingly empirical and practical. *Daigaku wakumon*, in short, is an outstanding example of *jitsugaku*[q] in the sense of *keisei chiyō no gaku*[r] (learning in the service of administration) distinguished by Professor Abe Yoshio.[s3] There was probably no contemporary Confucian better qualified to write such a work. Banzan brought to it an impressive and unusual combination of practical experience and Confucian learning. After a period in his youth as a page to Ikeda Mitsumasa[t] (1609–1682). the daimyo[u] of Okayama,[v] he had studied Confucianism under Nakae Tōju[w] (1608–1648) for some months in 1641–1642. Subsequently he had reentered the service of Ikeda Mitsumasa in 1647, and, partly on the strength of his Confucian learning had risen to occupy a "pivotal position"[4] in the domain administration. It was almost certainly during this period that he gained the familiarity with domain finance, administration, irrigation, and other topics reflected in *Daigaku wakumon*. During this period also, Banzan appears first to have attempted to alert the authorities to the danger of a Manchu invasion.[5] His career in Okayama, however, ended in frustration with his early resignation in 1657 at the age of thirty-nine, and the rest of his life was spent in study, teaching, and writing. Though subject to occasional persecution by the authorities, he produced a large body of written works, mainly in the form of miscellanies and commentaries, of which *Daigaku wakumon* is the climax. Many of its themes and the assumptions on which it is based may be traced in Banzan's other writings. It is in *Daigaku wakumon*, however, that their practical implications are most forcefully and dramatically expressed.

An inquiry into the Neo-Confucian background to Banzan's *jitsugaku* may, therefore, appropriately quote *Daigaku wakumon* as its point of departure. Although the work contains little in the way of exposition of Confucian doctrine, two passages suggest lines of approach to the Confucian thought behind the proposals. The first concerns Banzan's attitude to the body of objective, normative practices and institutions that constitute an important part of the Confucian tradition in any age.

Question: The methods of the Early Kings are recorded in the classics and commentaries. If the ruler is gifted with the ability to do so, why should he not employ them?

Answer: In the methods of the Early Kings there is expressed the ultimate good of [conformity with the principles of their own] time, place, and rank. This is impossible to put down on paper. A man born into the position of ruler of a province or of a state, unless he is a sage with the knowledge innate in him, cannot by himself apprehend this ultimate good. The man who knows it is the man born in a lower position who is familiar with historical change and human feelings, who has powers of learning, the requisite ambition and basic talent. (3:239–40)

Two aspects of this passage require comment. First, Banzan strongly affirms the principle of the subordination of political institutions to time, place, and social circumstance. Indeed, a strong sense of the relativity of all forms of action to their particular circumstances is a dominant feature of *Daigaku wakumon*. Banzan described the work as "for the salvation of the present" (3:233), inapplicable to other ages or countries, and the text is, for a Confucian work, rather free of doctrinaire appeals to Confucian precedent. Second, Banzan asserts that only those in inferior positions have the knowledge to determine appropriate measures of administration. Their qualification is that they are directly acquainted with the evolving conditions in society. Neither of these points is exceptionable or indeed original in Confucian terms. Most Neo-Confucians, however reluctantly, recognized that times changed and rendered many of the ideal institutions of the past impractical in their own society, and that knowledge of the feelings and attitudes of the governed was also an important principle of Confucian statecraft. The emphasis with which they are stated here, however, and the very real remoteness of early Tokugawa[x] Japan from the sources of the Confucian tradition, raise the problem of Banzan's view of the practical relevance of the whole Confucian tradition to his time. They suggest also a tension between Confucian tradition and action based on practical experience. It is natural, therefore, to ask how thoroughgoing Banzan's dedication to practicality and empiricism is and whether it remains compatible with Neo-Confucian orthodoxy.

The second passage concerns the role and importance of self-cultivation and, in particular, the traditional Neo-Confucian goal of sagehood.

The reason that the Han,[y] T'ang,[z] Sung,[aa] and Ming[ab] dynasties lasted for three or four centuries despite their lack of sagely or worthy rulers like those of the Three Ages was that they instituted the office of prime minister, made use of the wisdom and talent in the land, and, in prosecuting the tasks of administration as they arose, employed the appropriate codes of conduct. The prime minister was a man of basic talent. This basic talent is the most important in the land, but it is useless without virtue. The virtue of a prime minister, even though it may not be the divine virtue of a sage or worthy, is the virtue of heeding remonstrations and welcoming advice. (3:282)

This statement is again unexceptionable in broad Confucian terms: a ruler's choice and promotion of able subordinates represented an important aspect of Confucian statecraft. Viewed from the perspective of orthodox Neo-Confucianism with its central interest in the pursuit of self-cultivation leading to sagehood, however, Banzan's formulation requires comment. His definition of the virtue appropriate to a prime minister is remarkably precise and limited. It suggests at least a tacit assumption that sagehood is not a preeminent concern. It is as though the urgent practical need to ensure dynastic survival made the higher aims of spiritual achievement no longer of immediate importance. Such a view would constitute a significant shift of emphasis from the conventional Neo-Confucian view of self-cultivation and sagehood.

These two quotations thus raise questions in two different though complementary areas of Confucian thought: the outer realm of the objectification of Confucian values in society, and the inner realm of the pursuit of self-cultivation by the individual. Together they imply that, in *Daigaku wakumon*, Banzan may have been prepared in principle, indeed may have felt it necessary, to accept some accommodation of traditional Neo-Confucian imperatives to expediency. It is important, therefore, to ask with reference also to Banzan's other writings whether this is a consistently and consciously realized position, and whether it involved a deliberate attempt to reorder Confucian priorities or to restructure the tradition.

The argument of this paper is that though Banzan made some interesting criticisms of Neo-Confucianism, there is in his thought no attempt systematically to restructure Neo-Confucian philosophy. Banzan was not a systematic thinker and speculative thought was perhaps uncongenial to him. Rather, he belongs to that class of Tokugawa Confucian thinkers concerned primarily with the social and political utility of Neo-Confucian ideas. Nonetheless, at the level of Confucian practice, he made historically significant modifications of certain aspects of the Neo-Confucian system. These modifications were inspired by an approach that tended strongly to subordinate conventional priorities to the practical requirements of the contemporary political and economic situation, as Banzan perceived it. It is his choice of practicality that justifies use of the term "pragmatic" in this paper. By pragmatic here is meant a mode of thinking which, whatever its ultimate reference, determines questions of action on the basis of immediate practical criteria rather than the prescriptions of orthodox doctrine.

In theory, such an attitude is not necessarily irreconcilable with orthodox Neo-Confucian beliefs. However, in practice, if carried beyond a certain point, a dedication to pragmatism could be argued to distort commonly accepted assumptions and priorities relating to Confucian conduct. It could imply that men might act independently of the normative principles (*ri*)[ac] believed to be immanent in their own natures and in the external world alike. More obliquely, by focusing attention on the relationship of actions to the situations in which they are performed rather than on the moral qualifications of those performing them, it could in practice suggest that self-cultivation was no longer a prerequisite for political action. It is not claimed, however, that a developed pragmatic orientation is consistently realized in Banzan's thought, but rather that there are significant tendencies in that direction.

Banzan's pragmatism expresses itself in the two main fields suggested by the two introductory quotations from *Daigaku wakumon*. It is found first in his willingness, on the grounds that adherence to Confucian norms was impractical in contemporary Japan, to advocate or at least tolerate practices normally unacceptable to Confucian opinion and, secondly, in a less consistent and more subtle tendency to shift attention from the moral regeneration of the man in authority to the appropriateness of his actions in themselves. These two strands of Banzan's pragmatism derived in turn from different sources in his thought. The first is based on a reasoned conviction that history, geography, and social circumstance imposed practical limitations on the realization of the ideal society prescribed in the Confucian canon. The second, though this is harder to show, appears to be associated more directly with Banzan's belief in the deterioration of society and the need for urgent preventive action. In both cases, Banzan's arguments derived urgency from his belief in the imminence of a foreign invasion. What follows is an exploration of the Confucian background to these two facets of pragmatism in Banzan's thought, primarily through quotation from his written works. These works, which began to appear in the early Kambun[ad] period (1661–1673), about a decade and a half after Banzan's retirement in 1657 from active service under Ikeda Mitsumasa, are, from a Confucian viewpoint, casual and informal in style. They consist of miscellanies, discursive commentaries on the Confucian classics, and other works including *Daigaku wakumon* and a remarkable commentary on the *Tale of Genji*.[ae] Banzan's dialogues have not been used, since it is difficult to establish firmly which speaker presents the author's viewpoint in them.

BANZAN AND TŌJU

A convenient point of departure for a discussion of Banzan's pragmatism is his doctrine of the relativity of action to "time, place, and rank," introduced in the first quotation from *Daigaku wakumon* above. This threefold formula was not original to Banzan, but was a part of his inheritance from Nakae Tōju. It was, of course, to Tōju that Banzan owed his introduction to Confucian learning. His period of study under Tōju in Ogawa[af] in 1641–42 provided him with a basic orientation to the tradition which, though he later modified it to some extent, he never discarded.

At the time of Banzan's period of study with him, Tōju was in what has been called his "middle period." The thought of this period is expounded in his best-known work *Okina mondō*[ag] (Dialogues with an Old Man). After absconding from the Ōzu[ah] domain in 1634, his dedication to Confucian learning had expressed itself in an attempt to realize in his daily conduct the patterns of behavior appropriate to a sage. This attempt, however, had led to an impasse, and Tōju "conceived doubts as to whether the way of the sages, if this were its real character, was not beyond our attainment in the present age."[6] He solved this problem through a distinction between the internal, absolute source of a sage's actions, and their external, relative manifestation. This solution was first expressed in the *Rongo kyōtō keimō yokuden*[ai] (Introduction and Supplementary Commentary to the *Hsiang-tang* Chapter of the *Analects*), a commentary on the tenth chapter of the *Analects*[aj] written in about 1639. This chapter of the *Analects* purported to describe Confucius' ritual conduct on various occasions, and was clearly intended to be prescriptive. Tōju, however, interpreted Confucius' actions by positing a distinction between the "mind" (*kokoro*)[ak] of his actions and their objective manifestations or "traces" (*ato*).[al] The mind, Tōju suggested, could not be verbally transmitted and was accessible only through its traces. These traces, however, represented only the actions of Confucius at a particular time, and were not in themselves permanently prescriptive. The Confucian student should "not rely on the traces of the sage," but should "grasp his mind,"[7] and, by implication, adjust his conduct according to his own time. In defining time, Tōju used a phrase that was to become fundamental to his own and to Banzan's thought. "Time," he wrote, "has three dimensions: Heaven, earth, and man. These are called time, place, and rank" (*toki tokoro kurai*).[am][8]

Tōju's doctrine of the relativity of action to "time, place, and rank" was a persuasive reformulation of a principle accepted in some form by most Neo-Confucians. It solved for his Japanese followers the acute practical problem of the meaning for them of an important element of the Confucian tradition, its ritual prescriptions. The denial of absolute status to the objective institutions of Confucianism and the introduction of a strong element of subjectivity into the conduct of the individual undoubtedly greatly simplified the practice of what was, after all, an alien religious system in Japan. The very freedom introduced by this doctrine, however, created a potential source of practical difficulty. The distinction between "mind" and "traces" inevitably resulted in practice in a tension between an individual's perception of absolute values in his mind and the limitations imposed on their practice by time, place, and rank. In theory the "illumined virtue" (meitoku)[an] with which every individual was endowed would, if cultivated, provide an infallible guide to the correct course of action. This action would, in turn, express the universal principle of filial piety (kō)[ao] immanent in the external world. So long as the values in the mind were linked in this way to objective moral values in the external world, the individual's perception of the absolute "mind" of the sage's actions would express itself in turn in proper Confucian action in society, and the system would retain an orthodox emphasis. The danger was that in practice a separation between the two aspects of the distinction might develop and a disproportionate emphasis attach to one or the other aspect. Either emphasis, if carried beyond a certain point, would be regarded as heterodox. If the mind were overvalued and its ontological identification with the moral principles immanent in the external world became attenuated or lost, the individual might adopt a contemplative or fugitive pattern of conduct condemned by orthodox Confucian opinion as Buddhistic. Or, if too much weight were placed on time, place, and rank as conditions distorting the practice of conventional Confucianism, the student might find his conduct no longer recognizable as Confucian. It can be argued that, after his middle period, Tōju developed in the former direction. Banzan, on the other hand, developed towards a type of Confucianism in which limitations imposed by time, place, and rank, as he perceived them, tended to encroach on conventional Confucian values. It is this displacement of conventional Confucian norms and substitution of action determined by practical criteria that justify use of the term pragmatic in connection with Banzan's thought.

Nakae Tōju himself may be said to have realized an orthodox balance between the two aspects of his basic distinction in Okina mondō. In this work he combined a concern for the spiritual rewards of Confucian practice with a sense of Confucianism as a creed of social action. Emphasis is placed on the individual's fulfillment of his social role as a means to self-realization, and moral meaning is conferred on the external world through the immanence in it of the universal principle of filial piety. The balance achieved in *Okina mondō* however, proved unstable. If the persuasive analysis of Professor Bitō Masahide[ap] is to be accepted,[9] after Tōju embraced the teachings of Wang Yang-ming[aq] (1472–1529) in 1644, his thinking developed a quietistic and Buddhistic emphasis, falling into exactly that contemplative interpretation of Wang's doctrines that Wang himself had been anxious to prevent. For instance, Tōju interpreted Wang's activist doctrine of "extending good knowledge" (*chih liang-chih*)[ar] in the sense of "arriving at good knowledge" (*ryōchi ni itaru*).[as][10] "Good knowledge" thus tended to become an absolute source of goodness in the individual, to be apprehended through contemplation rather than realized in action. Tōju was also reported by a disciple to have remarked that once one knows the true happiness of a state of peace free from desire, "the wish to be a samurai or to have a stipend no longer exists."[11] In terms of the basic distinction in Tōju's thought, this position suggests a severing, or at least a weakening, of the link between the mind and the external world, and a disproportionate emphasis on the former.

In his mature thought, Banzan adopted an ambivalent attitude to Tōju. On the one hand, he was critical of certain aspects of Tōju's thought, charging that it was "immature" and had "heterodox faults" (2:108), and he claimed that it was a disciple's duty to renew his master's teachings in accordance with the demands of the times (1:340–41). He was critical also of Tōju's school, accusing its members of "heterodoxy" and "self-satisfaction with shallow learning" (1:270). On the other hand, Banzan protested that he did not differ "a hair's breadth" from Tōju in his interpretation of the "real meaning" of Confucianism (1:341). This ambivalence almost certainly reflects a basic loyalty to Tōju's teachings combined with a condemnation of the developments of Tōju's later thought and the attitudes of his followers. Banzan's mature thought may, in effect, be regarded as an attempt to recover the orthodox balance of Tōju's middle period. His interest in the objective, relative aspect of Tōju's basic distinction, however, together with his sense of impending crisis, led him, as will be shown, to a greater accommodation with the contemporary world than Tōju. Banzan also retained Tōju's interest in Wang Yang-ming, and his emphasis on introspection as a technique of self-cultivation particularly shows Wang's influence.

THE PRACTICE OF CONFUCIANISM IN JAPAN

Banzan accepted Tōju's fundamental distinction between "mind" and "traces," though he often rephrased it as a distinction between "truth" (*shin*)[at] and "traces." He also frequently employed a parallel distinction, probably also derived from Tōju,[12] between the "way" (*dō*)[au] and "law" (*hō*),[av] perhaps because "way" was a less subjective concept than "mind." Banzan was, however, a thinker of a very different temperament from Tōju. Where Tōju had dwelt on the emotional satisfactions and spiritual rewards of Confucian practice, Banzan, though by no means insensitive to such things, habitually viewed Confucianism from a wider, more detached, and objective perspective. From Tōju to Banzan there is a shift of emphasis from the individual to the social and political plane comparable to that between the thought of Itō Jinsai[aw] (1627–1705) and Ogyū Sorai[ax] (1666–1728). Further, Tōju had substantiated his doctrine of the relativity of Confucian institutions to time and place largely by the scholastic method of appeal to the Confucian canon and to the authority of later Chinese commentators on the tradition. Banzan also on occasion used a similar method (e.g., 1:350). Further, he justified the principle of relativism by appeal to what were basically conventional Confucian theories of history and geography. Banzan's theory of history may be summarized as a rather casual synthesis of the simplicity (*chih*)[ay] and refinement (*wen*)[az] alternation of Tung Chung-shu[ba] (179?–104? B.C.), the cyclical theory of the Sung Confucian Shao Yung[bb] (1011–1077), a modification of the belief stated in the *Shih-chi*[be] (Records of the Grand Historian) that "every thirty years there takes place a minor change and every five hundred years a major change,"[13] and a more original theory which related the rise and fall of political regimes to the condition of the nation's forests. These theories showed how time and cyclical change rendered particular institutions applicable only to the time of their inception. His theory of geography was based on a belief that the *ki*,[bd] the physical stuff of the world, varied from country to country and with it the moral and psychological disposition of its inhabitants and their capacity to observe ritual imperatives.[14] Banzan's practical temperament, political perspective, and an impatience with formal scholarship led him, however, to widen the scope of his discussions beyond theory and the conventional language of Confucianism to include his own observations and experience. This broadening of discourse is in itself significant, since it suggests an approach to the problem of Confucian practice in Japan that was more empirical than Tōju's.

On the basis of these theories, Banzan was able to argue that Chinese Confucian institutions and imperatives did not necessarily apply to Japan, and to point out that the integration of Neo-Confucianism (*dōgaku*)[be] and administration (*shioki*)[bf] had proved a practical impossibility (2:157). It is, however, in his extensive discussion of the practicability of particular ritual institutions in Japan that his application of Tōju's formula and pragmatic approach are best seen. Much of his writing is, in fact, taken up with this kind of problem, and with arguments against those whom he saw as offending his belief in flexibility. A good example is provided by his discussion of the problem of the proper form for the disposal of the dead. Confucianism, of course, prescribed earth burial, and the *Book of Rites*[bg] and later ritual manuals such as the Neo-Confucian *Wen-kung chia-li*[bh] (Domestic Ritual of Chu Hsi)[bi] gave detailed instructions for the number, size and decoration of coffins. In Japan, however, the Buddhist practice of cremation had become popular from the eighth century on and was widespread. To Confucians, the burning of a parent's body was an intolerable violation of filial sentiment. When Confucian ideas became influential in the seventeenth century, some attempt was made by idealistic Confucian administrators such as Ikeda Mitsumasa, Hoshina Masayuki[bj] (1611–1673) of Aizu,[bk] and Nonaka Kenzan[bl] (1615–1663) of Tosa[bm] to stop it. [15]

Banzan was opposed to the universal practice of Confucian burial, largely on economic grounds. The Chou[bn] dynasty regulations for coffin construction had, he argued, been laid down at a time of unprecedented peace and affluence (2:284). In the past there had been much space available, and the population had been small. Contemporary Japan, however, had little space and a large population. It would be possible for those of samurai rank and wealthy commoners to use board of two- to three-tenths of an inch thick for their coffins, but how could the very poor do this? (2:183–84)

At the present time, it is an impossibility for the populace down to the lowest of the common people to use coffins, erect tombs and practice burial. The people in the mountains who supplement their agriculture with gathering firewood and wood for salt kilns do not have three days' food supply. Those who are hired by the day do not have food for the morrow. There must be countless millions like this. Those better off than this are upper class among the common people, but many of them do not have the price of a single garment. They rarely eat rice. To such as these the ruler would have to present the materials for funerals. Since the amount involved is limitless, it would be impossible in the present circumstances. Even were the Way to be practiced, economies made, and the materials supplied by the ruler, within twenty or thirty years according to locality, the ground for burial would run out. Even if in each province distant sites were found, and with the backing of the authorities a hundred-year plan were made, the mountain forests would not stand up to it and the timber supply would run out. (2:287)

For most of the population, Banzan maintained, cremation was more suitable than burial. Cremation had come to Japan with Buddhism. It had been necessary in India to counter the tendency of the avaricious Indians to survive death as ghosts, a very rare phenomenon in Japan (2:278–79). Its simplicity and economy, however, had been among the reasons for the success of Buddhism in Japan (2:285). It would be an act of greater benevolence to retain Buddhist cremation than to enforce Confucian burial according to the *Wen-kung chia-li* prescriptions (2:286).[16]

Banzan's political perspective and sensitivity to the limitations imposed on Confucian practice by Japanese conditions led him to advocate, at least as far as a large part of the population was concerned, the substitution of a practice that most Confucians felt to be wrong. His justification for this course was the impracticability of adhering to the Confucian norm, and his choice of an un-Confucian alternative may be termed pragmatic. It might be objected that in the argument quoted and indeed elsewhere in Banzan's thought, for instance in *Daigaku wakumon*, the ultimate criterion determining the choice of action is the Confucian value of benevolence, and that therefore the question is not one of pragmatism but rather basically one of casuistry, the reconciliation of contradictory religious imperatives. It would seem, however that, mutatis mutandis, similar objections could be raised against the use of the term "pragmatic" in almost any context, since any deliberate action presupposes ultimate reference to some value. What is important here, rather, is the primarily practical character of Banzan's argument. There is a world of difference between his exposition of the economic factors preventing the universal practice of Confucian burial and genuinely casuistical Confucian argument such as is found, for example, in Hayashi Razan's[bo] (1583–1657) discussions of such questions as the conflict between loyalty and filial piety in his *Jumon shimon roku*[bp] (Confucian Problems).[17]

Banzan extended similar approval or tolerance to practices condemned by Confucian opinion, in such areas as marriage between members of the same clan, non-agnatic adoption, and sodomy. His tolerance of sodomy is particularly significant, since he consciously adopted an attitude of greater flexibility than Tōju, who had condemned the practice in *Okina mondō*.[18]

I have a friend who is a keen believer in Confucianism but is ignorant of time, place, and rank, and unfamiliar with human feelings and historical change. He quotes from Mr. Nakae's *Okina mondō* to the effect that sodomy is a great evil in order to shame and admonish people. My reaction is to say that in China, India, and Japan alike sodomy is a social practice and has long constituted something of a custom. Even if suppressed, it would not stop. One does not condemn as an evil something that has been a widespread practice in society over long years, even if it is immoral. (2:186)

The same principle of the suspension of conventional moral position from consideration of time, place, and rank could also be applied in judging standards of behavior in the past. This is most striking in Banzan's attitude toward the *Tale of Genji*. In his commentary on that work he attempted to exonerate the novel from charges that the hero's philandering made it unworthy of serious consideration. Genji's affairs, he argued, were the product of the times in which he lived and should be judged accordingly. "Everything," he wrote, "alters with the age, and should be viewed in its light" (2:542). Banzan's eagerness to exculpate Genji led him to claims which, if consistently held, would subvert one of the central values of Sung Neo-Confucianism, principle (*li*), whose permanence and immutability had been accepted as fundamental in the metaphysical thought of Chu Hsi.[19] In a somewhat tortuous argument showing how Genji's affair with Oborozukiyo[ba] could at one and the same time be the ground for his exile and yet not a serious crime, he wrote:

This was not a time in which an affair like that with Oborozukiyo was regarded as a crime. However, Heavenly principle and human feelings had changed from former times [in which such affairs had been tolerated], and so, when made the subject of a charge, it could be regarded as a crime. (2:543)

A passage such as this suggests a world in which even the central values of Neo-Confucianism are subject to the determining influence of history.

To some extent, of course, the principle of the relativity of political and ritual institutions to time and history was, as has already been suggested, built into the Confucian tradition, for Neo-Confucians were conscious that much from classical times was impracticable in their own age. Wang Yang-ming in particular adopted a relaxed attitude to ritual observance,[20] and it is clear that, directly or indirectly, the arguments of both Tōju and Banzan owed much to him. Nonetheless, it seems doubtful that many Neo-Confucians would have gone as far as Banzan in condoning contemporary practices such as sodomy. An acceptable balance between the ideal and the present was outlined by the Sung scholar Ch'eng Ming-tao (Ch'eng Hao,[br] 1032–1085) as follows:

Merely to adhere rigidly to the past and not to know how to apply the system to the present, to wish to follow the name of the system but to sacrifice its reality: this is the view of vulgar scholars. How can they be qualified to talk about the way of government? However, if it is said that human sentiments and customs today are all different from those of the past and that no trace of the system of ancient kings can now be seen, so that it is better to do what is convenient for the moment and not engage in anything lofty, such a theory, I am afraid, is something that will not lead to great accomplishments and it is something that can not remove great troubles today.[21]

Banzan's attitude, therefore, is not remarkable for the principle on which it is based. Rather, it is the developed form in which it is argued, its centrality to his thought, the empirical method of its application, and the lengths to which it is taken that set it apart from earlier Neo-Confucian attitudes and lend it historical significance.

That Banzan's pragmatism did indeed carry him to the very limits of acceptability to Confucian opinion is confirmed by the response of his contemporaries. It was suggested to him that if he were to be given responsbility for government, his administration would be "too lax, the rituals of human morality would be abandoned, and society would become indistinguishable from that of beasts" (2:117). His interlocutors also brought him reports that his teachings were being compared to those of Lao Tzu[bs] and Chuang Tzu[bt] for their total independence of laws (hō) (2:172). Ikeda Mitsumasa, the great Confucian daimyo of Okayama, also condemned Banzan's position from the standpoint of a less accommodating Neo-Confucianism. In a series of letters to his son Tsunamasa[bu] (1638–1714) which date from 1670, Mitsumasa, shortly to retire, criticized Banzan's tolerance of marriage with another from the same clan, sodomy, and infringement of mourning regulations. He argued that Confucianism involved "nothing other than seeking the perfect good that is immutable in past or present," and questioned the capacity of those who were not sages or worthies to decide merely on the basis of their consciences questions of moral or ritual conduct on which the sages had spoken clearly.[22] For him, as probably for most Neo-Confucians, the essence of the tradition was summed up in a saying of Tung Chung-shu quoted in the *Chin-ssu lu*[bv] (Reflections on Things at Hand): "Rectify moral principles and do not seek profit. Illuminate the Way and do not calculate on results."[23]

Banzan's defence against arguments of this sort was, in effect, a statement of his creed as a Confucian.

Unless rituals are so lax that, compared to the ritual systems of the Chou dynasty, they may be called Taoistic, it is impossible to practice them in the Empire in modern times. But in fact my Way is not Taoistic or anything else. It is the great Way of patterning oneself on Heaven above and conforming with the geographical environment below. (2:174)

Elsewhere Banzan made it clear that the Way, the content of which he defined as the Three Bonds and the Five Norms (*sangō gojō*),[bw] was eternal, transcendent, and a part of the order of nature (2:63). His defense of the moral core of Confucianism does not, however, diminish the significance of the considerable erosion of the conventional Confucian moral tradition that he was prepared to tolerate in practice.

EMPIRICAL KNOWLEDGE AND DESCRIPTIVE PRINCIPLE

If the practice of Confucianism and the conduct of administration were thus limited by time and place and social situation, it followed that awareness of the limitation thus imposed was of vital practical importance. Like other Confucians of the period, Banzan was concerned that the ruling feudal elite of his time was becoming isolated by its life style from the realities of contemporary society. In his thought, therefore, there is a particular insistence on the importance of knowledge. For him knowledge, particularly knowledge on the part of the man in political authority, was the most important of the three Confucian virtues of knowledge, benevolence, and courage. "A ruler's government of a state and exercise of power over the lands within the Four Seas," he wrote, "is based on knowledge. If his knowledge is illumined, he exerts control and his actions are appropriate" (1:392). The main object of this vital knowledge was precisely that area that was most free of Confucian values, "time, place, and rank," or, as Banzan also frequently called it, "human feelings and historical change" (ninjō jihen).[bx] Its importance was demonstrated in history. Ignorance of changing conditions in the outside world had, for instance, been the main cause of the court's loss of political power in the Heian[by] period (3:91). In his commentary on the *Tale of Genji*, Banzan pointed out specific symptoms such as the Emperor's fondness for pictures (2:523) which, he claimed, illustrated the growing isolation of the court.

The method by which it was to be acquired also indicates something of the empirical content of Banzan's knowledge. He set rather little store on such conventional Confucian sources of political and moral wisdom as the Chinese historical classics, remarking to his disciples that the *Tso-chuan*[bz] and other commentaries on the *Spring and Autumn Annals*[ca] were unnecessary and that the *Spring and Autumn Annals* itself was "of no value for psychological techniques" (6:12). By temperament he was, perhaps, more interested in action than in study, and, while he saw some use for erudition, he made no claim to it himself (1:89). His somewhat bibliophobic attitude resembles that of Wang Yang-ming, whose comparison of the acquisition of knowledge from books with the processes of digestion he quoted with approval (1:388).[24] He did, however, value texts which conveyed information on human feelings (ninjō),[cb] such as the *Book of Songs*,[cc] the study of which he described as *jitsugaku* (1:353). He also commended another highly unconventional text as a repository of knowledge of human feelings, the *Tale of Genji*. His enthusiasm for the novel, unusual among major Confucians, is one of the most original aspects of his thought, and deserves separate study.

Banzan evidently felt that conventional Confucian sources of knowledge were an inadequate guide to action in the contemporary world. He constantly stressed, rather, the value of questioning (mongaku),[cd] particularly on the part of those in superior positions. This technique was not, of course, new in Confucian terms. Confucius, for instance, extolled Shun[ce] in the *Mean*[cf] because he "loved to question others";[25] and in the *Analects* there was praise for K'ung Wen-tzu[cg] because "he was not ashamed to ask and learn from his inferiors."[26] In Banzan's thought, however, oral questioning goes far beyond lip service to a piece of Confucian convention, and was a matter of urgent practical necessity. A theme constantly reiterated in his written books, it became part of his style. It was said of him: "You are always questioning others and are never heard of as giving instruction to anyone" (I, 216). He himself attributed his success in constructing irrigation ponds during his period of office to this technique.

All I did was to extend permission to the work of others. Later I questioned other people, observed and was instructed, and achieved a little success of my own. Observation of the blunders made by those in charge of operations suggests that they mostly arise from failure to ask questions. If you ask a man reared in the capital about matters connected with the capital, a mountain peasant about the mountains, and if you consult about the flow of a river and the force of its floods with someone living on its banks, you will have few regrets. (1:437)

Banzan's approach to knowledge and his stress on questioning as a means to acquiring it thus laid strong emphasis on experience and may to this extent appropriately be called empirical. This empirical knowledge was the cognitive basis for his pragmatic attitude to action.

Banzan's empirical interest in the objective realm of time, place, and rank and in human feelings and historical change led to a need for a rational concept that would explain the structure and processes behind the functioning of the external world. Here he turned not so much, as Tōju had done, to filial piety, but to an orthodox Neo-Confucian concept that Tōju had tended to neglect, ri or principle. In reintroducing ri into his thought, however, he tended to emphasize its descriptive rather than its moral and normative aspect.

In orthodox Chu Hsi Neo-Confucianism, of course, ri was the fundamental cause, immanent both in man as his nature and in the external world. It was both moral and normative—prescribing how things should be—and descriptive—reporting how they were. "Exhaustive exploration of principle" (kyūri),[ch] the perception of principle as it operated in history, in the external world, and in the self, was one of the main techniques by which the student achieved insight into the fundamental identity of his own moral nature with that of the external world. In practice, in the Chu Hsi tradition, this technique acquired a moral and academic emphasis. Principle was valued more for its moral than its descriptive content; and Chu Hsu himself made it clear that the commended method of exhaustive exploration of principle involved the perception of principle as exemplified in the canonical Confucian classics.[27]

His interest in ri as a rational concept and the influence of Wang Yang-ming on his thought led Banzan to adopt a characteristically ambivalent attitude toward Chu Hsi. Chu, he argued, was "a great Confucian," "a worthy," who was the "most famous man in history for commentaries on the classics" (2:106). He himself, significantly, had gained insight into principle "in my spare time from self-cultivation," and he had "no doubts about the principles under Heaven" (1:221). Nevertheless, following the attitude of the Wang Yang-ming school, Banzan criticized the academic emphasis of Chu Hsi's thought. "Master Chu," he wrote, "has the fault of too extensive a reliance on texts" (2:107). He condemned also the practice among his own contemporaries of the exhaustive exploration of principle.

Modern exploration of principle is conducted from books and consists of lectures on texts or empty discussions. This is not exploration of principles with reference to things. (1:213)

Banzan used the term "learning of principle" as a pejorative expression for a learning that was insufficiently introspective (3:285). He discouraged his disciples from too exclusive a use of "exploration of principle," saying that it would be detrimental to their progress (6:67).

Rather than as a technique for self-cultivation, Banzan saw "exploration of principle" as a means to the understanding of the external world, necessary for effective administration. Defending himself against a charge that his interests in proletarian matters was "uncouth," he wrote:

The basis of the state is the people, and the basis of the people is food. Without deep familiarity with the latter, administration of state or district is impossible. I am not an administrator. However, the subject is an important one, and, for it, it is essential to know the learning of exhaustive exploration of principle. (1:455)

In the following exposition of the relevance of principle to administration, the sphere of exploration of principle is explicitly external to the self:

The important principles under Heaven are those concerned with "regulation of the home, administration of the state, and the establishment of peace in the empire." In connection with each matter in this field, there are talents and knowledge which are the gifts of Heaven. The ruler discerns his subjects' natural gifts and confers the appropriate office on them. . . . A man eager to cultivate himself, slow to blame others, quick of knowledge and sincere in deed, he chooses to take charge of education. . . . When a man has a talent for mountains, rivers, and the principles of topography, the ruler gives him charge over mountains, rivers, ponds and meres. The man quick in the understanding of the way things grow is given charge over agriculture. . . . The man who understands the principles of yin,[ci] yang,[cj] and the spirits, and who is familiar with human character and historical change is made to coordinate the hundred offices as chief minister.

There are many things under Heaven, and principle is infinite. Those mentioned are only two or three of the important matters. (1:214)

It is interesting also to note that chapters twelve to fourteen of Banzan's *Shūgi gaisho*[ck] are entitled *"Kyūri,"* (Exhaustive Exploration of Principle) a title it is reasonable to attribute to Banzan himself. They deal with a wide variety of subjects, including problems of administration, horsemanship, trade, contracts for engineering operations, astronomy, river silting, and flood control.

Such a use of the concept suggests that, for Banzan, principle was indeed primarily of external, descriptive significance, a key to the functioning of nature and human society, rather in the sense that Dazai Shundai[cl] (1680–1747) was to use it.[28] In Banzan's thought, it did not in practice, as it did in Chu Hsi Neo-Confucianism, or as filial piety did in the thought of Nakae Tōju, provide a moral link between the individual and the world external to him. In this way, the external world is deprived of something of its primary moral meaning to the individual. It is not fanciful to suggest that the resulting freedom created room for pragmatic action.

Banzan's attitude to knowledge and to principle thus suggests that his pragmatism was based on a spirit of empirical and rational enquiry. It is well to add that this spirit was largely confined to the sphere of administration and related problems, and did not reflect a radical empiricism. In this field he did not rival the proto-scientific empiricism of his younger contemporary Kaibara Ekken[cm] (1630–1714). Banzan accepted the basic Confucian world view, and seems to have felt that empirical verification of it would not be a worthwhile procedure.

Lord Shen-nung[cn] tasted vegetation and founded medicine and pharmacology. Thereafter men of knowledge identified correspondences between the human body and the vastness of the universe and thus discovered and transmitted the details of moxa, acupuncture and pharmacology. If one dissects a human body one gets spattered in blood, but it is a pointless exercise. Through principle (*dōri*)[co] one has, without stirring oneself, knowledge that is not a hair's breadth in error or a fraction mistaken. (2:45)

MORAL REGENERATION AND POLITICAL ACTION

The foregoing discussion has shown how Banzan was able, on the basis of Nakae Tōju's teachings and his own empirical attitude to knowledge, to adopt a pragmatic attitude toward political and ritual action in the external sphere of time, place and rank. It is now appropriate to examine Banzan's attitude to the internal aspect of Tōju's dichotomy, the mind, and to take up the problem of self-cultivation and sagehood suggested in the second introductory quotation from Daigaku wakumon.

For Nakae Tōju, the mind had been the absolute source of Confucian values in the contemporary world. Only when actions were based on a proper grasping of it would they be morally acceptable. Such a grasping, however, could in turn only be achieved through self-cultivation and the regeneration of the self. This premise, shared in some form by all orthodox Neo-Confucians, was symbolized in the order of the eight steps of the Great Learning.[cp] So long as Banzan accepted this premise, his thinking would not be genuinely pragmatic, for actions would be evaluated in relation not to their consequences so much as to the moral condition of those performing them. Conversely, any destruction of that premise would enhance the pragmatic character of his thought.

Two apparently inconsistent attitudes toward the subject of self-cultivation and its relation to action may be found in Banzan's thought. The first is conventional in its assumptions; the second is unconventional from the point of view of the practical priorities of orthodox Neo-Confucianism because it disregards the premise outlined above. Of these two views, Banzan gives more space in his writings to the conventional. In this view, moral regeneration, particularly on the part of the ruler, was necessary not only for action in society (1:212) but also for the proper functioning of both the human and the natural worlds. For him, as probably for all orthodox Neo-Confucians, the world was basically a moral-natural continuum, and the norms of human conduct were linked to the laws of nature. Banzan illustrated this belief with a series of diagrams, the Shinpō zukai[cq] (Diagrams of the Method of Mind) (1:132–47), which demonstrated the fundamental unity of the human and natural worlds. For Banzan, moreover, not only was there a fundamental unity of structure, but also a unity of the moral and natural worlds as process. This belief, called "cosmic reciprocity" by Joseph Needham,[29] was a very ancient one in Confucian thought. One of its purest expressions is found in the Mean, where the sage, the morally regenerate individual in possession of sincerity, is spoken of as "able to assist the transforming and nourishing powers of Heaven and earth."[30] This he was able to do because sincerity itself could "produce changes," "without any movement."[31] In the following passage, Banzan paraphrases the *Mean* to show how the moral conduct of the individual, particularly in this case the ruler, directly influences the functioning of the natural order:

To preserve an attitude of humaneness, righteousness, decorum, wisdom and good faith and to practice the path of the five moral norms is to assist [the creating and annihilating processes of Heaven and earth][32] . . . To lose one's nature of the five norms and to depart from their path is to damage [these processes]. The five moral norms are the paths of the five physical agents. Therefore to preserve them and practice them is to assist [Heaven and earth] through their responsiveness to the five agents. (3:136)

The logical implication of this belief would be the attribution of imperfections in the functioning of nature to human moral failure. Thus Banzan was able to attribute disease to moral evil.

Leprosy, epilepsy, smallpox, syphilis, and the like are diseases which did not exist in remote antiquity. They appear to be sicknesses produced by the obstruction of the creating and annihilating ether caused by the violent administration of Chieh,[cr] Chou,[cs][33] and the First Ch'in Emperor.[ct] (3:135)

Similarly, Banzan wrote of crop failure that, "If the state is immoral, the ether of Heaven is out of harmony, and the five cereals do not ripen completely. The people are accustomed to shortage and regard it as the norm" (2:12). Conversely, since the cause of disorder lay in the moral realm, moral perfection could effect perfect functioning of the human and natural orders. Banzan wrote that, "there are no eclipses of the sun or moon, or earthquakes in a moral age, nor are there fires, plagues, supernatural visitations, or noxious insects that destroy cereal crops" (3:134). In the human realm also, even the intractable problem of population pressure on natural resources was to be solved in the same way. Banzan claimed that if a morally illumined ruler were to appear "in response to the correctness of human morality, the ether of Heaven and earth too would be purified, there would be a return to spring, gradually fewer people would be born, and good men would come forth" (2:291). The logical implication of these beliefs was, of course, the Confucian ideal of the sage-ruler who did not rule, but who, by his own moral perfection, simply caused the human and natural orders spontaneously to function perfectly according to their own natural laws.

His experience and sense of realism, however, must have suggested to Banzan that the achievement of this ideal was a remote possibility, and his belief that a crisis faced Japan must have encouraged him to consider alternatives. Together with this conventional view, therefore, there occurs—sometimes in startling juxtaposition to it—the second view, based on apparently contrary, more pragmatic assumptions. Here the premise that moral regeneration is essential for political action is modified, sagehood is implicitly abandoned as an immediate goal, and the idea that the ruler's moral conduct directly influences the natural order is, at least temporarily, disregarded.

Even though the ruler may not yet have attained the state of mind of a worthy and remains in the unregenerate condition of taking pleasure in wealth and licentiousness, if only at the right moment, he enacts the measures that should be enacted and provides an administration and education that produce large numbers of good men, it cannot be denied that he is assisting the creating and annihilating processes. (3:68–69)

In this passage, the ruler's actions are evaluated primarily with reference to their results rather than to his state of mind. In so far as it is required that the policies produce good men, however, morality has not been completely eliminated. Nevertheless, the premise that regeneration was essential for political action has been overlooked. That Banzan was conscious of this is shown by the following passage in which both views are presented.

Assisting the creating and annihilating processes by means of virtue is a matter for sages and worthies. It involves harmonizing the ether of Heaven-and-earth on a grand scale through a sage-ruler and his worthy ministers. But there are times when this assisting is achieved by talent and knowledge and a man, even though he is not a sage or worthy, may, if he has some slight aspiration to morality, assist the creating and annihilating processes. Heaven and earth produce and grow things in an unregulated manner. In some years there are good harvests, in others, poor. It is the responsibility of human talent to extend the harvests of years of good crops to supplement years of crop failure. Here the creating and annihilating processes may be greatly assisted even if one does not possess the virtue of a worthy or superior man, by being unashamed of questioning one's inferiors, and by using the knowledge available in the land. (2:274–75)

The passage continues with Banzan's observation that heavy financial losses were frequently sustained by various social groups exchanging rice for cash in years of good harvest, a theme elaborated in Daigaku wakumon (3:281). It would be to the benefit of peasants and samurai, he claimed, if in such years, instead of selling at a depressed price, surpluses were spread out over following years. Such a measure would constitute "assisting Heaven and earth" (2:275). Here again, it is required of the ruler not that he pursue the goal of sagehood, but only that he have "some slight aspiration to morality," enough presumably to dispose him to question his inferiors. The conventional Neo-Confucian premise that regeneration is necessary for political action and that the goal of life is the achievement of sagehood has lost much of its force. There is a shift of focus from the state of mind of the ruler to the appropriateness of his policies. In so far as these policies are now judged primarily with reference to their practical results rather than their moral origins, they are pragmatic.

A similar and parallel ambivalence over the necessity of regeneration is to be seen in Banzan's discussion of "talent" (sai).[cu] Talent had two meanings in the Neo-Confucian tradition. In one of its uses, it had a technical and primarily moral sense and referred to an individual's "moral stuff,"[34] the capacity essential for the successful pursuit of self-cultivation. Significantly, Banzan seems not to have understood this technical meaning of the term, for he objected to an assertion in a subcommentary of the Ssu-shu chi-chu ta-ch'üan[cv] (Great Compendium of Commentaries on the Four Books) that the superior man must have talent (4:99–100). He understood the term, rather, in its vernacular sense of talent or ability, in practice often ability in administration. In orthodox Confucian thought, it was a normal assumption that talent in this sense must be subordinate to, or at least accompanied by, moral virtue. Confucians distrusted the exercise of talent uninformed by virtue as mere skills (jutsu).[cw] A negative exemplar in this respect was Kuan Chung,[ex] (d. 645 B.C.) chief minister to Duke Huan[cy] of Ch'i in the Spring and Autumn period of Chinese history, who had achieved fame by pursuing utilitarian policies and saving China from barbarian invaders.

As with regeneration and political talent, Banzan accepted the orthodox view that virtue was a prerequisite for talent, writing, for instance, that "for a person to have talent and no virtue is for him to be a monster" (1:338). Commenting on Confucius' remark that "Is not the saying that talents are difficult to find, true?",[35] he wrote that "basic talent" (hon-zai),[cz] which he defined as talent for administration, "necessarily includes Confucian virtues and learning" (4:119). It will be recalled though that his definition of virtue in this context was a narrow one. Side by side with this view, however, he also expressed the view that talent could be divorced from virtue. In the course of an elaborate classification of abilities and temperaments, he wrote:

There are also unregenerate men who have basic talent. Such a man as Kuan Chung had not escaped from an unregenerate state of mind, but had basic talent. With regard to his success in saving the empire from major disaster, there are aspects of him not inferior to humane men. (3:70)

In this passage, the separation of administrative talent from regeneration enabled Banzan to evaluate Kuan Chung's conduct positively and in terms of its results rather than his state of mind.[36]

Not only was regeneration no longer essential in the contemporary world, but in certain situations, Banzan noted, unregenerate conduct could be preferable to regenerate conduct, in terms of its result. In a remarkable but difficult passage which probably dates from the mid-1670s,[37] Banzan argued that it was better, in an immoral age, for government officers to be greedy and make large tax exactions from local rulers than it was not to do so. Such exactions eliminated the ten or hundredfold more wasteful entertainments and bribery which otherwise surrounded these officers and led to dissipation of the country's resources. Actions might be evaluated by truly pragmatic standards. Banzan's support for this argument, though logically inexact, is entirely empirical.

I first realized this in Miyako,[da] with the Ōhara[db] and Yase[de] firewood trade. In the mountainous terrain of Yase and Ōhara, there are few domestic dwellings. For this reason the place of sale is the small area around Imadegawa[dd] and westwards as far as Muromachi.[de] Even there the inhabitants do not rely solely on this supply. Since it supplements the wood brought up in the Takase[df] boats from Fushimi[dg] which they buy up for their fires, it does not amount to much. Thus the brushwood and firewood of Yase and Ōhara have lasted from the old days till now. If the residences of Yase and Ōhara were increased and the market area in Kyoto extended, the exhaustion of the mountains and disappearance of the woodsellers would ensue within a few decades. (1:155)

Banzan infers from this observation that on a national scale also a situation in which those in authority were greedy, as presumably the Yase and Ōhara wood-sellers were, but in which economic activities were restricted by transport difficulties, was preferable to one in which the rulers of society were regenerate in respect of greed but cities were large and the general rate of consumption was high (I, 154–55). Given a choice between alternatives involving Confucian or un-Confucian conduct on the part of those in authority, un-Confucian conduct might be preferable. Economic considerations, in short, might under certain circumstances outweigh moral ones.

Though unconventional from the point of view of traditional Neo-Confucianism, the shift of emphasis from self-cultivation to statecraft documented above need not be considered more than a reordering of practical priorities. After all, statecraft remained a legitimate Neo-Confucian concern; and Confucius himself had praised Kuan Chung's achievement in saving China from barbarians.[38] Rather, the two viewpoints expressed by Banzan may be seen in terms of the polarity, identified by Professor Benjamin Schwartz, between the inner realm of self-cultivation and the outer realm of ordering society.[39] Emphasis on one pole, of course, need not permanently exclude the other. Those who attached greater importance to objective policies and statecraft usually did so with the ultimate aim of achieving a moral and harmonious Confucian society; it was a question of practical priorities. Banzan himself would certainly have attributed the apparent contradictoriness of his views to the difference between a moral and an immoral age. He would have pointed out that in a degenerate age such as his own and in a remote country such as Japan it was necessary to make concessions to the limitations imposed by time, place and rank. Not least, he would have argued that, whatever the moral disposition of the contemporary rulers of Japan, it was of vital importance to adopt policies that would ensure national survival in face of the threat of imminent social disintegration and foreign invasion. But he would have denied that these practical concessions involved a radical change of goals or assumptions. His ideal remained a society in which the spontaneous practice of Confucian morality natural to man was the basis of cosmic and social harmony.

It would be a serious distortion of the overall emphasis of Banzan's writings to suggest that he consistently played down the importance of self-cultivation. It is clear that at least some of his disciples regarded him primarily as a teacher of a "method of mind" (shinpō)[dh]. In fact, his ideas on self-cultivation are an interesting adaptation of the introspective emphasis of Wang Yang-ming. He particularly stressed the technique of "watching oneself when alone" (shindoku),[di] or, as he explained it, "being cautious over private knowledge" (1:287); and he used the term jitsugaku with respect to the introspective technique of "honoring the moral nature" (sontokusei)[dj] (4:64). He also spoke vividly of the "sincerity of the will"—the end state reached through "honoring the moral nature"—

as a condition of enlightenment like that of William James's "cosmic consciousness."[40]

When this state is reached, the mind is spacious and the body enriched. Its flood-like ether fills the space between Heaven and earth, and the myriad creatures are endowed within one. Heaven, earth and the Supreme Vacuity are omnipresent within the self. (1:288)

Viewed from a wider perspective, however, it is possible to detect a certain contradiction and sense of unreality in Banzan's teachings on the subject of Neo-Confucian enlightenment. He professed the belief that if a sage, the enlightened individual according to Neo-Confucianism, were to be given appropriate rank, even his own degenerate times could be restored to the state of remote antiquity (4:23). But he also told his disciples that, though Japan might produce a worthy, the quality of her *ki* made the appearance of a "complete sage" impossible (6:70). The ultimate goal of Neo-Confucian self-cultivation was, it seems, beyond the reach of Japanese. At a different level, also, there is some evidence to suggest that those of Banzan's disciples most interested in psychological techniques and self-cultivation may have been drawn mainly from the *kuge*[dk] (court noble) class, precisely those whom Tokugawa society denied an important political role. For them, perhaps, Neo-Confucian self-cultivation was something in the nature of a private pursuit of enlightenment rather than the preparation for the public exercise of political authority implied by the high orthodox tradition.

It is appropriate, in summary, to express Banzan's position in terms of Nakae Tōju's distinction between the inner realm of the mind and the outer realm of time, place, and rank. Banzan, it will have become clear, attempted to preserve a balance between these two realms. He expounded a theory that showed, in accordance with orthodox priorities, how the moral conduct of the ruler directly affected the functioning of the natural order, and he taught a method of moral and psychological regeneration to his disciples. At the same time, he was prepared to suspend the premise that regeneration was necessary, and to focus instead on the practical appropriateness of the policies adopted by the ruler. This attenuation of interest in self-cultivation was the analogue in the internal realm of the great weight he attached to the external realm as a factor limiting the objectification of Confucian values in the contemporary world. Together, these themes of Banzan's thought suggest something of an imbalance, opposite to that of the later Tōju, in the direction of time, place, and rank.

CONCLUSION

In the foregoing discussion I have explored the Neo-Confucian under-pinnings to one of the major monuments of political economy to come from seventeenth-century Japan. I have shown how in Banzan's thought there is a strong tendency toward accommodation of the prescriptive aspects of the Neo-Confucian system to the practical realities and require-ments of contemporary Japanese society as he perceived them. This ac-commodation had two main aspects. In the external sphere it was ex-pressed as a rejection of certain established Confucian norms of conduct on the grounds of impracticality and substitution of non-Confucian alter-natives. In the internal sphere it was expressed as an implicit acknowl-edgement that Neo-Confucian self-cultivation leading to sagehood was no longer of overriding importance in a ruler. These modifications were made within the framework of the tradition. Banzan's pragmatism was derived from Neo-Confucianism by what Professor Chung-ying Cheng[dl] calls a "special focusing"[41] rather than by any radical restructuring of Confucian doctrine.

A special focusing, however, even if it does not imply radical restruc-turing, at least suggests an altered perspective on the tradition. It is not surprising to find that Banzan regarded Neo-Confucianism with a detach-ment inconceivable in the more fundamentalist of his Neo-Confucian contemporaries. He could claim, for instance, of Neo-Confucian in-terpretations of the classics that "neither Chu nor Wang grasped their en-tire meaning." (2:108), and he made interesting criticisms of both Chu Hsi and Wang Yang-ming over specific points of interpretation of the classics, particularly of the *Book of Songs* (2:367). He was critical also of the practice of Neo-Confucianism in his own society, condemning, in what must certainly be a reference to the Kimon[dm] school of Yamazaki Ansai[dn] (1618–1682), the fundamentalist belief in Chu Hsi (2:107). And, in a statement that shows his tendency to think above all in practical and political terms, he asserted that, "In the present state of Confucianism, neither the school of Chu Hsi nor the school of Wang Yang-ming would be of any assistance in the conduct of administration" (2:283). These in-teresting comments suggest a certain distancing from earlier Neo-Con-fucianism and the beginnings of a critical attitude.

Banzan's attitude to Neo-Confucianism thus appears the complex and ambivalent response of a practical and political mind to a diverse and flexible tradition. On the one hand, he appears to have been attracted to the conventional Neo-Confucian vision of the ideal world and man's function in it. Undoubtedly the rationality of the tradition, its subtle combination of spiritual discipline and constructive social action together with its promise of advancement and exercise of power to those intellectually and morally qualified, attracted him as they did many of his contemporaries. At the same time, Banzan was an experienced official, gifted with acute powers of insight and observation and convinced that both internally and externally his society faced a crisis. He sensed an incongruity between certain aspects of the Neo-Confucian tradition and the contemporary reality. Consequently, the ideal and empirical aspects of his mental life were, probably increasingly, at odds with one another. The ideal tended to assume an unreal character, often expounded in jargon and sometimes verging on cant. Banzan therefore focused on those elements of the tradition (its historicism and concern with statecraft) that could best adapt it to the contemporary situation as he perceived it. He attempted to modify the institutional aspects of Neo-Confucianism to accommodate contemporary political and economic realities, and he tended to become concerned with statecraft at the expense of the traditional Neo-Confucian commitment to moral regeneration and sagehood. His modification of Neo-Confucian priorities was attacked by his contemporaries as un-Confucian or presumptuous. However, it was not actually heterodox from a Neo-Confucian point of view, since Banzan made no serious assault on the philosophical structure of Neo-Confucian doctrine. Rather it represents in extreme form application of basically orthodox principles, in short, a "special focusing."

Nonetheless, it is possible to see in Banzan's thought at least the potential for development in the direction of heterodoxy. Had his empiricism and pragmatism, his belief in the determining influence of time, place, and rank, and his doubts about self-cultivation been pursued to their logical conclusions, they might have provided the basis for a challenge to orthodox Neo-Confucianism. Indeed, it could be argued that some such development lay behind the rise of the anti-Neo-Confucian schools of Soraigaku[do] and Kokugaku[dp] in the following century. In Banzan's thought, however, it can be said that the doctrinal structure of Neo-Confucianism remains intact, but that at the level of practice there is a certain tension between doctrine and experience accompanied by a critical attitude toward certain aspects of the tradition.

It is appropriate, finally, to glance at Banzan's thought in a broader historical context and to ask further whether it represents an eccentric or a typical phenomenon in the history of the period. First, it should be said that it is possible to see an objective historical basis for Banzan's sense of incongruity between Neo-Confucianism and contemporary Japanese society. Leaving aside the question of invasion, there was much in the historical evolution of seventeenth-century Japanese society that might encourage a sense of disillusionment in a Neo-Confucian observer, particularly one who, like Banzan, implicitly required of the tradition that it should be "of assistance to the conduct of administration." In the early seventeenth century, as Professor Maruyama Masao[dq] has shown,[42] Neo-Confucianism might well have appeared a persuasive interpretation of experience. Its stress on social harmony and optimistic belief in the basic perfectibility of human nature were suited to an age in which peace had newly been established. Moreover, in an agrarian society in which the means of production altered little and relatively little direct official supervision of agriculture was needed, the belief that moral regeneration and personal virtue on the part of those in authority rather than coercive rule by law held the key to social harmony probably had a certain cogency. This very optimism, however, made the theory fragile. If it became incongruous, the system would assume an air of unreality. During the course of the seventeenth century, Japan rapidly evolved from a more or less agrarian economy in the direction of a nationwide economy based on money and commercial capital. New forms of social relations, based on money rather than the old personal values, accompanied this development. The profit motive threatened the practicality of the Confucian model of political and social relations. The growth of the rice exchange and their own isolation from the rest of society deprived the feudal elite of economic initiative. These trends reached a peak in the Genroku[dr] (1688–1704) and Kyōhō[ds] (1716–1735) periods, but they had already been diagnosed several decades earlier by acute observers such as Banzan.

Like all Confucians of the period, Banzan saw these developments as a threat to society. His experience, together with the conviction he inherited from Nakae Tōju, however, ruled out for him any attempt at a formal Confucian solution imposed by political authority. Nor, as a follower of the tradition of Mencius, was the exercise of legal coercion acceptable to him. He was inclined, rather, to seek a solution in the moral regeneration of society. However, perhaps increasingly towards the end of his life, he seems to have had doubts as to whether this kind of solution was practicable, whether what he once likened to "a great sea" (1:153) could be dammed by purely internal moral restraint. His sense of crisis must have been further intensified by his belief in the imminence of a Manchu invasion, itself cogent enough in the light of the historical parallel between the Mongol and Manchu conquests of China. In responding to these threats, Banzan consistently rejected doctrinaire solutions, and relied rather on his own experience, even if doing so involved contradictions of conventional Neo-Confucian imperatives. His pragmatism was born out of a sense of crisis and a belief that the conventional practices of Neo-Confucianism could not provide a solution to the country's difficulties.

In terms both of its historical background and its internal emphases there is much in common between Banzan's thought and the strand of late Ming thought described by Professor de Bary as the "new 'pragmatism.' "[43] Apparent similarities in detail can be found, for instance, between Banzan's relativism and Chang Chü-cheng's[dt] (1525–1582) rejection of "eternally valid institutions,"[44] or between Banzan's ambivalence over the need for regeneration and the somewhat similar position of Ni Yüan-lu[du] (1594–1644) over the efficacy of virtue in administration.[45] Banzan's attempt to harmonize Chu Hsi and Wang Yang-ming (2:143–44) and his interest in ki also resemble well-documented tendencies in late Ming thought. Through his teacher, Nakae Tōju, Banzan was, of course, indirectly influenced by the late Ming Neo-Confucian Wang Chi[dv] (1498–1583). The most recent Chinese thinker mentioned by name in Banzan's written works is Wang Shih-chen[dw] (1526–1590), whose opinion on the relationship between principle and divination he quotes in his own commentary on the Book of Changes (4:339). The possibility that Banzan was influenced by late Ming thought independently of Tōju, therefore, cannot be ruled out, though it would be difficult to document. The features of Banzan's thought original to him, however, bear the stamp not of doctrinal influence so much as of a practical attempt to adapt Neo-Confucian thought to contemporary Japanese conditions. It seems more persuasive to see Banzan's thought in terms of a complex interaction between his intellectual inheritance from Chu Hsi, Wang Yang-ming, and Nakae Tōju and his own practical and political temperament. In this view, similarities in detail between Banzan and late Ming thinkers should be attributed not to direct influence, but to broader parallels in historical predicament and participation in a common intellectual tradition.

It is tempting to see in Banzan's strongly practical and political response to Neo-Confucianism an example of the primacy of political values that has been seen as a characteristic of Japanese society.[46] If Banzan's thought indeed articulated the underlying value system of the society, it would be reasonable to expect his contemporaries to have been in some measure receptive to his ideas. Banzan himself was subject to repression during most of the latter half of his life and appears to have exerted little influence on the society of his own time. However, he expressed the hope that his style of Confucianism, even if temporarily subject to repression, would find acceptance among later generations (1:296–7). This hope was perhaps fulfilled in two ways. First, it seems probable that his attempt to adapt Neo-Confucianism to the conditions of seventeenth-century Japan exercised an influence on the succeeding generation of Japanese Confucian thinkers. It does not seem fanciful to see in Banzan's pragmatism, his political perspective, his empiricism and historicism, and his ambivalence over the role of Neo-Confucian self-cultivation, intimations of some of the themes in the thought of Ogyū Sorai. Indeed, Sorai's expressed admiration for Banzan[47] suggests that he may have felt some such debt. Secondly, when more than a century after Banzan's death, fears of foreign invasion began once more to be aroused, some of his successors turned to Banzan's jitsugaku in their quest for a solution. The admiration for him of the Mito[dx] school and of Yokoi Shōnan[dy] (1809–1869) is well-known.[48] These scholars found in Banzan's attempt to adapt Neo-Confucianism to the practical needs of a nation threatened with crisis from within and without, a valuable precedent for their own attempts at reconstruction. Nor did Shōnan, for instance, accord his respect solely on the basis of Banzan's specific administrative proposals. He particularly esteemed Banzan's Shūgi washo (Japanese Writings on the Accumulation of Righteousness), a work in which many of the assumptions which found expression in Daigaku wakumon are expounded.

NOTES

1. Famous Chinese military leaders in the San Kuo[dz] and the Ch'in[ea] and Former Han[eb] periods respectively.
2. References in the text of this paper are to the six-volume edition of Banzan's collected works edited by Masamune Atsuo, *Banzan zenshū*[ec] (Tokyo: Banzan zenshū kankōkai, 1940–43). The titles of individual works from which quotation is made have been mentioned only when they seemed of particular importance.
3. Abe Yoshio, "Jitsugaku no shin-Jugaku ni okeru soin (Min oyobi Edo jidai),"[ed] Draft paper presented to the Conference on Neo-Confucian Sources of Practical Learning in the Ming and Early Tokugawa periods, p. 1.
4. Taniguchi Sumio, *Ikeda Mitsumasa*[ee] (Tokyo: Yoshikawa kōbunkan, 1961), p. 87.
5. In *Daigaku wakumon* Banzan refers to having discussed the threat of invasion "in earlier years with the Lord of Kii[ef] and others, but they have all since died" (3:249). The Lord of Kii was almost certainly Tokugawa Yorinobu[eg] (1602–71), one of the daimyo whom Banzan is said to have met in Edo[eh] during his period of office in the Okayama domain. Yorinobu was head of one of the *gosanke*[ei] or three collateral Tokugawa houses. Banzan's autobiographical description of a visit when in office to the house of one of the "three lords" (2:113–14) very probably refers to his discussion of the invasion threat with Yorinobu.
6. *Tōju sensei nenpu*,[ej] in *Tōju sensei zenshū*[ek] Katō Seiichi et al., eds., (Tokyo: Iwanami shoten, 1940) 5:20.
7. *Tōju sensei zenshū*, 1:405.
8. *Ibid.*, p. 410.
9. Bitō Masahide, *Nihon hōken shisōshi kenkyū*[el] (Tokyo: Aoki shoten, 1961), pp. 185–208.
10. *Tōju sensei zenshū*, 2:31; Bitō, *Nihon hōken shisōshi kenkyū*, p. 187.
11. Fuchi Kozan, *Kōzan sensei shikyōroku*;[em] *Tōju sensei zenshū*, 1:601; Bitō, *Nihon hōken shisōshi kenkyū*, p. 213.
12. *Tōju sensei zenshū*, 3:287.
13. *Shih chi, Po-na pen* (Ssu-pu ts'ung-k'an ed.)[en], ch. 27, 38b. For the historical theory of Tung Chung-shu, see Fung Yu-lan,[eo] *A History of Chinese Philosophy*, Derk Bodde, trans. (Princeton University Press, 1953), 2:58–71; for Shao Yung, see *ibid.*, pp. 469–76.
14. It was this belief that suggested to E. H. Norman that Banzan was "something of a geographical materialist." *Andō Shōeki*[ep] *and the Anatomy of Japanese Feudalism*, Transactions of the Asiatic Society of Japan, 3d series (Tokyo: Tuttle, 1949), 2:43.
15. For Ikeda Mitsumasa's attempts to convert the populace of Bizen to Confucian burial practices, see Mizuno Kyōichirō, "Bizen-han ni okeru shin-shoku-uke seido ni tsuite," *Okayama daigaku hōbungakubu gakujutsu kiyō*[eq]

(1956), no. 5, p. 74; for Hoshina Masayuki, see Taira Shigemichi, "Kambun roku-nen Yamaga Sokō hairyū jiken no shisōteki igi," *Bunka*[er] (1956) 20(5):798; for Nonaka Kenzan, see Yokokawa Suekichi, *Nonaka Kenzan*[es] (Tokyo: Yoshikawa kōbunkan, 1962), p. 60.

16. Banzan himself claimed the right to bury his parents according to Confucian ritual (2:183), and did not object to the use of coffins "however fine" by practicing Confucian scholars (2:13). This discrimination was probably exercise of the otherwise rather little mentioned factor of "rank" from Tōju's formula.

17. Text in *Zoku Nihon Jurin sōsho*[et] (Tokyo: Tōyō tosho kankōkai, 1930–33), vol. 2.

18. *Tōju sensei zenshū*, 3:233.

19. A. C. Graham, *Two Chinese Philosophers* (London: Lund Humphries, 1958), p. 14.

20. Wang for instance permitted his family to eat meat during the period of mourning for his father and also offered meat to old persons who came to offer condolences. For this he was censured by Chan Jo-shui[eu] (1466–1560). Takase Takejirō, *Ō Yōmei shōden*[ev] (Tokyo: Kōbundō, 1915), pp. 187–88. See also Tu Wei-ming,[ew] "Subjectivity and ontological reality -- An interpretation of Wang Yang-ming's mode of thinking," *Philosophy East and West* (1973) 23(1 & 2):195.

21. Wing-tsit Chan,[ex] trans., *Reflections on Things at Hand: The Neo-Confucian Anthology Compiled by Chu Hsi and Lü Tsu-ch'ien*[ey] (New York: Columbia University Press, 1967), pp. 220–21.

22. Nagayama Usaburō, *Ikeda Mitsumasa kō den*[ez] (Tokyo: Ishizaka Zenjurō, 1932), 2:1144.

23. *Ibid.*, p. 1145; *Han-shu*,[fa] *Po-na pen* (SPTK ed.), 56:21b; Wing-tsit Chan, trans., *Reflections on Things at Hand*, p. 57.

24. Wing-tsit Chan, trans. *Instructions for Practical Living and Other Neo-Confucian Writings by Wang Yang-ming* (New York: Columbia University Press, 1963), p. 198.

25. *Mean*, VI. In this paper the Confucian classics are quoted in the translations of James Legge.

26. *Analects*, V:14. For further remarks on questioning in the Confucian tradition, see Wm. Theodore de Bary, "Neo-Confucian Cultivation and the Seventeenth-Century 'Enlightenment,'" in de Bary, ed., *The Unfolding of Neo-Confucianism* (New York: Columbia University Press, 1975), pp. 147, 178.

27. *Chu Tzu wen-chi*[fb] ch. 59; quoted in Bitō, *Nihon hōken shisōshi kenkyū*, p. 57.

28. For Shundai's concept of *ri*, see his *Keizai roku*[fc] in Takimoto Seiichi, ed., *Nihon keizai sōsho*[fd] (Tokyo: Nihon keizai sōsho kankōkai, 1914–17), 6:16–18.

29. "Time and Eastern Man," The Henry Myers Lecture, 1964, Royal Anthropological Institute Occasional Paper No. 21 (1965), p. 14, footnote 5. The belief that a ruler's conduct influenced the course of events was taken seriously in seventeenth-century Japan. In 1663, the Emperor Go-Sai[fe] was

deposed on the grounds that his lack of virtue was responsible for frequent fires in Kyoto and Edo, earthquakes, and the burning of the Ise [ff] Inner Shrine. *Koji ruien*, [fg] 12:564–65; cited by Herschel Webb, "The Development of an Orthodox Attitude Toward the Imperial Institution in the Nineteenth Century," in Marius B. Jansen, ed., *Changing Japanese Attitudes Toward Modernization* (Princeton: Princeton University Press, 1965), p. 173). Compare also Ikeda Mitsumasa's introspection after the Okayama flood of 1654. Diary entry for the eighth day, eighth month, 1654, quoted in J. W. Hall, "Ikeda Mitsumasa and the Bizen[fh] Flood of 1654," in Albert M. Craig and Donald H. Shively, eds., *Personality in Japanese History* (Berkeley: University of California Press, 1970), p. 70).

30. *Mean*, XXII.
31. *Mean*, XXVI:6.
32. For this interpretation of the expression *zōka*, [fi] see *Banzan zenshū* 3:17.
33. Evil last rulers of the Hsia[fj] and Shang[fk] dynasties respectively.
34. Graham, *Two Chinese Philosophers*, p. 48.
35. *Analects*, VIII:20.
36. In the continuation of this passage, Banzan suggests that Kuan Chung had "powers of learning," but the context suggests that he is referring to knowledge of "human character and historical change" rather than Neo-Confucian style self-cultivation. For the attitudes of other Tokugawa Confucian scholars toward Kuan Chung, see Maruyama Masao, *Nihon seiji shisōshi kenkyū*[fl] (Tokyo: Tokyo daigaku shuppan-kai, 1952), pp. 59–60; and Tahara Tsuguo *Tokugawa shisōshi kenkyū*[fm] (Tokyo: Mirai-sha, 1967), pp. 496–500.
37. This dating is suggested by the fact that this passage does not occur in the first edition of *Shūgi washo* (1672), but is among the additional material included in the second edition of 1676.
38. *Analects*, XIV:18.
39. Benjamin Schwartz, "Some Polarities in Confucian Thought," in David S. Nivison and Arthur F. Wright, eds., *Confucianism in Action* (Stanford: Stanford University Press, 1959), p. 52.
40. William James, *The Varieties of Religious Experience* (New York: Mentor paperback ed., 1958), p. 306.
41. Chung-ying Cheng, "Practical Learning in Yen Yüan, Chu Hsi and Wang Yang-ming." This volume, pp. 45–46.
42. Maruyama Masao, *Nihon seiji shisōshi kenkyū*, pp. 7–19.
43. Wm. Theodore de Bary, Introduction, in de Bary, *Self and Society in Ming Thought* (New York: Columbia University Press, 1970), p. 23.
44. Robert Crawford, "Chang Chü-cheng's Confucian Legalism," in de Bary, *Self and Society*, pp. 367–68.
45. Ray Huang, "Ni Yüan-lu: 'Realism' in a Neo-Confucian Scholar-Statesman," in de Bary, *Self and Society*, p. 441.
46. Robert N. Bellah, *Tokugawa Religion: The Values of Pre-Industrial Japan* (Glencoe, Ill.: Free Press, 1957), pp. 13–15.

47. Ogyū Sorai, Letter to Yabu Shin'an,[m] quoted in Imanaka Kanshi, *Soraigaku no kisoteki kenkyū*[o] (Tokyo: Yoshikawa kōbunkan, 1966), p. 102.

48. Tamamuro Taijō, *Yokoi Shōnan* (Tokyo: Yoshikawa kōbunkan, 1967), p. 102.

GLOSSARY

a	熊澤蕃山	am 時處位	by 平安
b	矢田	an 明德	bz 佐傳
c	奈良	ao 孝	ca 春秋
d	稻葉彦兵	ap 尾藤正英	cb 人情
e	だつたん	aq 王陽明	cc 詩經
f	諸葛孔明	ar 致良知	cd 問學
g	張良	as 良知に至る	ce 舜
h	關東	at 眞	cf 中庸
i	老中	au 道	cg 孔文子
j	松平信之	av 法	ch 窮理
k	喜多見若狹守重政	aw 伊藤仁齋	ci 陰
l	德川綱吉	ax 荻生徂徠	cj 陽
m	大學或問	ay 質	ck 集義外書
n	幕府	az 文	cl 太宰春臺
o	古河	ba 董仲舒	cm 貝原益軒
p	仁政	bb 邵雍	cn 神農
q	實學	bc 史記	co 道理
r	經世致用の學	bd 氣	cp 大學
s	阿部吉雄	be 道學	cq 心法圖解
t	池田光政	bf 仕置	cr 桀
u	大名	bg 禮記	cs 紂
v	岡山	bh 文公家禮	ct 秦始皇帝
w	中江藤樹	bi 朱熹	cu 才
x	德川	bj 保科政之	cv 四書集註大全
y	漢	bk 會津	cw 術
z	唐	bl 野中兼山	cx 管仲
aa	宋	bm 土佐	cy 桓公
ab	明	bn 周	cz 本才
ac	理	bo 林羅山	da 京
ad	寬文	bp 儒門思問錄	db 大原
ae	源氏物語	bq 朧月夜	dc 八瀨
af	小川	br 程明道（程顥）	dd 今出川
ag	翁問答	bs 老子	de 室町
ah	大洲	bt 莊子	df 高瀨
ai	論語鄉黨啓蒙翼傳	bu 綱政	dg 优見
aj	論語	bv 近思錄	dh 心法
ak	心	bw 三綱五常	di 愼獨
al	跡	bx 人情時變	dj 尊德性

dk 公家
dl 中英成
dm 崎門
dn 山崎闇齋
do 徂徠學
dp 國學
dq 丸山眞男
dr 元祿
ds 享保
dt 張居正
du 倪元璐
dv 王畿
dw 王世貞
dx 水戶
dy 橫井小楠
dz 三國
ea 秦
eb 前漢
ec 正宗敦夫、蕃山全集
ed 阿部吉雄、「實學の新儒學
に於ける素因（明及び江戶
時代）」
ee 谷口澄夫、池田光政
ef 紀茘公
eg 德川賴宣
eh 江戶
ei 御三家
ej 藤樹先生年譜
ek 加藤盛一、藤樹先生全集
el 尾藤正英、日本封建思想史
研究
em 淵岡山、岡山先生示教錄
en 百衲本、四部叢刊
eo 馮友蘭
ep 安藤昌益
eq 水野恭一郎、「備前藩にお
ける神職請制度について」、
岡山大學法文學部學術紀要
er 平重道、「寬文六年山鹿素
行配流事件の思想的意義」
文化

es 橫川末吉、野中兼山
et 續日本儒林叢書
eu 湛若水
ev 高瀨武次郎、王陽明詳傳
ew 杜維明
ex 陳榮捷
ey 呂祖謙
ez 永山卯三郎、池田光政公傳
fa 漢書
fb 朱子文集
fc 經濟錄
fd 瀧本誠一、日本經濟叢書
fe 後西
ff 伊勢
fg 古事類苑
fh 備前
fi 造化
fj 夏
fk 商
fl 丸山眞男，日本政治思想史
研究
fm 田原嗣郎，德川思想史研究
fn 藪震菴
fo 今中寬司、徂徠學の基礎的
研究

Minamoto Ryōen

"Jitsugaku" and Empirical Rationalism in the First Half of the Tokugawa Period

I would like to begin by broadly outlining the contours of the problem I have chosen: jitsugaku[a] and empirical rationalism. In Japan today the term jitsugaku is usually understood to refer to learning which is empirical and rational and which is an aid in our lives. When jitsugaku is used in this sense, empirical rationalism is the philosophical statement of jitsugaku.

In early Tokugawa Japan, the identity of jitsugaku and empirical rationalism was never achieved. Although empirical rationalism was firmly established, jitsugaku was still bound by intellectual tradition and adhered to old forms, thus precluding their fusion. It was Ogyū Sorai[b] (1666–1728) who first developed a concept of jitsugaku which was ultimately to make the fusion possible, and yet the issue was not fully resolved in Sorai. While the possibility was enhanced in the late eighteenth century in the work of Sugita Gempaku[c] (1733–1817), who was influenced by Sorai's writings, it did not become a philosophical reality until the latter half of the nineteenth century, when Nishi Amane[d] (1829–1897) wrote Hyakuichi shinron.[e]

THE MEANING OF EMPIRICAL RATIONALISM

Readers may be puzzled by the expression "empirical rationalism," for it seems contradictory. Empiricism, of course, is the philosophic view

375

which has knowledge originate in experience, while rationalism sees knowledge based on experience as confused and argues that reliable knowledge originates in *a priori* principles which are immanent and self-evident. Empirical rationalism does not oppose rational principle to actual substance (or, principles to things), but seeks instead to clarify the rational principles of actual substances (or, the principles of things).

When we look at empirical rationalism in the Confucian context, we find that thinkers of the Chu Hsi school[f] thought in terms of the "principle of matter," and not "principle opposed to matter." Chu Hsi at times advanced the view "principle[g] first, then material force,"[h] but he was neither consistent nor clear about what he meant. For example, in one place, he admitted that it was impossible to say which is prior and which posterior, principle or material force. But he also wrote, "Before material force has agglomerated, principle has nothing in which to inhere." From this it may be inferred that principle presupposes the existence of material force. Thus I do not feel that it can be said, as it often is, that, for Chu Hsi, principle is the origin of all things. Yet Chu did say in other passages, "Before Heaven and earth existed, there was after all only principle," and "There is principle, and it gives birth to material force." Here the relationship of priority and posteriority is not temporal but logical, not generative but ontological. In these passages, principle is clearly made the ground of existence, so that, more than material force, it is principle which is fundamental. However, for Chu Hsi there is no existence without material force. He himself said that principle is the basis of material force, that is, of all things in the world. Principle, while it presupposes the existence of material force, is also the basis for material force.

But what exactly is this principle which is the basis of material force and of all things in Heaven-and-earth? In order to understand this, we should consider Chu Hsi's statement in the *T'ai-chi-t'u shuo chieh,*[i] (Notes on the *Diagram of the Supreme Ultimate, Explained*), "The Infinite and yet the Supreme Ultimate. Outside the Supreme Ultimate there is no Infinite." Chu Hsi also viewed the Supreme Ultimate[j] as principle and saw it as the principle which encompassed all things and which formed the universe. In addition to this Supreme Ultimate, he also envisioned the supra-sensible reality that he called the Infinite[k]. It is not that the Supreme Ultimate arises from the Infinite. The Supreme Ultimate—that is, principle—is nothingness and yet being, being and yet nothingness. This is the meaning of Chu Hsi's "The Infinite and yet the Supreme Ultimate." According to Yasuda Jirō, a more precise statement might be that principle is, in respect to concrete existence, non-being and, in respect to reason or significance, being.[1] Or as Shimada Kenji elaborates this view, principle is metaphysical. "If one speaks of principle as having existence, it is existence in the sense of meaning or significance. That is, it has transcendent character, but 'transcendent' in a sense other than that conveyed by saying that it lacks extension or dimension."[2] Stated in terms of its relationship with material force, this is not the "principle of material force," but "principle as opposed to material force." If we take note of different views of the relationship between principle and material force in Neo-Confucianism, we discover that this view of principle as metaphysical and transcendent in character is the one that was advocated by the Korean Confucian Yi T'oegye[l] (1501–1570), the central figure of the school that emphasized principle. In Japan this view was emphasized by Yamazaki Ansai[m] (1618–1682), Satō Naokata[n] (1650–1719), and Miyake Shōsai[o] (1662–1741) of the Kimon school,[p] who followed the same line as T'oegye and his school.[3]

If principle were adequately described by representing it as having a metaphysical character, there would be no justification for my hypothesis that the view of principle found in the Chu Hsi school was transformed into empirical rationalism. But we also find in Chu Hsi's writings the following:

To say that the extension of knowledge lies in the investigation of things means that when we desire to extend knowledge, we do so by plumbing the principle which is in things. However, there must be knowledge which is the spirit of man's mind. And, of course, principle must also exist in all things in the world. It is with this in mind that the first teaching of the *Great Learning* has scholars steadily pursue the knowable principle found in things, seeking it to its limits. One is to use one's power and proceed to the external, the expansive and all-pervasive; that is, to a broad knowledge of the external and the internal, the delicate and the coarse. This I consider proceeding to things and to knowledge. (*Ta-hsüeh pu-ch'uan*)[q]

From the Infinite and the Supreme Ultimate above to the minuteness of a single blade of grass, a tree or a crawling creature below, each has its own principle. (*Chu Tzu yü-lei*)[r]

The relationship of principle and material force as described here is not that of "principle opposed to material force," but rather that of the "prin-

ciple of material force." And if we push this even further, we might say
that Chu Hsi's notion of principle had the potential for becoming empirical rationalism.

In Ming China, Lo Ch'in-shun[s] (1465–1547) and Wang T'ing-hsiang[t]
(1474–1544) advanced a theory which also stressed material force in
terms of the principle of material force, and a similar theory was advocated by the Korean scholar, Yi Yulgok[u] (1536–1584). In neither
China nor Korea did the group advocating an experiential principle of
material force become the mainstream of the Chu Hsi school. In Japan,
however, Lo's K'un-chih chi[v] (Notes on Knowledge Painfully Acquired)
had an influence on many of the supporters of Chu Hsi's philosophy,
including Hayashi Razan[w] (1583–1657), Andō Seian[x] (1622–1701), and
Kaibara Ekken[y] (1630–1714), and may even have touched the Ancient
Learning[z] of Itō Jinsai[aa] (1627–1705). This influence was such that we
cannot overlook the importance of Lo Ch'in-shun in the formation of
empirical rationalism.

THE NATURE OF JITSUGAKU

If we examine how the word jitsugaku has been used, we find that
most of its various meanings and connotations are logically related, and
there is a common denominator. Jitsugaku, for example, is always contrasted with empty learning[ab] or false learning,[ac] and jitsu,[ad] which
means "real" or "true," is usually opposed to kyo,[ae] which means
"empty" or "false." So "reality" or "truth" is the essential meaning of
jitsu.

Yet there are no definite criteria by which to judge what is real or
empty and what is true or false. When the advocate of jitsugaku asserts
that his is a real and true learning, he bases his judgment on more than
strictly "intellectual" grounds. He bases it partly on performance, so that
the criteria for "reality" or "emptiness" change as his behavioral ends and
values do. They may also differ from period to period. Thus, the definition of jitsugaku is highly situational. It is the standard raised by those
who, dissatisfied with certain prevalent values and trends of thought, seek
to create new varieties of learning and alternate forms of thought.
Jitsugaku, therefore, in its origins, is highly polemical.

Chu Hsi speaks of jitsugaku in the following passage from his Chung- .
yung chang-chü[af] (Commentary on the Words and Phrases of the Mean):

At the beginning of this book, it speaks of one principle, and towards the middle, it speaks of this principle dispersing and becoming the myriad things, and near the end, it speaks of their in turn reuniting to become one principle. Release it, and it expands to fill the entire universe; recall it, and it is contained within one's innermost being. Its savor is endless. It is all real learning (*jitsugaku*).

Another passage in Chu Hsi's *Ta-hsüeh chang-chü hsü*[ag] (Preface to the Commentary on the Words and Phrases of the *Great Learning*) suggests the sense in which he used the word *jitsugaku*:

[Since the death of Mencius], ordinary Confucians have devoted even greater effort to textual studies than [is required by] the *Elementary Learning,*[ah] and yet their efforts have been useless (*wu-yung*).[ai] The heterodox schools have espoused doctrines of emptiness and quietude which are loftier than those of the *Great Learning*, and yet their doctrines are impractical (*wu-shih*).[aj]

It seems that Chu Hsi, when he systematized Confucianism so that it centered on moral practice, as opposed to the exegesis and commentary favored by Han and T'ang scholars, viewed his own learning as *jitsugaku*. In the same sense, his learning valued human relations and morality in this world as against Buddhist and Taoist attempts to transcend this life. He created the ethics and metaphysics for a secular learning of human relations. As a system of learning with a firm ontological basis, Shushi-gaku pursued, both theoretically and practically, the question of how men were to act within society. It was this that led Chu Hsi to claim that his system was *jitsugaku*.

Many of Chu Hsi's contemporaries, such as Lu Hsiang-shan,[ak] and successors, such as Wang Yang-ming,[al] called their own systems of thought *jitsugaku*, which suggests that the word *jitsugaku* had established itself among Confucians. Advocates of *jitsugaku* usually agreed in their emphasis on human relations, but their views diverged on the question of what was real (*jitsu*). This became the source of bitter controversies, in which each damned the views of his enemies with the epithet "empty" (*kyo*), while confirming his own as real. More fundamentally, however, there are two types of *jitsugaku*: the "moral-practical" and the "empirical." If the former involves questions of value, the latter scrupulously avoids them. The former includes those who, speaking of a "*jitsugaku* of moral consciousness" and of "the pursuit of human truth," emphasize individual concerns as well as those who focus on political practice. There is, in addition, what might be termed a "political-economic *jitsugaku*," which is not so much a third type as another expression of the two basic types of *jitsugaku*. In its more internal expression, political economy is related to moral self-realization, while in its external expression, political economy is divorced from interior concerns and aims at ruling the country and pacifying the people. If the former tendency is represented by the political-economic thought of the Chu Hsi and Wang Yang-ming[am] schools, the latter is found in the thought of Ogyū Sorai, Kaiho Seiryō[an] (1755–1817), and Fukuzawa Yukichi.[ao]

What I am calling the "moral-practical *jitsugaku*" might also be described as a "*jitsugaku* in pursuit of human truth." This should not be taken to mean that it is concerned solely with problems of individual morality as might be suggested by phrases such as: "cultivating the self and ruling others," "illuminating virtue and renewing the people (or, loving the people)," "aiding the country," "ruling the country," "preserving the world," and "forming one body with all things through humaneness." For it is in their concern with society and the country as a whole that Confucians differ from Buddhists, and these differences originate in the weight each accords the individual as opposed to society and the state, and on the balance that is struck between the individual and the larger whole. In abstract terms, the moral-practical *jitsugaku* leads to the internally-oriented political-economic variety of *jitsugaku*, while the empirical *jitsugaku* leads, in turn, to the externally-oriented political-economic variety of *jitsugaku*. The former seeks to govern the world and aid the people through the pursuit of human truth, while the latter would govern the country and pacify the people on the basis of standards quite dissociated from interior and personal considerations. To put it another way, the former view may be considered idealistic and the latter realistic.

The problem is complicated because it is bound up with the issue of principle and material force. One might suppose that the moral-practical and the internally-oriented political-economic conceptions of *jitsugaku* would be based on the concept of principle as *opposed* to material force, i.e., on a priori metaphysical and moral principle such as existed as one strand in the Chu Hsi tradition. In this view, the externally-oriented political-economic variety of *jitsugaku* would be based on an understanding of principle as the principle *of* material force, i.e., an empirically observable principle, which was a concept associated with another strand in the Chu Hsi tradition. The reality, however, is not so simple. For example, Kaibara Ekken, whose views correspond to the internally-oriented political-economic *jitsugaku*, can also be described as being empirical in his methodology, while the Wang Yang-ming school, which regarded principle as the principle of material force, falls into the category of an idealistic doctrine of the mind.

In this essay, I shall attempt to explain the major lines of development that *jitsugaku* followed in the early Tokugawa period. I shall do this by looking closely at how the concepts of *jitsugaku*, principle, and material force changed in the course of the period. In the process, I shall be testing three hypotheses. The first is whether the history of *jitsugaku* can be described as a "dialectic of substance (*jitsu*) and emptiness (*kyo*)," that is, as a progression from *jitsugaku* to *kyogaku* to *jitsugaku*. The second is whether the fundamental trend of *jitsugaku* was from concern with problems of value to approaches that may be considered "value-free." The third centers on the relationship of the internalistic and externalistic varieties of political-economic *jitsugaku*: was the internalistic type simply a transitional stage to the other externalistic type? Or were they antithetical?

THE CONVERSION FROM BUDDHISM TO CONFUCIANISM AND THE *JITSUGAKU* OF HAYASHI RAZAN

Nearly all Confucians before Ogyū Sorai believed that concern for morality in the context of everyday life was an essential condition of *jitsugaku*. We see this in the lives of Fujiwara Seika[ap] (1561–1619) and Hayashi Razan. Both had either been Zen priests or had had extensive contact and experience with Zen before they began to question the value of an other-worldly life and returned to secular life. *Seika sensei gyōjō*[aq] describes Seika's state of mind upon his return to secular life:

Our teacher studied Buddhism for a long time yet continued to have doubts about it. He then had an opportunity to read the writings of the sages and from that time on he believed their teachings to be true and never doubted them. And believing this to be the True Way, he questioned how the Way could exist outside human relations. Buddha extinguished the seeds of humaneness, ruining the moral principles of an ethical life. This is why Buddhism is a heresy.[4]

This might equally be taken as a description of Hayashi Razan's views. When the seemingly interminable wars ended and there once again was hope of social stability and order, Seika and Razan were attracted to Confucianism with its affirmation of a secular life and its denial of the ascetic and supramundane life of the Buddhists.

However, Razan and Seika rejected not only the traditional authority of Buddhism but also that of established Japanese Confucianism. At that time in Japan, a small circle of privileged families, such as the Kiyoharas,[ar] from whose ranks instructors at the government college had been selected in the Heian[as] period (794–1185), were officially recognized as "families of erudites." They and they alone were permitted to publish Confucian texts. These texts, which had been rendered into Japanese by means of conventionalized marks which allowed Chinese to be punctuated in a Japanese word order, were based on Han[at] and T'ang[au] annotations and commentaries. Anyone wishing to give a public lecture on Confucianism had first to receive permission from these families. In defiance of this rule, Seika published editions of the Four Books[av] and Five Classics[aw] using the annotations and commentaries of the Sung Confucians, and Razan delivered a public lecture on Chu Hsi's commentaries without the permission of the guardian families. Since this opposition to tradition directly affected their approach to *jitsugaku*, I would like to look more closely at Razan's view of it. In the following passage he addresses the issues of reality and emptiness:

Confucianism is real, and Buddhism is empty. Indeed there is great confusion now as to what is real and what is empty. If one were asked which he preferred, the real or the empty, who would choose the empty and discard the real? And so when people favor Buddhism, which is not the real, over Confucianism, this is only because they have not heard of the Way and cannot discriminate between the real and the empty. Ch'eng I says that Buddhist books are as beautiful as a seductive voice or a beautiful face which cause people to be easily deluded. Chu Hsi says that the teachings of stillness and annihilation are sublime but lack reality . . . Ah! what they call the Way is not a true way. What we call the Way is the true way. What determines whether it is the Way or not is whether it is real or empty, public or private.[5]

In Razan's eyes, Confucianism is real while Buddhism is empty. Though both speak of the Way, only the teachings of Confucianism, which offer a social and public morality, are real. Buddhism, which talks only of the salvation or enlightenment of the individual, is empty, though it seems lofty.

Yet Razan's conception of Confucianism was far from being as comprehensive as that of his teacher Seika. Though he recognized Shushigaku, for example, he refused to accept the ideas of Lu Hsiang-shan and

Wang Yang-ming. He criticized their ideas as "subitaneous" and charged that "they try to rise to the heights without climbing the ladder" and "try to go straight to the top without having learned the basics." From these criticisms we surmise that he rejected them because they were religious. They did not first proceed through Chu Hsi's "investigation of things and plumbing of principle," but instead sought to perceive reality directly and intuitively in their own minds. Razan apparently felt that to "honor the virtuous nature" without first exhaustively studying principle was to risk estrangement from society. In this respect, he was more deeply concerned with human relations than his teacher Seika had been. Though he believed that after exhaustively studying the principle in things one could experience a sudden realization of the oneness of all things, we may wonder whether he himself ever experienced this or simply took it on faith that it was possible.

That there were both subjective and objective dimensions in Chu Hsi's school is evident in phrases such as "preserving the mind and abiding in reverence" and "investigating things, extending knowledge and plumbing principle." Yet to do as Chu did and establish both dimensions within oneself required both breadth and depth. Razan, though he possessed considerable breadth in his knowledge of external things, was wanting in internal depth. Thus he lacked the ability to integrate these mutually opposed tendencies. Contrary to his own expectations, his fondness for investigating things and plumbing principle did not in the end deepen the tie between the internal dimension and his concern for human relations. This may have been because his concern for human relations was not the product of interior needs. Absent from the writings of the otherwise talented Razan is the element of human agony.

The focus of Razan's internal proclivities, such as they were, was on the concept of reverence. Unlike Chu Hsi, however, Razan does not seem to have attached much importance to quiet-sitting as a practical method of preserving one's mind and abiding in reverence. His pronouncements on reverence are little more than restatements of Chu Hsi's ideas. As his concern with social relations was not based on interior demands, it was easy for him to define reverence as an interior problem, on the level of ordinary self-discipline, just as it was easy for him to define it as an exterior problem as subordination to the actual social order and to the preservation of social standards. He wrote, for example:

Just as one washes off dirt and cleanses one's self, so too do we bathe today and tomorrow. And just as we wash our faces and use water to wash our hands, so too do we cleanse our minds.[6]

We glimpse in these words, which occur in his *Santokushō*,[ax] the development of the doctrine of cultivation within his definition of reverence. In spite of his rejection of Buddhism and his refusal to receive the tonsure as a youth, he later did accept the tonsure on order of the first shogun, Tokugawa Ieyasu[ay] (1542–1616), and was invested with the priestly rank of *minbukyō hōin*.[az] As Professor Sagara Tōru notes, Razan defended this act by invoking the example of Confucius, who, in his view, had effectuated the Way through following the existing order.[7] His submission to the existing order is also exemplified by his criticism of the school of Wang Yang-ming, which centered around Kumazawa Banzan[ba] (1619–1691) in Okayama. He saw the ideas of the Wang school as a variant of Christianity and plotted Banzan's downfall. All of this suggests that Razan not only submitted to the *Bakuhan* feudal system,[bb] but worked assiduously to strengthen it.

If there is any one idea which might be seen as the basis for Razan's scholarly pursuits, it is Chu Hsi's notion of investigating things and plumbing principle. Razan's ideas on principle fluctuated, however, and he appears never to have had a fixed conception of what it was. For instance, in a letter he wrote to a certain Yoshida Genshi[bc] when he was twenty, we find the following:

As regards the doctrine of the divisibility of principle and material force, though it goes against Chu Hsi's ideas, I have no choice but to discuss it.[8]

According to Professor Abe Yoshio, this doctrine of the indivisibility of principle and material force reflects the influence of Lo Ch'in-shun's *Kun-chih chi*.[9] If this is so, the view of principle and material force that Razan held at that time should be described as having involved a conception of an empirically observable principle which was the principle *of* material force. Later, however, he had a change of heart, as is evident in his *Myōtei mondō*,[bd] the record of his debate with the Jesuit Fabian, in which he argued that "principle is prior and material force posterior."[10] Thereafter Razan seems to have been perplexed over the relationship between principle and material force, and a number of exploratory essays which he attempted on the subject reveal the conceptual difficulties he experienced. In one place, for example, he referred to the conflicting views of Wang Yang-ming and Chu Hsi on the question of how principle and material force were related:

Principle and material force. Which is prior and which is posterior? Wang Shou-jen says that principle is the regularity in material force and that material force is the operation of principle.[11]

In another place:

Principle and material force are one and yet two, two and yet one. This is the view of the Sung Confucians. However, Wang Yang-ming claims that principle is the regularity of material force and that material force is the operation of principle. If we follow the latter view, then there is the danger that everything will be chaotic.[12]

The issue, however, is not simply the relationship of principle and material force, but also the relationship of principle, the emotions, mind, and material force, as we see in the following:

A youth of Ch'üeh who did not sit in a corner addressed an elderly Confucian, saying, "Though I know nothing at all, I would beg permission to talk with you. Some say, 'Human nature is principle.' Others say, 'Mind is principle.' And still others say, 'Principle runs through all things and is complete within the mind.' When [Confucius] spoke of 'following what his heart desired without transgressing the bounds of propriety,' he identified 'not transgressing the bounds of propriety' with human nature, which is principle. When he said of Yen Hui that '[for three months] his mind would never depart from humanity,' 'not departing from humanity' was identified as the nature, which is principle. Since the Sage spoke about the mind and yet also spoke in this way [about the nature and its relation to the mind], how can the mind and principle not be distinct? Originally the decree (ming),[be] the nature (hsing),[bf] the Way (tao)[bg] and instruction (chiao)[bh] were one. Therefore the Mean says, 'What Heaven has decreed is called the nature; what accords with this nature is called the Way; the regulation of this Way is called instruction. Where it speaks of 'the state before the emotions of pleasure, anger, sorrow and joy have been aroused,' it pertains entirely to the mind. Here the mind is identified with principle. If one speaks of principle as 'running through all things and also being complete within the mind,' this seems to divide the mind and principle into two. The mind and principle cannot have changed between ancient times and the present, and so I would like to know whether the mind and principle are the same or different?"[13]

A youth from Hu-hsiang made the following inquiry: "It is said that the 'four beginnings'[bi] emanate from principle and the seven emotions[bj] emanate from material force. But, once joy and anger have been aroused, they may then be properly regulated, and surely this regulation derives from principle? Is it not the case that 'propriety that is not proper and acts of righteousness that are not righteous' derive from material force? Is it then the case that principle is essentially good, while material force is essentially either clear or turbid? A Confucian of former times said, 'There is nothing in the world that lies beyond the realm of principle.' Do clarity and turbidity come within the sphere of principle or without? He also said, 'The mind that controls the nature and feelings is fundamentally one mind.' But if the 'four beginnings' emanate from principle and the 'seven emotions' emanate from material force, does this mean that there are actually two minds? A Confucian of more recent times said, 'Principle is the order according to which material force operates, whereas material force is the functioning of principle.' Was he right or not?"[14]

From these and other statements by Razan on the problem of principle and material force, we may draw the following conclusions. First, Razan vacillated in his ideas and never resolved this problem. Second, he came to entertain doubts about Chu Hsi's view of principle as prior and material force as posterior—a view which he himself had held earlier in his career—and also rejected the views of Yi T'oegye that the "four beginnings" were principle and the "seven emotions" were material force. Third, he was attracted by Wang Yang-ming's notion of principle as the "regularity of material force." Fourth, although he was not drawn to the idea of a "principle opposed to material force," but to the idea of the "principle of material force," we should not immediately infer that his position was an empiricism involving materialist assumptions, for he recognized this as Kao Tzu's view of "righteousness as external." Fifth, Razan avoided a decisive commitment to either an a priori or an empirical interpretation of the relation between principle and material force, and, unlike Kaibara Ekken, he did not ultimately arrive at a formulation in which the two were fused. Razan took great pains over the solution of the issue of the philosophical bases of the relationship of principle and material force. Given his preference for the idea that mind is principle, one might think that he was following Wang Yang-ming; but in the total context of his thought and scholarship, his view of principle and material force inclines more toward the empirical.

As Sagara Tōru has pointed out, Razan recognized that all objective things have within them their own principles. He also recognized the objective and external order as manifestations of principle.[15] Yet when he spoke of an objective and external order, he was thinking of culture and literature, though this was a culture and literature which did not exclude such objects of the natural world as a single blade of grass or a single tree.

Culture was the externalization of morality and it was through culture that the Way could be known:

Culture always expands the Way. The Way does not expand culture. The Way does not exist outside culture, and culture does not exist outside the Way. Thus it is said that culture is the vehicle of the Way.[16]

Culture is the vehicle which bears the Way. When we study culture, poetry and ritual, we are studying the Way, for it exists amidst all these things.[17]

Razan energetically pursued a practice of investigating things and plumbing principle which involved studying literature and the systems of ritual and music in literature.[18] When pursued, this view leads to that of Chu Hsi's most fervent Japanese critic, Ogyū Sorai. Sorai's study of literature began in the Neo-Confucianism of the Hayashi school, and on occasion he even praised its academic style, as, for example, in *Gakuryō ryōken sho*.[bk 19]

As Razan lived at a time when Sung Confucianism was just taking root in Japan, it would be unfair to expect his thought to be systematic and deep. Yet we find in his definition of the investigation of things and the plumbing of principle, hints of what was to come. First, there was the tendency, encouraged by the influence of Wang Yang-ming school, to internalize the pursuit of the investigation of things and the plumbing of principle and to deepen it as a "learning of the mind." Second, there was a deepening of the ethical and metaphysical aspects of the investigation of things and the plumbing of principle in one wing of the Chu Hsi school, a process in which the empirical tendency in Shushigaku was curtailed and the teaching crystallized around a devotion to moral practicality. Here the idea of reverence or seriousness became a central problem. Third, there was a movement toward precisely the kind of objectivity which Razan himself had been unable to achieve. This took the form of an empirical rationalism in that wing of Shushigaku which regarded the investigation of things and the plumbing (or exploring) of principle to be exploring the principles of things in the objective world. Finally, there was a tendency to view poetry, prose, ritual, and music as embodiments of the Way and to undertake the thorough study of them in a conceptual context quite different from that of Razan. The first of these tendencies was exemplified by Nakae Tōju[bl] (1608–1648) and Kumazawa Banzan, the second by Yamazaki Ansai and the Kimon school, especially Satō Naokata, the third by Kaibara Ekken, and the fourth by scholars of the

Ancient Learning school, especially Ogyū Sorai. In the remainder of this essay, I shall discuss each of these in turn.

THE *JITSUGAKU* OF NAKAE TŌJU

Hayashi Razan claimed that his learning was *jitsugaku*, but to young Nakae Tōju it was far from being that. When in 1629 Razan was given a priestly rank, in spite of his being a Confucian, Tōju wrote an essay entitled, "On Master Hayashi's Taking the Tonsure and Being Accorded the Highest Priestly Rank,"[bm] in which he criticized Razan:

Hayashi Dōshun (Razan) has a very good memory and is a man of erudition. Yet in preaching the Way of Confucius, he vainly embellishes his words. Also in imitation of the way of the Buddhists, he has had his head shaved and has abandoned his family duties. He has left the right way and does not follow it. He is what Chu Hsi called a parrot that speaks well.[20]

Tōju saw no value in Razan's moralistic side. In his eyes, Razan was merely erudite and endowed with a good memory, a clever parrot. His learning, moreover, was the "learning of mouth and ear,"[bn] merely seeking erudition and not a *jitsugaku* through which one illumines bright virtue and is close to the people. Apparent in such a criticism is Tōju's life-long belief in the truth of Confucianism, a Confucianism which for him was not objective learning but subjective truth.

It is said that when Tōju was eleven, he read the *Great Learning*, and after reading that a man can become a sage through learning, he set his heart on this goal. But, unlike other Japanese Confucians, Tōju sought neither to Japanize Confucianism nor to fuse it with Shinto. Not that he rejected Shinto, but in his mind it accorded with the Confucianism which he believed to be universal truth. In *Okina mondō*[bo] (Dialogues with an Old Man) we see manifestations of this belief in the universality of Confucianism:

The Confucian Way is the Shinto of the Supreme Vacuity [Receptivity]. Thus the vessels of the land and the sea run to it, all human commerce passes through it, Heaven and earth rest upon it, the sun and moon illumine it, and frost and dew settle on it. It is the habitat of all creatures endowed with blood and the vital spirit. There is nothing to which Confucianism is not applicable.[21]

Although as a youth Tōju believed in Confucianism as a universal truth, his understanding of Confucianism at that time was rather superficial and formalistic. According to his chronological biography, a certain Araki mocked the appearance of Tōju at the age of twenty-two, saying, "Here comes Confucius!"[22] Though obviously a caricature, the incident suggests that Tōju was so formalistic in his devotion to Confucianism that he had relinquished something of his spiritual freedom. How to escape from formalism without abandoning his faith in the essential truth of Confucianism was the problem that he faced.

A warrior in a small fief in Shikoku, Tōju was disgruntled over the situation prevailing in the warrior class at that time. Virtuous men were not always given high rank. Naive but sincere warriors, reminiscent of warriors in the Warring States Period, were passed over, with the clever and more calculating types getting the jobs.[23] In time, Tōju broke with his fief. Recent studies have shown that Tōju was actually involved in fief politics,[24] and suggest that the prevailing view—that his break with his fief can be explained in terms of his filiality to his mother—is probably erroneous. At any rate, his estrangement from fief politics profoundly influenced his thought. Whereas most Japanese Confucians placed great emphasis on loyalty to one's lord, Tōju tried in *Okina mondō* to build an alternate system of ethics around "filiality." This should not be construed as opposition to feudal society. Tōju envisioned a feudal society based on virtuous Confucian rule in which the ruling warrior class was responsible for nourishing the people and exemplifying Confucian ideals. This society stood in marked contrast to the feudal society taking shape in his time. Indeed, this is why Tōju devoted large sections of *Okina mondō* to a description of the Confucian Way of the Warrior, his ideal.

An understanding of Tōju's idea of *jitsugaku* as it appears in *Okina mondō* requires at least a brief description of the process by which he came to reject Shushigaku formalism. If any one idea stands at the center of Tōju's thought, it is that of "illumining virtue," a concept found in the *Great Learning* and common to both the Chu Hsi and Wang Yang-ming schools. A number of reasons may be adduced to explain the fact that, although he consistently stressed this idea, Tōju was not satisfied with his own Shushigaku affiliation and subsequently broke with Shushigaku. First, there is Tōju's own religiosity. Second, there is his affinity for the warrior and his admiration for the Warring States period, for an active mind and a dynamic life. Third, there is his preference for concrete and practical modes rather than general rules of an abstract or objective character.

Several works contributed to opening Tōju's eyes to his own interior being, among them, the *Analects*, especially the *Hsiang-tang*[bp] chapter, and the *Book of Changes*, especially the idea of "stilling in the back" and "responding to contraries"[bq] (in hexagram 52). Here we see a broadening of intellectual concern from the Four Books to the Five Classics. Another important work was the *Classic of Filial Piety*.[br] Finally, there was late Ming thought, received through the medium of the *Hsing-li hui-t'ung*[bs] (Comprehensive Anthology of Commentaries on the Nature and Principle). Tōju was most influenced by the thought of Wang Yang-ming and the left wing of the Wang Yang-ming school, including especially Wang Chi[bt] (Wang Lung-hsi,[bu] 1498–1583). We are told that in the winter of 1641, shortly after he had written *Okina mondō*, Tōju procured a copy of the *Wang Lung-hsi yü-lu*[bv] (Recorded Conversations of Wang Chi), and that four years later he made efforts to get a copy of the *Yang-ming ch'üan-chi*[bw] (Complete Works of Wang Yang-ming).[25] When considering Tōju's personal experiences, it is difficult to overlook his agonies over Chu Hsi's commentaries on the classics and the pedagogical methods of the *Hsiao-hsüeh* (*Elementary Learning*), methods which he saw as robbing their users of their "inborn nature and vigor."

Tōju's basic ideas in the period before he wrote *Okina mondō* included a religious conception of a higher power, *huang shang-ti*,[bx] an idea which first appeared in his *Genjin*[by] (Inquiry into Man) and *Jikei zusetsu*[bz] (The Diagram of Holding Fast to Reverence Explained) He also believed in *t'ai-i shen*,[ca] and Tōju's biography indicates that, under the influence of the *Hsing-li hui-t'ung*, which he read when he was thirty-three, he performed ritual observances on the first day of every month in homage to *T'ai-i shen*. His metaphysical perspective was expressed in terms of the "Supreme Vacuity" (*t'ai-hsü*),[cb] a concept which he apparently got from Chang Tsai's[cc] *Hsi-ming*[cd] (Western Inscription) and from the Wang Yang-ming school. It is of interest that Tōju did not use Chu Hsi's term "principle" in this connection. He also redefined the concept of seriousness or reverence. For Ch'eng I and Chu Hsi, reverence implied "concentrating on one thing without getting away from it"[ce] and "composing the mind so that it is undisturbed by anything external";[cf] for Tōju it meant "fearing the mandate of Heaven and honoring the virtuous nature."[cg] Tōju interpreted "fearing the mandate of Heaven" as fearing the mandate of *shang-ti*, which is an important example of how the rationalistic ethics of Shushigaku could be interpreted religiously.

Tōju also attached considerable importance to the active working of the mind and to actions appropriate to actual conditions. What links Tōju's religious and metaphysical thought is the idea of "stilling in the back" and "responding to contraries" from the *Book of Changes*. Tōju's special concern with this problem is indicated by the fact that the first volume of his complete works contains four essays on this issue. He interpreted "stilling in the back" in a number of ways. At one point, he described it as "preserving the spirituality and intelligence of the Heaven-endowed nature so it is never changed by environment or circumstances, never sullied by the feelings and desires, never confused by talent and knowledge." On "responding to contraries," he wrote, "Responding to yang on the basis of yang and to yin on the basis of yin is called 'responding to contraries.' In responding to events and encountering things, one must be without egotism and must respond to particular things as they are, acting appropriately without obtruding oneself." He then linked these two ideas to the idea of equilibrium[ch] and harmony[ci] from the *Mean*.[cj26] For Tōju there was nothing pragmatic about this way of responding to dynamic and changing conditions. Rather, through the "spirituality and intelligence of the Heaven-endowed nature" as manifested in "original unselfishness," or "the original mind in which all things form one body"—in other words, through the mental effort by which the "unaroused mind" is kept from being besmirched by material desires—it becomes possible to be natural and thus to act appropriately. This aspect of Tōju's thought also had a bearing on the formation of his views on "timeliness"[ck] and "time, place and rank"[cl] in *Rongo kyōtō keimō yokuden*,[cm] which he wrote when he was thirty-two.

Having done all this, Tōju wrote *Okina mondō*. He was never satisfied with it and kept revising it until the time of his death, but he never felt he had finished it. In spite of this, or perhaps because of it, *Okina mondō* is the most coherent of all of his writings.

In this work, Tōju set down ideas which had been brewing in his mind for a long time, ideas which coalesced around filiality, the central idea of the *Classic of Filial Piety*, a work he had studied assiduously. Though written in Japanese, *Okina mondō* advanced, not popular notions of filiality but rather a new conception of filiality as veneration for *huang shang-ti*, understood in the manner of an anthropomorphized Heaven. While not, in *Okina mondō*, opposing the existence of feudal institutions, he did introduce the ontological doctrine that Heaven and man are linked and that all men are brothers. He also developed the doctrine of

Heavenly-appointed offices as a means of filial action: everyone, from the emperor down to the common people, was to perform their appointed tasks. For him, learning was based on the illumining of virtue, and he suggested here that if this foundation could be established, actions appropriate to time, place, and rank would naturally become possible. In *Okina mondō*, Tōju was building his own system of ethics around Confucianism. He produced not an abstract ethical theory but an extremely compelling expression of the ideals and hardships of one man—a masterless samurai and warrior of good conscience who lived in the founding age of the *Bakuhan* system.

What kind of *jitsugaku* did Tōju describe in *Okina mondō?* The truth of the matter is that he did not use the word *jitsugaku* in this work. He did, however, make a distinction between "true learning"[cn] and "counterfeit learning,"[co] which corresponds to the distinction made by himself and other scholars between *jitsugaku* and *kyogaku*. The following is Tōju's description of "true learning":

> Both teaching and learning take the Way of Heaven as their primary goal. Anywhere in the world where it goes on, whether in China or in a barbarian land, the true teaching and the true learning which conform to the divine principle of the Way of Heaven are called Confucianism.[27]

"False learning" he defined as those teachings "which ignore the divine principles of the Way of Heaven," and among the practitioners of a false learning which resembles true learning he includes vulgar Confucians,[cp] the Mohists,[cq] Yang Chu,[cr] Lao Tzu, and the Buddhists. The vulgar Confucians "merely read Confucian works, master textual exegeses, focus on memorization and literary compositions and repeat whatever they hear. They neither know virtue nor execute the Way." The Mohists err in substituting universal love for Confucian public-mindedness and in reversing the order of root and branch, prior and posterior. Yang Chu and his followers misunderstand "studying for one's own improvement" (*Analects*, XIV: 25) and "watching over oneself while alone" (*Mean*, I) as an esoteric truth and miss out on the truth which is common to all." The Buddhists and Taoists "see only the external manifestations of the unfathomable change which is indeterminate and insubstantial and miss the underlying truth of equilibrium and harmony."[28]

Other categories of true and false learning applied strictly to Confucianism:

True learning requires that one abandon his ego and concentrate on righteousness. One is to make the absence of pride the focus of moral practice. One is to be filial to one's parents, loyal to one's lord, fraternal to one's siblings, and sincere and trustworthy with one's friends. One is to make study of the Five Classics one's first task.

False learning values only erudition. Its advocates are envious of those of high ability and obsessed with fame. They are given over to arrogance and self-conceit. Neither filiality nor loyalty is a central concern and they labor solely at the arts of memorization and literary style.[29]

When Tōju distinguished truth and falsity, he did so from a purely ethical point of view. Having examined his distinction between true and false learning, let us turn to his views on the content of true learning:

In the first place, the illumining of virtue should be one's goal. The Four Books and Five Classics should be one's teacher. By using the task of "responding to events and encountering things" as a grindstone, one should polish the gem of "illumining virtue." One should practice the perfect goodness of the Way of the Five Relationships and the five classes of filial deeds. If the Great Harmony is achieved, then everything profits and all in the four seas is rectified and the world is pacified and the work of Yi Yin and T'ai-kung is carried on. When the times are not propitious, one should see to one's self, exhaust one's nature and proceed to the mandate, spreading the teachings of Confucius and Mencius.[30]

At the outset Tōju explained that true Confucians and vulgar Confucians differ according to their manner of studying the Four Books and Five Classics. He then distinguished "mind," "traces," and "exegesis." He explained "traces" as the words and deeds of the sages and worthies, "mind" as the perfect goodness intended by the sages in what they said and did, and "exegesis" as the traces of the sages' words and deeds as recorded in the Four Books and Five Classics.

If one studies the exegesis of the classics, carefully learns the traces, applies it to one's own mind and models one's mind on it, and if one makes one's will sincere and one's mind correct, the mind of the sages will be one's own, and there will be nothing separating them. If this is done, then one's deeds and words will not violate the timeliness of the sages. Learning of this kind is true learning.[31]

In true learning, he tells us, one uses the mind of the sages and worthies and of the Four Books and Five Classics as a mirror to correct one's own mind. This is why he called it the learning of the mind. By diligently studying the learning of the mind, one could "rise from the common ranks to that of sage." Hence it was called "the learning of sagehood."[cs]

There is, however, another problem which is related to the essential practicality of his teaching. This concerns his views on "timeliness" and "time, place and rank" as they are found in works written prior to *Okina mondō*. The idea of time, place, and rank is introduced in his *Rongo kyōtō keimō yokuden*:

The appropriateness of the polity and economy is timeliness. In timeliness there are the three spheres of Heaven, earth and man. These are called time, place and rank. [32]

Shimada Kenji has argued that Tōju's idea of time, place, and rank is probably original and typical of Japanese Yōmeigaku as represented by Tōju and Banzan. [33] My feeling is that it may have been inspired by the *Book of Changes* where there is a similar tripartite division of Heaven, earth, and man. Timeliness means responding to the circumstances determined by time, place, and rank and conforming to the normative (or natural) laws dictated by various situations. Since this is beyond the average man, Tōju called it "the timeliness of the sage."[ct] To him, all learning aimed at achieving this timeliness of the sage. By closely examining the tenth chapter of the *Analects*, he hoped to show how Confucius demonstrated the "mystery of timeliness."[34] He probably understood from the descriptions of Confucius' personal behavior found in this chapter that true moral principles involved not fixed concepts but rather the most appropriate response to each situation.

In *Okina mondō*, Tōju offered two theories to explain the relationship between absolute principles and what might be called "situational ethics." In one place, for example, he wrote:

Even if one acts in such a way that his conduct accords in every detail with the ritual prescribed in Confucian works, if one lacks principles which are appropriate to the time, place and rank, one will not be practicing the Confucian Way but that of heterodoxy. [35]

In this case, absolute principles and situational ethics are two different things which must be united. Elsewhere he noted:

If bright virtue is illumined, the discriminations of time, place and rank, the duties of human affairs, and the degrees of fate—all will be as clear as reflections in a mirror. [36]

Here, once one is able to concentrate on the "illumination of virtue," one is naturally able to act in accordance with time, place, and rank. If the former theory is a dualistic one for the sake of those who have yet to illumine virtue, the latter is a monistic one which applies once virtue has been illumined. Describing the condition in which the two were integrated, he wrote: "When moral principles correspond to time, place and rank, this is known as the Mean."[37]

Tōju employed another concept, the "Way of adaptation"[cu] to unify the other two. Apparently he saw in the Way of adaptation a means of achieving a kind of theoretical integration analogous to that achieved by Wang Yang-ming through his doctrine of the "unity of knowledge and action."[cv] However, Tōju's interpretation differed from the conventional one based on Chao Ch'i's[cw] (A.D. 108–201) commentary on *Mencius* IVA:17, which explained that when Mencius used the term "adaptation" to characterize the act of saving a drowning sister-in-law, he meant goodness as opposed to conventional morality.[38] Tōju criticized this view, saying that, "to speak of 'adaptation' as conforming to the Way as opposed to conventional morality is a grievous error." His own definition was as follows:

"Adaptation" is the mysterious functioning of the sages and a general name for the divine Way.

To use the term "adaptation" for the divine way conveys the sense that the sage is of the same substance as Heaven; his utter sincerity is unceasing, he is unimpeded by things, unlimited by external traces, solitary in his coming and going, vigorous in his actions. His conduct is always in perfect conformity with the divine principle of the Way of Heaven. It has none of the rigid fixity of the steelyard. Through flexibility, it attains perfect accuracy in the weighing and measuring of all things.[39]

Tōju aims here at creative and timely deeds which are appropriate to each situation and which can be carried out freely and naturally in concert with Heaven. It is Tōju's understanding that sages are those who are consistently capable of performing such deeds. As he explains their spiritual significance:

Apart from adaptation there is no Way, and outside the Way there is no adaptation. Apart from adaptation, there is no learning, and apart from learning, there is no adaptation.[40]

We might characterize the idea of adaptation as the ultimate goal of the practical aspect of Tōju's *jitsugaku*. One senses that it is here that the religious and the practical elements in Tōju's *jitsugaku* are fused. But

while at the conceptual level the religious and the practical aspects of his
jitsugaku converged in the idea of "adaptation," he was unable to attain a
corresponding resolution in the sphere of practical life. As a masterless
samurai, Tōju, who had resigned the offices he once held, was not in a
position to carry out his ideas or execute his social goals. There is no
question that this dissociation between the idea and its realization was difficult for the conscientious Tōju to bear.

Tōju had his own version of Wang Yang-ming's idea of the unity of
knowledge and action, though it lacked the progressive aspect and the
conative emphasis associated with Wang's doctrine of "extending innate
knowledge." Whereas Wang's thought had both ethical and religious
dimensions, Tōju's concept of adaptation—especially his focus on free
and creative acts to be carried out in concert with Heaven—indicates that
he leaned more decidedly to the religious. In addition to social reasons,
there are also interior reasons which may explain why he modified Wang
Yang-ming's ideas and why he was so profoundly influenced by Wang
Chi. Contrary to what might have been expected, Tōju's thought in the
period after the age of thirty-seven, when he procured the *Complete
Works of Wang Yang-ming*, became less social and practical in character
and more religious. Why this occurred is not altogether clear. Wang
Yang-ming's thought cannot have prompted the change; the reason may
lie in Tōju's own introspectiveness or in the fact that he became acquainted with the thought of Wang Yang-ming through the interpretations of Wang Chi, which he had encountered previously, or perhaps in
still other factors. Since Bitō Masahide has already provided a detailed exposition of the characteristics of Tōju's later thought, I will not go into
detail here.[41] Suffice it to say that Tōju's thought developed around the
concept of innate knowledge.[cx] As indicated by his use of the term "mirror of innate knowledge" and his misreading of the phrase "extending innate knowledge" as "arriving at innate knowledge," Tōju understood innate knowledge to be passive and introspective in character. The conative
and activist emphasis involved in Wang Yang-ming's view of innate
knowledge receded. Tōju equated the idea of will in the phrase "making
the will sincere" with will as it appears in the phrase "the will necessarily
involves the sense of ego" and rejected the working of the will understood
as the "origin of the hundred desires and aversions."[42] It is significant
that the phrase "the unity of knowledge and action," which is so basic to
Wang Yang-ming's thought, rarely occurs in Tōju's writings.

Tōju established his own free spirit by severing his contacts with external society. The thought of his later years is characterized by the continued influence of Wang Yang-ming along with a rejection of Wang's activism. His concerns were directed almost entirely within. In his commentary on the Great Learning, Tōju noted in connection with the phrase "loving the people," that one should "practice in terms of the mind, for there is nothing to be seen in the traces of things."[43] Tōju's thinking in Okina mondō focuses on refining the mind through experience and action. In his last years, the religious nature of his thought deepened, and its universality grew. Such was his religiosity, that Tōju seems even to have transcended the Confucian framework itself.

THE JITSUGAKU OF KUMAZAWA BANZAN

After Tōju's death, his school broke up into two groups. The one centering around Kumazawa Banzan came to be known as the utilitarian group and the other, which was built around Fuchi Kōzan[cy] (1617–1686), was the eremitic group. While this division is historically correct, the appellation "utilitarian" for Banzan is inappropriate. True, Banzan is highly realistic, especially when he is compared with the eremitic and religious Kōzan, who became Tōju's disciple after the latter, at thirty-seven, had turned his attention inward. Yet to call Banzan "utilitarian" is to misread his real intent, for he scrupulously avoided the utilitarian. Some scholars feel that Banzan's weak point is that as a thinker he is rather unappealing and on this account, the vast majority of studies on Banzan have focused on his views of practical realities rather than on his philosophic ideas.[44] This is not altogether fair to Banzan, for he was, after all, Tōju's disciple. We should recall that with Tōju religious and metaphysical concerns coexisted with a concern for actual social problems, the latter having been expressed through his doctrine of time, place, and rank. It was in the difficult period when Tōju was struggling so intensely to integrate both elements, as he did in Okina mondō, that Banzan was his disciple, and Tōju's current intellectual concerns became the framework for Banzan's thought.

Although Tōju's religious and spiritual proclivities were considerably weakened in Banzan's thought, both men shared a philosophical concern for the ultimate, and were fundamentally devoted to the kind of effort of mind through which this concern could be furthered. Though Banzan's thought lacks the order and clarity of Tōju's, there is no denying that it has its own appeal based on the depth of his personal experiences. In *Shūgi washo*,^{cz} Banzan did two things: first, he developed and extended in the context of political economy the idea of time, place, and rank, an idea which had been central to Tōju's *Okina mondō* but which had vanished from Tōju's later work. Second, he discarded the metaphysics of filiality which appeared in *Okina mondō*, deepening instead the "method of the mind centering on equilibrium and harmony,"^{da} an idea which derived from the *Mean* and which was important in Tōju's later thought.[45] All this resulted from Banzan's attempt to recreate the kind of intellectual orientation found in *Okina mondō* in a context quite different from that of *Okina mondō*. Perhaps we should say that Banzan, rather than simply pursuing "traces," inherited the true spirit of Tōju's work, which is, of course, "true spirit." He described this true spirit thus:

What I have inherited unaltered from my teacher is [my regard for] true spirit (*jitsugi*^{db}). If one's learning, words and deeds are immature, when responding to time, place and rank, one should be patient and mature and adapt to the time. My successors should remedy the deficiencies of my learning, just as they should modify my words and deeds where they are inappropriate to later ages. As for the true spirit of the great Way, there is not even a hairsbreadth of difference between my teacher and me. . . .

[What is the true spirit of the great Way?] . . . True spirit is not gaining an empire by committing unrighteous acts and killing innocent people. It is holding fast to the bright virtue which abhors unrighteousness and is ashamed of inborn evil. It is the method of the mind by which one nourishes this virtue and illumines it day by day so it is not besmirched by human desires. This is the true spirit of the method of the mind.[46]

If we assume that Banzan worked to preserve the true spirit of his teacher's method of the mind and to carry out great works of political economy, and if we assume too that he pursued his scholarly activities with this intent, then our consideration of his *jitsugaku* should include his philosophical thought as well as the moral practice of the "method of the mind"^{dc} which rested upon it.

What then was Banzan's concept of *jitsugaku*? That it was essentially moral we see in the following:

It is difficult to call *jitsugaku* what does not exemplify a fondness for virtue.[47]

Jitsugaku consists in honoring the virtuous nature.[48]

In studying ancient literature, one starts with poetry, which expresses the will. Good and evil, the crooked and the straight are all the actual stuff of the human emotions. And the study of this is *jitsugaku*.[49]

The last passage, though obscure, probably refers to what Banzan spoke of as the "practical learning of the human quest for truth."[dd] Elsewhere he wrote:

Establishing the ritual of the sages begins with food and drink, male and female. It is with this that the actual practice of the art of the mind[de] should begin. Those who dismiss this as shallow and common and who adhere instead to high-sounding principles are chasing after miracles and forgetting *jitsugaku*.[50]

Here Banzan seems to be speaking of a *jitsugaku* of moral practice, one devoted to moral practice in the context of one's daily existence.

To speak and not act is emptiness. This is what brings shame to the *chün-tzu*. Humanity is real principle. The humane man reflects on the correspondence between word and deeds, so that there is no emptiness.[51]

Although the word *jitsugaku* does not actually occur here, Banzan often referred to the correspondence of words and deeds as a measure of what is real.

Banzan intended his *jitsugaku* of moral practice to perform the social function of ordering households and ruling the country:

Scholars have lost the moral principles transmitted by the sages and worthies, those which were commentaries on one's own mind. When they view the classics and commentaries as something apart from the mind, the classics become primary and one's mind becomes secondary. When they make sport of assaying the loftiness and the depth of the classics and commentaries, they are merely mouthing their principles and the mind is lost. The profound meaning of the classics then becomes a learning of the mouth and ear. If the function of ordering one's household and ruling the country has been neglected for a long time, it is because it is no longer the *jitsugaku* which corrects the mind and cultivates the person.[52]

There is here no separation of morality and politics, as was to be the case with Sorai. The first half of the passage shows that Banzan's teaching leans towards the Wang Yang-ming school and away from conventional Shushigaku. In addition, his ideas of the empty and the real reveal the special features of his *jitsugaku* as a learning of the mind.

A close friend asked whether the doctrines of "emptiness" and "nothingness" were found only in heterodoxy and whether sagely learning offered nothing but "reality."

Answer: "Emptiness is reality. For things with form and color are not constant, and things that are not constant do not have true reality. Things that lack form and color are constant, and what is constant is real. Heterodox learning does not exhaust 'nothingness,' but sagely learning does."[53]

Upon closer analysis, we see that *jitsugaku*, as he defined it, contained elements of emptiness. On the one hand, it shared these with the Buddhists and Taoists, but, on the other, it differed in its interpretation of them. Yet this is not the whole of the story. Banzan's own response to this issue is highly interesting:

A close friend asked. "Honored elder, you said that the Taoists and Buddhists are unable to grasp vacuity and nothingness, and yet indulge in detailed discussions of vacuity and nothingness, taking them as their way. Sagely learning does not take vacuity and nothingness as subjects of study. Why did you say this?"

Answer: "Our minds are the Supreme Vacuity. Our minds are without sound or smell, form or color. All things come from nothingness. In sagely learning there are vacuity and nothingness in the teaching of 'having no mind.' This is what we mean by 'the ultimate of vacuity and nothingness.' The Taoists and Buddhists have something in mind in respect to vacuity and nothingness, and thus theirs is not true vacuity or true nothingness. Using their minds, they speak of vacuity and nothingness, and so their learning is detailed. But they have their own purposes in mind. Master [Wang] Yang-ming said, 'Even the sage would be unable to add an iota of reality to the vacuity of the Taoist seekers of immortality. Their talk about vacuity is motivated by the desire for nourishing everlasting life. The sage would also be unable to add an iota of being to the nothingness of the Buddhists. Their talk of nothingness is motivated by the desire to escape from the sorrowful sea of life and death.' Kao Tzu's notion of an 'unmoving mind' is also like this. For him, the effort is directed to not moving the mind, whereas the original substance of the mind is at the outset unmoving, and movement naturally occurs when one's actions are not in conformity with righteousness."[54]

According to this account, the "nothingness"[df] conceived by the Taoists and Buddhists on the one hand, and by the sages on the other is not in itself different. The former, however, is nothingness with a purpose, with a goal, and thus is not true nothingness. Neither is Kao Tzu's idea of an unmoving mind, for it too is bound by this purposefulness. True nothingness is the Confucian idea of "having no mind" (i.e., no selfish intent). As a nothingness which is originally unmoving, it remains the same unless there is something incompatible with righteousness, in which case it moves. This nothingness is a nothingness which includes movement. It is not a nothingness which is removed from actual society. It is rather a nothingness which, within the confines of actual society, continuously comes into contact with different things, transforming itself into movement and then returning to nothingness. This, Banzan tells us, is the idea of "empty and yet real," which one finds in sagely learning. The characteristic of Banzan's *jitsugaku*, his learning of the mind and his learning of the Way, is that all are empty and yet real.

How then did Banzan structure the various elements of his multi-faceted conception of *jitsugaku*? His *Shinpō zukai*[dg] (Diagrams of the Method of Mind) in the sixth chapter of the *Shūgi washo* is instructive in this regard.[55] Influenced by Tōju's *Meitoku zukai*[dh] (Diagram of Bright Virtue), Banzan's piece has been simplified and abbreviated. Although his discussion of the "Way of Heaven"[di] and the "Way of man,"[dj] which is based on the *Book of Changes* and the *Mean*, is important for under-standing Banzan's ideas, the characteristic aspects of his thought are best revealed in his diagram of the "method of the mind." Here the ideas of equilibrium and harmony, indicating as they do in the *Mean*, the ideal condition of the mind, are discussed in relation to principle and material force. Equilibrium is referred to as "the original unaroused state"[dk] which is defined in terms of principle and human nature and characterized as the original substance which is without form, color, sound or smell. Harmony, in turn, is referred to as the functioning of material force and the emotions and is characterized as "action and non-action penetrating to the source of the world."[56] That is, when the unaroused, original mind (equilibrium) is stimulated and moves toward action, this action is always appropriate. Banzan, while fundamentally following Chu Hsi on the method of the mind, also differed from him in two respects. First, he defined equilibrium, the original substance of the mind, as "quiescent, unmoving and yet feeling," in contrast to Chu Hsi and the Ch'eng brothers who described it as merely "quiescent and unmoving." The in-troduction of the notion of "feeling" is the distinguishing feature of Ban-zan's concept of the original substance of the mind. As Tomoeda Ryūtarō has pointed out, Banzan's view is "holistic and vitalistic."[57] Perhaps Ban-zan wanted to make certain that the Buddhist, and particularly the Zen, concept of mind was not confused with his own. The second difference lies in his designating the area of contact between equilibrium and har-mony as the "spiritual intelligence of the mind."[dl]

The teachings of the sages are received, and scholars, fond of learning through inquiry, exhaust principle and enter into virtue. Thus the spiritual intelligence of the mind is shown within

equilibrium and harmony. "Watching over oneself while alone"[dm] is the essence of the method of the mind.[58]

In his *Shinpō zukai* Banzan considered the issue of the "spiritual intelligence of the mind" not only in terms of "being watchful over oneself while alone," but also in terms of "inquiry and study and the exhaustive exploration of principle."[dn] His fundamental attitude towards learning was an interiority which took "watching over oneself while alone" as a foundation. This inwardness, however, was "not the 'interiority' of 'inner' as opposed to 'outer' but the master of the universe which was prior to such an opposition."[59] If stated in terms of the relationship between Chu Hsi and Wang Yang-ming, we might say that Banzan based his philosophy on the teachings of Wang Yang-ming, while incorporating from Chu Hsi's teachings a sense of breadth and scope in which the internal and the external were united into one. Inquiry and study and the exhaustive exploration of principle play an important role in Banzan's over-all conception of learning.

Early in his career, Banzan, under the influence of Wang Yang-ming and Chang Tsai, had espoused the doctrine of the Supreme Vacuity as a monism of material force and joined this to the doctrine of forming one body with all things.[do] In the *Shinpō zukai* he espoused a theory of principle and material force as integrated, saying, "The Supreme Vacuity is simply principle and material force." In the second edition of *Shūgi washo* he described this integration of principle and material force as the Way:

When one speaks of "principle," material force is left out. When one speaks of "material force," principle is left out. One retains the terms "principle" and "material force" even though the two are inseparable; it is only when one speaks of "the Way" that neither is left out. "The Way" is a term for the oneness of principle and material force. In referring to its largeness, one speaks of emptiness and vacuity. In referring to its smallness, one speaks of minuteness and imperceptibility. In referring to its mysterious functions, one speaks of spirits. It is through the Way that Heaven and earth are positioned and that the sun and moon are bright; it is through the Way that the four seasons pass in turn and that all things are born.[60]

Underlying all of this is Banzan's vitalistic understanding of existence and his interpretation of equilibrium as "solitary and unmoving and yet feeling." He wrote in a similar vein,

In truth it is quiescent and unmoving; it is without sound or smell. This is called "the equilibrium before the feelings have been aroused." It is the great basis of the world. Though we speak of the Way as both natural and boundless, the constancy involved in the succession of yin and yang, the heat and cold of the sun and the moon, and the changes of day and night is the principle of "the Infinite and yet the Supreme Ultimate."[61]

Here there is ambiguity in Banzan's thought. Chu Hsi had distinguished between the principle of "things as they are," (as in "the Infinite and yet the Supreme Ultimate") and the principle of "things as they should be," (as in the rules governing the objective world). Banzan ignored this distinction, explaining normative principles in terms of the metaphysical principle of "the Infinite and yet the Supreme Ultimate." One explanation for this lies in his view of the exploration (or plumbing) of principle (kyūri).

Although his view of exploring principle generally followed Chu Hsi's, there was one important difference, as can be seen in the following passage:

A scholar asked whether exploring principles in direct relation to things means studying things and affairs one by one by studying the principles underlying them one by one.

I answer that it is. I do not know the meaning of questions like, "How does one understand the principle of each thing and affair?" My view is that things are affairs. Affairs are the functioning of things, and things are the substance of affairs. They are not a duality. If the things (objects) of the Five Relations[dp] exist, then so too do the affairs (moral relations). The things of the Five Relations are the relationships between lord and retainer, father and son, husband and wife, older brother and younger brother, friend and friend. The Five Relations as affairs involve the Five Relationships and the Ten Moral Obligations. Understanding them and carrying them out is called investigating things and extending knowledge. Knowledge is principle. What is presently considered exploring principle is done through books. It is explained in writing and argued in elevated discussions. This is not exploring principle in direct relation to things.[62]

Whereas Chu Hsi's theory of exploring the principles of things had included exploring the principles of things in their physical aspect, Banzan's statement suggests that, for him, principles were confined to the principles of the Five Relations. However, upon careful examination of Banzan's writings, exceptions to such a generalization emerge. For example:

For the most part the principles of the world have to do with ordering and ruling states and pacifying the world. Each and every one of these affairs involves knowledge and ability bestowed by Heaven. Rulers are to examine the abilities of their retainers and assign tasks accordingly. Retainers, in turn, are to exhaust their own endowments from Heaven. . . . If one has talent pertaining to the geography of mountains and rivers, he should manage mountains, rivers, ponds and bogs. If one has insight into the Way of growing, he should oversee agricultural affairs. . . . If one is well-versed in the principles of the pitch pipes, he should handle music. . . . Numerous are the affairs of the world, limitless are their principles. . . . One man cannot exhaust them. We must combine our strength and make plans collectively; we should utilize the knowledge of the world to carry out its affairs.[63]

Thus, exhaustively exploring the principles of mountains, rivers, ponds and bogs, the principles of growing things, and the principles of music, was to explore their empirical principles; this had no direct bearing on the Five Relations. As a rule Banzan limited principle to metaphysical and ethical principle, yet he understood that the exhaustive exploration of principle included the matter of empirical principle.

Banzan's experience as an administrator was such that, unlike Wang Yang-ming, he had to think in terms of exhaustively exploring the principles of things. Yet, unlike Chu Hsi, he believed the actual application of the pursuit of principle in the various things and substances of the world to be harmful. His acceptance of the idea of exhausting principle involved first, exploring principle in order to resolve the perplexities of the mind,[64] and, second, exploring principle in order to rule the state and pacify the world.

Ruling the country is the greatest of affairs. Exploring principle cannot but realize this.[65]

Given his viewpoint on political economy and statecraft, Banzan was obliged to pursue the study of empirical principles,[66] yet at a conceptual level, as a believer in the learning of the mind, he could not accommodate this idea. This forced him to link it to the principle of "the Infinite and yet the Supreme Ultimate." In other words, while he included the principles of things within the sphere of moral principles, he could not explain this relationship in philosophical terms. He maintained the rather optimistic view that if, on the one hand, one treated the problem empirically, and if, on the other hand, one pursued and realized moral principles with all sincerity, then one would naturally understand the principles of things. Herein lies the difference between Banzan and Kaibara Ekken and Arai Hakuseki[dq] (1657–1725), the practitioners of a Shushigaku variety of empirical rationalism.

Of his relationship with Chu Hsi and Wang Yang-ming, Banzan wrote:

I follow neither Chu Hsi nor Wang Yang-ming. I follow the sages of antiquity.[67]

It is from Wang Yang-ming's idea of the arising of innate knowledge that I derive my understanding of the effectiveness of self-examination and "watching over oneself while alone" for interior receptivity and the mastery of affairs. It is from Chu Hsi's idea of exhaustively exploring principle that I derive my understanding of how to overcome perplexity.[68]

In his *Shinpō zukai*, in which he attempted to systematize his ideas, Banzan was conscious both of his debt to Chu Hsi and his debt to Wang Yang-ming. Perhaps we should say that Banzan recognized the Shushigaku concept of investigating things and exploring principle even as he maintained an unmistakable Yōmeigaku posture.

At the heart of Banzan's "method of the mind" were his views on "watching over oneself while alone." As he put it:

"Being watchful over oneself while alone" is to have a mind which is watchful over its own knowing. It is the same whether one is with others or by oneself. Even when one is with others, one's private thoughts are not known by others. When pursuing the solitary knowledge of one's mind, there are no external restrictions. Having no depraved thoughts, allowing no self-deception, making the will sincere—this is the meaning of "being watchful over oneself while alone." When a thought arises in one's mind, one spontaneously knows if it is good or evil—this is knowing. Knowing is the spiritual intelligence of the mind. It is originally without good or evil. Thus, it illumines good and evil. It is like the mouth not having the five flavors, yet being able to distinguish them; or like the eye not having the five colors yet being able to distinguish them; or like the ear not having the five sounds and yet being able to distinguish them. To take solitary knowledge as one's ruler and to watch over it—this is the meaning of honoring the virtuous nature.[69]

This is why Banzan's *jitsugaku* of moral practice can be called a *jitsugaku* which honors the virtuous nature.

How did Banzan's introspective learning, which valued solitary knowing, become a learning devoted to political economic matters? The answer lies in the universalistic impulse expressed in the idea of "forming one body with all things." Still, there remains the question of how this was related to his learning of the mind. For Banzan, becoming free of distracted or desultory thoughts and images was an important method of cultivating the mind. However, he thought it useless to engage in such cultivation apart from the realities of daily life and human relations. If one were to expel all fleeting thoughts, and expunge all desires, stopping all thoughts of either good or evil in the mirror of the mind, and seeking out the original substance of emptiness, the effects would show immediately, yet they would be—like the intervals between paroxysms of malarial fever—little more than the momentary preservation of a sense of peace and quiet. It would be like clarifying water by causing foreign bodies to sink to the bottom; in that these bodies remain, the water, when stirred up, again becomes cloudy. Thus, there would be no real chance of changing one's basic temperament. Then what is one to do? According to Banzan:

As regards the things and affairs of the world, one is to realize where one's mind is clear and where it is unclear and to exert effort in actual practice. The world and the state are both things. Human relations are likewise things. As regards the things and affairs of the world, where my mind is confused, my knowledge is not clear.[70]

This is Wang Yang-ming's idea of self-polishing through experience. Though Banzan was a masterless warrior, he never lost interest in the problems of statecraft and continued to believe that he could eliminate distracted or desultory thoughts within himself in the process of solving this problem.

As we have seen, Banzan's *jitsugaku* was structured in such a way that a *jitsugaku* of moral practice could become a *jitsugaku* of political economy. The ideas that Heaven and man were integrally related and that all things formed one body were conducive to this shift. Here I will not discuss the actual problems his political economic *jitsugaku* was meant to solve, but rather will focus on its conceptual basis, which was the idea of time, place, and rank.

Fundamental to his conception of time, place, and rank was, first, a distinction between the Way and law[dr] and between the Way and ritual.[ds] If the Way is universal, law (or ritual) is limited to time, place, and rank. Errors occur when this is forgotten, and when law is viewed as the Way. He continued:

The Way consists of the Three Relations and Five Norms. These extend through Heaven, earth and man, and the Five Agents. Even before morality was given a name and before the teachings of the sages existed, this Way was already operating. So too was it working when man did not exist, and when Heaven and earth did not exist. It was working in the Supreme Vacuity. Even as men have died and Heaven and earth have returned to the void, the Way has not been annihilated. How true must this be for later ages as well. Law corresponded to the time, place and rank of the sages, creating appropriate deeds. The Way existed in that age too. Yet as the age and the rank of men have changed, even the law of the sages is difficult to employ, and carrying out what is inappropriate will bring harm to the Way.[71]

A second idea underlying Banzan's conception of time, place, and rank is talent,[dt] or basic talent.[du] Banzan speaks of those who possess talent for government as having "basic talent." If such men were also learned, the country and the world would be well-ruled. To have basic talent but lack learning is like walking on a dark night without a light; one is afraid and walks on only because it is the way one has already set out on. In contrast, government by men who have learning but lack talent will resemble the behavior of a blind man who, wishing to take a walk, has no choice but to walk as directed since he is utterly incapable of considering what is best in terms of time, place, and rank. It goes without saying that Banzan preferred the former to the latter, for he believed that, "though a man be endowed with wide learning and virtue, if he lacks the talent to know human emotions and changing circumstances, ruling will be difficult."[72] Evident in all of this are Banzan's own experiences as a political economist.

A third idea which figured in his conception of time, place, and rank is "sincerity,"[dv] which may at first glance appear to contradict the idea of talent. Though talent and ability are needed to act in conformity with time, place, and rank, this alone would result in mere pragmatic or utilitarian learning. As the following passage suggests, Banzan saw the need for action to emerge from sincerity as well:

In both funerals and ancestral worship services, one should consider time, place and rank. One should also concentrate on exhausting the sincerity of one's mind.[73]

A fourth element in Banzan's conception of time, place, and rank was a view of politics which preferred the natural to the artificial. About this preference he once wrote:

Man too follows the naturalne s of Heavenly principle, sometimes working and sometimes resting. Not intruding one's own selfish aims is to take no unnatural action. When rulers are not bent on achieving things but act in accordance with time, place and rank, the state and the world are at peace. This is called ruling through taking no unnatural action.[74]

Banzan's emphasis on naturalness involved the conviction that even the laws which might be deemed most artificial were, in their original state, responses to nature, and as such, without artifice.

When the Early Kings succeeded Heaven and established the ultimate standards, what did they make their basis: sincerity, work, naturalness or production? They needed only to make sincerity the foundation. With sincerity as a foundation, they responded to nature, and in accordance with time, they worked. Production also needed to exist. Sincerity is also established to control excesses. Responding to nature without artifice is the beginning of law.[75]

Here are the elements of a political theory diametrically opposed to that of Ogyū Sorai, for whom everything rested on artifice. It is significant that Banzan raised the issue of artifice here. In keeping with the idea inherited from Tōju that all men are equal, Banzan also created a new conception of natural law, one which differed from that of Hayashi Razan. In the Bakumatsu[dw] period, Yokoi Shōnan[dx] would inherit Banzan's idealistic view of politics.

There is, finally, one more idea which underlies Banzan's conception of time, place, and rank, that of the Great Way (or Great Unity).[dy] According to Banzan:

We should consider the man who exists alone in Heaven and earth. When he makes Heaven his teacher and spiritual intelligence his friend, he need not rely on externals or on other people. One who is like this is inwardly secure and imperturbable, outwardly harmonious and irreproachable.[76]

As is evident here, Banzan was himself highly independent in spirit. On the issues of politics and education, he believed that rulers and teachers should not extol what they alone can do and others would find difficult to do.

Those who stand apart from the ordinary, establish their own school and cease to do what is ordinary can in no way assist the transforming and sustaining force of Heaven and earth. In the end, theirs will be a petty Way.[77]

Thus the Great Way is to proceed together with what is ordinary and is to be carried out together with the people for "the Great Way is the Great Unity." It was Banzan's conviction that the Way could not be established apart from the people.

Why not choose the Mean of time, place and rank? Why use an incomplete law to thwart the people and obstruct the beneficence which would further the Way of the Great Unity?[78]

The "Mean" of time, place, and rank is the "great basis of the world" and the "truth of Heavenly principle and nature." Although he did not create the idea of the Great Unity, Banzan might be seen as a predecessor of the late Ch'ing thinker and reformer K'ang Yu-wei[dz] (1858–1927).

If we recall that the exploration or plumbing of principle, as he described it, was to have an empirical dimension and that "basic talent" was to be required of political leaders, then Banzan's *jitsugaku* may be seen as anticipating that of Ogyū Sorai. Sorai would reject certain aspects of Banzan's learning, built as it was on the Sung and Ming traditions in which the natural and the human were connected, all things formed one body, and the Way and its instruments were linked. Yet Banzan's political views were rich in new insights and offer an alternative model to that of Sorai.[79]

THE ESTABLISHMENT OF EMPIRICAL RATIONALISM IN KAIBARA EKKEN AND HIS VIEW OF *JITSUGAKU*

Kaibara Ekken is notable particularly for having turned Shushigaku toward empirical rationalism and formulated a moral and practical conception of *jitsugaku*. Ekken is representative of those who opposed the Kimon school, especially its preoccupation with the metaphysical and moral aspects of the Shushigaku concept of principle and an austere and introspective *jitsugaku* which focused on moral practice. Among those who were close to him on these issues were the Shushigaku thinker Nakamura Tekisai[ea] (1629–1702), the agronomist Miyazaki Yasusada[eb] (1623–1697), the Confucian doctor and botanist Mukai Genshō[ec] (1609–1677), Inao Jakusui[ed] (1655–1715), and Matsuoka Jo'an[ee] (1668–1746). We are told that Ekken communicated at some time with all of these men. And although he appears not to have had any relationship with Arai Hakuseki and Nishikawa Joken[ef] (1648–1724), there seems little question that as thinkers they too were very close to Ekken. That thinkers with a penchant for empirical rationalism should have emerged at this time was the result of the social stablity of the age, the development of agricultural technology, the impact of Ming treatises on science, and the influence of Hispanic studies. Philosophically, Ekken was profoundly influenced by the revisionist Shushigaku thinker, Lo Ch'in-shun, and his monism of principle and material force. Tekisai's teacher, Kinoshita Jun'an[eg] (1621–1699), is said to have had a copy of Lo's *K'un-chih chi*, and it seems probable that Tekisai and Hakuseki also had copies or that they were at least influenced by it.

Jitsugaku, as Ekken defined it, contained a major contradiction. Of learning he once wrote:

Those who carry out learning usually seek to perfect its utility. Consequently, learning has to be carried out in relation to affairs, and only then is it considered useful learning.[80]

We should recall that the *jitsugaku* of moral practice was expected to extend to the state and the world and to have a certain utility. Though Ekken scrupulously avoided pursuing utility directly—since this would have transformed learning into utilitarianism—he did create a new view of learning as "useful learning."[eh] It was this new ideal that inspired Ekken to write *Yamato honzō*[ei] (Herbs of Japan) and other works. When he described *jitsugaku* concretely, however, he did so in completely traditional terms, that is, as a *jitsugaku* of moral practice. And here lies the contradiction. He wrote, for example:

The Sage said to Tzu-hsia, "Become a scholar (*ju*) who is a superior man (*chün-tzu*). Do not become one who is a mean man." This means that the scholar who is a *chün-tzu* learns only for the sake of self-cultivation. This is *jitsugaku*. The Confucian who is a mean man learns in order to be known by others. He merely yearns after name and profit and cares little about cultivating himself. His is a vulgar learning.[81]

This contradiction in Ekken's view of *jitsugaku* is in a certain sense emblematic of his position in intellectual history. There is no question that Ekken broke new ground when he transformed Shushigaku into empirical rationalism, by discarding its emphasis on the metaphysical reality of principle and developing its empirical dimension. However, he did all this while remaining within the Shushigaku framework, and what impelled him to make these changes was a commitment to revising and correcting the Shushigaku in which he believed. The result was that the continuities in Shushigaku thought, particularly its tendency to equate physical and moral principle and to identify the laws of nature and moral norms, went unchallenged. The task of criticizing and refuting the structure of Shushigaku thought was left to the scholars of Ancient Learning.

How then did this transformation of Shushigaku into an empirical rationalism proceed? In *Taigiroku*[ej] (Grave Doubts), a work of his latter years, Ekken raised doubts concerning Chu Hsi's dualism and denied the concept of principle as prior and material force as posterior. Establishing a monism of principle and material force, he developed the view that principle was not opposed to material force, but was the principle of material force. Apparent here is the influence of the Ming scholar Lo Ch'in-shun,[82] who similarly had sought to revise and correct the thought of the Chu Hsi school in this regard. Yet Ekken, while he questioned certain fundamental ideas of Shushigaku, did not renounce the theoretical basis of the Shushigaku system, which lay in its commitment to moral practice. As Dazai Shundai[ek] (1680–1747) would later note in criticism of Ekken, he had doubts about Shushigaku without either rejecting it or managing to free himself from its influence.[83] Nonetheless, Ekken's thought and achievements reveal the birth of a new current, one which I have termed "empirical rationalism." This empirical rationalism was based on an empiricism which, while continuing in the pursuit of principle, was not limited to Shushigaku. From the middle of the Tokugawa period on, this new intellectual current, which had begun with Ekken, came to deny the speculative rationalism of Shushigaku and to espouse a form of positivism. This current should be distinguished from the one represented by Ogyū Sorai, who, by severing the link between morality and politics, established the basis for an independent realm of politics. Yet, it represented one more modernizing trend in the thought of the Tokugawa period.

Clues found in Ekken's major work *Shinshiroku*[el] (A Record of Reflective Thought) may help to elucidate the way in which empirical rationalism took shape within the framework of Shushigaku. Principle, he tells us in this work, is not distinct from the Way, and here Ekken was faithful to Chu Hsi. He also followed Chu Hsi in his views on investigating things and exhaustively exploring principle, as when he wrote, "The practice of extending knowledge begins with the self and proceeds to the principles of all things." [84] Ekken criticized Lu Hsiang-shan's advocacy of pursuing only "the principles that exist in the mind" and Kao Tzu's advocacy of pursuing only "the principles that exist in things," calling the former "a teaching which neglects external things,"[em] and the latter, "a doctrine which ignores ethics."[en] He criticized those who "speak of the Way as distinct from yin and yang" and those who "speak of the Way as confined to yin and yang," terming the former theory "heterodox and specious"[eo] and the latter "technical and mechanistic."[ep][85] Such criticisms were founded on the Shushigaku premise that the principles of things and the principles of the mind were united. Ekken advocated neither a pure idealism which would abandon the principles of things nor a thoroughgoing empiricism which would abandon the principles of the mind. It was the commitment to a view in which the two were integrated that attracted him to Shushigaku. What made this conceptually possible, according to Professor Okada Takehiko, was precisely the Shushigaku idea of total substance and great functioning.[eq][86]

The following provides some indication of the way in which Ekken's empirical rationalism emerged within the Shushigaku framework:

Those desirous of extending knowledge are to proceed to things. One makes one's mind clear through knowing the principles of things. To be unable to investigate things and therefore to focus only on one's mind is absolute stupidity. How is intelligence to be developed? One must surely extend his knowledge.[87]

Those who tried exhaustively to explore the principles of things, while ignoring the principles of the mind, Ekken called opportunists or "technicians"[er] who had deviated from the Confucian Way. In his eyes, if one were intent on developing the intelligence of one's mind, one should not exclusively pursue the principles of the mind, as scholars like Lu Hsiang-shan had done. One had to investigate things as well.

Breadth and precision were to Ekken indispensable both in book-learning and in exhausting principle:

If one's learning is broad, one will be conversant with the principles of the world. If one's learning is precise, all of the principles of the world will be clear. Breadth and precision should both be present as prerequisites for exploring principle. This is the Way of extending knowledge.[88]

Informing this conception of learning were the four principles of the *Mean* which Chu Hsi had adopted as the educational policy of his Po-lu-tung Academy: "broad learning,"[es] "extensive inquiry,"[et] "reflective thinking,"[eu] and "clear discrimination."[ev] On one occasion, Ekken explained that broad learning referred to the scope of one's learning, while "extensive inquiry," "reflective thinking," and "clear discrimination" had to do with inferring the principle in each activity. On another occasion, he identified a complementarity between "broad learning" and "extensive inquiry" on the one hand, and "reflective thinking" and "clear discrimination" on the other, with the former designated as "learning" and the latter as "thought." Ekken argued forcefully that both were indispensable to "extending knowledge and investigating things."[89]

One may wonder what breadth and precision in "investigating things and exploring principle" actually meant in concrete terms. Ekken tells us:

In the effort of extending knowledge one begins within one's self and proceeds to the principles of all things. If one is diligent in this, never avoiding what is troublesome or difficult, one will achieve true perception naturally and quite suddenly. Such is the effort of investigating things and exploring principle.[90]

Although this is a typical Shushigaku conception, we perceive in the phrase, "never avoiding what is troublesome or difficult," Ekken's intense interest in the external world of events and things.

It was in the context of his profound interest in actuality that Ekken made the statement, "There is in the world nothing that stands outside principle,"[91] and formulated the concept of "constant"[ew] and "changing"[ex] principles. In instances when something appears at first to stand outside principle or to be unfathomable by principle, wrote Ekken, it only seems to be so because principle has not been fully explored, and should be included in the category "changing principle." Yet even "changing principles" are within principle, for nothing in the world exists outside principle. That this thoroughgoing rationalism contained elements of empiricism and positivism is suggested by his emphasis on such terms as "broad learning" and "hearing and seeing widely."[ey] Yet, at the same time, his empiricism and positivism are shot through with rationalistic elements. Even as he formulated his empirical rationalism, Ekken related the pleasure derived from exploring principle:

Abundant are the events and things which fill the world, and inexhaustible are their principles. It is through study that one grasps the principle of each, of this there is no doubt. This is the greatest happiness in life. Boundless is one's pleasure.[92]

Even as Ekken uttered these words, he was deriving immense pleasure from his efforts to explore principle, not only in Confucianism, but also in botany, medicine, and other empirical science. The combined rationalism and empiricism of his thought culminated in his *Yamato honzō*, an epoch-making study in the history of botany in Japan.

In the preface to this book, there occurs the following significant passage:

All those who pursue studies such as this should be broad in their learning and of diverse experience. They should hear and see much so that their doubts and misgivings are dispelled. If their researches into the myriad things and their distinctions between the true and the false lack precision, accuracy will be wanting. They will see their own views as true and those of others as false. They will cling tenaciously to erroneous views.[93]

Having said this, Ekken went on to caution scholars against four pitfalls: first, insufficient observation; second, uncritical acceptance of what one sees and hears; third, exclusive adherence to one's own views; and fourth, hasty conclusions. This analysis, which recalls Francis Bacon's theory of idols, is perhaps the most striking discussion of scientific method in the early Tokugawa period.

Ekken bears another resemblance to Bacon. He too saw learning as advancing through the destruction of old habits.

Why is it that our learning does not advance? No doubt it is because we are content with our old habits and cannot break out of our set ways. The material force of Heaven and earth changes day by day, and its transformations are unceasing. This is why Heaven and earth have such great powers of nourishing and growth. Likewise the scholarly method and Heavenly virtue of the noble man are daily made new. This is why he is able to attain higher things. Scholars too should renew themselves day by day, abandoning their old habits and not clinging to old customs. . . . If this is done, their learning will make great strides.[94]

This is an unusual view for a Confucian since standards of truth were usually believed to reside in the sages of antiquity. The fact that Ekken was a natural scientist as well as a Confucian led him to develop to an extraordinary degree the concept of the "progress of learning."

The fact that Ekken's *jitsugaku* tended toward the practical and had its basis in empirical rationalism was related to the ethical and practical orientation of Shushigaku with its commitment to "cultivating the self and governing others,"[ez] and "ruling the world and meeting the needs of human society."[fa] Ekken also distinguished between "useful learning" and "useless learning" and chose the former, which, in his words, served to "clarify human relations, further human enterprises, cultivate the self and rule the people."[95] He wrote in a similar vein:

The arts of learning are the means of ruling the world. Yet why is it that the learning of latter-day scholars is rarely applicable in ministering to the needs of the world? Learning which pursues principle and knows the Way is the basis for ruling the world and meeting its needs. Learning should always be useful.[96]

If one is to fulfill the practical, moral, and political ideals of "cultivating the self and governing others" and "ruling the world and meeting the needs of human society," one must work to achieve an objective perception of things in the external world. When he wrote in the preface to *Yamato honzō* that, "All the affairs of the universe are affairs of the Confucian,"[97] he was drawing on the words of Lu Hsiang-shan. But when Hsiang-shan, as an idealist, had said that, "The affairs in the universe are my own affairs," he was discussing the issue of a Confucian's sphere of responsibility in an effort to clarify the principle of the mind. For this, Ekken substituted an empirical rationalism and worked instead to exhaust the principles of things in the world.

One other thing should be added concerning Ekken's view of *jitsugaku*. He emphasized what some other Confucians abhorred: the lowly and commonplace.[fb] One reason for this reevaluation of the lowly may be found in his idea of Heaven. Ekken differed from Hayashi Razan, who had sought to establish the a priori nature of high and low status relationships by finding an analogy in the relationship of Heaven and earth. Ekken interpreted Heaven as the "generative source of all things."[98] As creatures whose lives were engendered by the same Heaven, all men were brothers:

The people are all brothers. That even one person should not occupy his appropriate position in society is a source of great personal grief.[99]

Here we see the idea of all things forming one body, an idea Ekken shared with Chang Tsai, Chu Hsi, and Wang Yang-ming. Central to Ekken's thought was the notion of loving all people as one would the children of one's brother. Similarly, his conception of *jitsugaku* involved a sense of gratitude for one's existence (a gratitude which could also be expressed to Heaven), a recognition of one's dependence on the labor of others, and mindfulness of the importance of giving all one has for the betterment of human existence. Ekken was not ashamed of studying "the commonplace."[100] His *jitsugaku* has as its impetus or emotional foundation the moral ideals of Shushigaku, and as its philosophical base, the revisionist Shushigaku doctrine of a monism of principle and material force and the Shushigaku doctrine of total substance and great functioning.

However, a *jitsugaku* which united the exhaustive exploration of the principles of the events and things of the external world with moral practice, ironically, had the consequence of severing the link which Shushigaku had always maintained between ethics and intellectual perception. This is apparent in the relationship between an interior morality of "rectifying the mind and making the will sincere" on the one hand, and "extending knowledge and investigating things" on the other. In Ekken's words:

If scholars have not exhaustively explored external events and things, they will not understand the affairs of the world. Even if one is free of selfishness, one will be unable to respond to the principles of things.[101]

Ekken was trying to say that internal moral practices such as rectifying the mind and making the will sincere served to eliminate selfishness, but did not necessarily guarantee an objective perception of things. Wang Yang-ming, had he known of this view, would have protested. It is tempting to speculate about how Chu Hsi would have reacted. With this view, Ekken approached Sorai, though at the same time he remained, emotionally and subjectively, within the conceptual limits of Shushigaku.

When Ekken transformed Shushigaku into empirical rationalism on a practical level, he overlooked two important philosophical problems: the relationship of the Way and principle, and the relationship of "the principles of the mind" and "the principles of things."

That Shushigaku exhibited a propensity toward empirical rationalism is manifest in Chu Hsi's remark in *Chu Tzu yü-lei* (Classified Conversations of Chu Hsi), "Everything, even the most minute blade of grass, tree or insect, has its own principle." To Shushigaku thinkers, principle was simultaneously the principle of things and of the Way; it was a principle in which laws of nature were bound up with the ethical sphere. As Chu Hsi wrote in his *Ta-hsüeh huo-wen* (Questions and Answers on the *Great Learning*), "All things in the world always have a reason for their existence and a pattern of how they should be. This is principle." This should be distinguished, however, from Kant's view of reason as consisting of a sphere of perception dominated by necessary laws and a sphere of moral practice based on free will.

It was the scholars of Ancient Learning, especially Itō Jinsai, who paid special attention to this problem. Jinsai expunged the concept of principle from the moral sphere, where he felt only the concept of the Way was appropriate. Ekken, in turn, opposed Jinsai's view, describing Jinsai as that "advocate of heterodox learning who recently emerged claiming that the law of the moral world should be called the Way and not principle. How obstinate he is!"[102] To the end, Ekken never faltered in his defense of the Shushigaku idea that principle and the Way are one, though we do sense that he may have failed to understand fully the meaning of the problem Jinsai raised.

It was a problem, we should note, which was linked to Ekken's notions of a "principle of things" and a "principle of mind," the formulation of which was in itself a major advance in intellectual history. Although he failed to consider fully their relationship, he did go so far as to say that they differed from each other and yet were mutually necessary. He did not, however, explain whether the differences between the two kinds of principle resulted from differences between mind and the objects containing the principle, whether principle in both cases was actually identical, or whether the two kinds of principle were actually distinct categories. It may well be that Ekken, since he identified principle with the Way, would have explained the difference between the "principle of things" and the "principle of mind" as one which derived from differences in the things or the mind in which principle inhered, while, as principle, it was always identical. This is a view which would be conceived sometime later by Yamagata Bantō[fc] (1748–1821) and Sakuma Shōzan[fd] (1811–1864), whose Shushigaku was of the same sort as Ekken's. The philosophical answer to the problem would have to wait for the early Meiji philosopher, Nishi Amane (1829–1897). But even before this, the task of denying the

all-inclusiveness and continuity characteristic of Shushigaku thought
would be carried out by the scholars of Ancient Learning, and Ogyū
Sorai would offer a radical solution to the issue of principle.

SATŌ NAOKATA'S VIEW OF *JITSUGAKU* AND THE PLUMBING OF PRINCIPLE

Here I have chosen to consider the views of Satō Naokata (1650–1719)
from the Kimon school of Yamazaki Ansai, on *jitsugaku*, the plumbing
of principle, and principle itself. Naokata often spoke of *jitsugaku* and
was deeply concerned with the idea of principle and, of course, there is
an internal relationship between *jitsugaku* and the exhausting of principle.

The Shushigaku thinkers I have treated thus far have held various
views of principle. Hayashi Razan, for example, at first believed that
principle was prior and material force posterior. Later, under the influence of Lo Ch'in-shun and Wang Yang-ming, he advocated a "principle
of material force," though he died without having arrived at a definitive
view of principle. Kaibara Ekken, with his empirical orientation, recognized a "principle of the mind" and a "principle in the mind" as distinct
from a "principle of things" and a "principle in things." His achievement
was to join Shushigaku and natural science. Naokata's achievement, in
contrast, was to provide the metaphysical and ethical aspects of Shushigaku with a theoretical basis. His special emphasis on the ethical dimension of Shushigaku may be partially explained by the fact that he was following Ansai, but another more personal reason lay in the fact that
Naokata believed it was his mission to defend Shushigaku against
Yōmeigaku, which opposed the idea of the exhausting of principle, and
the Ancient Learning of Itō Jinsai.

Before beginning my discussion of Naokata, it will be useful briefly to
describe the main characteristics of the thought of Ansai and his
school.[103] Though broad in scope, the scholarship of Hayashi Razan, the
first Japanese to adopt Shushigaku systematically, lacked interior depth.
Razan did not internalize Shushigaku as a learning of personal experience, mind-cultivation, and ethics. This was the result of the manner in
which he studied Shushigaku: rather than attempting to study Chu Hsi by
reading his writings, Razan relied instead on the *Wu-ching ta-ch'üan*[fe]

(Great Compendium of Commentaries on the Five Classics) and the *Ssu-shu ta-ch'üan*[ff] (Great Compendium of Commentaries on the Four Books), works which were used as official primers in Ming China and Yi Korea. Although his advocacy of Shushigaku involved, for him, opposition to the Wang Yang-ming school,[104] Razan's intellectual interests were catholic: they included Confucianism after Chu Hsi, the Hundred Schools, history, literature, natural science, and law, and encompassed China, Korea, and Japan. Razan no doubt deserved his reputation as a man of wide erudition.

Yamazaki Ansai, in contrast, returned directly to Chu Hsi. He read Chu Hsi's writings, starting with the *Chu Tzu wen-chi*[fg] (Collection of Literary Works of Chu Hsi) and the *Chu Tzu yü-lei*, and including the *Ssu-shu chang-chü chi-chu*[fh] (Collected Commentaries on Words and Phrases of the Four Books) and other authorized works. In view of his highly subjective and interior understanding of Shushigaku as an ethical learning and his devotion to the learning of personal experience, discipline, mind-cultivation, and ethics, there is little question that he was the first Japanese Confucian really to understand Shushigaku. Yet his concerns were limited to Chu Hsi, and this led to a narrowing of his intellectual interests. Furthermore, as his knowledge of Chu Hsi's philosophy deepened, his notion of what was orthodox and what was heterodox became more intense and more exclusive. In his school, quiet-sitting was highly regarded as a means of moral practice, so highly regarded in fact that Tokutomi Sohō[fi] (1863–1957) once compared him to Calvin.[105]

While the distinctive features of Ansai's thought and learning reflected his own personality and his own internal needs, he was indebted to the Korean Shushigaku thinker Yi T'oegye for his particular view of Chu Hsi and Shushigaku. Yet there are aspects of his thought which distinguish him from T'oegye. For example, Ansai, together with Asami Keisai,[fj] one of his disciples, gave special importance to Chu Hsi's doctrines of respecting the king (*sonnō*)[fk] and of fulfilling one's fixed obligations (*meibun*)[fl]. He also fused Shushigaku and Shinto, creating a Confucian Shinto called Suika Shinto.[fm] It is noteworthy that Naokata and Keisai were expelled from the Kimon school for refusing to acknowledge Suika Shinto.

Ansai's thought is most readily understood in relation to the thought of his disciples. For example, his view of humaneness, an idea which was central to his thought, is more readily understood through Keisai's idea of humaneness, which was not only deeper but more explicit.[106] The same is true of Ansai's special focus on principle, an important assumption in the formation of his thought. It is more easily grasped through Naokata's more thoroughgoing explorations of principle.[107] This is because in Ansai's writings, all of this was still largely embryonic; there were hints of movement in a particular direction but never full development. Undoubtedly, Ansai's lectures were more lucid than his writings and thus served as a major stimulus to his disciples. This is the impression one receives from the lecture notes of his disciples which are cited in Abe Yoshio's study of the Japanese Chu Hsi school and Korea, *Nihon Shushigaku to Chōsen*.[108] Conventionally, Ansai is seen as a thinker preoccupied with reverence and as a man with a penchant for the most rigid kind of asceticism. Yet it is my feeling, especially in view of his description of humaneness as latent or unexpressed love, that this characterization is not completely fair and that there still is room for reconsidering his notions of humaneness and reverence.[109]

At the center of Naokata's thought was the concept of principle. Principle was the chief premise of Ansai's thought as well, but given his interest in the devotional and practical aspects of learning, he was not a skilled metaphysician. Thus Naokata's ideas tended in the same direction as those of his teacher, but he also developed what Ansai had neglected, especially in his consideration of principle.

I shall look at Naokata's view of *jitsugaku*, asking first what, in his eyes, was not *jitsugaku* and then what was. As to what was not *jitsugaku*, he spoke of the heterodox,[fn] the useless,[ai] and all those who were called and who called themselves scholars of *jitsugaku*. By heterodox, he meant the Buddhists and Taoists, individuals who, in his words, "lacked knowledge of principle." In his view, they knew only the world of material force, and not knowing what to do with themselves, they abandoned the world. When he used the term "useless," Naokata was thinking of:

scholars who know many things . . . [scholars who] compose poetry and prose, who record past events and history, who write inscriptions on Buddhist temple bells, and who create family genealogies. What is worse, they speak of good and bad fortune, and if unable to compose poems on New Year's they feel they have failed to preserve their honor as scholars. They are fond of the same things that mean men find pleasure in.[110]

He was thinking of men whose conduct bore not the least resemblance to that of the sages and worthies. It is possible that Naokata, when he wrote this, was thinking of Hayashi Razan.

When he condemned the Buddhists and Taoists and others who lacked principle, he was in agreement with the earlier advocates of *jitsugaku*. Interestingly, it is Naokata's criticism of "contemporary scholars of *jitsugaku*" which reveals the special features of his point of view. His criticisms of the various types of *jitsugaku* provide a key to his own definition of *jitsugaku* and to its significance in the intellectual history of the period. Consider the following:

Undiscerning Confucians, though they have learned that each principle has diverse particularizations, do not know the unitary principle, and are, as a result, confused by external things. The reason that many members of the Ch'eng school have gone over to the Zen Buddhists is that they would not become vulgar Confucians. Contemporary practitioners of *jitsugaku* worried little about the drift toward heterodoxy. This is why Chu Hsi said that contemporary Confucians had less vision than the heterodox. This is also why Ch'eng I often discussed the unitary principle but rarely the diverse particularizations.[11]

Heterodoxy here refers to those who dislike the exhaustive exploration of principle or the plumbing of principle (*kyūri*). Since those whom Naokata called "contemporary scholars of *jitsugaku*" did not reject the plumbing of principle, it is clear that he was not pointing to the Wang Yang-ming school. Rather he was referring to those Shushigaku scholars who were less concerned with the "unity of principle" than with its "diverse particularizations"—that is, those who followed Lo Ch'in-shun in their empiricism and whom Naokata called the "adherents of a ritualistic learning."[fo] This suggests that Naokata's primary concern was to grasp directly the unitary principle referred to in the phrase, "the unity of principle and its manifold particularizations," a principle which was identical with the Supreme Ultimate and also the Way. Likewise in the matter of plumbing principle, he also saw principle to have primarily a moral sense. Let us look at a second example:

The great virtue of Heaven and earth is called life, and the renewal of life is called the changes. Man is a living being. The substance of the Way in the *Reflections on Things at Hand (Chin-ssu lu)*[fp] is alive and flowing. Human desires are dead and do not flow with the current of Heaven and earth . . . Reverence enlivens man's mind, while losing one's mind is death . . . In these terms, one expects that the effort applied to the latent and manifest states of mind should never be interrupted. A man in a daze has lost his mind. No matter how well-mannered an individual is, if his mind is not alive, he is of no use. Contemporary scholars of what is called *jitsugaku* do not know this, and hence, do not understand the method of the mind. . . . Reverence is essential; it is the basis of sagely learning. If one does not proceed from reverence, there will be interruptions in [the living flow of] his humanity. There will be selfish desires. Courage will be lacking. Knowledge will be superficial and rootless. I am speaking here of honoring the virtuous nature and carrying on study and inquiry.[112]

What is being discussed here is a species of vitalistic philosophy which was current in the Kimon school. According to this philosophy, Heaven-and-earth and man are all alive. So too is the Supreme Ultimate (or the substance of the Way) which is their source. So too is man's mind, which is the Supreme Ultimate in miniature. The mind has its own obstacles, namely, human desires, and it is because of these desires that the minds of men often die. What keeps their minds alive is reverence. Thus reverence is absolutely essential; it is the basis of sagely learning. Scholars of *jitsugaku*, however, do not know that mind is preserved by reverence, and this is why they are ignorant of the method of the mind.

Evident here is the fundamental importance of reverence as the basis of Naokata's Confucianism. He was responding directly to an issue which had not been clarified in the writings of his teacher, Ansai—the relationship of reverence and humaneness. Naokata found humaneness in the ongoing processes of the universe; he found it also in the related processes of the human mind. In this view in which humaneness was understood as vital movement, reverence was regarded as the effort to ensure that this humaneness would endure forever, and it became, for Naokata, the essential basis of Confucianism. To a surprising degree, Naokata's idea of principle depended on this vitalistic philosophy, and in this respect, his views were similar to those of Itō Jinsai. Where they differed was that Jinsai limited principle to the world of objective phenomena and preferred the ethics of humanity to those of reverence. Here is Naokata's criticism of Jinsai:

Look at Itō Gensuke, who is not fond of preserving reverence and who speaks, instead, of practical action. He is a vulgar Confucian and there is nothing in him worth considering.[113]

A third criticism of contemporary scholars of *jitsugaku* appeared in various forms in *Ōgaku rondan*[fq] (Discussions on the Learning of Wang Yang-ming and His Followers), the twelfth chapter of his *Unzōroku*.[fr] What follows is representative of these criticisms:

As regards learning, since ancient times there have never been any fools among the sages and worthies. Fools are those who are ignorant of moral principle and who fail to cultivate new knowledge. This you should understand completely. Those simple, boorish scholars who speak of *jitsugaku* are like those whom Mencius called "your good, careful people of the villages."[114]

This is from Naokata's debate with one of Wang Yang-ming's followers. In his time there was no consensus as to what was sagely learning. Some argued that idiots and loafers were the exemplars of the real virtue of the *chün-tzu*. Others denied that the exhausting of principle was *jitsugaku*. To Naokata, such views were utterly lamentable. This was his reply to the claims of the Wang Yang-ming school that "there is one and only one method of honoring the virtuous nature," and his answer to their notion of the "task of introspection."[fs]

As was evident in his saying, "the central purpose in the thought of the sages and worthies was to stress knowledge," Naokata was thoroughly intellectual. He criticized Wang Yang-ming's theory of the unity of knowledge and action as follows:

When Wang Yang-ming speaks of the unity of knowledge and action, he includes knowledge in action. This is a Taoist and Buddhist view. For knowledge and action are naturally distinct, though their principles are one. This is manifest in the doctrine of the Ch'eng-Chu school. It is precisely because they are two that one speaks of unifying them. If they were one from the start, one would not use the word "unify."[115]

In spite of his viewing knowledge as the base, he also believed that knowledge and action progressed in tandem. The following passage affords a clear illustration of his criticism of the Wang Yang-ming school:

The key to Wang Yang-ming's thought is the extension of innate knowledge. In this view, book learning is believed to be useless. Why even consider morality and debate good and evil? All men are endowed with innate knowledge, and learning is carried out by means of this innate knowledge. To believe that innate knowledge renders unnecessary the pursuit of learning and the plumbing of principle is like believing that mirrors are always clear, and that even if they were not, they should not be polished. How absurd this is! Those who are misled by this are fools. Everyone knows that a cloudy mirror which remains unpolished is useless. There is no mistake about this. This is why we speak of illumining virtue. If scholars do not plumb principle, will their minds become clear? Polishing cloudy mirrors then is natural. To say that one has studied the sages and worthies when one does not understand this is insufferable. If what one knows is not clear, then one will not be able to act. Thus I do not doubt that Chu Hsi's theory of investigating things and plumbing principle commands the respect of scholars throughout the world.[116]

Only in the sages and worthies is the original innate knowledge unsullied. If what is sullied remains unpolished, scholars have no choice but to rely on methodical effort, for, unlike the sages, they cannot realize the innate criteria for judgment. This is because knowing things clearly is being able to weigh things and conform to moral principle. If one believes, as do the adherents of the Wang Yang-ming school, that because there is innate knowledge, there is no need for exercising judgment, then the Four Books and Six Classics will be useless.[117]

Naokata seems to have misinterpreted Wang Yang-ming's thought. Given Wang's idea that the principles in the mind are subject to correction each and every time the mind comes into contact with things, it seems unlikely that he would not urge that the metaphorical mirror be polished. In this respect, Naokata's criticism missed the mark.

The differences between the Wang Yang-ming school and the Chu Hsi school lay in the fact that Wang Yang-ming school emphasized correcting one's own mind through one's own experience and action, while the Chu Hsi school placed an equal emphasis on plumbing principle in things and on clarifying one's mind. Naokata's criticisms of Wang Yang-ming originated in his view that the plumbing of principle was indispensable for the clarification of the mind. It was unnecessary, he believed, only in the case of the sages and worthies, for they understand the nature of things. Naokata felt that, for those who were less perfect than the sages, the plumbing of principle was absolutely essential, and it was for their sake that learning existed. He also believed that the object of the plumbing of principle was the Four Books and Six Classics, for these provided the guidelines for the plumbing of principle. While the adherents of the Wang Yang-ming school did not reject research on the classics, it is undeniable that the view that the Four Books and the Five Classics were useless was one that might by logical extension be derived from their thought. This doctrine of the irrelevance of ancient texts was once expressed by Kumazawa Banzan:

Men of above-average ability, when they hear something of the unwritten teaching concerning the mind, make Heaven and earth their teachers. Learning from creation, they never look to books. They execute the Way and enter into virtue.[118]

This is indicative of a process through which thought was purified, but it also involved a denial of the Confucian system of learning and became a major problem for Tokugawa Confucian apologetics. Although both Shushigaku and Ancient Learning scholars advocated the preservation of the classics, Itō Jinsai established, on the basis of his textual criticisms of the *Great Learning* and the *Mean*, his preference for the *Mencius* and the *Analects* and came to venerate the Five Classics. Although Naokata was writing after Jinsai's criticisms of the *Great Learning* had been published, he simply dismissed Jinsai's views as "unfinished," adding, "Summer insects doubt the existence of ice." [119] This was before the advent of mid-Tokugawa textual criticism, and Naokata was not trying to cast doubt on traditional Shushigaku. He was mainly concerned with principle as the substance of the Way; in other words, as the Supreme Ultimate. To his metaphysical sensibilities, textual criticism must have seemed an exercise in trivia.

These criticisms also indicate, though indirectly, what Naokata thought on the subject of true *jitsugaku*. It is learning which centers one's concern on principle as the metaphysical substance of the Way (i.e., the Supreme Ultimate), clarifies one's mind by the plumbing of principle in things and affairs, and emphasizes reverence as a practical endeavor which ensures freedom from human desires. His view of *jitsugaku* also conformed to a Shushigaku which showed no interest in the empirical dimension of principle or, at least, made it secondary. On the basis of this view of *jitsugaku*, Naokata criticized the interpretation of principle in empirical terms by Lo Ch'in-shun and Kaibara Ekken, the rejection of the plumbing (or exhaustive exploration) of principle in things in favor of the pursuit of personal and internal matters by the Wang Yang-ming school, and the substitution of humanity for reverence by Itō Jinsai. [120]

The passages in which Naokata actually advocated *jitsugaku* have all been cited here; however, there are two other passages which reveal the character of his ideas. In the first he says:

The *Great Learning's* "making the will sincere" is the highest form of action. Carefully to judge each thought as it emerges is the basis for action. Applying effort to the discipline of the mind determines the realness of the action. [121]

What we learn from this passage is that Naokata's ethical learning focuses on the interior dimension of "each thought as it emerges," and not on the external dimension of language and appearance. In the second passage he says:

Scholars use discussion and debate as a means of correcting errors. A man who resents those who correct him is not a scholar. Those who aspire to the sages and worthies exult in the criticism they receive from others. Those who dread the criticisms of others are cowards. Those who correct their oversights and seek to do so are exemplars of *jitsugaku*. [122]

We see here that self-reliance and mutual criticism were basic to Naokata's conception of learning. In his words:

Scholars who depend on the example of their teachers will not be trusted by others. However you look at it, one has to stand on one's own. Thus, establishing one's purpose in life is of primary concern in learning. [123]

These ideas probably emerged out of Naokata's experience when he and Asami Keisai, having been expelled from the Kimon school for differing with Ansai, then broke off relations with one another because they themselves had divergent views. When Ogyū Sorai said of the Kimon school that its members were men of questionable character, [124] Naokata responded:

Considerations of character should not enter into discussions of the rightness or wrongness of reasons or teachings. If what a person says corresponds to reason, then even if he be a wicked man, it should be counted good. If what a man says diverges from reason, then even if he be a good man, it should be counted as evil. [125]

The internal link between a thought and the character of the person thinking it was not allowed for by Naokata's intellectualism and rationalism. That he did not lapse into sentimentality was one of the characteristics of Naokata's thought and one of its strong points. Yet if his rationalism culminated in a purely formalistic rationalism—as we see in his views on the Akō Rōnin Incident of 1702 [126]—it was because of this distinction between a thinker and his thoughts.

As I suggested earlier, Naokata's intellectualism and his rationalism were tied to his intense self-reliance, and this tendency in Naokata's speculation led him to the following conclusion:

If a scholar does not have faith in his own principles, he cannot be trusted. It is all well and good to believe in the sages, but it is not as good as believing in oneself. [127]

These are words which other Shushigaku Confucians in China, Korea, and Japan might have said but were never able to. We should recall that Sorai considered the Shushigaku idea of plumbing principle (*kyūri*) dangerous and foresaw its logical outcome, arguing in *Benmei* [n] that, "the ·

plumbing of principle will undoubtedly lead to the rejection of the sages." While Naokata did not go so far as to reject the sages, there is no denying that he came precariously close to fulfilling Sorai's prediction with his apotheosis of the "principle in the self." Or, at least, it was ideas like those of Naokata which aroused the fears expressed by Sorai in *Benmei*.

It should now be clear that at the heart of Naokata's conception of *jitsugaku* was the idea of plumbing principle, with principle here being understood in a metaphysical and ethical sense. In his view, the true *jitsugaku* was Shushigaku, in which the Supreme Ultimate (or principle) was identified with the sage, and in which one sought sagehood by transforming his physical nature; for him, the most essential form of practice involved combining abiding in reverence with the exhausting of principle.

How then did he conceive principle? As has been suggested, Naokata was one of the ablest expositors of the metaphysical and moral dimension of Chu Hsi's conception of principle. This is exemplified in his *Taikyoku kōgi*[fu] (Exposition of the Supreme Ultimate), found in the eleventh chapter of *Unzōroku*. Naokata argued, first, that it was a mistake to see yin and yang as emerging out of the Supreme Ultimate; second, that it was because Han and T'ang scholars perceived the Supreme Ultimate in concrete terms, as "a thing" (*i-wu*),[fv] that they could not correctly understand the Way of the sages; third, that Chou Tun-i's representation of the Supreme Ultimate in terms of "the Infinite and yet also the Supreme Ultimate" suggested its unfathomability, and it was on account of the unfathomability of the Supreme Ultimate that it could be seen as arising and functioning through being borne by the material force of yin and yang (the assumption being that it is erroneous to interpret the Supreme Ultimate as a thing that first exists and then activates yin and yang); fourth, that the Supreme Ultimate as an actual entity does not exist, for all that exists within Heaven-and-earth is yin and yang. The Supreme Ultimate, however, is the reason behind the operation and existence of yin and yang as yin and yang. As such it is the metaphysical substance of principle and the Way, and its existence is postulated as what ought to be.[128] His understanding of Chu Hsi's theory of the Supreme Ultimate was correct. As Tomoeda Ryūtarō observes, Naokata was one of the few Japanese Confucians to achieve this. Moreover, his understanding of Shushigaku was orthodox, and it should not be overlooked that an interpretation such as Naokata's represented the mainstream in Korea and China. The fusion of Shushigaku and Western learning, an integration based on an interpretation of principle that stressed its empirical aspect, was the characteristic achievement of Japanese Shushigaku, a fact which has not generally been recognized in the history of Shushigaku.

With his particular view of the Supreme Ultimate, it was natural for Naokata to accept both the theory that principle "neither arises nor disintegrates" (pu-sheng pu-mieh),[fw] and the theory that "principle is prior to material force" (li hsien ch'i hou).[fx] Like Sorai, he felt that the investigation of things and the plumbing of principle with respect to natural phenomena was unnecessary. However, he did not reject the investigation of things and the plumbing of principle by the sages in respect to their devotion to the livelihood of the people. According to Naokata:

If the Supreme Ultimate is inherent in the ten thousand principles, then if there were a sage who was in accord with the Supreme Ultimate, we would expect him to know the ten thousand principles.[129]

Although I have already introduced his views on principle, there remains the problem of the relationship between his vitalistic philosophy and his rationalistic thought. Asami Keisai is said to have noted, "Gorōemon (Naokata) is one of a kind. Though he is endowed with a frightening temperament, no one understands principle as well as he." When one considers Naokata's pronouncements on the Akō Rōnin Incident, one is struck by his severity. His attitude appears to have been that one should, in deciding such matters, deductively apply the logic of principle, dispensing with considerations of feeling. His view is unusual among Japanese. It is not that the conventional view that Ansai and Keisai were emotional, while Naokata was intellectual, is incorrect, yet one wonders nonetheless whether Naokata really excluded the emotions from his considerations. If they were really excluded, then what of their relationship with his vitalism? In his collected works, there are passages which seem to anticipate Motoori Norinaga's[fy] theory of the emotions:

There is nothing so purposeless as to be without a sense of sympathy. When one—and this is true of everyone—gives away a cherished possession, to give it away saying, "this is precious," or "this is exquisite," or "be content with it," is not to give it away with sympathy. Bad though it is, the desire between men and women is a feeling which arises naturally from mutual sympathy. Give something to someone with true affection, and statements like those described above will go unsaid. So too is this true with learning. One may read innumerable books, but if

one reads them without a sense of sympathy, they will be of little benefit. . . .
To think that learning is the way of men and to think that it suffices simply to
know humaneness, righteousness, decorum and wisdom is to consider them only
theoretically. To have one's heart utterly set on something, that is sympathy . . .[130]

This is just one example. In his mastery of the emotions, Naokata was
second to none. Yet why, in spite of his understanding of the emotions,
did he sacrifice the emotions to principle? As of this writing, I have no
fully satisfactory answer to this problem. I am inclined to the view that
his rationalistic thought, which was based on moral principle, had no
place in his vitalistic philosophy and was developed independent of the
context of life as a whole. I should not be too hasty in drawing conclusions as to whether this feature of his thought is idiosyncratic or whether
it originated in the form of Shushigaku. Perhaps this was one aspect of
Shushigaku, which, filtered through Naokata's peculiar vision, emerged
with new emphasis. At any rate, it was precisely the kind of Shushigaku
that Naokata championed that was opposed by the Confucians who
created the Ancient Learning school. Their criticism was that his position
was one in which concepts such as principle and reverence were used to
judge men cruelly. Jinsai, for example, placed special importance on
humaneness as the central virtue in place of reverence. But we should
not overlook the fact that the vitalistic philosophy which supported Jinsai's idea of humaneness was shared by Naokata. Ekken's Shushigaku,
which emphasized an empirical principle, and even Naokata's Shushigaku, which emphasized a metaphysical principle, were, at least in this one
underlying respect, linked to the Ancient Learning.

THE SCHOLARS OF ANCIENT LEARNING: THEIR IDEA OF JITSUGAKU AND THEIR CRITICISMS OF CHU HSI'S CONCEPT OF PLUMBING PRINCIPLE

The Quest for a New Attitude Toward Man—the Case of Yamaga Soko and Ito Jinsai

Here I would like to discuss Yamaga Sokō,[tz] Itō Jinsai, and Ogyū
Sorai, who were scholars of Ancient Learning. Although today we group
them as a school, they were not, in fact, tied by the customary master-

disciple relationships. Certainly, Sorai recognized Jinsai as his forerunner, though by criticizing Jinsai, he established his own standpoint as a thinker and scholar. Sokō and Jinsai, however, were neither related nor linked in any way. Sokō, a masterless warrior, lived in Edo, while Jinsai was a Kyoto townsman. Yet they set forth their views as scholars of Ancient Learning at roughly the same time—Sokō in 1661 and Jinsai in 1662.

What I am calling here "Ancient Learning" aimed at returning to Confucius and the other sages of ancient times. Its advocates claimed that the Confucianism of the Han and T'ang dynasties as well as the new Confucianism of the Sung and Ming dynasties had deviated from what they considered true Confucianism. And while the views of the three men differed in some respects, they were yet remarkably similar. For example, while Sokō and Jinsai started out in Shushigaku, both grew dissatisfied with it and were drawn either to Taoism and Buddhism or to Yōmeigaku, and both ended up returning to Confucius. Both Sokō and Jinsai spent long years searching for a new outlook on human nature. Neither was able to endure the rigidity of Shushigaku or the antiquarianism of Han and T'ang Confucianism. They sought the affirmation of man's desires, and as a concomitant of this, they believed that the refinement of man's desires should become the basis for morality. Although morality was a central concern for Chu Hsi, his approach was indirect— one either exhausted the principle of things or concentrated one's mind. What the scholars of Ancient Learning wanted was an active rather than a contemplative philosophy, and they found this in the teachings of Confucius. It was his teachings, in their view, which emancipated human nature.

Although the basic ideas of Sokō and Jinsai were similar, differences in personality and in the circumstances in which they lived made their learning and thought in some respects quite different. In the first place, Sokō, who was the son of a masterless warrior, remained acutely conscious of his special status and worked to blend Confucianism and military science and thereby transform Confucianism into a teaching for the warrior class. By contrast, Jinsai, who was the son of a townsman, and as such, generally freer, aimed at making Confucianism a universalistic teaching. In the second place, Sokō was far less concerned with methodological issues than was Jinsai. It might be expected that the scholars of Ancient Learning, in dissociating themselves from the followers of Wang Yang-ming, would have stressed the importance of the classics and have made them, rather than the mind, the basis for their learning. Sokō, however, did not feel that this was necessary. To deny the validity of Chu Hsi's ideas, it was necessary to discredit the Four Book-centered approach from which they derived. As Sagara Tōru has pointed out, Sokō stopped at "disputing Chu Hsi within the sphere of Shushigaku."[131] In this sense, it is probably more appropriate to consider Itō Jinsai the founder of the school of Ancient Learning. At any rate, it was the humanistic view of man formulated by Sokō and Jinsai which served as the basis for Sorai's philological research on the classics.

The *Jitsugaku* of Yamaga Sokō

Yamaga Sokō at one time called his learning *jitsugaku* and at another time, "Sagely Learning."[cs] He used the latter term to distinguish his views from those of the adherents of Shushigaku and Yōmeigaku who often called their own views *jitsugaku*. In Sokō's use of the term *"jitsugaku,"* we sense that what he meant was practical learning for everyday life. He wrote:

If what we learn is not practiced and reflected upon, it should be called the "learning of mouth and ear," and it is not a true and real learning.[132]

It is useless to compare those who read literary works and do not know *"jitsugaku"* with knowledgeable men who have experience with the affairs and things of this world. . . . Men of letters, because of their ignorance of current affairs, are familiar with neither the trends of the present time nor the affairs of ancient times. As a rule, if one does not study *jitsugaku*, literary knowledge can become inimical to daily practice.[133]

Sokō developed this idea of practical learning in what he called Sagely Learning:

In Sagely Learning, neither literary study nor scholarship per se is necessary. If each day we concentrate on implementing what we have learned in ordinary affairs, that is enough, and no special effort or method of holding to reverence or the practice of quiet-sitting is necessary.[134]

This is the standpoint from which he criticized the Confucianism of the early Tokugawa period. He believed that Confucianism in his day was of two types: *jitsugaku*, and what might be rendered as "vulgar learning." The latter referred to a Confucianism that centered on exegesis and commentaries in the manner of Han and T'ang Confucianism, while the former referred to the philosophies of Chu Hsi and Wang Yang-ming. Needless to say, he preferred *jitsugaku* to vulgar learning. His preference notwithstanding, Sokō was also critical of the kind of *jitsugaku* that was associated with the schools of Chu Hsi and Wang Yang-ming, as we see in the following:

Jitsugaku has the merit of discussing the Way, inquiring into moral principles through study of the classics, savoring the mind and human nature, discriminating the Way of the King from that of the hegemon, discussing humaneness and justice. It also considers as fundamental cultivating one's person, ruling the state and bringing peace to the world. Yet there are shortcomings in its aims and methods of inquiry.[135]

Sokō then pointed out five such shortcomings. First, the practitioners of *jitsugaku* were too fond of discussion and seemed merely to toy with learning. Second, they trifled with human nature and were interested in empty and distant things. Third, they respected only the Way of the King[ga] and deprecated the value of the Way of the hegemon.[gb] Fourth, they admired the revolts of King T'ang[gc] and King Wu[gd] while despising the arts of war. Here we see his desire to join military science and Confucianism. Fifth, these vulgar Confucians did not know the true meaning of humaneness, confusing it with the "compassion" (*jikei*)[ge] of the heterodox sects. What enabled Sokō to make this criticism was his view of Sagely Learning as an ethical theory for daily life. Asking rhetorically, "To what end does learning exist?" he answered, "It exists to extend itself to the ordinary things of daily life and to mend the Way." Needless to say, ethical practice in daily life, as he defined it, included the political function of ruling the state and pacifying the world as well as the military science which he viewed as one means of realizing this function.

One of the characteristics of Sokō's Confucianism is the affirmation of humanity. "Desire,"[gf] he once argued, "is an expression of human nature and the act of responding to external reality. If one lacks such feelings, he is not a man. In general, whoever has knowledge has feelings of desire." Or more briefly, "He who flees from desire is not a man."[136] Originally, Confucianism as a secular morality did not categorically deny ordinary human desires. However, Chu Hsi had advocated returning to man's original nature[gg] as against his physical nature[gh] and favored the principle of Heaven as against human desire. In other words, his view of human nature was rigoristic, as we see in the case of Hayashi Razan, an earnest devotee of Chu Hsi's teachings. If this is kept in mind, then Sokō's assertion that man's intellectual existence and his desires are inseparable and that one who lacks desires is not a man was nothing short of epoch-making. For Sokō, the admission that human desires were natural and acceptable raised the problem of how they were to be moderated. Here he suggested that this was possible through the investigation of things and the extension of knowledge. He explained that learning is the extension of knowledge, and that it is by means of this extension of knowledge that we can free ourselves from illusion and temper our desires.

Behind this idea was a new concept of principle, and Sokō's notion of plumbing principle differed from Chu Hsi's. While Sokō did not completely deny Chu Hsi's theory of the diverse particularizations of a unitary principle, he did believe that the transformation of principle into Heaven-and-earth and the myriad things cannot be grasped in terms of a single principle. That is, he saw Chu Hsi's idea of a unitary principle and diverse particularizations as a theory which placed excessive importance on a unitary principle, and thus reduced a complex world to the simplicity of the single principle. Against this, he formulated a new view which sought to see the complexities of the actual world as they really were, in the fullness of their complexity. In his view, principle was confined to the world of events and things. And as the world is the sum of the myriad things within it, the investigation of things and the extension of knowledge involved seeking the law (or particular principle) of each affair and thing. By grasping the law of each thing, he tells us, man can moderate his desires, for the law of each affair and thing is ritual. As Sokō put it, "If principle is in disorder, neither the prior and the posterior nor the root and the branch will be correct."

Self-cultivation, as Sokō described it, was not to center on the mind, but was to be accomplished when one achieved a responsiveness to everyday things. The embodiment of this ethical outlook which so emphasized outward activity was *Shidō*,[gi] the Way of the warrior—which, given its strongly rational character, should be distinguished from what might be called the "emotional *Bushidō*" of such warrior classics as *Hagakure*.[gj] Sokō endeavored to combine *Bushidō* with Confucianism. In his vision of what should be, the warrior—unlike the farmer, craftsman, and merchant, who were always busy at work—was spared from having to worry about making a living and could thus devote himself to serving as a model for the people. In Japan, warriors were to become gentlemen, an event virtually unimaginable in China where gentlemen were more highly esteemed than warriors.

The Idea of *Jitsugaku* and the Concept of the Way in Itō Jinsai

As far as I know, there are only two places where Jinsai actually spoke of *jitsugaku*. Further, it is extremely difficult to ascertain what he meant by *jitsugaku* from statements such as, "When there is *jitsugaku*, there is real virtue,[gk] and where there is true virtue, there is real talent."[gl][137] Owing to this difficulty, when scholars discuss the history of *jitsugaku*, they usually exclude Jinsai. Yet there are many places where Jinsai used the word "real":[ad] real principle,[gm] real words,[gn] real places,[go] real heart,[gp] real knowledge,[gq] real perception,[gr] and real virtue. Jinsai considered that after the time of Mencius, learning had become "empty," and he devoted his life to establishing true and real learning.

What then did he consider real? This is not an easy question to answer, but the following may be helpful:

You may think there is surely a supremely noble, supremely high, bright and shining and wonderfully felicitous principle apart from what you see and hear. But there is not. Within Heaven and earth, there is only one real principle. Apart from this there is no miraculous principle.[138]

As is clear here, to Jinsai, there is nothing real outside experience. He also noted, "If we do not study culture, then our wisdom is biased. This is the case with the learning of Buddhism and Taoism. If we do not practice it, then our learning is empty. This is the case with the learning of vulgar Confucians."[139] Jinsai's view is that those who do not study the classics but confine themselves to scrutinizing the mind are one-sided, while the learning of those who do not engage in actual practice is empty and unreal. Jinsai added, "When it is ordinary,[gs] it is real. When it is lofty,[gt] it is surely empty. Therefore learning does not scorn the ordinary and the familiar."[140] Reality, for Jinsai, exists in commonplace, ordinary, and familiar things. Phrases such as "fidelity and faithfulness[gu] are the real and true heart"[141] and "love emerges from the 'real and true heart' "[142] suggest that, for Jinsai, the term "real" implied not merely a name but a concrete reality and, at the same time, conveyed the sense of truthfulness and sincerity. His statement that, "The principle of equilibrium is empty, while the virtue of humaneness and righteousness is real,"[143] illustrates the fact that he saw the real as something determinate which could serve as a clear standard. In addition, Jinsai held that *jitsugaku*, as the learning of morality, was useful and that it rested on real virtue and real talent.

His use of the word, "real," reveals that it included a number of meanings ranging from morality to objective fact. Moreover, his statement that, "The essence of learning is moral and its function is seeing and hearing,"[144] suggests that his concept of *jitsugaku* represents a connecting link between the *jitsugaku* of moral practicality of the early Tokugawa period and Sorai's *jitsugaku* of objective fact. Yet Jinsai was also an independent and profound thinker, and the significance of his thought transcends whatever function it may have served in providing a conceptual link or conduit for ideas. We are obliged to look more deeply into what he was seeking when he endowed *jitsugaku* with so many meanings, and we should try to discover what was regarded as real in the context of his Ancient Learning as a whole.

Although Sokō asserted the concept of Ancient Learning before Jinsai, the latter, as I suggested earlier, may be considered its true founder. For unlike Sokō, who accepted Chu Hsi's view of the Four Books, Jinsai directly challenged this understanding of orthodoxy. In his eyes, the *Analects* was the best book in the cosmos; the *Mencius* he valued for the insights it offered into the *Analects*. But, contrary to Chu Hsi, Jinsai believed that the *Great Learning* was not attributable to Confucius and that the *Mean* was actually composed of passages taken from other works. His discussion of the heterogeneity of the Four Books, which Chu Hsi believed to be a single, unified corpus, and on which he based his system of thought, was tantamount to a reversal of Chu Hsi's point of view. Especially noteworthy in this regard is the reason for his evaluation of the *Great Learning*. Its denial of such passions as anger, fear, joy, and sorrow, he pointed out, does not agree with Confucius' expression of sorrow on the death of Yen Yüan as related in the *Analects*. From this, he proceeded philologically to the conclusion that the *Great Learning* was not attributable to Confucius.[145] His method cannot really be described as a scientific philology. It would be more appropriate to regard it as a kind of philosophical philology based on his understanding of man, an approach which reflects rather well the distinctive features of Jinsai's thought. We might even describe his learning as a kind of philosophical anthropology.

The basis of Jinsai's thought is his vitalistic view of the cosmos. "The sages," he wrote, "take Heaven and earth as a living and active thing, while the heterodox take it as a dead thing."[146] He considered the essence of the teachings of the sages to lie in a vitalistic understanding of the cosmos. For him, material force is the origin of the reality of the cosmos, for "within Heaven-and-earth, there is only one original material force."[147] And the Way of Heaven is the ceaseless movement of the coming and going of the two forces, yin and yang. From this point of view, principle is merely the organizing principle within material force itself.[148]

Jinsai carried his denial of Chu Hsi's ideas even further. He recognized, for example, the objection that could be lodged from the side of scholars of the Chu Hsi school against his idea that after the separation of Heaven-and-earth there might exist only a single primal material force, but that before their separation only principle exists, and this is the infinite or the Supreme Ultimate. Jinsai's point was that this view was based solely on the imagination, since no one has any knowledge of the time before the beginning of Heaven-and-earth. His cosmogony is reminiscent of Kant in that it argues that the same evidence can be used to establish either that the universe has a beginning and end or that it does not.[149] Therefore, he reasoned that there is no reality save for a developing cosmos, the features of which can be grasped by our senses. Jinsai also denied Chu Hsi's assertion that, "It is the Way that brings yin and yang into operation," when he wrote that "the ceaseless alternation of yin and yang is itself the Way."[150]

All of creation in this active and living cosmos must be apprehended in terms of the living beings which constitute it. In place of Chu Hsi's concept of "principle" which made living things into dead things, Jinsai offered a view of "the Way" in which living things are understood as living things. Furthermore, morality, in his eyes, was the supreme self-manifestation of life, and man, who was supreme among those things endowed with life, was a moral agent. The basic principle of behavior for man as a moral agent and the basic principle of life was "the Way." By contrast, "principle" was merely a principle of existence. At any rate, for Jinsai, the Way was a living word[gv] whereas principle was a dead word.[gw]

It should be clear from the foregoing that the idea of the Way occupied the most important place in Jinsai's thought. Faithful to the *Book of Changes*, he divided the Way into the Way of Heaven,[di] the Way of earth,[gx] and the Way of man.[dj] Each had its distinguishing qualities: yin and yang are the Way of Heaven; the hard and the soft are the Way of earth; and humaneness and righteousness are the Way of man. These qualities must not be confused. We also see in his separation of things into categories, a distinction between what ought to be and what is. And among the three Ways, it is the Way of man that he was most interested in.

In his discussion of the Way of man, Jinsai distinguished human nature, the Way, and teachings. The Way here means morality, or more concretely, the Five Relationships. As Jinsai himself noted: "There is no Way apart from man and man does not exist apart from the Way."[151] If one were to look only at this statement, it would appear that, for Jinsai, the Way was purely immanent in man. But the following explanation of the relation between the Way and man's nature reveals that this is not so, for the Way also possesses a transcendental character which puts it beyond man:

What is spoken of as human nature exists in ourselves; the Way extends throughout Heaven and earth. . . . Therefore when man exists, human nature exists. When man does not exist, neither does his nature exist. The Way exists of itself, regardless of whether man exists or not.[152]

It is in these terms that he criticized Chu Hsi's description of human nature as the root and the Way as the branch. In Jinsai's eyes, Chu Hsi reversed their proper relationship. Of human nature, the Way, and teachings, he placed the highest value on the Way. He did not believe, however, that the Way could transform men into sages. The evidence he adduced for this was the passage in the *Analects* which said that, "The Way does not enlarge man; it is man that enlarges the Way." Jinsai did argue, however, for the importance of teachings, and this presupposed an object capable of receiving them; and this, of course, was human nature. While he did not deny the importance of human nature, he placed greater store by teaching than by human nature since teaching establishes differences of superior and inferior among men who originally have similar natures.

Jinsai also believed that, contrary to what Chu Hsi had suggested, true moral practice cannot develop simply by abandoning the desires, quieting the mind and thus returning to the original nature. Jinsai defined moral practice in terms of the "enlargement"[gy] of which Mencius had often spoken, and he believed that this "enlargement" was possible only when

"human nature is fulfilled." Since he recognized that human nature is
limited and finite, merely fulfilling it would not be sufficient to assist in
the transforming and nourishing of the universe. What makes this possible is the power of education, and it is through education that essentially
finite human nature can be enlarged so as to help to transform and
nourish the universe. What makes education possible? It is Mencius' so-
called "four beginnings." Following Mencius, Jinsai argued that every
human being is endowed with a mind which contains the four beginnings. When we develop our natural sense of sympathy or commiseration,
shame and dislike, modesty and yielding, and our sense of right and
wrong, the virtues of humaneness, righteousness, decorum, and wisdom
are brought into play. In order to bring them into play, counseled Jinsai,
an active moral practice is necessary. Here we see that his theory of morality is essentially dynamic, which puts it in nearly diametrical opposition
to Chu Hsi's notions of "being free of desires and preserving tranquillity."[gz] and of "clarifying the mind so it is like a shining mirror and still water."[ha][153]

Among the four virtues of humaneness, righteousness, decorum, and
wisdom, humaneness was, for Jinsai, the central virtue.

The virtue of humaneness is great. If we summarize it in one word, it is none
other than love.[154]

Love emerges from the true heart. Therefore if the five virtues of human relationship emerge from love, then they are true. If they do not, then they are false.
Thus, there is no greater virtue than the compassionate love of the gentleman,
and there is nothing more miserable than cruelty and coldheartedness. This is
why humaneness is considered the chief virtue of Confucianism.[155]

Jinsai did not call humaneness the principle of love, as Chu Hsi had, but
said simply that humaneness was love.[156] Humaneness was not perceived
as an abstract principle which serves as the ground for the establishment
of love, but rather was seen as the love which issues from the very sources
of human life. Thus Jinsai's vitalism was inextricably tied to his understanding of humaneness.

Jinsai was at one with traditional Confucianism in taking the five constant virtues of human relationship to be a universal morality. But if these
virtues were merely external norms not supported by love, there was the
danger that the practice of them would be infected with hypocrisy. Seeing
this danger in Chu Hsi's idea of reverence, Jinsai wrote:

He who exclusively preserves the virtue of "reverence" has a particular interest in acting with dignity and in insuring that his appearance is proper. Therefore, although his mien may be that of a solemn and respectable Confucian, when we look into his inner nature, we find that his sincerity is hollow, that he is exceedingly concerned with himself, and that he is cruel in his accusations against others. It is impossible to list all his faults.[157]

In his conception of humaneness as love, Jinsai also reached new heights as we see in the following passage:

When the mind of compassionate love penetrates outward from within, when it is everywhere in the world, when there is no place where it does not reach, and when there is not even the smallest hint of cruelness or coldheartedness, this is humaneness. What exists in one man but does not extend to another is not humaneness. When the mind of humaneness exists in one's breathing and fills one's dreams and sleep, when one's mind does not depart from love and love fills one's mind, and when in the mingling of love and the mind a state of total unity is attained, this is truly humaneness.[158]

Jinsai's ideal world is a community of love, that state in which man feels, "I shall love others, and they shall love me."[159] He whose ideals do not go beyond self-purification, however sincere he may be, is not a man of humaneness. It is only "when love emerges from the true mind and extends to other people" that one can speak of humaneness.[160]

On the relation between learning and humaneness, Jinsai tells us that, "when learning attains 'humaneness,' it becomes real virtue."[161] And "when real learning exists, then real virtue exists. And when real virtue exists, then real talent follows."[162] In view of this, we can conclude that, for Jinsai, *jitsugaku* was a form of moral practice which was to be carried out in daily life and which was to expand an inborn sense of sympathy and commiseration that was to become an infinite love for others. His phrase, "real talent follows" suggests that this is a view which he shared with Sorai.

The Concept of the Way in Ogyū Sorai and his Idea of *Jitsugaku*

Sorai's ideas are not radically different from Jinsai's. Both men criticized the philosophy of human nature and principle proposed by Chu Hsi and both advocated a rediscovery of Confucianism. They differed in the nature of their criticisms and in their definitions of Ancient Learning. Jinsai's studies are usually called *kogigaku*[hb] and Sorai's *kobunjigaku*.[hc]

They are different in that the former aimed at philosophical explanations of the meaning of the teachings of Confucius, while the latter employed philological methods to clarify the teachings of the ancient kings (the sages). Behind these differences lie different concepts of the Way.

The following passage from *Benmei* illustrates Sorai's concept of the Way:

There is that which we call the Way of Heaven and that which we call the Way of earth. In their midst hang the sun, moon and stars; within them move the wind, thunder, clouds and rain; and heat and cold, day and night ceaselessly alternate.

What we call the Way of Heaven is impenetrable in its depth and profundity and unfathomable in its mystery. The ten thousand things begin from it, and good luck or ill luck, weal or woe seem to be destined by it, though we know it not. When we ponder it quietly, it is as if there is something from which these things derive. Therefore, we call it the Way of Heaven.

What we call the Way of earth bears up mountains but is not burdened. Making rivers and seas flow, it releases no water. It is so immense, its end cannot be reached. It is so deep, it cannot be exhausted. Though the lives of the ten thousand things issue from it, it does not diminish. Neither does it increase when the ten thousand things return to it in death. When we are close to it, we can know it though there will still be much that is unknown. When we carefully consider it, it is as if there is something from which these things derive. Therefore, we call this the Way of earth.

We call them this—the Way of Heaven and the Way of earth—in analogy to the Way of the sages.[163]

Whereas Chu Hsi thought of the Way as principle, Jinsai had divided it into the Way of Heaven, the Way of earth, and the Way of man. Sorai took Jinsai's views a bit further so that the Way of Heaven and the Way of earth are seen "as if" they existed—which is reminiscent of Hans Vaihinger's notion of *als ob*, or "as if."[164] For Sorai only the Way of man exists for certain; the existence of the other two Ways can only be inferred. His view of Heaven was agnostic: Heaven cannot be known but is merely to be the object of awe and respect.

Sorai's thought appears to have been influenced by Hsün Tzu's[hd] concept of ritual and music. The concept of ritual, which was central to the *Analects* was developed by Sorai, whose own thought centered on ritual and music and on the achievements of the sages whom Confucius venerated, especially Yao and Shun, the creators of ritual and music.[165] For Sorai the Way does not consist of the virtues attained through the "enlargement" of the mind of the four beginnings, and he criticized Jinsai for a "misreading" of Mencius on this point:

By misreading Mencius, Jinsai advocates achieving virtue by enlarging the four beginnings. What difference is there between him and Chu Hsi? . . . The point of contention between them is only whether virtue is complete after the process of cultivation or is complete in one's nature to begin with. Thus the term "virtue" must apply to what has yet to be accomplished, which means that it is name only and not reality. He reverts in the end to the moral theories of the Sung Confucians.[166]

Of course, the similarity between Jinsai's moral theories and those of the Sung Confucians is not as complete as Sorai would have us believe. Given Sorai's view of the Way as the concrete social morality of ritual, music, and government, the moral theories of Jinsai and Chu Hsi might seem to be similar. It is for this reason that Maruyama Masao sees the transition from Jinsai's moral theories to Sorai's as analogous to the transition from Kant's moral theory of *Moralität* to Hegel's theory of *Sittlichkeit*.[167]

We might say that, for Sorai, the Way was the Way of governing the country and making the lives of the people stable, and it consisted of "ritual and music, punishment and government," or in other words, the institutions and civilization created by the Early Kings. That Sorai chose to define the Way in these terms may reflect the fact that he was not a moralizer by temperament and that his view of the mind was rather pessimistic.

The mind has no form. We cannot regulate it by catching hold of it. Therefore, the Way of the Early Kings was to regulate the mind through ritual. To say there is a way to control the mind apart from ritual is narrowness and delusion. Why do I say this? The mind, in this view, is both that which rules and that which is ruled. Controlling the mind by means of the mind is like a madman controlling his own madness. How can he do so?[168]

A realist, Sorai had little faith in the good will of people at large, and even less in Chu Hsi's belief in moral politics and in Jinsai's assumption that man is fundamentally moral. What Sorai believed in was governing through institutions.

These institutions were to be fundamentally cultural in nature, not simply expressions of power. In his view, the Way was mediated by culture and included art and skill. He rejected both the unqualified naturalism of Lao Tzu and the moralism of Chu Hsi. He also differed from most Confucians in believing that the sages were sages because they created ritual and music and not because they embodied morality. In speaking of ritual and music he referred to the institutions first created by Yao and Shun and thereafter refined by succeeding generations of sages.

While he recognized the historical development of the Way, Sorai thought it had been completed with Confucius. Thus, there was a chasm between the Early Kings and the sages who were the creators of the Way on the one hand and modern man on the other. He felt that it was the task of Confucianism to elucidate the Way of the Early Kings—namely, ritual and music—through clarifying the language and the facts which were its concrete manifestations. Naturally his system of thought centered on the Five Classics or the Six Classics in contrast to Chu Hsi's focus on the Four Books or Jinsai's concentration on the *Analects* and *Mencius*. The rationale of Sorai's choice, of course, was that the words and actions of the Early Kings were described in the Five Classics.

Sorai's attempt to clarify the Way of the Early Kings was based on the assumption that, "the world changes, carrying with it language; language changes, carrying with it the Way."[169] Thus, reading the classics which were written in an ancient language as though they were written in a contemporary language should be prohibited. The underlying principle of his philology which sought to clarify the Way of the Early Kings through a reading of the classics was that, "What is essential in learning is humble attention to words and facts, not grandiose speculation about man's nature and destiny."[170] Sorai learned this from the Ming scholars Li P'anlung[he] (1514–1570) and Wang Shih-chen[hf] (1526–1590), but unlike Li and Wang, who worked mainly at writing literary compositions in the classical style, he aimed at developing methods which would permit a new philological interpretation of the Six Classics. He once contrasted his methods with those of the Sung Confucians:

In their commentaries, the Sung Confucians merely speak of the principle which they seek in their own minds, so that principle does not have a definite criterion. The minds of the sages cannot be fathomed. Only a sage can understand a sage. Are the Sung Confucians not arrogant in what they do?[171]

Speaking of Wang Yang-ming and Itō Jinsai, he wrote:

Yang-ming and Jinsai criticize the Sung Confucians but they do so only on the basis of their own minds; they do not know to inquire about word and fact, and because of this, they are of a kind with the Sung scholars.[172]

The Way is lofty and beautiful. A man as bereft of talent as I cannot possibly realize it. Therefore, I seek it with humility in word and fact. I believe that the task of the Confucian can only be accomplished adequately if he preserves the classics of the ancient sages and transmits them to future generations.[173]

In view of the foregoing, it is clear that Sorai's *kobunjigaku* was closely related to his political thought. However, a concern for political matters was shared by all Confucians. The uniqueness of this positivistic *kobunjigaku* and of Sorai's political approach may be categorized as follows. First, he did not view politics as an extension of morality as had the Shushigaku scholars. Second, eschewing subjectivism, he saw politics as a phenomenon of the objective world and insisted on taking an institutional view. Third, his institutional view was not limited to a narrow understanding of politics based on power, but concentrated on cultural elements such as ritual and music. It was not that Sorai ignored "punishments and governing"—the realistic aspect of politics; however, cultural elements such as ritual and music were at the heart of his institutional theory, and he believed that an institutional political model which was based on ritual and music had been established by Yao and Shun in ancient China. Fourth, he saw the psychology of the governed, or to use his word, *ninjō*,[hg] as an important component of politics. More crucial to rulers than illumining their own bright virtue was knowing the psychology of their subjects. Fifth, he distinguished the practitioners of politics from the scholars who studied it, and consciously counted himself among the latter. Unlike Kumazawa Banzan, Sorai neither lauded practitioners of a Confucian-style politics as "noble men," nor belittled professional Confucian scholars as "mean or small men." The functions of the politician and the scholar were differentiated. Confucians who were scholars were to understand correctly the "Way" of the Early Kings as described in the classics, transmit it to later ages, and offer the sources of political knowledge to politicians. Sorai wrote the political-economic *Seidan*[hh] and *Taiheisaku*[hi] from the standpoint of a scholar, which set him apart from Banzan, who always thought from the standpoint of a statesman.

Sorai argued that, "in general, the Way of learning does not exist apart from writing,"[174] and that "learning is confined to history."[175] The former shows the importance of the "word"[hj] in his idea of learning, and the latter the importance of "fact."[hk] He combined this view of "fact" with his concept of *jitsugaku*. Here he compared two styles of historiography, one of which was positivistic and the other moralistic. It is the former, he argued, that is written from the standpoint of *jitsugaku*, while the latter, as an essentially moralistic account, is not. Here he cited Ssu-ma Kuang's[hl] *Tzu-chih t'ung-chien*[hm] (Comprehensive Mirror for Aid in Government) as an example of a positivistic account and Chu Hsi's *Tzu-chih t'ung-chien kang-mu*[hn] (General Outline of the Comprehensive Mirror for Aid in Government) as an example of a moralistic account. He explained:

Although vulgar scholars think that they can understand moral principle by reading the *Tzu-chih t'ung-chien kang-mu*, this should not be called *jitsugaku*. . . . The discussions in this work verge on the stereotypical in their presentation of moral principle as something fixed and rigid. Though Heaven and earth are active, living things, as is man, they are bound up here as if in fetters. Learning like this is truly useless, serving only to increase a man's verbal acuity. The *Tzu-chih t'ung-chien*, which consists only of facts, is far superior.[176]

In this passage, Sorai advanced a new concept of *jitsugaku*: it is positivistic learning, free from value judgments and based on a recognition of facts.

Sorai's high regard for facts, coupled with his description of the Way as essentially diverse, evolved into the idea that, "The Hundred Schools and the Nine Teachings and even the deviations of Buddhism and Taoism are all offshoots of the Way."[177] Thus his research and his intellectual concern were not confined to the Five Classics but extended also to the Hundred Schools and to a wide variety of subjects, including theories of music, military science, law, and current affairs. His interest in language was no less broad. It is probably not too much to say that the flowering of arts and learning in the latter half of the Tokugawa period owed much to the influence of Sorai's ideas.

Before Sorai, moral action had always been seen as a crucial aspect of *jitsugaku*, although the concept of the nature of moral action differed from thinker to thinker. With Sorai, this traditional moralistic *jitsugaku* was transformed into a positivistic *jitsugaku*, which was truly a revolutionary development in the history of this concept.[178] Was it possible for Sorai to separate politics and morality and the public and private spheres and yet to remain within the framework of Confucianism? Or had his definition of *jitsugaku* carried him beyond the bounds of Confucianism itself? For Sorai himself there was no loss of theoretical consistency, for the indispensable element in Confucianism was faith in the sages:

To follow the Way of the Early Kings is called right and not to follow their Way is called evil.[179]

Sorai made the Way of the King an absolute criterion. He continued:

As a stupid old man, I believe deeply in the sages. Even when I think to myself that something cannot be, I tell myself that as it is the Way of the Sages, surely it cannot be wrong, and then I act upon it.[180]

I, a stupid old man, do not believe in Buddha. I believe in the sages.[181]

This faith in the sages was what kept Sorai's thought within the framework of Confucianism and what gave unity to his ideas.

The Problem of Principle in Sorai

Sorai's reinterpretation of *jitsugaku* was immensely important, but he himself did not accomplish the fusion of *jitsugaku* and empirical rationalism. To understand why this was so, it is necessary to review the development of the concept of principle in the context of Ancient Learning. Yamaga Sokō, it will be remembered, differed from the Chu Hsi school in that he did not believe that the myriad things with all their multiformity and diversity could be discussed in terms of a single principle. Neither did he agree that the plumbing of principle (*kyūri*) was equivalent to the investigation of things. For Sokō, principle was limited to the world of events and things, and he denied the applicability of the concept to human nature and Heaven. His was the first real challenge to Chu Hsi's notion of principle.

Sokō's idea of principle was, in turn, inherited by Jinsai who emphasized the Way more than principle and who, as the more philosophical of the two, delved more deeply into the problem. Jinsai abandoned the idea of the Way as a single continuous entity and chose to divide it into the Way of Heaven, earth, and man, allotting distinct and separate functions to each. For example, in the sphere of events and things the relevant function was to "plumb principle," in the sphere of man, it was to "fulfill one's nature," and in the sphere of Heaven, it was to "attain the mandate." Jinsai also followed Sokō when he confined the plumbing of principle to the world of events and things. But the reasons he gave for this were his own; we do not find them in Sokō's writings. Jinsai said that the idea of principle was not suitable as the source of production and reproduction.[ho] Underlying this view was his metaphysics of vitalism, or, in other words, his philosophy of *ch'i* or material force. In the formulation of this philosophy of *ch'i*, the essential cause lay in the affirmation of a vitalistic cosmology which grew out of the experiences of Jinsai's own youth and spiritual agony. For Jinsai, to discuss the Way of Heaven from the standpoint of principle amounted to "burning it to death." The idea of principle which Jinsai advocated was not "principle opposed to material force," that is, not an a priori and abstract metaphysical principle, but a "principle of material force," that is, a concrete experiential principle predicated on the vital and living reality of "primal material force." As Jinsai wrote in *Dōjimon*[hp] (Boy's Questions):

In living things, there is the principle of living things. In dead things, there is the principle of dead things. In man, there is the principle of man. In things, there are the principles of things. But a single primal material force is the basis, and principle is posterior to material force.[182]

In addition to the criticisms which stemmed from his vitalism, Jinsai adduced various other reasons for denying the Shushigaku idea of plumbing principle. First, the affairs of the world are complex, so complex that one cannot evaluate them, as Chu Hsi did, in the light of a single principle. Second, if we look for humaneness in terms of principle, we will actually move farther away from it, and it will, in turn, become more and more unknowable. Third, if we rely exclusively on principle in judging affairs, cruelty and coldheartedness are sure to overwhelm tolerance and humaneness. Finally, if we seek to plumb principle, we are actually deferring the fundamental task of Confucianism, the practice of virtue. For Jinsai, then, the practice of humaneness was the main task of Confucianism. Discussing humaneness as a love which flows steadily from the source of man's life rather as a spring flows and gushes forth, he believed that humaneness was to be grasped intuitively through daily application, not in lofty and abstruse discussions about the plumbing of principle.

Jinsai, however, did not deny the plumbing of principle itself. He merely asserted that it should not be the central focus of Confucianism. We see this in his view that,

People in ancient times did not neglect the investigation of the principles of things. However, they considered cultivating the self and governing the people as the main tasks of learning. They did not pour their energies into the investigation of the principles of things, but saw it as an ancillary task. In later times, people have made the "investigation of things and the plumbing of principle" the primary tasks of Confucianism. So today there are few who do not seek principle by assiduously investigating and probing things as diverse as astronomy, geography, law, calendrical science, military science, penology, agriculture, horticulture, medicine, and divination and things as minute as a tree and a single blade of grass.[183]

Jinsai's views conform, of course, to the original Confucian definition of learning as the practice of virtue. Yet that important element of modern thought—the idea of rational inquiry concerning things and events—did not emerge in Jinsai's thought as it had in that of Kaibara Ekken. Jinsai did not completely reject inquiry into the principles of things but saw this pursuit as one that required simultaneous attention. There was ample room in his thought for the accommodation of Western learning and the rational investigation of nature, though when we compare Jinsai's view of plumbing or explaining principle with Ekken's, we see that Ekken's thought, which combined inquiry into the "principles of the mind" and the "principles of things," was formally richer in possibilities than Jinsai's. This is true in spite of the fact that Ekken failed to reflect philosophically on the differences between these two kinds of principle, having gone no further than to establish a relatively simple distinction between them and to allow them to coexist.

We now turn to Ogyū Sorai, who was less concerned than Jinsai with the philosophical problem of the relationship of principle and material force, but attacked more strenuously than Jinsai ever had the Shushigaku notion of plumbing principle. Yet there is a kind of continuity between Jinsai's idea that, "Since the emergence of the philosophy of principle and nature, many Confucians have come to regard themselves very highly,"[184] and Sorai's conviction that, "In the plumbing of principle, Confucians will come to reject the sages."[185] On the other hand, there was also a world of difference between them, for Jinsai's approach was fundamentally moral, while Sorai's was undeniably political.

Sorai wrote:

Principle naturally inheres in each event and thing. Through extending our minds to consider these events and things, we may make inferences about what is necessarily proper for them and what is improper for them. We call this principle. In general, when people want to do good, they perceive the principle whereby it is possible and hence they do it. When people want to do evil, they perceive the principle whereby it is possible and hence they do it. In either case, our minds perceive what is possible and, on this basis, we do it. Therefore principle does not represent a fixed criterion.[186]

For Sorai, everything had its own principle. In order to know this principle, we are obliged to rely on our own minds to make inferences, and in so doing, we know what must necessarily be so and what must not be so. This is principle. Although principle exists objectively, it can only be known through the participation of the subject. And if principle is known in this way, it becomes purely subjective and can hardly be regarded as an objective criterion.

We should remember, however, that when Sorai described principle as subjective and said it cannot serve as an objective standard, he was speaking of the subjectivity of principle in respect to ethical problems. As evidence of this subjectivity, he cited the different responses of Po-i[hq] and Tao Chih[hr] on seeing some wheat gluten. The former felt it would be a suitable food for the aged, while the latter imagined it would be useful in breaking into a house since it could be used to muffle the sound of a door opening. As is clear from this example, Sorai was rejecting the *Shushigaku* idea that principle is the standard for thought and action. He did this by separating the principle of the ethical world, that is, the principle of what ought to be, from the principle of the natural world, that is, the principle of what is. Sorai's observation that for the most part the world of ethics is subjective is correct only as long as our view of ethics is empirical. Once the existence of transcendental value is admitted, it can no longer be considered correct. The issue, of course, is whether an ethical principle can be considered solely in empirical terms, and this is a problem which lies beyond the scope of this paper. The problem that confronts us here is how Sorai saw principle in the world of nature.

Kaibara Ekken and Nishikawa Joken, their differences notwithstanding, recognized the validity of Chu Hsi's conception of principle in the world of morality. Yet at the same time they also postulated the existence of an objective principle in the world of nature, one independent of Chu Hsi's essentially speculative principle. Sorai, in contrast, chose to deny the continuity of morality and politics and the objective existence of principle in the moral sphere. And at the same time, he was skeptical about the existence of objective principles, which meant that he was thoroughgoing in his denial of the possibility of a speculative principle in the world of nature.

Sorai's agnosticism, which led him to argue that we should not say we know Heaven, but rather that we feel awe and respect for Heaven, carried over to his view of natural phenomena. Of thunder, he once wrote: "As the phenomena of the miraculous and unfathomable Heaven and earth are in their origins unknowable, we had better leave the problem of thunder as it is." [187]

And in his criticism of the Shushigaku advocacy of the plumbing of principle in the world, he wrote:

Since the Sung philosophers erred in their understanding of the meaning of "the investigation of things and the extension of knowledge," men came to define learning as plumbing the principles of such things as the wind, clouds, thunder, rain, and even of a single tree or a single blade of grass. If we examine their motivations, we find that they are dedicated to becoming well-informed men who plumb everything in Heaven and earth and thereby leave nothing unknown." [188]

Sorai's criticism of a notion of principle which was bound up either with speculation or with value judgments was based on his rejection of a continuity between moral and natural principle. In a sense, this was a logical consequence of his positivistic definition of *jitsugaku*. But his rejection of the Shushigaku concept of plumbing principle was accompanied by a rejection of any attempt to explain natural phenomena. He was struck by the sheer stupidity of the theories of yin and yang and the five agents, and eschewed the search for laws governing natural phenomena. This means that his empiricism or positivism was, as far as nature was concerned, little more than an uncritical empiricism, or what might be called pure "factualism."[hs] There was no attempt to reconstruct experimentally the objects of perception. This, indeed, is the deficiency of Sorai's thought as modern thought.[189]

Why did he reject the possibility of plumbing principle? He gave a number of reasons for his choice. First, it is not possible for ordinary men to plumb the principles of the world, for this is a task reserved for the sages. Second, the term, "plumbing principle," referred originally to the creation of the *Book of Changes* by the sages. Classical Confucianism, furthermore, does not admit the possibility that ordinary men can plumb principle. Third, in his claim that if we plumb principles one by one, "we will suddenly achieve a great enlightenment," Chu Hsi had been influenced by Buddhism. Fourth, principle is minute. The Sung Confucians who wanted to proceed through study of the minute to attain a grasp of larger things failed to understand that minor misconceptions about small matters can easily grow to become major misconceptions about great matters. This was why the sages looked first at what was great and as a result, made almost no mistakes about what was small.

Sorai's last point is especially interesting since it shows that his methodology was based on an intuitive understanding of what was great, rather than on a process which moved from analysis to synthesis. It also reveals that his scholarly method was not that of natural science but rather was modelled on the methods of statecraft and on the experience of rulers in actual social and political affairs. The most important reason for his rejection of the idea of plumbing principle is revealed in the following:

The Way of the Early Kings rested solely on respect for Heaven and the ghosts and spirits. This is because its main concern was humaneness. Latter-day Confucians value knowledge and examine principle, thus destroying the Way of the Early Kings and Confucius. Owing to the shortcomings of this notion of examining principle, they have come to feel that it is no longer necessary to fear Heaven and the ghosts and spirits, and they pride themselves on occupying an independent place between Heaven and earth. This is a common failing among later Confucians. Aren't they saying [as did the Buddha,] "In Heaven and earth I alone am to be reverenced"? How can this infinite universe be investigated? How can we fully investigate all its principles? If I say that I know all principles in Heaven and earth, I am deluded. Therefore everything they preach, while outwardly respectful of the Early Kings and Confucius, actually opposes them. Their intention is to be able to express what the sages of antiquity left unexpressed, and they fail to realize they are actually aiming to surpass the Early Kings and Confucius. Yet the teachings of the sages are complete. How can they be surpassed?[190]

Here Sorai is saying that the examination of principle in Shushigaku is based on the self-assertion of the individual. This is dangerous because it can lead man to lose his awe and respect for Heaven and for ghosts and spirits, and if fear and respect for them, which are essential to Confucianism, are lost, the result will be nothing less than the denial of Confucianism itself. Given his view that Confucianism was a creation of the Early Kings and Confucius, the desire to plumb principle struck him as little more than an egoistic urge to surpass the sages. Elsewhere he concluded that, "The error of plumbing principle is that it inevitably leads to the rejection of the sages."[191]

Of course, Shushigaku did not actually lead to this. Yet if one were to extend to its logical conclusion the Shushigaku idea of plumbing principle, there is the possibility that the examination of principle would give rise to self-consciousness. As Yasunaga Toshinobu has observed, the following important passage occurs in the sixty-seventh *chüan* of the *Chu Tzu wen-chi*: "The mind is the means by which people govern themselves. It is one, not two. It is master, not guest. It commands things and is not commanded by them."

We must acknowledge, as Yasunaga does, that, "These are the signs of a fearfully precocious subjective self."[192] Whether Sorai was actually aware of this, we do not know. We might imagine that he had ample opportunity to see this in passages like the following, which was written by Satō Naokata:

If a scholar does not have faith in his own principles, he cannot be trusted. It is all well and good to believe in the sages and worthies, but it is not as good as believing in oneself.[193]

In such an attitude Sorai foresaw the abolition of the sages. In his call for belief in the sages, we see the refutation of the concept of plumbing principle. In his anti-intellectualism we may find a prognosis of the effects of Shushigaku intellectualism.

JITSUGAKU AFTER SORAI: A PERSPECTIVE ON THE PROBLEM OF PRINCIPLE

Among the empirical rationalists who followed Sorai, there were those like Yamagata Bantō and Sakuma Shōzan who held Shushigaku views, identified the empirical rationalism in Shushigaku and Western science as one and the same thing, and accepted the latter in the same terms that they accepted the former. There was also Miura Baien[ht] (1723–1789), a representative natural philosopher of the late eighteenth century who wrote from the standpoint of an independent empirical rationalism. Baien rejected Sorai's denial of principle as lacking standards at the same time that he abandoned the speculative rationalism of Shushigaku. He chose to seek his own way and eventually created his own system of natural philosophy.[194]

There remain a number of important problems related to Sorai's view of principle which may be clarified through a consideration of the ways in which he influenced the study of medicine. Sorai exerted some influence both on traditional medical practices, as illustrated in the case of

Yoshimasu Tōdō[hu] (1702–1773), and on modern Western studies, as indicated in the case of Sugita Gempaku.

On the subject of principle, Tōdō once wrote:

Those who speak of principle are determined to apply it to each thing and to explore it in every event. When there is something they cannot understand, they lay the blame on the fact that there are gaps in principle. It is not that there is any fault to be found with principle; the fault lies only with the gaps. They talk about a principle which underlies the hundred illnesses, and when it comes to the fact that it is difficult to cure them, this too is attributed to the gaps. Principle provides no definite standard, while the illness has definite symptoms. How can we expect to employ a principle which lacks any definite standard to treat a disease which has definite symptoms?[195]

With an anti-rationalistic "factualism" like that of Sorai, Tōdō here criticizes the medical practices of Li Shu[hv] and endorses the more ancient tradition of Pien Ch'üeh[hw] and Chung Ching.[hx] While he is to be praised for rejecting the fallacious doctrines and principles of Li Shu, it was precisely this disinterest in the search for the causes of illness that prevented medicine from becoming modern. In this respect Tōdō displays an affinity with Sorai, who likewise rejected the search for the causes of natural phenomena or of natural laws. We can probably conclude that Tōdō developed Sorai's basic concept of principle—a concept found in the latter's important philosophical works such as Bendō[hy] and Benmei—and applied it to the world of medicine.

Let us now turn to Gempaku. It was, oddly enough, Sorai's idea of military principles as developed in Kenroku gaisho,[hz] which exerted an influence on the formation of modern medicine. According to the research of Fujikawa Yū and Satō Shōsuke, Gempaku, one of Japan's pioneers in Western learning, first perceived the correctness of Confucianism after reading this work and subsequently started his own research on Western learning. Here it was Sorai's conception of the relationship between military principles and military techniques that was the intellectual stimulus for Gempaku. Sorai's argument was that in military science, techniques together with developments in weaponry change with the times, while principles remain constant. Yet because these principles do not exist apart from technique, which evolves historically, they must be perceived through an understanding of military works, and this understanding was to be based on objective and empirical methods like those employed by Sorai in philological research on the classics. Sorai's view that, after grasping military principles in this manner, "one considers the nature of the age and then devises changes in the patterns of military technique" made Gempaku aware of the errors of Chinese and Japanese medicine and led him to write:

I now know that true medical practices exist in the distant Western country of Holland. These medical practices exist because they take as the fundamentals of the Way investigating and knowing in detail the anatomical structure and the internal and external functioning of the human body.[196]

By contrast with Tōdō, who rejected the speculative character of Li Shu's medical studies by pointing out that principle afforded no fixed criteria and who saw the search for the root causes of illnesses as meaningless, Gempaku recognized that a perception of medical principles based on an anatomical knowledge of the body and its structure is the essential condition for curing illness. He also recognized the need for research on the causes of illnesses. What we see here in Gempaku is medicine emerging from a traditional into a modern form.

Upon reading *Kenroku gaisho*, which was published recently, we find that "military techniques"[ia] are given greater weight than the "military strategies,"[ib] which had been so prominent in military science up to then. And as descriptions of the relationship of "military principle"[ic] and "military technique" occupy only a very small part of this work, we also have some idea of Gempaku's perspicacity in noting the significance of these sections.

It is hard to deny that the major clues to Gempaku's new ideas are found within Sorai's writings. If this is the case, we should reexamine Sorai's view of principle. As was shown earlier, Sorai, for a variety of reasons, rejected Chu Hsi's concept of plumbing principle, proposing instead that man believe in the sages and feel awe and respect for Heaven. He also advocated, on the basis of his anti-rationalism, "factualism" and positivism. Up to now these elements have been considered fundamental to Sorai's thought. Sorai's influence on Tōdō and the description of him by Miura Baien as "the man who abjured principle" can be seen in this light.

Kenroku gaisho was an esoteric text. As long as it was transmitted only in handwritten copies, it was natural that Sorai was viewed as an anti-rationalist. On a cursory reading of *Bendō*, it seems that Sorai was an empiricist who rather self-consciously refuted Chu Hsi's view of the inves-

tigation of things and the exhausting of principle. If we carefully read
Bendō and *Benmei*, however, we find that Sorai also offers us a glimpse of
his rationalist side, as when he wrote, "Principle inheres in all events and
things." But, for Sorai, as we saw earlier, the sages and the sages alone
have the ability to plumb principle. He did not recognize the average
man's ability to do this, since to have done so would have meant the destruction of Confucianism. Sorai's anti-rationalism—namely, his denial
of the possibility of the plumbing of principle and his belief in the sages
and in the worship of ghosts and spirits—preserved Confucianism as a
system of thought. It was Sorai's fiction. Through his "veneration of word
and fact," he established his philosophy and a theory of government
rooted in the Way of the Early Kings. It was an indispensable fiction. Or,
if "fiction" seems too strong a word, let us call it a "necessary postulate,"
without which his system of ideas would possibly have collapsed.

If we assume that Sorai saw the sages as sages not because of their virtue but because they created institutions, then this belief in the sages is
not a simple idolization of the sages. Rather it manifests a tendency
toward a kind of utilitarianism. Even his worship of ghosts and spirits was
an attitude which, from the point of view of ruling and pacifying the
country, was in conformity with the sentiments of the people. Here too
we see a utilitarian tendency.

The view of principle which is found at various points in his works is
not always negative. I doubt that a man with Sorai's capacity for rationality could have altogether failed to recognize the possibility of
plumbing principle, and the following passage supports such a view:

Still, I do not want to see scholars abolishing, under my influence, the theories of
the Sung Confucians and the various schools. The past is distant from the present
and the Six Classics remain incomplete. We cannot but make inferences on the
basis of principle; and inferring on the basis of principle was first employed by the
Sung Confucians as an opening volley. But their principle was still far from being
precise, and because of this, principle became an impediment. We have to make
it more and more precise. Why should we consider this to have been an error on
the part of the Sung Confucians and the various schools?[197]

Exactly how "inferring by means of principle" is related to what Sorai
says about "investigating principle" is unclear, and this is deserving of our
attention. What is clear is that Sorai and Chu Hsi differed in their thinking about the investigation of things, which was linked with the plumbing
of principle. "To investigate things," for Chu Hsi, meant "to go to" or

"to reach" things. This was an extremely natural interpretation in the case of Chu Hsi who took the plumbing of principle as the aim of scholarly inquiry. But Sorai, seeing this as a kind of hubris on the part of men in thinking to plumb principle, said, "The error of plumbing principle is that it inevitably leads to the rejection of the sages." Thus he interpreted the investigation of things as "coming or arising from things." Sorai explained that things were the basic articles of teaching and spoke about the investigation of things as naturally grasping things from long familiarity with them, or studying things for a long time so they naturally become clear. In contrast to Chu Hsi's plumbing of principle, which involved the active pursuit of principle by the subjective self, Sorai's had a passive character. This view perhaps arose from his experience as a philologist who comes to an understanding of difficult terms after long exposure to them, sharing a common experience with those involved in scholarly studies of a linguistic character. It is a fine method for humanistic studies but certainly to be distinguished from scientific method. Within the limits of this methodological awareness, principle was not to be rejected. That he did not totally reject Chu Hsi's philosophy was probably because he recognized in Chu Hsi a superb textual critic. Sorai's scholarship itself reflected the influence of Hayashi family scholarship. What he rejected in Chu Hsi's philosophy was its natural scientific aspect and its speculative metaphysics, as well as the plumbing of principle, which supported them, but he did not totally reject Chu Hsi's rationalism which itself contained a positivistic character. While having a great sensitivity to the irrational side of human life, in his scholarly studies he did not discard rational methods.

Many, including his own successors, have been "blinded" by Sorai's rather forceful statements in *Tōmonsho*[id] where he wrote:

Whether with the Buddhists or the Confucians, all theory is a matter of conjecture, and matters of conjecture are not to be relied upon.[198]

As a fact of intellectual history, Sorai has been cast as an anti-rationalist and a "factualist" by all but those who have read *Kenroku gaisho*. Sorai, in fact, did not succeed in establishing an intellectual standpoint which fused, on the one hand, the positivism and empiricism which rested on the anti-rationalist fiction of his belief in the sages and his denial of the possibility of the exhausting of principle and, on the other hand, the rationalism found in his conception of military principles. What we conclude from all this is that there were two Sorais—the philologist Sorai and the speculative Sorai—interacting within the same person. Thus Sorai as a thinker is full of contradictions in his system of thought. What probably supported him as a human being was his feeling of awe and respect for Heaven and Heaven's mandate. For this was at the crux of his political thought. There was even a religious feeling supporting this personality with its many contradictions caused by the conflicting demands created by an insatiable intellectual appetite. With his death, a variety of movements which had been united only in his person, splintered. The fusion of Sorai's anti-rationalistic empiricism and positivism with his empirical rationalism was left to the *jitsugaku* thinkers who followed him. Its philosophical solution had to wait for the early Meiji philosopher, Nishi Amane.

Translated by Samuel H. Yamashita

NOTES

1. Yasuda Jirō, *Chūgoku kinsei shisōshi kenkyū*[ie] (Tokyo: Kōbundō, 1948).
2. Shimada Kenji, *Shushigaku to Yōmeigaku*[if] (Tokyo: Iwanami, 1967), p. 89.
3. Abe Yoshio, *Nihon Shushigaku to Chōsen*[ig] (Tokyo: Tokyo daigaku shuppankai, 1965).
4. *Seika sensei gyōjō*, in Koito Natsujirō and Ōta Heisaburō, eds., *Fujiwara Seika shū*[ih] (Tokyo: Kokumin seishin bunka kenkyūjo, 1941), 1:8.
5. *Razan sensei bunshū*[ii] (Kyōto shiseki kai ed.) (Kyoto: Heian kōkō gakkai, 1919–1922), 3:32–33.
6. *Zoku zoku gunsho ruijū,*[ij] Kokusho kankōkai, comp. (Tokyo: Kokusho kankōkai, 1906–1909), 10:76.
7. For example, Razan cited Confucius' statements indicating that he was devoted to the music of Shun (*Analects*, III: 25), the seasons of Hsia, the state carriages of Yin, the ceremonial caps of Chou (*Analects*, XV: 10, ii–iv), and yet that he "followed the Chou" (*Analects*, III: 14). See Sagara Tōru, *Kinsei Nihon ni okeru jukyō undō no keifu*[ik] (Tokyo: Kōbundō, 1955), p. 23.
8. Abe, *Nihon Shushigaku to Chōsen*, pp. 204, 520.
9. *Ibid.*
10. *Razan sensei bunshū*, 1:229.
11. *Ibid.*, p. 388.
12. *Ibid.*, p. 400.
13. *Ibid.*, p. 380.
14. *Ibid.*
15. Sagara, *Jukyō undō no keifu*, pp. 20–31.
16. *Razan sensei bunshū*, 2:372.
17. *Ibid.*, p. 373.
18. I have benefited immensely from Sagara Tōru's discussion of this in *Jukyō undō no keifu*.
19. In *Gakuryō ryōken sho*,[bk] Sorai praised the educational policies and style of learning of Hayashi Razan and Hayashi Gahō[il] (1618–1680). For in Razan's idea of the five curricula—the first is widely studying the various theories of the ancients, without overly adhering to Shushigaku; the second is reading for broad learning; the third is excellence in poetry; the fourth is excellence in prose as well; and the fifth is Japanese studies, which meant covering the whole range of things Japanese—there was special emphasis on talent and individuality, and peace and order were to be achieved by expanding what was each person's outstanding quality. Sorai referred to this as a "house rule passed on by Razan,"[im] and he thought to create theories of education based on it. Thus, we know that he conceived his own learning as an extension of Razan's, and the latter, of course, took broad learning as its base. Ogyū Sorai, *Gakuryō ryōken sho* in Yoshikawa Kōjirō et al., eds., *Ogyū Sorai zenshū*[in] (Tokyo: Mizusu shobō, 1973), 1:565–71.

20. *Tōju sensei zenshū*,[io] Katō Moriichi et al., eds. (Kyoto: Tōju jinja kyōsankai, 1928), 1:122–23.

21. *Ibid.*, 3:248–49.

22. *Tōju sensei nenpu*,[ip] in Yamanoi Yū et al. eds., *Nakae Tōju, Nihon shisō taikei*[iq] (NST) (Tokyo: Iwanami, 1974), 29:288.

23. For Tōju's views on these problems, see the third chapter of *Okina mondō*,[bo] *Tōju sensei zenshū*, 3:198–202.

24. Kaji Nobuyuki, in his article, "Kōkyō keimō,"[ir] in NST, 29:408–62, introduces Sakurai Hisajirō's "Iyo Ōzu-han Niiya-han no bunkyō,"[is] which is found in *Ehime ken kyōikushi*[it] 1:66–217 (Ehime: 1971).

25. The influence of Wang Yang-ming and Wang Chi on Tōju is discussed in Sagara Tōru, *Jukyō undō no keifū*, pp. 45–59, and in Bitō Masahide, *Nihon hōken shisōshi kenkyū*[iu] (Tokyo: Aoki, 1961), pp. 136–216. This author also benefited greatly from Yamashita Ryūji's "Chūgoku shisō to Tōju,"[iv] which is the first thorough study of the influence of late Ming thought beginning with Wang Yang-ming and Wang Chi on Japanese Confucians. It appears in NST, 29:356–407.

26. See *Tōju sensei zenshū*, 1:18–21.

27. *Ibid.*, 3:106.

28. *Ibid.*, 3:103–106.

29. *Ibid.*, pp. 170–71.

30. *Ibid.*, pp. 107–8.

31. *Ibid.*, p. 109.

32. *Ibid.*, 1:410.

33. In a private communication to the author.

34. Bitō, *Nihon hōken shisōshi kenkyū*, pp. 163–64.

35. *Tōju sensei zenshū*, 3:250.

36. *Ibid.*, p. 139.

37. *Ibid.*, pp. 192–93.

38. See Yamashita Ryūji's note in NST, 29:136.

39. *Tōju sensei zenshū*, 3:238–39.

40. *Ibid.*, p. 241.

41. See Bitō, *Nihon hōken shisōshi kenkyū*, pp. 185–94.

42. *Tōju sensei zenshū*, 2:14.

43. *Ibid.*, p. 24.

44. See for example Watsuji Tetsurō's view as presented in his *Nihon rinri shisōshi*,[iw] (Tokyo: Iwanami, 1953). Although Maruyama Masao in his *Nihon seiji shisōshi kenkyū*,[ix] (Tokyo: Tokyo daigaku shuppankai, 1952) does not deal with Banzan, he does characterize Banzan's ethical learning as "trite ethical teachings."

45. According to Gotō Yōichi's "Kumazawa Banzan no shōgai to shisō no keisei,"[iy] in *Kumazawa Banzan* in NST, 30:467–534, Tōju noted in a letter of 1643 to Banzan: "I think that, even if only temporarily, it is important to realize with utter concentration the method of the mind which centers on harmony. . . . .The absence of prejudice, willfulness, obstinacy and egoism

is the basis of equilibrium and harmony" (NST, 30:473). According to Gotō, Banzan inherited this particular aspect of Tōju's thought early in his career, as we see in *Jikkai no zu* and *Yamato nishi no mei* which were written when he was thirty-two. Later, after he had gained administrative experience, he wrote *Shūgi washo*, in which he revived Tōju's idea of time, place, and rank as discussed in *Okina mondō*.

46. NST, 30:254–55.
47. *Ibid.*, p. 394.
48. *Banzan zenshū*,[iz] Masamune Atsuo, ed. (Tokyo: Banzan zenshū kankōkai, 1940–1942), 4:64.
49. NST, 30:263.
50. *Ibid.*, p. 321.
51. *Ibid.*, p. 298.
52. *Ibid.*, p. 175.
53. *Ibid.*, p. 194.
54. *Ibid.*, p. 275.
55. *Shinpō zukai* in NST, 30:101–07. Watsuji Tetsurō argued that it had been really written by Tōju. He claimed that the explanations of metaphysical principles are rather dogmatic, and above and beyond the fact that they lacked the persuasive power of Banzan's other pieces, Banzan was not interested in such things. *Watsuji Tetsurō zenshū*, Furukawa Tesshi et al., eds. (Tokyo: Iwanami, 1961–1963), 13:166. If one carefully reads *Shūgi washo*, it seems that what Banzan is saying corresponds rather well with what he says in *Shinpō zukai*. In the latter, Banzan presented in abstract form the highly concrete ideas of *Shūgi washo*. Though metaphysics was not Banzan's forte, this does not mean that he was not interested in such problems.
56. NST, 30:107.
57. *Ibid.*, p. 106. Concerning *Shinpō zukai* and Banzan's theory of principle and material force, I have learned a great deal from Tomoeda Ryūtarō's notes to the texts in NST, 30, and from his "Kumazawa Banzan to Chūgoku shisō."[Ja]
58. NST, 30:106–07.
59. *Banzan zenshū*, 3:285.
60. NST, 30:299.
61. *Ibid.*, p. 300.
62. *Ibid.*, p. 159.
63. *Ibid.*, pp. 159–60.
64. *Banzan zenshū*, 6:67.
65. NST, 30:344.
66. In *Shūgi washo*, kan 12, 13, 14, Banzan developed the idea that the "exhaustive exploration of principle" was necessary for politicians.
67. NST, 30:141.
68. *Ibid.*
69. *Ibid.*, pp. 213–14.
70. *Ibid.*, pp. 163–64.

71. *Ibid.*, p. 380.
72. *Ibid.*, p. 10.
73. *Ibid.*, p. 81.
74. *Ibid.*, p. 177.
75. *Ibid.*, p. 195.
76. *Ibid.*, p. 157.
77. *Ibid.*, p. 78.
78. *Ibid.*, p. 97.
79. Ian James McMullen in his "Kumazawa Banzan and *Jitsugaku*: Toward Pragmatic Action" (this volume, pp. 337–74) views Banzan's *jitsugaku* as leading towards Sorai's *jitsugaku*. Although our perspectives are different, I learned much from his essay.
80. *Nippon rinri ihen,*[jb] Inoue Tetsujirō and Kanie Yoshimaru, eds. (2d ed.; Kyoto: Rinsen, 1970), 8:12.
81. *Ekken zenshū*[jc] Ekken kai, ed. (Tokyo: Ekken kai, 1910–1911), 3:60.
82. In *Taigiroku*[ej] Ekken gave the following evaluation of Lo Ch'in-shun: "The learning of Lo Ch'in-shun is not marked by adulation of the Sung Confucians. In his words, 'Principle is merely the principle of material force.' And again, 'Principle must be identified in the context of material force.' I venture to say that the Sung Confucians divided principle and material force into two things, and later Confucians slavishly adhered to the views of their Sung predecessors without being capable of differing with them. Only Master Lo honored the Ch'eng brothers and Chu Hsi as his teachers without subscribing uncritically to their views. His opinions should be considered most correct and appropriate." (*Ekken zenshū* 2:162)
83. Dazai Shundai, "Shundai sensei Sonken sensei no *Taigiroku* o yomu,"[jd] NRI, 8:206.
84. *Ibid.*, p. 14.
85. *Ibid.*, p. 101.
86. For Professor Okada's views on Ekken's idea of "total substance and great functioning," see his contribution to this symposium, this volume, pp. 281–82.
87. NRI, 8:95.
88. *Ibid.*, p. 24.
89. *Ibid.*, pp. 92–93.
90. *Ibid.*, p. 14.
91. *Ibid.*, p. 158.
92. *Ibid.*, p. 63.
93. *Ekken zenshū*, 6:18.
94. NRI, 8:144.
95. *Ibid.*, p. 12.
96. *Ibid.*, p. 11.
97. *Ekken zenshū*, 6:2.
98. NRI, 8:144.
99. *Kaibara Ekken shū,*[je] commentary and notes by Takigawa Masajirō, in *Kinsei*

shakai keizai gakusetsu taikei, (Tokyo: Seibundō shinkōsha, 1936), p. 130.

100. There is a famous anecdote which tells how Miyazaki Yasusada, when he was writing his Nōgyō zensho, asked Ekken's older brother, Rakuken (1625–1702), to write the preface for this work. Rakuken subscribed to the custom current among Confucians of not treating "lowly things," and thus refused, though later, upon more fully understanding its purposes, he contributed a supplement to the work.

101. NRI, 8:22.

102. *Ibid.,* p. 108.

103. For more on the characteristics of Ansai's thought, see Abe Yoshio, *Nihon Shushigaku to Chōsen,* pp. 253–69.

104. Hayashi Razan was dissatisfied with his teacher Seika's adoption of ideas from both Chu Hsi and Lu Hsiang-shan, and argued that one should distinguish between the two and accept only Chu Hsi's ideas. See *Razan sensei bunshū,* 1:12–15. For Seika's reply to all this, see Sagara Tōru, *Jukyō undō no keifū,* pp. 14–17.

105. Denki gakkai, ed., *Yamazaki Ansai to sono monryū*[jf] (Tokyo: Meiji shobō, 1941), p. 5.

106. See Abe Yoshio's discussion of this in *Nihon Shushigaku to Chōsen,* especially *Jinsetsu mondō shisetsu,* pp. 348–56, and *Kokoro no toku-ai no risetsu,* pp. 360–63.

107. Naokata's principle-centered theories were developed in works like *Gakudan zatsuroku,*[jg] *Taikyoku kōgi,*[fu] and *Ōgaku rondan,*[fq] all of which can be found in *Unzōroku.*

108. There is Miyake Shōsai's *Seiron meibi roku,*[jh] which is a transcription of Ansai's lectures. Abe, *Nihon Shushigaku to Chōsen,* pp. 325–26. Ansai's powerful influence can be seen in *Asami sensei gakudan,*[ji] *Kōshū yoroku,*[jj] *Jinsetsu mondō shisetsu,*[jk] and Miyake Shōsai's *Jinsetsu mondō hikki,*[jl] all of which are quoted in Abe's book.

109. *Naokata zenshū,*[jm] ed. Nihon koten gakkai, (Tokyo: Nihon koten gakkai, 1941), p. 19. According to Abe Yoshio, Chu Hsi used the phrase, "as yet unmanifested love,"[jn] in the last years of his life, though only infrequently. Ansai noticed this, and his phrase "the principle of love" is said to refer not simply to the substance of love, but also to this "as yet unmanifested love." Abe, *Nihon Shushigaku to Chōsen,* p. 347. For Ansai's theory see his *Bunkai hitsuroku,*[jo] in *Yamazaki Ansai zenshū,*[jp] 1:186.

110. *Naokata zenshū,* p. 19.

111. *Ibid.,* p. 21.

112. *Ibid.,* p. 22.

113. *Ibid.*

114. *Ibid.,* p. 226.

115. *Ibid.,* p. 221.

116. *Ibid.,* p. 222.

117. *Ibid.,* p. 223.

118. NST, 30:52.

119. *Naokata zenshū*, p. 223.

120. In Naokata's criticism of Tōju, Banzan, and Jinsai (*Naokata zenshū*, p. 220) there is the following passage: "Recently scholars like Nakae, Kumazawa and Itō have appeared, and their arguments ignore the teachings of Confucius, Mencius and the Ch'engs and Chu Hsi. They all seem to be of the Wang Yang-ming stream."

And of Banzan he once wrote (*Naokata zenshū*, p. 221): "Belief in the *Shūgi washo* is the result of its conforming to popular opinion."

121. *Ibid.*, p. 218.

122. *Ibid.*, pp. 216–17.

123. *Ibid.*, p. 22.

124. Ogyū Sorai explained that a fault of the followers of Shushigaku was an unpleasing personality, and he noted, "I have heard that by and large this is true of Yamazaki and Asami." Quoted in Bitō, *Nihon hōken shisōshi kenkyū*, p. 72. The original source of this is *Sorai sensei Tōmonsho*.

125. *Naokata zenshū*, p. 221.

126. For Naokata's criticism of the Akō Rōnin Incident, see Bitō Masahide, *Nihon hōken shisōshi kenkyū*, pp. 105–20. See also my article, "Jushatachi wa dō hyōka shita ka," in *Rekishi to jinbutsu*[jq] (December 1971) and Kojima Yasunori, "Akō rōshi uchiiri jikken," *Tetsugakkaishi*[jr] (October 1973).

127. *Naokata zenshū*, p. 32.

128. See Tomoeda Ryūtarō, "Kumazawa Banzan to Chūgoku shisō, NST, 30:549–50.

129. *Naokata zenshū*, p. 21.

130. *Ibid.*, p. 36.

131. Sagara, *Jukyō undō no keifū*, p. 94.

132. Yamaga Sokō, *Takkyo dōmon*,[js] in *Yamaga Sokō zenshū*,[jt] Hirose Yutaka, ed. (Tokyo: Iwanami, 1940–1941), 12:18.

133. *Ibid.*, p. 23.

134. Yamaga Sokō, *Haisho zanpitsu*,[ju] in *Yamaga Sokō zenshū*, 12:595–96.

135. Yamaga Sokō, *Chihei yōroku*[jv] in *Yamaga Sokō zenshū*, 14:583.

136. Yamaga Sokō, *Takkyo dōmon*, in *Yamaga Sokō zenshū*, 12:172.

137. Itō Jinsai, *Dōjimon, Kinsei shisōka bunshū*,[jw] in *Nihon koten bungaku taikei* (NKBT), Bitō Masahide et al., eds. (Tokyo: Iwanami, 1966), 97:91–92.

138. *Ibid.*, p. 60.

139. *Ibid.*, p. 68.

140. *Ibid.*, p. 73.

141. *Ibid.*, p. 82.

142. *Ibid.*, p. 84.

143. *Ibid.*, p. 99.

144. Itō Jinsai, *Gomō jigi*,[jx] NRI, 5:49.

145. What is described here can be found in Jinsai's "Daigaku wa Kōshi no isho ni arazaru no ben,"[jy] NRI, 5:64–68.

146. Itō Jinsai, *Dōjimon*, NKBT, 97:140.

147. Itō Jinsai, *Gomō jigi*, NRI, 5:11.
148. *Ibid.*, p. 12.
149. See *Ibid.*, pp. 12–13.
150. *Ibid.*, p. 11.
151. Itō Jinsai, *Dōjimon*, NKBT, 97:60.
152. *Ibid.*, p. 65.
153. Jinsai interpreted the character *tan* (*tuan*)[jz] in the concept of the four beginnings, *shi tan* (*ssu tuan*)[bi] as *tancho* (*tuan chu*),[ka] and in opposition to Chu Hsi viewed it rather positively as a "beginning and origin."
154. Itō Jinsai, *Dōjimon*, NKBT 97:84.
155. *Ibid.*
156. Chu Hsi's "humaneness as the principle of love" proved to be a stumbling block for the Kimon school as well. As long as their thought rested basically on a vitalistic philosophy, it was unlikely that they would interpret humaneness as an abstract principle which made love, love. However, unlike Jinsai, they were faithful to Chu Hsi and thus were unable to deny the phrase, "the principle of love." Ansai's solution to this issue was to interpret humaneness as "as yet unmanifested love,"[jn] whereas Abe Yoshio tells us that the theory that humaneness was "as yet unmanifested love" rarely occurred in Chu Hsi's later writings. Ansai also interpreted principle as it occurred in the phrase, "the principle of love" as referring to that which links the "substance" (*tai, t'i*)[kb] and "function" (*yō, yung*).[kc] Among those who subscribed to Ansai's basic ideas, Asami Keisai considered this problem most exhaustively. Here is what he had to say about the "principle of love":
  "What Chu Hsi called the princple of love does not refer to the external, but rather to that inborn and natural love which one possesses even before one begins to love. Love surely is an emotion, but people usually interpret the character *ri* (*li*)[g] as *dōri* (*tao-li*),[kd] and this is the principle of people loving as people should and parents loving as parents should, each in his own way. . . . Humaneness is pity. There are some who are unaware that humaneness is inborn and who describe the principle of love as an external act. This is lamentable. Chu Hsi himself saw the principle of love as inborn, as when he described it as substance and human nature. Chu Hsi said that when one looks at one's parents, the pity one feels before one actually utters the word "pity" is the principle of love. He was viewing love as a state of pure latency. Here substance and function separate naturally, though one cannot speak of substance apart from function, nor function apart from substance. This is the mysteriousness of the words 'the principle of love.' "
157. Itō Jinsai, *Dōjimon*, NKBT, 97:82.
158. *Ibid.*, p. 88.
159. *Ibid.*
160. *Ibid.*, p. 93.
161. *Ibid.*, p. 89.
162. *Ibid.*, p. 92.
163. Ogyū Sorai, *Benmei*, NRI, 6:32.

164. Hans Vaihinger in his major work, *Die philosophie als ob,* insisted upon the practical importance of fictions.

165. Yoshikawa Kōjirō has taken the view that Sorai's notion of ritual, music, governing, and punishment—a single concept in Sorai's thought—was influenced by Chu Hsi's *Chung-yung chang-chü.*[af] See Yoshikawa Kōjirō, "Sorai gakuan,"[ke] in Yoshikawa Kōjirō et al., eds., *Ogyū Sorai,* NST, 36:712 and 728. Yoshikawa does not altogether reject the prevailing view that Sorai was influenced by Hsün Tzu, but he attempts to show that Sorai's notion of ritual, music, governing, and punishment derived also from Chu Hsi.

There is a problem as to the ways in which Sorai was influenced by Hsün Tzu. Maruyama Masao emphasizes the differences between Sorai and Hsün Tzu. See Maruyama Masao, *Nihon seiji shisōshi kenkyū,* pp. 93–94, 116–17. I myself think that, while the influence of Hsün Tzu on Sorai cannot be ignored, there are also significant differences between them. Sorai did not agree with Hsün Tzu's view that human nature is evil. Furthermore, Sorai saw ritual and music as a means of transforming man and nature, whereas Hsün Tzu, with his theory that human nature is evil, believed that the people were to be controlled by the institutions of ritual and music.

166. Ogyū Sorai, *Benmei,* NRI, 6:35.

167. Maruyama Masao, *Nihon seiji shisōshi kenkyū,* p. 86.

168. Ogyū Sorai, *Bendō,* NRI, 6:22.

169. Ogyū Sorai, *Sorai sensei Gakusoku,*[kf] NRI, 6:121.

170. Ogyū Sorai, "Sei-hi Sui-shūsai no toi ni kotau,"[kg] NRI, 6:138.

171. Ogyū Sorai, "Hori Keizan ni kotauru sho,"[kh] NRI, 6:132.

172. *Ibid.*

173. *Ibid.*

174. Ogyū Sorai, *Tōmonsho,* NRI, 6:189.

175. *Ibid.,* p. 153.

176. *Ibid.,* pp. 152–53.

177. Ogyū Sorai, *Gakusoku,* NRI, 6:124.

178. Maruyama Masao sees the conception of *jitsugaku* undergoing a massive change—a "change of Copernican proportions"—in Fukuzawa Yukichi. He calls this the change from a Tokugawa conception of *jitsugaku,* one centering on ethics to one which centered on physics. Generally speaking, it cannot be denied that in many cases *jitsugaku,* in the Tokugawa period, had ethics as its core. But it is also worth noting that a view of *jitsugaku* took shape in Ogyū Sorai which defined *jitsugaku* as learning which is empirical—that is, resting on actual perception—which is free from value judgments, and which does not center on ethics. In Sorai's conception of principle, however, there is both "anti-rational factualism" and "rational experientialism." Given his failure to recognize the necessity of natural scientific perception, we cannot see his views as completely modern. However, it is not that the ethical *jitsugaku* of the Tokugawa period underwent a rapid

and revolutionary change, but rather that in Sorai it changed in one respect. This is an important consideration for our understanding of later Tokugawa thought and for our evaluation of the function the Tokugawa period played in the process of modernization.

179. Ogyū Sorai, Benmei, NRI 6:70.
180. Ogyū Sorai, Tōmonsho, NRI, 6:196.
181. Ibid., p. 172.
182. Itō Jinsai, Dōjimon, NKBT, 97:141.
183. Ibid., p. 169.
184. Ibid., p. 79.
185. Ogyū Sorai, Benmei, NRI, 6:99.
186. Ibid., p. 97.
187. Ogyū Sorai, Tōmonsho, NRI, 6:159.
188. Ibid., pp. 158–59.
189. Both the merits and defects of Sorai's thought are reflected in Yoshimasu Tōdō who applied Sorai's ideas to medicine. Tōdō's standpoint was positivistic. On the one hand, he denied speculative medicine, that is, medicine which adopted the principles of yin and yang and the theory of the five agents; this is his strength. On the other hand, he denied the necessity of scientifically exploring the causes of disease, and this is one of his weaknesses.
190. Ogyū Sorai, Bendō, NRI, 6:23.
191. Ogyū Sorai, Benmei, NRI, 6:99.
192. Yasunaga Toshinobu, "Onozukara naru mono—kinsei shisō ni okeru shizen to ningen," Bungaku[ki] (June 1973), 41:43. In my Tokugawa gōri shisō no keifū,[kj] (Tokyo: Chūō kōron, 1972), I wrote: "If Shushigaku had denied the unity, the connecting link between nature and norm, between nature and man, and made nature its object, and then turned to pursue the laws governing this nature, the birth of the self-consciousness of the self as the basis for the investigation of principle might have been possible. This is something that the history of modern philosophy in the West after Descartes teaches us. Sorai rather astutely recognized this possibility within the Shushigaku idea of exhausting principle and foresaw, logically, the results it would bring."
193. Naokata zenshū, p. 32.
194. Taguchi Masaharu, Miura Baien,[kk] (Tokyo: Yoshikawa kōbunkan, 1967), pp. 318–31.
195. Nihon tetsugaku zensho,[kl] Saegusa Hiroto, ed. (Tokyo: Daiichi shobō, 1936), 7:303.
196. Sugita Genpaku, "Keiei yawa,"[km] Nihon tetsugaku zensho, 7:398.
197. Ogyū Sorai, Bendō, NRI, 6:27.
198. Ogyū Sorai, Tōmonsho, NRI, 6:172.

GLOSSARY

a 實學
b 荻生徂徠
c 杉田玄白
d 西周
e 百一新論
f 朱子學
g 理
h 氣
i 太極圖說解
j 太極
k 無極
l 李退溪
m 山崎闇斎
n 佐藤直方
o 三宅尚斎
p 崎門學派
q 大學補傳
r 朱子語類
s 羅欽順
t 王廷相
u 李栗谷
v 困知記
w 林羅山
x 安東省庵
y 貝原益軒
z 古學
aa 伊藤仁斎
ab 虛學
ac 僞學
ad 實
ae 虛
af 中庸章句
ag 大學章句序
ah 小學
ai 無用
aj 無實
ak 陸象山
al 王陽明

am 陽明學派
an 海保靑陵
ao 福澤諭吉
ap 藤原惺窩
aq 惺窩先生行狀
ar 淸原
as 平安
at 漢
au 唐
av 四書
aw 五經
ax 三德抄
ay 德川家康
az 民部卿法印
ba 熊澤蕃山
bb 幕藩体制
bc 吉田玄之
bd 妙貞問答
be 命
bf 性
bg 道
bh 敎
bi 四端
bj 七情
bk 學寮了簡書
bl 中江藤樹
bm 林氏剃髮受位辨
bn 口耳之學
bo 翁問答
bp 鄉黨
bq 民背，敵應
br 孝經
bs 性理會通
bt 王畿
bu 王龍谿
bv 王龍谿語錄
bw 陽明全集
bx 皇上帝

by 原人
bz 持敬圖說
ca 太乙神
cb 太虛
cc 張載
cd 西銘
ce 主一無適
cf 其心收斂不容一物
cg 畏天命尊德性
ch 中
ci 和
cj 中庸
ck 時中の思想
cl 時處（所）位
cm 論語鄉黨啓蒙翼傳
cn 正眞の學問
co にせの學問
cp 俗儒
cq 墨家
cr 楊氏（朱）
cs 聖學
ct 聖之時
cu 權
cv 知行合一
cw 趙岐
cx 良知
cy 淵岡山
cz 集義和書
da 中和心法
db 實義
dc 心法
dd 人間的眞實追求の學
de 心術
df 無
dg 心法圖解
dh 明德圖解
di 天道
dj 人道
dk 未發之本然
dl 心之神明
dm 愼獨

dn 問學窮理
do 万物一体
dp 五倫
dq 新井白石
dr 法
ds 礼
dt 才
du 本才
dv 誠
dw 幕末
dx 横井小楠
dy 大同
dz 康有爲
ea 中村惕斎
eb 宮崎安貞
ec 向井元升
ed 稲生若水
ee 松岡恕庵
ef 西川如見
eg 木下順庵
eh 有用の學
ei 大和本草
ej 太疑錄
ek 太宰春台
el 愼思錄
em 遺物之學
en 義外之說
eo 異學空誕之說
ep 方技術数之説
eq 全体大用
er 術者
es 博學
et 審問
eu 愼思
ev 明辨
ew 常の理
ex 変の理
ey 多聞多見
ez 修己治人
fa 經世致用
fb 鄙事

fc	山片蟠桃	gr	實見
fd	佐久間象山	gs	卑
fe	五經大全	gt	高
ff	四書大全	gu	忠信
fg	朱子文集	gv	活字
fh	四書章句集注	gw	死字
fi	德富蘇峰	gx	地道
fj	淺見絅斎	gy	擴充
fk	尊王	gz	無欲守靜
fl	名分	ha	明鏡止水
fm	垂加神道	hb	古義學
fn	異端	hc	古文辞學
fo	儀式學問ノ徒	hd	荀子
fp	近思錄	he	李攀龍
fq	王學論談	hf	王世貞
fr	韞藏錄	hg	人情
fs	自反之工夫	hh	政談
ft	辨名	hi	太平策
fu	太極講義	hj	辞
fv	一物	hk	事
fw	不生不滅	hl	司馬光
fx	理先氣後	hm	資治通鑑
fy	本居宣長	hn	資治通鑑綱目
fz	山鹿素行	ho	生生
ga	王道	hp	童子問
gb	覇道	hq	伯夷
gc	湯王	hr	盜跖
gd	武王	hs	事實主義
ge	慈惠	ht	三浦梅園
gf	欲	hu	吉益東洞
gg	本然之性	hv	李朱
gh	氣質之性	hw	扁鵲
gi	士道	hx	仲景
gj	葉隱	hy	辨道
gk	實德	hz	鈐錄外書
gl	實才	ia	軍法
gm	實理	ib	軍術
gn	實語	ic	軍理
go	實處	id	答問書
gp	實心	ie	安田次郎，中國近世思想史研究
gq	實知		

if 島田虔次，朱子学と陽明学
ig 阿部吉雄，日本朱子學と朝鮮
ih 藤原惺窩集
ii 羅山先生文集
ij 續々群書類從
ik 相良亨，近世日本における儒教運動の系譜
il 林鵞峰
im 道春ヨリ傳來ノ家法
in 荻生徂徠全集
io 藤樹先生全集
ip 藤樹先生年譜
iq 日本思想大系
ir 加地伸行，孝經啓蒙
is 桜井久次郎，伊予大洲藩，新谷藩の文教
it 愛媛県教育史
iu 尾藤正英，日本封建思想史研究
iv 山下龍二，中國思想と藤樹
iw 和辻哲郎，日本倫理思想史
ix 丸山眞男，日本政治思想史研究
iy 後藤陽一，熊沢蕃山の生涯と思想の形成
iz 蕃山全集
ja 友枝龍太郎，熊澤蕃山と中國思想
jb 日本倫理彙編
jc 益軒全集
jd 春台先生読損軒先生大疑録
je 貝原益軒集
jf 伝記学会編，山崎闇斎とその門流
jg 學談雜錄
jh 性論明備錄
ji 淺見先生學談
jj 講習余錄
jk 仁說問答師說
jl 仁說問答筆記
jm 直方全集

jn 未發之愛
jo 文会筆錄
jp 山崎闇斎全集
jq 源了圓，儒者たちはどう評価したか，歴史と人物
jr 小島康敬，赤穂浪士討入リ事件，哲学会誌
js 謫居童問
jt 山鹿素行全集
ju 配所残筆
jv 治平要錄
jw 近世思想家文集
jx 語孟字義
jy 大學非孔子之遺書弁
jz 端
ka 端緒
kb 体
kc 用
kd 道理
ke 吉川幸次郎，徂徠學案
kf 徂徠先生學則
kg 対西肥水秀才問
kh 答屈景山書
ki 安永寿延，オノヅカラなるもの——近世思想における自然と人間，文學
kj 德川合理思想の系譜
kk 田口正治，三浦梅園
kl 日本哲學全書
km 形影夜話

David A. Dilworth

"Jitsugaku" as an Ontological Conception: Continuities and Discontinuities in Early and Mid-Tokugawa Thought

While we are prone, as are the Japanese themselves, to speak of the "modernization process" (*kindaika*)[a] as pertaining to the last century or so of Japanese history, we must not lose sight of the fact that the first half of the seventeenth century in Japan launched a full-scale "modernization process" in its own right. The Japanese take account of this fact in their periodization of their history when they refer to the *kinsei,*[b] the "modern age," as stemming from the seventeenth century. The *kinsei* and *kindai* stages of modernization are linguistically related, and it seems necessary to develop a heuristic model for understanding the relation between both moments in Japanese history.

The necessity for such a conceptual model is accentuated when we consider that the *kinsei* and *kindai* stages of Japanese history are intelligible only in terms of a larger, and consistent pattern of historical and cultural formation. For it is no less true that the Nara, Heian, Kamakura, and Muromachi periods were each a "modern age"—each brought forth a distinct style of cultural productivity—in its own time of social-historical formation.

In this regard, the philosopher Watsuji Tetsurō (1889–1960) has provided a productive heuristic model of the dynamics of Japanese cultural formation. In his essay, "The Stadial Character of Japanese Culture," Watsuji observes that a newly crystallized stratum of Japanese culture,

471

often the result of a vigorous assimilation of foreign values, tends not to displace, but to coexist with older cultural strata.[1] The dynamics of this equation exemplify what he calls the "stadial character" ($j\bar{u}s\bar{o}sei$)[c] of Japanese culture, that is, the synchronistic coexistence of various sediments of Japanese value traditions in a variety of integrative contexts. We have all been intrigued by how the Japanese so keenly assimilate the new, yet at the same time so loyally preserve the old. The Japanese cultural quantum-lattice, as it were, allows for the fact that transcended elements live on as transcended elements, and thus provide for a complex pattern of interflow among stadially inter-present levels and their potential energies, in a given context of integration.

In this model, the formative historical present—that is, modernization process—in the Japanese case entails the synchronistic inter-resonance of the various strata of the cultural lattice on the one hand, and the transformation of the multilayered cultural legacy into a new style of social-historical productivity on the other. I have shown elsewhere that Watsuji's own *method* of cultural phenomenology was grounded in such contemporary authors as Husserl, Heidegger, and Nishida Kitarō.[2] Here let me cite Husserl as the seminal thinker on this matter:

To be sure, the method of intentional explication had first to be developed, owing to the remarkable fact that Brentano's discovery of intentionality never led to seeing in it a complex of performances, which are included as *sedimented history* (Husserl's emphasis) in the currently constituted intentional unity and its current manners of givenness—a history *that one can always uncover by following a strict method.*[3]

In this paper I should like to suggest that the concept of *jitsugaku* contains such a sedimented history, involving the legacy of centuries of Chinese and Japanese thought and cultural formation. By employing Watsuji's model I hope to be able to create a clear enough focus to bring at least some of the variables into a coherent picture. I will suggest that the Edo period conceptions of *jitsugaku* were variations on an underlying metaphysics. Etymologically, *jitsu* means full, as opposed to empty, and real, in contrast to unreal. *Gaku* refers to learning, study, and, by extension, style of learning, doctrine, and theory. Together, as *jitsugaku*, both ontological and methodological claims are implied and co-implicated. On the one hand, we have a *theory* of what is real, or ontology; on the other, we have a philosophical anthropology, containing an essential reference to Confucian *practice*. Like the Marxist conception of praxis, the

Confucian theory of reality is inherently practical—a theory which calls for a lived unity of knowledge and action. The various Neo-Confucian styles of learning and schools of thought were simultaneously styles of being, and active involvement, in the world. Conversely, the various styles of Neo-Confucian cultivation and "practical learning" presupposed a specific theory of reality. They exemplified the "clear character" of the ontological and human orders in their most transparent state of integration.

THE SIXTEENTH-CENTURY HISTORICAL AND INTELLECTUAL BACKGROUND

Let me begin by referring to the changing climate of sixteenth-century Japanese intellectual and cultural history as providing one essential dimension to our understanding of the multi-nuanced conception of *jitsugaku* which evolved in the early- and mid-Edo period. In the broadest terms, the establishment of the Edo shogunate climaxed a longer historical process in which the samurai class, after a period of decline, reconsolidated its political base. The resurgence of the samurai class caused the political energy of the rising *chōnin* class of the later Muromachi period to be deflected into the aesthetic productivity of the Azuchi-Momoyama culture. This rechanneling of the energies of the common people continued as the deep undercurrent of culture in the Edo period.

Tokugawa Ieyasu's victories thus brought to completion a larger historical process referred to as *gekokujō*, [d] the "overthrow of the higher by the lower," which took place on many levels of Muromachi society. Ieyasu, following in the path of Hideyoshi, decisively set back the political rise of the *chōnin* class; yet both Hideyoshi and Ieyasu were themselves examples of the *gekokujō* process in respect to the older order of warrior families whose prestige they eclipsed in the process of reunifying Japan.

Considered in terms of the stadial dynamics of Japanese culture, the Tokugawa settlement effected a new configuration of *bun* [e] (the cultural sphere) and *bu* [f] (military rule) that repossessed an earlier integration of *bun* and *bu* realized in the time of the early Ashikaga shoguns. The "modern" Edo style of cultural productivity was thus achieved by the reconstruction of the whole social order, beginning with the samurai class, around the turn of the seventeenth century.

Needless to say, this process entailed the elevation of Neo-Confucian philosophy to the status of the dominant spiritual authority of the Edo social order. The varieties of Neo-Confucian philosophy were not simply the predominantly ethical teachings of classical China, but represented a complex metaphysical synthesis of Confucian, Taoist, and Buddhist elements worked out in Sung and Ming China. On the Chinese side, Sung and Ming Neo-Confucianism had already evolved into the spiritually dominant form of thought by virtue of having negated, yet retained as negated, the considerable heritage of Taoist cosmology and Buddhist dialectical thought that had flourished between the Six Dynasties and T'ang periods. In Japan, too, there had been a long development of Buddhism as the major form of spiritual experience in the Heian, Kamakura, and Muromachi cultures. In the background of the claims of the various strains of Edo Neo-Confucianism that they were *jitsugaku*—namely, "real" as opposed to "empty," and "practical" in the sense of being historically and socially productive—there was always this dimension of Neo-Confucian philosophy having replaced Buddhism as the dominant spiritual form at this juncture in Japanese cultural transformation.

A perhaps less obvious aspect of the same process was that Sung and Ming Neo-Confucian philosophy served the historical function of checking the incursion of Christian ideas at this point in Japanese history. The Sung Learning had been imported into Japan during Chu Hsi's own lifetime in the thirteenth century. Traces of the Sung Learning are clearly evidenced in such works as the *Taiheiki*, which was widely known among the classes of Japanese society, including the common people, during the Muromachi period. Under the influence of Buddhist monks, however, the Sung Learning suffered a reamalgamation with Buddhism, and was never able to emancipate itself as a distinct metaphysical conception during this time. It became a vested interest of the leading *hakase* families at court and of the Buddhist establishments of the older order which was struggling to survive in the *gekokujō* process. Christian ideas for a time had an appeal to the leaders of the new order that was forming. It was only after a fresh wave of continental influence, which came in as a result of Hideyoshi's Korean campaigns, that the Sung Learning was able to evolve into a position of dominance over Buddhism and Christianity.

As another instance of the same phenomenon, let us recall that the central figure of Ming thought, Wang Yang-ming, died in 1529. Wang Yang-ming thought was imported by the Zen monks who dominated the

Gozan bungaku movement of the latter half of the sixteenth century. The coming of Wang Yang-ming's philosophy to Japan, therefore, roughly coincided with the coming of Francis Xavier, and the subsequent waves of Christian missionaries, at the time Japan was making its initial contacts with the Western world. But it was only during the first half of the seventeenth century that Yōmeigaku was able to establish itself as an independent form of Edo thought.

The story of the initial successes and eventual failure of the Christian missions in Japan is well known. But it is worth pursuing the story from the side of intellectual history since it will shed some light on the "modernization process" taking place at the time. For internal political reasons, coupled with not entirely unwarranted fears that the Christian missionaries were the vanguard of military and economic aggression from the West, edicts expelling the missionaries and active persecution began in Hideyoshi's time. In 1614, fifteen years after the first great martyrdoms, Tokugawa Ieyasu issued another expulsion edict and set in motion another wave of persecution. The effective suppression of Christianity was completed under Tokugawa Iemitsu by 1637.

It is germane to our topic to note that even after Hideyoshi's expulsion edict the missionaries were able to propagate their teachings through an underground strategy, and for a time the printing of Christian documents was able to flourish in this way. The strengthening of the persecutions against the faith caused these documents to be eventually swept out of the provinces, so that they had no influence on later generations of Japanese in the Edo period. However, from the kinds of documents that were preserved abroad, we can take note of the fact that they were already, from the point of view of contemporary sixteenth-century Western history, "medieval" in character. They included such works as the *Doctrina Christiana*, a book of instructions begun by Xavier; a *Compendium of the Acts of the Saints*, translated by the missionary Vilela with the aid of Japanese converts; a translation of the *Imitatio Christi*, attributed to Thomas à Kempis; a translation of the famous *Contemptus Mundi*; and such works as the *Introduccion del Simbolo de la Fe*, a great summa of the faith, written in 1582 by the Spanish scholastic, Luis de Granada, and the same theologian's *Guia de Pecadores* (A Guide for Sinners).[4]

The progressive Japanese of the late sixteenth century, such as Oda Nobunaga, had been looking for the spirit of modern Europe, as evidenced in their interest in Western firearms and technology, acquired through their initial contacts with the Portuguese traders. They were looking for the broad range of knowledge and expertise with which the Europeans had been able to cross the Pacific Ocean. The missionaries, however, were facing backward into the "medieval" world from which the progressive elements in Japanese society were trying to emancipate themselves.

The leaders of the newly forming historical moment in Japan were demanding, in other words, a release from the then repressive and destructive influence of the older religious establishments. This demand was expressed in such forms as the reckless burning of Mt. Hiei by Nobunaga. Unfortunately for the Christian movement in the late sixteenth century, its apocalyptical theology was in some respects not entirely different from the Buddhist world view which the politically resurgent samurai class was now attempting to destroy. By contrast, Sung and Ming philosophy offered the Japanese a fully articulated secular humanism, based on the more "modern" ideas of the free development of man's nature and mind.

The careers of the pioneer Edo-period Neo-Confucians such as Fujiwara Seika, Hayashi Razan, and Yamazaki Ansai have been cited by historians as typifying the process of emancipation of the new intellectual class from Buddhist influence. Their conversions to Neo-Confucianism, in turn, reflected the epochal decision by Tokugawa Ieyasu to shift the spiritual authority from Buddhism to the metaphysical and humanistic thought of Neo-Confucianism. In so bringing about the spiritual collapse of Buddhism, which had held sway over both the older warrior families (such as Hōjō Sōun, Takeda Shingen, and Uesugi Kenshin, who were all pious Buddhists) and the common people of the Muromachi period, Ieyasu and his Confucian advisors set in motion new social and intellectual variables characterizable as a genuine modernization process. Among those variables, and decisive for both the *kinsei* and *kindai* stages of modernization in Japan, was the possibility of the new secular humanism permeating the lives of the common people. Thus while the political rise of the incipient Japanese bourgeoisie was delayed for two and a half centuries, the Japanese people as a whole underwent a process of spiritual modernization by internalizing the Confucian value system.

In the mid-Tokugawa period, exponents of a *jitsugaku* which repudiated the earlier matrix of Sung and Ming Neo-Confucianism of seventeenth-century Japan appeared in the form of the intellectual movement called Kogaku. It was an intellectual movement oriented toward textual and historical criticism which paralleled a similar development within Ch'ing Confucianism. My suggestion here—to be elaborated below—is that the Kogaku scholars were presumptuous, and even guilty of some malicious nonsense, when they attacked the mainstreams of Neo-Confucian thought as being a species of mere "private wisdom" and therefore deficient in the character of *jitsugaku*. The fact is that the metaphysical and humanistic philosophy of the Sung and the Ming—both in the form of official Tokugawa Shushigaku, and in the forms of Shushigaku and Yōmeigaku which appeared in the domains and among the Confucian teachers of the common people—played a formative and productive role in creating the intellectual matrix in the *kinsei* stage of modernization. Throughout the *kindai* stage of intellectual modernization, which has been characterized by the importation of Western conceptual values since the Meiji period, the *kinsei* intellectual matrix has coexisted as one of several strata of sedimented intentionalities available to the Japanese. But my argument will be that those scholars who trace the *kindai* stage of Japanese modernization to the Kogaku movement of the eighteenth century, to the neglect of the wider intellectual order, do so at the risk of falling prey to what Whitehead has called the "fallacy of misplaced concreteness." As one corner of the multivariate and dynamic matrix of Tokugawa Confucianism, Kogaku placed its own role in the slow transition from *kinsei* to *kindai* stages. But as a variety of *jitsugaku*, its role and significance have been much exaggerated.

HAYASHI RAZAN, SHUSHIGAKU, AND *JITSUGAKU*

Tokugawa Ieyasu first summoned Fujiwara Seika to lecture on the *Chen-kuan cheng-yao*,[g] a T'ang dynasty compilation of political philosophy, in 1593.[5] The significance of this was that while Hideyoshi was dreaming of invading Korea, Ieyasu was beginning the final phase of his career by promoting learning in the Confucian style. Hideyoshi died in 1598. The very next year Ieyasu was ordering such works as the *K'ung-tzu chia-yü*,[h] containing the teachings of Confucius and his discussions with his disciples, and the *Liu-t'ao san-lüeh*,[i] a Chinese classic on military strategy, to be printed on moveable type. Copies of the *Analects, Great Learning,* and the *Mean* were completed by Ieyasu's order in the same year. He had the *Chen-kuan cheng-yao* published in 1600. In 1601, he built a library at his castle in Sumpu. In 1602, he also built a library within the Edo castle, to which he moved the books of the archives at Kanazawa. In 1605, he summoned Funahashi Shūken, and in 1606, Hayashi Razan to lecture on Confucian philosophy. In 1608, Razan was formally summoned into the Bakufu as Confucian advisor to the shogun Hidetada. Ieyasu, who is said to have especially loved the *Book of Mencius*, thus cast the deciding vote in favor of Neo-Confucianism as the intellectual motive force of the Edo modernization process.

Hayashi Razan is credited with writing most of Ieyasu's edicts, including the *Laws Governing the Military Households* (1615).[6] He served the first four shoguns and wrote over one hundred and fifty books. Through the perpetuation of his influence in the official shogunate university, the Shōheikō, he exerted a lasting influence on the intellectual life of the Edo period. His sons, Gahō (Shunsai) and Hōkō, continued the tradition of prodigious scholarship in the tradition of Sung Learning, and were supported by the shoguns Iemitsu and Tsunayoshi. A temple dedicated to Confucius was erected on the Shōheikō grounds, where the sage was honored at regular intervals. The shoguns came once each year to such ceremonies, at which the head of the Hayashi family acted as master of ceremonies. The curriculum of this school consisted of the full range of Confucian classics of philosophy and history, the Sung Learning, and Japanese histories. While largely restricted to the Edo area, the example of the Hayashi school soon attracted attention in the domains, where many daimyo imitated the shoguns in employing Shushigaku scholars.

Through this means the intellectual resources of the Sung Learning were put at the service of the newly forming Edo social order. By any criterion, the relatively successful translation of the many facets of Shushigaku into the fabric of the Edo social order must be accorded the palm for exemplifying the meaning of *jitsugaku*, that is, real, timely, and productive learning in its broadest connotation. But as Shushigaku functioned in this way to define what we might call the central value system of the new order, it also served as a vector for the stadial coexistence of earlier strata of ethical values in Japanese culture. In Robert Bellah's terminology, universalistic commitments and vertical loyalties took precedence over individual values, and there was a subordination of integrative to goal-attainment values. The high prestige of the military class, and of "performance values" generally throughout the society, was symbolized in terms of *Bushidō*. Japanese family values remained central to this value system, but in the official Shushigaku interpretation, "filial piety" was subsumed under the more generic obligation of "loyalty"—again bearing witness to the exigencies of the feudal heritage.[7]

Social stratification took place in terms of the central value system. Tokugawa society was organized into a legal and hereditary class system in which prestige was correlated with power. Power, in turn, was based on family origin and particularistic relations. Economic and legal stratification coincided with prestige stratification, with recognizable differences in income, sources of income, patterns of consumption, education, and political power.[8] In actual practice, the internal pressures of the feudal system—pressures generated, for example, by the alternate attendance system (*sankin kōtai*)[j] enforced on the various daimyo by the Tokugawa shogunate—worked to impoverish the samurai class and to enrich the urban merchant class. Together with the leadership roles assumed during the long period of Tokugawa peace, this forced the samurai into non-traditional areas of economic support, such as the pursuit of learning and of various bureaucratic skills. But, significantly, the impoverishment of the samurai class as a whole did not lead to an attack on the central value system from either the samurai or merchant classes, the latter also enjoying a kind of "economic vassalage" within the social order.[9] Rather, dissatisfaction among the samurai led to an intensification of vertical loyalties within the system, and, when the attack on the shogunate finally came, it was in terms of its inability to live up to the central value system.[10]

While these sociological details are of particular interest to institutional historians, they are germane to our understanding of the *jitsugaku* concept as well. For if Shushigaku was taken over, if only by the Tokugawa shogunate itself, as symbolizing, in ideal form, the basic political and moral structures of the newly emerging social order, then the later Kogaku critique that Shushigaku was a species of book-learning and "private wisdom" divorced from the concrete political process is exposed as being largely fallacious. I have emphasized that the social order was not merely so *interpreted* by the Tokugawa shogunate, but also *concretely formed* according to the same conceptual model.

Shushigaku was able to play this central role in the intellectual and social ordering of seventeenth-century Japanese culture because it was officially sponsored and promoted by the Tokugawa shogunate. But we must guard against the fallacy of reading into the word "official" in this context the various critiques of "orthodoxy" levelled against the Sung Learning from the standpoint of the rival Confucian schools of Ming and Ch'ing China. Of course, the various reconstructions of the Sung Learning worked out in Ming and Ch'ing thought immensely broadened the range of philosophical variables, and thus produced a richer distribution of intellectual resources accessible to the scholars of the Edo period. And given the feudal distribution of power in the Edo period, it was entirely natural that institutional and ideological differences emerged, and that the scholars of the various domains—especially the scholars who arose from the common people—were drawn to forms of Chinese Confucian thought which had arisen in opposition to the "official" status accorded the Sung Learning. However, the total contextual framework of what constituted the "official" and "orthodox" in China and Japan at this historical juncture should warn us against accepting a one-sided interpretation from the standpoint of any of the rival schools involved. Each of the main schools of Edo-period Confucianism made claims to being the "real" and "practical" Confucian learning, and each school could back its claims with arguments and reasons more or less valid in its own context. The intellectual historian is thus presented with a multidimensional and inter-resonating pattern of variables.

My point is that the officially sponsored Shushigaku of the early Edo period was a true form of *jitsugaku* insofar as the practical domain of experience was concerned. I would also contend that the Tokugawa shogunate's promotion of the Sung Learning was not entirely arbitrary, but based in some measure at least on a valid perception of the centrality of the Sung Learning in the evolution of all forms of Neo-Confucian thought. Professor Wing-tsit Chan has written of Chu Hsi's metaphysical synthesis as having "completed" Neo-Confucianism in its essential structure.[11] This evaluation seems correct, if only in the sense that the forms of Ming and Ch'ing Confucianism necessarily developed their positions in reference to the initial formulations of Chu Hsi, and are ultimately unintelligible apart from that reference. We can add to this consideration the fact that the Tokugawa shogunate, as a stable *political* structure, was hardly dependent upon the Shushigaku philosophy as some absolutely indispensable revelation. It always had the option to sponsor (and cosponsor) other schools of thought. That the Shushigaku philosophy continued to enjoy official patronage throughout the Tokugawa period leads me to suspect that leading minds within the power structure found the Sung Learning to be an intelligible, appealing, and also productive philosophy.

Let us now inquire into the intelligibility of the Shushigaku position. It was a philosophy possessed of a broad cosmological and metaphysical range; it represented a synthesis of the Sung masters (Chou Tun-i, Shao Yung, Chang Tsai, and the Ch'eng brothers), and incorporated classical Confucian philosophy, Buddhist dialectical thought, and Taoist cosmological speculation. At the same time it had a focus, as originally formulated by Chu Hsi, on the humanistic and ethical concerns of Confucianism, and worked out that focus in terms of a doctrine of the inner relationship between subjective and objective, personal and public domains of experience. It goes without saying that this was no mere eclectic mixture of philosophical variables, but a highly original and sophisticated thought structure. (And it must have appealed to the Japanese as such.)

In working out his synthesis, Chu Hsi interpreted Chou Tun-i's conception of the Supreme Ultimate (wu-chi erh t'ai-chi)[k] as the absolute Principle (li),[1] which was further identified with Heaven's Decree (ming)[m] and human nature (hsing).[n] The concept of human nature was then articulated into a metaphysical formulation of the dialectical relation between the Nature-as-Principle and its manifestational energy and embodiment (ch'i).[o] This doctrine of the co-inherence of li and ch'i undergirded Chu Hsi's elaboration of a multivariate and internally consistent structure, according to which the personal and public domains of Confucian experience, as expressed in the Analects, Mencius, Great Learning, and the Mean, were seen as dynamically unified by the mind.

In metaphysical terms, Chu Hsi's thought revolved around this dialectical structure of li and ch'i. Li is the universal, or what the classical Greek philosophers called the archē, the formative and generative universal; ch'i is the aspect of individuation, and therefore particularization and process. To borrow the language employed by Professor T'ang Chün-i, Chu Hsi's thought involved both vertical (transcendental) and horizontal (human) planes, and their synthesis.[12] Each plane constitutes a generic structure of li and ch'i (and as such, allows for any number of particular substructures); but the vertical and horizontal planes of li and ch'i intersect, forming an endlessly dynamic and creative pattern. Therefore, while absorbing Buddhist metaphysical and logical structures of the "interpenetration" of universal (li)[1] and particular (shih),[p] and of "substance" (t'i)[q] and "function" (yung),[r] and further drawing upon Taoist cosmological conceptions of *ch'i*, Chu Hsi grounded his system in the doctrine of "sincerity" (*ch'eng*)[s] of the *Mean*. For Chu Hsi interpreted this sincerity as the concrete structure of the intersection of the horizontal and vertical planes of *li* and *ch'i* (including their sub-planes). Sincerity is thus the meeting point of the cosmic and human orders.

All the variables in Chu Hsi's system must be understood in terms of this dialectical co-inherence of vertical and horizontal planes. Chu Hsi's brilliant perception was that the theoretical and practical, transcendent and immanent, and cosmic and human orders, while distinguishable in their separate intentionalities, can nevertheless be seen as one lived reality. This is what he meant by "reality" and the "real" (*jitsu*). Thus, by repossessing, as he did, the centrality of the conception of "self-realization" or "self-completion" (*tzu-ch'eng*)[t] which was conjoined with the doctrine of "sincerity" in the *Mean*, and bringing these notions into further synthesis with the teaching of the innate moral mind in the *Book of Mencius*, Chu Hsi was able to bring into one architectonic, metaphysical configuration the subjective and objective, cognitive and moral, personal and public intentionalities of the Confucian value tradition.

The *Great Learning* and the *Mean* were conjoined with the *Analects* and *Mencius* by Chu Hsi for their exemplification of circular, dialectical balance. Thus we read in the classical text in the *Mean*:

While there are no stirrings of pleasure, anger, sorrow, or joy, the mind may be said to be in the state of equilibrium. When those feelings have been stirred, and they act in their due degree, there ensues what may be called the state of harmony. This equilibrium is the great root from which grow all the human actings in the world, and this harmony is the universal path which they all should pursue. (*Mean* I:4, James Legge translation.)

Chu Hsi subsumed this dialectical structure of "equilibrium" (*chung*)[u] and "harmony" (*ho*)[v] into his doctrine of the co-inherence of *li* and *ch'i*, and thereby worked out the relation between the emotional and aesthetic orders (*ch'i*) and the rational and moral orders (*li*). He also worked out the relationship between personal cultivation (the immanent plane) and the moral and cognitive domains (transcendent planes) in terms of the same logic, and based it also on such texts from the *Mean* as the following:

The possessor of sincerity does not merely accomplish self-completion of himself. With this quality he completes other men and things also. The completing himself shows his perfect virtue. The completing other men and things shows his knowledge. Both of these are virtues belonging to the nature, and this is the way by which a union is effected of the external and internal. (*Mean* XXV:3, James Legge translation.)

I will take up at a later point the Sung Learning's doctrine of the "investigation of things" as one specific intentionality within the broad metaphysical logic of Chu Hsi's position. Suffice it to say here that both cognitive and moral dimensions of experience (each a structure of *li* and *ch'i*) were interrelated by Chu Hsi through a higher dialectical structure that laid the foundation of Wang Yang-ming's conception of the "unity of knowledge and action."

Here let me return to the notion of "self-realization" formulated by the Sung Learning, and note its contribution to the notion of *jitsugaku* as real, dynamic learning *grounded in the ontological order*. As we read in *Sources of Chinese Tradition*:

In this type of self-cultivation, broad learning went hand-in-hand with moral discipline. The "things" which Chu Hsi had in mind to investigate may be primarily understood as "affairs," including matters of conduct, human relations, political problems, etc. To understand them fully required of the individual both a knowledge of that literature in which such principles are revealed (the Classics and histories) and an active ethical culture which would develop to the fullest the virtue of *jen* (humanity or benevolence). It is through *jen* that the individual overcomes his own selfishness and partiality, enters into all things in such a way as to fully identify himself with them, and thus unites himself with the mind of the universe, which is love and creativity itself. *Jen* is the essence of man, his "humanity," but it is also the cosmic principle that produces and embraces all things.[13]

There is no reason to suppose that the intellectual leaders within and without the official circles of Tokugawa society could not understand Chu Hsi's thought in these terms, or to suppose that they did not regard the Sung Learning as a rich and multivariate ontology involving a balanced synthesis of personal and public, and cognitive and moral horizons of experience based on the legacy of classical Confucian thought. The cultural resources implicit in this grand synthesis were, by a combination of historical contingency and native genius, exploited to a considerable degree by the same Japanese at the crucial juncture of the seventeenth-century modernization process.

Finally, let us return to the figure of Hayashi Razan to get a better sense of how the Sung Learning was internalized by the Japanese at the beginning of the Edo period. (The fuller picture, of course, requires study of the whole Shushigaku movement, as depicted in Inoue

Tetsujirō's *Nihon Shushigakuha no tetsugaku* [1905] and subsequent scholarly writings.)

While being the representative figure of the early development of Shushigaku in the seventeenth century, Razan's thought manifested personal and idiosyncratic elements. In contrast with his mentor, Fujiwara Seika, who was possessed of a broadly cosmopolitan mind—even to the point of tolerance for Chu Hsi's contemporary rival, Lu Hsiang-shan —Razan was an advocate of a more "orthodox" interpretation of the Sung Learning. Professor Abe Yoshio has shown that Razan was influenced in this regard by Korean Neo-Confucianism, both through the imported writings of Yi T'oegye (1501–1570) and through Yi's disciple, Kang Hang (1567–1618), who became a war captive as a result of Hideyoshi's expeditions. The same scholar has pointed to the influence of the Ming thinker, Lo Ch'in-shun (1465–1547), on Razan and several other early Tokugawa Confucians. [14]

Lo Ch'in-shun quarreled with Chu Hsi over the precise formulation of the relation between *li* and *ch'i*—placing higher priority on *ch'i* in both the cosmological and human orders, and apparently arguing for the inseparability of *li* and *ch'i* one-dimensionally, in contrast to the Sung thinker's formulation of the dialectical interplay of vertical and horizontal dimensions of *li* and *ch'i*. Therefore, Lo's position seems to bear some resemblance to the *ch'i-hsueh*[w] (philosophy of the monistic identity of *li* and *ch'i*) worked out in the Neo-Confucian schools of the Ming. But in his own writings, Lo had criticized Wang Yang-ming, his younger contemporary, for departing from Chu Hsi over the issue of the serious investigation of things. [15] And Lo followed Chu Hsi in his teaching of the difference between the innate moral nature (*hsing*)[n] and the manifested mind (*hsin*), [x] thus retaining in his thought at least one sub-structure of *li* and *ch'i* as dialectically related. [16] Consequently, Razan's affinity with Lo Ch'in-shun's position did not imply a break with, but rather a reinforcement of, his adherence to the Sung Learning.

Razan was only twenty-five when he was brought into the Bakufu in 1608. He had been born into a town house on Shijō in Kyoto and educated at the Kenninji. After refusing to become a monk he devoted himself to private study, including Chu Hsi's commentaries, and came to adhere to the Sung Learning. He must have read Lo Ch'in-shun when he was no more than twenty. He began lecturing on Chu Hsi's commentary on the *Analects* at the age of twenty-one, one year prior to becoming

Fujiwara Seika's disciple. By this point (1605), Razan was already mounting an attack on Buddhism, as evidenced in his "letter to Yoshida Soan" (*Den Genshi ni yosu*)[y] written at this time. About this same time Razan also wrote a letter to the haikai master Matsunaga Teitoku (*Juyū ni yosu*)[z] which advocated the teaching of the *Great Learning* as a refutation of Buddhism. Following Chu Hsi, he argued that "the doctrine of nirvana is lofty but not real."[aa][17] He attacked Buddhism in the Sung master's terms as being false and selfish, and thereby negating the true way of human relationships.

Commentators have pointed out that Razan never went beyond this line of attack on Buddhism even in works which were presumably more mature. For example, his later works, *Shakurō*[ab] (The Buddha and Lao Tzu). *Zento ni tsugu*[ac] (Admonition to Zen Buddhists), and *Sannin ni satosu*[ad] (Advice to Three Men), have the same thought.[18]

Razan was possessed of an equally abiding antipathy to Christianity. In 1607, the year prior to his invitation into the Bakufu, Razan visited the Christian Fukansai Fabian in a mission church at the persuasion of the above-mentioned Matsunaga Teitoku. His work, *Hai Yaso*[ae] (A Critique of Christianity), recorded the dialogue between himself and Fukansai Fabian. In it, Razan betrays an extreme intolerance not only for the Christian doctrine, but for Western scientific lore as well—in sharp contrast with the enlightened attitude of such later Shushigaku figures as Arai Hakuseki, and with the Shushigaku-supported interest in Rangaku (Dutch Studies), in the eighteenth century.

Commentators have pointed out that, if anything, Razan's enthusiasm for attacking Christianity grew in intensity over the years, as did his wrath against "unorthodoxies." His own "orthodoxy" developed to the point of using the pretext of the insurrection of Yui Shōsetsu in 1651 to condemn the then leading scholar of the realm, Kumazawa Banzan. Was this due to the fact that he stood in the position of representing the official orthodoxy of the Tokugawa shogunate's university, or was it due to personal, psychological idiosyncracy on Razan's part?

Whatever the reason, Razan's antagonism to Buddhism and Christianity entered as a negative element into his advocacy of the Sung Learning's metaphysics of the Supreme Ultimate. The conception of the Supreme Ultimate served as absolute Principle, on which to ground his critique of the rival absolutes of Buddhism and Christianity, and thus Razan's thought recapitulated the late sixteenth-century historical process, in which Neo-Confucian philosophy won out in the struggle with Buddhism and Christianity for spiritual ascendance. From this metaphysical basis Razan went on to expound the Sung Learning's teaching of the primacy of human relations in such colloquial works as his *Santokushō*[af] and *Shunkanshō*. [ag]

But Razan's anti-Buddhist and anti-Christian attitude was also based on a positive religious standpoint of his own, which was manifested in his endeavor to link the metaphysics of the Supreme Ultimate with Shinto. Given the vertical parameter in the Sung Learning, this did not necessarily represent a "mythological" and "irrational" departure from the metaphysical structure of the Sung Learning. Rather it was another possible horizon within the architectonic dialectical structure of *li* and *ch'i* (here, the metaphysical and religious domains, respectively).

Since this mythological, or religious element is a common thread running through such diverse figures as Razan, Tōju, Ansai, and Banzan in the seventeenth century, and even Ogyū Sorai and Kokugaku in the eighteenth century, it is worthy of our attention here. Various amalgamations of Shinto, Confucianism, and Buddhism had already been worked out in the Muromachi period. Razan, under the influence of the Sung Learning—which nevertheless included Buddhist metaphysics as a negated element—proclaimed the exclusive unity of Shinto and Confucianism in such works as his *Shintō denju*[ah] and *Shintō hiden setchū zokkai*. [ai] According to the former work, Razan seems to have read the *Nihon shoki sanshō*, [aj] written by Ichijō Kanera, a leading aristocrat and scholar of the Muromachi culture. But the direct influence on his thought came from the Yuiitsu Shinto of the Yoshida school, founded by Yoshida Kanetomo (1435–1511), a younger contemporary of Ichijō Kanera. Kanetomo's work, the *Shintō tai-i*, [ak] took the form of expounding the *Shintō Yuraiki*, [al] which was supposedly the work of Kanetomo's ninth-generation ancestor, Urabe Kanenao, but more probably was written by Kanetomo himself, or someone of his generation. On the first page of the *Yuraiki* there is the passage:

Kami[am] does not mean the usual kami; it is the kami that precedes Heaven and earth. The Way is not the usual Way, but the Way that transcends Heaven and earth. The divine nature moves without moving; the spiritual substance takes on form while being formless. This is the unfathomable divine substance. When it exists in Heaven and earth it is called kami; in the myriad things it is called soul (*tama*); in human relations it is called mind (*kokoro*). Mind is the dwelling place of the divine brightness, the shrine of the original chaos. The original chaos is the reality before the division of Heaven and earth, yin and yang, and before the emotions of joy and anger, pleasure and sorrow have arisen. These are all the essence of the mind. The mind is the essence of the one kami. The one kami is our Kuni-Hitachi-no-Mikoto. Kuni-Hitachi-no-Mikoto is the form of the formless, the name of the nameless; it is called Komu-o-moto-no-mikoto-no-kami [Nothingness, the Great Source, the Exalted Deity]. From this Great Source the vast three thousand worlds are formed, and a thousand forms are distinguished from one mind.[19]

While expounding the Shinto conception of the divine kami, Kuni-Hitachi-no-Mikoto,[an] the passage is a striking amalgamation of Confucian, Taoist, and Buddhist elements as well. For example, the Taoist notion of "original chaos" is noteworthy, and it returns in the thought of Nakae Tōju in Razan's time—although Tōju also discovered the notion in the writings of the Ming thinker, Wang Chi. We note also the doctrine of *chung*,[u] the "equilibrium" of the mind before the emotions are aroused, deriving from the *Mean* and incorporated into the Sung Learning. And the concluding sentence reflects Buddhist influence.

Razan did not take over wholesale the teachings of Kanera and Kanetomo. But he did incorporate many of the above elements into his own Confucian-Shinto syncretism. Among these were such notions as the "one kami," mind as the "dwelling place of the divine brightness," and the notion of the "form of the formless." He also identified, as did Yamazaki Ansai's conception of Suika Shinto, the "one kami" with Kuni-Hitachi-no-Mikoto, and fused this with the Sung Learning's metaphysics of the Supreme Ultimate as the absolute Principle.

In this way, metaphysical and religious elements coexisted in Razan's thought. Did not, then, Razan's notion of the "one kami" embody his own religious answer to the sixteenth-century conceptions of Amida Buddha and the Christian God, which had been negated by the rise of Sung Learning under his own influence around the turn of the century?

We have already seen that Shushigaku crystallized in the early Edo period as a multidimensional matrix of metaphysical, cosmological, and ethical notions. We must now add to this equation the religious dimension. Each of these dimensions, in turn, repossessed earlier strata of values from both the Japanese and Chinese cultural legacies. Their synchronistic inter-resonance in Razan's thought is a vivid example of the stadial character of Japanese culture.

NAKAE TŌJU; YŌMEIGAKU, AND *JITSUGAKU*

If we turn our attention to Razan's younger contemporary, Nakae Tōju, and trace the initial formation of the Yōmeigaku (Wang Yang-ming school) of the Edo period, we shall note the same pattern of integration of historically sedimented conceptual values. And we shall see that the Yōmeigaku tradition imposed various changes on the thought pattern of Shushigaku, but did not depart from the fundamental ontological conception of *jitsu* as the ground of the notion of *jitsugaku*. Indeed, the profound internal relation between Shushigaku and Yōmeigaku was recognized in due course, when in the late Tokugawa period the so-called Shin Yōmeigaku (New Wang Yang-ming school) formed as a synthesis of both traditions. The Shin Yōmeigaku school, in turn, functioned as one of the major vectors in the successful transition from the *kinsei* to *kindai* stages of Japanese cultural modernization.

The initial formation of the Yōmeigaku school in the early Edo period also bears witness to the rapidity of the intellectual modernization process in the *kinsei* stage. As in the case of the Meiji-period assimilation of Western forms and values, the Japanese of the seventeenth century were able to internalize, in the space of only a few decades, thought traditions which had taken centuries to work out in the Sung and Ming. Nakae Tōju, in fact, responded to the thought of Wang Chi (Wang Lung-hsi, 1498–1583) one of the most sophisticated forms of Wang Yang-ming philosophy developed in the Ming.

According to the *Tōju nenpu* (Chronological Biography), Nakae Tōju (1608–1648) first came in contact with Wang Yang-ming thought through reading the *Hsing-li hui-t'ung*[ao] and later Wang Chi's *Wang Lung-hsi yü-lu*[ap] in 1641 when he was thirty-three. He is said to have adhered to the teaching of the Wang Yang-ming school after discovering the truth of the unity of the three religions (Confucianism, Buddhism, and Taoism), under the influence of Wang Chi. If the historical record is correct that Tōju first read Wang Yang-ming's own works in 1645 when he was thirty-seven, then Tōju's first major work, *Okina mondō*[aq] (1641) takes on added significance as a work reflecting Wang Chi's influence. Wang Yang-ming's key phrase, "the extension of innate knowledge" (*chih liang-chih*),[ar] does not appear in the text. Tōju does, however, speak of *liang-chih* as the Supreme Vacuity (*t'ai-hsü*),[as] a phrase derivative from Wang Chi.

We must bear in mind, however, that Nakae Tōju turned to the Yōmeigaku only in the last seven years of his life. Before this he participated in the intellectual modernization process of the early seventeenth century as a student of the Sung Learning. As for Tōju's intellectual conversion from Shushigaku to Yōmeigaku, we must also note that Tōju had become a *rōnin* and returned to his mother's village in 1635 when he was twenty-seven, and this must have been reflected in his later attitude toward the Sung Learning. Because of his choice of this life-style, he was in a position to recapitulate in his own experience the spiritual egalitarianism of the Wang Yang-ming school, and to emphasize the vertical dimension of religious transcendence which was already contained in the Sung Learning, but was further developed in the Wang Yang-ming schools of the Ming.

One of the dimensions of Tōju's thought can thus be appreciated in terms of the fact that he was the first of the Confucian teachers who arose from among the common people in the Edo period. The charismatic status accorded him by later generations is probably related to this fact, as well as to the religious quality of his teaching. But as the Yōmeigaku school developed, it manifested contrasting attractions for both "inner contemplation" and "outer activity," as exemplified in the two direct disciples of Tōju, the retiring Fuchi Kōzan (1617–1686) and the active Kumazawa Banzan (1619–1691). We have already seen that both these intentionalities were brought into a structure of dialectical relationship in the Sung Learning's teaching of the balance between "inner reverence and outer righteousness."

Although Tōju later rejected the authority of the Four Books, he did not depart from the *Great Learning*'s doctrine of the centrality of personal cultivation. On the contrary, he developed the essential dialectic of inner and outer domains of experience by centering his teaching on the notion of filial piety.[20] This position was not a departure from the logic of the Shushigaku position in that Tōju elevated "filial piety" (*kō*)[at] into a metaphysical *principle*. For it became, in Tōju's system, the *absolute principle inherent in the existential mind*—which exemplified Chu Hsi's dialectical logic of the co-inherence of *li* and *ch'i* as well.

According to Yamashita Ryūji, Tōju's conversion to the vertical dimension of religious transcendence apparently came as a release from his own rigoristic adherence to "formal patterns of conduct" which he had understood as enjoined upon the individual by the Sung Learning.[21] The

Yōmeigaku position, particularly that of Wang Chi, thus served the function of mediating his own psychological emancipation. When Tōju later repudiated the "rigorism" of the Sung Learning, however, he was only repeating a misunderstanding of the essential standpoint of the Sung Learning. As he developed his own standpoint in his later years, Tōju in fact took a position which involved both Shushigaku and Yōmeigaku elements. Like Razan, he brought the vertical dimension contained in the Neo-Confucian conception of *jitsu* into further alignment with Shinto.

We can go further and say that Tōju's conception of "filial piety" functioned in the same way as the concept of "sincerity" did in Chu Hsi's thought—as the point of intersection of the vertical (metaphysical, religious) and horizontal (moral and cognitive) orders. It would be incorrect to say that Tōju, under the influence of Wang Chi, emphasized the vertical plane to the neglect of the horizontal, because in the final analysis his thought was a stadial repossession of Shushigaku and Yōmeigaku elements. Tōju's teaching of filial piety thus exemplified a religious conception of *jitsugaku* based on the insight of the interpresence of immanent and transcendent planes of experience.

Unless we see this dialectical quality of Tōju's thought, and the profound internal relation it had to the essential logical and ontological standpoint of the Sung Learning, we shall be at a loss to interpret the multifaceted character of Tōju's teaching. Inoue Tetsujirō has shown that Tōju's teaching involved a full array of cosmological, psychological, ethical, and religious elements, all brought into a structure of the unity of theory and practice, by virtue of his ontological conception of filial piety.[22] He has also shown that Tōju's conceptions of government, learning, and education, issued from the same ontological ground.[23] The upshot is that the apparently simpler philosophical standpoint of Tōju, supposedly based on his own devotion to his mother in the village of Ōmi, turns out to be an extremely multidimensional perspective.

We can get a glimpse of this complexity when we note that Tōju's emphasis on the ethical intentionality of service to one's own parents simultaneously implied, for him, devotion to one's ancestors, to the greater ancestors of Heaven-and-earth, and finally to the "ultimate ancestor," the *absolute principle* which he termed the "Supreme Vacuity." Thus, what begins as an ethical teaching derived from the *Classic of Filial Piety* ends as a metaphysical teaching of experiential reversion into the presence of absolute reality. He expressed this doctrine syncretically in terms of Wang

Chi's teaching of the unity of the three religions, but especially in the Shinto vocabulary of the "Divine Way of the Supreme Vacuity." He further identified this absolute principle with Wang Yang-ming's and Wang Chi's doctrine of *liang-chih*, the innate essence of the mind—the center-point of the intersection of cosmic and human, ontological and personal planes.

Inoue Tetsujirō has criticized Tōju for not having adequately explained how the conception of *liang-chih* functioned as the point of intersection of the theistic and monistic, human and cosmic, and religious and moral orders.[24] Inoue's critique is a valid one from the point of view of the Sung Learning, in which an attempt had already been made to work out all these variables in a more complex thought structure. But if we bear in mind that Tōju began his career by thoroughly absorbing the Sung Learning, and included Shushigaku elements in his own mature thought, it becomes possible to see Tōju's Yōmeigaku as stadially repossessing Shushigaku. In this way his position already contained the seeds of the later integration of Shushigaku and Yōmeigaku thought in the Bakumatsu period.

I have argued above that this essential co-inherence of the two major schools of seventeenth-century Japanese Neo-Confucianism produced a distinctive ontological conception of the unity of theory and practice. Tōju did not differ essentially from Razan in envisioning this unity of "knowledge" and "action" in the social context of the forming Edo world. His notion of filial piety as the supreme manifestation of, and experience in, the absolute order cuts across the feudal ideology of status distinctions; but at the same time Tōju affirmed what he called the *saburai no michi*, or *saburaidō*.[au] He even elaborated his own concept of *Bushidō*[av] as the unity of civil and military spheres, and thereby contributed to the Tokugawa symbolization of the samurai as the Confucian gentleman.

Because of the historical contingency that Yōmeigaku played the role of rival to the established "orthodoxy" of the Sung Learning, Tōju's thought can be looked upon as having injected a "restorationist" variable into the intellectual life of the Tokugawa period. The institutional affiliation of Shushigaku with the Tokugawa Bakufu meant that Shushigaku took on an identity—entirely accidental to its pure philosophical character—as representing the actual social order, while Yōmeigaku could flow on as a deep undercurrent of potential reconstruction of that order. It was, in fact, the Yōmei tradition that played a large role in the restorationist ideology of the *shishi* patriots of the Bakumatsu period who challenged the authority of the Bakufu. But in the final analysis, the restorationist ideology was grounded in a thought tradition held in common by both Shushigaku and Yōmeigaku.

Therefore we should not fall prey to the error of confusing ideological with philosophical dimensions when assessing the quality of *jitsugaku* contained in the Yōmei tradition. In essence, this tradition stood on the bedrock of personal moral restorationism in the intentionality of the unity of knowledge and action. And personal moral restorationism to the adherents of the Yōmei school necessarily involved the existential exemplification of the ideal Confucian values upon which the Tokugawa social order had been established. In the context of the Bakumatsu-period transition from *kinsei* to *kindai* stages of modernization, the Yōmeigaku "restorationism" had an accidental greatness thrust upon it.

Let me briefly trace the evolution of the Yōmei school from its origins in Tōju to the last clearly identifiable Yōmei scholar of the Tokugawa period, Ōshio Chūsai. For even in such an inadequate way we shall get a better sense of continuous flow of the Yōmei line throughout the Tokugawa period, and its eventual confluence with Shushigaku thought as well.

We have already mentioned Fuchi Kōzan, Tōju's direct disciple; the line of Fuchi Kōzan is traced by Inoue Tetsujirō through several generations of scholars totalling sixty-four names. Other disciples directly associated with Tōju were Izumi Chūai, Nakagawa Kenshuku, Nakamura Toshitsura, Kase Suehiro, and Shimizu Kikaku. The greatest of Tōju's direct disciples, of course, was Kumazawa Banzan. Banzan was a samurai who studied under Tōju for about eight months. He took the point of departure of his teaching from Tōju's doctrine of the innate knowledge and innate capacity as the activating source of the moral mind's spontaneous responses to the times, the situations, and men's stations in life. As both teacher and administrator of the Okayama domain of the lord Ikeda Mitsumasa, Banzan emphasized a practical learning of this kind.[25] He shared with Tōju an interest in the *Book of Changes* and attempted to elaborate a cosmological teaching concerning the sixty-four hexagrams which coincided with the Way of Man of the fundamental Confucian relationships. He also took over the doctrine of "sincerity" as the horizon in which the Way of Heaven and the Way of man interpenetrate. Banzan also stressed the unity of Confucianism and Shinto, but at the same time was often severely critical of scholars of his day, both Confucian and Buddhist alike.

After Tōju's death an independent line of Yōmei thought was established by Miyake Sekian (1665–1730); this school, transmitted through Nakai Shūan (1693–1758) and Nakai Chikuzan (1730–1804), evolved into the historically influential Shin Yōmeigaku of the end of the Tokugawa period. Other early Tokugawa schools of Yōmei thought developed from Kitajima Setsuzan (1636–1697) and Mie Shōan (1674–1734).

The impact of both Tōju and Banzan was felt by Miwa Jissai (1669–1744), who renewed the scholarly spirit of the Yōmei school in the eighteenth century. Jissai furthered the interest of the Yōmei tradition in Shinto, and Tōju's interest in medicine. Jissai's disciples included many persons of the rising merchant class. He gained his reputation as a great scholar of Wang Yang-ming's own writings, and produced commentaries on Wang's teaching of the Four Maxims, and on the *Ch'uan-hsi lu*. This scholarly direction was developed in the early nineteenth century by Satō Issai, who promoted studies of the *Ch'uan-hsi lu* on the side of exhaustive textual research.

Satō Issai (1772–1859) studied in the Hayashi school of Shushigaku as a colleague of Hayashi Jussai, who later became head of the official Bakufu school. For this reason the latter could not officially promote Yōmeigaku; but Jussai was deeply interested in Wang Yang-ming thought. Issai himself effected a synthesis of Shushigaku and the orthodox Yōmeigaku tradition, and was critical of the left-wing transmission of Wang Yang-ming thought as represented in his contemporary, Ōshio Chūsai. Issai continued many of the emphases of Tōju, such as the doctrine of the centrality of the mind, the unity of knowledge and action, self-realization as the dialectical identity of substance and function, and the equation of mind with Heaven and the "Supreme Vacuity."

Ōshio Heihachirō (Chūsai) (1793–1837) has been enshrined in literature by Mori Ōgai's historical novel, *Ōshio Heihachirō*. In addition, he has often been co-opted by both the Japanese political left and right as a "revolutionary hero" at various stages of modern history. But in historical retrospect his rebellion has been over-mythologized, and his scholarship and philosophical talent neglected. The historical fact is that his rebellion was not "revolutionary" in any sense of the term that departed from the "restorationist" moral activism of Tōju's essential teaching. But even if we grant that his rebellion was not ideological in the classical Marxist sense, serious questions still remain. One concerns the nature of his charisma, in comparison with that of Tōju. Although Chūsai may have sincerely and authentically translated religious and ethical sensibilities down to the level of direct action, his charisma seems to have had a malignant quality. His rebellion of 1837 grew out of his deep sensitivity to the desperate condition of the poor people in Osaka; it ended with more than one-fourth of the city in flames, the poor people worse off than before.

Prior to 1837, however, Ōshio Chūsai established his reputation as a representative scholar in the Yōmeigaku line. He knew Satō Issai, but diverged from the latter's interest in effecting a synthesis of Shushigaku and Yōmeigaku. He followed Wang Chi's interpretation of the Four Maxims as the Four Negatives, and, under the influence of Tōju as well, emphasized the teaching of ki taikyo, [aw] "return to the Supreme Vacuity." Chūsai resigned from the Osaka police force in 1829 to devote himself to study and teaching. He is said to have experienced an enlightenment while travelling on Lake Biwa to Tōju's shrine in Ōmi. He became particularly learned in the tradition of commentaries on the Great Learning in the Wang Yang-ming school, and devoted his research to over one hundred commentaries on the Great Learning from the Han dynasty on. He produced five philosophical works centering on such ideas as the "return to the Supreme Vacuity," "the extension of knowledge as the rectification of the mind," "the transformation of the physical disposition," "the unity of life and death," and "sincerity as the elimination of artificiality." Thus, as in the case of Tōju and other Yōmeigaku thinkers, we find a confluence of metaphysical, religious, and ethical ideas in Chūsai's writings. They bear witness, at the end of the Tokugawa period, to the vitality of ideas first internalized by the Japanese thinkers of that school at the beginning of the period. Chūsai seems to have shared a mystical strain with Tōju in his emphasis that the human mind is the Supreme Vacuity, the absolute principle of both the existential self and the universe. He also identified the Supreme Vacuity with innate knowledge (liang-chih). As one's innate knowledge spontaneously responds, the moral order is established. Thus the fundamental task and effort of life, Chūsai taught, is to cultivate the inner light of one's innate knowledge by "preserving the solitude of the self." Since the inner light of innate knowledge is deathlessly one with the absolute principle of the Supreme Vacuity, Chūsai taught that one must act fearlessly in the depths of one's own resoluteness and sincerity—that is, in the horizon of the unity of knowledge and action.

Given the continuing vitality of the Yōmeigaku line of thought in both Satō Issai and Ōshio Chūsai, it is perhaps not amiss to suggest that an exhaustive study of the whole school will reveal a substantial, enduring form of *jitsugaku*.[26] The tradition of the Yōmeigaku scholars was in fact multivariate, involving "existentialistic," "restorationistic," and "left" and "right" tendencies—in fact, the full spectrum of variables. Their *jitsugaku* did not involve a break with the essential structure of Shushigaku thought. On the contrary, as Professor T'ang Chün-i has made clear, the development of the doctrine of the active, moral mind in Wang Yang-ming and Wang Chi presupposed the main categories of the Sung Learning.[27] On the Japanese side, the common philosophical bonds between Razan and Tōju were forged by their stadial inheritance of the two Chinese schools at the beginning of the Edo period modernization process. Thus while personal, institutional, and conceptual differences remained, both Shushigaku and Yōmeigaku styles of thinking were implanted in the same soil of the early Edo period, to be nourished and to grow in reference to each other for two centuries.

THE CHALLENGE OF EIGHTEENTH-CENTURY *JITSUGAKU*

I should like finally to take up the question of the relation between the ontological conceptions worked out in the seventeenth-century Shushigaku and Yōmeigaku traditions, and the eighteenth-century formulation developed in the Kogaku[ax] line of Confucianism which culminated in the school of Ogyū Sorai (*Soraigaku*).[ay] According to the influential study of Maruyama Masao, the eighteenth-century formulation resulted in no less than a "dissolution" of the essential elements in the seventeenth-century metaphysical synthesis.[28] By taking up this thesis—which seems by and large to have adopted the assumptions of the Soraigaku standpoint—we shall perhaps be able to shed further light on the content and significance of the seventeenth-century conceptions.

According to Maruyama, the process of establishment of the Sung (Ch'eng-Chu), Ming (Wang Yang-ming), and Ch'ing (historical criticism) styles of Confucianism was repeated on the Japanese side in the Tokugawa period, but the quality and intellectual significance of the lat-

ter were different, in fact, unique, by virtue of the "internal development" of Tokugawa Confucianism that culminated in Japanese Kogaku.
This internal transition was brought about by the dissolution of the
"moral rationalism" of Shushigaku; and this dissolution called forth the
"irrationalism" of the schools of Ogyū Sorai and of Kokugaku,[az] the National Learning school centering around Motoori Norinaga. Maruyama's
thesis does not bring the Yōmeigaku tradition into the picture except as a
variation on the Shushigaku position.

To state briefly the results of Maruyama's analysis: the "internal reconstruction" of Japanese Confucianism achieved in the Kogaku line "dissolved" the original Shushigaku rational synthesis by a multivariate shift
in emphasis from "subjectivity" to "objectivity"—all the variables involving a further shift in emphasis from the "private" (shi)[ba] to the "public"
(kō)[bb] intentionalities of Confucian thought. The main points of dissolution of the seventeenth-century position effected by the evolution of Kogaku thought are as follows: (1) the Soraigaku severed the Shushigaku
link between the "private" moral and the "public" cognitive domains,
placing priority on the latter; (2) it severed the Shushigaku relation between "private" self-cultivation and the "public" political domain; (3) it
repudiated Neo-Confucian metaphysical speculation in favor of historical
criticism, philology, and a general positivistic methodology; (4) it did so
by challenging the Sung Learning's position on the authority of the Four
Books in favor of the paradigms of civilization found in the Six Classics;
(5) it distinguished the area of emotion (aesthetic and moral) as pertaining
to the domain of "private wisdom" from the "public Way" of the Sages,
as found in the Six Classics. As Maruyama has pointed out, this shift in
the philosophical variables in Soraigaku was not entirely "rational," since
Sorai grounded his position on a religious belief which took the mythological sages of Chinese antiquity as absolute personalities. This fideistic
element was coupled with a complete rejection of the Sung Learning's
teaching of sagehood through personal cultivation.

Maruyama went on to interpret the emergence of eighteenth-century
Kokugaku as an internal development within Soraigaku, by a further
shift from absolutizing the ancient Chinese sages to absolutizing the ancient Japanese kami, as rediscovered in the ancient Japanese classics. The
Kokugaku movement thus exemplified a further release of the emotional-
aesthetic sensibility that was supposedly suppressed in the seventeenth-
century Shushigaku formulation.

According to Maruyama, this dissolution of the elements of the Shushigaku position also led to the development of the "modern consciousness" in Japan. He contends that the "irrationalism" of Soraigaku and Kokugaku bears some analogy to the role played by the fourteenth-century European schools of Duns Scotus and William of Ockham, which attacked the universal, theological, and metaphysical syntheses of the thirteenth-century Schoolmen by placing significant restrictions on the power of human reason and consigning many items to pure faith.[29] Thus the "modern," but "irrational" investigation of principles through empirical, scientific methodology commenced only after the "premodern" and "medieval" legacy of "rational" thought was overturned. Similarly, the dissolution of the "systematic moralism" of Shushigaku called forth the independence of various cultural elements—the seeds of the modern "pluralistic consciousness."

It is apparent at a glance that Maruyama's thesis does not put much emphasis on the seventeenth-century modernization process (*kinseika*) which I have outlined above. As a heuristic model, its strong point has been in clarifying the internal relation and continuity between eighteenth-century Soraigaku and Kokugaku. But its guiding assumptions are *linear* (as opposed to stadial), making the case for a radical discontinuity between seventeenth- and eighteenth-century forms of Japanese thought. It does not seem to be inaccurate to characterize it as a kind of *bunmei kaika*[bc] thesis reminiscent of, if not indebted to, the "progress" assumptions of Fukuzawa Yukichi, Nishi Amane, and other "civilization and enlightenment" figures of the first decade of the Meiji era.

My suggestion is that the Maruyama thesis—and the Kogaku position—are vulnerable to attack from the standpoint of the "stadial character" of Japanese culture. In this latter standpoint, the "pluralistic consciousness," involving a broad spectrum of cognitive, moral, religious, aesthetic, and metaphysical intentionalities, can be thought to have already crystallized into one coherent matrix within the Sung-Ming philosophical world, and then become internalized to a considerable extent in the seventeenth-century Tokugawa context. I would argue that the same synchronistic (as distinguished from linear) Neo-Confucian framework continued to provide the spiritual *basis* of the eighteenth-century schools of thought, and of the *kindai* stage of Japanese modernization in the late Tokugawa and Meiji periods. The *kindai* stage of modernization, of course, further involved a large-scale importation of Western values. But the peculiarity of the Japanese case, as possibly distinguished from other cultures making their initial contacts with Western forms and values, was that the waves of Westernization in the Meiji period did not overwhelm and displace indigenous Japanese elements. The strength of the Japanese *kindai* modernization process was provided by the deeply rooted and widely deployed Neo-Confucian value matrix.

In my view, therefore, Kogaku did not amount to an entirely unique development and culmination of Tokugawa thought. The Kogaku movement seems to have been a half-philosophical and half-philological movement that was the Japanese counterpart of the transition to Ch'ing historical criticism on the Chinese side. There are ample cases of a similar shift from philosophical to philological and positivistic concerns at various stages of Western thought. But if we take a position outside of the institutional identity which this school took on, there seems to have been no significant "dissolution" of the metaphysical conceptions of the seventeenth century. And strictly speaking, how could there have been? For philological and positivistic *methodology* presupposes, but does not conflict on the same level with, philosophical *thought*. Such a methodology may have implicit (or even explicit) philosophical assumptions of its own, but then it becomes a question of the adequacy of its *philosophical* assumptions over against rival *philosophical* assumptions, and of the adequacy of the patterns of *articulated reasons* presented by the rival positions. The only half-philosophical position of Soraigaku was, in my opinion, no match for the sophisticated, and internally inter-resonating matrix of Shushigaku and Yōmeigaku thought.

Maruyama's study has attributed the rise of the Sorai school to the change in social conditions taking place within the Edo culture of the early eighteenth century.[30] Taking the Genroku period (1688–1704) as an historical "watershed," he has described that period as a "highpoint" of luxury, taste, and the arts, based on the economic rise of the *chōnin* class. It was the time of the flourishing of the Horikawa school of Itō Jinsai, and, shortly thereafter, of the Ken'en school of Ogyū Sorai as well. The priest Keichū labored on his studies of the *Manyōshu*; Bashō appeared as the consummate master of *haiku* poetry; Saikaku grew out of the *haikai* tradition to write stories of the floating world; the theater and gay quarters boomed; Chikamatsu developed the *jōruri* puppet theatre; Sakata Tōjurō in the Kansai, and Ichikawa Danjūrō in the Kantō, dominated the *kabuki* stage. In painting, anti-conventionalism was developed by Hanabusa Itchō, challenging the orthodox Kano school; Hishikawa Moronobu became the father of *ukiyo-e*; and Ogata Kōrin challenged the styles of the shogunate-sponsored masters of *makie* such as Kōami and Kōmarō. "Genroku style" kimono and other extravagant luxuries swept both samurai and *chōnin* classes. "The sounds of laughter and music filled the mansions of the wealthy and the narrow lanes of the gay quarters, clearing the air of the bloody memories of the Sengoku period" —this was the *"pax edona"* (*goseiyō no miyo*)[bd] of which Saikaku spoke.[31]

However, the same cultural efflorescence put a heavy strain on the *bakuhan* system. It produced a travel and money economy, drew the samurai off the lands, and created a "dynamic" situation in the midst of feudal "staticism." The process brought the samurai class and the Bakufu to the brink of bankruptcy. Continued coinage debasement, and a series of natural disasters, also weakened the *bakuhan* system, and strengthened the *chōnin* class. Ienobu employed Arai Hakuseki, who worked on currency reform. Yoshimune's "Kyōhō reform" was the first thoroughgoing effort at financial retrenchment. This did not have the desired effect. The *sankin kōtai* system was partially relaxed, then restored in 1730. In the "Tanuma period" of Ieshige and Ieharu, there was further financial irresponsibility, to be followed by periods of economic austerity in the Kansei (1789–1801) and Tempō (1830–1844) reforms. The samurai declined in self-prestige, while the *chōnin* grew in self-consciousness. But lacking a social base for upward mobility, the *chōnin* spent his wealth in conspicuous consumption, and thus underwrote the aesthetic efflorescence of the Edo culture.

In the peasant villages, there was tension between increasing tax burdens and the rise in standards of living. Peasant uprisings doubled from the Hōei to Kyōhō periods. The picture worsened by the Hōreki period (1751–1764). Infanticide (*mabiki*) among the peasants, who comprised over eighty percent of the population, increased after the Kyōhō period.

According to Maruyama's study, the rise of the Soraigaku reflected these transitions in mid-Tokugawa society. Sorai is depicted as developing the *political* side of Confucianism because of his sensitivity to the decline in "public" values that had weakened the government and the whole *bakuhan* system. And Sorai is credited with separating out the sphere of "human emotions" in the *private* sphere as well, after the Genroku culture.

As to the former, Sorai made precise analyses of the economic difficulties of the *bakuhan* system that were created by the *sankin kōtai* arrangement. He proposed such measures as temporary inflation through coin mintage to relieve the samurai, then the return of the samurai to the lands, control of travel, and elimination of the "world of inns." He also proposed the "regulation of desires" according to status to bring supply and demand into balance (that is, by returning to a natural economy). To do so he wanted to apply the principle of "ritual and music" as social *controls*. He conceived this Confucian reconstruction of society, therefore, on the principle of *fukko*, be "restoration of antiquity," and this dimension appeared in Sorai's mythologizing of the ancient Chinese sages. He even recommended that daimyo be limited to 30,000 *koku* estates to create a more harmonious "public order" on the highest samurai level.[32]

As even this brief summation suggests, Maruyama's study has made a substantial contribution to the "sociology of knowledge" reflected in the emergence of the Sorai school of the eighteenth century. The point at issue, however, is whether this rise of the Soraigaku must be interpreted in the linear way in which Maruyama's thesis is cast—at the expense of the Shushigaku metaphysical framework. I would argue, on the contrary, that the Soraigaku, and by extension, Kokugaku, schools represented, from a philosophical point of view, a considerable narrowing of the original seventeenth-century Neo-Confucian structure—but not a departure from, displacement, or dissolution of that structure.

For one thing, the above-cited program of social reform aimed at the "regulation of desires" based on rational principles does not seem to be any departure from the essential Shushigaku position. Indeed, the *pax edona* which blossomed in the Genroku culture was a product, not of the Sorai School, but of the Tokugawa political settlement and its official symbolization by Shushigaku in the seventeenth century, as I have indicated above. During the same Genroku period the Hayashi school enjoyed the patronage of the shogun Tsunayoshi. It is possible to go further and note the "stadial character" of the distinct cultural expressions of the mid-Edo period. Bashō, in a famous passage, related his art of the *haiku* to the aesthetic sensibilities of Saigyō, Zeami, and Sen no Rikyū. Both *jōruri* and *kabuki* transcended, yet preserved as transcended, the aesthetic of the nō. The movement in art of the Sōtatsu through the Kōrin school involved the repossession of the aesthetic of the *Tale of Genji Scroll*. In short, the synchronistic structure of the Japanese cultural lattice, as exemplified in mid-Edo culture, did not necessarily indicate a departure from, displacement, or "dissolution" of earlier cultural strata, but rather involved the inter-resonance of older and newer forms in the cultural climate of the time.

I suggest that the Sorai school was no exception to this equation. Sorai in fact began his career in the Shushigaku school. He was already forty-eight in 1714, the year of Kaibara Ekken's death, when Sorai published his *Ken'en zuihitsu*, a work which bitterly attacked Itō Jinsai's Kogaku from the standpoint of the Sung Learning. Three years later in 1717, his *Bendō* and *Benmei*[bf] appeared, laying the foundation of his kobun-jigaku[bg] (literally, "study of ancient culture and texts"), as a development of Kogaku. In this duration, Sorai had supposedly gone through an intellectual conversion, entailing the rejection of the Sung Learning in favor of *jitsugaku* as "empirical rationalism" in the cognitive domain, and as "political science" in the public domain. But in actual fact, neither his intellectual methodology nor his concern for the political domain constituted a real departure from his own training in Shushigaku. As we have already seen, both were integral moments in the heritage of Shushigaku scholarship and moral concern.

According to Maruyama, however, there is an issue here. Sorai came to hold that the "Way of the Sages" had been glossed over by the metaphysical accretions of the later centuries. He thus felt it necessary to return to the "facts" (*koto*) by studying the "words" (*kotoba*)[bh] which expressed them pristinely. The Six Classics were taken as expressing the "facts," that is, the institutions and civilization of Yao and Shun, and of the three dynasties of Hsia, Shang, and Chou. In Chu Hsi, on the other hand, the Four Books were given the central position, especially the *Great Learning* and the *Mean*. Jinsai had contributed the argument that the *Great Learning* was not a work written by Confucius, and recommended the *Analects* and the *Mencius*. Sorai wrote: "The Six Classics give the facts (*mono*),[bi] the *Book of Rites* and *Analects* give their meaning (*gi*).[bj] The meaning must be related to the facts, only thereafter can the way be determined."[33] He criticized even the *Mencius* (which Jinsai extolled) as inferior to the *Analects* in giving the true meaning of the Six Classics. The *Mencius* and the *Mean* were, to Sorai, born of later controversies and were too polemical.

It becomes at once apparent that this implied criticism of the Sung Learning was more scholastic than substantive. The Shushigaku position contained, as one of its moments, an emphasis on "the investigation of things." It is clear from the above-cited passage that Sorai was not suggesting that we have knowledge of the "facts" (the institutions and civilization found in the Six Classics) apart from a *principle*, that is, a *basis of interpretation* (namely, the *Book of Rites* and the *Analects*). In Chu Hsi's terminology, this implied "plumbing the principles of things," that is, interpreting the particular (*ch'i*) in terms of the universal (*li*) in the cognitive domain. (As for Sorai's supposed empiricism, we should bear in mind that Kant has well clarified the point that scientific inquiry is not a pure "factism." Science is an ongoing *interpretation* of facts, involving the subsumption of the single "fact" into a system of "facts" of the same order, by the application of the universal categories of the understanding.)

The main thrust of Sorai's polemic, then, was undercut by the Sung Learning's own scholarly moment, and its epistemological advocacy of the plumbing of the principles of things. In transferring the authority from the Four Books to the Six Classics, of course, Sorai was following the Yōmeigaku line, as Professor Yamashita's paper brings out. It was a teaching already present in Nakae Tōju. As presented in this context of extolling the "facts" of the Six Classics, however, Sorai's argument makes little philosophical sense. In fact, as Maruyama has pointed out, Sorai's claim for the superiority of the Six Classics was not properly a philosophical claim so much as an element in his *belief* in the absolute character of the mythological Chinese sages. In this respect Sorai's "empirical rationalism" was neither empirical nor rational. It seems to have been a continuation of a religious moment found in Razan's and Tōju's thought—or was it a *tariki*[bk] element?—and to have served as a halfway house to the remythologization of the ancient Japanese kami in the Kokugaku school. How could Sorai's own belief in the ancient Chinese sages not eventually "dissolve" into a belief in the ancient Japanese kami in the midst of Japan's *sakoku* policy?

Of course, one may take a mythological, or fideistic position. And such a position is irrefutable as a subjective, psychological, or religious experience. We can even assert that, for the man of religious experience, there is nothing more real (*jitsu*) than what comes to him in his personal religious life. But it would simply be a confusion of standpoints to take one's own religious experience as a criterion of truth in the philosophical or scientific domains. Religious, philosophical, and scientific domains are each distinguishable domains of experience, each with its own structure and intentionality. However, both religion, as personal realization of the sacred, and science, as the ongoing process of exhausting the principles of things in a limited plane of facts, presuppose a larger whole—an ontological universe, in which the relation between the sacred and the human and natural, and between the knower and known, are ultimately real (*jitsu*). The Sung Learning was primarily a *jitsugaku* in this sense, a *jitsu no gaku* or theory of reality, containing a broad speculative thrust concerning the ultimate predicates we can apply to the whole ontological universe and presuppose in the more particular domains of experience.

Chu Hsi's dialectical structure of *li* and *ch'i*, worked out on both vertical and horizontal planes, and their intersection involved such a generic metaphysical structure of the co-origination and mutual determination of "substance" and "function"; of "principle" (*archē*) and manifestational energy and embodiment; of reality as ontological ground and reality as appearance in human subjectivity; of nature (*hsing*) and mind-and-heart (*hsin*); in short, of the universal and particular. We can even say that Chu Hsi's position represents a penetrating articulation of the Confucian insight of the unity of Heaven, earth, and man as a structure of *Natura-naturans*. His philosophy thus *allowed for* the particular domains of experience—emotional, moral, cognitive—and at the same time *gave reasons for* their co-inherence in a wider ontological whole. But it would again be a confusion of perspectives to take one's subjective stand on a particular intentionality of experience, and then invoke that particular form of experience to "dissolve" the general ontological whole of which it is a part. Whitehead, following the metaphysical analyses of F. H. Bradley, has called this the "fallacy of misplaced concreteness."[34]

Because of Chu Hsi's metaphysical integration of the various domains of experience, the Sung Learning was dedicated to exemplifying a style of "practical learning" based on the perception of the intrinsic relationship between the cognitive and moral orders. As expressed in the formula, "the extension of knowledge through the investigation of things," intellectual inquiry was emphasized as an important link with moral self-realization. The uncovering of principles (*li*) in the objective order was at the same time the process of "clarifying" and "realizing" one's own subjective moral nature. And hence, as we have seen, the Sung Learning's conception of the cognitive and moral life was essentially dynamic, grounded on the dialectical structure of inner reverence and outer righteousness.[35]

Chu Hsi's formula ko-wu chih-chih[b1] was a variation on the dialectical theme of "fully developing one's mind and knowing one's nature." The Wang Yang-ming school often criticized this formula as being "intellectualistic," that is, as connoting a one-sided intention of book-learning and the exhaustive exploration of the objective principles in things at the expense of the personal, moral domains of experience. But this criticism was itself one-sided, failing to account for the fact that Chu Hsi's extension of *objective* knowledge simultaneously co-implied the revelation of the whole domain of *subjective* moral realization, that is, the domain of self-realization which is concretized in the Five Relationships.

Soraigaku attacked the Sung Learning from the other side, accusing Chu Hsi of reducing the cognitive to the moral orders, and of thereby creating a "moral monism." But this polemic was also one-sided, failing to take account of Chu Hsi's dialectical formulation of the relation between immanent and transcendent planes of consciousness (as grounded, for example, in the *Great Learning* and the *Mean*). Chu Hsi may not have worked out these intentionalities in the terms of precise philosophical articulation, but they were implicit in his position. The cognitive intention involved the plumbing of principles in the objective world in the form of objective judgment. Objective judgment has the structure of the predication of the universal (*li*), of the particular(s) (*ch'i*), and, in the form of scientific inquiry, becomes the basis of a systematic configuration of a given type of predicate into a coherent and ever-widening field of such interrelated predicates. The subsumption of the particular under the universal in the process of *objective* judgment, however, simultaneously involves the noetic activity of the knowing *subject* and its innate principles; and thus knower and known, subject and object, are co-implied in the cognitive structure. The objective transcendence of judgment has, in other words, taken place within the active, immanent field of consciousness. It is precisely at this juncture that Chu Hsi's conception of the dialectical structures of experience can lead us to understand that the process of plumbing objective principles simultaneously co-implies the clarification and realization of the *moral* nature. For the *real subject* of experience is not a merely transcendental plane of abstract predicates—the plane of impersonal, general truths—but the individual, whose ongoing activity knows, wills, and realizes the good. The person knows, wills, and realizes the good by "transforming" the *ch'i* of his subjective physical-emotional existence under the guidance of his moral nature (*li*). This means, not to repress and eliminate the *ch'i* of subjective, emotional, and volitional disposition, but to channel the same energy in the light of ideals and principles of the moral capacity (*hsing*).

We might say, then, that the moral plane involves the cognitive plane as one of its moments; but this does not imply a simplistic reduction of the cognitive to the moral order. Rather, as exemplified in the Sung Learning, the cognitive and the moral domains were understood as distinguishable, but essentially interrelated domains of experience, in a wider ontological universe.

With this as background, let us return to Maruyama's claim that Soraigaku severed the various links between "private" and "public" intentions in the Sung Learning. Sorai taught that the "Way of Heaven" is to be understood symbolically, not metaphysically, because, as Confucius taught, Heaven can only be reverenced but not known. As Jinsai said, the emphasis should be on the Way of man. But Sorai went on to reject both the Sung Learning's *rigaku* and Jinsai's *kigaku*, in favor of a conception of the Way as exclusively connoting the public Way of the Sages, which concerned itself entirely with the Way of governing the realm and bringing peace to the world. It had nothing to do with governing one's own mind, Sorai contended. He thus relegated the Sung Learning, Yōmeigaku, the Jinsai school, together with Buddhism and Taoism, to the domain of merely "private wisdom"—techniques for the governing of one's subjective mind.

In severing the continuity between personal morality and government Sorai even attempted to treat personal morality as a mere political means—a position later taken by Fukuzawa Yukichi in his *Bunmeiron no gairyaku* (1875). He rejected Mencius' theory of the innate moral nature in favor of his objective Way of the Sages. In so doing, he shifted the *criterion* (*li*) of value to that of faith in the Way of the Sages, but at the cost of glossing over the entire legacy of interiority in the Confucian value tradition. The question then became one, not of becoming a sage and cultivating one's moral nature, but of *following* the Way of the Sages. If this was not a shift in emphasis so radical as to return to the position of Hsün Tzu—or Machiavelli—Sorai nevertheless left unanswered the key question of "who would educate the sages." He also left open the question as to why the people should reject the interiority of self-realization as the ground of the Five Relationships in favor of following the irrational "Mandate of Heaven."

As noted above, Maruyama's study saw in the variables in the Soraigaku of the eighteenth-century Tokugawa world the seeds of the modern, "pluralistic consciousness." He has portrayed the process of transition from the premodern, universal system of Shushigaku to the modern consciousness as an intellectual process which paralleled the societal transition from the "freezing" of the Tokugawa value system in the seventeenth century to its "dissolution" after the Genroku period. In contrast with this perspective, I have tried to suggest above that the metaphor of "highpoint" and "watershed" as applied to the Genroku culture can only be taken so far; there are grounds for viewing the whole Edo culture as forming one dynamic piece, the stadial coexistence of whose parts continued as one stable complex from the beginning to the end of the period. In the philosophical realm, Kogaku, Soraigaku, Kokugaku, and various eclectic schools appeared to have coexisted, too, in the eighteenth century, but none of these schools, or their combination, displaced the metaphysical matrix of Neo-Confucian values articulated in the seventeenth century by Shushigaku and Yōmeigaku.

It has been pointed out that a particular deficiency of the Maruyama study was its neglect of the Yōmeigaku tradition as an independent current of Tokugawa thought. But we have seen that the Yōmei tradition already contained many of the variables that emerged in the Kogaku and Soraigaku lines. I refer to the emphasis on ch'i-hsüeh (that is, the monistic identity of li and ch'i), the rejection of the authority of the Four Books, the element of political restorationism, and so forth. Tokugawa Neo-Confucianism was continuously enriched by the importation of several strains of Ming and Ch'ing thought. In the short run, this produced the phenomenon of different schools emphasizing discontinuous elements that helped refine their positions and advance the general intellectual atmosphere. But in the long run, the Ming and Ch'ing emphases, and their Tokugawa counterparts, do not seem to have conflicted with, but were actually the outgrowths of, the original ontological universe created by the major Chinese thinkers of the Sung and Ming. The genius of the Japanese thinkers was their ability to assimilate these conceptual values within the multileveled structure of Japanese culture, with its distinctive indigenous elements. Razan and Tōju were two such Japanese thinkers who created the possibility of the varieties of *jitsugaku* in the Tokugawa period.

Concerning the indigenous Japanese elements, the *ch'i-hsüeh*, we have already seen, was present in one form or another in the Muromachi amalgamation of Shinto, Buddhist, and Confucian elements. It was resurrected in that way through the Shinto-Confucian syncretism of such figures as Razan, Ansai, and Tōju. Tōju also came in contact with the *ch'i-hsüeh* of the Wang Yang-ming school, initially through the thought of Wang Chi. And Lo Ch'in-shun's *K'un-chih-chi* had its own influence on the thought of Razan, Ekken, Ansai, Sokō, and Jinsai—through whom it must have also been transmitted in some form to the Soraigaku and Kokugaku. My hypothesis here is that the *ch'i-hsüeh* must have functioned to support the Shinto religious tendency in some of these thinkers. It became the vehicle for affirming the value of the emotional life in others. Itō Jinsai's statement in this latter regard was exemplary: ". . . Human emotions are the Way, and desires are the source of righteousness. What evil do they have?"

But unfortunately for this apparent critique of the Sung Learning's position, the "source of righteousness" as subjective emotion (*ch'i*) is confused with the rational criterion of righteousness (*li*). Spinoza has also said that the emotions and desires are *good*—but he added that some are *better* than others. Yamaga Sokō, under the influence of the *ch'i-hsüeh*, also attacked the Sung Learning's position on "having no [selfish] desires" as the extreme error. But when he said that what is to be rejected is emotional "disorder," which arises from "going too far or not far enough," Sokō was simply reiterating Chu Hsi's own position without fully understanding it.

Lo Ch'in-shun's stress on the cognitive "fact" also reoccurs in Sorai's positivism. But Lo's own *ch'i-hsüeh* can be construed as based on an epistemological misunderstanding of Chu Hsi's position. For, as stated above, the *particular* fact (*ch'i*) presupposes the *universal* system of facts and their interrelation. An analogous problem, as Inoue Tetsujirō has indicated, exists for *ch'i-hsüeh* in the form of the Yōmeigaku position of the *hsin* (mind-and-heart), and *liang-chih* (innate knowledge), functioning as both universal, cosmic principle and subjective, existential embodiment. In Chu Hsi's own ontological structure, the principle (*li*) of the individual existence (*ch'i*) becomes the point of relation with the wider field of principles (predicates) required for its intelligibility as an item in the larger universe.

Thus, from the point of view of the Sung Learning, Lo Ch'in-shun's "monism of *ch'i*" is hard pressed to account adequately for the dialectically interrelated aspects of individuation and intelligibility. Lo can talk of the "particular" *ch'i* and the "universal" *ch'i*, but that would hardly be an improvement over Chu Hsi's terminology. Lo's thought, at any rate, came as a refinement of some aspects of the Sung Learning from within the Sung Learning. The Wang Yang-ming school of the Ming attempted further reconstructions of the fundamental structure of Chu Hsi's position. My tentative conclusion is that the eighteenth-century Ch'ing historical criticism and its counterpart, the *jitsugaku* of the Kogaku-Soraigaku-Kokugaku line of development, were also attempted reconstructions of the basic matrix of conceptual values of the Sung Learning. They may be viewed as interesting ways of refocusing those variables. But the eighteenth-century conception of *jitsugaku* seems philosophically limited in its one-sided shift in emphasis to the externality of cognitive and social values in the Confucian world view.

Japanese thought in the Edo period was heir to the several strains of Sung, Ming, and Ch'ing thought. According to Professor Okada Takehiko, it was the Yōmeigaku scholars of the Bakumatsu period who strove again to synthesize the Ch'eng-Chu and Lu-Wang schools, while the orthodox Shushigaku scholars were more committed to the distinctions between them. In so doing, the Shin Yōmeigaku scholars of the late Tokugawa period—such as Hayashi Jussai, Satō Issai, Hayashi Ryōsai, Yoshimura Shūyō, and Ikeda Sōan—were in fact closer to the original spirit of Fujiwara Seika, the father of Tokugawa Neo-Confucianism. Professor Okada points to their integration of personal and public Confucian values when he writes:

Some of the Bakumatsu scholars we have discussed were followers of the teachings of Wang Yang-ming and some were followers of Chu Hsi, but all regarded both a diligent self-examination (*hansei jigaku*)[bm] and a deep, personal self-realization (*tainin jitoku*)[bn] as essential to learning. This sort of scholarly attitude had, of course, existed in the past also, but it became much deeper and more thorough with these scholars. Why is it that their scholarly tone at least with respect to personal realization, reached a depth and intensity that could not have been achieved previously? The chief reasons for this would seem to be: (1) having been born into a period of troubles, both within and without the country, which had no parallel in history, they underwent deep and poignant personal experiences; (2) they imported and enthusiastically accepted the teachings of the Chu Hsi and Wang Yang-ming schools of the Late Ming period which emphasized the importance of deep personal self-realization in the midst of the same sort of chaos and misery. They thought that since the fate of the country and the well-being of the people ultimately depended on the individual's mind and disposition, the rise and fall in the popularity of the study of moral cultivation (shinsei no gaku)[bo] was importantly connected to the life pulse of the country. This meant that moral cultivation which they advocated was for them a matter of life and death—it was something on which one wagered his life. Thus it is not surprising that they concentrated on the cultivation of a deep and thoroughgoing personal experience and self-realization. Neither is it surprising that this dedication allowed them to bequeath some of the brightest accomplishments in the history of modern Japanese thought.[36]

In these terms, there appears to have been a profound internal relation between the intellectual dimensions of the nineteenth-century (kindaika) and the seventeenth-century (kinseika) stages of Japanese history. Far from giving evidence of the dissolution of the seventeenth-century conceptions of jitsu and gaku, the mid-nineteenth century gives evidence of the stadial inter–resonance of the two layers of Japanese Neo-Confucian tradition.

POSTSCRIPT: THE MEIJI STAGE
OF NEO-CONFUCIAN JITSUGAKU

As a postscript to the question of modernization and jitsugaku discussed in this paper, I should like to close by briefly taking note of the "Meiji stage" of Neo-Confucian tradition in Japan. While this will take us far beyond the explicit focus of this symposium, I think it will shed further light on the various issues.

We have seen that a marked feature of the late Tokugawa thought was its syncretic tendency, as the various schools of Confucian learning established by the great teachers of the seventeenth and eighteenth centuries came to merge with one another. I have pointed to the significance of the Shin Yōmeigaku school of Satō Issai as having effected a synthesis of Shushigaku and Yōmeigaku lines during the Bakumatsu period. In the Meiji period, Neo-Confucianism lost its institutional character, as Japan set itself the task of catching up with the West. But the rich legacy of Neo-Confucian thought acted as the vector through which Western values were introduced into the Meiji context and continued to permeate the cultural and intellectual life of the Japanese people. During the early years of historical change, the Shin Yōmeigaku even provided a major thrust towards the modernization process. Far from sinking into oblivion with the dismantling of the feudal system, the synthesis of Shushigaku and Yōmeigaku variables energetically reappeared in what I term the "Meiji stage" of Neo-Confucian tradition.

I suggest that this Meiji stage of Neo-Confucianism must be taken into account in any complete assessment of the various claims of *jitsugaku*. There is overwhelming evidence of the contribution of the Neo-Con-fucian schools to the formation of the consciousness of the *han* samurai and *shishi* loyalists—both "reformers" and "restorationists"—whose careers were central to the story of the fall of the Tokugawa regime and the restoration of imperial rule. The influence can be traced, for example, in such figures as Hayashi Shihei, Yamada Hōkoku, Kasuga Sen'an, Ikeda Sōan, Yoshimura Shūyō, Hayashi Ryōsai, Azuma [Higashi] Takusha, Yanagawa Seizan, Sakuma Shōzan, Yoshida Shōin, Yokoi Shōnan, and Saigō Takamori. Most of these figures can be linked to the Shin Yōmei school of Satō Issai, and some even to the school of Ōshio Chūsai. Saigō Takamori, in particular, was an admirer of Chūsai, although he studied in a school deriving from Satō Issai. We should remember that Saigō's death in 1877 occurred only forty years after Chūsai's death in 1837, and only eighteen after Issai's in 1859.

The Shin Yōmeigaku values of Satō Issai, Sakuma Shōzan, Yoshida Shōin, Saigō Takamori, and others were in some measure retained by the first wave of modernizers in the Meiji period. Itō Hirobumi and Yamagata Aritomo were disciples of Yoshida Shōin. Shōin, in turn, was the disciple of Sakuma Shōzan, who was himself a disciple of Satō Issai. Shōzan's disciples also included Katsu Kaishū (1823–1899), father of the Japanese navy in the Meiji period, and such prominent figures of the Meirokusha as Nishimura Shigeki (1828–1902), Katō Hiroyuki (1836–1916), and Nakamura Keiu (1832–1891). All of the Meirokusha figures came out of a common background of Confucian learning and the officially sponsored Dutch Studies. The full story has not yet been told of the degree to which the Meirokusha figures responded to the challenges of modernization from the strengths of their Confucian heritage.

However complex the tapestry of Meiji intellectual life becomes, we never lose sight of the threads of Neo-Confucian influence. Since we are here dealing with a multivariate spiritual heritage in the process of expansion and transformation, it becomes increasingly difficult simply to identify variables in terms of their pre-Restoration forms. But consider, for example, the deep sense of interiority in the spirituality of Uchimura Kanzō, Ebina Danjō, Uemura Masahisa, Kozaki Hiromichi, and other figures of the Japanese Christian movement of the 1880s on. Their self-consciousness as "Christian samurai" bears witness to the repossession of many Neo-Confucian values and their integration in the Meiji context. Uchimura particularly loved Nakae Tōju, and wrote chapters on both Tōju and Saigō Takamori in his *Japan and the Japanese*, published in 1894. For another example, consider the writings of Miyake Setsurei, Kuga Katsunan, Tokutomi Soho, and the other "new youth" of the 1890s who similarly repossessed Yōmeigaku values as they identified with the Bakumatsu *shishi* in their critiques of the Meiji bureaucratic establishment figures, whom they indicted for having betrayed the spirit of the Meiji Restoration.[37]

Indeed, forms of liberal and left thinking in the Meiji 20s and 30s—the Christian liberalism of Uchimura and Ōnishi Hajime, the Christian Socialism of Abe Isō and Kinoshita Naoe, even the radical socialism of Kōtoku Shūsui—can all be studied in reference to the conscious identification of these types with the ideals of the *shishi* tradition.[38] But this was part of a still larger pattern, involving all fronts of Meiji-period intellectual modernization. As the great establishment figures of the late Meiji—Mori Ōgai, Inoue Tetsujirō, Natsume Sōseki, Nishida Kitarō, and others—came to play a formative role in the articulation of the modern Japanese identity, they too, in varying manners and degrees repossessed the historically-sedimented legacy of Confucian thought.

I suggest in closing that the Neo-Confucian values which such figures inherited and integrated into the Meiji context functioned as archetypes of the unconscious, as it were, through which they were able to respond creatively to the pressures of Westernization. They bear witness to the continuity between *kinsei* and *kindai* stages of Japanese modernization.

NOTES

1. Watsuji Tetsurō, *Nihon bunka no jūsōsei* (The Stadial Character of Japanese Culture), first published in *Gūzō saikō* (The Revival of Idols, 1919). The essay is found in *Watsuji Tetsurō zenshū* (20 vols.) (Tokyo: Iwanami Shoten, 1963), 17:377–86.
2. David Dilworth, "Watsuji Tetsurō: Cultural Phenomenologist and Ethician," *Philosophy East and West* (January 1974), 24(1):3–22.
3. Richard M. Zaner and Don Ihde, eds., *Phenomenology and Existentialism: An Anthology* (New York: Capricorn Books, 1973), pp. 131–32. The selection is from Husserl's *Formal and Transcendental Logic* (1927), ch. 6.
4. Watsuji Tetsurō, *Nihon rinri shisōshi* (History of Japanese Ethical Thought), (2 vols.; Tokyo: 1952; rev. ed., 1965), 2:365.
5. *Ibid.*, pp. 368–69.
6. Ryusaku Tsunoda et al., eds., *Sources of Japanese Tradition* (New York: Columbia University Press, 1958), pp. 335–38, and ch. 16, "Neo-Confucian Orthodoxy," pp. 344 ff.
7. Robert Bellah, *Tokugawa Religion: The Values of Pre-Industrial Japan* (Glencoe, Ill.: Free Press, 1957), pp. 13–15.
8. Bellah, *Tokugawa Religion*, pp. 15–18; Bernard S. Silberman, *Ministers of Modernization: Elite Mobility in the Meiji Restoration, 1868–73* (Tucson: University of Arizona Press, 1964), pp. 7–31.
9. Silberman, *Ministers of Modernization*, p. 17.
10. Bellah, *Tokugawa Religion*, p. 25; Albert Craig, *Chōshū in the Meiji Restoration*, (Cambridge: Harvard University Press, 1961), p. 353.
11. Wing-tsit Chan, "Chu Hsi's Completion of Neo-Confucianism," in *Études Song: In Memoriam Étienne Balazs*, Françoise Aubin, ed., ser. 2, no. 1 (1973), pp. 59–90.
12. T'ang Chün-i, "The criticisms of Wang Yang-ming's teachings as raised by his contemporaries," in *Philosophy East and West* (January and April 1973), 23(1–2):177.
13. Wm. Theodore de Bary et al., eds., *Sources of Chinese Tradition* (New York: Columbia University Press, 1960), pp. 534–35; Wing-tsit Chan, "Chu Hsi's Completion of Neo-Confucianism," p. 73.
14. Abe Yoshio, *Nihon Shushigaku to Chōsen* (Tokyo: Tokyo daigaku shuppankai, 1965), esp. pp. 491–519.
15. T'ang Chün-i, "The criticisms of Wang Yang-ming's teachings," pp. 175–77.
16. *Ibid.*, p. 183.
17. Cited in Watsuji, *Nihon rinri shisōshi*, 2:386.
18. *Ibid.* The following account of Razan is drawn from the same source, pp. 386–95.
19. *Ibid.*, p. 395.
20. *Ibid.*, pp. 403–4; *Sources of Japanese Tradition*, pp. 369 ff.

21. Yamashita Ryūji, "Nakae Tōju's Religious Thought and its Relation to *Jitsugaku*," this volume, pp. 316–20.
22. Inoue Tetsujirō, *Nihon Yōmeigakuha no tetsugaku* (Tokyo: Fuzanbo shoten, 1900), pp. 33–56.
23. *Ibid.*, pp. 77–84.
24. *Ibid.*, p. 96.
25. *Sources of Japanese Tradition*, p. 385.
26. See the *Yōmeigaku taikei* (Compendium of [Wang] Yang-ming Thought), a twelve-volume series being published under the supervision of several outstanding Japanese scholars of Yōmeigaku thought, including Araki Kengo, Uno Tetsuto, Okada Takehiko, Yamashita Ryūji, Yasuoka Masahiro, and Yamanoi Yū.
27. T'ang Chün-i, "The Development of the Concept of Moral Mind from Wang Yang-ming to Wang Chi," in Wm. Theodore de Bary, ed., *Self and Society in Ming Thought* (New York: Columbia University Press, 1970), pp. 93–120; see also Okada Takehiko, "Wang Chi and the Rise of Existentialism," *ibid.*, pp. 121–44.
28. Maruyama Masao, *Nihon seiji shisōshi kenkyū* (Study of Japanese Political Thought) (Tokyo: Tokyo daigaku shuppan-kai, 1953), ch. 1, section 1, pp. 20–70.
29. *Ibid.*, pp. 183–90.
30. *Ibid.*, pp. 118–30.
31. *Ibid.*, p. 123.
32. *Ibid.*, pp. 134–38.
33. See Olof G. Lidin, trans., *Ogyū Sorai's Distinguishing the Way [Bendō]*, (Tokyo: Sophia University Press, 1970), p. 10. Cited in Maruyama, p. 79.
34. Alfred North Whitehead, *Process and Reality* (New York: Macmillan, 1929), preface and *passim*.
35. *Sources of Chinese Tradition*, p. 554.
36. Okada Takehiko, "The Chu Hsi and Wang Yang-ming schools at the end of the Ming and Tokugawa periods," in *Philosophy East and West* (January and April 1973), 23(1–2):151–52.
37. Cf. Kenneth B. Pyle, *The New Generation in Meiji Japan: Problems of Cultural Identity, 1885–1895* (Stanford: Stanford University Press, 1969).
38. Frederick G. Notehelfer, *Kōtoku Shūsui: Portrait of a Japanese Radical* (Cambridge: Cambridge University Press, 1971).

GLOSSARY

a	近代化	am	神
b	近世	an	國常立尊
c	重層性	ao	性理會通
d	下剋上	ap	王龍谿語錄
e	文	aq	翁問答
f	武	ar	致良知
g	貞觀政要	as	太虛
h	孔子家語	at	孝
i	六韜三略	au	士の道，士道
j	參勤交代	av	武士道
k	無極而太極	aw	帰太虛
l	理	ax	古学
m	命性	ay	徂徠学
n	氣	az	國学
o	事	ba	私
p	体用	bb	公
q	用	bc	文明開化
r	誠	bd	御靜謐の御代
s	自成	be	復古
t	中	bf	辨道，辨名
u	和	bg	古文辭学
v	氣学	bh	事，言葉
w	心	bi	物
x	寄田玄之	bj	義
y	寄頌遊	bk	他力
z	寂滅之說高而無實	bl	格物致知
aa	釋老	bm	反省自覚
ab	告禪徒	bn	体認自得
ac	諭三人	bo	心性の学
ad	排耶蘇		
ae	三德抄		
af	春鑑抄		
ag	神道傳授		
ah	神道秘傳析中俗解		
ai	日本書紀纂疏		
aj	神道大意		
ak	神道由來記		

Index

Index

531

NEO-CONFUCIAN STUDIES

Instructions for Practical Living and Other Neo-Confucian Writings by Wang Yang-ming, tr. Wing-tsit Chan   1963

Reflections on Things at Hand: The Neo-Confucian Anthology, comp. Chu Hsi and Lü Tsu-ch'ien, tr. Wing-tsit Chan   1967

Self and Society in Ming Thought, by Wm. Theodore de Bary and the Conference on Ming Thought. Also in paperback ed.   1970

The Unfolding of Neo-Confucianism, by Wm. Theodore de Bary and the Conference on Seventeenth-Century Chinese Thought. Also in paperback ed.   1975

Principle and Practicality: Essays in Neo-Confucianism and Practical Learning, ed. Wm. Theodore de Bary and Irene Bloom. Also in paperback ed.   1979

TRANSLATIONS FROM THE ORIENTAL CLASSICS

Major Plays of Chikamatsu, tr. Donald Keene   1961

Four Major Plays of Chikamatsu, tr. Donald Keene. Paperback text edition.   1961

Records of the Grand Historian of China, translated from the Shih chi of Ssu-ma Ch'ien, tr. Burton Watson, 2 vols.   1961

Instructions for Practical Living and Other Neo-Confucian Writings by Wang Yang-ming, tr. Wing-tsit Chan   1963

Chuang Tzu: Basic Writings, tr. Burton Watson, paperback ed. only   1964

The Mahābhārata, tr. Chakravarthi V. Narasimhan. Also in paperback ed.   1965

The Manyōshū, Nippon Gakujutsu Shinkōkai edition   1965

Su Tung-p'o: Selections from a Sung Dynasty Poet, tr. Burton Watson. Also in paperback ed.   1965

Bhartrihari: Poems, tr. Barbara Stoler Miller. Also in paperback ed.   1967

Basic Writings of Mo Tzu, Hsün Tzu, and Han Fei Tzu, tr. Burton Watson. Also in separate paperback eds.   1967
The Awakening of Faith, Attributed to Aśvaghosha, tr. Yoshito S. Hakeda. Also in paperback ed.   1967
Reflections on Things at Hand: The Neo-Confucian Anthology, comp. Chu Hsi and Lü Tsu-ch'ien, tr. Wing-tsit Chan   1967
The Platform Sutra of the Sixth Patriarch, tr. Philip B. Yampolsky. Also in paperback ed.   1967
Essays in Idleness: The Tsurezuregusa of Kenkō, tr. Donald Keene. Also in paperback ed.   1967
The Pillow Book of Sei Shōnagon, tr. Ivan Morris, 2 vols.   1967
Two Plays of Ancient India: The Little Clay Cart and the Minister's Seal, tr. J. A. B. van Buitenen   1968
The Complete Works of Chuang Tzu, tr. Burton Watson   1968
The Romance of the Western Chamber (Hsi Hsiang chi), tr. S. I. Hsiung. Also in paperback ed.   1968
The Manyōshū, Nippon Gakujutsu Shinkōkai edition. Paperback text edition.   1969
Records of the Historian: Chapters from the Shih chi of Ssu-ma Ch'ien. Paperback text edition, tr. Burton Watson   1969
Cold Mountain: 100 Poems by the T'ang Poet Han-shan, tr. Burton Watson. Also in paperback ed.   1970
Twenty Plays of the No Theatre, ed. Donald Keene. Also in paperback ed.   1970
Chūshingura: The Treasury of Loyal Retainers, tr. Donald Keene. Also in paperback ed.   1971
The Zen Master Hakuin: Selected writings, tr. Philip B. Yampolsky   1971
Chinese Rhyme-Prose: Poems in the Fu Form from the Han and Six Dynasties Periods, tr. Burton Watson. Also in paperback ed.   1971
Kūkai: Major Works, tr. Yoshito S. Hakeda   1972
The Old Man Who Does as He Pleases: Selections from the Poetry and Prose of Lu Yu, tr. Burton Watson   1973
The Lion's Roar of Queen Śrīmālā, tr. Alex and Hideko Wayman   1974
Courtier and Commoner in Ancient China: Selections from the History of The Former Han by Pan Ku, tr. Burton Watson. Also in paperback ed. 1974

STUDIES IN ORIENTAL CULTURE

COMPANIONS TO ASIAN STUDIES

INTRODUCTION TO ORIENTAL CIVILIZATIONS
Wm. Theodore de Bary, *Editor*

Sources of Japanese Tradition	1958	Paperback ed., 2 vols.	1964
Sources of Indian Tradition	1958	Paperback ed., 2 vols.	1964
Sources of Chinese Tradition	1960	Paperback ed., 2 vols.	1964